Lester Leaps In

Lester Leaps In

THE LIFE AND TIMES *of* LESTER "PRES" YOUNG

Douglas Henry Daniels

Beacon Press
Boston

Beacon Press
25 Beacon Street
Boston, Massachusetts 02108-2892
www.beacon.org

Beacon Press books
are published under the auspices of
the Unitarian Universalist Association of Congregations.

Printed in the United States of America
06 05 04 03 02 8 7 6 5 4 3 2 1

This book is printed on acid-free paper that meets the uncoated
paper ANSI/NISO specifications for permanence as revised in 1992.

Text design by Dean Bornstein
Composition by Wilsted & Taylor Publishing Services

Library of Congress Cataloging-in-Publication Data
Daniels, Douglas Henry.
Lester leaps in : the life and times of Lester "Pres" Young /
Douglas Henry Daniels.
p. cm.
Includes bibliographical references and index.
ISBN 0-8070-7102-1 (alk. paper)
1. Young, Lester, 1909–1959. 2. Jazz musicians—United States—
Biography. I. Title.
ML419.Y7 D36 2002
788.7′165′092—dc21
[B]
2001037387

for Claudine

CONTENTS

PART I

Many Moons Ago

In a world where everybody's twins, [Pres] was different. . . . It takes a whole lot of courage to be different. You know, anybody can follow the crowd.

Jimmy Heath

CHAPTER 1

The President of the Tenor Saxophone

LESTER "Pres" (or "Prez") Young (1909–1959) was without question one of the most influential tenor saxophonists of the twentieth century. While Coleman Hawkins is justly recognized as having been the first to popularize the tenor saxophone in jazz, Young revealed an entirely new dimension to the instrument. Then, too, Young was a genuine cultural hero to many fans and other musicians, partly because of his unique musical style, but also because he was a real rebel—or individualist, depending upon one's point of view. His refusal to bow to the dictates of popular opinion regarding his playing, or to the military authorities after he was drafted (eventually leading to his court-martial in early 1945), only enhanced his stature among his fans in an age of patriotism and conformity.

He was, as guitarist Barney Kessel maintained, perhaps the most controversial as well as one of the most gifted of musicians. Besides denying having been influenced by Coleman Hawkins, he was notoriously aloof, at once shy and uncommunicative, relying on his own unique jargon, jazz slang, and witty comments when he did speak. He was described by more than one writer as elusive and, in his later life, suspicious. Even some of his fellow musicians found him strange, with some likening him to an extraterrestrial. The saxophonist was a musical legend, one of those colorful jazz characters of the 1940s, but he also had a serious drinking problem that ultimately robbed him of his health. Only his inner circle and a few hangers-on knew his private side. He was actually gentle, sensitive, and quite chivalrous toward women; he never spoke ill of anyone and was generous to a fault with loans and gifts. And there was yet another dimension to his private life: like Louis Armstrong, he smoked marijuana daily and unashamedly, in the solitude of his hotel rooms.

Despite his controversial character, he was, in the opinion of everyone who played with him, of his family, and of many fans, first and foremost a superior musician. Both his virtuosity as a soloist and his actual compositions were singularly influential among musicians besides saxophonists, and his manner of speech, style of dress, and general demeanor all led the Beat Generation to lionize him. He first came to the notice of the public with the Count Basie band in 1936, and the title by which he became known, "Pres," or "Prez"—short for "President of the Tenor Saxophone"—would last long after his passing in 1959. Moreover, acclaim for his musical prowess was the rule for him for over two decades. His popularity among his fans endured despite his poor health toward the end and in spite of the considered opinion of many critics and reviewers that his playing had diminished in quality.

This book deals with the life and significance of this brilliant saxophonist, but it is not the usual type of jazz biography. When I started working on it, no full-length biography of Young had ever been published, but as other such volumes began to appear, I became even more firmly convinced that there was much more to the history of Black folk and to the evolution of jazz than could be found in these or many other books about Black musicians. I had always admired those earlier jazz biographies that were based on interviews with their subjects and that were thus, in a sense, autobiographical, such as Alan Lomax's *Mister Jelly Roll* and Larry Gara's *The Baby Dodds Story.* But that was a model I could not follow, since I myself never met Young (I was just a teenager when he died), and no one else ever interviewed him at length, as Lomax and Gara did Jelly Roll Morton and Dodds, respectively. The problem was daunting: how does one write the biography of someone who left only a few interviews but hundreds of hours of recorded music, when readers are so accustomed to reading about people who kept diaries, scrapbooks of clippings, and other kinds of written records?

Further complicating matters was the fact that Young himself did not often contribute to the clear presentation of the details of his own life; he not only was careless about dating events but, as his nephew James Tolbert has noted, could be "kind of frosty" toward interviewers and people he did not know. Lee Young claimed that the writer Ralph Gleason got close enough to his brother to appreciate his sterling worth, but Gleason was alone among critics in this regard. Nonetheless, the saxophonist did stick to the facts in some areas, notably when it came to his early musical training, and such information, corroborated to the extent that it can be, provides some insights that can be compared to the recollections of other musicians of his generation.

What this work attempts to do is in some ways very simple. My object has been, first, to uncover historical evidence that may shed new light on the details and significance of the saxophonist's life, utilizing published interviews with him as well as public records, archives, and oral histories; and then, second, to interpret that within the context of what we know about his family, about the careers of other, contemporary musicians, and about Black history and culture. This necessitates taking into account the views of Young's family members as well as his fellow musicians, an approach that in itself seems reasonable enough, until one considers that often the opinions of Black folk are not taken seriously, both in the United States in general and in jazz scholarship in particular. Only then does it become apparent just how controversial such a strategy might be.

Many writers interview jazz musicians to glean details of their lives, discographical information, and accounts of specific incidents, especially humorous ones, but these writers are usually journalists, not historians. Also of significance is the fact that on those occasions when musicians speak of the philosophy behind their music, such ideas are rarely analyzed or even commented upon by writers. While I have relied to some extent upon evidence and opinions from some critics (some of whom are superb at what they do), the writings of other journalists have more often carried the day because their ideas are in better accord with prevailing beliefs about Black musicians. Where I have made use of the pronouncements and opinions of critics—or of relatives and sidemen, for that matter—I have been careful not to blithely accept them as the final word on a matter, a failing that is seen in far too many histories, in my estimation.

I wanted, in this work, to place Young and his experiences front and center and within their appropriate historical context, a context that has changed considerably thanks to the efforts of scholars over the past generation. The music culture is far too important to be neglected by those interested in its various manifestations, from songs and dances to slang, dress, and lifestyles. Also, jazz audiences—dancers, fans, and other various jazzophiles—tend to interact with "their" music to a much greater degree than those who favor European classical works. Black music, including jazz, involves significant audience activity; beyond dancing, audience members offer vocal encouragement, and the music itself often serves as a backdrop for partying, conversation, and carrying on. As the composer and pianist Thomas "Fats" Waller once explained, swing was "just a musical phase of our social life."[1] This fact, however, is largely lost on the wider public and on many writers, who remain oblivious to the new scholarship in the field of Black Studies on the complex dynamics of both African and African American history and culture.

I myself have always felt this very strongly. The music (a term I prefer to the word *jazz*) has been a part of my life since I was in my teens. As a child, I listened to the Hit Parade on the radio in Princeton Park, the Black community on the far South Side of Chicago where I grew up, and memorized songs by whites—especially Bill Haley and Hank Williams—along with ones by Blacks such as Little Richard and Chuck Berry. My older sisters liked the Platters, Ray Charles, and Johnny Mathis, and thanks to their record collection, I also discovered jazz as it was played by Ahmad Jamal, the Three Sounds, and Ramsey Lewis, all of whom were very popular in Chicago.

As I reflect upon it now, I realize that my passion for music came from my father, who was born in New Orleans but grew up in Chicago's Black Belt in the 1920s, and who along with his childhood friends saw the former heavyweight champion Jack Johnson when he was a nightclub owner and heard tales of the battles among King Oliver, Louis Armstrong, and other trumpet players. The fact that my father could identify Clark Terry's trumpet playing from just a few notes really impressed me, but I was even more in awe of his ability to mimic singers such as Billie Holiday and Dinah Washington, which suggests to me now that he was much closer to the music than I ever realized at the time. During my last years of high school, I felt transformed by my discovery of the music of Charles Mingus, Thelonious Monk, and Miles Davis. I knew that their music and their lives would be of major importance to me, no matter what I ended up doing.

One other autobiographical note is relevant here. Two years spent teaching primary school in Tanzania, in 1965 and 1966, introduced me to the Kiswahili language, the history, and the peoples of East Africa. I also became acquainted then with the worldviews of Tanzanians and the ethos of a newly independent and Socialist government. During my second year there, the government prohibited foreigners like me from teaching history and geography. The reasoning behind this was that only other Africans could provide African children with the proper perspective, one in which the "great explorers" such as Livingstone and Stanley were regarded as mere "visitors."

I became sympathetic to this anticolonial outlook, and after I came back to the United States, my new insights were sharpened by the uprisings of 1967, a summer of considerable unrest and awakening on the part of African Americans. I entered graduate school at Berkeley that fall, avidly interested in African American history and convinced that once I had developed my research skills, I could set about discovering a historical perspective that would do justice to African Americans and jazz, in much the same way that African historians and government officials were recasting the teaching and conceptualization of African history from an anticolonial point of view.

From the outset of my research on Lester Young, I learned to question the once-prevailing notions promoted by the jazz journals, especially in contemporary record reviews, highlighting Young's successes with Basie and exaggerating his decline after 1945. The critics' Eurocentric emphasis—as when they likened Young to Mozart, for example, in reviews of reissues of the saxophonist's work in the 1980s—was also troubling, both in and of itself and because it carried such bald connotations of racial superiority in the suggestion that the saxophonist was worthy of comparison with this or that European master.

When I first began doing research for this book, I did not really notice how frequently my sources were giving me—often in just a few words—verbal snapshots of Young that challenged existing conceptions. For example, when he was asked if the saxophonist had played differently after being discharged from the military, Wilbur "Buck" Clayton expressed the heretical opinion that he had played *better*, even though according to jazz legend, Young's playing had suffered after his stint in the army. Clayton also recalled that Young's father had been a professor of music, pointing to the development of talent within the family over multiple generations. In another instance, in interviews with me, several Blue Devils with whom Young had played in 1932 and 1933 took credit for naming him Pres, contradicting the widespread belief that Billie Holiday had given him that nickname. In other words, his identity as "Pres" had preceded his meeting the singer or joining Count Basie's band, despite hallowed folklore and testimony to the contrary.

In interviews and casual conversation, both family members and fellow musicians questioned the prevailing wisdom about Young in ways that were not only tactful and insightful but profound. I remember how the late Connie Kay, drummer in the Modern Jazz Quartet, responded to allegations that Young had had bad nights, or hadn't played as well, or had failed to meet his own artistic goals in the 1950s: he said that as a sideman, he couldn't make those kinds of judgments about Young, or about Charlie Parker, either, for that matter, because those two men had been artists, not imitators. To paraphrase Kay, when an imitator plays something differently, you can conclude that he doesn't have it together, but how can you tell with a musician of the caliber of a Pres or a Bird, both of whom were always experimenting? I rarely encountered comments as thoughtful as this in the printed jazz literature.

Kay told me of another drummer, Carl "Kansas" Fields, who had been with Young during his last days in Paris and who in 1981 was living on Chicago's South Side. Fields was an unassuming gentleman who responded that he was *still* learning—and was enrolled in a local college—when I asked him when he had learned to play the drums. He very patiently explained what was then a new idea to me, that Young's music reflected the man himself, and that his personality was expressed in his music. In other words, the saxophonist had been a total artist, whose life was submerged in his art. This concept merely puzzled me at the time, but it made me want to go deeper into the subject matter in an attempt to understand Fields's notion and the perspective that had fostered it.

From the musicians I learned to be highly skeptical of received wisdom about Pres. I also came to appreciate their often quite scientific approach to questioning people's ideas about such things: Were you there every night? they would ask. Did you play or travel with him? Did he himself tell you that? Such questions deal with the very essence of the respondent's knowledge about jazz and are therefore essentially epistemological, touching on the nature of opinion and on how we know what we know.

This kind of skepticism was, I thought, quite healthy. In my own interviews, I noted a certain tendentiousness on the part of a few musicians, who disagreed with whatever I suggested about the music's history and indicated that it was *always* greater than expectations or preconceived notions. This was one way they had of resisting the labels and ideas that were commonly assigned to them, regardless of their opinions. Furthermore, it reflected a measure of intelligence not generally attributed to jazz musicians.

Still, I wondered, why are the opinions of musicians so readily discounted by critics, and why do writers so rarely secure the cooperation of family members in jazz biographies? These were some of the questions I pondered over the years as I interviewed musicians. Family connections are seldom examined in any detail in jazz biographies, but as Jo Jones pointed out, African Americans have family traditions just like the Rockefellers and the Kennedys. Many jazz writers seem to ignore this fact, for whatever reason. In this respect, the Young family's oral tradition was particularly rich, and it was not one they always shared with writers. They were typical Louisianans, a tightly knit family presided over by a patriarch, Young's father, and *his* father before him. They had their own unique perspectives on the saxophonist and on other family members. For example, Young's father, the music professor, impressed upon his children the importance of a work ethic, punctuality, self-discipline, sticking to one's principles, and standing up for something—specific values that were adopted by his children, including Lester, but that have often been overlooked by those writing about Young.

Moreover, important spiritual truths and traditions were a part of the family heritage for generations. Jacob Young, Lester's paternal grandfather, was a pillar of Allen Chapel, the first African Methodist Episcopal (A.M.E.) church in Lafourche Parish, in the bayou country of Louisiana about sixty miles from New Orleans; his name is listed on a memorial plaque in the church's vestibule. Martha, his wife, was a missionary. The saxophonist's father conducted church choirs. The women of the Young family sang and gave recitations in church; Lester's aunt Mamie married the minister of Allen Chapel late in the nineteenth century. Unlike the Baptists, the denomination to which the majority of African Americans belonged (and still belong), the members of the A.M.E. were quite cerebral in their spiritual demeanor, not given to jumping up and shouting or dancing with joy, as many of their Protestant brethren did.

The pianist Sadik Hakim, a Young sideman (and one of the first such I interviewed), stressed that he had seen Young as a spiritual leader—another of those opinions that have gone largely unpublicized. Hakim's assertion was quite perplexing to me at the beginning of my research because Young had usually been portrayed as a rebel, an iconoclast, and an alcoholic—qualities not generally associated with spiritual leaders. Nevertheless, a memorial service has been held for him at Saint Peter's in Manhattan every March since the 1980s.

Whenever I told musicians that I wanted to ask them about Lester

Young, they invariably corrected my use of his name: "You mean Pres?" His identity as President of the Tenor Saxophone was so compelling that long after his death, this term was still presented as his rightful title, representing the essence of his stature in the jazz world. Of course, it was some time before I understood the significance of their correcting me: it was tantamount to their saying that he was a giant who should be spoken of in a manner befitting his singular contribution. This habit of theirs impressed upon me the permanence of the mark Young had left upon music.

Revealing though they were, however, the insights that Young's sidemen provided were limited to some degree. I knew I needed to get a better sense of the historical, social, and cultural influences that had shaped Young, and so I began archival research in Louisiana parishes and other places where his family had lived prior to his going out on his own, in around 1929. Eventually this research led to Lester's father, Willis H. Young, who Buck Clayton said had taught music and voice, played every kind of instrument, led bands all over the country, and trained not only his children but his grandchildren and generations of other musicians.

Some old-timers, such as Le Roy "Snake" Whyte and Charles "Truck" Parham, helped me re-create the Minneapolis milieu (oddly neglected in histories of jazz) in which Young had spent nearly a decade of his career. I also bore down on the U.S. Manuscript Census, which turned out to be of less use than I had hoped: I could never find any listing for Willis Young after 1900, and the identification of Lester, his sister Irma, their mother, and their stepmother was problematic, too. But it was through the census that I discovered Aunt Mamie, Willis's sister, living with her husband in Washington Parish, Louisiana, in 1910, and without that piece of information it would never have occurred to me to search that parish's records for her brother's marriage license.

Throughout my years of research on this book, I felt a sense of responsibility toward the members of Young's family, who took me into their confidence; above all, I wanted to remain true to their trust rather than betray it with a quick publication that would add little to our knowledge of the saxophonist or, even worse, contribute to the all-too-prevalent misinformation and misunderstandings about him. During his life and after his death in 1959, rumors circulated that led to a persistent and unsympathetic depiction of him as an aging alcoholic, a has-been whose artistry had declined precipitously after he was drafted into the U.S. Army, court-martialed for possessing marijuana, and dishonorably discharged in 1945. Then, too, I often recalled the words of advice that Young once gave a sideman, Valdo Williams, who paused in a solo as if uncertain whether to take another chorus: "Never give up. . . . Don't ever give up."[2]

I felt obliged to write a sympathetic portrait because I believed it would permit a better understanding of my subject than any other kind of approach. One reader's response to an early draft of my manuscript typified the reactions of those who wanted me to make judgments about Young—to condemn him for being irresponsible and a bad father, for abandoning his wife and children when he went to live at the Alvin Hotel in Manhattan toward the end of his life.

Such opinions were never voiced about Lester by his family members or sidemen, who were in fact puzzled and sometimes troubled by attempts on the part of the press to portray Young as anything but a gentle, sensitive artist who was misunderstood and maligned during his lifetime. One Blue Devil, Ernie Williams, rather cryptically remarked to me, "It was a damn shame what they did to Lester." (Williams did not consent to be interviewed.)

I came to reject the conviction of some writers that those closest to Young were hiding some deep, dark secret about him. Furthermore, the portrait drawn by family members and fellow musicians seemed to contrast so sharply with published descriptions of Young as to require a revisionist portrayal of the saxophonist, undertaken in much the same spirit in which historians have revised African, African American, and U.S. history over the past generation.

Eventually I came to appreciate why so few people really did or could know Young: like many musicians, he had a rich social life outside the world of commercial entertainment, a life that he guarded closely because he valued it as private. For him and others like him, relations with spouses, children, other family members, and musician friends and their families were particularly important because they were their own and they were real, intimate, and sustaining, different in character from the tinsel and hullabaloo of show business. Young, for one, often visited with what he called his "waybacks"—friends he had known for years—when he traveled on the road with his combo. At other times, in a world of his own making, he would "hold court"—to use saxophonist John "Zoot" Sims's expression—with sidemen and local musicians in his hotel room or backstage. This jazz musicians' universe of family and close friends, and its meaning to the musicians themselves, would have been invisible to outsiders and writers unless, for example, they were regularly invited to dinner in a musician's home or, an even rarer occurrence, married into his family.

African American musicians in general, and Young himself in particular, were remarkably adept at hiding their private lives from strangers. Tactful responses to pointed questions, the use of vague metaphors and jazz slang, and a host of other techniques all kept people out of their business. When interviewed in private and asked to tell their story, however, in the comfort of their own homes, musicians may sometimes reveal their special insights, wisdom, and criticism. Had I invested less time in this project, such glimmers of Young's interior life would never have shown themselves to me.

My respect for the opinions of Young's family and sidemen extends to the precise words they chose to express them, which is why I have elected to quote them at length in this work and to provide an interpretive context that does them justice. Young's reputation and memory are safe in the record (now CD) grooves that he etched, and I suspect that his music will continue to be heard forever. I am not so sure that the same will be true of the testimony of the musicians who revered and loved him, so I hope to make some contribution to its longevity by taking it seriously and reproducing it so that others can consider it, too. These witnesses deserve to be heard along with those whose opinions have so often been voiced in the trade journals, books, liner notes, and record reviews.

CHAPTER 2

Shoeshine Boy

Way Down Yonder, 1909–1919

BECAUSE Woodville, Mississippi, was where he was born, on August 27, 1909, it is the logical place to begin an account of Lester Young's life. Located in the southwestern part of the Magnolia State, about thirty miles south of Natchez, Woodville is closer to New Orleans than its actual distance of 125 miles suggests. One of the first railroads in the United States, the West Feliciana, linked Woodville with St. Francisville, Louisiana, on the cotton shipping route to the major southern port city. At the turn of the century, Mississippi cotton workers also migrated seasonally to southern Louisiana's cane fields, further underlining the close ties between the two locales. It was said that both of Young's parents, Willis Young and Lizetta Johnson, were teachers in or near Woodville. Willis, who was also a musician and bandleader, even earned the title of professor.[1]

Louisianans had begun settling in southern Mississippi a century prior to the birth of the saxophonist. Wilkinson County, of which Woodville was the county seat, was in fact one of the state's oldest settlements; its hardwood forests and rich soil had early on attracted white slave owners, and its major cash crop, cotton, had dominated the economy for generations. Before the Civil War and for several decades after it, wealthy slave owners and their descendants controlled the politics and economic life of the region.[2]

Woodville's twelve hundred residents were obsessed with cotton. Early in the twentieth century, the boll weevil presented a formidable problem for cotton farmers, wiping out nearly the entire crop in 1908. Recovery was slow, but in the late summer of 1909, a local farmer claimed the honor of bringing the year's first bale of cotton into town for sale. Regional news and reports on the boll weevil, on drought, and on the town's first automobile filled the columns of the *Woodville Republican* that summer.[3]

Young was not exactly proud of having been born in Mississippi, considering its history of oppressive race relations. Of course, he probably did not remember anything about the place, given that he left it as an infant, but his mother must have carried with her memories of the state's tragic past. Lizetta had been born on October 3, 1888, in Woodville.[4] Her parents, William and Cornelia Johnson, were very likely farmers near that Mississippi town, which was also the birthplace of Jefferson Davis, president of the Confederacy; in any case, they do not appear to have been property owners like Willis Young's parents. Information about Lizetta's family is scant: the Young children knew very little about their mother's early life because they were taken away from her when they were quite small and did not see her again for some twenty years.[5]

Opinions of Woodville varied considerably along color lines. Whites viewed it as "the home of year-round hospitality," and according to a local tradition, it was studied by Harvard University anthropologists precisely because it "best typif[ied] and preserve[d] the traditions, customs, and culture of the antebellum South." In 1909, the center of town was "a courthouse island entirely surrounded by banks, drugstores, and merchant establishments [and] fruit stands." The *New Orleans Picayune* characterized Woodville's citizens as "good people" and idealized the countryside around it as "a scenic dream undescribable."[6]

But the romanticism of these portraits masked the racial hatred and the violence visited upon whites or Blacks whenever custom or intimidation failed. Local histories as a rule concealed the rather singular fact that in Wilkinson County, Blacks outnumbered whites two to one. White supremacy manifested itself in many ways; the month before Lester's birth, for example, the *Woodville Republican* announced that the local merry-go-round would be run for whites only on Monday afternoons and evenings. This new rule was proposed so "that the best order will prevail."[7]

Blacks in this state who insisted on equality put their lives in danger in these years and over the next several decades. The mere threat of retaliatory violence often sufficed to maintain the prevailing racial order. In Greenville, in the heart of the delta, a Black bishop ran into difficulty and had to leave the state after he appealed to the manager of the local telephone company, asking that his daughter, who had been educated at Oberlin College, be addressed as "Miss" by the local telephone operators. After a mass meeting, the white citizenry informed the bishop and his daughter "that Greenville was not a very healthful place for them to remain." The *Republican* editorialized that "this disturbance is only one of the results of the social equality practice that prevails in the North." Furthermore, it insisted, "Mississippi is no place for any negro, whether man or woman, who so far forgets himself or herself as to make the demand that the prefix by which a gentleman or lady is designated be added to their names."[8]

Local elections often provoked violence among white Mississippians, and 1909 was no exception: the national guard was called in to suppress unrest around election time, in late summer. That same summer, in Meadville, not far from Woodville but in the adjacent county, the national guard responded to the sheriff's summons to halt a riot that followed an attempted assassination of the newly elected chancery clerk, whose father had held the same office until *he* was assassinated along with others in the political violence. The son had been "badly wounded" by the same gunfire that killed his father, and then, after winning the election, was shot again one Sunday evening at his home. Such incidents in the last month of Lizetta Young's pregnancy illustrate the level of repression in the region. The lynching of Blacks represented but one facet of the violence used against anyone who defied the dictates of white supremacy and the prevailing social order.[9]

This oppressive racial supremacy influenced the life and culture not only of the Young family but of everyone in the state. It gave some whites an unfounded sense of superiority even as it sought to crush any feelings of well-being or pride among Black Mississippians. Black pride hid behind the facade of the patient, submissive sharecropper in the same way that hope, optimism, and the sheer joy of living resided in the blues, a genre often thought to harbor precisely the opposite qualities. The coping strategies of southern Blacks were expressed in song:

Got one mind for white folks to see,
'Nother for what I know is me;
He don't know . . . my mind.

Lester Young's alleged inscrutability, or more accurately, his ability to prevent outsiders from penetrating his mask, was an indication of just how well he had learned and lived the lesson that all Black southerners were taught in their earliest years. His story should help us, nearly a century on, to understand why the blues meant so much to so many African

Americans in the Deep South and later, as they migrated, in the North and West as well.[10]

In his own account of his childhood, Young glossed over his Mississippi origins to romanticize New Orleans, where he spent his early years. Willis Young wed Lizetta Teresa Johnson in Washington Parish, Louisiana, on Tuesday, December 1, 1908. The ceremony probably took place in the home of Willis's sister, Mary, and her husband, the Reverend W. W. Hunter, since the local A.M.E. church had not yet been built at that time; in any case, the Reverend Hunter performed the ceremony. We do not know for certain how Willis and Lizetta met, though the fact that both were reportedly schoolteachers suggests some professional link. They also had musical interests in common, as Lizetta sang and later in life would run a music school in New Orleans.[11]

Very little is known about Willis and Lizetta Young's relationship. It certainly lasted no more than ten years, and possibly only five or six. In naming their two eldest children, Willis Lester and Irma Cornelia, they clearly chose to honor the professor himself and Lizetta's mother, Cornelia. Rather inexplicably, despite Lester's testimony concerning his family's New Orleans residency, no written evidence exists to indicate that Willis ever lived with Lizetta in New Orleans between the time of their marriage in 1908 and their final separation around 1919. His name never appeared in the City Directory, nor did New Orleans residents of the era recall the family's presence in the city. Indeed, in the William Ransom Hogan Jazz Archive, which contains scores of interviews with people who would have known him if he had been active on the New Orleans music scene, Professor Young's name is mentioned only a few times, and then not in the context of that city.[12]

To understand Lester Young's early years and his musical development, we need to examine what few details we have about where he lived, both in New Orleans and outside it. Despite statements made by Lester and his brother and sister about the family's living in the Crescent City, other evidence suggests that the Youngs in fact resided in one of the outlying parishes and visited New Orleans only intermittently, or sojourned there for just a few years around World War I. In other words, their roots in this port city were not as deep as their roots in the southern countryside.

The saxophonist himself maintained that he and his mother, sister, and brother had lived across the river in Algiers, and rather mysteriously insisted that he did not "meet my father until [I was] ten years old. I didn't know I had one." Perhaps to assert his independence from the professor's influence, he added, "I didn't know my father was the musician" until 1919, when Willis took the children from their mother.[13] No one else in the family knew quite what Lester meant by this, unless he was implying simply that his father was on the road a great deal during his childhood. It might also mean that Willis Young did not visit the family after Lester reached the age—four or five—when he could remember such episodes.

The saxophonist's account of his New Orleans childhood had him selling newspapers and shining shoes, both typical jobs for youngsters of the day. He asserted that he would "never" steal—a rare statement for big-city boys, and one that suggests he harbored an intense moralism from an early age. He stressed, furthermore, how impressed he had been by the vitality, dynamism, and majesty of the city's music: "I loved this music so well."[14]

He recalled with some relish how involved he had become with that music, and claimed that it was this tradition, and not his father's tutelage, that was his first musical influence. He helped local bands with publicity by passing out handbills and recounted how "every time they'd start to play, anything I was doing, they['d] start playing some music—Boom! I'd run there." He knew all the band routes, so he could always find them. The power of New Orleans music was such—"this excited me"—that it set him "running behind those [band]wagons until my tongue was hanging out." At a young age, he was initiated into the second-liners, the fans who followed the bands while dancing and cavorting on the sidewalks and in the city's streets. He concluded this account of his New Orleans years by saying, "So that's about it. Then my father came, and he taken us away from the family, and all."[15] He said this happened when he was ten, meaning sometime after his birthday in late August 1919, or perhaps even in the first half of 1920.

Although Young reported that the family had lived in Algiers, across the river from the city proper, no written documentation or family tradition supports this claim. In fact, all the evidence points to several "uptown" or "back-o'-town" residences in New Orleans itself. One such address, 2235 Eighth Street (actually renamed Harmony Street in 1893), appeared on the birth certificate of Lester's younger brother, Lee, in 1914. He must have been one of the first residents to have his birth recorded on such a document.[16]

Other documentation, namely the City Directory, lists a Lizzie Young at a number of different addresses in the city's working-class districts between 1914 and 1919. All were within a mile or two of one another—1028 Bordeaux (in 1914), 517 Second Street (in 1918), 515 Third (in 1919), and 2309 Second (also in 1919)—and all but the Third Street house are still standing. These dwellings were all double shotgun houses, allowing occupancy by two families and thus affording the possibility of close relations between adjacent occupants. Front steps or porches permitted children safely to observe the street life, while private backyards provided the intimacy that families with young children also desired. But if Lester's mother was the Lizzie Young who lived in these homes, we must wonder why, for directory purposes, she did not list her husband, Willis, as living at the same address. The answer may be that the marriage began to break down around the time of or shortly after Lee's birth.[17]

It is significant that the sole Lizzie Young listed in the City Directory during this decade lived at these back-o'-town Second and Third Street addresses. (There is no Lizetta Young to be found in the directory.) Although no employment was cited for her until the 1920s, the two 1919 listings may in fact have been home and work addresses for the same person. In the early 1920s, she listed her occupation as laundress and lived at the same Third Street residence (515) as in 1919; by 1925 she had moved to 634 Felicity. In subsequent years she was listed most of the time, and then she married the barber Levi Gray in around 1926.[18]

Relatives on both sides of Lester's family lived in New Orleans, so there were plenty of people around to take care of him and for him to stay with. In 1920 his paternal cousin Austin resided with his family—his wife, Angela, and two children, Austin Junior and Lawrence—at 3509 Tonti Street, more than five miles from the back o' town. Moreover, Alice, the professor's oldest daughter from an earlier relationship and thus Lester's half sister, stayed with her mother, Martha, in a boardinghouse at 2028 Felicity Street. Cornelia Johnson, Lizetta's mother, also appears to have lived in the city on the eve of World War I.[19]

Assuming that Lizzie and Lizetta Young were one and the same person, she and her children—like most of their relations—lived uptown, in the horseshoe-shaped portion of the city, bounded on three sides by the river. None of the addresses given for Lizzie Young in the City Directory was downtown in the French Quarter, or Storyville, the district traditionally associated with jazz, where longtime inhabitants and Creoles lived. Still, the back o' town was hardly the musical sticks: in 1918, the trombonist Edward "Kid" Ory resided at 2330 First Street, just a block away from Lizzie Young's 1919 Second Street address, and Joe "King" Oliver also lived nearby, at 2714 Dryades.

It is not at all clear how long the children were in the Crescent City with their mother. All of the other places where their parents are known to have lived were outside New Orleans: Thibodaux, Willis's and Irma's birthplace; Bogalusa, in Washington Parish, and Natalbany, in Tangipahoa Parish, where Willis stayed with his sister, Mary Hunter (Lester's aunt Mamie), and her husband; and Woodville, where both Lester and his mother were born. The Mississippi hamlet was the farthest from New Orleans, and Natalbany was the closest, about fifty miles out on the Illinois Central rail line; Thibodaux was sixty miles distant on the Southern Pacific line.

The Manuscript Census does not corroborate a New Orleans or Algiers residency for the family as a whole; in fact, the 1920 census lists a girl named Irma Young living with a family at 1120 General Taylor.[20] This remarkable piece of information raises the possibility that Lester, Irma, and Lee spent time apart from one another and, at least in Irma's case, away from both parents.[21]

The couple's marriage in Washington Parish late in 1908 and Lester's birth in Woodville the following summer further suggest that New Orleans did not figure in the Youngs' lives at first. The family did not appear in the 1910 census, and, following Irma's birth in Thibodaux in 1912, it evidently took another year or two for Lizetta to move to the South's largest port city (again presuming that she and Lizzie Young were the same person). By the time of the next census, in 1920, the children (with the possible exception of Irma) were no longer in New Orleans. Indeed, in the latter year, the only Lester Young listed in the Louisiana census at all lived, inexplicably for us, in Madison County, some miles upriver from New Orleans and just across from Vicksburg, Mississippi. He was living in a Black household of three generations headed by one Henry Young, an illiterate but self-employed farmer from Mississippi who was described as his "grandfather."[22]

The Lester in question had been born in Louisiana, but it is unclear exactly who his parents were or if they were even in the same household, since the eligible candidates, Henry Young's three children, were all single adults residing with Henry and Ida, his wife, another Mississippian. Also, the boy's age was given as five, or six years younger than our

Lester would have been—raising further doubts about the identification (though this may, of course, have been simply a clerical error).

The Irma Young listing for that same year is likewise puzzling, though here again she was the only Louisianan of that name in the census. Thomas Murley, the head of the household that included this Irma, located at 1120 General Taylor Street, was a longshoreman, sixty-nine years old and literate. His wife, Mary Ellen, a washerwoman who worked at home, and three grandchildren—John Gray, age seven, Irma Young, age fifteen, and Marian Young, age fourteen—lived there with him. Again, either an incorrect age was recorded (our Irma was only seven and a half at the time) or this was a different Irma Young.[23]

Still, if we suppose for a moment that these children were indeed our Lester and Irma, we must assume that this was during an interlude before they went on the road with their father and in which they were temporarily separated from him, their mother, and one another. Irma stressed that when they left their mother's house, "we was very small," which also suggests that more than sixty years later, the details might understandably have been less than perfectly clear in her memory.[24]

During her marriage to Willis, Lizetta may well have been content to let her children spend time with their relatives while she worked, especially with her husband's touring keeping him away from home so much. And then later, when Aunt Mamie took them away, she may have simply bowed to the will of Willis Young, who was older than she and used to having his own way. No doubt she was heartbroken by the loss of them, but we have no record of how she reacted.

For his part, Lee Young, who would have been about five at the time of his parents' separation, had only a vague memory of the transition from his mother's care to his father's: "Now there is a gap between there that I have no recollection of, never have because I'm not sure if there is a gap. Because all I can ever remember is the next thing I knew, I was traveling . . . and singing and dancing."[25]

It is plausible that Willis Young left his children with relatives or foster parents until he could take them with him on the road. In Lester's case, if he was indeed the Lester listed in Madison Parish, he may have been with relatives of his father's. One specific detail indicates that both this and Thomas Murley's families would have met with the professor's approval: in both households the children attended school.

The fragmented evidence suggests that for a time Willis did rely on an extensive network of relatives, and perhaps others as well, to care for

Les, Irma, and Lee. This accords with recent research done by historians into the many and impressive systems developed by African Americans for raising children, based upon relationships with actual and fictitious "grandparents," "aunts," "uncles," and other relatives during slavery—customs that persisted for generations after emancipation. So Lester's contention that he did not know his father until he was ten may indeed have been a statement of fact. This was a condition common to other Black boys, some of whom—including Louis Armstrong and Jelly Roll Morton—never really got to know their fathers.[26]

Very likely Lester's not recalling his father's presence during his first ten years had to do with the fact that the professor's touring kept him on the road and away from his family. Then, too, until 1913, Willis Young had a family homestead in Thibodaux, Louisiana, not to mention a brother and sister in neighboring parishes. His omission from the City Directory listings for the household of "Mrs. Lizzie Young" points to the marriage's ending around the time of Lee's birth, in 1914; we will probably never know this for sure, however. Significant for our understanding of Lester is the possibility that he lived variously with his mother, with his aunt Mary Hunter and her husband, with his grandmother Martha Young, with his mother's mother, and with other relations in both the city and the country. Thus he was introduced to Black people and Black culture in all their variety in urban and rural settings in southern Louisiana.

From the life stories of Sidney Bechet, Danny Barker, Joe Darensbourg, and Kid Ory, we know that music culture along the lower Mississippi was quite fluid, flowing with the current and against it, crossing parish and state boundaries as well as breaking down barriers between races and classes. Neither Wilkinson County nor Madison Parish would have boasted anything like the number or variety of people and bands to be found in New Orleans, and of course the port city's European operas and classical singers and musicians were rarely seen in the small towns and bayou communities. But itinerants and musicians with medicine and tent shows, minstrels, vaudeville acts, and brass bands offering up the popular music of the day circulated in abundance, and these troupers inspired young and old listeners alike, causing Young and others to become lifelong devotees of Louisiana music in general and blues and jazz in particular, with all the latter two's rhythms and rhythmic surprises.[27]

Young's early musical tutelage was connected with his New Orleans years; drummers and drumming provided the bridge between his hometown and the road. The professor started Les out on drums, probably with the aim of imprinting upon him a solid musical foundation via the rhythms that were such an integral part of the performances and the culture. Irma Young reported that her older brother was "crazy" about drummers, and in one interview he himself mentioned his admiration: "Here was the onliest person that I liked, it was these drums, you dig?" By his own estimate, he acquired some proficiency on his first instrument: "And I really played them! I could play my ass off. I'm playing for a year."[28]

He quit because he got tired of them—"bein' lazy, you know." He explained, "Carryin' all them drums got to be a real grind. I decided I'd better get me a lighter instrument. That's all there was to it, man." On other occasions he remembered that he could not pack up his drums quickly enough to go with the girl of his choice after the performance: "All the other boys got little clarinet cases, trombone cases, trumpet cases, and here I am wriggling around with all this shit."[29]

He was talking about the jazz drum kit when he said that "it was too much trouble to carry the traps." Lee Young, however, recalled that his brother played the *bass* drum—"with that strap around up here." The saxophonist reminisced, reliving his drumming years one last time in the winter of 1959, making the sounds "ivey, divey, oobie, doobie. . . ." The reporter interrupted, "Like military drums," to which Young responded, "No. Everything but that." He did not reveal that he held one drumstick differently from the way it was supposed to be held.[30]

Even with the change of instruments from drums to saxophone, Willis Young gave him only a few music lessons, Lester claimed. Yet Lee insisted that it was highly unlikely that the professor would have permitted his oldest son to get by with minimal lessons; his regimen was much too strict for that. Lester preferred to give the impression that he was self-taught and that he had learned primarily from records—in other words, he sought to present himself as a reluctant pupil under his father's tutelage, as a way of asserting his individuality and denying that he had had a solid musical foundation.[31]

Although Lester's father's influence cannot be refuted, his mother must have had an impact on him, too. Yet Lester later downplayed her contribution during these years, rarely mentioning her in interviews. This is a revealing omission. It seems rather improbable, given his devotion to music, that Willis would have married someone who was not herself a singer or musician, and indeed, Lee Young remembered that his mother had a beautiful voice. Irma Young maintained that Lizetta had played the piano; in fact, the New Orleans directory for 1926 had her running the Lizetta Gray School at 1307 Magnolia—quite possibly a music school. Her singing of lullabies and hymns was in all likelihood Lester's first musical influence.[32]

So it was not the Crescent City bands but rather his family that first introduced Lester to Black music traditions—and not just his father and mother but also his father's sister, Mary Hunter, who sang in church, and others in his extended kin network. In this fashion, the boy became familiar with hymns, lullabies, and popular music and with the culture that nourished them before he was even old enough to go out into the streets to follow the bands passing through the neighborhood. From sources outside the home, he absorbed ideas about "hot" rhythms and rhythmic displacement, stop-time and breaks, call-response and blues harmony, and the vocal conception of instrumental playing. He also acquired values concerning rapport among band members, fellowship with the audience, and the profound power of music. All of these things shaped his sensibilities and determined the goals he would pursue throughout his life.

Both Young's compositions and his solos reflected the African American heritage, a heritage in which rhythm was foremost. Within European classical traditions, melody and harmony are both considered more important than rhythm, the third element of music, but in African, West Indian, and African American cultures, the order is reversed.[33]

The interlocking rhythms of Louisiana dance and brass bands gave the music a singular dynamic and emotional quality that excited and literally moved audiences, turning fans such as little Lester into secondliners running after the band, then high-stepping or dancing to the music and snaking behind the musicians to their destination. In New Orleans in particular, but in other areas as well, the music was full of rhythmic surprises—notably breaks and stop-time (a succession of breaks)—that delighted audiences. Genuine "musicianers," as Paulo "Polo" Barnes and others asserted, were "interested in making *you* play, making *you* dance." These bandsmen were said to "play with so much feeling that even a little baby in your arms would jump like that to the music."[34]

The meagerness of Young's testimony on the role drumming played in his musical education forces us to turn to other musicians' experiences for insight into not only the importance of drummers in Black American society but also the nature of their apprenticeships and, by extension, Lester's own. Experts on the bass and snare drums enjoyed considerable respect in this entertainment world. Two such percussionists, "Shadow" (bass) and Benny (snare), played with Professor Young in 1924, and Lester likely admired and learned from them. Another New Orleans drummer, Black Benny, was immortalized in autobiographies by several different musicians, who singled him out for his prowess in the bands and for his status and exploits in the nighttime resorts.[35]

New Orleans native Warren "Baby" Dodds, reviewing his own learning experiences in interviews and in his memoirs, recalled the living African heritage that influenced apprentice drummers such as Lester. Baby Dodds and his clarinetist brother Johnny both performed and recorded with King Oliver and Louis Armstrong. One of Baby Dodds's drumming teachers had placed him squarely within ancient African traditions by explaining that "the right hand was 'mammy' and the left 'daddy.'" The metaphor not only introduced familial relations but also expressed the symbioses between one rhythm and the other, between the rhythm and the melody, and finally between the musician and the audience. On this basis, the young drummer "learned how to get my two hands working differently . . . after I [had] mastered having both hands doing the same thing."[36]

It did not take long for apprentices to realize that drumming was more than simply beating. Dodds conceded that what he had learned contradicted commonplace notions: "Somebody is going to say this sounds foolish, but I would say again, 'It's music.' Even though it's out of drums, it's still music." A professional musician almost until he died, in 1959, he said, "My intention has always been to bring melody out of drums." In the same spirit, Joe René actually "tuned his bass drum to various pitches while playing dances," to match the key in which the pianist was playing.[37]

Apprentice drummers also learned social responsibilities, including the importance of pacing the bandsmen. Dodds's advice to snare drummers applied equally to all other marching-band musicians: "If you are out of step when you hit your stride, you can't half play, because you are going to be off-beat." Moreover, he said, "it's the stride that you walk in that puts you in the right beat. It's all taken from the snare drum," which "keeps everybody in time." The drummer made the band walk slowly or quickly or even run. During funeral marches, he had to maintain subtle rhythmic differences, because "he's got to break the time. . . . You don't walk as slow after you get through playing as when you're playing." Finally, the snare drummer was a leader: "Nobody called the band but the drummer. The snare drummer alone."[38]

Such rhythmic conceptions gave Young an essential foundation for his musical education. Throughout his career he would remain a master of rhythm—"fantastic," according to the late Connie Kay, a sideman of Young's in the early 1950s. This percussionist who was known for decades for his matchless precision with the Modern Jazz Quartet recalled that Lester "had perfect time. He could play anything and know where the time was."[39]

As a saxophone player, Young approached the goal of turning rhythm into melody from the opposite direction, as his up-tempo compositions and solos were always rhythmically charged. Many of the tunes for which he is best known—"Lester Leaps In" is a good example—and the climactic moments in his solos are drum patterns as much as they are melodies. His compositions often manifested an energetic and dynamic quality associated with drumming, street parades, and New Orleans band music. Such exuberance is heard in "Lester Swings," "Afternoon of a Basie-ite," "Neenah," and "Up-'n'-Adam," and is announced even in certain song titles, including "Movin' with Lester," "Lester Blows Again," "Jumpin' at Mesner's," "Jammin' with Lester," "Lester Smooths It Out," and "Pres Returns."[40]

But Young was more than a former drummer; there were other dimensions to his rich cultural heritage. The Creole legacy of southern Louisiana as well as blues and country traditions also influenced the youngster. As an adult he would say little on these topics directly, but his family, and his own statements about the importance of the blues, would nonetheless reveal a great deal. The rich New Orleans tradition, his mother's Creole background, and his own bayou or country (as distinct from urban) ties all help explain the saxophonist's complexity. Thanks to his mother's and father's origins in small towns in the countryside of Mississippi and Louisiana, respectively, he was quite familiar with the roots of the nineteenth-century Black culture that spread to the city.

The term "Creole" has a long history, over which it has carried different meanings for different people. Both whites and Blacks have claimed the word. For the former, it denotes native-born white Americans of Spanish or French ancestry; for the latter, it refers to native-born African Americans, the *gens du couleur* ("coloreds"), who were free before the Civil War, and encompasses their French heritage, their skilled positions as artisans, and their membership in a class above the slaves and freedmen but still below the status of whites. At the end of the nineteenth century, white segregationists reconstituted this three-tiered society as a two-tiered hierarchy, lumping the Creole African Americans together with all other Blacks, regardless of their social or economic class.[41]

Willis Young's family came from a region settled by Cajuns—that is, "Acadians," or French-speaking migrants from Canada, thus "Creoles" in the white sense. While Lester's paternal grandparents were undoubtedly affected by the cosmopolitan character of Lafourche Parish, which was inhabited by French, Italian, German, Cape Verdean, and American settlers, they themselves did not speak French. (Nor do we have any reason to think that Lizetta's family did, either.) Then, too, the Youngs were A.M.E. Methodists, not Catholics like most French Creoles. Nevertheless, they took over some of the customs of this latter group. Irma Young remarked, for example, that the family referred to a godfather as a "pieram," recognizable as a pronunciation of the French *parrain,* indicating that the Youngs adopted not only the singularly important custom of appointing godparents but also a variant of the actual word used for "godfather" by Francophones throughout the world. Years later the saxophonist would continue the practice by asking his manager, Charlie Carpenter, to serve as godfather to his son, Lester Junior.[42]

The cultural heritage of Lizetta Young's family is more problematic. Both Irma and Lee maintained that their mother was Creole or part Creole, and the name Lizetta is in fact an Americanized version of the French Lisette. For whatever it is worth, she was light-complexioned, as were both of her sons, and she was recalled as having very long and straight hair—not exactly typical of African American women but common enough among Creoles and, of course, among Native Americans, who made a more sizable contribution to African Americans' cultural and genetic heritage than has generally been recognized.[43]

A number of Young's fellow musicians attributed a Creole character to the saxophonist and his playing. Norwood "Pony" Poindexter, an admirer of Young's and himself a New Orleans saxophonist, described him as a Creole and a nonconformist: "Lester was a rebel in a sense that he was a Creole . . . hanging out with the black cats from uptown." For Poindexter, Creoles were synthesizers who, finding themselves unable to compete with such Black cultural heroes as Buddy Bolden and King Oliver, had reacted by creating a music that combined African American dynamism with the format of the European march. Creoles were also the innovators of Dixieland and the most successful merchandisers of African American music, Poindexter contended, until whites came along and appropriated from them the tradition that the Creoles themselves had borrowed from the African Americans.

Poindexter made the same observation as the musicologist Alan Lomax about the Crescent City's music: both noted that in the newly segregated urban milieu shared by Creoles and Blacks at the end of the nineteenth century, the Creoles had to learn the style of the Blacks—how to play "hot" and emotionally—while the Blacks had to learn to read music like their Creole counterparts. Young's tenor style, Poindexter believed, "was a mixture of the black cats' vigor and preoccupation with the blues format and his [own] Creole background of a taught respect for technique and European conception of the march form."[44]

In a similar vein, the critic Ross Russell argued that "it is this synthesis of opposing attitudes and ideologies—the profound tradition of the blues combined with the infusion of European harmony and white romanticism—that gives Lester Young's music its special appeal." The synthesis, he added, was a thorough one: "The various materials are combined in a style which has no eclectic qualities, but is fused, integrated, and intensely personal."[45]

Like Sidney Bechet and Jelly Roll Morton, Young possessed the ability to blend seemingly contrasting styles in a new and imaginative fashion. He played "sweet" (or "cool," in modern parlance), meaning ethereal and detached, as well as "hot," with rhythmic intensity, drive, and passion—and often both at the same time. The guitarist Irving Ashby, who recorded with Young in the 1940s, claimed that the saxophonist combined these two opposing qualities so well that even when he played with "fire," it was cool, something few other musicians could accomplish.[46]

Young's playing was reminiscent of that of the Creole reedmen, who generally started out on the clarinet. His sister claimed that Lester "loved clarinets." He was mainly a saxophonist, however, and yet even on this instrument he strove for a purity of tone and a "superbly fluent style of playing" recalling the music of the New Orleans Creoles. Musicians who befriended Young in the late 1920s maintained that he was then playing C-melody or alto style on tenor, but the New Orleans influence suggests that the saxophonist's tone was more directly shaped by clarinetists. His interest in the instrument was corroborated by his pianist

Sadik Hakim, who remembered Young's frequently performing on the clarinet in clubs in the late 1940s.[47]

Young's roots in New Orleans music have gone unacknowledged in the recent spate of writing by musicians and musicologists on the tenor saxophonist. He himself stressed his New Orleans heritage in his interviews, but writers have been prone to overlook that and to characterize him instead as an exemplar of Kansas City jazz.[48]

In addition to the Creole influence, the complexity of Young's music also reflected a strong country influence. It does not matter all that much precisely where in Louisiana he lived during his first decade; whenever he resided in or visited Lafourche and Tangipahoa parishes, or Woodville, Mississippi, for that matter, he would have been exposed to the origins of the music and the Black culture that blossomed in New Orleans.[49]

While he himself emphasized that he had spent his childhood in the South's largest metropolis, many among the Crescent City's population were in fact newcomers from the country. Young's "country" beliefs point to a profound southern tradition concerning the power of music, manifest in the language and music of the blues and in other forms of expression that are generally discussed under the heading of folklore. "Signs" in nature, by which seemingly ordinary things or occurrences augur what will happen to a person in the future, are a part of this African American tradition and stem from the African heritage. Likewise, storytelling and the use of falsetto, voice inflections, occasional braggadocio, dramatic pauses, and proverbs to convey opinions and to impart wisdom, specific superstitions, and other aspects of Black culture were so embedded in southern culture as a whole that they became second nature for whites as well as Blacks.[50]

Young was thus partly "country" because his people were newcomers to New Orleans, because his father's roots lay in the outlying parish communities, and because his mother came from Woodville. Lizetta was steeped in these traditions. During the ten years they spent together, mother and son were very close; as her daughter remarked, "She sure loved Lester." We can see something of the intimacy of this bond in a photograph taken of Lizetta and her firstborn when he was about two: rather than sitting in her lap, in the classic pose for photos of mother and child, Lester is perched on a chair or stool, his face on exactly the same level as his mother's (see photo insert).[51]

Young's claim of a Mississippi birth and a New Orleans childhood testifies to a dual country-city heritage at a time when mass migration to the city, industrialization, and the emergence of a new music were all occurring simultaneously. Even Algiers, where he said his family lived, was known as a center of hoodoo or vodun, the legacy of West African religions that honored and respected ancestors and spirits that has been maligned in the West as a kind of sorcery devoted to evildoing. In this neo-African belief system, adherents served the deities and revered their ancestors through drumming, offerings, song, and dance, and read signs in nature that foretold or commented upon fortune or misfortune.[52]

To cite one instance of belief in such signs: Lizetta Young was convinced that the sound of bells tolling meant that a person had just died. It did not matter if there was no belfry in the region, and the "bells" were merely "psychological," as one might say; their knell inevitably signaled the demise of someone close to whoever heard the sound. At Lester's funeral in New York City in March 1959, Lizetta told his widow and son that she had known of her firstborn's death when she heard bells ringing near her home in Los Angeles, three thousand miles from the scene of his passing. Her grandson Lester Junior recalled her description of this experience as being rather frightening to him; he was just eleven at the time.[53]

Irma Young remembered that her older brother was "*very* very" superstitious—a result, she claimed, of his particularly close relationship with their mother. Someone had tried to poison Lizetta before her marriage, Irma said, suggesting that she had angered an enemy who then sought retribution by a means not uncommon in that culture. Lester shared some of his mother's beliefs. As his sister explained, "What you call them things in New Orleans, . . . like cross the rivers, voodoo, or something? . . . Lester, being the oldest, . . . knew about that." "Crossing the rivers" was a reference to the boundary between the world of the living and the world of spirits, a profound and well-known divide in West African and Afro-Caribbean religions as well as in vodun. One of Lester's favorite nicknames for anything or anyone he liked, "Pound Cake," points back toward this heritage, as pound cake was used for conjuring in the Deep South; that he called his sax by this name in the early 1930s indicates how closely he connected it with his Louisiana roots.[54]

Young also believed in signs, which he called telegrams. In his lexicon, a bird alighting on a nearby windowsill or a butterfly resting on your hand meant that someone loved you. Moreover, he used his saxophone to call to birds and felt inordinate affection for stray animals and pets.[55] These were not simply personal idiosyncrasies peculiar to the tenor saxophonist, but aspects of something larger that he shared with millions of others, not all of whom were African Americans.

Besides suggesting Young's orientation toward a world laden with discernible meaning, these behaviors draw attention to his sensitivity and permit glimpses of what the world must have been like when wildlife and waterfowl were still abundant and people paid attention to them, observing their habits and imitating their sounds. It also helps us to understand Lester's attachment to his cats and his dogs Pimpy, Tonics, and Concert, even as it reminds us of the Black oral tradition in which animal tales played such an important role.

Young was quite familiar with Louisiana bayou folklore, which is very similar to Haitian and West Indian oral traditions, with tales of zombies and loopgarou (from the French *loupgarou*, meaning "werewolflike") figuring prominently.[56] In an area as fantastic as that encompassing southern Mississippi and lower Louisiana—where two devastating floods occurred in September 1915 and April 1922, submerging solid ground in just a few hours' time and carrying away people, wild animals, cows, chickens, and entire houses—it was not at all difficult to believe in a spirit world that dominated the material existence of the living.

As he sat on the steps of the uptown shotgun houses where Lizetta may have lived, or stood on street corners selling newspapers and shining shoes, Lester would have been exposed to another sort of oral tradition, hearing the latest gossip and local lore from frequenters of the neighborhood stores, barbershops, and saloons—the places where men gathered to converse and to tell "lies" about their heroes and their own adventures. For most youngsters—in fact, for most *people*—in the Deep South, these sites were more important than church or school or any other public venue.

Storytelling, the use of proverbs, and other oral means of instructing and imparting wisdom enriched the lives of Black Americans and most other southerners. Among African Americans in particular, proverbs, ballads, "toasts," and blues songs conveyed knowledge and feelings as effectively as, or more effectively than, speeches. Young's rather oblique slang "I feel a draft" (meaning "I'm getting bad vibes") was in some ways a continuation of this tradition. It typified one of the ways in which Black Americans hinted at an idea that was (and remains) anathema to many Americans: the notion that life in this segregated nation was a supreme tragedy rather than a progressive tale of forward and upward movement into an ever more just and democratic society.[57]

Young lived this oral tradition during his Louisiana childhood and adolescence, and his vocabulary as an adult, as we know it from interviews, reflected a country aura. Sometimes he used proverbial expressions such as "To each his own" or "Seeing is believing" or "Until death do we part." Other usages were the essence of country—as "I reckon" and "onliest"—while still others, employing the double negative ("I don't bother nobody" and "If they don't know no blues, they can't play shit"), exemplified Black English. His highly personalized jargon was laced with images of home and southern hospitality—for example, "Have another helping" was an invitation for a sideman to solo for another chorus. Young's high regard for family was evidenced by his choice of endearments for band members, as when, on one recording, he is heard yelling out, in a joyous moment, "Cousin Willie!" during the solo of the white pianist Bill Potts. Home and family ties thus provided the basic vocabulary and values for many of his cryptic expressions, though others were more generic. When one reporter asked him about Billie Holiday, for instance, he responded in pidgin English: "Many moons, no see. Still nice!" Often his words conjured up a primeval epoch far away in time and space—that "many moons [ago]" was a favorite expression of his, and in 1958 he distinguished his years with King Oliver from Louis Armstrong's stint in the 1920s by explaining that Armstrong was from "a older tribe than me."[58]

But if Young's use of slang stemmed from the Louisiana heritage, West Africans and Black southerners (and northerners) are equally well known for their love of verbal contests, their punning, their lengthy toasts and boasts, and the delight they take in the spontaneity of creative language. Young's highly developed sense of humor was remarked upon by friends no less often than were his storytelling abilities. In his hotel room and backstage before performances, he would "hold court." On long bus rides with his sidemen, he would engage in comic warfare with some passengers and keep others in stitches with his commentaries. Otherwise, he was quiet and felt uncomfortable about speaking, as some Blacks do when they are around officials or journalists or white strangers. Young also had a southerner's dislike of written contracts: the saxophonist who maintained that he had never stolen as a child had grown up in a society where a man's word was his bond, and neither was to be questioned.[59]

New Orleans urbanites seem to have been pioneers in the creative use of language, at least as far as jazz culture was concerned. Armstrong, for one, acquired a reputation for both his scat singing and his jazz slang. He popularized the terms "cats" (for "men"), "chicks" (for "women"), "gate" (for "brother" or "man"), and "alligators" (referring to denizens of the jazz world) and used all manner of greetings and sign-offs in letters, including "Redbeans and Ricely yours." Both Armstrong's letters and his conversations were liberally sprinkled with these words. Inquiries to others about the origins of this language have provoked responses such as "That's the way they talk in New Orleans."[60]

Young's attachment to the culture of his youth was also reflected in his love of the New Orleans working-class diet. We know nothing about his mother's cooking, though we can assume it was probably typical Mississippi and Louisiana fare. Even the professor, who was always proper in every way, loved the dishes known as soul food, which, though regarded highly today, were once looked down upon in some circles. For breakfast he especially liked "hoecake," a kind of biscuit whose very name suggests its down-home origins: it was a flour-and-water mixture cooked over a fire or in an oven, the humblest sort of bread. The saxophonist Buddy Tate related how early one morning, he and Young went to a Kansas City diner for breakfast. Without bothering to ask Tate what he wanted, Young informed the waitress that they would both have red beans and rice. For Young, his heritage was a badge of pride, and appropriate at any time—breakfast with an old friend being no exception.[61]

Throughout the Deep South, Black show people and bluesmen, Crescent City residents, and plantation workers in Louisiana's sugar and rice fields were Young's real teachers. As a product of these instructors, he embodied a specific southern Louisiana heritage, with all its Creole and blues traditions. Everything he said and did expressed the values he had learned about how people should live and treat one another. Behavior should always be guided by conscience, which should in turn be grounded in standard Christian doctrine—the Ten Commandments, doing unto others as you would have them do unto you, and so forth.[62]

Young also seemed to feel that music had a special power. At an early age he learned that the music promoted remarkable closeness and fraternity among band members, singers, dancers, and the listening audience; the fact that it could do that across race and class lines during a period of intense class conflict and racial segregation, migration, and urbanization gave impressive evidence of its inherent power. More than mere sounds, it was the embodiment of a living, breathing reality or history that could accommodate people of different racial and national origins.

Young admired and respected the humanity of southern Louisianans and the way their music bonded people. The music, the cuisine, the dances and parades, the good times, even the lighter moments after funerals when the mourners sauntered back into the city from the cemetery behind the bands, which jazzed the same music they had played in a more traditional fashion earlier in the day—all were an integral part of this culture. In interviews, the saxophonist sometimes claimed New Orleans as his birthplace; the city's music produced in him a sense of warmth, solidarity, and vibrancy that he memorialized with the famous standard "Way Down Yonder in New Orleans," which he recorded in 1938.[63]

Undoubtedly, the strong sense of loyalty among fellow Louisianan musicians (and loyalty to the music itself) explained why the trumpeter Thomas "Papa Mutt" Carey, who recalled walking Lee Young to school in the Crescent City, took him on as a drummer in Los Angeles in the late 1930s without even requiring him to audition. Much the same thing happened to Lee and Lester's nephew James Tolbert back in Louisiana: he was allowed to sit in with Oscar Celestin's band and others when the leaders learned he was a cousin of Boots and Sport's.[64]

While Lester does not seem to have visited New Orleans again as an adult until the late 1930s, his love for the city and its traditions was evident his entire life. For him, making music was more real than any other aspect of existence: "Seeing is believing," he said, "and hearing's a bitch—that's a sound, that's real." When his interviewer claimed, "My business is the musical thing," Young responded, "Mine is too—all the way. *Real* musical thing!"[65] The degree of warmth experienced in the music was in some ways truer and more lasting than anything he experienced in the outside world.

Similar values inform the reminiscences of other New Orleans musicians. When the Louisiana bassist "Pops" Foster recalled the different settings in which he played in that developing urban milieu, for example, he stressed the intensity of the fellowship in the bands: "We had plenty of fun together and there was music everywhere. If the rest of the world was like musicians, this would be a great world. You should see musicians backstage when one band comes to see another. Jesus, there's some noise and talk."[66] Likewise, in his reminiscence of the Black self-help society the Zulu Social Aid and Pleasure Club, Louis Armstrong fondly recalled the fraternity that existed across the different ranks of Black citizens of a cosmopolitan port city. The Zulu society was, like the music, democratic to the extreme, consisting of "coal-car drivers, bartenders, waiters, hustlers, etc.—people of all walks of life. Nobody had very much . . . but they loved each other." That the music and the fellowship both enriched the lives of the poorer urbanites to whom racism had denied the opportunities of an expanding city is indicated by Armstrong's contention that "we were poor and everything like that, but music was all around you." Moreover, "music kept you rolling." As a result of the beliefs acquired in such a milieu, Lester Young's generosity, like Armstrong's, was legendary, and he would help out friends and sidemen in need his entire life.[67]

Lester Young and the others grew up in an era when Louisiana musicians had to forge strong bonds among themselves and with their fans to protect themselves from the materialism of the business world and the racism of American society. Baby Dodds described the treatment a new band member received: "When the leader of an orchestra would hire a man, there was no jealousy in the gang. Everybody took him in as a brother, and he was treated accordingly. If a fellow came to work with anything, even a sandwich or an orange, the new man would be offered a piece of it. That's the way they were. They believed in harmony."[68]

The same spirit carried over into the music itself. In short, these musicians strove for social as well as musical harmony—or to express it yet another way, the music was the people. "If those men would happen to like you enough to pick you up, they would either make a musician out of you, or you wouldn't be any musician. In their way, they were rough, but in a way they weren't rough. Everything they told you they would make you do for your own benefit."[69]

Typically it is the competitiveness among band members and bands that is highlighted in histories of jazz, which too often fail to consider the sense of community that was so important to these musicians. This strong cooperative and fraternal spirit within a culture of rampant materialism and unfettered individualism was remarkable because it ran against the dominant ethos. Sidney Bechet understood this; he bemoaned what business had done to the music he loved. Like Young, he despised that aspect of the music industry and of leading a band. The New Orleans artists who became tragic heroes, Bechet maintained, "didn't know how to keep up with all this commercializing that was happening to the music." He added, "If it could have stayed where it started and not had to take account of . . . all that making contracts and signing options and buying and selling rights . . . it might have been different."[70]

In a statement that could have been made by Young in his last years, Bechet lamented, "In a way, all that business makes it so a man don't have anything left to give. . . . If all I've got is a contract, I've got nothing to give." Young's commitment to the humanistic values in jazz culture made him ambivalent about achieving fame and fortune—material success alone could never satisfy his needs for beauty, for individual self-expression, and for a life dedicated to music.[71]

Dedication to jazz traditions was of fundamental importance to Young in particular and to musicians and audiences in general because of the music's affective component, its ability to promote harmony and fellowship among different classes, races, sexes, and nationalities. While the greatest refinements were achieved in New Orleans and in the carnivals and festivities of the West Indian port cities, the testimony of Black musicians suggests that the music was also a profound and integrative force throughout Black America and abroad. Lester Young entered his teens just as jazz and blues mesmerized American society in the carnivals and on vaudeville stages. The second stage of his musical development began with his immersion in this milieu, as he traveled with the band conducted by his father from the spring to the late autumn of each year.

CHAPTER 3

The Professor

The Louisiana Heritage

LESTER was Willis Handy Young's most famous pupil, and the son, in turn, was very proud of his father. Willis, he said, had "studied at Tuskegee [Institute] and he knew so much. He tried to teach me *everything*." Then he paid homage to him: "I really appreciated what my father did for me." The bandleader could "play all instruments, although he liked trumpet best." As versatile as he was talented, he "taught voice, too, and kept up . . . teaching music until he died in the 1940s." Willis was, his grandchild Lucille Tolbert recalled, "just steeped in music."[1]

Lee Young added another dimension to his father's commitment to music, remembering that he "always told us that we were going to play music so that we wouldn't have to work hard like *his* father had done as a blacksmith." Moreover, the professor "didn't want his kids to be segregated." He wanted them to become musicians—"that's all he used to tell us . . . 'I don't want my daughter working in someone's kitchen [or] carrying someone's bags, being a porter, shining someone's shoes.'" The professor would have been pleased to learn just how effective that lesson was: Lee Young emphasized, "That's what I tried to do with my own son."[2]

Racism and Jim Crow were not abstractions for the professor and his family. He grew up under the legacy of Reconstruction, which, while it officially ended in Louisiana a few years after his birth around 1872, meant genuine liberties for the freedmen during his youth. They formed churches, schools, and societies and enjoyed the right to vote and other civil rights through the 1880s. In 1887, however, the professor's family witnessed what would become known as the "great strike" or "great massacre," right in their hometown of Thibodaux, Louisiana, when some thirty-odd African Americans were shot and killed during a strike of more than ten thousand sugarcane cutters in Lafourche Parish. Having been intimidated or temporarily driven away, Black Louisianans were then denied the right to vote and forced to suffer Jim Crow segregation by law in all state and local institutions.[3]

Willis Young survived these painful historical realities by leaving Thibodaux and eventually the South altogether. In the course of his lifetime, he achieved considerable success as a professional musician at a time when racist whites closed other professions to Black Americans. His remarkable influence spanned generations, including not only two nephews and the three children he had with Lizetta—Lester, Irma, and Lee—but several of his grandchildren as well; his next wife, Sarah, also played in his bands. If you lived with him, you studied music; it was as simple as that. Only his older sister, Mary Hunter ("Aunt Mamie"), who stayed with him and Sarah in the 1930s after they moved to Los Angeles, was exempted, but then, she was a church mother who sang in the Ward African Methodist Episcopal choir.[4]

His devotion to teaching both church and show-business idioms, on all instruments and voice, earned him the title he bore so proudly: "Professor." That a Black musician would be honored with such a title during the early twentieth century may strike some readers as unusual, but in fact it was not an uncommon practice at the time. For one thing, during the winter, when he was not on the road, he was a schoolteacher. His nephew the Reverend John W. Young recounted how the professor "taught school right down this bayou [Lafourche]. There are a lot of people down here—men who was deacon of my church back then; of course, they all passed now—they referred to him as Professor Young." Moreover, education was an integral part of Willis's program of uplift: "He always would say that education would become the key of social life. . . . If you didn't have it you going to be a slave."[5]

In the jazz age, the nickname Prof was given to the alto saxophonist and arranger Henry "Buster" Smith and a number of other Black bandleaders who read music, notated it, arranged, and composed—talents lacking among most musicians. The possession of such highly specialized skills was the musical equivalent of the mastery of Latin and Greek among ministers and academics. It often meant familiarity with European classical traditions or at least with light classics and the music of John Philip Sousa's Marine Band, which was quite popular at the time.[6]

For Willis Young, the term also meant something more, signaling that there was a certain profundity to everything he stood for. Even in his music lessons he taught principles of living, ethics, and the importance of individual integrity. So for Les as for all of the professor's students, music was integrated with a philosophy of life emphasizing specific Christian values such as honesty, personal responsibility, and reliability; this philosophy and the music were always connected to each other. The Youngs remained true to these ideals all their lives.

Willis Young attained the very special status of professor sometime in the early twentieth century. He came of age in the 1890s, just before African American music, in the form of ragtime, blues, and jazz, became the nation's music and won international acclaim. Of the same post–Civil War generation as the ragtime composer Scott Joplin, he found himself in a unique position to capitalize on this major change in American culture. While Young himself was not a composer and never achieved Joplin's fame or success, the two no doubt received similar musical training, at church, in school, from local teachers, and from traveling bandsmen; Young may have spent his youth, like Joplin, touring with vocal groups or bands. If we consider the musical environment in which Willis Young grew up and his approach to the music business, we can better understand the origins of jazz and the values that would later inspire Lester, Irma, and Lee as well as subsequent generations.[7]

Willis Handy, the third son of Jacob and Martha Young, was a man of mystery in some respects. His children were not only vague about the details of his early years but uncertain as to whether William or Willis was his actual given name, since he was called by, and himself used, different variations. He was known as Willie when he was a child, which must have been a bit confusing, considering that his oldest brother's name was William. (He also shared that brother's initials—W. H. for William Henry.) His stage name was Billy Young, leader of carnival and dance bands; to his acolytes, however, he was Professor Young or simply Fess. To his children and grandchildren he was Papa Young, while Sarah, the woman he married in 1919, was, of course, Mama Young.[8]

The family knew that he started out as a blacksmith and attended Tuskegee; he was often described as a "traveling man," that figure known in African American folklore as a wanderer with many identities that were to be simply accepted rather than questioned. But the professor was a traveling man with a mission, and he was never too busy to provide for the needs of the less fortunate members of his extended family. His nephew the Reverend Young recalled, "So many times after my uncle left the bayou, to get on the road to travel, he was the traveling person . . .

and once in a while, he would always, we lived on a farm, he [would] always send my daddy a box of clothes for us . . . because it was pretty rough on the farm. . . . He was the person that was on the move all the time, because he . . . had one of these shows."[9]

The written historical record yields only a few precious details of the professor's life before the 1920s. Indeed, he left only a few clues as to where he lived between 1900 and 1927. In 1900 he was listed by the Lafourche, Louisiana, census enumerator just outside of Thibodaux, on the family homestead. Apparently Willis was then taking care of his first wife, Amelia, and his mother, Martha, plus the extended family of his late brother Jacob—seven people in all.[10]

Late in November 1921, he purchased a parcel of land in Natalbany, Tangipahoa Parish, virgin land north of Lakes Maurepas and Pontchartrain. This was the first property known to have been bought by his family since 1872, and as such it indicated a period of prosperity for Willis Young. His older sister, Mary Hunter, purchased the lot next door in 1923, which suggests that the siblings were committed to living in the South in the 1920s. However, in 1927, Willis turned up in the Minneapolis City Directory—his first listing in any directory. He showed up a second time in Albuquerque, New Mexico, in 1929, and in 1930 he appeared in both the Albuquerque and Los Angeles city directories. From that point on, the West Coast city directory listed him nearly every year until his death, in 1943. The Los Angeles addresses were the only ones where Willis Young could be traced over succeeding years.[11]

Marriage and courthouse records provide a few bare facts about the professor's residences and his brides. He married for the first time in Lafourche Parish, in 1897. In 1904 he and other family members assembled at the Thibodaux courthouse, five years after his brother Jacob's death, in order to set up a tutorship for the deceased's children; the professor gave his address as Lafourche. This was in early August, a time of year when a traveling musician would very likely be out on the road somewhere, miles from home. Near Bogalusa, late in 1908, he obtained a license to marry Lizetta Teresa Johnson. He appeared again at the Thibodaux courthouse with family members in January 1911, at which time he was said to be a school principal in or near Bogalusa, a new lumber town on the Pearl River near Louisiana's border with Mississippi.[12]

The births of Lester, Irma, and Lee in—by their accounts—Woodville, Thibodaux, and New Orleans, respectively, indicate where their mother was at the time of delivery but tell us little about their father's whereabouts. At best, this information suggests that after a season of touring, he was in southern Louisiana when they were conceived—in late 1908 and late 1911 for Lester and Irma (born on August 27, 1909, and July 18, 1912), respectively; Lee's birth, on March 7, 1914, does not so easily fit the pattern of touring, because it would mean a visit to southern Louisiana in the late spring of 1913, when the professor ordinarily would have been on the road. After that, he disappears from the historical record entirely until 1919, except for one citing.[13]

Around this time he played trombone in a seven-piece band led by Arthur and Albert Verrett in Houma, Louisiana, in the bayou country south of Thibodaux, according to the trumpet player Amos White, who was also in the band. White claimed they "played up and down the bayou" at this time. His recollection of Willis Young's presence in Louisiana in 1917 seems to contradict the contention of Willis's daughter, Irma, that her father played in Texas and Mexico during World War I.[14]

However, Irma may have been correct about his Texas stint after all, as he showed up at the Pittsburg courthouse in Camp County Texas in late May 1919 to obtain a marriage license to wed the woman he would live with for the next twenty-four years; according to his children, her given name was Sarah. He also appeared in southern Louisiana in 1919 to take his children from their mother, Lizetta. Actually, Irma explained, he had his sister pick them up: "Momma was at work when she [Aunt Mamie Hunter] came and got us. She told us she was taking us down [to Natalbany] for a visit, but when we got in there Papa got us and he taken us with him wherever he was going." They spent the next decade traveling with him from spring until fall, "a week in each town," often wintering in Natalbany, where, in 1920, Willis's mother and the Hunters, his brother-in-law and sister, resided at 534 Tangipahoa Road. This is probably where Lee Young recalled the family's running a country store.[15]

The professor remained a man in motion even as he entered his sixth decade, in the 1920s. Despite his purchase of a home in Natalbany in 1921, early in 1924 he and his family spent the winter in Warren, Arkansas, where he taught music to several promising students, including Otto Jones and brothers Leonard and Clarence Phillips; he also conducted his band at local dances. Family oral traditions recounted the move to Minneapolis late in 1926, but within a year or two ("We never stayed anyplace") they were on the road again, heading west to Los Angeles, all except for Lester, who had other plans. They performed along the way, sojourning in Albuquerque for as long as a year, and in Phoenix, too, at the end of the jazz decade. Willis and Sarah would reside on Los Angeles's East Side for the remainder of their lives, sending for other members of the family and helping them to relocate and find jobs.[16]

The story of Willis Young's family life is complex and often murky. He married at least three times, and oral traditions indicated that he fathered children by yet another woman besides Lizetta. The first ceremony took place on Monday, June 7, 1897, when he wed Amelia Rhoden in Thibodaux. It is not clear what became of her—whether she died in childbirth or succumbed to disease, or whether they simply divorced. None of Willis's children knew of his first marriage.[17]

Willis Young also had two children with Martha Anderson, who kept a boardinghouse in New Orleans early in the twentieth century. How they met is unknown, as is whether they married and lived together; the professor may already have been touring by that time. Their first daughter, Alice, married Hezekiah Tolbert in the late spring of 1919 and bore five children. The second daughter, Lillian, married several years later and moved out to Los Angeles with her husband during the Depression; with the professor's help, she got a job at Gold's Furniture Store.[18]

Willis and Martha split up for reasons unknown, though we may speculate that perhaps he wanted to make a new start in life, to have a family with a new wife. Lizetta Johnson was young and striking, and she had a beautiful voice; the professor believed, like other Black southerners, that the eyes were windows to the soul, and Lizetta's eyes were particularly enchanting. He wed her in 1908, and they had three children together, a bond that would link them together long after their marriage ended.[19]

Willis Young's sense of family obligation was especially strong, and of course he passed these values on to his children, including Lester. Willis and his oldest brother, William, took on responsibility for the wife and children of their middle brother, Jacob, after his death in 1899. When Willis Young assumed charge of his three young children Lester, Irma, and Lee in 1919—no small matter for anyone, at any time—he was already in his late forties. That he did it while living on the road eight to nine months a year is even more impressive. On June 18 of that same year, Alice, his oldest daughter, had married, thus freeing the professor of his paternal responsibility toward her. But for Willis, family was a lifelong commitment: fourteen years later, after Irma's husband, Crawford Brown, was killed in an auto accident, the professor and Sarah took in his newborn grandchild, Crawford Junior ("Brownie"), along with his sister,

Martha, then about five years old. And in 1936 Willis sent to Louisiana for his Tolbert grandchildren (the offspring of Alice and Hezekiah) to come and stay with him and his wife after their mother was seriously injured in another car accident. His sister, Mary Hunter, also came to live in her brother's Los Angeles household, where three generations resided together until Irma and Lee went out on their own.[20]

After his second marriage ended, Willis wed Mattie Stella Pilgrim in Pittsburg, Texas, on Sunday, June 1, 1919. His bride must have changed her name to Sarah, because that was what she was called by everyone in the family until she died, shortly after her husband, in Los Angeles in the late winter of 1943; nor did they know her by any other name. We know a great deal more about this marriage than we do about the others because Sarah Young took over the role of mother to Willis's children, who said they had called her Momma and still spoke of her lovingly years later, even as they acknowledged that she had really been their stepmother.[21]

The professor and his new wife soon became a team, both as professional musicians and as heads of their household. She toured with him and the three children, played saxophone and banjo in the bands, sewed clothing for the personnel, and managed the troupe of singers, dancers, and comedians who constituted the show for which her husband conducted the band. She delivered Irma's first child, Martha, who was born in the late summer of 1927 in Lexington, Nebraska. When the Tolbert children, the professor's grandchildren, came to stay with them on the West Coast in 1936, she saw to it that they were cared for and involved in the band as well.[22]

As much as he relied upon Sarah's assistance, Professor Young was clearly the family patriarch, described by one of his grandchildren as "absolutely the autocrat of all times." His personality was as impressive as his musical accomplishments. He presided over the family by blending his worldly experience with wisdom and humor; he was, in fact, not only much older than Lizetta but also old enough to be Sarah's father: his third wife was born in around 1896.[23]

Only Willis's mother and his sister, Mary, known as Aunt Mamie to Lester, seemed to have the advantage of seniority over him. Otherwise, he knew more about the world than his younger spouses or most of the other people he came into contact with, and his experience, versatility, confidence, and business acumen enhanced his authority. He was prudent enough, however, to consult with his mother, wife, or older sister, knowing that such consultations were essential to the proper functioning of the household as an economic and domestic unit. Under his roof, of course, children knew their place and spoke to adults only when spoken to; after he reached the age of ten, Lester became familiar with both his father's character and his penchant for discipline.

The nature of Willis Young's music education was unknown to his family; nor does the historical record yield much on this subject. Instead, a likely scenario must be pieced together from the few facts that can be gathered about the music culture in the bayou parishes west of New Orleans in the late nineteenth and early twentieth centuries. In a few rare instances the professor's name may be found in the reminiscences of musicians in the Hogan Jazz Archive at Tulane University. Given the meager nature of the evidence, much of the portrait that follows must necessarily be subject to reinterpretation if and when new material comes to light. The research of William Russell, Alan Lomax, Rudi Blesh, Al Rose, and Karl Koenig on the evolution of ragtime, jazz, and blues in the South and in New Orleans, fortunately, is particularly rich.[24]

Willis Young's reasons for entering the music profession can be deduced from fundamental political changes that occurred in southern Louisiana, where, beginning in the 1890s, African Americans' right to vote was taken away, along with their civil rights. Jacob Young, Willis's father, enjoyed high status in the community as a blacksmith and cooper as well as a property owner; he and his wife, Martha, were stalwarts at Allen Chapel. In the aftermath of Reconstruction, however, they lost their economic security and political rights, though they did manage to hold on to their property. Lester's grandfather's skills soon became obsolete in an age of industrialism and monopoly business enterprise, even as the family's economic prosperity was threatened by the restrictions placed on certain kinds of new jobs—that is, the ones most desired by white men, those resulting from industrialization, urbanization, and the formation of cadres of office workers, managers, and commercial, highly skilled, and industrial workers. Then, too, the death of their brother Jacob, in the prime of his life, meant that Willis and his older brother William had to share responsibility for providing for Jacob's widow, two children, and mother-in-law.

The careers of Willis Young and his family illustrate how African American music, which had always been of primary importance among Black American slaves, assumed even greater significance in the lives of freedmen and in the national arena after the rise of white supremacy. The Black musical influences on a youngster growing up in Lafourche

Parish were both sacred and secular. When his parents took him to Allen Chapel, the young Willie heard Methodist sermons and songs, both features of a profoundly rich Black oral tradition. His father, Jacob, may have been prosperous enough to afford an organ or piano, and quite possibly Allen Chapel possessed one suitable for a precocious youngster. Willis probably started out as a singer in church, or as an accompanist for his sister, Mary, who sang in Methodist choirs for much of her life. He may also have traveled with his mother, Martha, in her work as missionary, providing musical accompaniment.

For church members such as the Youngs, the spirituals and hymns of Allen Chapel had an important extramusical significance as a response to bondage and a basis of group pride, a portrait of triumph over adversity. This feature distinguished Black Americans' relationship to the music from the relationship of others who sang the same religious songs. Outside the church young Willie would have had the opportunity to hear the full range of African American work songs, field cries, shouts, and hollers echoing from the sugar plantations and rice fields and during the loading and unloading of boats along Bayou Lafourche, the major transportation route until the arrival of the railroad. In Thibodaux ballads, marches, popular songs, and very likely blues as well as the music of Acadians, French, Germans, and Italians were heard by Willis Young and were a part of his music education.[25]

Black folksongs also embodied memories of what were for African Americans the most distinctive and central aspects of the nation's history: the Civil War, emancipation, and racial segregation, alongside the cruel, unremitting, unrewarded toil they endured both before and after freedom. Charged with the martial spirit of war and the exhilaration of liberation, Black American brass bands were made up of freedmen. White folk in southern towns also organized bands late in the nineteenth century, so Willis Young had access to instruments and to teachers of both secular and religious music. Whether his music instructors were white as well as African American is a matter of conjecture. In the winter of 1887, when he was in his midteens, Thibodaux boasted at least two "crack colored bands," the Excelsior and the Eureka, which "came down to participate in the [New Orleans] fireman's parade."[26]

Willis Young no doubt played in different brass bands in the bayou country. We know the names of one or two of these, but perhaps more important than those details is the fact that the style and militant spirit of the brass bands were "not of the battlefield or the church, but of the political arena," meaning that they echoed the gains of emancipation and Reconstruction. These characteristics carried over into Professor Young's determination to raise his family up by training his children to be musicians, and they carried over into Black music in general, which was a reservoir of pride, hope, and faith in a better life. This was another thing that for Lester, just as for his father, made music far more than mere music.[27]

Willis, his children claimed, attended Tuskegee Institute. His father, Jacob, may have financed his education with his two oldest sons' assisting him in his cooper/blacksmith shop and in the family garden. Members of the community may have contributed as well. Since Tuskegee included a grammar school as well as a normal school (for training elementary-grade teachers), young Willis would have entered one of the institute's first classes in his midteens, in the 1880s, during which period Tuskegee did not keep particularly good records. But then, music education at the institute consisted primarily of the singing of spirituals in the tradition of the Fisk Jubilee Singers, who, while publicizing these songs, raised funds for their institution by traveling around the nation and abroad.[28]

Unlike Fisk, however, Tuskegee was not a liberal arts college that offered music as a part of its curriculum. Tuskegee's founder, Booker T. Washington, instead advocated industrial education for Black Americans—meaning skilled trades, such as those practiced by Jacob Young. Nevertheless, Willis Young's life and career personified the Tuskegee mission, which was based upon race pride, racial uplift, thrift, and hard work. Other influences shaped him as well, of course: besides Allen Chapel, these included Lafourche's public schools and the cooper/blacksmith shops of his father and other African Americans in Thibodaux who worked in the same skilled professions.

The members of the Black electorate, composed of teachers, skilled craftsmen, and some agricultural workers, most likely supported the brass bands during the professor's childhood years, but otherwise little is known of these musicians. The existence of a colored brass band in Lafourche Parish was mentioned as early as 1877, when Willis was about five. Two years later a benefit concert was held at the Thibodaux public school for what may have been the same band. In 1886 African American musicians performed "several delightful airs in an artistic style" at the Thibodaux firemen's hall.[29]

That the professor's preferred instrument was the trumpet suggests that he may have been a bandleader for a time, since the leaders of brass bands were typically cornet players. His instrumental versatility, moreover, mirrored the demands of brass bands, which customarily dropped some of their horns in favor of strings and became dance orchestras for polite evening affairs; in fact, by 1901, string bands seem to have replaced brass bands in Thibodaux. In the string bands, the leader usually played violin, and it is worth noting that one photograph of the professor with his dance band shows him wielding a violin bow as a baton (see photo insert).[30]

The professor cut a singular figure in southern Louisiana in the early decades of the twentieth century, not because there were no other musicians around in those years—on the contrary, they abounded—but because he was one of the very oldest of the post–Civil War generation of musicians. He was not only versatile, equally able to conduct church choirs and lead instrumental bands, but also long-lived, and his influence was considerable, thanks to his longevity, his constant touring, and his residency in different parts of the nation. His career was similar to those of other professional music teachers such as Captain Walter Dyett, Major N. Clark Smith, and Zelia Breaux, who instructed generations of Black youth in high schools in the Midwest and Southwest.[31]

Unlike those music professors, however, Billy Young chose show business over teaching in high schools, which were virtually nonexistent for Blacks in the Deep South, aside from the schools associated with Black universities such as Fisk and Atlanta. Besides introducing his extended family to minstrelsy, vaudeville, jazz, and show tunes, he taught music fundamentals to numerous students, some of whom would go on to become professional musicians, among them Ben Webster, Cootie Williams, and Clarence Williams.[32]

His life in music provided a healthy income for the professor at about the same time that Black Americans such as Louisiana's John Robichaux (b. 1866) and Florida's Johnson brothers, James Weldon and James Rosamond, were emerging as accomplished musicians and entertainers who played for both white and Black audiences. Each of these men made the decision to pursue a career in music on the stage for reasons related to the rise of white racism. This was one way in which African Americans could take advantage of industrialization, the enrichment of elite white groups, and the growth of American cities—by providing entertainment for the nation's expanding urban audiences. As the professor himself emphasized, it was also a way of avoiding having to take menial jobs.

Willis Young appears to have been the only one of his father's three sons who pursued a musical career.[33]

The professor's career, furthermore, may be seen as an illustration of how the music came from the countryside into the city, and then went from city to city—from Tulsa to Minneapolis to Los Angeles and then eventually to London, Paris, and Shanghai. This is an essential part of the music's history. In addition, Willis's claimed connection with New Orleans helps us to understand why he took its name for one of his bands and also why his children loved the city so much. Bayou folksongs and music from various ethnic and national groups played an important role in the emergence of New Orleans jazz and in Black family traditions, not only of the Youngs but of the Jileses, the Humphreys, the Bechets, and countless other families. The remark made by one New Orleans musician, Willie Parker, concerning Sam Morgan's band is equally applicable to many small-town outfits that made their way to New Orleans: "They had a band before they came to the city, that's where it started, in the country."[34]

Many important African American musicians migrated to the Crescent City from the communities strung along Bayou Lafourche. Besides John Robichaux, its best-known native son, Thibodaux also produced Joe Gabriel (b. 1880), Lewis James (b. 1890), and Isaiah Robinson (b. 1892). Other small bayou towns such as Donaldsonville and Napoleonville and the countryside around them are likewise associated with singularly significant musicians, including the trumpet players Joe "King" Oliver, Oscar "Papa" Celestin, and Claiborne Williams.[35]

It is noteworthy that with the exception of Robichaux and James B. Humphrey (b. 1868), who hailed from Reserve, on the eastern bank of the Mississippi, all of these bayou musicians were younger than Willis Young, a fact that underscores his uniqueness and makes it more difficult to ascertain the source of his music training. When they migrated to the South's largest urban center, and to other cities beyond, these musicians carried with them a profound musical heritage that permeated every institution and every aspect of their lives: music was ubiquitous during work and play, indoors and out, preceding and following sermons and stump speeches, and at marriages and funerals, welding together generations of Americans.

What little has been written about Willis Young's early musical career either is inaccurate or cannot be corroborated. In 1904 he evidently played in Thibodaux's Eureka Brass Band, which is known to have performed at local fairgrounds and events—for example, the ball of the Woodmen of the World, a fraternal organization. Eureka's members that year were Lewis Farrel, Joe Banks, and Willie Young (cornets); Bud Green (clarinet); Lawrence Jiles (valve trombone); Albert Jiles Sr. (snare drum); and Clay Jiles (bass drum). The professor is also believed to have been a member of Henry "Red" Allen Sr.'s brass band in Algiers, though the person identified as him in a band photograph bears little resemblance to the Willis seen in other snapshots. The leader's son, also known as Red Allen, did maintain, however, that his father and Lester's played together in New Orleans. Finally, while family oral traditions place Willis Young at New Orleans University (called Dillard after 1937) as a professor, a search of that institution's records failed to confirm his employment there, though it may be that he taught only part-time and so went unrecorded.[36]

The achievements of the professor's contemporary John Robichaux were an indication of the heights that Black musicians could reach. A left-handed violinist, Robichaux led a dance band and sustained for decades a degree of success unmatched by anyone else of his generation. As a child, he had been raised by a white family and "given an excellent musical education." He performed with his band in the bayou town late in the nineteenth century before coming to dominate New Orleans society functions as "the most continuously active dance-band leader" of the early twentieth century, playing at "fashionable social gatherings" where composed music was the preferred choice. Robichaux's commercial success stemmed from the fact that his orchestra catered to white society dances; in fact, "most Negroes didn't care for his music," which was said to be "more classical." His men read sheet music and typically performed a one-step, a schottische, and a mazurka, then a rag, a waltz, and a quadrille, the whole sequence constituting a set—with six to eight such sets, each followed by a brief intermission, making up an evening's engagement. Robichaux's New Orleans unit featured cornet, clarinet, trombone, mandolin, guitar, bass, and drums—a lineup similar to those presented by early jazz bands such as the Creole and Original Dixieland Jazz Bands.[37]

Musicians who played to the tastes of African American audiences were less successful than Robichaux. One such was A. J. Piron, leader of a popular New Orleans unit that was of similar composition to Robichaux's but that performed more new material. Thibodaux's other bands were, according to Albert Jiles, more like Piron's. Such outfits constituted yet another model for the professor. Significantly, a great deal of their music was played by ear. In this fashion, these versatile musicians quickly learned to play a variety of songs and styles to accommodate the preferences of both small-town residents and new migrants to the city.[38]

Another local orchestra that served as a model for the professor was Joe Gabriel's, one of the leading bands in Thibodaux; Austin "Boots" Young, Willis's nephew, was a member at one time, and Willis himself may have been one, too. Its versatile character and music have been preserved in the Hogan Jazz Archives. Joe Gabriel, the leader, played violin in the dance band and switched to bass drum in the brass band. Gabriel's eight-to-ten-piece orchestra performed "any kind of music, waltzes, quadrilles, blues, [and] stock music" and rearranged commercial arrangements of popular songs—such was its individuality as a band. W. C. Handy's "St. Louis Blues" and the New Orleans specialty "High Society" were likewise in the Gabriel band's repertoire.[39]

Research by Sam Charters and others has shown that many parish musicians moved temporarily to New Orleans or else visited the city for special events, such as Mardi Gras, while maintaining their permanent residence in outlying districts. In all likelihood this was precisely what Willis Young did, as we know that Thibodaux's Eureka and Excelsior bandsmen went to the Crescent City in 1887. It was merely a few hours away by boat or train, and New Orleans musicians would put them up and see to it that they had plenty to eat. The festivity and camaraderie of it all, not to mention the tips, made the sojourn worthwhile for the parish bands, and they in turn provided newcomers to the city with familiar music from the places they had just left.[40]

Although Willis Young probably led dance bands in his early years, just like Robichaux, Piron, and Gabriel, he did not remain in Louisiana. By the 1920s he was conducting and touring with carnivals and bands on the Black vaudeville circuit, the Theater Owners Booking Association (TOBA or TOBY). African American entrepreneurs organized this circuit in 1921 and operated Black theaters in major urban centers from Kansas City and Oklahoma City to Atlanta, Philadelphia, and Baltimore. Playing these venues gave bands the opportunity to travel, to learn the music of different regions, and to meet musicians, singers, dancers, and comedians along the way.[41]

Willis may have been the first among the Youngs to take up a career in music, but he was soon followed onto the bandstand by his oldest brother's sons. Austin Young's experience was perhaps typical of the next generation of musicians after his uncle's; while he was an able student of Willis's, his approach to music was different from the professor's, and he would become known for his improvisational skills. His father, William H. Young, worked as a cooper in his youth before turning to farming around Napoleonville, where his first two sons were born in 1890 and 1898. Austin, the elder son, initially gave his occupation as butler and then laborer, but by the 1930s he was listing himself as a musician in the City Directories. We know from William Russell's interview with him that he learned to play the guitar and mandolin before taking up the string bass in around 1909. Music may not always have provided him with enough income to support his family, but it enriched his social and cultural life.[42]

Several sidemen who played with Austin Young mentioned him in the Hogan interviews. One New Orleans musician described him as "a perfect musician [who] could read anything at sight"; another admired his remarkably smooth tone on the trombone. His first professional job was in Napoleonville's Imperial Orchestra, led by John Nelson, a violinist. Subsequently he played in Earl Foster's first band, having left Sidney Desvignes's band to take the job. He joined the Verrett brothers' band and moved to nearby Houma, Louisiana, in around 1915—two years before his uncle Billy Young was said to have played in the same band. Austin switched to trombone when another band member quit. During World War I he played baritone horn in a battalion band.[43]

After his discharge from the military, Austin traveled around Louisiana and Texas before joining his younger brother, William ("Sport"), a saxophonist, in their uncle's carnival band in around 1920. They stayed with it for a year or two, and then Austin went back to playing in New Orleans and on the road. He traveled to Milwaukee with the Pettiford family's band in 1929, then returned to New Orleans for good in 1931; the Budweiser, a jitney dance hall, was one of the places where he performed regularly in the years that followed. His brother, William, played in New Orleans taxi dance halls for a number of years after leaving the professor's band, but beyond that, little is known of his career.[44]

Giving further evidence of the Young family's deep roots in New Orleans music, Austin recorded on string bass with the legendary Bunk Johnson in 1942 on William Russell's American Music label. The session was part of an effort to preserve for posterity the original New Orleans sound, which had been overshadowed by the commercial music of the swing era. It was also prompted by the New Orleans revival that was then taking place.[45]

In southern Louisiana, important differences distinguished older bands such as Professor Young's and John Robichaux's, composed of readers of music, from younger ones with their many nonreading musicians who had never had the benefit of a professor for a music teacher. These differences began to show up in the music itself by about 1910. The elders' maxim was "You'd better learn how to read," and their ranks included trumpet players, for example—"your sweet trumpet players [who] played real well in a band. . . . They really played beautiful tones, but they wouldn't make their own breaks off the melody[;] it had to be written for them." The bassist George "Pops" Foster, from Donaldsonville in the bayou country, placed Manuel Perez, Oscar Celestin, and Bunk Johnson among the "sweet" players. The "hot" trumpet players, in contrast, were those who understood the essence of jazz and "made the band swing" with their "nice peppery style"—a group that included Joe Oliver, Buddy Bolden, and Freddie Keppard.[46]

With his students, Willis Young focused on the fundamentals of music and professional behavior rather than specific genres or styles of music. Family members differed on whether he played jazz. Irma said he was clearly of the old school, meaning that he "played what was on the sheet. [He] stuck to the letter." Lester, however, averred, "My father could swing," and Martha Young agreed that her grandfather emphasized "swinging, playing with a beat."[47]

This capacity to swing, perhaps the most essential quality of jazz, could be heard in the professor's music whenever and wherever he conducted his band, whether for the show or for dances or, later, in Los Angeles, in the 1930s, for the large and devoted following of Father Divine, an extremely successful religious leader whose organization fed and sheltered thousands of urbanites from coast to coast during the Depression. In such a venue, Willis Young's band presented music that "was not of the church, really, but not necessarily of the world either." Sometimes Willis himself played piano in the "stride" style associated with Harlem pianists such as James P. Johnson and Willie "the Lion" Smith. In his last decade he listened to big bands on the radio, orchestras such as those led by Fletcher Henderson, Jimmy Lunceford, and especially Count Basie—the last partly because Lester was its star saxophonist at the time.[48]

Willis Young's versatility and depth of training enabled him not only to play any instrument the band might be lacking but also to write and arrange for all instruments and combinations of instruments. In this respect, he possessed a special genius. One New Orleans musician, Lawrence Douglas Harris, described the professor as the "most terrific guy I ever knew to do anything" with sheet music. Harris referred to him as "old man Billy Young," and recalled that he played saxophone and "a little piano."[49]

What impressed Harris most was the professor's ability to notate parts even as he saw to the details of his various music and business enterprises: Billy Young, he said, "could write an arrangement while in conversation, writing the parts before he wrote the 'cue sheet' [score], which he *might* write after he had written the parts." All the while notating, Professor Young would direct someone to "take [this] and run over to [so and so, and then would warn someone else to] watch that part in B"; Harris found it "just amazing how he could do that." While unclear on the year he played with him, Harris related how the professor's band was part of a stock company and had a name that had something to do with New Orleans.[50]

Of course, Billy Young's approach to notational music differed from the approaches of the African American bluesmen and the "hot" players in southern Louisiana, who followed an oral tradition of improvising, playing by ear and from memory; yet it was just these itinerant musicians who so profoundly influenced the improvisers, Lester among them. Pops Foster noted the blues ramblers' ubiquitous presence in southern Louisiana and the fact that they were invariably African American: "Up around [Port Barre] there were a lot of guys who played blues on guitar. All of them were colored, you never saw a white man with a guitar or a mandolin."[51]

The existence of Louisiana's anonymous bluesmen underlined the state's close ties to the delta country in the northwest part of Mississippi, where Willis's contemporary W. C. Handy and others first heard blues singers in the 1890s. "The good ones," Pops Foster remembered, "come out of the little backwoods places like the plantations and cotton fields of Mississippi and the railroads." New Orleans, meanwhile, was a haven for itinerant blueswomen. Foster claimed that in that port city, "women sang the blues and no men sang them." Armstrong, Morton, and other influential jazz musicians would later stress their fascination with these ramblers and their songs.[52]

Blues provided not only relief but also a home of sorts for a migratory people buffeted by increasing racial violence and segregation, industrialization, and urbanization and driven from the countryside by large planters and insect pests such as the boll weevil, which devastated the cotton economy and small Black-owned farms. The blues assumed a singular importance in song, music, and instrumentation by sustaining African Americans and permitting them to share their woes, their trials, their hopes, and their loss of family and loved ones, homes, and fortunes.[53]

The gospel singer Mahalia Jackson, who grew up in New Orleans and was so devout that she refused to perform anything but religious songs, understood very well how "Negroes all over the South kept those blues playing to give us relief from our burdens and to give us courage to go on and maybe get away." Red Allen Jr. maintained that the blues were important because "the feeling of the beautiful things that happen to you is in the blues[;] it's a home language." Country folk and city dwellers liked the new music equally, because "it's the language everybody understands."[54]

In the bayou country, at least one version of the blues was recalled by Oscar Celestin, who pointed out that "Froggomore Blues" was "a popular dance tune of the French people of Thibodeaux." As a youngster, Celestin, who would go on to become one of the Crescent City's most famous trumpet players, used to hear Claiborne Williams's band perform at the Donaldsonville fair and all up and down the bayou. The fact that "Froggomore Blues" was one of the band's selections suggests that blues blended with local ethnic traditions in a variety of permutations; it was not so much a repertoire of songs as an approach to music. But despite the growing popularity of the blues, "professors" such as Willis Young maintained the reading tradition, earning a livelihood and supporting their families by providing music for every occasion.

If the blues were not of great interest to Professor Young and members of his generation, they had a significant influence on the younger musicians, and on Lester Young in particular. For him as for Armstrong, Morton, and Bechet, blues shaped the very foundations of jazz by providing techniques (including special fingerings and lip and tongue movements as well as the use of bottlenecks on guitars and of various household items as mutes for brass instruments), blue notes and harmony, and a tradition of improvisation, of varying the melody and the verses endlessly and stopping only when inspiration ran out. The famous clarinetist "Big Eye" Louis Nelson DeLisle, who was credited with transforming "the coolly calculated legitimate Creole clarinet style" into a "breathing, living expressive voice," contended, "Blues is what cause the fellows to start jazzing." Like Bunk Johnson, DeLisle selected Austin Young to record several blues with him in the 1940s on William Russell's American Music label.[55]

Professor Young's involvement with the oral tradition had less to do with contemporary blues than with the tradition's roots in the church. He would conduct church choirs right up until his death, in 1943, and trained his students with all the rigor of a minister or Sunday-school teacher who was absolutely certain as to the profound truth underlying his text. He was, after all, the son of a church stalwart and an evangelist, the brother-in-law of one minister, and the uncle of another, John W. Young. As Irma Young reminisced, "Papa made us go to church. . . . People [would] say Papa should have been a preacher" because of the way he used to get up before the congregation and talk. Lee Young explained, "I would have to say he was religious. I had to go to Sunday school, eleven-o'clock service, Baptist Young People's Union [meetings], and eight-o'clock service." The professor's wives were also devout, as were his daughters from his relationship with Martha Anderson, Alice and Lillian, who performed and sang in church in Louisiana and, in the case of Lillian, after moving to Los Angeles; on the West Coast, the professor's grandchildren sang in the choir at St. Paul's Baptist Church and performed in the family band for the Peace Mission of Father Divine.[56]

Lester's preference for blues affected his playing on several levels. He liked to know the words to songs; was fond of using two contrasting "voices," high and low, in a call-and-response pattern; and often phrased and fingered the keys in such a way as to produce a talking sound. His marvelous ability to accompany singers such as Billie Holiday reflected the fact that Young, like many other musicians, thought of the human voice as a musical instrument. The aesthetic of the oral tradition reinforced the foundation of Young's very conception of instrumental music.[57]

Along with his musical talents, Willis Young possessed a remarkable business acumen. The band and the show were both his, and he dealt directly with booking agents, carnival owners, and theater managers. Clarence Phillips explained how in 1924, Billy Young "got the contract for Clark's carnival for the minstrel show. He . . . produced the show. Got his own performers and his own *band.* And he got a percentage out of the proceeds, and owned the show."[58] Billy Clark's Broadway Show "furnished everything *but* the performers and the band. It was furnished by this . . . white man that owned the [carnival] show. . . . He furnished the tent, the stage, and . . . the seating and everything."[59]

When not appearing with a specific show, Billy Young would write ahead to arrange bookings for the band, making use of contacts he had made in the course of earlier travels. Sometimes the professor and his retinue traveled by car. Occasionally his payment took the form of a house or car; in Minneapolis, Albuquerque, and Los Angeles, he and his extended family lived in large two-story homes. One of his employers, Irma Young contended, "told Papa if he would come to L.A., he would give him a car . . . and he did. He gave Papa a car and the house we lived in. Momma and Papa had a room and I had a room. A big, big house on the corner. . . . He gave it to Papa."[60]

When it came to music and money, the professor could be very persuasive. His ability to convince salesmen to provide him with musical instruments acquired the status of legend in family oral traditions. Lee Young noted that his father never had any trouble finding him instruments, even though, as a youngster, he frequently switched from one to another. James Tolbert explained, "My grandfather was the kind of guy who could go down into the music stores with no money, and the proprietor would already have told [the salesmen,] '*Do not let this man have any credit.*'" Professor Young's winning ways and silver tongue "would mesmerize them" nonetheless, and as a result, anyone who studied under him always had "a *very* good instrument."[61]

People, it seems, could not help but like this man who "*always knew exactly what to say*" even in the most trying circumstances. When asked what he liked about the professor, Clarence Phillips answered, "I'll just put it in one word: his personality. He was a kindhearted man, soft-spoken. . . . He could win you over confidentially. [But he was not] a *con* man." Lee Young recounted how when words failed him, his father might show his Masonic emblem—he was a thirty-third-degree Mason—or give the Masonic sign to request help from a train conductor who was himself a Mason, and in this way get around Jim Crow restrictions. (Although Masonic societies were strictly segregated in this era, members often viewed all other Masons as brothers and felt obliged to help them, despite racial differences.) The professor's powers of persuasion rarely let him down. Once, near Bogalusa, when his pupils needed uniforms or instruments, he walked into a gambling den and spoke to the owner, who explained to his customers that the cut from the next round would go to the professor for his school.[62]

Willis Young's charisma was such that he had a devoted following all his life, not only among his family but among musicians, show folk, and others in his retinue, such as Mr. White, the loyal gentleman who lived with the professor as late as the 1930s and whose job it was to see to it that he was driven wherever he needed to go. Mr. White "cannibalized" old touring cars, taking parts from one car or another to ensure that the professor could travel about southern California.[63]

His professional aura—or mystique, if you will—demanded a certain protocol. On entering the professor's studio, for example, visitors were expected to knock politely to announce their presence. Each of his pupils was handed a piece of sheet music "every single day"—something he had prepared especially for that student, "some new arrangement of an old song, or sometimes a completely new song." He was not only very formal but "absolutely intolerant about mistakes." An errant pupil who made "even the slightest mistake [in music needn't bother to] even try to apologize [but instead should] just go back to [his] room." After a student had his lesson, he might be tested on it at any time; moreover, under the professor's regimen, "nobody in the house could eat until everybody had their part." After dinner and chores, "everybody came together . . . and the whole family would play [their respective parts]." In the spirit of the day, Professor Young professionalized generations of musicians, teaching them that dressing properly, taking dutiful care of one's instrument, and arriving at the job on time were all integral aspects of musicianship.[64]

Of course, the professor himself dressed the part of a man who had been in show business for generations. Whenever he went out, he invariably wore a suit, shirt, tie, and hat. He never wore a coat that was not of the same material as his trousers—it "always had to be a suit." He had more than a hundred suits, and a number of silk shirts as well. Around the house, he wore "one of those fancy robes" that one associates with distinguished gentlemen. His wardrobe indicated that he enjoyed a measure of prosperity and that, in the best tradition of show business, he was of a somewhat different cut from the average person. In Los Angeles, even deep in the Depression of the 1930s, he not only visited the barber shop every day but somehow managed to get a daily shave and head massage there (he was bald).[65]

Himself a stern disciplinarian, the professor had no vices, other than his love of sweets and desserts, especially ice cream. He never swore—the closest he came was an occasional "Dadgummit!"—or drank or smoked. "Music, music, music; music, music, music, music" was the dominating passion in his life, and he instilled the values that he personified in his children and grandchildren as well as countless others. He believed, like other Black professors including Scott Joplin and W. C. Handy, that through music, African Americans could rise to the levels of prosperity they deserved and, moreover, maintain a sense of dignity in the face of continual racial assaults on their character and potential. His education of his children Lester, Irma, and Lee had to wait until the end of World War I, when they were finally old enough to accompany him on the road, but from that point on, he instilled in them the rich cultural heritage that was the legacy of the freedmen, along with specific ideas about morality, punctuality, chivalry, and decorum that embodied values held by his family in the late nineteenth century.[66]

CHAPTER 4

Big Top Blues

On the Road, 1919–1926

THE years on the road were particularly noteworthy in the history of the Young family, as this was the period when their father, a man they hardly knew, took the Young children under his tutelage. Unfortunately, we must rely almost entirely on the testimony of Lester, Irma, Lee, and the Phillips brothers in reconstructing these experiences because virtually no written data and only a few property records and photographs exist for this period. Presumably because of all the traveling the siblings did, much of the oral testimony is fragmented and anecdotal—for example, Irma's recollection that Lester used to suffer terribly from asthma and once, in Shreveport, contracted pneumonia. She remembered that their father had to send to New York to get medicine for his son's asthma.[1]

During this period, the professor assumed a significant role in combating racial stereotypes and in instilling in his charges a set of values that would facilitate their development as outstanding musicians and sustain them all their lives. For instance, Billy Young named one of his bands the Busy Bees, challenging the minstrel stereotype of the lazy Negro and claiming a work ethic with its very name. Another of his bands, the New Orleans Strutters, evoked the proud Crescent City heritage.

As late as the 1920s, blackface minstrelsy—in which entertainers, white and Black alike (but never together), blackened their faces with burnt cork, danced on stage, told jokes, and sang in what was alleged to be Negro dialect—was such a vital part of American culture and show business that it gave many bands and individuals who would play important roles in the history of jazz their start. The professor did not participate personally in the farce, only provided the music and saw to it that his children learned to perform, sing, and dance; but Billy Young's dancer-comedians wore blackface, and his stage backdrop was decorated with minstrel stereotypes, including blackface comedians seated in the traditional semicircle, dancing pickaninnies, and Negroes throwing dice. Then, too, the band and performers were African Americans working in white carnivals, and their very presence, not to mention their blackface roles, invited the kind of ridicule and humiliation from whites that were enacted on the minstrel stage (see photo insert).

Lester's, Irma's, and Lee's first memories of show business were inevitably connected with this particular tradition. Focusing on minstrelsy helps us to comprehend one way in which Lester and the rest of the Young family developed the new music and carried it to the small towns, the prairie and plains cities, and the hinterlands. Its history also clarifies the role of race in the entertainment of the nation, thereby illuminating the social and cultural contexts that are so essential to an understanding of Young's early years in show business.[2]

Long before the Young family went on the road, white men performing on stage "blacked up" to present and to mock African Americans and their culture. The institution had its beginnings in around 1840. Even before the Civil War, African Americans joined the tradition; afterward, they sometimes promised the genuine article in place of spurious imitations, and often satirized white minstrels. By the end of the nineteenth century, white and African American minstrels were offering a collection of both imitative and more authentic versions of African American song, dance, music, humor, heroes, and villains on stages and in back lots in large cities and small towns, in the United States and abroad. To show their adaptability, blackface minstrels also performed popular songs and dances from vaudeville, Tin Pan Alley, and successful shows and musicals. The proliferation and popularity of the minstrelsy tradition ensured that in this one context, African Americans could appear on the stage without violating social taboos and risking physical violence.[3]

Black minstrels toured small towns and hamlets across the nation; some of the more fortunate, such as the famous vaudeville stars Bert Williams and George Walker, drew crowds of city-dwellers in the late nineteenth and early twentieth centuries with their cornball humor, double entendres, and song and dance. Moreover, African American comedians in blackface were stock characters in shows at New York City's famous Cotton Club and in Black musicals of the 1920s. Minstrelsy also appeared in the new show-business medium of film and would shape the racial stereotypes perpetuated by Hollywood as well. In the movies' first decades, legions of white stars wore blackface at some point in their careers, from Al Jolson to Mickey Rooney, Judy Garland, Jack Benny, Bing Crosby, and John Wayne.[4]

From the vantage point of the early twenty-first century, it is difficult to appreciate the hold that minstrel stereotypes had on the American mind and on the show-business tradition that Lester Young became part of. Ridiculous though these stereotypes were to African Americans, contemporary white audiences found them sufficiently convincing that few whites at the time could even conceive of African Americans as being human and thus capable of romantic sentiments and heroic actions, much less accomplishments in song and music that were worthy of the designation "art." Count Basie drummer Jo Jones recalled that "the only way a black person . . . played the RKO or . . . Keith's . . . or the Pantages [vaudeville] circuit [was if he] put on a bandanna. . . . There had to be a cotton scene." The stereotypes included dumb, shiftless plantation characters (Sambo, Uncle Tom), overdressed urban dandies (Zip Coon), cute pickaninnies (Topsy), and sexless mammies (Dinah).[5]

Young and other musicians remembered their early experiences in such venues with a certain fondness and gratitude for the training they provided, but with clear ambivalence, too. In his first interview, in 1946, Young was reported to have regarded his carnival-minstrel days with a measure of nostalgia, but no direct quote expressing this sentiment was printed. Neither Lester nor Irma nor Lee ever recalled any specific skits, presumably because so much time had passed, but also, I suspect, because such material was often embarrassing.

The pianist and composer Mary Lou Williams maintained that her own carnival experience was "the worst life that anybody could ever [have]—oh, my goodness . . . we played some really rough places." Remembering the small jazz combos of the 1920s, she contended that "all they did was clown"; there was a lot of music, yes, but "there was [also] a lot of clowning." In much the same vein, the first recordings to introduce "jass" or "jazz" to the world, by the Original Dixieland Jazz Band (composed entirely of white musicians), featured barnyard and other unusual sounds—not exactly the type of introduction that was likely to bring dignity to the musicians or to the people who created and supported the music.[6]

While on occasion they traveled to points as far east as Baltimore, the professor and his entourage for the most part stayed in the American heartland, playing in places like Carbondale, Tulsa, and Oklahoma City. In his early years Lester Young visited countless towns in numerous states, becoming as national in his own identity (as opposed to parochial or regional) as was the music he played. In other words, during his teens he received an extensive education not only in American music but also in the geography of the United States and the psychology of white racism.[7]

Although the Youngs' precise travel routes in the early 1920s are unknown, we have, thanks to the recollections of Leonard ("Deke") and Clarence Phillips, some idea of their itinerary for 1924, when they toured with Billy Clark, and 1925, when they were with Lachman and Carson. In late 1923 and early 1924, Lester and the rest of the family wintered in Warren, Arkansas, in a large rented apartment. In around March, the professor and his family left to perform in a small road show before moving on to a larger one in April. Four musicians whom Young had befriended in Arkansas, the Phillips brothers, Otto "Pete" Jones, and Jesse "Ham" Hamilton, got the call to join them in Billy Clark's carnival. The itinerary that year included Lexington, Bowling Green, and Harlan, Kentucky; Knoxville and Chattanooga, Tennessee; and Roanoke, Virginia.[8]

Several incidents on this tour were quite troubling and seared themselves into the young troupers' consciousness. In Harlan, Leonard Phillips recalled, "the policeman had to escort us from . . . our Pullman car to the show ground . . . 'cause they didn't like Black people." The crowd called them names and groped at the female dancers; "I'll never forget that," Phillips observed, remembering the racial hostility. Somewhere in the South, young Lester smuggled a gun to one of his cousins, either Boots or Sport, who was hiding from a lynch mob. Texas was another place where white racism was particularly virulent; in fact, Lester left the band in his late teens when he learned they were heading to that state. His brother, Lee, and W. C. Handy, who had himself traveled with a minstrel troupe at the turn of the century, likewise singled out Texas for its hostile crowds, which would sometimes threaten to break up a show and thought it good sport to "riddle [the troupe's railroad] car with bullets as it sped through their town."[9]

Such incidents reminded members of the professor's entourage where they were: in Dixieland, where Blacks had no rights that whites were bound to respect. Most of the time, however, the performers and their music were welcomed, just so long as all involved conformed to the laws mandating racial segregation—which meant separation of the audiences, though "everybody would listen to the same music." Up north, they played for integrated audiences.[10]

In the fall of 1924, the teenage saxophonist accompanied his father's band to Palatka, in the heart of the Florida peninsula, where the show closed. At this point the professor probably began making arrangements for another Florida tour early in 1925. The family and other members of Willis's entourage had no time off at all: even before the show closed, they "got together a band and rehearsed [for] a vaudeville show." They immediately went on the TOBA circuit, playing the 81 Theatre, at 81 Decatur Street in Atlanta, for a week, and then performing in different vaudeville houses, traveling by train and spending a week each in Greenville, South Carolina; Pensacola, Florida; Columbus, Georgia; and Tampa, Florida. Early in 1925 in Lakeland, Florida, they joined another minstrel tent show, which traveled around the state, to De Land and Sarasota, before heading north again to Flemington, Alabama.[11]

Billy Young's cohort of fifteen—counting band members and a scaled-down show—was not really large enough for this last job, however, since a genuine minstrel troupe usually numbered about fifty entertainers. When the Phillips brothers and others left the band, it marked the end of the minstrel tour for the professor, who then enlisted new recruits in Mobile. His itinerary for the remainder of 1925 is unknown.[12]

The Phillips brothers rejoined the band in Carbondale, Illinois, in the spring of 1926, at which point the record becomes clear again. Lester played in a band conducted by his father in what was known as a "gilly" show—"a small show that travels . . . like a circus"—while his stepmother, Sarah, led a show that accompanied Lachman and Carson, a larger carnival. Lester was no doubt glad to see his friends the Phillips brothers and Pete Jones again. He learned what a gamble show business was when the gilly show failed; the professor sent his older son ahead to Sarah (who already had Irma and Lee with her) and then, along with the Phillips brothers and Jones, eventually joined them. That year, 1926, the show closed in November in El Reno, Oklahoma.[13]

We can only guess what impact the road experiences and racial incidents must have had on Lester, for he rarely spoke about the details, but obviously he was deeply affected by the race hatred he saw. In New Orleans with his mother, he was less exposed to it than he would later be on the road traveling with his father; he was also more observant and knowledgeable during his teen years. Writers and friends alike recalled his speaking out against white racists and racial discrimination, sentiments that many celebrities of his day chose not to voice. Other emotions and feelings of Young's, however, found their expression only in the music and in his loyalty to his family and friends.

Many sidemen and friends commented on Lester's sensitivity, not just to racial incidents but to a whole range of experiences. Lee Young indicated that all the Young men were this way and said they also cried easily. He maintained that his brother was "an extreme introvert . . . not out[going] at all. Very few people knew him. I'm positive of that . . . [even when he was] a youngster." Their mother, Lizetta, once remarked that Lester was shy about religion as a child. These rare recollections of Young in the first years of his life suggest that the tenderness and emotion of his playing grew out of his personality, and were qualities that lay deep inside him—or as he himself put it, "This [music] was in me, I reckon."[14]

He himself never said anything in interviews about what it had been like to leave his mother in 1919, but Irma recalled his crying for some time afterward. So far as we know, he did not see Lizetta again for at least ten years, and maybe considerably longer. We can only speculate that perhaps his rebelliousness and penchant for running away from his father were in part a result of the abrupt separation from his mother; it is pure conjecture to suggest that he may have gone to see her during the periods when he was away from the professor. Because he was, at ten, the oldest, he conceivably suffered most when the children lost what was presumably the sole parent in their life until then, and a parent who, Irma reminisced, "was crazy about *him.*" The exciting world of entertainment that he entered was thus in some ways a mixed blessing.[15]

Of course, after the professor took them away from Lizetta, Lester still had his brother and sister as well as their father and stepmother to ease the pain of the separation. He and Irma were particularly close, sharing a bed as small children until Lee was old enough to bunk with his brother. Although he himself was light-skinned, with light-colored eyes (known as "cat eyes"), Lester was not one of those Louisianans who looked down upon dark-skinned African Americans. In fact, he confided to his sister that he would prefer to have her complexion, which was a rich brown tone, and stood up for her against other children who taunted her by calling her "Blackie." The bond lasted their entire lives; in California in the early 1940s, and around 1955, when she moved to New York

City, they saw each other frequently. Years after his death, she continued to revere his memory and defend him against detractors.[16]

In a sense, when Lester went on the road, he acquired a new family—not only his father and stepmother, but the community of traveling entertainers. This was one of the more attractive features of this show-business period: the specific attachments that he formed with his family, the band members, and everyone else involved with the show. He acquired a strong sense of the identity that he would maintain all his years, becoming a trouper, which meant total dedication to show-business tradition and to life on the road.

One indication of the troupe's sense of family and community was the nicknames they all gave one another. Lee called Lester Bub, short for "Bubba" ("Brother"), commonly used for Southern boys; the saxophonist would be "Uncle Bubba" to his nieces and nephews all their lives. To his sister and Clarence Phillips, however, he was always Lester or Les, while he was known as Red to territorial musicians in the early 1930s because of the reddish tinge to his hair. Then there were Boots and Sport (Austin and William Young), Deke (Leonard Phillips), and Pete (Otto Jones), Irma's future husband. Shadow, named for the character in the act he presented, also played bass drum, and Dirty Red was a dancer and blues singer; both men's real names are long forgotten. The relationships reflected by these affectionate monikers were essential in helping Young and the others deal with the degradation of minstrelsy and the challenges of Jim Crow segregation.[17]

In the fluid popular-culture milieu of the early twentieth century, the minstrel show merged with vaudeville, the urban exponent of the stage show: "We was on a carnival," Leonard Phillips explained, "but it was more of a vaudeville show." Lee Young's recollections also stressed the flavor of variety: "They would have like, maybe ten or twelve acts, and they would put on a two- or three-hour show with intermission." A photograph from this era shows the New Orleans Strutters in front of their decorated backdrop at the 1924 state fair in Lexington, Kentucky (see photo insert).[18]

Perhaps because Lester was the oldest of the three children, Irma recalled that initially he "was the only one playin' [an instrument] in the carnival. Lester played, but Lee and I didn't. Lee worked under cork [in blackface], and . . . I tried to dance. I liked to dance." She recounted that before the show, someone would shout "Ballyhoo!" and "you get in the carnival, the music playing back there, and you sing or something." This was a teaser intended to get people's attention and draw them into the tent.

The entertainers would then come out onto the platform in front while the band performed behind the tent, out of sight, until the audience had entered and sat down; they might play, for example, "Runnin' Wild" or other songs from New York musicals by Noble Sissle and Eubie Blake. A barker would spiel to the crowd, "'There's a guy in there so funny . . . he made a mule laugh,' and all that," Deke remembered. "Then you go inside the tent, all the time the band is playing, right inside the door, they're playing until we [entertainers] get through, and then we go inside and put on the show." While the audience was taking its seats, the band might play the latest hits of the day, such as "Wang Wang Blues" and "How Come You Do Me Like You Do?"[19]

In acquiring a solid show-business education, Lester learned to tap dance, though he preferred to play rather than dance or sing. Jack Wiggins, "really a great dancer," was the children's teacher. Tap was his specialty; he always stressed the relationship between rhythm and dance and the precision of the rhythm in tap dancing. Sometimes he would stand underneath the stage to judge a dancer's artistry so that the visual aspect—the "flash" of the act, as it was known—would not interfere with his assessment of the aural element, the percussive sound of the dancer's feet.[20]

Having learned the fundamentals, Lester, and eventually Irma and Lee, performed on a variety of instruments commonly used in jazz bands, whose composition was strongly influenced by the instrumentation of brass and dance bands; violins, violas, and cellos were out of the question in this milieu. The personnel of Billy Young's New Orleans Strutters was as follows:

Trombone:	Otto "Pete" Jones
Bass horn:	Clarence Phillips
Baritone sax:	Sarah Young
Alto horn:	Jesse Hamilton
Tenor sax:	Lester Young
Trumpet:	Willis Young
Clarinet:	James Clark
Cornet:	Leonard Phillips
Snare drum:	Benny [last name unknown]
Bass drum:	"Shadow"

With five brass and three reeds, this ensemble resembled a typical swing band's brass and reed sections; it lacked only the larger bands' string bass, guitar, and piano in the rhythm section.

The Strutters company included the "show"—that is, the blackface comedians, dancers, and singers. A photograph of its members (see photo insert) pictured, from left to right in the second row:

Blackface comedian/singer:	"Dirty Red"
Dancer:	Beulah Lee Clark
Dancer:	Julia Wise
Dancer:	Irma Young
Blackface comedian/singer:	Ed Lee
Blackface comedian/singer:	Lee Young
Blackface dancer:	Unknown
Blackface dancer:	Tony ?
Blackface comedian:	Herbert?
Blackface comedian:	David Wise
Ticket seller:	George Kitchener

While no program or music survives for the Strutters' shows, we do know that the Young children opened with an act in which they sang, danced, and played; that six or so chorus girls danced to popular songs; and that blackface comedians sang, maybe danced a bit, and told jokes.

Contemporaries' programs give an idea of the character of the presentations. J. C. Rockwell's Sunny South Co., Inc., for example, offered up a blend of genuine examples of African American music and stereotypical presentations of Black dance, music, song, and humor, comprising an impressive variety of different class and cultural traditions at a peak time of mass migration of African Americans from the Deep South to urban areas in the North and Midwest. "Everybody Is Crazy over Dixieland," "'Carolina Sunshine' with interpolations," original songs by the Sunny South Quartet, banjo selections, and a "Plantation Buck and Wing Contest" evoked the old-time traditions, while "operatic selections" appealed to listeners who enjoyed European classical music. The closing numbers, "Hot Time on the Ol' Plantation" and "Mammy's Wedding Day," took the audience back to the original Dixie setting of blackface minstrelsy.[21]

The creativity of Black musicians and show people was not completely limited by stereotypical songs and skits. Some in fact realized that minstrelsy's focus on Black people gave them a marvelous opportunity to explore representations of a Black diaspora at precisely the moment when the United States was acquiring Caribbean and Pacific Island territories and European imperialists were dividing up Africa.[22]

One African American presentation in 1915, for instance, revolved around a character mistaken for the "president of Haiti"—just a few months before the United States invaded that Caribbean nation. In 1919, the famous company of African Americans Salem Tutt Whitney and J. Homer Tutt presented *Children of the Sun,* a musical whose title indicated its focus on nonwhite characters. Several African American actors dressed up as Mandarins and Japanese; others represented "the spirit of the Nile" and "a nobleman of India." The plot carried the actors "from the Swanee River to Japan, India, Persia, Thebes in Egypt and the site of ancient Ethiopia." In a full-page ad in the *Indianapolis Freeman,* members of the company were pictured wearing various national costumes, indicating that this particular production was trying to break out of the stereotypical Black mold by portraying historically ancient and noble people of color. In 1920 Whitney and Tutt presented a new show claiming jazz as an integral part of ancient Black history and culture. *Bamboula,* a "Jazzonian Operetta," was supposed to trace "the origination of Jazz back to the ancient Ethiopians." The company also boasted its own "Jazz orchestra."[23]

Professor Young's almost evangelistic championing of music as a means of uplifting a people was very much akin to Whitney and Tutt's promotion of jazz as part of a proud and ancient heritage. These showmen harbored a vision of colored people that was far more complex than the minstrel stereotypes, and their shows were an important aspect of their quest for dignity and civil rights as they challenged the parochialism of American race relations and connected African Americans' suffering to the suffering of people of color around the world.[24]

During his adolescent years, Lester benefited from daily exposure to Billy Young's teachings and show-business ideas. The professor displayed considerable creativity in featuring jazz musicians and performers in fascinating combinations. He not only presented jazz and dances such as the Charleston, the rage that began in 1923, but also helped to popularize the saxophone, a relatively new instrument in dance music in the 1920s (and one that today epitomizes this music). All of the Youngs played the saxophone (as well as several other instruments), but by 1923 it was clear that Willis and Lizetta's oldest child was a virtuoso.

Lester came along just about the time of the saxophone's peak popularity, and it is significant that he did not play another melodic instrument before he took up the sax. In the 1920s, the typical lead jazz instruments were cornet (or trumpet); trombone, and clarinet. The saxophone was actually a latecomer to jazz bands; though dating from the mid-nineteenth century, it was used primarily in military bands and only occasionally in vaudeville before World War I. Most reedmen started on the clarinet before switching over to it, because the fingering is similar, but this does not seem to have been the case with Lester. He went straight from drums to saxophone, becoming one of the multitude of Americans who played the one hundred thousand saxes made and sold in the United States between 1919 and 1925.[25]

The professor covered all the angles in introducing the sax. Sometimes, in a delightful kind of exponential of family, two different kinship units figured in the professor's presentations, the Youngs and the saxophone family: Lee on soprano; Irma and Willis on C-melody; Lester on alto; Sarah on baritone; Sport on tenor; and Boots on bass. As Lee Young recalled, "It wasn't a saxophone trio with Lester, my sister and Lee . . . all of us played saxophone. It was a saxophone band of seven." "Bugle Blues" was one of the featured compositions.[26] Likewise, ever alert to social currents, the professor freely tapped into women's-rights sentiments with publicity photos that promised women and children performing on saxophones. After the show, audiences could purchase souvenir stills of the band; if the photos were staged, and not always literally accurate, well, this was show business, after all.[27]

Lester was a daily witness to his father's business savvy and willingness to try out instruments and sounds that were foreign to the European classical tradition and new to American audiences. Once the professor learned that his children could touch the hearts and pocketbooks of audiences, he made certain to capitalize on their presence; Lester, Irma, and Lee soon became child stars on the circuit, like Judy Garland and Mickey Rooney.[28]

Contradicting his sister's contention that Lester only played an instrument, Lee Young maintained, "All three of us danced and sang," and he said they quickly became aware of their impact, exemplified by the vaudeville adage "[Never] follow a kid act or a dog act." Lee recalled, "My dad used to always say, 'Who's gonna close the show?' . . . He would say, 'We'll open it.' [Then] they could not get on stage . . . not when the kids got out there and started singing and dancing and jumping all over the place." When a child was talented, he explained, "the other acts just couldn't get on stage." And as Leonard Phillips observed of Les, Irma, and Lee, "They all was gifted."[29]

As child stars, according to Irma, they learned how to "milk" the audience, getting one ovation after another. "Lee used to do knee drops. He danced on his knees all the time . . . both of us did. We sang together and danced together. Both of us." When performing his knee drops, the youngest of the child stars would stop to pick up the coins that appreciative audience members had thrown onto the stage. Irma, for her part, gave up the alto saxophone when she discovered a convenient way to increase audience participation and contributions: "I switched to baritone because Papa used to play a lot of dances, and people at that time would put money in the bell of the horn." The larger baritone would, of course, hold more money in its bell.[30]

Young Lester's versatility as well as his precocity contributed to his ability to "milk" the audience. After drums and saxophone, Billy Young "made Lester learn to play clarinet," telling his elder son, "You must learn to play the clarinet, because the day is coming . . . when, if you cannot play clarinet . . . you will not be able to get a job." The professor emphasized flexibility: "You have to play clarinet, you have to play piccolo, you have to play flute." Under their father, said Lee, "you had to learn all of the instruments that were in the house. You . . . had to sort of fill in for anybody who may not be there to play their instrument."[31]

His friends' recollections indicate that Lester's virtuosity was apparent from the beginning. When they met in winter of 1923–24, Leonard Phillips was just mastering his scales, and while he knew some marches, he could not play any popular songs. His new friend, he said, "was way in advance of us. He could play anything he wanted to play." Lester's ear was such that "anything he'd hear, he could play." Moreover, "he was playing like he'd been playing for years. . . . He was just that far ahead of time. He was *way* ahead of time, man. He was a little boy with short pants on playin'. [People] said, 'Look at that boy! He sure can play, can't he?' "[32]

"Baby, Won't You Please Come Home?" and "Jadda" were the rage at the time, and Phillips explained that at first he himself "was just listening to them; I couldn't play them." Les, though, "was *playin'* them tunes." Indeed, both Phillips brothers and Jones practiced scales, but Les, "any time he'd practice his horn, he'd be playing some tune." And he improvised all the time: "Anything that he played, he would dress it up."[33]

On "How Come You Do Me Like You Do?," "Les . . . would go crazy." "Shoutin' Liza" was another of his specialties; "on the end of the trio, it's a pell-mell at the end . . . , man, he'd tear them up." On "Yes, Sir, That's My Baby," he would slap tongue, making a loud popping sound while playing, a novelty that delighted audiences. According to Leonard Phillips, "Everything a saxophone could be, he played." Lester not only improvised but had "his own ideas. See, he was creative . . . he had a hell of a style!" As for other influences, "there wasn't many cats out there playin' nothin' in them days. . . . They wasn't playin' nothin' he wanted to hear, because he was playin' more than they was playin'." At this time he was performing mainly on alto on stage and for his father's dance band, but on tenor in the show band for the performers.[34]

In a bit of showmanship, he would improvise on saxophone and then "turn it around like he's smoking a pipe [and] play it that way." He did this "to sell himself . . . People [would] go crazy for him playing a horn like that." As Leonard remembered it (again contradicting Irma's testimony), he combined this with his dancing abilities. The youngster "used to dance and do the Charleston and play the saxophone . . . and skate [a dance]. He used to take [the sax] and put it between his legs and play it like that." Young became thoroughly adept at presenting an act worthy of a real trouper; after all, this was in an era when "cats used to get all up on top of the piano. . . . [The] trumpet player would take his mouthpiece out and take that mute like I got and blow . . . through it." But then finally, one day, jaded by this type of clowning, Young said, "To hell with the floor show . . . just [let me] blow."[35]

We can never be certain exactly how Lester sounded in these early years, but we do know that the zest and virtuosity of his presentations amazed his colleagues. Clarence Phillips tried to explain his friend's talent: "Les was a gifted musician. You know some people just have a knack for their instruments. . . . Like music was just . . . easy for Les." Charles "Cootie" Williams, who joined the band in 1925, was unstinting in his praise for the teenager. Billy Young had a "legitimate tone," he said, but he was "nothing like Lester," who "could play all [the] different saxes"; he "was the greatest thing I'd ever heard in person."[36]

Sometimes musicians playing the same kind of instrument would "duel" with one another like the New Orleans masters, with the audience deciding the winner by its applause. In the spirit of this tradition, Lester was a saxophone champion who took on all comers. "Anyone who picked up a saxophone . . . Lester wanted some of it. . . . He really wanted to see who was the better man; it would be just like a prizefighter or wrestler." Once, when he was still underage, he sneaked into a place where his cousin Sport was performing and "just absolutely killed him" with a matchless display of virtuosity, causing his older relative considerable embarrassment. Sport wanted to punish the precocious upstart, but Sarah Young intervened, so he had to content himself with admonishing Lester, "Just remember, the same man [Willis Young] that taught you taught me!"[37]

In around 1924 the adolescent virtuoso battled Louis Jordan, another bandleader's son, in a saxophone duel in Greenville, Mississippi; once again he defeated his adversary. By the time he was fourteen or fifteen, he was teaching others to play. Clarence Phillips was the first of a number of people whom he would assist, including Ben Webster and Paul Quinichette. The professor gave the older Phillips brother a saxophone and only a few lessons. "I got most of my instruction . . . from Les," Clarence reported. "Les was playing a lot of saxophone then."[38]

To his contemporaries, Les seemed just naturally gifted, but his talent was also a result of the professor's meticulous instruction. Like other students of Black music professors, he learned many a lesson he would never forget, but one of them was especially painful. As Irma put it, her older brother "hated to read," preferring "to improvise all the time."[39]

Lester soon discovered, however, that "there was no way not to learn with my dad." At first he got around his father's requirement that every student follow the written score: having "marvelous ears," he simply accompanied his sister. Growing suspicious, the professor set a trap for his son, playing a written passage incorrectly and insisting that Lester play what was written on the blackboard just the way he had done. If his prize pupil repeated what he had heard instead of playing what was written, then the professor would know he was an utter illiterate in terms of his ability to read music.[40]

In this way Professor Young determined that his older son, the apple of his eye, had purposely deceived him. The revelation made him "so mad he hit [Lester] with his yardstick" and told him he could not come back to the band until he learned how to read. Chastened but undaunted, Lester complied—teaching himself, he claimed—but nonetheless continued to play in his former style, depending on ear and inner feelings. He never forgot the humiliation of being struck by his father and suspended from the band—"That hurt me real bad," he said. He must have been about thirteen when this happened, because Leonard

Phillips, who met Lester when he was fourteen, did not know about the incident, indicating that it occurred sometime prior to late 1923. By the time Phillips got to know him, the young saxophonist "could read pretty good, [but] he wouldn't read like his father wanted him to read."[41]

Lester made up for his deficiency with constant practice. In this respect, it is clear that his father's discipline instilled in him a strong sense of professionalism. "I don't think you ever heard a musician practice more or [more] diligently than Lester did," Lee Young contended. He would "lock himself up in his room and practice. . . . You had to *stop* him playing. All day, and records, too . . . phew!" It was probably about this time that, like Lionel Hampton, who also went from drums to a melodic instrument (vibes), Lester mastered "his scales and chords in all keys . . . so that they [were] at his fingertips—then practice, more practice and always practice." Lester also acquired from his father other values that were essential to the business of being a musician, not only discipline but punctuality, neatness in dress, and proper decorum.[42]

Young's early training in his father's band was typical of the way in which generations of jazz musicians learned their fundamentals. Looking at Lester's first years in music helps us to understand how Black cultural values, skills, and a sense of professionalism were preserved over generations. Because we usually think of churches and schools as the main training grounds for Black musicians, we may pay too little attention to family instruction, whose importance is rarely recognized except by the families themselves and by knowledgeable devotees of New Orleans music. The Heath, Jones, and Marsalis brothers are contemporary examples, but in addition to the Youngs, Eddie Durham, Roy Eldridge, Gene Ramey, Marshal Royal, Britt Woodman, and numerous others also started in family bands. The saxophonist Buddy Tate once noted, "Too many people look at Kansas City and think of Moten and Basie and that's all. . . . There were a flock of great bands out there then, not just in Kansas City but throughout Texas and Oklahoma." He emphasized that "many of them were what we called family bands, with . . . brothers and cousins and nephews." Tate's own relatives performed in two different bands. He observed, "Music was a big part of the Southwest then, and families saw to it that musical training was not only provided but pushed. You went to college [as Tate himself did] and more often than not, you studied music."[43]

As would be the case later in swing bands, a family atmosphere prevailed in these extended kinship groups. The professor's entourage, for example, included not only immediate family but cousins and their spouses, too. Moreover, others besides relatives were taken in and treated like members of the family. After Billy Young promised to give Leonard Phillips a Holden trumpet and said, "I'm going to show you how to play jazz, [how] to get on to it," Phillips was ready to go with the band, but his mother objected, saying, "You're too young to be going out in the world." Having introduced her sons to music, Mrs. Phillips was reluctant to lose them this way: "You stay," she urged them. "You play all right here. You play in the church."[44]

But Professor Young knew how to reassure nervous parents that their children would be guarded from harm and not led into a life of sin. He advised Leonard's mother, "You better let him go. Don't hold him back. . . . Let him get out that way, and hear people play and see people." To help to convince her, her son informed her that the professor "was going . . . [to] take me just like he'd take his children." Six decades later Leonard explained, "That's the way he did [it]. When the table was set, we all eat together . . . me and Pete [Jones]. Me and Pete was just in the family like his family."[45]

Cootie Williams and his older brother joined Billy Young's band in the spring of 1925, replacing the Phillips brothers, who went with Sidney De Paris's father. Worried about what might happen to his son, Williams's father had insisted that the boy's brother accompany him on the road with the Youngs. Nor were the Phillips and Williams brothers the only family groups in the professor's entourage, which at one time or another also included the Clarks (Beulah Lee, a dancer, and James, a clarinetist) and the Wises (David, a comedian, and Julia, a dancer), as well as Boots Young and his wife, Angela.[46]

Often the band and show featured former students and colleagues of the professor's. Ora Dee, one of the saxophonists pictured in a photo with Sarah, Irma, and Lee, "went to school with Papa. Papa taught her at school. She had a brother played sousaphone. Played bass. She came from someplace in Texas." Her brother Tom, the bass horn player, also "went to school under Papa." Of course, friendships developed between band members and the Young children. Irma reminisced, "I know the first pair of teddies I had, [Ora Dee] bought them for me. Women used to wear them, teddies, underwear. [Laughs.] She bought them for me."[47]

Knowing the character of potential recruits and supervising them closely were not matters to be taken lightly. In the era of TOBA, elders took precautions to protect youngsters on the road, screening candidates carefully. In the 1920s, a recruit had to be recommended by a minister, and "you had to be twenty-five years old before you drank alcohol." A new troupe member "just didn't come out and say, 'I'm eighteen, I'm eligible to drink.'" Jo Jones observed, "You didn't go into no nightclub. . . . You had a whole lot of fathers and uncles and mothers out here . . . and what was so remarkable about it, they taught us moral and civic discipline." Furthermore, Jones related, anyone who violated the rules would be blacklisted and barred from employment for a year.[48]

While Young learned much about the world in his show-business travels, he nonetheless also led a sheltered life, protected by the pious professor, who was at pains to provide a family atmosphere for his children and his other young charges. Leonard Phillips claimed that the professor taught him important things "about life," such as how to avoid "trashy women" among the fans and audience members. "Professor Young said, 'Anytime you see . . . those first women come up to the bandstand . . . you don't want them. 'Cause they do that to every band that come in town.'" These were the women Willis Young called the "dance rats," and he warned Leonard to keep his distance from them; instead, he advised, "You want to get that girl that stands way back and looks."[49]

As a result of the give and take of fatherly advice and traveling and living together, the entourage's personal and professional relationships fused, producing a society bound more tightly than one held together only by professional relationships could ever be. Such bonds protected the traveling community from the outside world. "Those carnival people were really, really together, because you go into a lot of places and the roughnecks in the cities . . . would try to destroy certain things . . . on the midway," Lee Young recalled. The cry of "Hey Rube!" coming from a carnival person would alert everyone to danger from townsfolk and outsiders. "When they hollered 'Hey Rube,' guys would jump from over the stands and drop their horns and run to the fight . . . and . . . come out swinging with everything."[50]

The professor and his wife managed to provide a measure of comfort and independence for the members of their entourage. Paradoxically, the level of comfort and style that the family and the troupers enjoyed also served to isolate them. The family's good fortune was evidenced by the fact that with Lachman and Carson, in 1925, they traveled by Pullman car, just as the more affluent swing bands such as Ellington's and Calloway's would do in the 1930s. Irma recalled, "Papa had a stateroom . . . and with a stateroom, you could cook and live there, too. The whole train. A whole car [with] berths upper and lower, so my two brothers slept together and I slept by myself. Mamma and Papa [were] down . . . in the berth, downstairs."[51]

The self-sufficiency afforded by the Pullman car meant that the family never had to seek meals or accommodations in the outside world. Like Duke Ellington and Fletcher Henderson, the Young children grew up relatively well off, and they were also insulated, to some extent, from the ravages of a racist society. When not with the carnival, the band traveled by train or in automobiles from one location to another. "Papa always had cars," Irma said. Billy Young himself did not drive, so sometimes he hired a chauffeur; trombonist Pete Jones, Irma's first husband, also did much of the driving. This measure of comfort enjoyed by Billy Young, his family, and the Black comedians and dancers who toured with them was thus additionally a means of enjoying the proverbial freedom of the road.[52]

The privileges available to Lester and his siblings, in particular, were considerable even if the professor's regimen was demanding. Willis Young adored his oldest son and purchased numerous new suits for him; he was "the apple of my daddy's eye," Lee Young contended, though both parents—like other members of their generation—were strict in disciplining the children.[53]

Papa Young "was the spare-the-rod-and-spoil-the-child" type of parent, and both of his sons were subjected to physical whippings that he inflicted with a razor strap known as "Greasy Jim." The effects were different for the two boys. Lee felt that he himself "needed" or benefited from the whippings, but he said that "Lester was the type of child that, I think if my dad had put more time in psychology [he] would[n't] ever have touched Lester, because every time he whipped Lester, Lester would run away from home."[54]

A model teenager, "Lester was never going to do anything wrong." He did not smoke, drink, or curse the whole time he was with his parents, or for several years thereafter. His strong sense of right and wrong was, he believed, sufficient to keep him on the right track; accordingly, he "would not let anyone beat on him." He always spoke to and treated the professor and Sarah with respect, and so if his father overreacted to something and struck him, as happened now and then, he felt the affront deeply. It was on such occasions that he ran away. He was not at all confrontational in this sense. Lester's isolation and privilege ended whenever he ran away from home; it was then that he developed the spirit of independence of which he was so proud—"I've been earning my own living since I was five, shining shoes, selling papers," he later boasted.[55]

Sarah Young's responsibilities included disciplining Irma—a division of labor typical of parents of that day. "Papa never whipped me, but [laughs] my stepmother would wear me out," Irma recalled. Greasy Jim was strictly for the boys; when it was Irma's turn, Mama Young would order her, " 'Go get a switch. And don't give me no *little* switch.' " She would then hit her on the legs, a common punishment for girls.[56]

Papa Young's discipline extended beyond his immediate family. Ed Lee, a singer and blackface comedian in the troupe who had the reputation of being a slick dresser and hustler, introduced Leonard Phillips to marijuana one night in the mid-1920s as they were walking along the railroad track some distance from the Pullman cars. The two musicians must have giggled uncontrollably as they returned and climbed into their respective berths, because later that night Phillips was awakened from his sleep by a "Boom! Boom! Boom!": "And we all jumped up and went up there to see what was wrong with [the comedian] and he said, 'Oh, oh'—he called Mr. Young 'Fess'—he said, 'Oh, Fess, I ain't going to smoke no more of that reefer.' And I [was] laughing so, Mr. Young looked at me and he didn't say anything."[57] The next morning, however, Professor Young invited Phillips out for a private chat: " 'Deke, come on let's take a walk.' " He spoke kindly to his young charge, informing him that he knew why he had been acting strangely the night before. Phillips reported his words: " 'Now don't you never do that no more. I'm going to give you this chance. But if you do it anymore, I'm going to send you home. . . . What would your mother think if [she knew] you was out there smoking that stuff?' " Then he added, " 'You got no business hanging out with [Ed Lee]. . . . [He] ain't your type.' " Phillips, who was about nineteen or twenty at the time, heeded the professor's advice.[58]

The patriarchy that Lester worked under would have been similar even if his employer had not also been his father—as witness the troupe led by the famous dancer Bill "Bojangles" Robinson. The *Kansas City Call* praised Robinson's company and his leadership for the fact that "in the dressing rooms and wings [there is] none of the vulgarity and profanity that usually characterizes stage shows." Here again, the company was modeled after a family: "Robinson is called and looked upon as 'father' of the troupe" and had "signed a paper promising the parents to take good care of their girls." Moreover, "all of the troupers adore Bojangles [and] look upon him not as boss, but as 'father.' " This held true regardless of the vaudevillians' age: "Even some of the oldest men in the troupe speak of Bojangles as 'father.'" Robinson, Young, and other patriarchs created a familial atmosphere in which youngsters and older troupers alike could focus on their craft and their professional roles without the distractions or temptations of the outside world.[59]

The values and discipline that Lester Young acquired in this milieu take on new meaning when we consider how much he must have chafed under these restraints. The road appealed to him and to other youngsters like him who sought to be grown up and independent, to follow the bands that promised them so much, to enjoy friends of their own choosing, and to see more of the world. Whenever this well-protected son of a bandleader ran away, he was testing his wings and learning about life; when the going got tough or homesickness set in, he returned to his family.[60]

During these years on the road, the young saxophonist developed close relationships with his father, stepmother, siblings, and cousins. Despite his later reputation as a carefree bohemian and hipster, his concern for his parents and family was always apparent. His father and Sarah were a model couple for him, loving and devoted. He remained with them until he was in his late teens, despite receiving attractive offers to join other bands and despite the professor's discipline. He kept in touch with them after he left, and visited them on occasion. Even years later in Los Angeles, his respect for them remained such that once he actually punched his good friend Le Roy "Snake" Whyte for cursing within earshot of Willis, Sarah, and Aunt Mamie. Then, too, the only time he is known to have missed a gig was when he took Sarah to the hospital.[61]

Lester and his close friends the Phillips brothers and Pete Jones finally escaped the minstrel tradition when the Young band became a dance band in 1927, but eventually they realized that the professor's travel plans did not coincide with their desires. Billy Young was intending to go down South—possibly to spend some time with his wife's relatives—but Lester wanted to avoid Jim Crow, so he left the band in Salina, Kansas. Leonard Phillips and Pete Jones followed his example the next day, complaining that Professor Young treated them like boys.[62]

Yet for Young and other musicians, minstrel and family traditions would leave a lasting mark, one that would long outlive both the family companies and the institution of minstrelsy. These troupers had established a network of friends and acquaintances everywhere they had toured, and furthermore, they would continue to rely on the contacts they had made in their earlier travels to find new jobs after they went out on their own. The honking noise Young often made in his solos reflected the humor of jazz's roots in minstrelsy and the TOBA circuit, and the way he held his horn up or out and to the side stemmed from the floor-showing he saw and did as a youngster. Similarly, his wearing of "masks"—poker-faced at some times, smiling and friendly at others—his "put-ons," his exclusive use of jive talk, and his mannerisms and affectations both onstage and off all had their roots in the show-business tradition that had been such an integral part of his family's history.[63]

Lester's well-known tolerance of other people's eccentricities and personal foibles—his philosophy of "live and let live"—was characteristic of old-time show business, and perhaps especially of carnivals and circuses, whose personnel were famous for accepting individual differences. Young's intense dislike of Jim Crow and racial prejudice was probably based as much on memories of the humiliations of blackface minstrelsy as on injustices experienced directly, either by the family in Louisiana or by Lester himself in his travels.[64]

In touring carnivals, Lester Young was introduced to the complexities of the nation and the varieties of its music culture. He mastered an entire battery of saxophones and reeds before taking them into dance bands and performing on them at parties and elite social affairs. In his travels, he saw some of the "greats"—Bill Robinson, Ida Cox, and others—and became acquainted with popular-culture traditions emanating from New York's Tin Pan Alley and from Broadway as well as off-Broadway shows. He also heard some of the nation's most creative performers playing those new instruments the saxophone and xylophone, which would assume singular importance in the swing era after first being introduced in these earlier milieus.[65]

Minstrelsy not only introduced him to new sounds and instruments, but also provided invaluable training for him and innumerable other musicians. Lester Young learned from the minstrel tradition in its last years, just before the era of record players, radios, and jukeboxes, whose increasing popularity in and domination of American culture were more or less contemporaneous with the virtual disappearance of the old-time minstrel stage show in the 1930s. While it continued in new arenas—in musicals and films depicting the "good old days," for example—minstrelsy had by then lost its connection to jazz and was associated primarily with older songs thought to be synonymous with an idealized version of Negro contentedness and southern life.[66]

Still, the minstrel bands' early links with jazz ensured that a comic dimension would always be found somewhere in the jazz tradition—a fact that helps explain not only Lester Young's subtle humor, but also the more extroverted antics of musicians such as Louis Armstrong and Dizzy Gillespie. Buck Clayton emphasized Young's talent for cracking people up with the witty remarks he made during rehearsals and in private. The music's association with minstrelsy, and even the stereotypical roles accorded Blacks in the United States, taught many musicians never to take themselves too seriously and always to be ready to poke fun at other performers, the audience, and themselves.

Both Young's sense of humor and his witty statements must be seen as a part of the show-business tradition in which he was raised. Even a composer as dignified as Duke Ellington understood the full effects of this tradition: during one radio interview, he contended that Europeans regarded jazz too seriously, while Americans, plagued by the minstrel heritage, considered the music to be "too lowbrow." It was a difficult task to straddle these vastly different kinds of reception, but as Ellington maintained, "You have to have a good sense of humor before you're a really great jazz musician."[67]

For Young, this early phase of jazz's history also had other long-lived effects. Beyond actual family ties, quasi-familial connections promoted harmony and fellowship among musicians in the territorial bands, in Basie's outfit, and in Young's own combos. Many such relationships lasted for a lifetime. In some cases the solidarity was a result of playing together as teenagers, of course, but more often it grew from and was deepened by sharing a life of adventure and hardship on the road. That life could be particularly trying for Black musicians forced to confront hard-core racism in the larger society or in the entertainment industry itself. Such encounters served to strengthen their bonds with one another and to convince them of the basically unjust and perverse nature of white racism.

Lester Young's beginnings in minstrel bands serve to illustrate the fact that jazz's origins cannot be separated from other aspects of African American or American culture. Black American culture is integral to the American culture, not separate from or marginal to it, and lies at the heart of many aspects of entertainment, including minstrel songs, dances, humor, ragtime, jazz, swing, and rock and roll. It is this centrality of Black culture that accounts for the presence of jazz in so many cities and towns at such an early date. It also explains why Young's playing anticipated so many later developments in popular music—why, in other words, one can hear in his playing the seeds of bop, cool, and rock and roll.[68]

Lester Young would eventually become internationally famous, but he got his start in a tradition that was much less well known, supported by anonymous musicians and fans who were engaged in creating the very essence of Black American music culture. The singer-bandleader Cab Calloway made an important point concerning an unrecognized aspect of the music when he noted that the best-known jazz figures were not in fact the primary purveyors of the music to the public. In a statement similar to Buddy Tate's lament that "too many people . . . think of Moten and Basie and that's all," Calloway observed, "You hear about the Duke Ellingtons and the Louis Armstrongs, the Jimmy Luncefords and the Fletcher Hendersons, but people sometimes forget that jazz was built on the backs of the ordinary ones—ordinary musicians from down South who carried the music to the corners of the country, to little speakeasies in little towns where they played honky-tonk music for five dollars a night. Or less . . . [or] for drinks, and the sheer love of it."[69] It was these struggling anonymous musicians, he said, who should be credited with disseminating the music: "That was the way jazz spread in America, not through the big concert halls, not through the big fancy clubs like the Cotton Club . . . but through small cafés and gambling houses and speakeasies."[70]

We can conclude from Calloway's remarks that close analysis of lesser-known bands—the Youngs are a good example—and of the early years of musicians such as Lester Young should prove as fruitful for the history of jazz as exhaustive study of the individual stars and name bands after they became famous. African Americans in particular have always been quite conscious of the fact that fame is too often a hit-or-miss affair, and that bands every bit as good as those in the spotlight have frequently remained in the shadows. The *Kansas City Call* confirmed in 1939 that "throughout the country, playing in smaller aggregations of little or no importance are musicians . . . who have not only had the schooling but have had [the] experience [to] merit their ranking alongside the Goodmans, Armstrongs, etc. Unfortunately, they have not received the so-called 'break.'"[71]

Focusing on the anonymous minstrel and family bands, and the early experiences of musicians, gives us a better idea of just how widespread or popular jazz was, and why: as staple fare in numerous families and households, it had a life of its own—one relatively independent of the fluctuations in commercial music circles—for at least some period of time in each generation. Young's artistry developed in relatively humble but historically important circumstances before he, his friends, and his father entered the dance halls and ballrooms of the jazz era.

CHAPTER 5

Jump Lester Jump

Winter Homes, 1919–1929

WHEN Lester Young and his family weren't on the road touring, they spent their winters in Natalbany, Louisiana, where Willis and his extended family owned property, and at least one other southern town. Lester's whereabouts during the off-season were important for his formal education and his musical development, because the professor would "winter somewhere every winter." In late 1923 and early 1924, the fourteen-year-old saxophonist stayed with his father and immediate family in Warren, Arkansas, where he met the Phillips brothers and Otto "Pete" Jones, who would become his lifelong friends. Other winters the family visited with the professor's mother, Martha Young, in Natalbany and listened to her sing and tell stories about her missionary work. Southern Louisiana was also "where Lester and them went to school."[1] Not far from the Natalbany home was the Napoleonville farm where Les's uncle William worked and provided for his second family—a new wife, a daughter, and twin boys.[2]

Late in 1926, the Youngs would settle in Minneapolis. The 1920s were a decade of development and transition for Lester, and the move from the Deep South to Minnesota marked significant changes: from playing for blackface performers to entertaining dancers in exclusive hotel ballrooms, and from the Dixie of legislated racial segregation, where Blacks were a majority in some counties, to this northern state where racism was not based in law, and African American families were few, both within and outside the city. The seasonal touring and the northward migration enriched Lester's music education even as they broadened his perspective on the world; assuming a pivotal role in disseminating jazz during his teens and early adulthood, he laid the foundation for the status he would later attain as a premier tenor saxophonist.

Although he remarked in one interview that the family went to Minneapolis after leaving New Orleans, it was actually more complicated than that. In the interim, the Youngs maintained their roots in the South, with the professor's purchasing a house in Tangipahoa Parish, as we have noted, late in 1921. This family tradition of owning one's own home continued with Lester, who bought at least two houses in Los Angeles and New York in his lifetime.[3]

In 1923, after the death of her husband, Willis's sister, Mary Hunter ("Aunt Mamie"), bought a house next door to the professor and his wife, whose own home ownership indicated their prosperity in the aftermath of World War I. It is likely that they settled in southern Louisiana because Willis and Mary's mother was there, and because the region offered economic opportunities for the professor.[4]

The family's Tangipahoa residency in the early 1920s was recalled only vaguely by Lee Young. Their grandmother "was an evangelist. . . . I just remember her—I think maybe I saw her once or twice, in Natalbany. . . . My auntie and my uncle and my grandmother and grandfather lived there. . . . They lived on a farm."[5] He seems to have been wrong about his grandfather Jacob, who died at the turn of the century, but the 1920 census corroborates the remainder of his recollections, listing his grandmother Martha, his aunt Mary and her husband, and a Texas visitor in the house on Natalbany Road.[6]

As a youngster, Les was adored by the childless Aunt Mamie, who was referred to so often by the familial that one almost forgets her given name, Mary Elizabeth. She was also close to his father and lived with him from time to time. Lester's later use of the name Mary in relating anecdotes about various girlfriends is noteworthy, but even more interesting is the fact that his second and third wives were both named that—an indication, however unconscious, of how much his aunt Mamie and her Christian name meant to him.[7]

Natalbany was probably the first place where the professor, his new wife, and his children settled. Like countless other rural communities of less than twenty-five hundred inhabitants, this small town was hardly even a whistle stop and was not included in published census statistics. It was located just west of the Illinois Central railroad route and about ten miles north of Hammond, a town of 1,279 Blacks out of nearly four thousand total residents in 1920.[8] Amite, the Tangipahoa Parish seat, lay about twelve miles to the north, and New Orleans was about eighty miles distant, south of Lake Ponchartrain. Baton Rouge was thirty miles west, and Bogalusa about seventy miles northeast—familiar territory to the professor, who had once taught there.

For Lester and his family, wintering in the Louisiana back country in the early 1920s meant being close to rural African American traditions. Nearly one third (28 percent) of the parish's population of thirty-one thousand was Black, as were exactly one third of Hammond's residents. The Natalbany and Tangipahoa river valleys were poor compared to the Louisiana sugar parishes, comprising many small farms instead of a few large plantations. A rustic aura pervaded the settlements of Tangipahoa, while Lafourche had a distinctly urban and industrial character. Most Tangipahoa residents were native-born, though a group of Italian immigrants moved into the parish and were quite successful in raising strawberries.[9]

The Youngs' property-holding status suggests that local Blacks were relatively well off in Tangipahoa. Many owned their own farms: in 1920, out of nearly two thousand (1,980) farms in the parish, 239 were owned by Black (and other nonwhite) proprietors, more than the combined total of Ascension's, Assumption's, and Lafourche's African American property owners. Farmers grew cereals, nuts, and most especially sweet potatoes and strawberries. Other parish residents worked in the lumber and canning industries.[10]

The Natalbany Lumber Company dominated the area's economy; headquartered in Hammond, it employed fully 90 percent of the workers in the region. It was in response to the needs of its employees, expressed by some seventy-seven parents, many of them African Americans, that the company constructed (and furnished) a school in about 1911. That first year, sixty-six Black children attended. The Tangipahoa Parish Colored Training School was built at about the same time. These two institutions offered potential employment for Willis Young and an education of sorts for his children during the winter months when school was in session.[11]

Leonard Phillips pointed out that the professor "had degrees to teach school, too. He taught [Lester, Irma, and Lee] until they went to high school. . . . He started them off in school. Every day they had to go to class with him." Every morning he would announce to his children, "All right, come on, it's school time."[12] His elder son later said that during his early teens, his education had depended entirely upon his father, of whom he remarked, "He tried to teach me *everything.*" Lester's formal education, like that of many Black southerners in the early twentieth century, was limited; he himself said, "I got to the third or fourth grade at school." Unfortunately, we have no records documenting his attendance anywhere.[13]

Tangipahoa school records of the 1920s and Young family oral traditions raise a few points that are worth considering before we examine Lester's brief academic life. Willis Young, educated two generations earlier during a period of optimism, must have been sorely disappointed by the deteriorating racial and political situation in Louisiana just at the time when his youngsters were growing up. This was undoubtedly part of the reason for his educating them himself and for his working so hard to train them as professional musicians. Tangipahoa's schools offered African Americans very little in the way of serious education in this era.

The school year of about three months coincided with the professor's wintering in Natalbany, making teaching a perfectly practical option for him. Conversely, considering the low salary paid to Black teachers, it is understandable that he should have sought to augment his income through touring. Like most other communities in the South, where racial segregation was the law of the land, Tangipahoa provided its Black schoolteachers and pupils with the barest essentials at best. Whereas white parish schoolteachers earned $99.61 (men) or $49.98 (women) per month, African American teachers were paid only $31.43 (men and women). Compounding the discrepancy was the fact that the school year lasted seven months for whites but only three for Blacks.[14]

Nor did Black schoolchildren's education compare to whites' in quality: the average yearly expenditure for a white child was nearly twice ($1.47) that for a Black one ($0.79). The situation was much the same at the local Colored Training School. It must have been particularly painful for Willis Young to learn that of his 1922 property tax—$16.38 on an assessed value of $550.00—the largest single amount, $4.40, went to the school budget.[15]

Having (we presume) attended school in New Orleans when they lived there, the Young children must have been struck by the overall poor quality of education in Tangipahoa. In Louisiana, the state with the nation's highest illiteracy rate at the time, the differences would have been especially pronounced between the schools in one of the region's largest and most cosmopolitan cities and those in a rural, relatively newly settled parish. Nonetheless, illiteracy rates of Blacks in Tangipahoa were fairly low, at 33.9 percent—still twice the rate for the same group in New Orleans (15.7 percent).[16]

Lester's sole commentary on school provides only a little insight into his formal education. In New Orleans, assuming that he started school at six or seven, he would have gone to McDonogh #6 from Lizetta's home at 1028 Bordeaux. A few years later, when the family lived on Second or Third, he may have enrolled in either the James Lewis or the Thomy Lafon School, or both. No records corroborate his attendance at any of the three.[17] He later recalled how he "used to fall asleep in school, because I had my lesson, and there was nothing else to do." The teacher worked "with those who hadn't studied at home, but I had, so I'd go to sleep. Then the teacher would go home and tell my mother. So I put that down." Precisely when and where this occurred went unsaid, but it was probably in New Orleans. In any case, the episode certainly was a factor in bringing his formal education to an early end: Lester was an able and maybe an advanced student bored by the slow pace.[18]

One thorny issue concerning Young's public-school education has to do with exactly when the family moved to Minneapolis, where Irma and Lee attended the Blaine School. Irma enrolled late in December 1926, according to local school records. It is unlikely that Lester would have had much reason to do the same, being seventeen by then; the Minneapolis school system, furthermore, has no record of his registration.[19] Yet it is not as simple as all that.

In particular, the conclusion that Young was educated mainly in Louisiana is hindered by his own testimony that he "was raised mostly in Minneapolis . . . trying to go to school and all that."[20] It is possible that the Youngs visited the city frequently before settling there in 1926, but more likely this was merely another one of Lester's typically careless statements about his past. Leonard Phillips's testimony and the Minneapolis City Directory both confirm that the family moved there at the end of 1926, by which time, even if he *had* enrolled, it would have been too late for the local schools to make a difference for Lester. Music had won out over school for him.[21]

Since he was apparently educated primarily in Louisiana, his dislike of school may perhaps be understood as a reaction to the quality of education and the discipline within the Jim Crow school system. His sister contended, "Lester hated school. He'd run out. He wouldn't study." In this respect he resembled Count Basie and Charlie Parker, for whom music provided a context in which to reveal considerable talents and through which to acquire a more exciting and doubtless more meaningful education by traveling to places that other youngsters could hardly imagine.[22]

Probably because he felt he could make up for anything his son might miss, Willis Young often took Lester out of school to play dates—"time off" during which, ironically, the boy was still under a teacher's supervision. In fact, not only Willis but also both Lizetta and Aunt Mamie were schoolteachers, giving assurance of Lester's early familiarity with institutional demands and discipline. Their influence was so profound that he often used the metaphor of school and the methods of teachers in other settings. The "Basie [band] was like school," he once explained, and there was always "someone who didn't know his part"; he hated having to sit and wait while that person learned it. Then, too, a close friend recalled a distinctive habit of Lester's: he kept an "imaginary scoreboard on people and sometimes they'd get a mark and sometimes if they'd get something wrong, he'd erase the blackboard [and say,] 'Well, that's all she wrote,' you know, it's the bottom line"—almost as if he were marking down grades or taking attendance.[23]

Lester was far more comfortable with his saxophone than with a pen. Perhaps understandably, he rarely wrote anything aside from the occasional postcard, preferring the musicians' grapevine, telegrams, and the telephone for long-distance communication. Music was his main means of displaying his rather considerable talent and intelligence; he musicalized everything, often quoting relevant song lyrics or playing an appropriate melody in both social and musical settings. His lack of formal education did hamper him, however, in his business dealings, because he preferred oral agreements—which are fine between gentlemen, a word that didn't exactly describe everyone he dealt with—to written contracts. Furthermore, he felt uneasy around people he did not know; he needed to establish a special rapport with someone before he would open up. His lack of formal education also affected his social life: he seemed to prefer the company of working-class folk to that of the core Black bourgeoisie of teachers, doctors, and ministers.

Unattractive though the public educational system of Tangipahoa Parish must have seemed from Young's perspective, the area furthered his music education in his early teens by immersing him in rural southern Black culture. Migrant workers, including itinerant blues guitarists, descended upon the lumber towns and camps to earn good money around Natalbany after picking cotton in Louisiana and Mississippi in early autumn and cutting Louisiana sugar cane late in the season. Lester heard the soulful work songs, blues, ballads, and spirituals that rang out from the logging camps and churches of such communities, evidence of a profound oral tradition.[24] Even in the big cities, he liked to listen to street-corner musicians; a friend reported that he would give them his last dollar when he heard them perform. As Lester himself once remarked, "Just any kind of music you play for me, I melt with all of it." This love for different kinds of music may have originated in New Orleans, but it was reinforced by his winter seasons in the back country.[25]

The Natalbany Lumber Company had unintentionally enriched the music culture by providing jobs for Blacks, who comprised an available and migratory labor force at a time when native-born whites shunned mill jobs as too arduous and dangerous. Moreover, the felling of trees in the South was often done by convicts, many of them African Americans. Song leaders such as the twelve-string guitarist Huddy "Leadbelly" Ledbetter abounded in logging camps. The cotton and sugar field workers, who traditionally sang as they toiled, came to Tangipahoa every winter to labor in the mills; the season as well as the place coincided precisely with the employment needs of Willis Young and his family during their off-season. The Youngs were, in effect, migrant workers themselves, familiar with the ways and music culture of other migratory people.[26]

The professor's band traveled frequently to logging towns and other newly developed areas. In Wilkinson County, Lester's birthplace, lumbering was an important part of the economy, and Bogalusa itself was founded by the Great Southern Lumber Company, which built a huge model sawmill there in 1907. In the winter of 1923–24 the Youngs stayed in an Arkansas logging town with "five big mills" in which the Phillips brothers worked as teenagers. The town of Palatka, where the Youngs closed late in 1925 with Billy Clark's Broadway Show, was situated in the middle of a rich Florida forest.[27]

In fact, the Youngs spent so much time in lumbering communities that it seems reasonable to speculate that the saxophonist may have worked in a mill as a youth. The professor's own decision to pursue a career in music presaged a lesson his son would learn years later out west, near Albuquerque or Phoenix in around 1930, when he and Ben Webster (at the time a pianist but later a saxophone student of Willis's) labored in a sawmill. Weary from such dangerous toil, Lester Young was reported to have vowed upon leaving the job, "I never pick up nothing but my horn."[28]

With his father's personal contacts, professional reputation, and winning ways to obtain good jobs for the band in churches or at dances, as the occasion demanded, the aspiring young saxophonist managed to enhance his musical skills and expand his repertoire even in the off-season. His knowledge of spirituals, anthems, and songs sung in the rural Black churches increased, as the small towns the family wintered in had African American populations of sufficient size to warrant the existence of a few institutions in which the professor could conduct the chorus and his band.

In 1926 the Youngs joined the Great Migration, as the northern exodus of African Americans from the South is termed. The move was prompted by a number of factors, some of which were directly related to the worsening economy and the sorry state of race relations in the South. Northern Black urban communities—in Chicago, Detroit, and Cleveland, for example—were growing due to industrial development in the region, and country towns like Woodville, Hammond, and Thibodaux simply could not compete with these cities or their southern counterparts, where jobs were plentiful and salaries much higher. In the 1920s the African American populations of many of Louisiana's rural districts—including Wilkinson County, Lafourche Parish, and Assumption, where Lester's uncle William resided—declined. (Tangipahoa and Washington parishes were exceptions in this respect—their Black populations nearly doubled in these years, and the number of whites living there increased as well.) Nor were Blacks alone in leaving the South: the white populations of numerous southern parishes and counties also declined during the 1920s, as the nation as a whole became more urbanized.[29]

The state of labor and race relations in nearby Bogalusa in 1919 gives us an indication of developments that must have seemed alarming to families such as the Youngs; one incident in particular was remarkably reminiscent of the Thibodaux strike of 1887, though the casualties were not so great. Labor unrest disturbed authorities throughout the United States in that later year, and labor organizers, among them one African American, came to work in Bogalusa, a town whose mayor was also the general manager of the lumber company.

An explosion at the mill led to its temporary closure, a situation that made workers desperate. For the first time in the town's history, Blacks marched in the Labor Day parade, and company officials accused the union of intimidating Blacks into joining its ranks. The mayor augmented the local police unit with his own special forces from the company's "Loyalty League"; when they clashed with workers, three white organizers were killed, and federal troops had to be called in. There were investigations and trials in which the Black organizer testified along with others, but the union failed to get indictments against the lumber-company officials.[30]

This kind of violence deeply troubled the Youngs and motivated them, like many other African Americans, to migrate north. Lester's dislike of being in the South can be traced in part to his father, who "had a real thing about [i.e., dislike for] segregation." Even before migration, when they toured, the Youngs went "mostly to the North . . . because Papa didn't want to go up and down the South . . . not with Jim Crow."[31]

A factor in the Youngs' migrating after the winter of 1925–26, and not sooner, may have been the death of Willis Young's mother, Martha, who was often away for certain seasons of the year, like her son. As late as 1925 she was still traveling for her missionary work. Then she evidently had a premonition that she was about to die, one that pointed to the role religion played in her life. The Reverend John W. Young, Boots and Sport's younger brother, recalled their grandmother's last days: "In the month of October, coming to the cold part of the year, she made it home. I'll never forget that year, 1925, that she came home. . . . During the harvest time, us two twin brothers, she would sit us on each one of her knees and she would read to us and sing."[32] When the boys' parents returned home that night, "my grandmother looked at my mother and said, 'Well, let me tell you my daughter (she'd call my mother her daughter) . . . I'm going to tell you . . . I has made my last mission.' She said, 'My mission is over,'" adding, "'when I leave here . . . you're going to have to carry me. I won't go anywhere, this is my last mission, 1925.'" She died in November of that year; she was said to be eighty-eight. The same sense of dutiful service that shaped her life also motivated her son Willis, except with him, it manifested itself in music.[33]

Family ties and loyalty to the band may also have contributed to the decision to move to Minneapolis; a cousin, Cleo Young, lived there at 6th and Lyndale, in a hotel that her relations managed.[34] Then, too, Lee Young remembered that they were stranded by TOBA in Minneapolis or somewhere nearby; he cited his father's refusal to scale down his band as the reason he never moved up to the Orpheum circuit.[35] The Youngs performed in a Minneapolis dance hall on November 1, 1926, and made "pretty good money . . . ten dollars, which was a lot of money then," but then they "didn't have no jobs right then, after that job."[36] For a time the professor could find little work and had to settle for playing the small towns in the northern prairies, all because of his unwillingness to abandon his principles and his allegiance to his band members. His strong sense of loyalty to the group no doubt impressed his son Lester as much as it did other members of the entourage; it was typical of the way the professor taught by example, in life as in music.

There may have been additional reasons for the family's ending up in Minneapolis, a large midwestern city in a distant state with a very small Black population in the 1920s. Perhaps it was just that it was as far away from the South as one could get and still stay in the United States. Also, Blacks in other cities, notably East St. Louis, Chicago, and Tulsa, had suffered considerably in the race riots of 1917, 1919, and 1921, respectively. Minneapolis's prosperity, too, was a draw. Its robust economy held special appeal for southerners, coming as they were from a region gone stagnant; the city had grown considerably in the early twentieth century and now dominated a vast agricultural hinterland encompassing the largest flour-producing, linseed-products, tractor, and agricultural-implement-manufacturing centers in the world. Minneapolis's citizens were proud of their fine paved streets and their water-supply system, one of the most modern in the nation.[37]

The city's physical setting probably reminded the Youngs of their home state: situated on the banks of the Mississippi, its forty-three square miles included six large natural lakes, part of a beautiful park system reminiscent of the blue lakes and verdant forests of Louisiana. Likewise recalling the South, bands in Minneapolis performed on river steamers for moonlight cruises, and there were free municipal band concerts at Lake Harriet on summer evenings.[38]

A month after the show closed in El Reno, late in 1926, the Youngs took up residence at 573 Seventh Avenue North, Minneapolis. They "had a big [two-story] house" and a maid to take care of it.[39] Electrical wiring had been installed just the year before. David Haas, the former resident, had died late in November, about the time of the family's arrival in the city;[40] his brother, Charles, worked in a local music shop. The connection suggests another dimension of Willis Young's business dealings: "Some people who was on one of his shows before, he knew them, and they was taking care of the house," remembered Leonard Phillips.[41]

The Youngs' new neighborhood was racially mixed, with a number of African Americans dispersed among the white residents. Lester would remain in North Minneapolis for nearly ten years, and every day he was there he would travel past local Black institutions, evidence of an organized and committed community. Black church services and fraternity and sorority dances required song and music, and the Youngs provided plenty of both. One denomination, the Church of God in Christ, met at 622 Lyndale Avenue North; Union Baptist was located at 616 Lyndale; and there was an A.M.E. church at 808 Bassett Place—all three within a few blocks of one another. These and several other churches looked after the spiritual and social needs of Black residents in the 1920s. Minneapolis's African American community also included the fraternal orders of the Free Masons, the Scottish Rites, and the Elks, and, for women, the Order of the Eastern Star, all of which regularly sponsored social dances for various causes. This community was not a Black ghetto like the ones forming in some of the larger industrial cities in the North, such as Chicago and Detroit.[42]

In this integrated community, race relations were decidedly better than they were down south. Leonard Phillips and Charles "Truck" Parham, a semiprofessional athlete at the time and later a musician and composer, both emphasized that Minneapolis was a place where Black men could date white women without fear of the lynchings that such pairings provoked in the South; two of Billy Young's band members, in fact, had white wives. Still, Minnesota in the 1920s was not completely free of the white racism that the Youngs thought they had left behind in Dixie: in Duluth in 1920, for example, three Black men charged with rape were forced to "confess" and then lynched, and two years later Black residents of St. Paul protested proposals to create a segregated employment bureau and build a segregated children's playground.[43] And if Black men in Minneapolis did not risk death by dating interracially, they were nevertheless subject to police harassment should they be seen merely speaking to white women on certain street corners. In the early summer of 1922, there were frequent encounters between African American men and police in North Minneapolis. "A crowd of 500 was held at bay by a Negro at Sixth and Bryant Avenues North last night who, armed with a policeman's revolver, backed slowly away and escaped," reported the *Morning Tribune* for June 21, 1922. The man had wrested the weapon from the officer rather than submit to arrest for "disorderly conduct after complaints had been received that he had been speaking to white girls." He may or may not have been propositioning them, but in any case, according to the reporter, "the incident caused the police to take immediate action to end simmering race troubles which have arisen in that district recently." Black nightclubs were ordered closed, and extra policemen were assigned to the area. "No serious troubles have occurred so far, but police say the race feeling there is such as to warrant precautionary measures." This particular clash "marked the third call to that territory in the last twenty-four hours." The day before, early in the morning, "a crowd [had] formed while two policemen had trouble arresting four Negroes for disorderly conduct." A few hours later, another crowd gathered. The *Tribune* claimed that local citizens had refused to help the police subdue the man who escaped, "although they did not openly hoot [i.e., cheer] him."[44]

The solidarity and vitality of the Black community—despite a modest African American population of under four thousand in Minneapolis in 1920—were reflected in the city's music culture and jazz. This must have been part of its attraction for Young and other musicians. Moore's Jazz Orchestra and the Famous Rogers Café Jazz Orchestra promised the new music at the start of the jazz decade. George Butler's Jazz Orchestra played in St. Paul in 1921, and the Railroad Men's Association presented Moore's Jazz Band every Monday night that summer at the South Side Auditorium. Several different jazz bands also performed for moonlight boat excursions, picnics, and receptions, for balls sponsored by various Black organizations, and for such affairs as the Grand Picnic of the Men's Episcopalian Club. These outfits included Moore's Jazz Knockers, Professor Stevens's Full Jazz Band, the same professor's Jazz Canaries, and the New Jazzland Orchestra.[45]

Twin Cities residents in the 1920s enjoyed big shows, territorial bands, and popular blues records. The troupe from Noble Sissle and Eubie Blake's *Shuffle Along*, a hit Black musical set in a small southern town at election time and featuring characters whose speech and actions were shaped by the minstrel tradition, appeared at the Metropolitan for a week in the early autumn of 1923. The Acme Palm Garden, at 317½ Wabasha Street, hosted the company every evening and invited patrons to follow the *Shuffle Along* crowd there for "Special Entertaining and Special Features"—probably humor, song, and dance reflective of the musical. The Nu-Way Jazz Hounds, "an all-star seven-piece" band from Kansas City, entertained at the November Dance at the South Side Auditorium, on the corner of Twelfth Avenue South and Third Street. Recordings on the famous W. C. Handy label, Black Swan, among them "St. Louis Blues," "Yellow Dog Blues," and "He May Be Your Young Man,

But He Come to See Me Sometimes," were sold at the Peyer Music Company, at 64 East Sixth Street.[46]

The city boasted a number of clubs, including several "black and tan" (integrated) nightspots where white slummers could listen to jazz and, furthermore, dance and drink in an interracial atmosphere, and where musicians such as Lester Young, Le Roy "Snake" Whyte, and Eddie Barefield could earn good money performing. Some of them were "chicken shacks," or modest restaurants serving "down-home" dishes, the best known being the Cotton Club (named after its New York counterpart), where Young would perform in the 1930s. Others were after-hours spots, such as the Kit Kat Club, at Sixth Avenue North between Highland and Aldrich; the Nest, also on the North Side; and the Musicians' Rest, "a black and tan ribs joint" in an old Victorian building on Sixth Avenue near Lyndale, not far from the Youngs' house. At Roy Langford's, a nightspot preferred by women, in Minneapolis's red-light district, the entertainer Charley Siegals held forth nightly in 1927, in an unusual act that had him playing the piano like Earl Hines with one hand while blowing and fingering the trumpet like Louis Armstrong with the other. Still other resorts were roadhouses outside of town and in neighboring counties.[47]

On the eve of the Depression, the photographer and composer Gordon Parks moved to St. Paul and began playing blues piano at Pope's, a brothel on Minneapolis's North Side. He wrote vivid descriptions of the nighttime characters there, including Red, the house drummer; the beautiful Casamala with "the honey skin, black hair, and doe eyes," and her identical twin, Carmanosa; Jimmy with the powdered face and "pencil line moustache"; and Pope, the proprietor, who "moved in the manner of one who definitely had everything under control." Parks's account also relates the sudden violence that resulted in the stabbing of a customer and the end of his own piano-playing job at Pope's.[48]

Minneapolis's civic and police officials were quick to crack down on any establishment that sold alcohol during Prohibition (1920–1933), and saw to it that all dance joints were closed by midnight—thus the proliferation of after-hours nightspots masquerading as private clubs. In 1923 a spokesman for local ballroom proprietors joined with public officials in objecting to jazz dancing, proclaiming, "The day of the 'jazz' music and dance is passing"; henceforth, he said, dance-hall proprietors would encourage waltzes and fox trots. They never could have guessed that the music they were trying to ban would become the most popular choice of the next few decades. The periodic closing of resorts[49] nevertheless prompted an exodus of musicians from Minneapolis, as it had done in other cities, and Lester was among the casualties when he worked in such clubs.

Although there was little work for the professor's band late in 1926, still, Leonard Phillips recalled, "we had a good time. Plenty of good food to eat. We rehearsed. . . . Then he started booking things, then we started working in Minneapolis, man. We got work. We played all the time. Every weekend we was playing at a place called the South Side Ballroom." Leonard Phillips reminisced, "We had a good band . . . a good entertaining band." Besides playing, the band "used to sing together" songs such as "Ain't She Sweet." After a while, Phillips said, "we were a pretty big name in Minneapolis . . . because we got most of the good work." At the time "there wasn't no big bands there—not no big white bands."[50]

Rare "sightings" during this period help us to reconstruct Lester's musical movement through the northern prairie states. The Iowans Eddie Barefield and Snake Whyte happened to encounter the Young family at the Patterson Hotel in Bismarck, North Dakota, in 1927. Barefield, a saxophonist and clarinetist about the same age as Lester, was with the Virginia Ravens at the time and recalled that Lee, dressed in a tuxedo, conducted the band while Irma and the professor played saxophones, Sarah was on piano, and Lester performed on alto and baritone saxophones.[51]

Trumpet player Snake Whyte remembered that the Youngs "performed for dances . . . like . . . an ordinary lodge hall or something like that," adding, "Maybe it wasn't a thousand people in the whole town, . . . that's the kind of a band [they were]. . . . There was not enough people there to hire a big band." Their versatility enabled them to take requests from the audience: "It was one of those kind [of bands]. . . . You name one of the old pieces, they play it for you."[52]

Eddie Barefield befriended Young that winter, and years later would recall him as a young man who led a very sheltered life—"a very naive quiet guy. He didn't curse, didn't smoke, he didn't do anything." Staying in the Patterson Hotel in North Dakota, Young and Barefield used to listen to records together; both admired the saxophone artistry of the white musician Frankie Trumbauer, a midwesterner and associate of Leon "Bix" Beiderbecke, an influential cornetist. At the time, Young maintained that "as soon as he got good enough his father was going to buy him a Selmer" (the brand name of a first-rate saxophone); until then he had to make do with a Buescher, the professor's usual brand.[53] In Barefield's estimation Young was quite "a good alto player, too."[54]

In Minneapolis, and maybe even earlier, Young and his colleagues sought to become part of the newest craze, the jazz dance band. Professor Young formed a dance band in which his son Lester, Leonard Phillips, and Pete Jones were the heart of the front line. Phillips contended that this band "was playing jazz . . . the same kind of music what [King Oliver was] playing—[though] maybe different tunes." He explained, "Everywhere you go, everybody was playing the same kind of music. Jazz." Initially the genre was monopolized by Black bands; in fact, "white people didn't start playing jazz till *way* late, I mean real jazz."[55]

As Young and his father's band gained popularity and respect, they moved from dance halls to hotel ballrooms. Their flexibility and new format reflected the professor's ability to adapt to the changing scene. While a few minstrel shows would continue to perform in rural areas through the 1930s, Druie Bess, a Blue Devils trombonist, maintained that in general, minstrelsy "went out around 1925," a development "that throwed me out of . . . show business." Bess "started looking for other things . . . and [concluded], 'Well, I got to learn how to jazz.'" Billy and Sarah Young's road show survived until 1928 or 1929, but they must have known its days were numbered.[56]

Les was on alto and soprano sax in the new band—"He used to play that soprano all the time," according to Leonard Phillips; "that's what he used to take his solos on"—while Phillips played trumpet and Jones was on trombone. Performing in first-class hotels in Minneapolis and St. Paul, the band members sang and offered up waltzes ("You had to play a waltz if you played a dance, or people would think you was crazy," said Phillips)[57] and renditions of "Charleston," "I Wanna Little Girl," "If I Could Be with You," "Bye Bye Blackbird," "Blue Skies," "My Blue Heaven," "Melancholy Baby," and the jazz pieces "I'm Coming Virginia," "Stampede," and "Tiger Rag." Such hits as "Baby, Won't You Please Come Home," "Jadda," "Runnin' Wild," "Wang Wang Blues," "Last Night on the Back Porch," and "How Come You Do Me Like You Do?" were included in their repertoire as well.[58] This jazz band lasted from late 1926 to late 1928, an exciting period in the history of the music, when Beiderbecke and Trumbauer were recording, and recordings by Louis Armstrong's Hot Five and Hot Seven and Ferdinand "Jelly Roll" Morton's Hot Peppers were released.[59]

In 1927 Lester and Willis Young's band "played at the Radisson Hotel, St. Paul Hotel, South Side Ballroom . . . all over Minneapolis."[60] The Radisson and the St. Paul were among the Twin Cities' finest hotels. The twelve-story Radisson, at 33–55 South Seventh Street, featured several different venues; it is unknown whether the Billy Young band performed for dancers in the Flame Room or for café patrons in the Teco Inn or the Viking, Fountain, or Chateau rooms. In 1928 the hotel advertised its Flame Room as being open for dancing on Saturday evenings from nine-thirty to midnight; admission was two dollars per couple, the high price an indication of the exclusiveness of the affair. Afterward Lester and his friends would socialize and play in the after-hours clubs.[61]

In photographs taken of Lester, his father, and the rest of the band in 1927 (see photo insert), an astonishing array of instruments stands at the ready for the tuxedoed musicians: eight reeds (mostly saxophones), a violin, a trumpet, a trombone, a tuba, a banjo, a piano, bass and snare drums, and a single cymbal. All of the band members face the camera, except Professor Young, who is standing in profile and pretending to conduct his sidemen with a violin bow. A northern landscape—pine trees, a river or lake, and a frame house—decorates the bass drum.[62]

At age seventeen and eighteen Young was a featured soloist on soprano, displaying an impressive virtuosity. He was a "born musician," a "born genius" who played "ungodly jazz" and was "way ahead of his time," in Phillips's words. Indeed, the professor's elder son so amazed listeners that his father insisted he take up the tenor, in the hope that it would slow him down. At the time, tenors typically "moaned," while sopranos and altos soloed.[63]

Lester was nevertheless the star of his father's jazz band, and audiences and other musicians admired him primarily for his solos. Leonard Phillips said he "was the band! . . . That's what people were looking at. They weren't thinking about his reading. They were thinking about them solos he played."[64] And as the band's hot soloist, he rode the crest of the Jazz Age, spreading the new music throughout the northern prairies and the Great Plains and taking it to places as distant as North Dakota, Nebraska, New Mexico, and Arizona. Young's dance-band apprenticeship enabled him to advance musically, and it has much to tell us about how jazz culture became an integral part of American life.

Historians who claim that jazz moved more or less directly from New Orleans to Chicago and New York and then on to Kansas City fail to recognize that young musicians took the music and dance on a more circuitous route, to small towns in outlying areas of the midwestern prairie, the Great Plains, and the mountain states, not to mention the West Coast. Nor do the standard histories acknowledge the resourcefulness of musicians or their willingness to accommodate various audiences' likes and dislikes by playing waltzes, popular songs, jazz, and blues, as necessary. Having penetrated the countryside as well as the city, it was itself influenced by different cultural traditions in different milieus, with the result that it became more complex and diverse over time. As Thomas J. Hennessey has argued, by the late 1920s jazz was "nationalized."[65] In short, jazz did not simply migrate north to Chicago; there were also other waves to other points, including Minneapolis, Tulsa, Phoenix, and Los Angeles.[66]

Thanks to Lester Young's virtuosity and the versatility of the Billy Young jazz band, communities such as Bismarck and Minot, North Dakota, were familiar with the music from at least 1928. Certainly this phenomenon cannot be attributed to the presence of a large Black population: in 1930 Bismarck would claim only forty-five African American residents out of a total population of 11,090.[67] If Lester Young and Black dance bands were popular in such settlements, it was precisely because they appealed to different groups, not only among whites but also among Native Americans, of whom Phillips remarked, "They was into everything . . . they knew what was going on." Of the region as a whole he observed, "All them bands [Eli Rice, Grant Moore, Andy Kirk, and Benny Moten] played up all through where we [were] playing." Phillips conceded that there "wasn't many Black people up in North Dakota, but they still like . . . Black music. I mean, they like to have the Black band come and play the dances."[68]

Billy Young's band took the music along the North Platte River to the small communities of Broken Bow, Grand Island, Lexington, and Scottsbluff, Nebraska, and Sioux City, Iowa. All of these towns, like Bismarck and Minot, were located on railroad lines or main highways, permitting the band easy access via train or automobile.[69] In most places there were African American families who welcomed the travelers and were glad to feed and house them, as well as local Black churches that sustained the Youngs spiritually, musically, and materially. Isolated Black teenagers from these towns, starved for any live African American music culture outside of church, awed by the glamour of show business, and drawn by allure of a jazz life, were willing recruits for the band or for the show. The professor's personal contacts were undoubtedly a major factor on these tours, just as they had been down south. Later, when they were with Art Bronson's Bostonians, Lester, Leonard, and Pete would fall back on experience, retracing the same routes they had traveled with Professor Young.[70]

While Lester learned from live performances of various kinds, he belonged to a generation of musicians for whom recordings would assume an unprecedented role in music education. In the unlikely surroundings of Bismarck, where temperatures reached fifty-five degrees below zero (Fahrenheit) that winter, Eddie Barefield introduced the young saxophonist to Leon "Bix" Beiderbecke's famous recording of February 4, 1927, "Singing the Blues." Beiderbecke was of German descent and from Iowa; in his youth, instead of attending the military academy that his parents sent him to near Chicago, he had spent his time listening to King Oliver and Louis Armstrong in the city's nightclubs. After that initiation, Lester "used to buy all the Bix and Trumbauer records as they came out, and copied Trumbauer's solos."[71] He and Barefield didn't even need to go to a music store to purchase them—"we used to get together and send off from a catalog and get all of Frankie Trumbauer's records." It was Barefield's contention that "that's where Pres got the basis of his style."[72] Young would invariably recall that important introduction by playing "Singing the Blues" in greeting whenever he met Barefield in later years. We do not know for certain what records he may have listened to before Bismarck.

In Minneapolis, as in other cities at this time, stores sold the latest devices for listening to commercial forms of jazz and blues. The Youngs and the members of their band may have had a special arrangement with the Majestic Music Shop, where Charles Haas worked as a repairman, enabling them to obtain the newest records and record players. Located downtown, at 14–16 South Seventh, the Majestic dealt in "Columbia, Brunswick and Victor Phonograph Records and Pantropes and Orthophonic Music Instruments." Music lovers could purchase Silvertone, Nordica, Edison, and Brunswick machines at reduced prices, with shopworn, rebuilt, and demonstration models going for as little as a dollar down and a dollar per week thereafter.[73] These record players were so popular among the musicians in 1927 that "most everybody in the band had one."[74] Recordings by African American performers on the Black Swan and Okeh Records labels were available in Minneapolis at the

Talking Machine Repair Shop, at 1027 Hennepin Avenue; blues lovers could find records by Mamie Smith and other artists at the Sonora Shop, at 20 West Sixth Street.[75]

The discs allowed Lester to compare his own talents with those of musicians fortunate enough to have recorded. He heard new songs and developed his skills by listening to the current recording artists—not only Oliver, Armstrong, and Morton but white performers such as the Original Dixieland Jazz Band, Ben Birney, Red Nichols, Coon-Sanders Night Hawks, and Vincent Lopez.[76]

Young later explained to interviewers how he had learned to play by ear: "I'd get to listening to a lot of music and I'd goof off and play everything but the scales," he recalled. After being forced to learn how to read, the competitive youngster "pretty soon could cut everybody and . . . was teaching other people to read." When giving advice to others on how to play jazz, he drew from his own early experiences: "A good way to learn is jamming with records. Find somebody you like and play with his records." Besides figuring out the melody by repeating the record as often as necessary, apprentices with sharp ears could learn key signatures and harmony from their favorite musicians. And as Young and Buddy Tate realized at about the same time, "if [the melody] isn't in the key you like, you can slow it [the phonograph] down [to change the key]."[77]

Discussing the early "influences" that writers invariably asked about in interviews, Young confessed, "I have great Big Eyes for Bix." He elaborated, "I used to confuse between him and Red Nichols, but finally had to put Bix on top." Beiderbecke's lyrical lines and beautiful tone moved the young saxophonist. Young alluded to his perceptions of an African American aesthetic in his statement that "Bix . . . sounded just like a colored boy sometimes."[78]

While in Bismarck and Minneapolis, Young copied the cornet solo on "Mississippi Mud" and "used to play [along] with . . . 'Singing the Blues,' 'A Good Man Is Hard to Find,' and 'Way Down Yonder in New Orleans'"—Trumbauer and Beiderbecke recordings made in 1927. Young and Phillips were especially fond of "In a Mist," a Debussyesque piano composition of Beiderbecke's.[79]

But it was Frankie Trumbauer who *really* impressed him. Raised in St. Louis, Trumbauer was the musical director of Jean Goldkette's organization, which consisted of several bands that played and recorded regularly with Beiderbecke. Young reminisced, "Frankie Trumbauer and

Jimmy Dorsey were battling for honors in those days, and I finally found out that I liked Trumbauer. Trumbauer was my idol." In 1927 and 1928, the apprentice bought "all his records" so he could learn to play along with his new hero. For Young, part of Trumbauer's appeal was that he "always told a little story." He also admired "the way he slurred his notes" and, finally, the fact that "he'd play the melody . . . then after that, he'd play around the melody." The Chicagoan Lawrence "Bud" Freeman was another saxophonist who made an impression on Lester: "Nobody played like him. That's what knocked me out." It may surprise some fans to learn that Black musicians were influenced by whites, but this kind of exchange was central to Young's musical development and to the creation of jazz and American culture.[80]

Leonard Phillips remembered the influence these musicians had on Young, describing him as being "crazy about Bix [and] about Frankie [Trumbauer] and crazy about Benny Goodman." "Miss Clementine," recorded by Jean Goldkette's band, featured solos by Beiderbecke and Trumbauer that Phillips and Young particularly liked, as did "Louisiana." Young's training and intelligence were abetted by the fact that he had a superb ear and a phonographic memory. "All he'd do was listen to [a record] once," Phillips said. "That cat had a *perfect* ear." He recalled how in Minneapolis, the two of them "used to go to the record store [and then] maybe a month later . . . he'd say, 'Hey, Deke!' 'Yeah?' 'Do you remember this?' He'd play it, and I'd forgot what it was. . . . And he'd play it [again]. I'd say, 'Yeah, man.' He'd say, 'We gon' learn that.' "[81]

The saxophonist's knowledge of the musical terminology did not match his ear. "He didn't know what note [was what]. He wouldn't say, 'Man, you play D-flat' or 'You play so-and-so,' breaking the chord in two, what you call. . . . He'd just say, 'You play this note here,' and he'd make it on his horn, 'And you play this note.' Then we'd hit it." Phillips would tell him, " 'That's my so-and-so [note],' " to which Young would respond, " 'That's the note I want you to play.' "[82]

White artists were not Young's sole influences. He was so impressed with Armstrong's artistry, for example, that he learned all of his cornet and trumpet solos by ear. He played the lead from these records first, followed by the harmony, which he also picked out by ear. (This ability to work out the harmony suggests just how well he had been trained by his father.) In the end, though, Young's tone was distinctly his own. As he explained it, "I tried to get the sound of a C-melody on a tenor. That's why I don't sound like other people."[83]

In later years, Young's repertoire would include some of the most frequently recorded songs from the first half of the twentieth century. In order of their popularity, they were (rank in parentheses): "Tea for Two" (2); "Body and Soul" (3); "After You've Gone" (4); "I Can't Give You Anything but Love" and "The Man I Love" (tied at 13); "Somebody Loves Me" (20); "I Got Rhythm" and "On the Sunny Side of the Street" (tied at 23). "St. Louis Blues" held the top spot, but Young seems not to have liked it.[84] Many of the songs came from New York shows: "Tea for Two" from *No, No, Nanette,* "Body and Soul" from *Three's a Crowd,* and "I Can't Give You Anything but Love" from *New Leslie's Blackbirds of 1928.* Two other well-loved songs released during Young's adolescence were also show tunes—Hoagy Carmichael's "Stardust" and "Indiana"—and they, too, joined his repertoire. Young himself often recorded songs by George and Ira Gershwin, the most memorable example being "I Got Rhythm," which Pres reworked as "Lester Leaps In."[85]

Despite Young's reputation as a seminal jazz and blues musician, his fondness for these songs indicates that in his late teens, he listened to and liked the popular music of the day. (Similarly, as an adult he would claim to be a fan of Frank Sinatra's, praise the talents of Jo Stafford, and keep up with various kinds of American music.) Significantly, he learned many of these popular songs during his Minneapolis decade, before he went to Kansas City.[86]

By regularly presenting show tunes and popular songs, Young became part of, even as he helped to develop, the nation's musical tastes. It is unclear why he passed over Andy Razaf and Thomas "Fats" Waller's "Ain't Misbehavin'" and "Honeysuckle Rose," which tied for eighth place among the most frequently recorded songs, and why he failed to include in his repertoire two other popular numbers with beautiful melodies: "Blue Skies" (6), which was played by his father's dance band, and "Sweet Lorraine" (tied at 23). Neither did he perform Gershwin's "Summertime," which first Sidney Bechet and then John Coltrane were famous for playing; moreover, Young's liking for some of Gershwin's songs evidently did not extend to the light opera, *Porgy and Bess,* if the fact that he never recorded anything from that work is any indication.[87]

Their repertoire of popular songs prepared Young and his companions for careers as professional musicians. Lester's superior musical talents provided him with lucrative opportunities by his midteens, not an unusually early age for a gifted youngster to play professionally away from home. As a precocious jazzman, he was clearly a match for many adult musicians. Leonard Phillips reminisced that he "set them people on fire up there, yeah. They never heard nothing like that. White bands up there offered to give . . . him a hundred dollars a week" to leave his father's band.[88] And from the mid-1920s, Cootie Williams recalled, "Lester wanted to leave. He had plenty of offers during the period of time I was there, to go with white bands."[89] Of course, the young man's desire for independence was not encouraged by his father.

The professor's punishments continued into the Minneapolis years, but as before, they backfired, making Lester more rebellious rather than more submissive. "Anytime my dad would take off his belt and whip Lester," Lee remembered, "[Lester] would split. He was gone." The young saxophonist "must have run away from home ten or twelve times" —so often that "you just got tired of it . . . out the window . . . sometimes for two or three months."[90] Such departures were typical of both Americans and African Americans, who for centuries had been running away from intolerable working conditions and societal restraints. Many other jazz musicians did the same as teenagers, including Sidney Bechet, Buck Clayton, Snake Whyte, Eddie Barefield, Freddie Moore, Jabbo Smith, and Alberta Hunter, the singer, who left Memphis at the age of twelve.[91]

One disagreement with his father prompted Lester to leave his family in El Reno, Oklahoma, late in 1926, just before they all moved to Minnesota. The incident revealed Young's developing sense of manhood as well as his ongoing sensitivity to the professor's slights and blows. The seventeen-year-old wanted to take a woman along with him when the entourage traveled, but Willis objected and slapped him, whereupon Lester immediately took off. Not realizing how much he had hurt his elder son, the professor either sent after him or himself asked him to return. While Les eventually did come back, he continued to protest his innocence, maintaining, "Papa did me wrong." He felt humiliated by the episode for some time; it was one more in a long catalog of injuries. Later, in the Southwest, father and son would clash again when Willis Young sent back the gift of a clarinet from his son's lady friend; the professor then replaced it with one he himself had procured.[92]

On one occasion, without furnishing any explanation, the runaway returned to the family after an absence of seven or eight weeks. As Lee recounted, "My dad had just gone up to the [railroad ticket] window to buy the tickets for us to go back to Minneapolis . . . and my [step]mother was just crying because she was going to leave Lester there . . . and hadn't seen him in ages, and my dad went up to the window and says . . . 'Give me two halves and two wholes'—those were tickets, you know. . . . And so my [step]mother said to my daddy to look around, and Lester was standing over by the door, and he said, 'Make that three halves.' "[93] Willis and Sarah were so relieved to have Lester back safe and sound that subsequently they acted as if he had never left, and life went on as usual. "He just picked up where he left off," Lee said. Extraordinary though this may seem, it typified the kind of treatment the young saxophonist was accorded. His father "never did question him—never questioned him . . . and you're talking about when men really would question their kids," Lee noted.[94] Willis's relative silence concerning his son's comings and goings may in fact have confirmed Lester's own belief that he had done nothing wrong, thus enhancing his sense of independence.

Over time the northern climate did its part in persuading the professor to leave Minneapolis, though the harsh winters do not seem to have been a negative factor for Les. Like many New Orleanians, Willis Young found himself drawn to the warmer climes out west, and in any case, he had "always said that he wanted to end up in California."[95] Los Angeles's rapid expansion during and after World War I promised new opportunities for Black migrants and for musicians as well. Will Johnson's Creole Band was in that city by the end of the century's first decade, and by the end of the second, New Orleans musicians Jelly Roll Morton, Papa Mutt Carey, and Kid Ory were calling it home or at least sojourning there for a time, often to return years later to settle down.[96] By 1928, too, Billy Young may have been finding life on the road a little too demanding for a man his age—he was then about fifty-six, which, while not old by today's standards, was old enough for African Americans born in the nineteenth century.

Other factors accounted for both Willis Young's leaving Minneapolis and Les's intermittent touring and returns to his family. One factor was the gangsters and rackets that so profoundly affected nightclub life during Prohibition. Minneapolis had its few gangsters, notably Kid Cann (alias Harold Bloom), and as in every city, Black nightclub men ran their own resorts or fronted for whites. Ben Wilson, whose unofficial title was "Mayor of North Minneapolis," had this part of the city "tied up" with respect to bootleg whiskey and women, running both the Nest, at 731 Sixth Avenue North, and the Kit Kat Club. His "mouthpiece" was another African American, Ted Crockett. In subsequent years, Wilson and at least one of the town's musicians would be sentenced to prison for their involvement in the rackets and prostitution.[97]

Early in 1928, two policemen investigating a brawl were shot—one seriously—at the Cotton Club, at 718 Sixth Avenue North, only two blocks from the Youngs' home. Kid Cann was also slightly wounded. The assailants got away. One was said to be a bootlegger and former South Dakota sheriff; a warrant was issued for his arrest. In the aftermath of this incident, the police chief ordered the Cotton Club (which was already temporarily closed anyway) and every other nightclub and café in town to put a stop to all "singing and dancing and the like" at midnight. Either the shooting or the reform efforts following it, or both, may have been sufficient reason for the professor and Lester to depart Minneapolis around that time. Lester would return, only to leave again after similar episodes early in 1932 and in 1936.[98]

Upon leaving Minneapolis, the dance band and the show appear to have diverged, with plans calling for Sarah and Willis Young to reunite in Texas, Mrs. Young's home state. In the interim, perhaps sensing his son's imminent departure with his friends, Billy Young enlarged his band to eleven players and performed for a year or so in the Southwest. In the mid-1930s, he would revive his band with his grandchildren in Los Angeles.[99]

Despite the shift to jazz and dance music, Willis and Sarah Young maintained links with the road shows. In around 1928, Sarah Young went out on her own with the show and its band, as evidenced by a photograph taken in Minot, North Dakota (near the Canadian border), showing her with Irma, Lee, and a number of other musicians, singers, and blackface entertainers, along with Irma's daughter, Martha, then a toddler (see photo insert). They are still the New Orleans Strutters, standing before the familiar backdrop, with its grinning Negro stereotypes playing dice beneath the caption "Rattlin' Good Bones" on one side, and a pickaninny next to the legend "A Popular Dance" on the other. The fact that Willis and Lester Young are missing from the photo confirms that they were playing elsewhere.[100]

When his father finally headed for Texas, Les decided to strike out on his own. The saxophonist recalled that "I told him how it would be down there, and that we could have some fine jobs back through Nebraska, Kansas, and Iowa, but he didn't have eyes for it. He was set to go."[101] On this occasion the professor sent a policeman after his son, either to persuade or to force him to return, but this tactic only postponed the inevitable. When they reached Salina, Kansas, Lester left the band. Leonard Phillips and Pete Jones followed his example the next day in Wichita;

they doubled back by bus to Salina and found Les playing pool in a café. "'What are y'all doing here, man! Oh, I'm so glad to see you,'" he said. He told them of Art Bronson: "'There's a guy got a band here said he want to enlarge his band to a ten-piece band.'"[102]

For Young, Phillips, and Jones, staying with the minstrel show meant moving "backward" and "down." Phillips explained, "We didn't want to go back to no damn carnival. That's going back. . . . I wanted to go *up*, [not] back. None of us . . . you didn't get no prestige playing on a carnival. . . . It's just a low-class . . . down-class show." They wanted to continue playing the more respectable jobs in hotel ballrooms and dance halls. So Pete, Leonard, and Lester all joined Bronson's band, which was headquartered in Denver. Besides the leader, pianist Art Bronson, the Bostonians included a number of musicians about whom little is known except that they were pioneers in early jazz in the region. The first altoist was a Jamaican by the name of Albert Walters, who had once held the same chair with the professor and "could read like mad"; they got him out of Omaha.[103] Buford Boswell was on third alto, and Lester completed the sax section. Trumpet player Ted Williams and Young's companions, Phillips and Jones, made up the brass. George Hudson (bass), Herb Hanners (banjo), and Percy Walker (drums) were the heart of the rhythm section along with Bronson.[104]

Years later Phillips would contend, "Mr. [Willis] Young . . . God bless him . . . see[,] money was always short with him. . . . He *had* money, but I mean he didn't give . . . *you* no money. . . . He wanted to work you for *nothing*." He and Pete Jones had learned a little bit about bandleaders in 1925, when they left Billy Young's band for a time to join Sidney De Paris. Part of the problem was the apprenticeship system, but of course, musicians in the professor's band were not the only performers who ever griped about low pay; that has been a perennial complaint of sidemen. When they were first recruited, Phillips and Jones were still teenagers, inexperienced and eager to play for little, but a few years on the road developed their abilities and gave them a better idea of their worth. As Phillips explained it, "[Professor Young]'d get a bunch of young guys [who'd say] 'I don't care if they give me nothing . . . I want to be out there playing.' [But] sooner or later, you wake up to that, you say, 'This ain't nothing. . . . Man, I'm playing out and I ain't getting nothing.' So we left."[105]

Even before this particular departure, in 1928 (it would not be his last), Lester had gigged in Minneapolis clubs and occasionally toured with the Bostonians and other local bands. In addition to Eddie Barefield and Snake Whyte, Frank Hines, Rook Ganz, Paul Cephas, and Oscar Pettiford all performed with him at one point or another in Minnesota in the late 1920s and early 1930s. These performers and such dance bands as Eli Rice's Cotton Pickers and the Virginia Ravens also toured the surrounding territories as the jazz and dance-band craze swept the nation. Such road experience allowed Lester to develop as a musician and to prepare for the big time, the ultimate goal of most territorial musicians.[106]

When Eddie Barefield met up with him again after North Dakota, this time in Minneapolis in, by Barefield's recollection, early 1928, Young did not have the Selmer his father had promised him, but he did have a tenor. "He was playing this alto style on tenor," Barefield recalled. The two teamed up to play school dances, with "just two saxophones, no rhythm section, no piano or anything." Barefield explained that they were learning from each other at the time, each developing his rapport and ability to work with and support the other, alternating lead and harmony roles.[107]

Late in 1929 or very early in 1930, Les left the Bronson band in Grand Island, Nebraska, to go to the Southwest, where his family was sojourning. His first-ever printed notice was a listing in the Albuquerque City Directory, revealing not only the saxophonist's mobility but the extent to which the music had penetrated the American heartland by the end of the jazz decade. He lived only a few blocks from downtown.[108]

Initially he moved in with his family, who appear to have settled in the city for a time in 1929. In fact, Willis and Sarah were both listed in the Albuquerque City Directories of 1929 and 1930. These rare printed references to the family's southwestern sojourn point to the elder Youngs' adaptability and suggest why Lester may have joined them in New Mexico.

In 1929 the professor and Sarah operated Young's Music Store at 115½ West Gold, near downtown Albuquerque and close to the railroad depot. The professor befriended local Black leaders and became comanager of the local Black newspaper, the *Trend.* Dr. James A. Lewis, a physician and surgeon, was the other manager of the semimonthly, whose offices were located at 211½ West Gold, one block up from the music store. The newspaper shared this address with the Rio Grande National Development Society, a joint real estate venture of Henry Outley, S. T. Richard, and Dr. Lewis.[109]

Given his father's contacts and standing in the community, it was easy for Les to resume his place in the band and settle in with the family in the large two-story house at 216 Stover, south of downtown. Meanwhile, Albuquerque held another attraction for him: the woman who would become his first bride resided in that New Mexico city in 1930. So Les had a compelling reason to stay in the Southwest, playing around town in Phoenix as well as in Albuquerque, even after his family left for southern California.

Whether he was with his father or on his own, Young remained highly mobile, a pattern that would characterize much of his adult life. Even after leaving his father's outfit in the late 1920s, Lester maintained the mobility of a territorial musician, alternating a Minneapolis residency and performances in local clubs with touring as a member of other dance bands. With Bronson's band, Young, Phillips, and Jones crisscrossed what were for them familiar routes in Kansas, Nebraska, and the Dakotas. The Bostonians were hardly alone out there, as the prairies were filled with dance bands: "We ran into Guy Lombardo, he was up through there [the Dakotas] when we ran into him. Lawrence Welk . . . lived up there," Phillips recalled. He and Young "used to see Lawrence Welk . . . plying wheat in the daytime, and playing at night."[110] The Bostonians also shared this dance-band territory with the Dixie Ramblers, Nat Towles, Bennie Moten, Eli Rice, Grant Moore, and Andy Kirk. All that traveling, of course, meant that Lester was constantly away from his family, which was hard on at least one of its younger members. When, in 1930, after performing at a place called East Lake Park in Phoenix under his father's leadership, "Lester left home . . . he and Ben Webster left home together,"[111] Irma Young wept at her elder brother's departure. Years would pass before she saw him again.

PART II

The Spark in My Heart

Prez invented cool. Rather than state a melody, he suggested it. He barely breathed into his horn, creating an intimacy that gave me chills. They talk about abstract painters; well, Prez was an abstract jazz man, and he taught me the beauty of modern art. He taught me to use the minimum amount of notes.

B. B. King, *Blues All Around Me: The Autobiography of B. B. King*

CHAPTER 6

Red Boy Blues

The Territorial Years, 1929–1932

TWO opposite poles attracted Lester Young beginning in his adolescent years: the road, with its constant change and adventure, and home, with all its comforts and security. This had been a pattern in his family for three generations. It probably started with his paternal grandmother, Martha Young, who traveled as a missionary spreading the gospel every spring through fall, a routine that was continued by her third son, Willis, on the musicians' circuit. Touring and being at home were not necessarily incompatible; their alternation constituted, rather, the satisfying rhythm that people on a mission prefer, and Lester was one of their number. Many entertainers enjoyed that rhythm for a while and then, due to the demands of family or their own road-weariness, elected to opt for a more settled life. Subsequently, if their marriages or families broke up, they might choose to go out on tour again. Recognizing this pattern will help us understand Young's career in the early 1930s, because the few details we have about his life and whereabouts during this period are confusing and contradictory at best.

We know that Young left Art Bronson's Bostonians temporarily in either late 1929 or early 1930 to go to Albuquerque; an old friend from the Strutters, the saxophonist Clarence Phillips (Leonard's brother), replaced him in the band, then touring in Nebraska. One reason, and probably the main one, for this sojourn in the seat of Bernalillo County can be gleaned from local marriage records: on a late-winter day in that New Mexico city nestled in the Rio Grande Valley, Lester Young wed Beatrice Toliver. He also played around town about this time, according to the pianist John Lewis, who grew up in Albuquerque. The saxophonist resumed his chair with the Bostonians in May or June of 1930. Later the same year he returned to Minneapolis with Beatrice, and there he stayed until 1936.[1]

The marriage was significant because, besides amounting to a new stage in Lester's adult life, it gave him reason to stop going out on the road and settle down. Of course, he still occasionally toured both locally and elsewhere in the Midwest, with both Minneapolis and name bands, especially from 1932 to 1934. But he spent extended periods in Minneapolis before moving to Kansas City in 1936. The northern prairie city, and not Kansas City, as is usually argued, was his home base during these years.[2]

Giving Art Bronson his final notice in Scottsbluff, Nebraska, in the fall of 1930 marked another kind of departure for Young. Tired of touring, he "wanted to go to Minneapolis where he could just sit down and play. He didn't want to travel," Leonard Phillips reported. Le Roy "Snake" Whyte, the son of a minister who was also a bandmaster, confirmed that for a couple of years the saxophonist "stayed in Minneapolis; he wouldn't move because . . . I guess that was the first steady job Lester had." Before he agreed to tour with the Blue Devils in 1932, it took some convincing on their part to pry him away from home.[3]

His new bride provided good reason for him to stay in Minneapolis. He was very attached to her, and their marriage would last for nearly a decade. Several musicians mentioned a wife named Bea, but neither they nor Lester's family knew how the couple met, when they decided to marry, or what became of her after 1942. The marriage records inform us that Beatrice Toliver, the first Mrs. Lester Young, was born in Perry, Oklahoma, on August 3, 1911. She was thought to have been in show business at one time. In 1930, like so many Black women in the United States, she worked as a domestic; she was fortunate enough to be employed, in that Depression year, in the home of an Albuquerque physician, at 221 North Dartmouth, only a few blocks from the University of New Mexico. She was later listed in the 1930 City Directory as residing with Lester at 311 North Seventh, about half a mile from the Coal Avenue A.M.E. church of the minister who married them. She was eighteen when she wed her betrothed on Sunday, February 23, 1930. Besides these bare facts, there are a few other details given in the marriage documents that shed some light on the groom's maturation.[4]

The saxophonist's name was actually Willis Lester Young, as indicated by his signature on the marriage application; this was also the name that appeared on the marriage license. Because this is the first bit of written information to come directly from him, the documents have a certain authority. Lee Young verified that Willis was indeed his brother's given name. Later he would drop it in favor of his middle name, even for official purposes such as the Social Security application he filled out in the late 1930s and subsequent property records.[5]

He gave his date of birth as August 27, 1908, making him twenty-one in early 1930. Since by all accounts he was actually born a year later, we may infer that he was marrying without parental permission, which was required in New Mexico for prospective grooms under twenty-one. His white lie suggests that he must have been really eager to get married right away rather than wait until August, when he would be of age. His father and stepmother were by then either headed for or already in California, and he likely would not have wanted to ask their permission in any case, so he simply did what he had to do to start his own family by marrying and setting up a place of his own.[6]

Rosie Toliver, presumably a relative of the bride, witnessed the marriage; no one from the groom's family joined her as a witness. It is doubtful that the Youngs even knew Lester was getting married. In some sense it must have been his way of declaring his independence after he separated from the family for the last time.[7]

For a person who would come to personify the archetypal rebel and hipster in the 1940s and 1950s, a man indifferent to legal niceties, Young appeared to pay surprising attention to following the proper procedure in his first marriage, aside from adding a year to his age. He obtained the license on Thursday, February 20, 1930, and wed Beatrice three days later in the seat of Bernalillo County. The couple probably took their vows in Albuquerque's oldest A.M.E. church, at 311 Coal Avenue West, just south of downtown, or perhaps in the parsonage next door, home to the minister who performed the ceremony, the Reverend Elias C. W. Cox, a doctor of divinity. The newlyweds rented their own place in a boardinghouse on North Seventh, less than a mile from the church, where they stayed at least long enough to be listed in that year's City Directory.[8]

Later in life, Young would offer the statement "I just wanted to be grown" as his reason for leaving his father's band. This adds a further dimension to the marriage record. Many of his near-contemporaries, including his sister, Irma, and fellow musicians Ed Lewis, a Bennie Moten/Count Basie trumpeter, and Charlie Parker, married in their midteens and immediately tried to assume the responsibilities of parenthood. Marrying and having his own place enabled Young to live his life as he saw fit at a time when he was still developing as a musician.[9]

The bridegroom wanted to do things right and make a new start in life. He could have simply married Bea before a justice of the peace in the local city hall, but instead he sought out an A.M.E. minister. He also could have gone straight back to Minneapolis with his bride, but he stayed in Albuquerque for a time, perhaps with the intention of putting down roots along the Rio Grande. The lack of legal discrimination against African Americans in New Mexico no doubt played a role in his staying on. Furthermore, not only was he married now, but he had made a number of friends in the city's African American Community. The pianist John Lewis recalled that Young "knew my whole family"—a family that had been in New Mexico for some time.[10]

In fact, the Youngs lived in the very same adobe boardinghouse where Aaron Lewis, John's father, had stayed in 1921. A porter at the Franciscan Hotel by the name of Lester Burt (or Burke) had resided at this North Seventh Street address in 1929 with Lottie Burt, who may have been his wife or a relative; the owner appears to have been still another person. Several other people with the name Burt (or Burke) lived nearby, which may mean that Lester and Beatrice had connected with a large extended family that, like the Lewises, had established a beachhead for other African Americans in this city on the Rio Grande.[11]

Perhaps because Beatrice lost her job as a domestic, the newlyweds decided to move on from Albuquerque later that same year. In spite of his subsequent reputation as a loner and vagabond spirit, Young now settled down in Minneapolis, where he and his wife lived from 1930 to 1932 and then again from late 1934 to 1936. Beatrice undoubtedly had some stabilizing effect on him, providing him with a home, comfort, and emotional as well as financial security during his early years as a professional musician. The fact that she worked as a domestic, instead of, say, a teacher, tells us something about Young's devotion to her regardless of the low social status that attended her line of work. By all accounts, she was a down-to-earth person—"kind of country," in one friend's depiction—and Lester's relationship with her underlined his penchant for judging people by standards other than social status. Her importance in his life, like their Minneapolis residency, has often been overlooked.[12]

Friends recalled that Lester and Bea were constantly together whenever he was not on the job. In Minneapolis they set up house on the North Side, near where he had lived with his family. Still, the Youngs were listed only once in the Minneapolis City Directory, with the 1935 edition giving 715 Sixth Avenue North, Apartment 1, as their address. This was a two-story flat building six houses down from the Nest, at number 731, where Lester performed in 1931, and just across from the Cotton Club, at number 718, where he played from 1934 to 1936. Even after his friend and sideman Snake Whyte went on tour as a Blue Devil, Young stayed in Minneapolis because he liked having the comforts and the sense of security it afforded him. "He had a home, steady. . . . He had a room, and he knew that money was coming in. So nobody could *budge* Lester," Whyte reminisced.[13]

The hardships that Young had experienced as a territorial musician in the late 1920s may have contributed to his desire to have a stable home and a regular job. Just as minstrelsy and vaudeville began to fade, radio broadcasts, sound movies, and documentary film shorts featuring jazz bands enlarged audiences for future tours. Yet as the Depression worsened in the early 1930s, record and phonograph sales and live-performance attendance plummeted. Jazz bands with national reputations could obtain bookings in large theaters, but local bands lost out—which was not good news for Lester and musicians like him. Some name bands profited while others languished until mid-decade. According to one historian, "In two short years, 1929–31, jazz bands, and particularly black bands, [became] a major element within the established structure of the national entertainment industry."[14]

Young's time on the road with the Bostonians, from around 1928 to 1930, was a difficult period for him. He later claimed to have been with Art Bronson for "two or three or four years," blurring time or admitting that he joined and then left the band on at least two or three different occasions. He also recalled, "Sometimes I used to go back to my father's band." The Bostonians rode around the prairies of the Midwest in a seven-passenger Buick followed by a truck filled with their instruments. They earned ten to fifteen dollars each, on a 70/30 percentage basis, but times were hard: "We're waiting for ninety years to get us a gig," Young remembered.[15]

Despite the difficulties and his eventual (final) departure from the band, however, the Bostonians played an important role in Young's career: it was with them that he switched from alto to tenor. Not long after he left Bronson, his reputation as a tenor saxophonist was so impressive that he was actively sought after by various swing bands. Exactly why he switched to tenor and why he sounded the way he did have been the subjects of endless speculation. Like many reedmen, he played different saxophones and occasionally even the clarinet from the early 1920s on, despite fans' and critics' assumption that he played only one instrument, either C-melody or alto, before adopting the larger, deeper-toned tenor saxophone. The reality was more complex. For one thing, he often soloed on soprano with his father's dance band. Moreover, he seems to have alternated between two instruments in 1930 and 1931, first playing tenor with Bronson and then going back to alto after rejoining him.[16]

Young's own accounts of his change of saxes may have reflected his ambivalence about whether to play alto—better known for its stylists at that time—or tenor, a relatively new instrument for jazz soloists. His statements, charming though they are, shed little light on the switch. In his first published interview, in 1946, he said he had played alto for five years; as for the change, "it was a funny deal. . . . [The] tenor player in the band [would] get high and never show up for the dates. . . . Kept messin' up." Young complained to Bronson, who responded by buying him a "beat-up tenor" that caused him to hesitate: "When I saw [it] . . . I almost changed my mind. It was an old Pan-American job. But I played it and liked it, what's more." The change did not present a problem. The reporter, Allan Morrison, explained in this interview that Young's "approach . . . to tenor playing was essentially an alto approach. . . . Before he knew it he was playing tenor, alto style."[17]

Later Young would tell the story differently, maintaining that he had played baritone as well as alto with the Bostonians. His explanation for the changeover recalls his reasoning for giving up drums: "I was playing the baritone and it was weighing me down. I am really lazy. . . . So when the tenor man left, I took over his instrument." Still later, he returned to the first account, asserting that he had replaced his "first instrument," the alto, with the tenor "when I was with the Bostonians": "The tenor player kept grandstanding all the time. So I told the leader, if you buy a tenor for me, I'll play it." Elaborating on the show-off's background, and in doing so revealing his bias against bandsmen from affluent families, he remarked, "The regular tenor was a boy from a well-to-do family. . . . He didn't have to play. I got sick of it."[18]

Other musicians' recollections of Lester's switch varied. Eddie Barefield and Snake Whyte both said that Young was an altoist when they first met him, in North Dakota. Barefield added that back in Minneapolis, Young had been "playing tenor and . . . playing [Trumbauer] style on *tenor* . . . the first part of [19]28." Whyte recalled that in the professor's band, Lester "was [playing] real light on his alto . . . so I was surprised when he put it down and went to tenor"—but then again, "he still was playing the alto style on his tenor."[19]

Benny Carter, himself a distinguished alto stylist as well as an arranger, believed that Young excelled on the alto and, furthermore, played it differently than he did the tenor. Carter reminisced about the winter McKinney's Cotton Pickers visited Minneapolis: "One night when we were on the road, word went around that band that this guy called Young was playing in [Minneapolis]. . . . He was a different man with a completely different style from his tenor." In his opinion, Lester "was a real flash on alto. Like Parker, what he was playing was entirely different from anything I'd heard." McKinney's arranger went on to admit, "He scared me—and at that time I was considered a pretty good alto player." Years later he could reflect, "It's too bad more people couldn't have heard Lester play alto sax. . . . It was the greatest thing I'd ever heard." Carter's final word on Young was that "he had a definition and a mastery that I don't think he ever felt necessary to display on the tenor."[20]

The tenor saxophonist Albert "Budd" Johnson, a friend of Young's from the late 1920s on, elaborated on Carter's evaluation: "Pres played two different styles at that time. He'd get up and play pretty on alto, and then he would really blow on the tenor, and this would break up the house." Moreover, he added, Young turned down the opportunity to join McKinney's band because the leader wanted him to play alto while he himself preferred the tenor chair, which belonged to Prince Robinson—then considered to be second only to Coleman Hawkins on the instrument.[21]

It is possible that the young saxophonist adopted the tenor because it was an instrument on which he felt he could excel at a time when there were few tenor men, at least compared to alto stylists, of whom there were quite a number—Johnny Hodges and Willie Smith, to name only two. Despite opinion to the contrary, Young was no match for some of those other alto players, according to Snake Whyte: "He couldn't touch nobody like Eddie Barefield." Moreover, Young himself "knew he wasn't an alto player . . . a Willie Smith or one of those guys . . . Scoops Carey. So I think that's the reason [he switched]." Whyte added another insight: "At that time a tenor didn't have as much a play as Lester *made.*" Young contributed to the legitimacy of tenors as soulful soloists in the jazz orchestra: "Lester made the way for tenors to blow a lot. 'Cause he kept *originating things.*"[22]

Confusing things even further, Leonard Phillips insisted, "Lester never did play no alto with Bronson," because "any time he left his father, his father was taking everything he had . . . all the horns . . . a clarinet, a baritone and an alto . . . and a soprano." Young was therefore lacking any instrument at all in Salina. With Bronson, Phillips said, Young "played tenor the whole time"; as to Young's contention that he had played alto first, then tenor with the Bostonians, Phillips commented, "I don't see how he could say that." But then Phillips seemed to contradict his own assertion, saying that Young first played on tenor with Bronson but that when he came back after getting married in New Mexico, "he was playing alto." Later, Phillips explained, he switched back again: "He started playing tenor after he went to Minneapolis. . . . He got started playing tenor again." Whatever the real story may have been, Young's adoption of the tenor became permanent by the early 1930s. Phillips recalled that Young "always told me . . . 'One of these days I'm going to play just tenor. I like it.' "[23]

As the instrument's popularity grew in the early 1930s, several tenor saxophonists left their mark on younger players. Besides Hawkins, Phillips noted, there was Bud Freeman, but "didn't nobody listen to him much." As for Freeman's influence on Young, "he didn't care nothin' about Bud." Phillips asserted that Young was an original in his own right who in turn influenced a number of prospective tenor men. "When Les came along, he started playing tenor. . . . That's when guys started playing tenors."[24]

Young's influence on other players was very clear to Ben Webster, who played piano with Professor Young in the Southwest in 1929–1930. Webster also played violin, but he joined the professor's band to learn the up-and-coming instrument: the tenor saxophone. Phillips recalled, "Ben said, 'I used to hear ol' Les in the room, man, playin' that horn, and I'd get in there and try to run over and play, but that cat was *gone.*' " Phillips himself was touring with Bronson at the time, but Webster and Young must have told him stories about this period in jazz history when Webster "stayed with Mr. Young I guess about a year . . . playing piano, and then he was practicing on the saxophone at the same time." After that he joined Jasper "Jap" Allen's band, "and Ben was a sensation. Cats wasn't blowin' tenor like he was blowin' then." For his sound and basic conception, however, Webster chose Coleman Hawkins as his model rather than Lester Young.[25]

In the 1930s, Young performed in several Minneapolis bands and clubs. The saxophonist Eddie Barefield fronted a band made up of Young, Snake Whyte on trumpet, and the pianist Frank Hines early in 1931. Young was also in the Nest Orchestra that year. The Nest, promising "Entertainment Supreme," was, Whyte recalled, "run . . . by the famous gangster of the North Side at that time, called Kid Cann," and managed by D. C. Ampey.[26]

The Nest's show featured "Kitty," a singer and the wife of Ben Wilson, the "Mayor of the North Side"; Genevieve Stearns, also a singer; and comedians Pedro Lane and Arcola Hill. El Herbert, on trumpet, directed the seven-piece Nest Orchestra. Its other members were Jack McVea (first alto), Buddy Harper (guitar), Johnny Wheeler (trumpet), Willie Burrell or Bell (tuba), Young (tenor), and an unidentified drummer. The Nest's tenor saxophonist also performed in the bands of the Minneapolis trumpet player and leader Reuben "Rook" Ganz and the arranger Boyd Atkins; occasionally he toured—into Wisconsin, for example—but he never strayed far from Minneapolis until 1932.[27]

Young's musicianship developed as he performed in the local after-hours spots. At the Nest and the Kit Kat, the bands played in the manner of many small jazz bands of the era in clubs in Kansas City and Oklahoma City, on Chicago's South Side, and in New York's Harlem—that is, without written arrangements. "It was five, six pieces, it was mostly heads [memorized arrangements]," Snake Whyte recalled. They bought piano scores at the dime store, "then we'd get the melody off of that, and then either [we'd] fake the harmonies or somebody [would] write the harmonies."[28]

By most accounts, Young was devoted to his wife and to music during his Minneapolis years. As both Barefield and Whyte observed, he had no vices; furthermore, "he was strictly a Bea man." Members of the Blue Devils, the next big band he would join, concurred, maintaining that Young displayed no interest in any woman besides the one he was currently going with, who was invariably his wife. Buster Smith, his section leader in the Blue Devils, said, "I never did see him talk to no woman. . . . He didn't pay no woman no attention." Smith recounted how "some of them tried to talk to him, [but] he just stand off and look at them . . . and they'd see he looked like he didn't want to be bothered, and they'd walk on away from him."[29]

According to these reports, he not only was loyal to his wife but at least at this point in his life still followed his father's example by abstaining from smoking, drinking, and using profanity. The actual story of his domestic life at this time, however, seems to be more complicated than his colleagues knew. Either he left Beatrice in Albuquerque for a time or else he broke up with her temporarily late in 1930, because in July 1931 he had a child with Bess Cooper of Minneapolis, who died soon afterward. Beverly, their daughter, was raised by her godparents. She later claimed that Young had married her mother, who was white, and been grief-stricken by her tragic death. He made arrangements with her godparents for her care, she said, sent money to provide for her when he was touring, telephoned her frequently, and stopped by to visit when he was in town. When she was about four years old, he bought her a baby grand piano. Sometimes she accompanied him on the road.[30]

Unfortunately, all documentation—marriage, death, and birth certificates as well as photos—relating to this aspect of Young's life was destroyed by a fire in Beverly's home, and no confirmation has been discovered in any official records. Compelling though Beverly Young's story is, until we have more evidence, we cannot easily reconcile her account of her parents' relationship with the lack of official records and the testimony of sidemen that Young was strictly a one-woman man. Lee Young, for one, doubts the story because he believes his brother would have told him about the marriage and especially about a daughter. Nevertheless, Young's concern for Beverly might help explain why he stayed in Minneapolis on and off for nearly ten years.[31]

In any case, touring still held its appeal for Young, and for much of 1932 and 1933 he would be on the road again. Young's friend Snake Whyte had joined the Blue Devils and eventually persuaded the saxophonist to take a chance and leave town again in 1932. The Oklahoma City band's reputation for having a large repertoire ranging from up-tempo or "jump" numbers to slow blues, and for defeating all contestants in battles, probably influenced his decision as well. The drummer Jo Jones felt that the band whose banner proclaimed that it had "Never Lost a Battle" was "the greatest band I ever heard," and Count Basie designated it as his favorite, too.[32]

Whyte recalled that when he first tried to recruit Young, he appealed to his desire to improve his financial status as well as his playing. "So when I came back there" to Minneapolis with the Blue Devils, Whyte recounted, "I was looking the part . . . had money, dressed [up], and everything. . . . 'Look,'" he told the tenor saxophonist, "'I got a chance for you to get out of here and get [with] some other saxophones.'" Whyte reminded him, "You been playing by yourself"—referring to the fact that Young was often either the only reedman or one of the few in the local bands he performed with. He continued, "You need to get somebody else. . . . Kansas City [has] all kinds of musicians . . . and that's where we're heading."[33]

Still Young resisted the lure of success. Finally, realizing what the problem was, Whyte offered to take his own wife, Cecile, along, and suggested that Beatrice accompany them. The Whytes had been married since the late summer of 1929. Whyte promised the Youngs, "You stay with me and Cecile . . . and see how you like it. And if you don't, I'll guarantee you I'll bring you back here." The two women had each other for company, which was especially welcome when their husbands went away for a few days; Bea was, in fact, said to be like a "big sister" to Cecile, who could use a friend's help in taking care of her son, Leroy Junior.

Such small comforts were important to both the musicians and their spouses, for the Blue Devils often played some distance away from any big city. Even when their wives went on the road with them, some physical separation was inevitable. Whyte explained, "When we'd move into a territory, it would be for six weeks or eight weeks. . . . We'd have a headquarters . . . we'd be in Sioux City, we might play Des Moines. Then Lake Okoboja, but we'd go back into Sioux City every two or three days."[34]

The band often traveled and played in predominantly white towns, so obtaining accommodations was part of the problem and sometimes the reason for the separation, because many citizens of Oklahoma, Missouri, and Kansas shared the racial prejudices of the Deep South. Whyte, Young, and the other Blue Devils turned to the Black community for help when no hotels would accept them. Black Americans commonly took in boarders; they had nothing against musicians.

In 1932, Lester, Bea, and Leroy and Cecile Whyte and their son "lived together all the time around Kansas City" during the band's sojourn there. The Kansas City jobs lasted only a few weeks, however. As they toured, Snake Whyte regularly found them places to stay: "In those days," he recalled, "if you got a wife, you could rent a room for two dollars and fifty cents a week, and you had kitchen privileges. There was no apartments. . . . People were honest those days. They'd open up their house to you." Whyte had a system: "All the time I was with the Blue Devils I'd find a minister of the town and I'd tell him I had my family with me (if I had 'em), and I would want a nice place to stay and he'd . . . call up somebody [and get a welcome reception:] 'Yes, we'd be glad to have them.'" As a matter of fact, "in those days musicians were respected just like doctors and professional people. People were always inviting us to their homes. And we liked that."[35]

In Oklahoma City, the next stop on their 1932 tour, they made similar arrangements. Whyte's kin were helpful in this instance: a cousin provided accommodations for the two couples. "Everywhere we'd go that's the way it would be," Whyte remembered. Occasionally they were "lucky enough to get a house with two bedrooms. They'd have a bedroom [and] we'd have one. Then our wives would go in the kitchen and *cook.*" Home-cooked meals and a soft bed appealed to bachelors and married men alike—not to mention their wives.[36]

For a time the Whytes and Youngs managed to avoid the problems so typical of the life of the traveling dance-band musician, but the deepening Depression made matters increasingly difficult for the band. Numerous other territorial bands broke up or became stranded in 1933, when the public could no longer afford this form of entertainment. Buck Clayton, for one, went to Shanghai, and other musicians left for European sojourns during these hard times. It was precisely the vicissitudes of the economy and the desire for greater success that led the Blue Devils to expand their territory, emulating their Kansas City arch-rival Benny Moten, who "went down South [and] made lots of money."[37]

Two known factors affected the Youngs' domestic life: the Blue Devils' need to keep touring over an increasingly large area, and their routine of making forays from a home base where their wives stayed. "You didn't have a chance to do much resting, and it was really a godsend when we got two or three nights in one place," Whyte said. For a while the band was able to achieve a measure of stability by playing the Ritz in Oklahoma City in the winter and the Cinderella Gardens in Little Rock during the summer, but in 1932, "most of [our work] was road work."

The expansion of the territory covered by the band caused a conflict when it was suggested that they tour the South in 1932 or 1933. Snake Whyte objected. The Iowa native explained, "I had been down South with a show and prayed that if I ever got away from down in there, they'd . . . have . . . [real] trouble getting me back down there." Also, he said, "I was married . . . my family was first. I turned down a lot of jobs and whatnot . . . to be with my family." So Whyte left the Blue Devils in Cincinnati and moved to Columbus, Ohio, settling there with his wife and son. Later he would join Eddie Barefield's band in Los Angeles, where he would reside for more than three decades. Wherever he lived, he made sure he told locals, such as Earle Warren in Ohio, of the prowess of Lester Young.[38]

Despite his objections a few years earlier to traveling in the South with his father's band, Young stayed with the Blue Devils through their Upper South tour. It is not clear exactly when Beatrice returned to Minneapolis, but no Blue Devils recalled her being on the road with them in 1933. After this episode, the tenor stylist's relationship with his first wife became an even more private matter. Little is known about the state of their marriage during Young's last years in Minneapolis—1934, 1935, and early 1936—before he relocated to Kansas City. He later made a rather cryptic reference to her in discussing this move: "So [Basie] sent me a ticket, and I left my madam and went on my way."[39]

In fact, the strength and longevity of their relationship—if not of their actual marriage—were evident in Beatrice's presence, eleven years after their Albuquerque wedding, in Los Angeles, where Lester played with his brother's combo in 1941. By then he was married for the second time, to Mary Dale, a white woman from New York, but he and his first wife remained on good terms. Aunt Bea, as she was known to the saxophonist's nieces and nephews, was described as "a very portly, very shapely dark lady" who took care of Les. Such matters as his breakup with Beatrice, and eventually with Mary Dale as well, were shrouded in the privacy Young preferred.[40]

In the touring bands of the early 1930s, Young became a leading member of a society of performers who made big-band blues and jazz so powerful and convincing as American cultural statements that immigrant and native white Americans assimilated the music and dance fads with enough enthusiasm to create a major market in the entertainment industry. The society of traveling musicians included both Black bands and white ones, though there was no integration of performers on the bandstand. There was a distinct hierarchy within this society, from the territorial bands that stayed in the Southwest or Midwest to the "big-time" orchestras that went everywhere, some even to Europe during the Depression. The main idea in touring, of course, was to get to the Big Time.[41]

Young's regional mobility reflected his desire to learn and to move up, and the touring he did in his early years would enhance his legendary status after he became famous. His virtuosity impressed musicians from Albuquerque to Minneapolis in the Depression years. As a matter of fact, he seemed to be everyplace at once, but perhaps as a way to simplify matters, his apprenticeship, musical influences, and sources of inspiration have all been mistakenly attributed to Kansas City. This focus, combined with Young's own indifference regarding specific dates and details and his desire to protect his privacy, makes it easy to lose sight of his actual geographic location at different times. Moreover, such a simplification offers little information on his comings and goings with various bands or on the development of his art and craft, nor does it tell us much about his devotion to family and his attempts to live a normal existence, with all the comforts of a settled life. Indeed, his years with Beatrice and his subsequent spouses exemplify aspects of his life—a loving wife, a nice place to live, and the security of a regular job in one place—that have been neglected in biographies of the saxophonist.[42]

Yet the commercialism that is such a driving force behind jazz journalism touted Young as a Kansas City musician, and so this belief has fixed itself firmly in jazz literature and in the popular mind. He in fact resided for longer periods in Minneapolis than he did in Kansas City. While he visited and played in the latter city, there is little evidence that he ever actually lived there for any length of time before joining Count Basie in 1936.[43]

The portrayal of Young as a Kansas Citian by writers such as John Hammond is contradicted by the saxophonist's own testimony, which puts him there only occasionally during these years. More definitively, he was not listed in Kansas City's City Directory for 1933 or 1934 (though he did have a listing in the 1936 edition). Here it may be useful to review Young's recollections, even though they provide only a rough sketch of this period. He recalled that it was in Salina, Kansas, that he joined Art Bronson's Bostonians in 1928; then he lived in Minneapolis from 1930 to 1932; after that, he reported, he went with King Oliver's band, followed by a stint with the Blue Devils, which he dated to 1934 and 1935 (in fact, it was two to three years earlier). He never mentioned his sojourn in the Southwest.[44]

He first toured with Basie's band in early 1934, after the Blue Devils' breakup and the King Oliver tour. He was with Basie in Little Rock, Arkansas, that spring when he received an invitation to join Fletcher Henderson, an interlude that lasted from spring to summer. He played with Andy Kirk's Kansas City band that summer, but not for very long, and then worked with Rook Ganz and Eli Rice in their Minneapolis-based bands from late 1934 to 1936. He rejoined Count Basie in 1936, a few months before his band members left for Chicago and New York.[45]

Other musicians' testimony makes it clear just how mobile Young was, and some of this information can be worked into his chronology. Barefield and Whyte, for example, performed with him in Minneapolis both before and after his Bronson stints, in 1928 and 1931. Leonard Phillips put him with Bronson in the late 1920s, in Albuquerque in 1930, back with Bronson later that year, and then in Minneapolis before he joined the Blue Devils and Oliver. However, Phillips contended that contrary to Young's own account, he played with Oliver *after* the Blue Devils, not before.[46]

The writer Ralph Ellison recalled seeing Young in Oklahoma City in 1929 and claimed that he was a Blue Devil then, but more likely he was with Bronson. John Lewis remembered Young's performing in Albuquerque, and Paul Quinichette placed him in Denver, where Art Bronson lived, at about the same time—sometime in the early 1930s. Benny Carter heard him in Minneapolis on his way through that city in the winter of 1931 or 1932.[47]

It is not easy to reconcile the sometimes conflicting recollections of when Young was with the Blue Devils or in Kansas City. Fortunately, city directories have been of some help in the reconstruction of his whereabouts, as those of Albuquerque, Minneapolis, and Kansas City corroborate his residence in those cities in 1930, 1935, and 1936, respectively. He was listed only the one time in each city. It is important to keep in mind that a more accurate itinerary may never be pieced together for this phase of Young's career because as a swing musician, he enjoyed considerable freedom to come and go as he pleased; he may very well have left the Bostonians, the Blue Devils, and King Oliver more than once, which could certainly account for the competing chronologies offered by different musicians.[48]

But if his movements during his territorial years are veiled by contradictory reports of his whereabouts and band membership at various times, his personality and behavior, as described by his former sidemen, appear fairly clear. He was a very different person from the character he would present to reporters who interviewed him more than a decade later. Young came from a comparatively privileged and sheltered background, not from the poverty of the ghetto, as reporters typically assumed of all Black musicians. The vicissitudes of life suffered by, for example, Billie Holiday—who was raped and abused as a youngster and worked as a teenage prostitute—were foreign to him. Nor was he familiar with the hardships endured by his fellow Blue Devil Buster Smith, who had spent his childhood and adolescence picking cotton near Dallas, Texas.[49]

Several musicians offered insights into what Young the man was like before he became famous. To Snake Whyte, he was a soft-spoken, well-mannered youth who had no vices and no blemishes on his reputation: "I never saw him indulge in nothing. Never." Moreover, Whyte averred, "I never heard him cuss." Yet neither did Young seem to him particularly religious: "I never heard him talk church, never . . . anything like that." Most remarkable of all, Whyte "never heard him really get *mad*"; "*nothing* excited *him*," he recalled. This even disposition would stay with Young all his life and was one of his more endearing traits, according to his friends.[50]

Blue Devil Leonard Chadwick corroborated Whyte's memories of the saxophonist: "He didn't smoke, he didn't drink, he was just a clean-cut young man." Chadwick saw Young as being, relatively speaking, "just off the farm [or] away from home." And there was still another quality of his that stood out: the introversion that his brother noted when he said, "Lester would keep you out there." Chadwick reminisced, "His ways were just strange in those early days . . . very *strange*." Young "wasn't effeminate," but "he was very well mannered," Chadwick added, whereas "we were supposed to be hard drivers . . . you know, musicians."[51]

Possibly to compensate for his introversion or shyness, Young became known for his witty remarks and keen sense of humor, which earned him the respect and admiration of sidemen. He never talked much, but the Blue Devils recalled that when he finally did say something, it was often funny. Humor was a crucial element among bandsmen barnstorming during the Depression, as it permitted them to endure the hardships of insecurity and anonymity and to confront challenges with a measure of dignity. It was during these years of scuffling as a Blue Devil that Lester Young acquired a reputation as an outstanding soloist, as well as a new nickname.

CHAPTER 7

Blue Devil Blues

1932–1933

DURING the period when he performed with the Oklahoma City Blue Devils, in 1932 and 1933, Young was one of their most faithful sidemen, remaining with the band until its breakup in West Virginia. He was the star soloist, replacing Oran Page, the trumpet player, who left to join Bennie Moten's band. In the Blue Devils, Young made a name for himself as a leading tenor stylist, worthy of comparison with eastern rivals. In recognition of his prowess, the other band members bestowed on him a new title: "Pres," for "President of the Tenor Saxophone." His reputation as a Blue Devil stalwart was the reason he was later hired by the bandleaders Count Basie and Buster Smith, themselves both former Blue Devils, at Kansas City's Reno Club. In some respects, the Basie-Smith combo was a reincarnation of the Oklahoma City band.[1]

Young had only fond memories of and kind things to say about the Blue Devils. He remarked on how much they traveled, how little they earned, and what sheer pleasure it was for them to play together. In some respects, touring with them was a blues life, combining troubled times and joy. Allan Morrison, an African American journalist who interviewed Young in 1946, reported the saxophonist's recollections that while musically "there were kicks in abundance," "financially, [Young] was broke most of the time." The saxophonist explained, "We got around everywhere . . . but we starved to death. . . . We had no capital, no bookings, no nothing." He was referring here to the rough times the band experienced in 1933, but he also unstintingly praised the Blue Devils as "one great band that played some fine music." No doubt that was part of the reason he stayed with them until the end.[2]

Other band members' versions of how Young got recruited differed from Snake Whyte's account. Buster Smith recalled that when the Blue

Devils visited Minneapolis and heard Young play with the pianist Frank Hines, they were so impressed that they immediately began to discuss "stealing" him. Reuben Roddy, then the tenor saxophonist with the band, was described by Smith as being "a good sax player . . . but no *hot* saxophone player"—unlike Young, who "was playing tenor and baritone; in fact, he played so much baritone that Walter Page [laid] *his* baritone down and said he wasn't going to play it anymore," vowing, " 'We're going to steal that boy.' "[3]

They returned to Minneapolis in 1932 to pry Lester away from his home. Buster Smith gave the Blue Devils' version of the oft-told story: "Ernie Williams went up there and talked with him, says, 'We still want you in the band, man.' " Young responded, 'Well, I don't know. . . . The wife don't want me to go.' " They tried another ploy: "We'd gotten this new Ford and [we] drove up in front of his house and said, 'Man, come on, let's go. We going to play so-and-so tomorrow night, and we going to make some good money down there.' " On viewing the new Ford, Young reconsidered: "He looked and saw the brand-new car and he said, 'I guess them Negroes is doing something. Got a brand-new Ford here, smacking brand-new.' " The recruit packed his bag and horn, "got in the car . . . and that's the way he left [—he] come right on out, he got in the car, and stayed with us."[4] Smith's account made no mention of his wife's going along, as in Snake Whyte's rendition, but Beatrice and Cecile Whyte may very well have joined their husbands later, after they found accommodations.

Once he had become a Blue Devil, Young remained committed to the band and its principles until its demise the next year. The new recruit, besides being a fine soloist, could "read good" and possessed the discipline and level of commitment the Blue Devils needed. The band's extensive repertoire required rehearsals that lasted "sometimes a whole half a day," but this was not a problem for Young. He told Smith how, prior to joining, "he'd sit around [and] blow and practice on his horn all day. . . . He didn't do nothing but play music. That's all he was studying."[5]

Besides complimenting Young's baritone playing, Buster Smith revealed something that no one else has ever spoken of: Young played piano. "Oh, . . . it was nice . . . ," he recalled. "He liked to play in E flat. E flat and B flat. F." Some piano players stuck to one or two keys, but not the saxophonist, who, according to Smith, could "play anywhere [in any key]." Unlike other horn men who played a little piano, both Young and his friend Ben Webster "played a whole lot of piano. And [saxophonist] Tab Smith [too]."[6]

This new information testifies to the depth of Young's musical education, which was clearly impressive and certainly has never been sufficiently acknowledged, despite the fact that Professor Young's students stressed that he instructed them on all instruments. Lester's interest in the piano is documented in a photo showing him "intently observing Joe [Sullivan]'s keyboard skills" at the Village Vanguard in Manhattan late in 1940.[7]

Collectively, the Blue Devils, led at that time by Buster Smith and Ernie Williams, were truly a phoenix, surviving the travails of show business and changes in personnel to rise again and again over a period of ten years. The band's mythic status stemmed from its being more than one band—in fact, three or four. There was the original band of the mid-1920s, which had its roots in the TOBA minstrel heritage; then the one led by Walter Page and featuring Jimmy Rushing, Count Basie, Eddie Durham, and Oran Page, late in the same decade; and finally another incarnation, in the 1930s, under Ernie Williams and Buster Smith. It was this revival that Young starred in, enhancing the band's legendary reputation.[8]

The band was remarkable as a resourceful collective of working-class musicians in an era when bands were known primarily for their stars —King Oliver in New Orleans and Chicago, Bennie Moten and Andy Kirk in the Southwest, and Fletcher Henderson and Duke Ellington in the East. In this respect, the Blue Devils went against the grain of developments in the music industry; moreover, they possessed a special character that served the needs of relatively anonymous musicians and working-class audiences. As a territorial band, they toured a specific geographic region from their base in Oklahoma City, covering several states and venturing as far north as Minneapolis and eventually as far east as the Virginias, where their efforts to sustain themselves as a band finally failed.[9]

In the Southwest, territorial bands were frequently organized along commonwealth principles. In accordance with the Blue Devils' motto, "All for one and one for all"—probably taken from the early movie version of the Alexandre Dumas classic *The Three Musketeers*—each and every band member had some say and one vote; the majority ruled. "They didn't want nobody getting no more than he had," explained Buster Smith. "Everybody got the same thing." When Page was the titular leader, after every performance he would take out money for expenses, divide the remainder into thirteen piles, and give an equal share to each member. Young must have liked this practice, for he would follow the same custom with his own combo years later. The commonwealth scheme also ensured that band members would keep hustling for jobs, since there was no guaranteed regular salary.[10]

Unlike Bennie Moten's or the big-time East Coast bands, the Blue Devils were strictly a grass-roots organization, part of the loose social network of African American urbanites in the Southwest. Their popularity prompted Oklahoma City's Black businessmen to lend them financial support when they faltered at one point. The band played for the Oklahoma City Negro Business League and the Pythian Grand Lodge in 1925, and in 1931 performed at an Elks charity ball, successfully raising nearly two hundred dollars to assist homeless and impoverished Black Oklahomans during the Depression. This community service helped to spread the band's name, with one local Black newspaper reporting, "The whole [Elks] affair would have been impossible but for the unselfish service of Mr. Walter Page and his famous Blue Devils." The next month they played for the Elks again, at Slaughter's Hall, one in a series of entertainments that culminated in the order's national convention in Denver in mid-1931.[11]

The Blue Devils' political sympathies and beliefs concerning racial integration were evident when they accepted an invitation from the Young Communist League to perform at an interracial dance in Oklahoma City in the spring of 1932. More than three hundred whites and Blacks turned up to dance at the Forest Park date. Said to be "the first interracial dance ever staged in Oklahoma City," it was successful "far exceed[ing] expectations." In a state where the Ku Klux Klan was quite active and the Black district of another city (Tulsa) had been bombed and burned to the ground by whites little more than a decade before, the affair went off "without any sign of friction." With the money it raised, the Young Communist League was able to send delegates to its party convention in Chicago. Around the same time, in May 1932, the Blue Devils also played at a ball and at a contest for the best yo-yoist, demonstrating that they were a band for all occasions.[12]

Differing from more prestigious bands in another respect, the Blue Devils provided opportunities for younger musicians to trade expertise with them. The author Ralph Ellison recalled that as a band student at

Douglass High School in Oklahoma City, he had loaned his mellophone to Oran Page, and other Blue Devils likewise borrowed mellophones from high school bandsmen "in order to play special choruses." Ellison explained that "in exchange I'd insist upon being allowed to sit in on trumpet during a Blue Devils rehearsal"; he would also "be asked to arbitrate when they got into arguments over interpretation." Occasionally he even played solos with them at weddings.[13]

In the spirit of a collective, the band arranged all of its own bookings at first, but as the Depression worsened, they hired the National Orchestra Service, an established agency in Omaha, and not only expanded their territory but were exempted from having to seek permission from local bands to play that territory. (Whether the latter was a union requirement or merely a custom is unclear.) Thanks to the agency's efforts, the Blue Devils traveled extensively, performing in dance halls, at state fairs, and at summer resorts. The little towns they depended upon for their livelihood often numbered as few as four or five hundred people, "but they had beautiful ballroom[s] in those days." Around dusk, "you'd see those car lights lining up and coming in to the Corn Palace in Mitchell, South Dakota, and the state fair in Huron, [South Dakota]." Leonard Chadwick, who had studied at Fisk to be a dentist but became a trumpet player and a Blue Devil instead, asserted, "These were bookings that we never would have gotten without the booking agency. . . . They kept us working."[14]

Young, who had rebelled against his father's strong hand, must have found both the grass-roots character and the commonwealth principles appealing. Also, in a larger band such as this, he had the opportunity to develop as a tenor soloist and, moreover, to team with the sax section, an important step in a saxophonist's career, and one that was crucial to playing in a major swing band. He became the fourth sax in what was no doubt the best sax section he had played in up until that time, made up of Buster Smith and Theodore "Doc" Ross on altos and Reuben Roddy on tenor. (Roddy did not stay with the Blue Devils much longer; he does not appear in the famous 1932 picture of the band, which shows only three in the sax section.) There were five brass—three trumpets and two trombones—and four musicians in the rhythm section.[15] Knowing how to team up in a section for ensemble passages, and with the brass and rhythm, enhanced a soloist's value—and even more so when the soloist was someone like Young, whose tone on tenor was unconventional and difficult to combine with the tones of other saxophones.

In the Blue Devils, Young was able to learn from one of the seminal saxophonists in the Southwest. In spite of his spending nearly a decade with this Oklahoma City band, Henry "Buster" Smith has been regarded as the "spearhead of the movement to be called [the] Kansas City style of jazz."[16] Born in Ennis, Texas, near Dallas, he arrived in Kansas City in around 1933—rather late compared to native Kansas Citians Bennie Moten and Charlie Parker, and after the Blue Devils had folded. Like many bluesmen, he was self-taught. Early on, Smith was one of a number of talented saxophonists—Eddie Barefield, for example—who could not read music even though they were accomplished soloists.[17] "Most of our musicians were not trained musicians . . . they just learned through practice and effort," Leonard Chadwick remembered. Often a band had a member "who could do some writing [and] they began to look for that type of person because that was the coming thing instead of everybody going their own way."[18] In 1925, in Dallas, the Blue Devils invited Smith to join them because of his virtuosity; moreover, they promised to teach him how to read music. Smith learned well enough to become the band's arranger. One of its most loyal stalwarts, he was a prime example of a bluesman's metamorphosis into a jazz sophisticate.

Young spoke warmly of his section leader and admired his abilities: "Buster used to write all the arrangements, and he could play crazy alto and clarinet," he recalled. "Oh, he could blow."[19] Not only Young but Snake Whyte as well acknowledged his influence, and Charlie Parker also fell under Smith's spell for a time. Whyte asserted that Smith "was a guy I don't think [has] ever been given the credit [he's due]."[20] His nickname, Prof, used by his fellow Blue Devils and other musicians, was an indication of their esteem.

Smith himself was a modest man despite his musical significance and accomplishments, which included mastery of the clarinet, alto sax, piano, and electric bass in a career that would span seven decades. He began his musical education by listening to Blind Lemon Jefferson and other itinerant bluesmen in the cotton fields of his home state and in Dallas's Deep Ellum, the district where musicians played on street corners and in saloons. A pianist as well as a reedman, Smith "always . . . made a lot of chords . . . in playing"; as he put it, "I'd run all them notes," a technique that influenced Young and Parker in the 1930s and, in subsequent decades, saxophonists such as Sonny Rollins and John Coltrane.[21] Both Young and Smith loved the blues and relied on that tradition for their solos, for their interpretations of songs, and for new melodies, riff improvisations, and their overall tone or mood. That both men excelled at soloing suggests how important a knowledge of the blues was in the swing musician's ability to "get off."[22]

With the Blue Devils, Young began experimenting with rhythmic line and tone. His thin, vibratoless sound was well adapted to innovations of this kind in up-tempo selections, which was precisely what the Blue Devils were seeking. Thanks to his "exciting" playing, Young "became a sensation overnight," according to Snake Whyte. In 1932, Blue Devils fans and newcomers flocked "to hear the outstanding tenor man play so much tenor."[23]

He was the band's featured performer and its exciting soloist, and it was always an ecstatic moment when he played—in much the same triumphant tradition, as we will see, as African American dance bands' playing of blues at midnight. Because of him and others like him, the tenor saxophone became a popular new solo instrument as jazz bands gradually increased in size from six or seven to thirteen or more. "All bands had tenors," Snake Whyte explained. "All the mediocre bands, any kind of band, they always had a tenor player"—in fact, "the reed section was not full unless you [had] a tenor in there . . . two altos and one tenor." Along with Coleman Hawkins, Young is credited with popularizing the tenor and revealing that it was well suited to competition: "Lester . . . played things nobody else thought about playing," Whyte asserted. He was chock-full of ideas. Despite the dominance of Hawkins and his disciples on tenor sax, by 1930 or 1931, "Lester had a style on his own." To embellish and add showmanship to his experiments, he turned the neck of his horn around so the saxophone bell was facing him.[24]

At first the new recruit experienced some adjustment problems. He complained about how hard it was to play Smith's innovative arrangements; the brass agreed with him. Smith quieted Young "by telling him that I was playing them right alongside of him"—in other words, if Smith himself could play the arrangements, then the others should be able to as well. Smith often pointed out another problem that he shared with Young and the altoist, Doc Ross: "The reed section couldn't blow loud enough to stay with them cats [the brass section, consisting of two trombones and three trumpets]. . . . They would drown us out." The three reeds were also outnumbered by the brass. They eventually came up with a solution, Smith recalled, "Ross and I would buy a C-melody [reed], that's a little bigger saxophone between the tenor and the alto, and we used them reeds and put them on alto. And Lester Young put a baritone reed on his tenor." As a result, they "blew just as loud, the brass couldn't get louder than us."[25]

Young quickly learned how to team with Smith and Ross. Moreover, he and Snake Whyte "both used to watch Buster" to get ideas for their own solos. "We all watched [Smith] . . . like you take a solo and you in front of me, I'm not going to miss a thing you doing [because] I got to follow you. . . . And so you preparing me for my solo," Whyte explained. The one who led off in the solos "was setting a pace for them that was going to follow him."[26]

The band's unity and the musicians' empathy were such that they could play together without using signals: "They all [knew] when to come in." The same would be true of Basie's band a few years later precisely because it was composed of many former Blue Devils. Snake Whyte stressed how their living and struggling together played a role in their musical teaming: "That was the advantage to . . . sitting down in those jam sessions. Blowing and blowing hour after hour with those guys." He added, "Lester knew everything Buster's going [to] do. . . . Lester and I lived together . . . roomed together. We practiced together." When one ended a solo with a particular musical phrase, the other would repeat it at the beginning of his solo, a technique called connecting or tying lines that would later be a frequent custom among Basie soloists. Whyte emphasized how the Blue Devils' lives and music mirrored each other: "That's the way we lived. We lived that horn."[27]

Whyte recalled their practicing "all day. . . . Like you'd hum something to me: 'Hey, let's try this!' . . . [Then] four or five of us [would be] sitting in some old nightclub, just *blowing*, for kicks." Whyte told how they developed their ideas: "OK, you take a solo, I'd hear you, pretty soon, it'd get good to me. I keep on, get the harmony to it. Next one, he'd get the harmony, pretty soon there's a riff going." The riff was the rhythmic motif that inspired everyone and got things swinging as it set the stage for the powerful soloist. Once the band took off, "Lester [would] probably take eight or nine choruses or something if it got good to him."[28]

Swing was so powerful because it was contagious, inspiring instrumentalists and dancers to take everyone to greater heights, to the climax or high point of a session: "Then maybe something hits the guy and he wants to show off a little more," Whyte recounted. For territorial musicians, swing was an integral part of African American culture, and an end in itself; not until a few years later would it begin to earn a few select musicians and promoters fortunes as well as national and international popularity. In those early years, "there was no big salaries"; instead, according to Whyte, compensation came in the form of "getting everything that was in that horn out. That was the height of our ambition." This distinctive music provided creative opportunities and supporting roles for band members, young musicians, and fans; it shared older traditions found in spirituals, New Orleans music, blues, and gospel. Its proponents were idealists—artists, really—almost (but not quite) oblivious to becoming rich.[29]

With the Blue Devils, Young became known as a stylist, one whose distinctive playing was recognized by knowledgeable listeners and debated in the contexts of both Black cultural aesthetics in general and other players' styles in particular. Rival tenor saxophonists suffered when they were matched against him in blowing contests. "Budd Johnson cried when Pres walked into Kansas City," Whyte remembered. "Pres blew him out the hall. See, Budd had been the king around there on the tenor—in the modern style of tenor." Young, with his sax artistry, his unique style, and his tone, had finally won wide acclaim as an innovator rather than an imitator.[30]

In recognition of his new status in their jazz world, and according to common custom among Black musicians, the Blue Devils bestowed upon their star reedman a fitting title. He became "Pres," short for "President of the Tenor Saxophone," around the same time that Franklin D. Roosevelt was elected president of the United States, late in 1932.

When asked what they had called Young in those years, former Blue Devils invariably thought for a second before responding, "Pres." Buster Smith reported: "We named him Pres." He laughed. "We gave him that name. . . . [Doc] Ross . . . and Abe Bolar [bassist] and all of them around there got to call[ing] him, and Ernie [Williams] got to calling him, Pres—'That's the President! Ol' Pres'—and Walter Page, too. That went on that way, and he got to New York, and all the cats around there heard us, some of the old members, calling him Pres." Young, of course, accepted the honor. Chadwick and Whyte agreed that *they* gave him his title, and neither ever went to New York City or in fact ever saw much of Young after the band broke up. Abe Bolar maintained that the nickname also paid homage to the young man's verbal abilities and wit. He explained that there was "a little game that was played around here [in

Oklahoma City], when you get burned [after] you say something. That's how he got to be named Pres. Something like that." This was probably a reference to what others have called signifying or capping.[31]

(Of course, this version of how the saxophonist got his title contradicts the repeated testimony of both Billie Holiday and Young himself, each of whom took credit for coining the other's nickname—Lady Day and Pres, respectively—after they met in New York City early in 1934, when Young was with Fletcher Henderson's band. It is conceivable that both accounts are true: Young, having received the name in the Southwest, may have told Holiday about it, whereupon, as a kind of badge of their close friendship, she took credit for it while he went along with the story and gave her *her* name—actually a longer form of her previous nickname, Lady—in return.)

The Blue Devils' extensive repertoire broadened Young's musical horizons, allowing him to think in terms of, for example, different audiences and settings and having several versions of a song to choose from, instead of just one. Like earlier territorial bands, the Blue Devils needed a number of different arrangements to appeal to a variety of audiences—and now, moreover, that variety was even greater, encompassing midwesterners and southwesterners, Black southerners and Scandinavians in the northern prairie communities, urbanites and farmers, in settings ranging from state fairs to club benefits, outdoor barbecues, and social dances. The band, Smith explained, "had about three repertoires, and that's to catch all the people, depending on the kind of music they like. . . . We had one repertoire that wasn't nothing but sweet music, and we had one that had a lot of waltzes in it and some of the country music—like 'Turkey in the Straw' and all that stuff."[32]

What Smith called the "uptown music"—the selections that whites preferred and that were, incidentally, easier to play—permitted the Blue Devils to perform for audiences on the circuit they shared with the bandleader Lawrence Welk. Another dimension of their repertoire was the blues, which, of course, appealed especially to African American listeners. With Black audiences, conceded Chadwick, "we had a little more feeling into it . . . and we got more when [we] look[ed] out and saw [our own people]."[33]

Young undoubtedly learned from the Blue Devils' penchant for having two or three separate arrangements of the same song in their repertoire to impress their audiences. This was "the thing that knocked everybody out about that band," one veteran said. "We played different things every night." Audiences "would hear us play a tune one night, and the next night we might play the same tune entirely different." Their rival Bennie Moten had several arrangers, an advantage over the Blue Devils, who had no more than one or two. "So we *had* to play a lot of [our own] stuff. We needed about forty numbers to play a dance without doing a lot of repeating." In keeping with its commonwealth principles, the band depended upon the contributions of each band member to enrich its repertoire.[34]

Immersed as he was in uptown and downtown musical traditions with the Blue Devils, Young also learned to love the blues and jazz heritage of Oklahomans and Texans. He would later contend that he had always had "great big eyes" for the blues; they were the foundation of jazz and the inspiration for his generation. "If you play with a new band like I have . . . working around," he said, "if they don't know no blues, they can't play shit." He also noted the connection between art and life: "Everybody plays the blues, and *have* 'em too!"[35] Knowledge of the form, its philosophy, and its techniques enabled Young to become an inspiring soloist, but it is not clear that he ever actually played slow blues in the Blue Devils, given that he was the "hot" tenor, known for his velocity and the excitement he created.

The Blue Devils diversified their repertoire by having their own arrangements—known as "head" arrangements—as well as the standardized kind; they alternated these, "always play[ing] . . . head numbers in between [written ones]." Certain tunes, one Blue Devil said, "let everybody play what they want[ed] . . . let everybody get off . . . where they want[ed] to get off." This constituted the very essence of swing music in the territories, where bands were democracies in which every instrumentalist had first a supporting role and then a leading one when he soloed or when his composition was featured.[36]

Appreciating the differences between standard stock and head arrangements is fundamental to understanding both the unique character of the Blue Devils and important developments in swing music. "Hundreds of thousands" of stock arrangements were sold in music stores throughout the United States at the time. When "Sweet Sue" was popular, Whyte recalled, "a band in Chicago playing [it] and one in New York had the same arrangement." Fletcher Henderson's, Duke Ellington's, and Jesse Stone's bands were pioneers in creating arrangements customized specifically for the distinctive talents of their members.[37]

While the Blue Devils bought the same over-the-counter music sheets as other bands, for the most part they used head arrangements, or memorized compositions based on the originals, which were worked out in lengthy practice sessions and were unique to them. "We didn't care what the song was . . . we bought stocks [stock arrangements] . . . and we'd play those, then branch off into something we could feel as though it had a little jump to it, and we'd do some solos, then go back to the ensembles," remembered Whyte.[38]

At one extreme, this process resulted in entirely new songs, but in the main it functioned as a method of arranging popular numbers. Head arrangements permitted sections to team up to play melodies or riffs together, thereby not only enlarging the sound but increasing the swing impetus that was so central to the music. The latter feature differentiated swing bands from the New Orleans ensembles in which each cornet or trumpet, clarinet, and trombone went for itself, alternating the melody with countermelodies, first leading and then playing a very similar countermelody as another instrument took up the main melody. Jelly Roll Morton's clarinet trios of the 1920s were precursors of swing sections. Eventually, as head arrangements became more complicated, it became increasingly difficult to distinguish them from written sections.

In the Southwest, Buster Smith was one of the first, along with Jesse Stone and T. Terence Holder, to take into account individual differences among musicians in his arrangements. Smith knew how to arrange in such a way as to highlight Young's unique talents as an explosive but soulful soloist. "Buster's arrangements were a little different because he knew the capabilities of his men, and he wrote for that effect," explained Snake Whyte. Like Ellington and Redman, Smith "started writing four- and five-part harmony. . . . In those days that was very [innovative]. . . . Buster began to add the sixth part to the chord . . . spreading the harmony throughout the band." This was "one of the things that made our band so unique, because we were one of the *first* bands in that area [to carry] five brass . . . two trombones and three trumpets." Smith's arrangements also caused some controversy, for as one band member observed, "White bands wouldn't use [four-part harmony] 'cause they thought it was out of tune." When Smith and other daring arrangers introduced the sixth note, "they'd make a chord sound different. [It] didn't have that pure triad." We must rely here upon musicians' recollections of Young's contributions and of how the band sounded because the Blue Devils recorded only two of their compositions—"Squabblin'" and "Blue Devils Blues"—and both of those before Young became a member.[39]

When Young and other Blue Devils veterans later joined Bennie Moten's and Basie's and other southwestern bands, they brought with them a rich fountainhead of blues and jazz compositions, many of which were based on American popular songs. Such reworkings took these songs to another level of musical development and made them swing. The Moten specialties "Moten Swing" and "Toby," for example, had their origins in the popular song "You're Drivin' Me Crazy" and the harmony of "Sweet Sue," respectively. The Basie anthem "One O'Clock Jump," meanwhile, was typical of many selections in that it began with a Fats Waller phrase and went through several permutations. Young's own "Lester Leaps In" was another of many jazz standards based on "I Got Rhythm," while his composition "Lester Swings" was based on "Exactly like You." Singers in territorial bands popularized "Good Mornin' Blues," "Until the Real Thing Comes Along" (also known as "The Slave Song"), and "When My Dreamboat Comes Home." These songs provided a foundation not only for the so-called Kansas City swing of the 1930s but for the rhythm and blues and rock and roll of at least the next three decades.[40]

In the Blue Devils—who, as we have seen, were as much part of a dynasty as they were an individual band—Young was introduced to southwestern musicians who recognized him as a stalwart, a serious musician, and a genuine trouper, ready and willing at any time and in any place to jam and to compete with all comers. They were, as many of them claimed, a band of brothers, bound by the hardships and joys they experienced in a time of national depression and during a period in their lives when they were particularly impressionable: all were then still in their twenties. For Young, distinctions among bands were blurred by the constant movement of band members, and the society of musicians, the collective, was at least as important as the bands' individual identities. This may have been part of the reason so many specific details were matters of indifference to him.[41]

Testimony from Young and other Blue Devils suggested that the sense of shared identity was as essential to the band as the arrangement techniques, the inventions of soloists, the propulsive swing, or the blues harmonies. During Young's stint, numerous individual sacrifices and displays of solidarity ensured the Blue Devils' survival as well as their future stature in the folklore of territorial musicians. When circumstances reduced the band's membership to four or five musicians, its ever-loyal stalwarts always revived it. Buster Smith stepped up after Eddie Durham, Walter Page, Oran Page, Jimmy Rushing, Bill Basie, and Dan Minor left to join Moten in 1929: "Ernie [Williams] and I kept that band. . . . Sometimes there wasn't but five pieces in it," he recalled. The same thing happened again late in 1932 or early in 1933, when Chadwick and Whyte left. Still, Williams and Smith refused to give up and "always kept adding one and bringing the band back to where it was supposed to be—twelve or thirteen."[42]

Young stood out as one of the faithful. "In Kansas City . . . Lester Young fed the whole band off the fourteen dollars a week he made [playing] at the Subway [Club]," Leonard Chadwick remembered. Fortunately, for the mere sum of fifteen cents a hungry Kansas Citian could dine on steak and rice with gravy at one of the Twelfth Street cafés. And when times got even tougher and a musician was down to his last few cents, Chadwick said, "there was a penny lunch there in Kansas City where if you had a little money you could go and buy vegetables . . . such as red beans, cornbread, greens, and things like that."[43]

Then there was the story about the time "Abe Bolar put his bass horn up so we could get out of town" after a job fell through one night in Des Moines.[44] Such unswerving loyalty enabled the Blue Devils to survive for a time in early 1933, but it was not enough to overcome their mounting hotel and meal debts in Bluefield, West Virginia. The hotel manager feared they were going to leave town without settling their accounts, so he put them out. Angry and impatient taxi drivers who had shuttled them back and forth from the hotel to their job also waited anxiously for payment of the accumulated fares. To keep the musicians from running away (a common out for debtors), rather than lock them up, the cabdrivers had the courts attach their instruments, which were released to them nightly so they could play and then immediately confiscated again after the dance by the sheriff. One by one, band members began leaving, and Young, George Hudson, Jap Jones, Doc Ross, Smith, and Bolar were stranded.[45]

Around this time, Young also made a court appearance that very nearly got him sentenced to a chain gang. As Leonard Phillips heard it, "They got out there and got stranded [in Virginia], and he messed around with some cat that used to be on old man [Willis] Young's show, driving a car. . . . He bought an automobile and he had this guy chauffeuring for him." But then the driver was caught selling bootleg whiskey.

Probably facing a lengthy prison term because of previous convictions, Young's old friend begged him, "'Les, you ain't got no record, ain't got nothin'. I want you to go up and stand [up in court] for this for me.'" Perhaps naively, Young agreed, according to Phillips. It is not altogether clear just what was going on in this episode; maybe the assumption was that Young, as a first offender, would be given a lighter sentence. It wasn't a safe bet, Phillips recalled: "They said they had a *hell* of a hard time to try to keep them from sending him on a chain gang."[46]

Young himself later provided a stark account of the Blue Devils' last months in West Virginia: "Those were tough times. The band was getting bruised, I mean really bruised, playing to audiences of three people. One time all our instruments were impounded . . . and they took us right to the railroad track and told us to get out of town."[47] Very likely their plan had been to tour the Upper South, following in the footsteps of their rival Bennie Moten, who had done the same tour the year before. The Blue Devils thought they would eventually get to the East Coast and make another recording, just as the Moten band had done late in 1932. Then, too, the banjoist, Reuben Lynch, came from Lynchburg, Virginia, and Ernie Williams was from Winston-Salem, North Carolina—both relatively close to some of the towns they played, including Martinsville and Newport News. They may have taken advantage of being near home to utilize their contacts.[48]

In any case, in less than one year's time, Young and his fellow Blue Devils had been reduced from impeccably dressed bandsmen in matching summer suits in Little Rock to virtual destitutes in Bluefield, hundreds of miles away from the band's home base in Oklahoma City. Young recounted their departure from West Virginia: "There we were sitting with these hobos [in a railroad yard], and they showed us how to grab the train. We made it—with bruises." Abe Bolar, who had regularly hopped trains as a youngster, tutored them in technique, and fortified with a few sandwiches for the ordeal ahead, they jumped a freight train drawn by a Mountain Jack, two powerful locomotives locked together to climb the steep Appalachian grades.

The stragglers arrived in Cincinnati with "no loot, no horns, all raggedy and dirty . . . trying to make it to St. Louis or Kansas City," recalled Young. Someone loaned him an alto saxophone, and he earned a little money playing a few jobs. It was hardly enough to support everyone, though, so "finally we all had a meeting . . . and we decided it was 'every tub'—every man for himself." After they arrived in St. Louis, Bennie

Moten sent a car for them, and several Blue Devils joined him, while Young went on to Kansas City and eventually got a job with the assistance of his former brother-in-law, Pete Jones, who was then with King Oliver.[49]

In the considered opinion of a number of them, the Blue Devils had missed their chance at fame late in 1932 or early in 1933, when they were playing around Cincinnati and Fats Waller attempted a takeover, a common practice for name musicians in need of bands. His attempt failed because some band members thought the salary he was offering for radio work was too low, and their vote prevailed. Smith himself later conceded, "We missed our best opportunity around that time when Fats Waller wanted us to work for him." Then, in West Virginia, the bandleader Zack Whyte had come over the mountains from Cincinnati to make them an offer, but he had needed only nine musicians; the band had turned him down, insisting that he take everyone or no one. Their motto, after all, was "All for one and one for all."[50]

Their many adaptive strategies and grass-roots ties to Oklahoma City were of little use to them in West Virginia. Looking back on those times, a wiser Buster Smith would rue the commonwealth philosophy because it had prevented the band from garnering the success it deserved. "We fooled away a lot of good opportunities. And most of us never got much out of it," he lamented. The surviving Blue Devils learned that there was truth to the folk saying "A commonwealth band never do no good," at least during the Depression. All the territorial bands abandoned this form of organization by 1933 or 1934. Smith noted, "After I joined Moten, we got rid of that. We just decided that somebody had to be the one boss. That was the only way to get anywhere."[51]

Young probably found the commonwealth structure particularly appealing because it eschewed the legalism of commercial show-business circles; cooperative endeavors of this kind were rather common among workers. When this band broke up, he left a world where, Smith said, "a guy could be hired today, and tomorrow would be gone and it was still OK," to enter a new epoch of contracts and union membership, surveillance and grievances. The Blue Devils' rival Bennie Moten succeeded in this arena even as others failed, though his band, too, experienced problems in 1932 and 1933. He had strong political connections to men in the Kansas City machine, especially Tom Pendergast, the urban boss whose regime made possible that Missouri city's rich nightlife. On one occasion, after the Blue Devils had defeated some band in a battle, Moten approached them and explained that he "liked our music . . . the way we played, and he made us a proposition. If we would provide the music, he would provide the jobs." Moten controlled "all the good jobs and choice locations in and around Kansas City." The Blue Devils were not agreeable to his offer, but he persisted and finally lured away several of the band's leading musicians.[52]

Moten prevailed once again when he hired several of the remaining Blue Devils following the band's 1933 demise. "Bennie was a businessman first and last," Oran Page observed. He actually had several bands that all played under his name—he was "stronger than MCA [the Music Corporation of America]," Page asserted—and as a result of his takeover, "the Blue Devils became the nucleus for the best band Moten ever had." After Moten died during a minor surgery gone awry in the spring of 1935, Basie and Smith's Barons of Rhythm became his bands' successor in the Kansas City dynasty.[53]

The Blue Devils' loyalty and sense of solidarity reflected their success in creating and perpetuating a tight-knit society of swing troupers for whom the joy of playing and the commonwealth system of organization went hand in hand. The rewards of learning to team, swinging the dancers, and defeating band rivals more than made up for the hard times and years of scuffling: "Back in them days . . . we played for nothing," recalled the trombonist Druie Bess. He explained, "I've played so many jobs for nothing, it's pitiful." Sounding a little like Armstrong talking about New Orleans jazz, Bess went on, "But it was the enjoyment to play. . . . I just loved [to] play." He was not the only Blue Devil to claim that the band's significance stemmed from the fact that "it was a whole lot of brotherly love." Moreover, Bess asserted, "I've never been with a band [that had] that since."[54]

This band and others like it served as quasi–extended families and played an important role in helping musicians survive the Depression. The sense of family not only fostered their musicianship by providing the intimacy and solidarity they needed to play head arrangements well, but also made up for their separation from their real families and alleviated some of the hardships they suffered on the road. Like a family, band members lived and traveled together and shared the chores of running the organization and keeping it intact. Ross and Smith often cooked for the bachelors in the group, while trumpet player James Simpson and Ernie Williams assisted in selecting uniforms, and Ross saw to it that they were cleaned. Ross and Simpson did much of the driving, and Page's knowledge of gasoline engines came in handy when one of the cars broke down. The solidarity among the Blue Devils was such that a stalwart such as Walter Page was seen as their "musical father," whose influence continued to be felt in the band long after the man himself had left. Chadwick, for example, credited the bassist with helping him with his reading; similarly, Jo Jones claimed that Page had taught him drums. Page would later become a mainstay in the Count Basie Orchestra's rhythm section, along with Jo Jones.[55]

Both as a Blue Devil and afterward, Lester Young symbolized the persistence of the unknown, archetypal struggling Black musician, overcoming formidable odds to earn a living, to raise a family, and to satisfy his own aesthetic needs through his saxophone artistry. In the Blue Devils, Young could swing with considerable enthusiasm and solo at great length, creating as he did so triumphant moments in the lives of a people subjugated by racism, discrimination, and economic oppression in the prairie and plains states west of the Mississippi. In serving his apprenticeship with them, Young demonstrated that he was worthy of the Basie band when it re-formed in 1935 under the direction of Basie and Buster Smith. By staying with the band as long as he did, Young demonstrated his stamina, his conviction, and his willingness to take a chance on his music and to cast in his lot with a group whose very existence was a symbol of the vitality of a people.

Young's reputation as a leading soloist with Basie actually began in the Blue Devils, where it soared, assuming legendary proportions because he was the star in a band that itself would have considerable influence on musical traditions and on the folklore that accompanied them—in spite of the fact that it left behind virtually no written record. Both Basie and Jones singled the band out for singular praise. When it came to explaining the rhythmic drive, verve, and uniqueness of Kansas City or Basie musicians, their accounts invariably cited the band whose evolution and ill-starred career became part of the legend about music in the Southwest.

CHAPTER 8

Big Eyes Blues

In the Court of the King, 1933

AFTER arriving penniless in Kansas City, Young was badly in need of a job—one that would begin immediately. Fortunately, he ran into his old friend and former brother-in-law, Pete Jones, who was then King Oliver's band manager. He did not know it at first, but Jones happened to be looking for a tenor saxophonist, and so was particularly glad to see Young and learn that he was available. The orchestra's previous tenor, Francis Whitby, had "got mad at the cats and . . . just *quit* . . . left. . . . We were just using two saxophones," recalled Leonard Phillips, who was also with Oliver at the time.[1] "So Les saw Pete [in Kansas City]. He says, 'Hey, Pete!' Said, 'Man, if you ain't got a job for me, I'm gonna take one. I ain't workin'. I'm in bad shape. I just came back. . . . I hoboed all the way back from [West] Virginia.'" Young admitted, "'I'm broke. I ain't got no money, ain't got no clothes, ain't got nothin'.'"[2]

The tenor stylist had first impressed Oliver's musicians during his stint with the Blue Devils, one time when they had all met up and jammed together at the Ritz Ballroom in Oklahoma City. He more than satisfied their needs for a hot soloist over the next several months. Their veteran leader, for his part, was undoubtedly relieved to get a stylist as talented as Young, who moreover came highly recommended by the band's manager.[3]

The new recruit let the bandleader know that his tenure would be temporary, from May until November, in light of the fact that Oliver's schedule took the orchestra south each winter. Sam Allen, the alto saxophonist, recalled that "[Young] couldn't see going south. Period!"[4] Leonard Phillips explained, "He couldn't go down to Nashville on this regular job we went on every year," and instead planned to join Bennie Moten and Count Basie in the late fall.[5] Until then, however, he was eager to get reacquainted with his old friends Phillips and Jones and to play for this orchestra leader whose bayou-country birthplace was not so far from Thibodaux.

Because the new sideman needed a matching suit, Sam Allen lent Young one of his to start with. Then, Phillips recounted, "We took him down, got him clothes, got him lookin' good—like we was, you know." All of the orchestra members had at least two suits—English tweeds. Evidently Young looked the part after that: when he finally joined the others in Joplin, Missouri, Phillips reported, "Cats said, 'Man, we got it made. We *got* a tenor player now.' "[6]

Young had "big eyes" for Oliver's band. His stint with the legendary bandleader would be similar to his Blue Devils experience in that both strengthened his ties to blues and jazz traditions; but it was more directly linked to New Orleans, the city where Oliver had won his title as King. Oliver was a blues veteran, a trumpet player and mentor to Armstrong, and a major inspiration for many musicians. With his orchestra, Young developed his skills as a section man, increased his knowledge of music and its presentation, and polished his considerable abilities as a show-stopping improviser and swing stylist. As Young's reputation grew, Oliver and others spread the word about his magnificent talents.

Oliver was a shamanlike figure among musicians, as the jazz historian Neil Leonard has suggested; his powers to transform audiences seemed almost magical. Folklore also played an important role in his life, according to a sideman, who noted, "He could tell some funny tales."[7] Indeed, in terms of his beliefs in the superstitions and customs of Louisiana, Oliver was a veritable archive. His legendary status as an outstanding soloist dated from the time he outblew Freddy Keppard, the New Orleans trumpet king, a generation earlier; five decades after his death, his sidemen still referred to him as King (often pronounced "Kang"). His reputation was enhanced by his majestic bearing and by the profoundly tragic quality of the blues life he led during his later years.[8]

Oliver's ordeals exemplified the philosophy of blues people, the notions that the human condition was filled with hardships and suffering that were almost unbearable; that music was one of the few things that made it all worthwhile; and that too often a person's real reward came only after the end. By the early 1930s Oliver was already a tragic figure, cheated by conniving bookers and businessmen who would eventually strand him by selling him inferior and broken-down band buses. His last few years would be even more sorrowful, as, impoverished and in poor health, he eked out a living at various jobs in Savannah, Georgia.[9]

Following his death near the end of the 1930s, Oliver was praised by African Americans who maintained that many Black and white musicians, especially those of the swing era, were deeply indebted to him. One tribute credited him with being "the real swing king"—a veiled critique, of course, of that title's bestowal on clarinetist Benny Goodman. Oliver had actually started "what is currently called swing" around World War I, his eulogists claimed. Louis Armstrong paid homage to his "Papa Joe," contending, "There isn't a riff played today that he didn't play more than fifteen years ago." Earl Hines agreed that Oliver had "featured [swing] exclusively years ago," and that the contemporary "kings of swing" were "mere imitators"; Cab Calloway concurred.[10]

The reminiscences of Oliver's sidemen permit us to reconstruct the path his career took in the Southwest during the bleak years of the Depression. After setting out from New York City to tour in early 1931, the bandleader was stranded when he became ill in Wichita, Kansas, and his New York sidemen left him. With the remnants of his group, he made it to Kansas City, where the singer James "Tiny" Taylor assumed responsibility for the faltering Oliver orchestra while its leader recuperated.[11]

Oliver was about to send for more New York musicians, but then he heard a band he liked, and as bandleaders were wont to do in such situations, he made its members an offer. In this case, the object of the takeover was Art Bronson's Bostonians.[12] Oliver was so impressed with the Bostonians that he came right out and said, "You all ain't going nowhere. . . . Why don't you let me take this band over?" He was relying upon his national reputation and tremendous popularity in the Southwest to sway them. According to Phillips, a disagreement erupted between Bronson and his sidemen; the leader, understandably, "didn't want to give the band up. But all the guys said, 'This is the time for us to get somewhere.' So everybody left [with King Oliver] but Bronson; Bronson wouldn't go. . . . [And so we] made money and more *name*, too. . . . King is a big *name* band, he's playing everywhere."[13] Young was in Minneapolis when the band was reorganizing, rehearsing, and getting measured for new uniforms in late 1931 and early 1932, so he did not join Oliver with the others.[14]

For years, Oliver was plagued by pyorrhea, a gum disease that was quite common among those of his generation. For brass and reed instrumentalists, losing teeth could be disastrous because it hindered their ability to earn a living. After being fitted with a bridge or plate of false teeth, Oliver resumed his role as the star of the show and featured soloist on a few numbers, though of course, when his teeth or his plate gave him trouble, it affected his playing. He also had stomach problems—"Oh, he could eat!" Phillips exclaimed.[15] His reputation suffered when he was ill or unable to play, and booking agents passed over him because of it.

Phillips, a stalwart in Oliver's trumpet section from 1932 to 1934, remembered that the bandleader was so famous that "the Buescher people gave him a gold-plated trumpet, a special trumpet. They had it built for him."[16] While the sideman loved Armstrong's playing, he really admired Oliver's tone: "He had a tone that big. His tone was bigger than Louis's. He had a *big* tone." Armstrong was, by comparison, faster and "had a more modern feeling on his horn." During his years with the orchestra leader, Phillips would often find Oliver in his room, "blowing over exercises and things"; he was particularly "crazy about diminished chords." Moreover, "he used to play little cadenzas on his tunes. He'd run a diminished chord and then come back to the tonic."[17]

Oliver differed from the other bandleaders Young had worked with prior to this: not only was he a full generation older than Art Bronson or Buster Smith, having been born in 1885, but he could play some deeply moving blues on his horn, in a style that was quite memorable to Louisianans and then, later, with white and Black urbanites from coast to coast. Fans in the Southwest flocked to hear him in the early 1930s; "wherever we played," one sideman recalled, "the audiences went crazy." His outfit was "one good-sounding band . . . [with musicians who] all knew the latest music, and that's what the public wanted."[18]

When Oliver was at his best, he knew it, and he made sure everyone else did, too. "King Oliver still played more and was more exciting" than most of his adversaries, claimed a member of his brass section. "Sometimes he was feeling terrific. [He would say,] 'Goddamn it, I feel *good* tonight! . . . I'm gonna play you all a 1923 solo.' And knocked everybody out." He did it "every time."[19] Leonard Chadwick, former Blue Devil who had joined Oliver's orchestra, confirmed that the leader "still could play—he couldn't play as well as I'm sure [he could] when he was in his prime, but he could still attract attention." Moreover, "he could play a *beautiful, beautiful* tone, and could play *high*."[20]

Oliver drew upon the African American blues aesthetic when playing both popular songs and jazz standards, thus enhancing Young's understanding of the power of this idiom. Slow blues that were intensely emotional and majestic, sad on some occasions but joyful on others, typified the bandleader's best performances. When he played these, the effect was "magnetic." He used three different mutes and "sounded like he was crying and moaning. . . . The horn really talked," trombonist Clyde Bernhardt reminisced.[21]

His repertoire was broad enough to appeal to different audiences and provide them with the variety they might have heard at a vaudeville show. "Sugar Blues" was one selection on which the trumpet stylist cried and moaned through his instrument; "Tiger Rag," in contrast, allowed his soloists to show off. Handy selections including the "St. Louis Blues," "Beale Street Blues," and "Memphis Blues" were also featured regularly, as were special requests such as "Wild Irish Rose," "Lazy River," "Stardust," and even "O Sole Mio." New tunes were often sent to Oliver even before they were published.

Like many blues men and some of the younger New Orleans musicians, Oliver himself did not like to read music, but since his orchestra usually numbered ten to twelve during this period, he insisted that everyone be able to read the arrangements, whose variety and modernity were part of the band's appeal. By late 1931, he was said to have more than three hundred selections in his book.[22]

The orchestra's head arrangements showcased its soloists. The New Orleans style of soloing—which Oliver, of course, preferred—consisted of "a little bit of this, a little bit of that," as the trombonist Clyde Bernhardt explained, adding, "Soon it set me up with a style of my own." In one of his first performances with Oliver, however, Bernhardt got carried away: "I took some long solos, got off some extra triple tongue passages . . . showing the King all my tricks and that I was worthy of him." After the set, Oliver counseled his new trombonist, "'Son, you don't have to do all that shit to impress me. You got a good swinging style and all them snakes you makin', loses the flavor. It don't mean a damn thing.'" He then assured Bernhardt, "'I like the way you was blowin' before, otherwise I wouldn't of took you.'" The style that Oliver, and eventually Young, favored—simple, emotive, and soulful playing—exemplified the profundity of the blues aesthetic.[23]

The New Orleans leader developed close relationships with some of his sidemen, and it is likely that Young was among them, considering his Louisiana roots and the fact that Oliver praised him as a musician. That the bandleader could still recruit younger musicians and take them under his wing years after his most glorious days had passed is remarkable testimony to the strength of his reputation.[24]

Oliver's sidemen also recalled the warm fraternal relationship they had with one another, reminiscent of the Blue Devils' camaraderie. Phillips stated quite simply, "We was like brothers." Baby Dodds claimed that the orchestra members "had known each other so long we felt that we were almost related," adding that Oliver's outfit "had more harmony and feeling of brotherly love than any I ever worked with." In any case, for Dodds, "playing music [was] just like having a home."[25] It was precisely this affective element that kept musicians loyal to Oliver and in his band. This held true for Young, too, though for a shorter period of time.

Despite his playing the dozens (exchanging insults in a joking fashion), his penchant for bullying musicians, his frequent use of profanity, and his no-nonsense demeanor on the bandstand, Oliver was quite a lovable leader. In all likelihood, he was a father figure for Lester Young. After all, he was regarded in that light by both Armstrong, who called him Papa Joe, and Bernhardt, who testified, "I respected King Oliver and learned a lot from him. He usually called me 'son' and I called him 'pop'—spoke to him just like I did my Papa and my family. . . . Regardless of his nasty words, I respected him."[26]

With the help of recollections by Oliver's sidemen, we can piece together a crucial episode in Young's development. During his months with the Louisianan, the tenor saxophonist glimpsed the ordeals endured by an aging jazz king, hardships that gave an authentic ring to the blues he played. Significantly, Oliver's situation in the 1930s in some ways prefigured what would happen to Young himself in the 1950s. The rise of new music styles to which each had contributed in his day, as well as poor health, including dental problems, were very real issues for both men near the end of their respective careers.[27]

The saxophonist's tour with Oliver ran from the spring to the fall of 1933, a period that was notable insofar as it marked a high point in Young's career up to that time. Phillips supplied some picturesque details concerning his old friend's stint with King Oliver.[28]

It does seem rather remarkable, in view of the sharp distinctions that are so often made in jazz histories between swing and New Orleans styles, that Young was willing to associate with an old-timer who was still quite popular in the Southwest. But the saxophonist's own comments on his six months with Oliver gave no hint of any musical condescension: "He had a very nice band and I worked regularly with him . . . around

Kansas and Missouri mostly. . . . He was playing well." Young noted that Oliver "was old then and didn't play all night, but his tone was full when he played. He was the star of the show and played one or two songs each set. The blues. He could play some nice blues." The tenor stylist found him to be "a very nice . . . old fellow" who "was crazy about all the boys"; he emphasized that "it wasn't a drag playing for him at all."[29]

Young's musical skills and reputation were enhanced by his work with this leader who has often been credited with launching the swing style. Although King Oliver was then in his twilight years, he remained a charismatic veteran who loved to recount the battles of the first blues and jazz artists. Young listened to his stories about Buddy Bolden and Freddy Keppard, and about horn battles in which the contenders had blasted away at one another for hours. In his midtwenties, the tenor saxophonist had in a real sense arrived in the big time with Oliver, performing in the huge ballrooms of the Southwest. He was a featured soloist as well.

Their common roots in southern Louisiana gave the two men considerable reason to spend time together talking; moreover, Oliver probably knew Lester's father, if only by reputation. As a rule, Oliver hired New Orleans musicians—Polo Barnes, Johnny and Baby Dodds, and Armstrong are only a few examples. The relationship between Oliver and Young must have been a very special one, reminding the saxophonist of both his musical roots and the Professor's early training. Young's good friend Leonard Phillips would make a similar connection when he stated that Willis Young and King Oliver were the "two guys who taught me the most of what I know and [who] are responsible for [who I am] on and off the stage today."[30]

From Oliver, Young learned how an extensive repertoire could satisfy a variety of audiences, a particular concern for dance-band musicians of different generations. He noted how the master showman alternated playing ballads and popular songs, slow and up-tempo blues. Then, too, Oliver offered white listeners "smooth, sweet modern numbers," while for Blacks, Bernhardt explained, "which was often on our Mondays off, we played a lot of blues and jazz numbers" and requests. Just as he would with Basie a few years later, Young enjoyed playing with a leader who "knew just the right songs, just the right tempo and just the right length to make those people get up off their behinds and fill the floor."[31]

There were numerous similarities between the two Louisianans. Oliver's soloing, mastery of blues, and highly emotional and speechlike playing all appear to have inspired the saxophonist, who would often finger the same notes in different ways, varying their tone and density to mimic the sound of human speech. In this fashion, nuance assumed a prominent role alongside instrumental virtuosity. Later in his life, his frequent use of profanity among friends would recall the trumpet player's repartee.[32]

In accordance with their devotion to blues and the oral tradition, both men made abundant use of musical space, giving themselves time to collect their thoughts and allowing the audience an opportunity to hear the rest of the band. This was a conscious strategy, and an especially important one in Black music traditions. If contemporary assessments of Oliver are any indication, his alternation of blues riffs and silence must have impressed Young as the essence of soulful music.

Young's playing exhibited precisely this same characteristic after he left Oliver. The bassist Gene Ramey claimed that the tenor saxophonist had "a very spacey sound *at the end of 1933*" (italics added), which in turn influenced Ramey's own bass playing. Young would, he said, "play a phrase and maybe lay out three beats before he'd come in with another phrase." Count Basie's solos likewise showed that a minimalist approach could serve as the basis of a unique style and a successful career.[33]

Young relied not only on blue notes and blues harmony, but on the breaks, stop-time, exchanges between soloists, and other musical devices typically associated with Oliver and Jelly Roll Morton. In staying close to the main theme, meanwhile, or even in creating an entirely new melody, he adhered to the tradition that was so important to both Morton and Bechet: to always have the melody going on. And finally, in keeping the melody simple, varying a note ever so slightly and repeating it rhythmically, he maintained the blues tradition of Mississippi and southern Louisiana, adapting the same techniques Oliver used on the trumpet, and Lonnie and Robert Johnson used on the guitar, to his own tenor saxophone.

Oliver's influence over Young extended to some of his eccentric habits and mannerisms, as well as the storytelling abilities that the impressionable young sideman found so captivating. Both men kept mostly to themselves. Phillips observed that Oliver "didn't never hang out with nobody. He always stayed to himself. . . . He didn't drink, he didn't do nothing like that. So he wasn't like the cats, drinking and smoking a little pot and all of that."[34] When he got older, Young likewise stopped hanging out and jamming around town. Moreover, each man's willingness to communicate with the public off the bandstand was hindered by his shyness. But the loyalty the two of them engendered among musicians was also remarkable, causing their former sidemen to speak reverentially of them years after their deaths.

A love of wordplay, storytelling, and New Orleans dishes was another trait shared by the two stylists. And then there was Oliver's liberal criticism of his musicians, a harsh scrutiny that he did not spare even himself. Bernhardt's explanation of Oliver's sharp rebukes also held true for Young: "Some New Orleanians have peculiar ways. You just have to understand them—they [are] critical of others and very critical of themselves."[35]

In the Southwest, Young was reacquainted with the Louisiana heritage that ranked supreme in Oliver's repertoire. One of the New Orleans leader's last recordings, "Shake It and Break It," was a good example of a jubilant Crescent City stomp, while "New Orleans Shout" embodied the spirit of the brass bands and the elation of emancipation and jubilee songs. "I'm Lonesome Sweetheart" and the legendary "Frankie and Johnnie" pleased the romantics, and "St. James Infirmary," "Too Late" (a blues number), and "Stingaree Blues" took listeners back down to the Deep South.[36]

Young's understanding of the blues as a vehicle for improvisation was deepened and broadened during his tour with Oliver, and he would continue to pay homage to New Orleans and southern blues traditions throughout his career. The pianoless Kansas City Six recordings harked back to that city's heritage in their instrumentation and mood; "Way Down Yonder in New Orleans" was a direct reference to it. The recorded version of the up-tempo standard "Sweet Georgia Brown," on which Young played, ended with a collective improvisation typical of New Orleans bands.[37]

Some of the similarities between the trumpet king and the President of the Tenor Saxophone would take some time to emerge. For example, Young would later choose a varied selection of blues and popular songs for his repertoire, much as Oliver had done before him. Then, too, both men became legends during their lifetimes, and both were known for their genuineness, their signifying, and their sense of humor. Finally, as we have noted, each one's reputation was eclipsed by the rising popularity of new musical fads—swing in the thirties, and cool and rock and roll in the fifties.[38]

One characteristic Young did not share with Oliver was the trumpeter's famed tendency to eat enormous amounts of food in one sitting; in fact, the saxophonist was known for hardly eating at all in his last years. And as much as he admired the bandleader, by 1933, unlike Oliver, Young had stopped practicing. In Phillips's words, "He never practiced. He'd [just] take his horn and play. He warmed up." Rather than rely on exercises like Oliver and many other musicians, "he'd pick it up and just play whatever I guess was in his mind. He didn't do it that long." Phillips emphasized, "I never heard him [sitting] around blowing a horn and practicing. I never heard him practice. He'd just blow."[39]

The tenor stylist acquired a growing reputation not only as the band's special feature and hot soloist, but as a crowd-pleasing showman. No numbers were written specifically for him, but he could solo as much as he wanted.[40] On "Tiger Rag," his specialty with the orchestra, his solo might last as long as ten choruses. To get over with his presentation, Young "used to take his mouthpiece off the horn and turn it around, and play it like he was smoking a pipe," according to Phillips. In other words, he "turned his mouthpiece upside down so the bottom of the reed would still be on his lip" and the bell of his horn was "pointing straight down to the floor." At the climax of his solo, he would throw in an acrobatic stunt: holding "his left arm behind his back . . . he would finger the bottom of the tenor saxophone, and his right hand would be in the front, fingering . . . the top."[41]

Phillips recounted how "whenever we played 'Tiger Rag,' we'd feature him. . . . And we played it way up in temp, too. He'd play [the saxophone] this way and make all the breaks up this way, then after we'd get down to the trio part and go back in the chorus again, he['d] put it behind him and ma[k]e the breaks behind him." At the conclusion of this old warhorse, Young would "make a cadenza on the end with [the saxophone] behind him, and then come out. He'd break the house up. I mean, the house went down everywhere that he did that," Phillips added, "because you didn't see nobody doin' nothin' like that."[42]

Young's longtime friend recalled Oliver's praising his new tenor man as being "finished," meaning "ain't nobody [could] tell him nothin' about that horn," because he "*knew* that horn." The bandleader particularly liked to hear his hot tenor player on "Good Night, Sweetheart," which was "his going-home tune [finale] in them days." On that number, Young would "tear it up . . . like in North Dakota."[43]

The King Oliver tour offers us a window into jazz culture in the early 1930s and its effects on Lester Young. Young's life was more than just the story of a famous swing musician who came up through the territorial bands; the changes that he experienced as a person and as a member of jazz society in those years were the same ones faced by millions of swing fans all over the country as they followed and danced to their favorite bands in large dance halls and small, suffocating, smoke-filled clubs. Young was highly respected by these fans—people who often were not educated or famous or prosperous—as well as by his fellow musicians. They were, along with the musicians themselves, the core constituency of swing culture, its most faithful and dedicated advocates.

In part because of King Oliver's success in the 1920s, swing music pulsated through a generation of city dwellers in the 1930s, just as jazz and blues had done after World War I. Swing was thought to have replaced jazz, just as in the previous decade jazz and blues had supplanted ragtime. Yet as the pianist Earl Hines observed, swing really "was nothing but New Orleans jazz dressed up." At first the territorial bands played in the two-beat mode popularized by Oliver, but then gradually the Blue Devils, Bennie Moten, and Count Basie developed the style that would be introduced as a new idiom in the mid-1930s.[44]

The swing fad was more than just music: there were fashions and dance steps, a new lingo, and other trappings to go with it. To be sure, being a swing musician required having the ability to play, which in turn demanded considerable knowledge and training, not to mention talent. But the song lyrics, slang, dances, and hip clothing and hairstyles of swing were readily accessible to prospective adherents of the jazz life, giving them opportunities to show off and to become popular among friends and swing zealots of different social classes and hues.

If Young became famous because of his saxophone prowess, he was eventually idolized because he identified so thoroughly with his fans, who likewise saw themselves in him. Jazz culture—the name bands and the anonymous ones—and all that went with it, transformed the lives of numerous fans. The story of Young's life during this era illustrates and illuminates that larger trend.

In the 1930s, the saxophonist became the consummate hipster in his clothing as well as his general demeanor. As he developed his own personal style, he added special accessories, including a porkpie, a soft saxophone case, a liquor flask, a ring consisting of three bands linked together, and cuff links engraved with Egyptian hieroglyphics. The singer Sylvia Sims recalled, "He was a beautiful dresser and his accent was his pork pie hat worn on the back of his head. He used cologne, and he always smelled divine." Along with his hat, his shoes were particularly important style-wise: he liked Cuban heels and was so fond of suede that he used to buy pairs of suede shoes in different colors to match his suits. Young acquired these accessories only gradually—he did not add the porkpie hat until around 1940, for example—but the process, starting with the suit, contrasting or matching shirts and ties, handkerchiefs, and shoes, began in the early 1930s, if not earlier. Of course, he was hardly alone in his concern for fashion: clothes were important not only for musicians but also for dancers, who held the spotlight, and for swing fans on the sidelines as well.[45]

From his childhood, dress uniforms and musical presentations were closely connected in Young's mind, beginning with the marching bands in the New Orleans parades. In the Strutters, he wore a band coat and cap with gold braid like the other musicians. The members of his father's dance band, meanwhile, often sported tuxedos. Young was photographed in business suits while he was with the Bostonians and the Blue Devils; a circa 1930 photo of Art Bronson's sax section—Young, Odie Cromwell, and Sam Allen—shows him in a double-breasted suit jacket, his tie blowing in the breeze, while the other reedmen are in pullover sweaters and matching striped slacks. Their pants appear to be flared at the bottom, if not actually bell-bottomed.[46]

Black men in show business often straightened their hair, and Young seems to have followed suit, possibly even as early as 1927, to judge from a photograph of the Professor's band in that year. The reddish tinge to his hair also suggested a mixed racial ancestry. But Martha Young, the saxophonist's niece, emphasized that his hair was not processed; she recalled it as being "kind of a sandy red. . . . It wasn't conked, he had that hair that was straight, and he'd wear what they called a duck[bill] . . . like the hippies . . . [but with] no rubber band or anything holding it."[47]

In their grander days, in 1932, the Blue Devils invested in three sets of suits for the band. A photograph from that year shows the musicians in matching light-colored coats, slacks, shoes, handkerchiefs, and ties: "*Every*thing matched," Leonard Chadwick confirmed. Ernie Williams is the exception in this shot, wearing a dark suit—possibly because he directed the others. The musicians look equally sharp in other photos taken the same year.[48]

Territorial musicians remembered Young's style of dress as being tasteful, neat, and somewhat conservative when they knew him, suggesting that far more than just clothing was involved. Druie Bess reminisced, "We stayed clean. . . . When I came along . . . you had to be clean . . . you had to have a tie, shirt, and everything—be immaculate . . . clothes pressed and everything—make that a point. Shoes shined." The latest fashions were required—"Everything was right up to date"—though the appearance of prosperity could be deceiving: "You'd think you'd have a pocket full of money. . . . You'd think everybody was well off. You had to make that appearance."[49]

As show-business people, the dance bands likewise had reason to focus on how they presented themselves; Chadwick emphasized, "We felt very strongly that our appearance was [an indication of our] organization." Gray, blue, and dark-green band suits showed that "we weren't new members [the band was] picking up anywhere . . . we were a group that had been together long enough to . . . dress alike and have uniforms." Stylish apparel was "a very important factor[—]part of our salesmanship." Band members obtained the latest styles from an Oklahoma City tailor; Raymond Howell, one of the Blue Devils in the 1932 photograph, reported that they wore pegleg drapes—wide, flowing pants with narrow cuffs, which would later become the rage for jitterbugs and zoot-suiters. This band must have been among the very first to adopt the style.[50]

In the 1930s, people dressed up to go to church or out on the town, and most of all to hear and dance to swing orchestras, meet old friends, flirt, woo, and make various kinds of important connections in nightclubs and dance halls. Swing bands could be heard in vaudeville theaters and movie houses, with shows or musicals and before feature films, yet their primary purpose, and their genesis, lay in social dancing. This specificity permits us to see how the swing audience affected other jazz fans as well as the musicians themselves.

All of the bands that hired Young played for dancing; this is a simple fact, but one that is often overlooked in musicological studies. The ability to jitterbug to the latest jazz hits distinguished swing fans from "lames," "hicks," or country folk—that is, new arrivals in the city. In fact, jitterbugging revitalized the national culture and expressed the dynamism of the music, highlighting its riffs and rhythms and enhancing them with a visual component. Dancers orchestrated the music in ballrooms and on dance floors in cities throughout the United States, underscoring the interdependency of dance and music and demonstrating that in African American music culture—and increasingly in the nation's as well—the two art forms were inseparable.

Dance itself is often trivialized in popular histories romanticizing white dance bands, yet it has been essential to popular music and social life in the United States. (To cite one obvious example, the term "jazz" was at first synonymous with dance.) The commercial success of certain swing bands has invariably been emphasized to lend weight to something that has not otherwise been taken very seriously: African American dance and music styles. Thus we are told by an article in *Down Beat* that in 1938, American audiences "paid 90 million dollars for the privilege of listening to dance bands."[51] But jazz dance was much more than a money-maker; it reflected two typically African aspects of music: a visual component that was integrally related to what was heard, and a participatory role for the audience, who were a vital part of the whole event.

The writer Ralph Ellison emphasized the reciprocal character of African American music and dance and also pointed out that during an evening of dancing, blues selections marked a particular mood and moment: the climax of the night's affair. "During public dances . . . when the band was swinging the dancers and the dancers were swinging the musicians—usually around midnight—*that's* when the blues were evoked," he noted. Jazz dance, in other words, raised musicians' performances to new heights. The swing impulse traveled from the musicians to the dancers and back again, and then it peaked in the blues. First the musicians tried to discover what the listeners liked, then they sought to please the dancers, and finally, themselves inspired in turn, they played blues at a particularly special hour, a moment of triumph for the blues tradition and its faithful, who exhibited their ecstasy in dance.[52]

In their first few hours, African American dances were not much different from white events. "But when the hour got a little later and the drink got to hitting just right, the people would do the type of dancing that suited them," the journalist Nat Williams explained. "You did what the spirit told you. If it said, 'Jump and kick,' you jumped and kicked. If it said, 'Turn around,' you'd turn around." He stressed the self-expression that was so much a part of Black dance culture: "The polite movements of white people's creation—Negroes could do them. But when they got [to] the place where they felt they could relax, just go on and enjoy themselves, they'd give you a show."[53]

In the Young family, the dance heritage was especially strong. We know that Lester did the Charleston while playing the saxophone during his carnival days, and Lee moreover described his brother as "the only one of us who can really jitterbug."[54] In the 1930s, the tenor stylist joined his colleagues in playing for the jitterbug fans of the territorial and leading swing bands.

Young was, of course, steeped in an awareness of dance's significance, and he understood the differences among specific dance audiences and how they shaped a performance. He revealed the extent to which his basic music conception was rooted in dance when he mentioned his love of it and how it affected his playing: "The rhythm of the dancers come[s] back to you." He added, "I have a lot of fun playing for dances because I like to dance too. . . . When you're playing for dancing, it all adds up to playing the right tempo." Early on in his career, he learned that each jazz performance was an experiment in finding the right tempo: after trying out "three or four tempos, you find the tempos they like," a preference that he said "changes from dance date to dance date."[55]

Few of his sidemen in the 1940s and 1950s ever saw Young dance, aside from a bit of clowning around backstage, but the drummer Connie Kay, offering a subtler definition of the art form, maintained that the tenor saxophonist danced on the bandstand when they played together. Unlike other musicians who could not stand still while they performed, Young was invariably flat-footed and otherwise immobile. However, when his sidemen soloed, Kay claimed that Young danced in a very "hip" way. Insofar as it made a strong visual statement, his outthrust saxophone was also a gesture reminiscent of dance.[56]

Since it was so important for him and so integral to the swing musician's aesthetic, we must consider the likelihood that when Young thought about music, it was inseparable from dance. Dancing figures were in his mind, whether or not he saw actual dancers before him; dancers were in his fingers as they pressed the shiny saxophone keys. Dancers spilled out of his golden horn when he played, particularly on the uptempo numbers, and jumped to the rhythms that he spun out so effortlessly above the blues riffs and swinging motifs of the various band sections night after night. Visions of New Orleans parades, memories of his own apprenticeship as a drummer, and images of dancing couples in ballrooms across the nation all figured into his saxophone artistry.

Dance and dance bands not only provided vocations for musicians but shaped their cultural and social life as well. For many urbanites, both Black and white, swing music and dance were favorite accompaniments to all manner of social activities, formal and otherwise. Some lived to dance, while others were thrilled just to attend and watch the spectacular shows. Proscribed by racial barriers, limited by a lack of formal education, and unable to attend college, or to play in symphonies, or to rise in white society, Lester Young and other African Americans nonetheless found ways of overcoming all that. In this new dance era, musicians and audiences created arenas in which their talents and intelligence could find expression in accordance with their own aesthetics and needs.

The tenor stylist's use of swing slang dated from the 1930s, when the lingo was very much a part of all that was going on in the music culture. Although several Blue Devils would later deny that there was ever any jive talk among band members, their emcee, singer, and drummer, Ernie Williams, who had spent the mid-1920s in Harlem, had adopted the idiom of those who would come to be known as hipsters or hip cats, and band members sang rhythmic chants, another innovation in popular song borrowed from the oral tradition. Young's speech was soft-spoken and polite in those days—his fondness for jazz slang was not noted until he became a Basieite—but he was already familiar with the special show-business language used on the TOBA circuit and in carnivals, having been exposed to it as a youngster. The saxophonist's later creativity in terms of language would be legendary.[57]

Among the millions who used the swing argot were marijuana smokers, who developed their own jargon within this world of coded meanings. In 1931 or 1932, Young himself had started smoking marijuana, which was then legal in many states. The herb (often called mary jane, reefer, or pot) would become popular in select jazz circles over the course of that decade. This was an aspect of the life that was not available to everyone, in practice if not in theory. Smokers, however, were not disturbed in the least that not everyone smoked. They believed in "Live and let live," and besides, marijuana use would doubtless lose some of its appeal if everyone indulged. Young was renowned among musicians for regularly smoking it and for preferring the company of those who shared his tastes.

In the United States, the use of marijuana (though not always for smoking) dated from the colonial era in Virginia; from there it spread to Kentucky and Tennessee and the prairies of the Southwest, where it grew wild and proliferated without cultivation. Louis Armstrong was known for popularizing what he referred to as "New Orleans gold leaf." During Prohibition, marijuana use increased among city dwellers; because the herb was legal, at least under federal law, until 1937, it was often smoked in public and on the bandstand before performances in the early 1930s.[58]

The tenor saxophonist Budd Johnson, a native Texan, took credit for introducing Young to marijuana in the late 1920s. He also revealed its importance in Armstrong's band: before recording sessions, he said, Armstrong "would like to get high, and he'd like for the band to get high," so no one was allowed to attend the sessions except for "real personal friends." The herb was also smoked during an early recording session featuring Billie Holiday, an occasion on which Young performed as a supporting musician.[59]

Not all musicians smoked marijuana, but the swing era was commonly associated with marijuana songs such as "The Reefer Man," "Chant of the Weed," and "The Stuff Is Here," and barely concealed references to getting high were rife; the argot of "vipers," as the smokers were known, enhanced their sense of identity and the distinction they drew between themselves and nonvipers. Use of the herb had taken hold in eastern cities during the jazz decade (Billie Holiday, for example, started smoking while still in her teens, in the late 1920s), and by 1935, Chicago's *Defender* was deploring the "amazing rapidity" with which "tea pads," or marijuana smoking parlors, had spread over the South Side, permitting "both young and old [to] inhale the system-destroying weed."[60]

Young was an occasional marijuana smoker by the early 1930s; by 1936, and very possibly sooner, it had become a daily habit for him in the privacy of his hotel room or behind clubs during breaks. In an account that contradicted Budd Johnson's claim, another Oliver sideman recalled that Young's initiation into the vipers' society occurred in Tulsa, Oklahoma: "We was with King Oliver. There was a cat that came by had been playing in King's band, and [when] he heard [where] we was at, he said he just had to come by and see King and talk with the band. He was a drummer, and he brought some good shit with him from California. And at intermission, we all went out, and we was talking, and he lit up. So we got high, and Pres said, 'Let me try some of that stuff. . . . You all been talking about you all getting *high* and all that stuff, I want to see if I can get high.' "[61]

After a minute, Young said, " 'You know one thing? . . . I feel good. . . . I feel like going in there *now* and picking up old Pound Cake and blow it till the bell come off.' " Phillips claimed Young "blew so much horn that night [that] people stopped dancing" in order to come up close to the bandstand and watch him play.[62]

Many bandleaders and musicians, of course, did not approve of this smoking. On nights when Oliver's bandsmen would get high and afterward boast about how "we'd played like hell," the leader would tell them, " 'You *think* you played something. That stuff make you think you're doing something when you ain't doin' nothin'.' " He reprimanded them: " 'You all get full of that shit and think you're playing something. You ain't playing a damn thing!' "[63]

Perhaps its association with Armstrong attracted Young, or maybe it was its slightly forbidden air. Billy Young had once reprimanded two of his musicians, the younger of whom was Lester's good friend, for smoking marijuana, and had physically assaulted the older one for leading the younger astray. The conspiratorial aspect of obtaining and smoking the weed after it was made illegal in 1937 may also have appealed to Young. The change of law did little to stop the trend: marijuana use was so common in Harlem by late 1937 that for Young and Billie Holiday it became, along with the music, another basis of their fraternization.[64]

In truth, marijuana smoking was more than a quaint custom or habit for the Armstrong and Young cliques; both men used it to initiate sidemen and fellow musicians into the deeper levels of the swing culture. Buck Clayton recalled undergoing such an initiation or test when he joined the Basie band in Kansas City. Young took him out to the "yard" behind the Reno Club and, without saying a word, pulled out a joint, lit it, eyed Clayton, offered it to him, and closely observed as he inhaled. The trumpet player was hardly surprised by this; after all, Louis Armstrong had introduced him to the herb in Los Angeles. What did surprise him, however, was that earlier in the evening at the Reno, "somebody [had] pulled out a stick of pot and lit it up right there in the club," at Basie's table—something they "wouldn't dare do . . . in Los Angeles."[65]

Marijuana smoking was but one facet of the jazz culture that some American urbanites found so attractive and others so repellant. When marijuana became illegal, it lent an outlaw character to jazz culture, years before heroin addiction grew widespread. In some ways the habit was associated with what years later would be termed an alternative lifestyle—alternative, that is, to the straight life and sobriety of the workaday world.

Having gained admission to the inner circles of various cliques through their music, Young and his colleagues behaved and dressed in a manner appropriate to their new roles, and they took their acquired tastes back to their own social circles and with them wherever they traveled. An acquaintance with the manners and customs of different cliques and national and ethnic groups became a part of the swing musician's persona. Musical tastes, dress styles, jazz slang, and dance all figured in the "hip" philosophy epitomizing the worldview first of the musician, then later of the sophisticated urbanite, and eventually of the teenage jazz fan who modeled himself after Lester Young or Dizzy Gillespie. For the generation that played in and followed the territorial bands and, moreover, survived the Depression, the specific music culture and attendant styles and customs represented a legacy worth preserving. That legacy nurtured people's spirits, enriched urbanites' lives, provided musicians with income, and served as an antidote to the pernicious effects of materialism, commercial music, and racism.

CHAPTER 9

No Eyes Blues

More Than Just Music, 1934–1936

BEFORE swing became a national craze with the popularity of Benny Goodman in 1935, the harsh realities of the Depression caused many territorial bands to flounder and break up. Toward the end of 1933, when he left the Oliver band, Lester Young, like other territorial musicians, had to make some important career decisions. Stranded on the road by the demise of their bands, many musicians found havens in Minneapolis, Kansas City, and Oklahoma City, where they formed small groups of between five and nine members that toured only occasionally (and even then not very widely). Some considered other kinds of employment. Young, for his part, went back to Minneapolis, where he and Beatrice stayed until 1936. Leonard Chadwick, a veteran of both King Oliver's band and the Blue Devils, worked at Bishop's Waffle House in Oklahoma City by day and at night provided "hotcha rhythm" at the Ritz Ballroom; later he moved to Denver, where he gradually rose through the ranks to head the city's housing authority, all the while continuing to perform on weekends. Clarence Phillips made Kansas City his home and quit music altogether in 1936; he worked in the meat-packing houses until his retirement, when he moved to Berkeley, California. His brother Leonard finally left a beleaguered King Oliver in Charlotte, North Carolina, in July 1934, and the next year found his way to Washington, D.C., where he would remain for nearly six decades, until his death. He, too, got out of the entertainment business, though in 1983 he would work at a popular Washington club. King Oliver himself did a few more tours, but he was sickly and declining, and he died in the spring of 1938.[1]

The territorial musicians kept alive their heritage and, significantly, the music culture and values, even if they lost some of the freedom to improvise, the economic independence, and the sense of solidarity that the early swing bands had afforded them. The tradition survived not only in the music, songs, and dances but in dress styles and slang, as well as in the memories of warm camaraderie among musicians and fans, family and friends, in different nightclub settings over the years throughout the land. The blues life they lived gave real meaning to Duke Ellington's contention that "jazz is a state of mind."[2] Blues and jazz idioms and slang, humor, folklore, dance, and dress styles, along with the standard melodies and traditional riffs, all became significant expressions of their ethos.

The musicians who stayed in the territories kept close track of those who went on to successful careers in name orchestras, and they waited eagerly for them to come to town on tour, so they could relive the territorial days and catch up on what was happening to former bandmates. These were the old friends—"waybacks," he called them—whom Young preferred to spend his free time with when he traveled with his combo in later years. His persistence in the music business in 1934 and 1935, despite the hardships of the Depression years and the specific problems he encountered in the different bands he played with, testified to his commitment—a commitment based on deeply held beliefs.

Young's transformation from an aspiring saxophonist into a tenor legend was not a matter simply of his learning his craft or adopting the latest swing slang. Certain fundamental values instilled in him as a child steeled him for the ordeals he would face as a territorial musician and allowed him to reinterpret his own basic beliefs and adapt them to jazz society. The specific Protestant values acquired by the saxophonist when he was a youngster—a strong sense of morality and unbending ideas about how people should treat one another—were part of a larger religious framework that was quite familiar to many, if not most, African Americans.[3]

We know that Lester grew up in a devout African Methodist Episcopal household; Martha Young, his paternal grandmother, was an evangelist, and her husband's support of Thibodaux's Allen Chapel was recorded for posterity on a plaque in the church's vestibule. His aunt Mamie married Allen Chapel's minister. His father conducted choirs and often spoke before congregations during his travels. Moreover, a blessing always preceded every meal in Professor Young's home. These facts all suggest that Lester Young was very likely quite familiar with basic Christian precepts—the admonishment to love all humankind regardless of race or status, for example.

To fully understand his values and views, we must bear in mind that jazz, like Black music culture in general, drew upon a rather profound southern Protestantism and, ultimately, upon African religiosity. The musician and writer Francis Bebey observed that West African music is among the most difficult musical traditions for Westerners to comprehend. More than mere entertainment, such music is, according to Bebey, "a challenge to human destiny; a refusal to accept the transience of this life; and an attempt to transform the finality of death into another kind of living."[4] The music cannot be isolated from art, or life, or religion. These qualities are particularly important for African American jazz musicians and their audiences, as well as for Black churchgoers in the United States, the West Indies, and Africa.

Certain aspects of West African culture are valuable for the study of jazz inasmuch as they are keys to African thought. The art historian Robert F. Thompson has stressed that Black heritages combined moral objectives with entertainment and blended the sacred with the profane. On both sides of the Atlantic, in churches and popular-culture settings, the study of dance and music offers a means of understanding philosophy and values.

Lester Young was a moralist, a man with strong opinions about right and wrong—in regard to telling the truth and stealing, for example. Like his father, he believed that music was far more than mere music or light entertainment; rather, it was closely linked with life and one's very essence and sense of self-worth. But it was not just an individual or private matter, for the jam sessions that he sought out in the 1930s recalled West and Central African worship in which drumming, song, and dance united the community with its ancestors and spirits and reaffirmed the values that gave meaning to its worldview. In jazz society, jam sessions became sacred milestones in a musician's career, and after death, memorial concerts served a specific function for the community.[5]

Failing to comprehend the relationship between art and belief, the public, most critics, and even some musicians fundamentally misinterpreted Young and viewed him and other Black artists as enigmatic. Young himself explained that music played a singular role in his life—"all the way," he said[6]—but the profundity of jazz from the musicians' standpoint has gone both unappreciated and unexplored. The saxophonists Eddie Barefield and Budd Johnson shared Young's depth of feeling about the music; like him, they knew they were very much a part of something that was bigger than any one or even all of them. This knowledge is a basic part of religion.

As Barefield put it, "Whatever you're doing . . . this never leaves you, you're always thinking of it, of something that you might do with your instrument. It is a way of life." Once, when asked to join the Baha'i faith, Barefield responded, "I already have a religion . . . music. I don't have time for the Baha'is . . . for anything. . . . When I say 'music,' I mean jazz music."[7] Budd Johnson maintained that the future of the music was eternal and that its origins were primeval and lay in nature itself: "Music started out by the winds, the waterfalls falling . . . the grunts and groans of the different beasts . . . and the birds that sing."[8]

This belief in the spirituality of music was so successfully instilled in Lester and his siblings, and in many other African Americans of their day, that certain values and forms of behavior were simply assumed. One did not have to go to church or practice religion in any obvious fashion. For Young and his colleagues, as for Duke Ellington, maintaining and developing jazz traditions were special missions in life, and their faith was reflected in much of their behavior as swing musicians, dancers, and fans.[9]

Jazz is rarely viewed as part of an African American religious base, perhaps because so many musicians came from strict, God-fearing households in which blues and honky-tonk music were considered to be evil incarnate. W. C. Handy, Jelly Roll Morton, and Buck Clayton, among others, risked parental censure because they chose careers in music or because they played the kind of music they did. Nonetheless, few writers have considered the humanitarian dimension of the bands or the ethos of the young urbanites who made careers for themselves in jazz. When it was possible for them to do so without paying a terrible and immediate price, they defied the dictates of Jim Crow and the traditional ranking of social classes. They were indeed among the faithful in the sense that they believed in the true worth of every person and were often highly tolerant of individuality, be it in the form of artistry, eccentricities or vices, or even outright criminal behavior. Their society offered companionship and solidarity to Black and white urban dwellers persecuted by those possessed of deeply entrenched prejudices against African Americans, musicians, and members of the demimonde. Nor have scholars considered the fact that African American religious ideals have often found expression outside of church. For example, the very vocabulary used to describe good music or to characterize specific bands, or particular musicians, or the mood of certain songs—the word *soulful* comes to mind—reveals the singular influence of religion on jazz.[10]

As one who had grown up in church society, Young tried to find ways of following Christian morality in personal relationships, notably by observing the Golden Rule and respecting others' beliefs. He was also an idealist who strove to make life better, to dispel evil and racism—things for which he had "no eyes." Furthermore, he liked to hear and see beautiful things, and that search for beauty lay at the heart of the aesthetic of his saxophone artistry. As the pianist Billy Taylor noted, "Lester's approach to everything he did in life was concerned with beauty."[11] In many ways he succeeded in leading a life in which he abided by his principles, spoke no evil of others, and showed genuine sympathy for all living creatures.

Yet Young's religiosity was not readily apparent, disguised as it was by his eccentricities and by jazz culture generally. His sidemen and family pointed out that he was not religious in the strict sense of attending church or reading the Bible. But—and more important to the faithful—he was described as having "a good heart" and as being "sincere . . . never had any animosity." Moreover, "if he couldn't say something good about you, he said nothing."[12]

The pianist Sadik Hakim, a sideman with Young and later with Buddy Tate, regarded Young as "deeply religious" and recalled that the tenor stylist "was more religious than *all* of those people who [attend church] just to be seen. He was, in his head, a religious man."[13] Bobby Scott, the pianist in the Gene Krupa Quartet, echoed Hakim's opinion, asserting that Young was religious "without . . . saying anything about it." That God existed was taken for granted—the way it was taken for granted that the grass was green and the sky blue. Scott further believed that Young had an "equilibrium [that] had something to do with a certain kind of peace."[14]

Young masked his faith with an aura of rebelliousness, a device not uncommon among individuals from devout households. He also displayed his spirit of independence and individuality in different ways—not only by choosing a career in dance halls and outside the church, but by his insisting on paying little heed to the dominant tenor style of the day, in using jive slang almost exclusively, in maintaining that 13 was his lucky number, and so on.[15]

Young's quest from adolescence to adulthood, to become a stylist with his own unique tone and conception, was rooted in certain ideas he harbored about purity and the inherent value of himself and every individual. Whether or not he was always conscious of them, these beliefs appear to have originated in his Protestant upbringing, in his forebears' religiosity, and in African American and African music traditions. These legacies were an integral part of his identity and life.

We see the links in the purity of his tone and conception, qualities that were often emphasized by musicians; an allegedly spiritual element was occasionally noted in his playing as well. His very sound and power to move people were likened by the guitarist Barney Kessel to "classical music . . . like Mozart. It's spiritual. It's very pure . . . linked to a person's soul."[16] The tenor saxophonist Paul Quinichette, known as the Vice Pres because of his admiration of Young and the similarity of their musical approaches, accounted for his hero's tone and his ethereal conception by relating that "[Young] used to tell me, 'You're still up here in the air with me, instead of going down there in the mud. Don't go down there in the mud below you.'" Quinichette recalled Young's assessment that "most of these guys . . . all sounded like Coleman Hawkins, playing out of their bellies. . . . [They] got this heavy, muddy sound . . . [whereas Young's sound was] up in the air . . . light, and airy, and flexible."[17] Dizzy Gillespie likewise described Young's playing as "ethereal-like."[18]

Basie trumpeter Harry "Sweets" Edison, an avid Bible reader and witty raconteur from Columbus, Ohio, detected a spiritual element in Young's performances. Young had a "way of showing that he was a believer in a Supreme Being. It wasn't like a preacher. . . . Pres gave his message through his horn, like a reverend. . . . He had a strong belief because it was heard in his playing." Edison, characterized Young's playing as soulful in addition to simple. It had deep feeling because soul music "is mostly spirituals. . . . Reaching somebody's soul is reaching their inner feelings . . . conveying . . . your absolute inner feeling, the way that you have suffered."[19]

The tenor stylist reached out to everyone with his message because he "had a great love for *everybody*. . . . He didn't pick out no race of people. . . . he loved everybody," Edison recalled. An entertainer, he added, "looks *forward* to doing a performance. [He or she] can't *wait* to get on stage." Edison noted that soulful entertainers were in fact "healers" and explained, "You get up there, if you're sick, it makes you well, and you're making somebody happy out there, which is our aim in our business."[20] In the same vein, the alto saxophonist and Basieite Earle Warren contended that music was "the fruit of life," elaborating, "It's something that revives you."[21] Buddy Tate believed that music was spiritual in that it "makes you love people."[22]

Young's first interview, "You Got to Be Original, Man," published in *Jazz Record* in the midsummer of 1946, suggested that he felt the relationship between a person and his Creator was a very private matter, known primarily in the person's heart. A supreme sense of inner worth and deep convictions about originality accounted for Young's self-confidence. Although the actual words sounded more as if they had been written by Allan Morrison, the Black interviewer, they nevertheless conveyed the message that Young would repeat throughout his life: he explained that he believed "passionately" that "originality should be the highest goal of art and life. Without [originality] . . . art or anything else worthwhile stagnates, eventually degenerates." Playing was in some ways like prayer or confession: Young was adamant that "musicians wishing to say something really vital must learn to express their inner feelings with a minimum of outside influence." At some point early in his life, he had decided that "he was going to play music the way he felt it and not the way the other musicians played it." In the spirit of the rambling bluesmen whose lived truths had set popular music on its course in the twentieth century, he asserted, "You got to have a style that's all your own. A man can only be a stylist if he makes up his mind not to copy anybody."[23]

Another statement from this interview reminds us of Protestantism, with its emphasis on the piety of the individual rather than the pronouncements of the clergy. Young continually spoke of his heart as being the seat of his inner feelings—using the phrase "What was in my heart" frequently. This was the real source of his inspiration, he said, not some other saxophonist. He disliked talking about outside influences, as he felt that "a real musician doesn't need influence outside of his own imagination and responsiveness to life." Asked to name his greatest influence, he replied, "Nobody, really."[24]

His philosophy of life was clearly expressed in other interviews as well. He kept his own counsel—"I stay by myself. So how the fuck do you know anything about me?"—and believed in his own version of the Golden Rule: "I don't bother nobody."[25] For people who were concerned mainly about what others might say, he had some advice: "Whatever they do, let them do that, and enjoy themselves—and get your kicks yourself. Why you envy them because they enjoyin' themselves?"[26] And when asked about some musicians' preferring the music of the old days to that of the high-fidelity age with all its microphones and emphasis on recording techniques, Young responded with an aphorism exalting the freedom of the individual: "To each his own."[27]

On one occasion he simultaneously expressed his belief in a life of constant struggle, showed his familiarity with biblical language (or at least marriage vows), and referred to an afterlife: "But it's the same way all over, you dig? It's fight for your life, that's all. Until death do we part, you got it made."[28] Such quotations corroborate what we have inferred about the religious sources of his ideas.

Young's thoughts on the importance of having a unique musical identity—such that one's very "sound" was immediately recognizable to those in the know—echoed what Louis Armstrong wrote in one of the first books on jazz, *Swing That Music*. Partly autobiographical and partly an explanation of the new music, the volume includes a chapter entitled "I Hope Gabriel Likes Our Music," which informs the swing musician that if he wants to be the very best, "he must try always to originate and not just imitate."[29] While there is no evidence to indicate that Young actually read this work, the language he used a decade later in his interview—that is, his statement about originating rather than imitating—is so similar as to suggest either that someone told him about these words of advice from Armstrong or that this was an oft-repeated axiom in jazz culture.

Young believed that a musician's tone and style were so closely associated that they were all but patented; but because they could not be registered, imitators followed in the wake of stylists, copying them in ways that extended beyond their conception of music to various details of the jazz culture and even their personal habits. For the true artist, of course, an individual style remained the most sought-after goal and was the end result of years of practice, choice of equipment, physiognomy—for horn men, the structure of the jaw, alignment of the teeth, and so on—and aesthetic values. As the saxophonist Bert Etta Davis, from San Antonio, Texas, explained, in order to reach this objective, "one just keeps playing."[30]

During the key years of his artistic development, in the early 1930s, Young was part of a community that shared his ideals, though that did not preclude some misunderstandings and sharp disagreements about his saxophone aesthetic. The Kansas City and southwestern jazz fans who stuck by Young appear to have been faithful disciples; their social harmony recalls the fellowship of "love feasts," those ritual teas and dinners of the nineteenth and twentieth centuries at which Black Protestant churchgoers practiced goodwill and fraternity. Through late-night and early-morning jam sessions, musicians and jazz citizens created a sense of community and introduced a sacred dimension into a world that was invariably viewed as secular, if not profane. In these sessions, bands as well as individuals also competed with one another to see who would wear the crown, just as their musical forebears had done in New Orleans. In some ways, with his singular and all-encompassing vision—a vision that sharply clashed with the dominant tenor style of Coleman Hawkins—Young served as a prophet, launching a new musical conception that affected many young people who were serious about music, not all of them saxophonists.

Young's reputation among territorial musicians rested from his unparalleled success in numerous jam sessions and "cutting contests"—tests of an artist's mettle and ability to outplay others in terms of original ideas and staying power—from the late 1920s through the 1930s. The writer and Oklahoma City native Ralph Ellison referred to these competitions as "ordeals, initiation ceremonies, or rebirth," in which musicians vied for local titles and honors.[31] By such means and by becoming familiar with "the traditional techniques of jazz," a musician "must . . . 'find himself,' must be reborn, must find . . . his soul."[32] In other words, the musician's search for spiritual truth was like a quest, and the suffering endured in the course of the pilgrimage was an inevitable challenge posed for the pious believer.

For Ellison, Young's artistic conception and stylistic individualism were the most daring he ever heard. His introduction to Young's talent came when he saw him "jamming in a shine chair, his head thrown back, his horn even then outthrust, his feet working the footrests," in Hallie Richardson's shoeshine parlor at 308 East Second Street, in Oklahoma City's African American district. "To us he was the future . . . that melodic line, so swinging, so sinuous, so unpredictable! . . . A line so clearly—as you could hear—based on chords, but far-out chords that could lift a blues or a ballad out of sight!" As early as 1929, Ellison claimed, the tenor stylist "with his battered horn upset the entire Negro section of Oklahoma's capital city."[33]

It was around then that Buddy Tate came to a similar conclusion about Young's impressive virtuosity, after hearing him for the second time in his life, in an African American hotel—probably the Washington—in Tulsa, Oklahoma. The proprietor encouraged jam sessions in the lobby, and during one such event, Tate learned that "there was a tenor player upstairs, Red Young," and went up to his room. He found him sleeping, woke him up, and informed him, "We're having a session downstairs, why don't you come along and play because I haven't heard you play tenor?"[34] Young gladly accepted the invitation. Tate's account revealed how much Young had progressed since they first met, in Sherman, Texas: "I'll never forget that sound—light, very light, but aah! Everybody put their horns down on the floor and left. He scared everybody to death!" Tate was expecting Young to sound different on a larger horn: "He played like that on alto, too, but I thought the tenor would slow him down some, but it didn't." With some humor, Young informed the awed musicians, "Look—I didn't come here to do a concert."[35] Tate recalled, "Anytime there was a jam session, man, he was ready, man. . . . I never heard anybody play tenor like that in my life. . . . He was swinging like mad." On at least one occasion, the other musicians shrank from the competition: "We just stopped and just—and he says, 'Look, somebody else play something.' "[36]

Budd Johnson was another avid admirer of Young's competitiveness and ability to prove his mettle. He reminisced, "Pres used to come and get me, wake me out of a deep sleep, pour whiskey down my throat, and say, 'Get up! So-and-so just came into town, and he's over there blowing. Let's go and get him.' " But Johnson also stressed Young's willingness to help some fellow saxophonists; the two of them, for example, constantly "schooled" each other, sharing knowledge: " 'Dig this. Here's what I learned today.' " When they were in the same town, Young would find Johnson and confide, " 'Look, I found out how to do all this in one breath.' We were eager then to show each other what we learned. There was no gap between musicians."[37]

Young earned recognition for being not only a stylist but a saxophone "freak"—not a pejorative term at all but rather a comment on his unparalleled virtuosity. He "could make a note anywhere" on his instrument. Certain notes were usually produced by depressing specific keys or combinations of keys on the saxophone (or valves on the trumpet and cornet), but "freaks" found ways to defy convention and orthodoxy by means of "false fingerings" and adjustments of the mouth and lips, or embouchure. The trombonist-guitarist Eddie Durham explained that "Coleman Hawkins and Chu Berry and those guys, they fingered it correctly with what they were doing. Lester and those guys [e.g., Herschel Evans] didn't." Furthermore, Young and Evans "could do anything they wanted to do with a horn, anywhere."[38]

It is against this background, then, that we should reinterpret accounts of the most famous saxophone cutting contest in the history of jazz. Legend has it that Young proved his worth in competition with Coleman Hawkins, bandleader Fletcher Henderson's biggest star, at the Cherry Blossom at 1822 Vine Street in Kansas City, Missouri. Mary Lou Williams, the pianist and arranger with Andy Kirk's band, was one of the first to tell the story of the local tenor men—Dick Wilson, Herschel Evans, Herman Walder, Ben Webster, and Young—triumphing over Coleman Hawkins, who lingered so long trying to get the best of the Kansas City stalwarts that he blew the engine on his new Cadillac while racing to the next Henderson date in St. Louis. In Williams's words, "Hawkins was king until he met those crazy Kansas City tenor men."[39] Gene Ramey, from Austin, Texas, maintained that Young "tore Hawkins so bad. . . . Seemed like the longer Pres played, the longer they had that head-cuttin' session, . . . the better Pres got."[40] The drummer Jo Jones and other musicians also related the tale, but few claimed actually to have been there to witness the dethronement.[41]

It is difficult to verify the date of the battle or, as we shall see, whether it even occurred the way Williams and Jones recalled it, because though it was often recited as fact, it was witnessed by only a few people who left records of their recollections. In 1934, only about four months after the alleged cutting contest, the *Chicago Defender* not only praised Young as "one of the most celebrated tenor sax players in the music world" but also noted that he was "rated by many to be the equal of the old master [Coleman Hawkins]." The article made no mention of the Kansas City battle.[42]

Perhaps the much-discussed event occurred after a "Night Club Party" advertised in the *Kansas City Call* in December 1933, shortly before Prohibition officially ended. As a matter of course, newspapers would not have documented a jam session, but *Hendersonia*, the definitive survey of the band's activities, did list a December 1933 date in Kansas City.[43] Then, too, the St. Louis portion of the story is corroborated by ads in the *St. Louis Argus* announcing that Fletcher Henderson and His Roseland Orchestra would play a December 1933 date at the People's Finance Ballroom.[44]

Noteworthy among the problems of verifying the battle royal is the fact that no less a personage than Count Basie himself challenged the actual story, maintaining, "I really don't remember that anybody thought it was such a big deal at the time." Basie admitted to having been in the Cherry Blossom and having witnessed the jam session among the city's tenor players, but he insisted, "I don't remember it the way a lot of people seem to and in all honesty I must also say that some of the stories I have heard over the years about what happened that night and afterwards just don't ring any bells for me." He recalled that after repeatedly being asked to play, Hawkins "decided to get his horn" and went across the street to his hotel to get it. When he returned, several people commented on his unusual behavior, because as John Kirby stated, "I ain't never seen that happen before"—that is, "Nobody had ever seen Hawk bring his horn somewhere to get in a jam session."[45]

In his autobiography, Basie related how Hawkins went on the bandstand, "and he started calling for all of those hard keys, like E-flat and B-natural. That took care of quite a few local characters right away." Basie did not recall Mary Lou Williams's presence, but he conceded that he left early and she might have come later. (She did.)[46] But the very fact that he went home to go to sleep, he emphasized, suggested that no real battle was taking place: "I don't know anything about anybody challenging Hawkins in the Cherry Blossom that night," he reiterated.

Basie acknowledged how subjective such undertakings could be when he mused, "Maybe that is what some of those guys up there had on their minds," adding, "but the way I remember it, Hawk just went on up there and played around with them for a while, and then when he got warmed up, he started calling for them bad keys." He concluded, "That's the main thing I remember." Williams's version of the story is neater and more dramatic than Basie's, and perhaps closer to what Kansas Citians wanted to believe. But as Basie pointed out, sometimes it was a matter of opinion as to who won a cutting contest.[47]

There is another problem with the accepted version of the tale: Young also told it differently, without making any mention of a cutting contest. He explained that he and Herschel Evans and others were standing outside a Kansas City club one night, listening to the Henderson band: "I hadn't any loot, so I stayed outside listening. Herschel was out there, too." Coleman Hawkins had not shown up for the date, so Henderson approached the crowd of hangers-on and, according to Young's account, challenged them, asking (in Young's words, which were not necessarily Henderson's own), "Don't you have no tenor players here in Kansas City? Can't none of you motherfuckers play?"[48]

Since Evans could not read music, Young accepted the challenge at the urging of his friends. Young recalled how he had always heard "how great [Hawkins was] . . . grabbed his saxophone, and played the motherfucker, and read the music, and read his clarinet part and *everything*." Then he hurried off to play his own gig at the Paseo Club, where a mere thirteen people made up the audience. Young nonetheless savored the memory of his triumph, observing, "I don't think he [Hawkins] showed at all."[49]

By Young's account, his success that night was highly symbolic, given that Hawkins was not even present. After all, with no rehearsal, he sat in the great saxophonist's chair and played his part, reading the music on sight "and everything." The basic point of the Williams and Young versions is the same: the new stylist with a local following defeated or matched the champion tenor player from the premier New York City jazz orchestra. Williams's retelling of Young's triumph sought to legitimize a new tenor stylist; the detail about Hawkins's ruining his new car was very likely an embellishment designed to enhance the taste of victory by stripping the loser of a prized possession.

Mary Lou Williams's account served to validate not only Young himself but also what would become known as the Kansas City style or school. It made the tenor saxophonist's subsequent attainment of the Hawkins chair in Henderson's band more meaningful, since this particular jam session was said to have convinced the orchestra leader that he needed to hire Kansas City men such as Young. However, the reputation that Young had earned with King Oliver and his sidemen may have played just as great a role in Henderson's recruitment of him as the famous story of Young's defeating Hawkins. King Oliver, Snake Whyte, trumpet player Herman "Red" Elkins, and others spread word of Young's impressive abilities among fellow musicians. Some time later, for example, Elkins ran into Red Allen and asked him, after he had heard Young play, "What did you think of Lester?" "Oh, he was all right, but he wasn't no Hawk," Allen said. Elkins responded to the lukewarm statement by exclaiming, "I know he's not no Hawk. Prez will set Hawk down in a jam session and blow him clear out the room!"[50]

Another interesting aspect of the story is the fact that because Young refused to play like Hawkins, Henderson's reedmen snubbed him. The tale of the victory of the Kansas City style goes some way toward explaining the poor treatment Young would receive from Henderson's men after he joined the band a few months later: they were generally uncooperative and probably jealous of the upstart. Because of his unique, un-Hawkins-like tone, Young was ostracized and resented by the New York musicians during the few months he was with the band, from spring to summer 1934.

In spite of the importance of his stint with this swing band that for many Black musicians epitomized the pinnacle of success, Young provided remarkably terse accounts—at least in published interviews—of his decision to join Henderson and his experiences in the big-name outfit. Henderson started his band in New York City in 1923, and before long it was studded with such stars as Louis Armstrong, Coleman Hawkins, Don Redman, Jimmy Harrison, and Horace Henderson, Fletcher's brother, an arranger and pianist. Together they recorded some of the first big-band jazz records in the 1920s.

Young's involvement with Henderson's band began in Little Rock, Arkansas, where the tenor saxophonist was playing with a contingent led by Count Basie in the spring of 1934. The Basie outfit featured a number of former Moten men and to some extent still operated under his name. Explaining in one interview how he came to join Henderson, Young claimed that the famous bandleader "offered me more money."[51] Basie released him, and off he went.

Buddy Tate's version supplied a few more colorful details. Young received a telegram, Tate recalled, inviting him to replace Hawkins after the star tenor went off to England. Tate was visiting Little Rock at the time and performing with Victoria Spivey's band, and he remembered that he and Young sat up all night "drinking whiskey out of a fruit jar" and discussing what Young should do. In this account, Young's ambivalence surfaced: "I talked to him, I said, 'Pres, take it.' He said, 'I think I could make it, but I understand the band is full of cliques and I just don't know how they'll treat me.' 'Anyway,' I said, 'go ahead and take it because if you don't like it, you can always come back.' He said, 'Yes, but the part that hurts is to go and be a failure and come back and face your friends.'"[52] His reluctance on this occasion recalls the time when Snake Whyte had to convince him to join the Blue Devils. In any case, he eventually overcame his doubts and once again took a friend's advice—in this case, Tate's.

Young toured with the orchestra from New York City to the Midwest, leaving it near Kansas City that summer. At first he avoided recounting any problems he had had during that period, in one early interview stating simply, "The band wasn't working very much."[53] But subsequently he recalled how the leader's wife, Leora Henderson, "would wake me early in the morning and play Hawkins's records for me so I could play like he did. I wanted to play my own way, but I just listened." Perhaps with some irony, he explained, "I didn't want to hurt her feelings."[54] In sharp contrast to territorial musicians, who always helped newcomers, Henderson's men refused even to tell the saxophonist the titles of the numbers they were about to play; furthermore, they ridiculed him because his tone was so different from Hawkins's.

Young's later account was detailed, and his complaints were substantive: "I had a lot of trouble there. The whole band was buzzing on me because I had taken Hawk's place." Finally he decided to leave because, he said, "I had in my mind what I wanted to play and I was going to play that way." He maintained that this was the only time in his career when someone tried to get him to play differently.[55]

Young showed a degree of business acumen in asking for, and receiving, a letter from the orchestra leader explicitly stating that he had not been fired. Around this time, Henderson called in the rest of the reed section—Hilton Jefferson, Buster Bailey, and Russell Procope—and informed them, "I'm going to fire this boy. . . . Actually, I don't want to. But I'm going to fire him because of you, because he'll never be able to play nothing in here, and he'll never have any place here. He won't be happy. . . . But before he goes, I want to tell all three of you something. He can outplay you, you, and you. One of these days, you're going to hear about him."[56] The bandleader had sought Young out because he recognized his remarkable talent, and nothing—not even the opinions of the remainder of his sax section—could persuade him that the tenor player was not destined for greatness.

The newcomer retained Henderson's respect by sticking to his own style and staying true to his beliefs; to employ Ellison's metaphor, his faith was tested, and he passed the test, refusing to succumb to the money and fame—not to mention the acceptance by the New York cliques—that went along with playing in someone else's style. This particular experience was, in religious terms, one of the trials that a faithful pilgrim must face when attempting to follow his or her heart or inner voice. In other words, the price of Young's future crown was his having to suffer through numerous such tests and ordeals.

First Chu Berry and then Ben Webster took over Hawkins's chair; their tones, unlike Young's, were modeled after that of the accepted tenor sax stylist. As for the switch from Young to Webster, it was basically a matter of two bandleaders, Henderson and Andy Kirk, exchanging their tenor men: Young joined Kirk's band in Kansas City in the summer of 1934.[57]

The criticisms and the hardships that Young endured in the early 1930s clearly took their toll on him; for two years after the Henderson debacle, he did not commit himself for any length of time to a big-name band. Tate maintained that "Lester never got over being fired from Fletcher Henderson because he couldn't play like Coleman Hawkins."[58] Perhaps Young was once again reliving that earlier experience with his father's band, when he had been humiliated and left.

But there was also a lesson here for Tate and other territorial musicians who felt that Henderson's sax section had unfairly prevented one of their own from assuming a position that he was rightfully due. Young's stance was based on self-respect and loyalty to his inner convictions, but it was also related to the kind of tolerance that was practiced among evangelical Protestants, who believed that one must always follow one's conscience. Tate explained that "a thing like that . . . taught me never to put anybody down, especially in music," because "everybody has his own way in jazz, his own approach." Whether or not you liked someone's music, "you should respect . . . the other man [and give him] the respect you would want him to give you as a man, as a jazzman."[59]

That Young had the same standards is suggested by the way he spoke of the other members of Henderson's reed section, in deprecating terms but without denying them a measure of respect. He could have named names, but he didn't. Even more significantly, he lived these ideals; his passionate belief in the importance of an individual's developing his or her own style carried with it a commitment to tolerance, which he made such a part of his life that other musicians rarely voiced critical comments about *him.* Tolerance was the keystone of a fundamental humanism that contrasted sharply with prevailing conditions in commercial music and all throughout American society; through it all, Young triumphed, though personally it had its costs.

The trials imposed by the Henderson band did not end with Young's resignation. That summer he toured with Andy Kirk's Clouds of Joy, and characteristically, the saxophonist's account of this period was terse: "Kirk was wonderful to work for," he said.[60] As the bandleader would explain nearly fifty years later, "I took him for his musicianship, and I wasn't looking for a copy of anybody's sound." But then Kirk added, "He didn't stay with me long because the things that I had were mostly . . . written arrangements, and there wasn't too much *freedom* of choice for a musician . . . like Lester, who had many ideas different from other saxophone players and other musicians." The Clouds of Joy "played for the society people where we had to play waltzes, not only three-quarter waltzes but six-eight waltzes"—a harsh constraint for musicians such as Young and Mary Lou Williams, who were "thinking of new ideas all the time."[61]

After a few weeks, Young left Kirk and returned to his home in Minneapolis to play with Rook Ganz and Boyd Atkins in local clubs. In 1935 he auditioned for a job with Earl Hines, playing "Tiger Rag"—Young's own choice—but was not hired. The reason for Hines's rejection is not known, though Charlie Carpenter, a Chicagoan and the lyricist for "You Can Depend on Me," was present for the audition and complained that the prospect "sounded like [he played] soprano saxophone to me." Carpenter would become Young's manager in the late 1940s, but at the 1935 tryout he was unable to understand the saxophonist's conception or why he held his instrument out and to the side. Carpenter realized, however, that Young "must have been doing something because, man, all the cats were listening to him."[62]

Afterward, discussing his concerns with Hines, Carpenter asked, "Why doesn't he play soprano? . . . What he's doing is the funniest thing I ever saw. Why does he hold it out there like that?" Hines responded with considerable insight: " 'Son, that's a peculiarity of his . . . and he does it to be different, I guess. What he's doing is way ahead of our time. The average musician doesn't conceive of what he's doing, because they're all on the Coleman Hawkins thing, but one day . . .' "[63]

Young's memories of such experiences matched those of other musicians, whose careers invariably involved some failed auditions, disappointments, or humiliations at the hands of their colleagues, especially when they were just starting out. In fact, many musicians vividly recalled some particularly humbling event from their youth, sometimes perpetrated by other musicians and sometimes by the larger community.[64] Earl Hines once asserted that what he, a big-name bandleader, had endured "makes me Christ-like; and my humiliation can't be as great as the suffering of my people in the South."[65] Young's own hardships and memories were quite vivid as he related them, and painful as well. Given the importance of religion in the Young household, he may well have viewed these trials in much the same way as Hines.

But we need not rely upon Christian traditions to understand that the tenor saxophonist was a striving musician who saw opportunities to perform with the leading swing bands as chances for fame and fortune. This commercial dimension of Young's early years added a certain complexity to his view of his career, since he could interpret his success in music as evidence that he possessed a God-given talent, on the one hand, or a virtuosity that would lead to wealth, on the other. Winning accolades yet barely getting by—Young's lot in life, as well as that of most of his fellow band members until around 1939—was a very difficult burden to bear.

It would be a mistake to dwell too much, however, on the struggles of these difficult years, because they were also full of "kicks," as Young himself conceded. The sheer joy, not to mention the triumphs, of jam sessions, of the mastery of his instrument, and of the fellowship among band members kept him in the music business. Then, too, he was gaining the confidence that came from playing in a town where he was known, respected, and recognized as an artist by his peers and some fans.

Despite the doubts he felt from time to time, Young possessed a remarkable determination to persevere in the Midwest and Southwest—and sufficient self-confidence to wire Count Basie, whose Kansas City band he had heard on the radio in Minneapolis, and offer his services as a tenor-sax replacement around February 1936. Born in Red Bank, New Jersey, Basie had come to the Southwest in the late 1920s with a road show, and after hearing the Blue Devils in Tulsa had eventually joined them, staying until he was recruited, along with several other Blue Devils, by Bennie Moten. Even before Moten died, in 1935, some of the band members who had disagreed with the bandleader formed their own band under Basie.[66]

Young's overture was prompted by the fact that Basie's current tenor, Slim Freeman, seemed completely inadequate to the bandleader's needs. Basie wired Young back, inviting him to join the band. While he knew Basie, having played with him in 1934, it still took a measure of confidence for Young to leave Minneapolis in this fashion. In moving to Kansas City, he probably never anticipated that the band would soon go on the road to such places as Chicago and New York, or have a radio setup in a Broadway club in two years' time; but then the lure of joining Basie's band in the first place was strong enough to overcome his aversion to a region he had spent his entire adult life trying to avoid.[67]

To deal with the hardships of a struggling musician's career and life on the road, sidemen required unusual amounts of self-confidence, considerable faith in their own resourcefulness, and extraordinary equilibrium. Faith in the profundity of their undertaking, combined with the need to earn money, drove them. In the course of their careers, Black musicians endured humiliations and trials that whites rarely faced; for them, the simple fact of their continued existence in a hostile society constituted a feat in itself. For Black musicians, composure and self-restraint were invaluable attributes in encounters with white racists and suspicious sheriffs. Accounts of southern tours by big bands are filled with incidents of violence between aggressive whites and defiant Black jazzmen.[68]

The Depression years were in many ways white racism's last gasp as official government policy in Europe and the United States. For the next two decades and more, Jim Crow and racial segregation would dominate life in the Deep South, and they would persist in practice, if not in the law, outside the South—in New York City, Chicago, and Los Angeles, for example, especially in jobs, housing, and education—for decades more to come. Even as millions of Americans prepared to fight Nazi racism abroad in the 1930s, many approved of retaining some kind of racial hierarchy at home, and a number of people fought to maintain white supremacy in the United States. They did so in the time-honored manner, relying upon both custom and law and using both legal and illegal means.

The relevance of all this for Young lay in the fact that his new home, Kansas City, Missouri, had the reputation of being "really prejudiced."[69] When Mary Lou Williams arrived there in around 1930, the city's streetcars were segregated; African Americans had to sit in the rear. Blacks and whites were forbidden to drink alcohol in the same house unless they kept their coats on. Roy Wilkins, a new reporter for the *Kansas City Call* and a future head of the NAACP, came to the Missouri city from St. Paul, Minnesota, in the late 1920s and, like the tenor saxophonist, quickly learned that "neighborhoods, schools, churches, hospitals, theaters and just about everything else [were] as thoroughly segregated as anything in Memphis." For Wilkins, "white Kansas City was a Jim Crow town that nearly ate my heart out as the years went by." The young journalist concluded that "in its feelings about race, Kansas City might as well have been Gulfport, Mississippi."[70]

Some contemporary readers may think Wilkins must have been exaggerating, but Blacks as young as twelve years old were shot and sometimes killed during that era by white policemen who placed little value on life in the African American neighborhoods. According to one historian, "Getting Kansas City's police to enforce the law in black neighborhoods was almost impossible": Blacks who murdered Blacks were rarely prosecuted. And if an African American tried to move into a better, white neighborhood and "took a stand against this system [, he would have] had to make [his] bed among bombs."[71]

Young faced such dangers daily. His stoicism, combined with a measure of skepticism and the fact that he rarely seemed to let anything bother him, helped him to cope with the trials of a stylist, the demands of cutting contests, the shady bookers and businessmen, and the hostility of white southerners. That the Black section of Minneapolis was immobilized by the Great Depression may also have accounted for Young's willingness to move on. "The Negro slum on the north side of town" was described by Nelson Peery, a Black resident, as "the most destitute part" of the city, where "hundreds of ragged unemployed black men stood up and down Sixth Avenue and Lyndale looking for a drink, to talk, to joke, and to laugh away the hunger cramps."[72] In graphic terms, Peery described in his autobiography how Black domestics "lined up at the 'slave market' [for a chance to be] selected and taken out to white people's homes . . . [where they] scrubbed, cleaned, and cooked for ten or fifteen cents an hour." Their men were depicted as being "cruel to their fellow men because only the cruel survived." In Young's neighborhood, pedestrians encountered "whorehouses, broken whiskey bottles, mean cops who fleeced the whores who had money and beat those who didn't, ashes in the streets, rats that walked boldly in front of the skinny alley cats, houses without running water . . . [and] black streetwalkers cursing the white ones for cutting in on their trade."[73] Basie's invitation offered the tenor saxophonist an escape from such misery.

Young said he "left [his] madam" when he joined Basie, but his separation from Beatrice may have been only temporary.[74] As we have noted, in 1935 the couple was listed in the Minneapolis City Directory, and in 1936, the directory for Kansas City indicated that they resided in apartment 14 at 1413 East Eleventh Street.[75] Although Young has frequently been portrayed as a Kansas City musician, this was in fact his only appearance in that city's directory. It is also significant that he was listed as living with his wife, suggesting how their relationship endured during his territorial years.

Past memories of earlier trials and chances for greater security, fame, and money all came into play in a conversation Young had with Count Basie the night the bandleader told him, sometime in the late summer or early autumn of 1936, of the new record contract to which he had signed the band. The saxophonist was quite skeptical when Basie shared with him the good news about the contract and about plans for the band to travel first to Chicago to play the Grand Terrace and then to New York City. Things had happened quickly: when Decca executive Dave Kapp came to Kansas City claiming to be a friend of producer John Hammond's, Basie had reportedly jumped at the opportunity to sign and in his eagerness neglected to read the recording contract closely—thus failing to notice that it made no provision for royalties for the promised twenty-four Decca recordings. Right around this time, Buster Smith, then Basie's coleader, and the blues singer–trumpet player, Oran Page, left the band; both had been around too long to take the promises of fame and fortune at face value. Page signed as an individual with Joe Glaser, Armstrong's manager, and Smith joined Claude Hopkins, with whom he would earn more than three times what the Reno Club had paid him. Basie recalled, "I guess Prof didn't really think we were going to make it into the big time."[76]

In this context, Young's rather skeptical response to, or incredulity at, Basie's news can be better appreciated. The bandleader told his other sidemen about the contract before Young arrived that night at the Reno Club. They had been enlarging the band and working on new arrangements in expectation of a tour and contract. When Young entered the club, the pianist took him "outside the doorway to the back alley, where we usually went when we wanted to have a little private sip and a little personal chat." Basie told him the "great news" about their taking "a Pullman into Chicago . . . [to] do some recording for Decca."[77] Transportation costs would be covered by management, and the fact that they were to travel in greater style than they were accustomed to impressed some band members considerably.

Young's reaction somewhat puzzled Basie, who remembered that "all he did was just sort of stand there looking into space like he hadn't heard . . . because he was listening . . . or thinking about something else." Young emerged from his reverie for long enough to ask, " 'What did I hear you say?' " When Basie repeated the news, Young "just stood there and looked at me and looked away and then looked at me again." Basie explained that his tenor saxophonist then "went into his sweet-talk thing: 'Listen, Lady B, you all right?' "[78]

Basie told him about the plans yet again, but the saxophonist still "just stood there nodding his head, thinking about it, and then the next thing he said was like he was talking to himself: 'Well, okay. So now we'll find out what happens.'" Having finished his drink, Young "looked at me and mumbled and went back into his sweet-jive thing again," reiterating his disbelief: "'Hey, look. I tell you what, Lady B. Let's go back in there and get us another little taste, and maybe you'll tell me that again.'"[79] (The bandleader's mention of Young's "sweet talk," a satirical raising of the voice to a girlish pitch, is the earliest reference we have to the tenor player's hipster facade. Such techniques were characteristic of the narrative mode in the African American oral tradition, in which the storyteller would mimic not only the voices of the characters but the sounds of footsteps, the whistling of the wind, and the rustling of leaves and branches—in effect, the entire soundtrack for the tale.)[80] Young's past tours with the Blue Devils and Henderson's orchestra had likewise promised fame, but both had ended in disaster, sending him back to the Midwest. Why should the Basie experience be any different?

He took his chances with Basie's band, traveling on the road, even down south, because with these sidemen he found the kind of fellowship that he sought and valued. These musicians appreciated and encouraged him, and as a group they reached spiritual heights they had rarely attained on their own before. Sweets Edison compared Basie's and other territorial bands to the church organists and singers in Baptist services who made people "get up to shout." In the same way, "Basie's band would make a person get up and dance. *That's moving you spiritually*" (emphasis added). In a remarkable commentary on the band's powers and the importance of dance, Edison boasted, "I've never played a dance with Basie [where] people would *sit down*."[81] This statement also indicated how much of an African sensibility, wherein the spirit moved listeners to dance, remained in the swing musician's consciousness, in the audience itself, and in the very essence of the night's celebration.

Jo Jones, Basie's main drummer after 1936, commented on the kinds of relations that existed among bandsmen. While he was speaking particularly of the rhythm section, the same held true for the rest of the band. He stressed the interdependency of the members of his section, and the fact that they were more than just piano, guitar, bass, and drums, but a band within the band: "We never played with the band; we played with ourselves. . . . If three people [in the rhythm] were down, one person was up. If two people, if three people [were down], put one person on four cylinders."[82] They were a quartet within the choir, the very heartbeat of the orchestra.

The Basie band's playing could only reflect the lives its members led, and when he focused on this aspect, Jones revealed the extent to which, in his opinion, their collective life was fused with their art. "We started the first spiritually. . . . You have to live the spiritual ingredient." Their unity stemmed from the common experiences they shared: "We incorporated our personal lives and we put it on our instruments." Similarly, Jones maintained that "the elbows that we had touched out and reached . . . we brought that on the bandstand and we were strong enough to go through these things."[83]

Jones explained that he stayed with the band for over a decade partly because it presented a challenge but also because it "operated on a strange spiritual and mental plane." The band members, he insisted, never argued among themselves, and they managed to congregate in the same bars and hangouts almost automatically every evening, as if the same spirit had transported them there. Harmony prevailed in the musical realm because the collective will of the bandsmen leveled any differences: "A new man would come into the band and we'd start to play [with no auditions]. . . . If he was a musician, he'd be playing with us pretty quick."[84]

Jones was not the only Basieite who noted the unusual spirit of fellowship within the orchestra. Tate also remarked on the "closeness" among band members and, like Jones, observed that there was "no animosity with each other."[85] Yet this characteristic was not exclusive to the Basie orchestra. The same sense of fraternity could be found in other southwestern outfits, such as Jay McShann's, in which the personality of the pianist and leader produced "a happy band." McShann's band members, too, "were like family . . . a happy family."[86] This specific quality reflected a highly developed sense of fellowship and a powerful moral ethos that ultimately traced back to the religious upbringing of band members and the importance of religion in their native communities.[87]

Young's skepticism regarding the lure of the big time and his single-minded devotion to his own musical conception and artistic goals recalled the attitude of Protestants toward the trappings and glitter of the material world, as well as the abiding faith of Black Americans in the existence of a spiritual order higher than that of their temporal society, with all its crass materialism and racial discrimination. This faith permitted them to persevere in spite of the troubled times and hardships they continually faced. Significantly, when Young later recounted his experiences as a struggling young musician, he presented himself almost in the guise of a pilgrim suffering the trials and tribulations of a true believer: "I know I got a good heart, man," he said.[88]

Despite his skepticism and the first rather trying years endured by the Basieites, this orchestra would provide him with a springboard to international fame. In fact, in the music's history he would always be associated with the Basie band, even though he would be one of their number for only five years or so. It was to become one of the most legendary bands in the history of jazz, and the 1930s version, showcasing Lester Young, would set the standard for comparison both with other swing orchestras and with subsequent reincarnations of the same outfit.

CHAPTER 10

Poundcake

The Holy Main, 1936–1940

IN the late summer or early fall of 1936, after signing his record contract with Decca, Basie booked a tour for his orchestra under an arrangement with John Hammond and the Music Corporation of America (MCA). The band went on the road that autumn and played in Chicago and New York City; early in 1937 they performed in Philadelphia. In between dates in big-city dance halls, ballrooms, and hotels, they toured the hinterlands, often venturing down south as Europe edged toward war.[1]

Young had played under Basie once before, in 1934, after the bandleader assumed command of one of Bennie Moten's bands (the members had rebelled and voted Moten out).[2] Young tended to gloss over such details in his own accounts, however; in one interview he maintained that Basie knew him because the Nest nightclub band "used to go back and forth between Minneapolis and Kansas City."[3] On another occasion he said Basie had known of him through "people [who] had gone up to Minneapolis for various shows."[4]

The story of Count Basie's most famous soloist and his band's rise to commercial fame is one of the most enduring in the annals of jazz; in fact, it is difficult to separate Young's history from that of Basie's orchestra between 1936 and 1940 because the two were so closely linked. Previous accounts have, however, overlooked the band's special importance for African Americans and misinterpreted both Young's relationship with Billie Holiday, the band's singer, and the rivalry between him and the other tenor, Herschel Evans. There has also been some disagreement about the band's origins, and about whether the Reno Club combo or the Oklahoma City Blue Devils served as the original model for the orchestra. The significance of some of the Young and Basie recordings as early expressions of rhythm and blues has been widely emphasized, and in a few very insightful articles, jazz critics have praised the music of the orchestra and of Young's later combos as foreshadowing developments for the next two or three decades. It is my belief, though, that the Basie musicians' opinions of Young provide the best understanding of the tenor stylist and his playing.

No single episode or formula guaranteed the success of either Young himself or the band. The latter was formed when Basie took over the Reno Club's combo in 1935 and staffed it with his own men, at which point Buster Smith also agreed to join as coleader. According to Basie, Oran Page was actually the club's emcee and blues singer as well as the combo's trumpeter; singer Jimmy Rushing was not technically with the band, either.[5] Over subsequent years, the core of Basie, Young, Jo Jones, Carl "Tatti" Smith, and Walter Page, augmented by Wilbur "Buck" Clayton, Herschel Evans, trombonist Dan Minor, and Claude "Fiddler" Williams on guitar and violin (later to be replaced by the guitarist Freddie Green), continued to develop the band's repertoire and expanded it to include popular songs, to increasing acclaim.

Later, as either replacements or augmentations, Earle Warren, Harry Edison, Buster Smith (for the second time), Ed Lewis, Al Killian, Eddie Durham, Dicky Wells, and Vic Dickenson joined, bringing the total number of band members to about fifteen. First Billie Holiday and then Helen Humes sang with Basie, in addition to Rushing. Nearly as important as the personnel was the band's management, overseen by John Hammond and Willard Alexander of MCA, whose goal was to enlarge and modify Basie's outfit so it could compete with the other swing orchestras that were then catering to white audiences in leading downtown hotels of the nation's metropolises. As far as the public and the media were concerned, 1935 was the beginning of the swing era.[6]

In describing the 1936 Reno Club combo, which was originally known as the Barons of Rhythm (the name did not stick), musicians stressed its rhythmic swing and excitement. The band literally entranced listeners, taking them to new heights—the specific ecstatic state sought by swing devotees. Buck Clayton asserted that he had "never heard such swinging music in my life and was spellbound from the very first minute I heard them." There were only nine musicians then, he noted, "but [those] nine could outswing anything that I'd heard."[7] Basie himself agreed that the band was "strutting, really strutting. . . . We had a ball every night." Fats Waller, for his part, "was *crazy* about that band" when he heard it. "*That's* what I want," he told his personal manager, and he offered the band the opportunity to accompany him on the road.[8] John Hammond also insisted that Basie's "was the most exciting, inventive band I had ever heard, and Lester was only one of several superlative soloists."[9]

The Reno Club combo was often cited by Basie as the model for his orchestra after its expansion in 1936. When the bandleader recalled his objectives in taking over that band in his autobiography, however, he emphasized the singular importance of the first predecessor to his orchestra, the Oklahoma City Blue Devils. His original goal at the Reno was to "bring some Blue Devils in there," he wrote, expressing his conception of a swinging unit; he also repeated the maxim "Once a Blue Devil, always a Blue Devil," indicating the permanence of the bonds formed in that band.[10] He sought out Jack Washington on baritone sax, the bassist Walter Page, Joe Keyes on trumpet, Buster Smith as his coleader and sax-section leader, and the drummer Willie McWashington, who would later be replaced by Jo Jones.

As for Young, who joined them a few months later, Basie claimed that he never thought much about the tenor stylist's unique tone: "I knew it was special, but everything he did was special," he explained. He simply "liked the sound [Young] got on his horn. It sounded right for what I wanted in there. It just sounded natural to me." And besides, Young had another qualification—"After all, he had been in the Blue Devils."[11]

When Basie traced the band's origins for reporters in the late 1930s, however, he reverted to the Reno Club version of its genesis. As the band expanded, he said, his goal was to re-create the unity of the Kansas City combo, whose members had "coordinated every move, every solo, perfectly." Given the orchestra's playing of show tunes and popular songs by 1937, it was significant that this earlier model of a swinging band full of soloists, a band that played "heads," remained his ideal: "We used to ride 'em down easy in those days. There was a lot of freedom, we felt completely relaxed and we got accustomed to playing with one another, and it was easy to work out on-the-spot arrangements which really jumped," he recalled. As for the larger orchestra, he maintained, "I want my fifteen pieces today to work together just like those nine pieces did." The small combo would be Young's preference as well, after he left Basie.[12]

The Kansas City slant on the Basie orchestra obscured both its Oklahoma City roots and the fact that because it was a territorial (rather than an eastern metropolis) band, its commercial success held special meaning for African Americans from the heartland—its biggest fans. But wherever the band's precise origins lay, Black Kansas Citians appreciated that it had achieved its success in spite of having to deal with racial discrimination in the very place from which it had been launched—the downtown Kansas City Reno Club, which practiced Jim Crow (as did New York's Cotton Club).

There was another reason that the band had a very special meaning for African Americans, who not only heard it perform under different circumstances than whites but also had their own unique customs for celebrating with it. Black entertainers and their friends attended the "spook dances" put on by Basieites at the Reno every Saturday night, which lasted until early Sunday morning. Basie started this tradition at the club, basing it on his memories of a similar custom among Black show-business people in New York City. Black locals thus had an especially specific reason for becoming boosters of the band.[13]

In much the same way, the Basieites' bonds with other members of the Black urban community developed even before Hammond wrote about the band in *Down Beat*.[14] Black Kansas Citians heard the Reno Club combo perform during the Musicians Ball at Paseo Hall on May 14, 1936, and at the Labor Temple on Labor Day of the same year. The combo was one of many bands that took turns playing at such events, including the Paul Banks, Harlan Leonard, Pete Johnson, Andy Kirk, and Bus Moten (Bennie's brother) orchestras. In late October 1936, it was Kansas City's African American community that feted the Basie band with a Halloween dance farewell party at Paseo Hall a few days before they left for Chicago. The following Monday-night date was "a very special night for everybody," the *Kansas City Call* claimed, because the band shared the bill with Duke Ellington's orchestra at Paseo Hall; the famous bandleader extended his good wishes for the Basieites' success. The band was a vital part of Black Kansas Citians' social life and entertainment, and it would continue to enjoy a close connection with African American urban communities throughout its lifetime.[15]

The *Kansas City Call* was one of the band's chief supporters early on; later other Black newspapers chimed in. The *Call* reserved particular praise for two Basie soloists, Lester Young and Buck Clayton, whom it hailed as "little short of sensational." The African American weekly followed the band's career and attempted to explain its music, maintaining that Basie's orchestra was different from its rivals insofar as it possessed a "perfectly coordinated rhythm section and the ability to improvise collectively for infinite periods."[16]

The band's reputation among African Americans was strengthened whenever it played for Black audiences, as it did in New York City engagements in 1937 at the Savoy, where Black dance traditions were developed, and the Apollo. The musicians could interact much more freely with Black audiences than with white ones, of course, and this was a key to their popularity among the most devoted swing fans; their adoring audiences included new and old friends, relatives, and well-wishers. Enhancing the sense of community was the fact that the band members resided in Harlem, the northern Manhattan enclave that housed thousands of Black newcomers and longtime residents. By the Depression decade, parts of Harlem were a ghetto, and a major riot had occurred there in 1935.[17]

In addition to living and playing around Harlem, Basie's band traveled the African American circuit, called the Around the World Theatres, which included the Howard in Washington, D.C., the Royal in Baltimore, and the Nixon-Grand in Philadelphia. Such appearances permitted the Basieites' fame to spread among African Americans in East Coast cities. Bands such as Basie's played these theaters one after another between dates at big hotels and forays into suburban ballrooms and southern towns; in their interactions with Black and white audiences, they influenced American slang, styles of dress, and urban culture in general, in addition to tastes in swing music.[18]

When the band began performing in early November 1936 at the Grand Terrace in Chicago, the famous South Side venue whose house bands had at one time or another included Earl Hines's and Fletcher Henderson's, some Basieites found the shift to the big time to be a difficult one. Perhaps this was the period Young was referring to when he compared the band to school and recalled falling asleep out of boredom while waiting for others to master their material. The band needed better instruments, more rehearsals, and more musicians who could read music comfortably. Some of the bandsmen balked at playing the complex arrangements for the floor show, something they were not prepared for.[19]

Some of the Basieites, and Young in particular, became better known among African American fans when they jammed in South Side nightspots with the trumpet player Roy Eldridge and the guitarist John Collins. In such sessions and on other occasions—for example, when they marched in the Bud Billiken parade on the South Side during the Thanksgiving holidays—they gave Black Chicagoans a chance to hear what was billed as "a new style of jazz." In late November the *California Eagle*, another booster of Basie's orchestra, even recommended that its Grand Terrace contract be extended, suggesting that the band had improved, probably thanks to Horace Henderson's generosity—he had given Basie some of his arrangements.[20]

During that same month, Young's and Basie's joint recognition was aided by the recording of four Vocalion sides featuring the saxophone stylist and the pianist along with Carl "Tatti" Smith, Jo Jones, and Walter Page. Recorded under the name "Jones-Smith, Inc.," due to contractual issues, the selections were "Shoe Shine Boy," "Evenin'," "Boogie-Woogie," and "Oh Lady, Be Good." Of course, "Shoe Shine Boy" had special meaning for Young because he, like many other African Americans, had shined shoes as a youngster. One critic acknowledged the song's historic racial overtones when he asserted that Young "rubs the bowl of his sax and his genius banishes forever the image of that Uncle Tom shoeshine boy." These recordings became legendary for introducing not only Young but also Basie's other musicians to a wider audience. Reviews from the press were laudatory, and when they were reissued a generation later, the selections were touted as landmarks.[21]

The Basieites arrived in New York City, the nation's capital of entertainment and finance, in time to play a Christmas Eve 1936 date at the famous Roseland Ballroom, an elite all-white nightspot. The tenor stylist's most avid supporter, John Hammond, could not praise him enough for his performances on the bandstand and in jam sessions. Describing his soloing at the Black Cat nightclub with Benny Goodman, Harry James, Basie, Clayton, and Jones soon after the band's arrival in Manhattan, Hammond wrote that Young "was not only the star of the evening but without doubt the greatest tenor player in the country"—in fact, "the most original and inventive saxophonist I have ever heard." Goodman, too, was sufficiently impressed with the new tenor stylist to present him with his clarinet on the spot; this was no minor statement, coming as it did from the "King of Swing." In a sense, Goodman was passing on his scepter.[22]

Popularity among white audiences was difficult for a Black musician to attain, and having earned it, Basie discussed his good fortune with a reporter between Sunday shows on an October afternoon in Baltimore in 1937. The engagement at the Chatterbox, in Pittsburgh's William Penn Hotel, had been the band's greatest success to date—"a very special deal," Basie conceded,[23] with an audience consisting of "mostly stiff rich and dignified socialites," the kind of people the Basieites did not know, did not fraternize with, and were unlikely to befriend (and vice versa). The band had had to experiment to discover what worked with these listeners: "First, we had to sell them [on] a Negro band and then sell them [on] our brand of music." He noted, "Oh, boy, did we receive a chilly reception." Significantly, on the third or fourth night, a younger generation—college students—"crashed in and demanded we give them swing of the wildest variety." So the Basieites "started going to town," and before long everyone "in the place was swinging . . . the stiff shirts, too." That was the turning point, Basie said; "from then on we could feel our popularity."[24]

Combining head arrangements with written selections, the orchestra mastered Broadway tunes but never lost sight of its blues roots or its loyalty to an African American blues aesthetic. Basie bowed to commercial pressures when he included pop tunes and novelties such as "London Bridge Is Falling Down" and "Let's Make Hay While the Moon Shines." Even those were jazzed, however: "When we play pop tunes, and naturally we must, I want these pops to kick!" the bandleader explained. "Not loud and fast . . . but smoothly and with a definite punch." The band did not rely on written arrangements for its own standards—"that way we all have more freedom for improvisations," Basie observed.[25]

The orchestra's recordings of the popular songs "Pennies from Heaven" and "Honeysuckle Rose" and the Basie hits "Swingin' at the Daisy Chain" and "Roseland Shuffle" helped to publicize the band in early 1937. This was a key to the Basieites' appeal to different audiences, and a sign of growing sophistication on their part. That summer they recorded five classics out of the African American blues tradition: "One O'Clock Jump," "John's Idea," "Good Morning Blues," "Time Out," and "Topsy." The recording of a WOR-Mutual broadcast from the Savoy in Harlem offered the territorial anthem "Moten Swing" as well as "Shout and Feel It," "The Count Steps In," and the romantic numbers "I'll Always Be in Love with You" and "When My Dreamboat Comes Home." New recordings in 1938, including "Sent for You Yesterday," "Every Tub," and "Swingin' the Blues," once again revealed the band's distinctive blues roots and helped spread its message and its influence.[26]

The singular effect of these recordings on Black musicians was perhaps best illustrated by the example of the Kansas Citian Charlie Parker, who woodshedded with (that is, isolated himself and studied) a stack of Basie discs featuring Young in the Ozark Mountains in the early summer of 1937. The hours he spent practicing along with the records and learning his idol's solos by heart marked a turning point for Parker, who likely could not have guessed at the time that his hero had done the same thing just ten years earlier with Armstrong and Trumbauer recordings. Inspired by Young and Buster Smith, Parker went on to develop the tradition, becoming one of the most important instrumentalists in American music.[27]

Buoyed by the success of their recordings, the Basieites battled Chick Webb's band at the Savoy early in 1938 and Benny Goodman's band later in the year. In mid-July they began performing at the Famous Door, a club on Fifty-second Street known for its live broadcasts. This engagement provided the setting they needed to draw a larger audience and thus obtain a measure of security, enabling them finally to settle into the city; their popularity was such that their original six-week stint was extended through mid-October. Also of significance in 1938 was that Basie signed an important radio contract with BBC, which arranged to broadcast a summer series of short-wave transmissions from the CBS studios.[28]

As the band gained visibility in New York City and particularly in Harlem, the Basieites became better acquainted with the philosophies of both racial integrationism and Black nationalism. The band members favored integration and the equal treatment of Blacks and whites, but their political involvement was limited by their devotion to the music and their constant touring. They did, however, develop an unusual degree of solidarity among themselves—a solidarity that had its roots in blues and jazz traditions, in their blues aesthetic and their sartorial splendor, and in their roles as style setters in different areas of Black music culture. Metaphors of home and family were constantly used to describe their relationships. Young and Billie Holiday became close friends (they were not romantically involved), and with Buck Clayton as their third, they often referred to themselves as "the unholy trio." Together they frequented Harlem nightspots between road trips.

Although the Basieites would later recount the early days of the band with nostalgia and warmly recall their camaraderie, neither Young's sidemen nor his relatives volunteered much detail on his personal life during this period, other than to mention his relationship with an

Italian-American woman named Mary Dale. Beatrice evidently was not on the scene in New York City when Young met Dale at the Roseland Ballroom, in around 1937; before long the two were living together at the Woodside Hotel in Harlem. Lee Young believed they were married and recalled his brother's bringing Mary out to Los Angeles with him in around 1941, after he left Basie. She appears to have helped the saxophonist out financially when the Basieites were struggling to become a name band in 1937 and 1938; by the late 1940s she seems to have disappeared from his life. Married or not, they doubtless faced the same problems that all interracial couples encountered in those days in the United States.[29]

The new stature Young enjoyed thanks to his success with Basie was diminished by the old prejudice that surfaced when any famous Black musician attempted to enter a white club or theater as a patron, even with white friends, or traveled down south on tour. Paul Robeson, Billie Holiday, and John Hammond became famous for their outspokenness and their willingness to fight rather than swallow the indignities of racism,[30] but the silence of others did not suggest that they did not confront the same issues or that they felt any differently about them. Many bandleaders—Fletcher Henderson and Duke Ellington, for example—followed another course by striving to present their outfits as models of proper deportment as well as exemplars of swing music; in this way, they hoped to improve the treatment they were accorded. Fletcher Henderson's views on the origins of the music were subtly phrased, reflecting the politeness of a southerner and an Atlanta University graduate: "Jazz music began as a racial expression," he wrote. This had helped to set the goal of the "genuine hot band," which Henderson described as "constantly seeking to better its technique and enrich the tradition which lies behind jazz music."[31] For Lester Young, however, there was no way to accommodate or compromise with racism, which he viewed as a kind of sickness that was ultimately incomprehensible. So he withdrew from the larger racist society and took refuge in his music, his family, and his friends in the swing subculture.

He shared the antiracist sentiments of the most outspoken individuals, though he might disagree with them on the best means of dealing with the problem. He often mentioned his refusal to go down south with his father's band, but with Basie, southern tours were fairly common despite the segregation the bandsmen encountered. He became well known by reporters for his dislike of racists, for his suspicion of whites, and for sometimes speaking out, as he did to Leonard Feather about the management at Kelly's Stable, a club on Fifty-second Street: "The boss was a crow, he didn't like mixing."[32] This was a rare critical statement from a jazz musician at this time.

Young's niece Lucille Tolbert "got the feeling that [he] felt that music should have been for everybody." Moreover, "it should have been shared with everybody, and this business of Black bands and white bands and all . . . the [prejudice] makes you sick inside when you are trying to do certain things [musically]." Others corroborated Young's belief that music should not have to observe racial boundaries.[33] He liked the work of certain white singers—among them Jo Stafford and Frank Sinatra—and among white saxophonists, he respected the "Four Brothers" of Woody Herman's band, though in one interview he gave some indication that he may have thought of white musicians in a separate category from black ones. After persistent probing by the interviewer, Young mentioned Wardell Gray as a contemporary saxophonist he admired, and then observed, "If you're talking about gray boys, Allen Eager can blow."[34]

Discrimination and other racial issues were occasionally discussed in print by musicians, usually in African American newspapers and other commercial publications. More recently, some rather candid opinions have been voiced in oral histories, identifying white racism, along with creativity and pride, as a source of Black musicians' originality, which in turn offered them a way of striking back at society's injustices. The saxophonist Marshal Royal, Basie's sax-section leader in the 1950s, maintained, "Most all jazz in every form is a Black heritage," adding, "New ideas come from jazz guys out of frustration and pride and other things that go toward trying to be inventive." Like Young, Royal stressed the importance of originality. African Americans, he explained, "have so much pride about themselves that once the other people start finding out and start mimicking them," they put a new twist on the music's evolution: "Rather than go back and play what the other guy has learned how to do and is mimicking well, [the Black musician will] get himself something new to play and go into a different phrase [phase?], just to screw them all up, so they don't know where they are."[35]

Royal's description of this source of African American creativity should be viewed in the larger context of American race relations. Young and his colleagues were, of course, deeply offended when white Americans almost invariably sanctioned Jim Crow restrictions. At New York's Roseland Ballroom, as at the Cotton Club, African Americans were excluded except as entertainers. In another unusual statement from a jazz musician, Mary Lou Williams complained about New York establishments' taking advantage of the business generated by Black artists. She, Young, and other Count Basie musicians, she charged, "[would] go all over [New York City] opening up new places and the minute the business was going well they'd throw us out, wouldn't allow us to come in any more."[36]

Young's recording associates of the late 1930s, Teddy Wilson, Billie Holiday, and Count Basie, were notable for stressing their commitment to racial equality and uplift. In 1938 Wilson, who had attended Tuskegee and was one of the first Black musicians to be featured in a white band, criticized Black Kansas Citians for not doing more to combat discrimination. Following in the footsteps of Wilson and Lionel Hampton in Benny Goodman's band, Billie Holiday "integrated" Artie Shaw's orchestra when she joined it after leaving Basie; according to the ideology of the times, she expressed her conviction that integrated groups improved social relations: "I really think that something has been started by the creation of mixed musical groups—something that will be of benefit to all of us—the whole race," she said. Her singing with a white band, she contended, helped dispel the notion that racial prejudice was invincible. Holiday, who was particularly renowned for performing the antilynching song "Strange Fruit," was identified in the Black press as "one of the few top singers who is 100 percent for the race. She'll bug anybody who tries to play her people cut-rate or get out of line on a Tom kick."[37]

Significantly for Lester Young, Count Basie was quite conscious of the need for Black bands to advance as originators in the swing idiom and in society in general; in 1937 the bandleader stated that his band was making significant steps in this direction: "We are proud to say we have opened several new avenues to Negro bands." In short, Basie, too, was an integrationist. He claimed that Carnegie Hall's "Spirituals to Swing" concert in late 1938 amounted to official recognition of the merits of African Americans in a decade when notions of racial supremacy were becoming identified with nazism. This concert was sponsored by John Hammond, the *New Masses*, and other left-wing supporters, all staunch opponents of the Third Reich's propaganda. Basie maintained that "music is still the universal language, and no greater proof is necessary than the Carnegie Hall concert," adding that "the fact that members of the colored race are invited to sing or play in this citadel of American art speaks well for the system that fosters it." As for the hall's management, Basie concluded, "Art has no color line."[38]

The African American urban community's efforts to honor and defend Black culture and to overthrow racial segregation were aided by a number of swing-era bandleaders, musicians, businessmen, jazz critics, and fans who were serious about combating racism. Left-wing and liberal whites opened integrated jazz clubs such as Café Society, in Greenwich Village, which sustained artists such as Young, Holiday, and Wilson and like-minded fans. While the saxophonist did not actively participate in electoral politics, he befriended and socialized with the integrationists, agreed with their objectives, and benefited accordingly.

Basieites and other African Americans displayed their pride in Black culture as well as their dissatisfaction over the state of race relations in the United States by mixing with whomever they pleased. Then, too, Harlem nightlife in the late 1930s offered neighborhood clubs and taverns that appealed to whites as well as Blacks, giving them the chance to mingle, converse, and dance—opportunities not permitted downtown until the opening of Café Society.

While Café Society is invariably given credit as an integrated haven, it was not the first club of its kind. Such resorts also existed in Harlem, where some depended heavily on white customers; others served different segments of society. In 1937, one Harlem restaurant, the Partridge, catered primarily to downtowners (as whites were sometimes known), while another, the Alhambra Grill, at 2120 Seventh Avenue, was geared toward entertainment and show people. The Hot Cha Bar and Grill was, along with Clark Monroe's Uptown House and Pod and Jerry's, among the many nightspots where Holiday sang before she went downtown to Café Society. Clark Monroe's, at 198 West 134th Street, was particularly important for upcoming musicians; the owner was Holiday's brother-in-law, and in May 1937 his establishment was said to be a place that "jumped from real hot rhythm." Jam sessions were held there on Sunday afternoons. It was one of numerous resorts that reopened under new names after the authorities closed them for one reason or another.[39]

The Basie band's New York City engagements marked many members' introduction to integrationism as well as to the racial awareness and political philosophies of socialist and radical African Americans. Black politics in New York in those years had a militant international character thanks to the speeches, articles, and organizing of W. E. B. Du Bois, Paul Robeson, and various African, Muslim, and other Black nationalists. The effects of the Great Depression, combined with the antilynching crusade and the Scottsboro and Angelo Herndon trials, galvanized Black folk, causing them to abandon the Republican party, their bastion for several generations, and form alliances with other political parties and causes ranging from the Democrats to the Communists.[40]

The activities that Basieites heard about, witnessed, or participated in furthered their racial consciousness and pride and added a cosmopolitan and even a kind of activist veneer to newcomers from the Midwest and the Deep South. (Presumably it was this socialization process that Basie's star soloist was referring to when he later explained how Billie Holiday had shown him around when he first came to New York.) When entertainers such as Holiday and Basie's and Artie Shaw's band members traveled down south, they braved the hostilities of the mob, thereby revealing to the world the barbarism and injustices of racism. Basieite Harry Edison contended, "We started integration." It is significant that in later days he and his colleagues would see themselves as having been the first of the freedom riders, promoting integration in their own way.[41]

Besides being the "Holy Main," or mother ship, for a number of other musicians' careers, the Basie orchestra served as Young's springboard to national and international acclaim. The tenor stylist became known as the featured soloist, according to radio outtakes; in early July 1938 the band played its anthem, "One O'Clock Jump," along with "Every Tub," "Song of the Wanderer," "Oh Lady, Be Good," and Duke Ellington's "I Let a Song Go out of My Heart" on CBS's "America Dances" broadcast. Young soloed on all but one of these selections, a clear indication of his importance in the orchestra. A few weeks later, he displayed his prowess on a Famous Door broadcast, soloing on three out of seven numbers—"Jumpin' at the Woodside," "Oh Lady, Be Good," and "Everybody Loves My Baby." During a Basie broadcast of "Wo-Ta-Ta," "Indiana," "Love of My Life," and "John's Idea" in mid-September, Young soloed on all but the second song.[42]

Nineteen thirty-nine was a turning point for Basie's orchestra, and particularly for its premier soloist. Young was ranked seventh on hot tenor in the *Metronome* poll early in the year; the white saxophonists Eddie Miller, Bud Freeman, George Auld, and Tony Pastor held the first four positions, followed by Chu Berry. Significantly, Young outpolled the expatriate Hawkins by 78 to 57 votes. Such polls should not, of course, be taken too seriously, but they do give a rough idea of the growing recognition of Young's talents during that period.[43]

Also in 1939, the orchestra recorded many of its classics, including "You Can Depend on Me" (recorded on February 2), "Cherokee" (February 3), "Jive at Five" (February 4), "Rock-a-Bye-Basie" and "Taxi War Dance" (both March 19), "Poundcake" (May 19), and "Clap Hands, Here Comes Charlie" (August 4). It was an important year, too, for small group recordings, among them Young's signature piece, "Lester Leaps In," and "Dickie's Dream" (both September 5).[44]

The orchestra had a second Famous Door booking that summer; the Basieites packed the house, and this time their stint was longer than before. They left in early September—"in the same blaze of syncopated glory in which they re-opened their engagement there several weeks ago," according to one Black weekly—and headed for the Hollywood Palomar in southern California. Both the star tenor soloist and the bandleader appeared in *Down Beat* advertisements that year, posing together for Martin clarinet ads in the spring and then again in the late summer. It was yet another breakthrough for Young, Basie, and Basie's orchestra, in the nation's most popular dance-band magazine.[45]

Young's talents as a saxophonist were praised by both Black and white critics in 1939. Frank Marshall Davis, a Kansan journalist, poet, and reviewer for the *New York Amsterdam News*, lavished accolades on recent Young performances, noting of one in particular that he "[outdid] himself on tenor sax." The review was altogether favorable: "Although the Count himself sounds too Fats Wallerish on the piano, he [Basie] and every soloist are positively thrilling," Davis wrote.[46]

Of "Lester Leaps In," *Down Beat*'s reviewer "Barrelhouse Dan" enthused, "[Young] plays the most unusual and stirring tenor he's shown on record." Reviewing recent releases in the late spring of 1939, Gordon Wright raved in his "Discussions" column, "Lester Young steals the show, blowing prodigious tenor on all four sides: *If I Didn't Care, And the Angels Sing,* and the two-sided *Cherokee.*" The last number was unique in that it continued on the second side of the 78 rpm record, forcing the listener to turn the disc over—in the middle of Young's solo, in fact. Wright praised its "great rhythm figures," adding that "this band improves with each session."[47]

Young starred on several Basie big-band recordings, including "Jive at Five" by Harry Edison, a cut that testifies to the strength and swinging quality of the band's rhythm, the tight integration of the sections, the players' interactions and repartee, and the responsorial nature of African American music. Taking its title from the name of a jazz radio show, the number was recorded in the winter of 1939 by the full band, though the recording gives the feeling of a combo because the sections play and blend so well.

The piece, which is essentially an extended series of riffs, begins with a brief introduction by Basie, and then the trumpet and trombone sections play alternating riffs of two bars each in the A section of the melody. Meanwhile, the baritone saxophonist, Jack Washington, provides a soft *obbligato* until the last eight bars of the A melody, at which point he looms into the foreground, playing counterpoint against the trumpets. The trumpets and trombones are responsorial—the latter commenting on the trumpets' opening like the singers in a church choir or the guitar of a bluesman—and frequently overlap.

In the third eight-bar passage (B), the sections exchange roles, with the trombones leading and the trumpets assuming the responsorial role, though their line is longer here. The trombones also introduce the B section, starting just before A is completed. In this way, and by modifying the trombone responses, variety is achieved with relatively simple material.

Young is the lead soloist, swinging in a very relaxed improvisation that many would try to imitate. In sixteen bars, he plays long lines while the brass complements his statements with short bursts. (Analyzing Young's solo for *Down Beat* in 1989, Julie Lyonn Lieberman suggested that students could use it to learn "new playing skills.")[48] Harry Edison continues for eight bars, then Young returns for eight more, followed by Basie; trumpet figures sustain them. Jack Washington next solos on baritone sax, playing a counterpoint to the melody and making a statement of eight bars. The melody is stated again, and then the composition fades out.

The roles played in this recording by the different sections are noteworthy because they underline the egalitarian nature of the orchestra; the switching-off of the lead riff between the trumpets and trombones underscores that democratic element. The sheer number of soloists, meanwhile—the quartet of Young, Edison, Basie, and Washington—points to a gathering of virtuosos. Young's two solos offer evidence of his unique status and of the fact that the orchestra was a showcase for his talents. The overlapping of riffs and the alternation of two-bar parts in the ensemble further highlight the degree to which the band, though composed of four different sections—two brass, reed, and rhythm—was a complex yet highly integrated unit in which nearly everyone got a chance to solo at some point, and everyone, of course, provided accompaniment for the others. "Jive at Five" illustrates how the small-combo format that Young would favor late in his career permeated even the big-band presentations.[49]

The Basie orchestra made other recordings in 1939 and 1940. Several of these, notably "What's Your Number?," "Five O'Clock Whistle," and "Broadway" (recorded in October 1940), indicated a dependence on long rehearsals, written scores, and complex arrangements, whereas other, small-group recordings featuring six or seven sidemen preserved the simple, basic swing emphasis, relying on riffs for melodies and backing—a legacy of the territorial heritage. A few years after Young's departure, the combo's rhythmic drive and effervescence on 1944's "Six Cats and a Prince" and "After Theatre Jump" would foreshadow the evolution of popular music—rhythm and blues as well as rock and roll—for at least the next two decades.[50]

Young's playing with Basie has often been romanticized and oversimplified by critics. Admittedly, he soloed most frequently on the orchestra's up-tempo numbers, but the Kansas City Six recordings would reveal his virtuosity on romantic tunes ("I Want a Little Girl" and "Them There Eyes"), and the Wilson-Holiday recordings, on which he accompanied the singer, would demonstrate his familiarity with love songs. Just as the seeds of bebop and rhythm and blues are evident in the early Basie recordings—those by the combos as well as those by the big band—so the trajectory of Young's subsequent development can be followed back to the same point.[51]

The tenor stylist's reputation was enhanced by the superior quality of the combo recordings he made with Basieites and various sidemen. His recordings with Nat Cole on piano and Red Callender on bass (1942), with his own quartet (1943), and with the Kansas City Seven (1944) have received considerable acclaim and been hailed as simply masterful. But perhaps the most important small-group performances in which he took part were those by the Kansas City Six, recorded in the fall of 1938 and the spring of 1944. The group comprised Young, Buck Clayton, Eddie Durham, Freddie Green, Walter Page, and Jo Jones (Basie was excluded for contractual reasons).

The first Kansas City Six sessions took place in late September 1938. The use of two guitars, electric (Durham) and acoustic (Green), was noteworthy, as these were among the first jazz records to feature an electric guitar. In one of the few times he ever recorded on the clarinet,

Young won the critic Martin Williams's praise because his playing so closely resembled counterpoint standards of the New Orleans tradition. This also caught fans' attention and served as a reminder to the saxophonist's family that he had taken to heart his father's teachings about reed versatility.[52]

Critics and radio disc jockeys have often singled out these selections for their swing, subtle phrasing, and alternation of blues and popular songs, and they have noted, furthermore, the absence of a piano, significant because that instrument usually provided the harmony. Less likely to be mentioned is the soft rendering of the selections, as if it were supper-club music. Clayton's muted trumpet and the three strings—guitars and bass—provide a very soft, sweet, sometimes poignant sound of the kind that Young, in particular, often preferred. In this respect, the Kansas City Six recalled the pianoless New Orleans string bands that played for polite social affairs, and the street "strollers" who serenaded passersby and selected urban dwellers outside their homes; the combo also prefigured the Modern Jazz Quartet of the 1950s, which Young would admire—though that group had a piano.[53]

With the Kansas City Six, Young brought a sweet and soulful sound to the blues selections, which included "Countless Blues," "Pagin' the Devil" (featuring Walter Page on bass in an era when the bass was rarely spotlighted), and "Four O'Clock Drag." Buck Clayton's trumpet solo on "Countless Blues" quotes the melody from an Eddie Durham composition, "Sent for You Yesterday," and blues fans can recognize the familiar phrase, "Don't the moon look lonesome, shinin' through the trees?"

These recordings re-created the smoke-filled rooms and late, late hours of Harlem parties and other occasions on which soft music was preferred. This combo contrasted with Basie's blaring orchestra and bore a resemblance to the Benny Goodman Quartet in that it was a band-within-a-band that swung freely, depended upon head music, and gave each member the opportunity to solo. It was also a precursor of so-called bebop as well as rock-and-roll bands in its instrumentation, freedom of expression, reliance on rhythmic motifs, and emphasis on the interplay between soloists and supporting rhythm.

"Lester Leaps In" was first recorded in September 1939 and became Young's signature tune. He had probably been using it for some time already before he recorded it; as early as 1937, for example, at the beginning of his solo on the recording "Shout and Feel It," he played a version of the familiar motif. The composition was a showcase for his considerable talents, and its breaks and stop-time choruses kept alive the principles of rhythmic variation and surprise—the elements that Jelly Roll Morton had once maintained were the very essence of good jazz. Call and response integrated the number, with the opening riff answered by silence and then a subtle piano response. The riff itself consisted of syncopated notes alternating with silences that constituted the downbeat; its heavily rhythmic motif recalled the drums that had been the saxophonist's first instrument.[54]

The classic for which Young became known was based on George Gershwin's "I Got Rhythm," whose chords were also used for numerous other jazz standards. The original version, "the most-played jazz classic of all time," came out in the fall of 1930, when Young was just beginning to develop into a mature stylist. In one Gershwin biographer's judgment "a song of confidence and connection in spite of it all," it was an appropriate anthem for a veteran of the territorial bands. And insofar as it marked the finale of the musical from which it came—*Girl Crazy*—it was fitting material for a climactic saxophone solo.[55]

Gershwin's song of celebration drew upon jazz traditions for its sheer exuberance, the syncopated rhythmic motif in its melody, and, equally important, its reliance upon the pentatonic scale, which lies at the heart of all blues. (Its motif and pentatonicism would be reused by Gershwin in other compositions.) Ira Gershwin wrote the lyrics, and the two brothers liked their song so much that George dedicated an orchestra work, "'I Got Rhythm' Variations," to the lyricist.[56]

"Lester Leaps In" was not merely the trademark tune of Lester Young and a standard of the swing era; it was also a classic example of the exchange that took place between jazz and popular-music traditions, each one influencing and being influenced by the other in a cycle of appropriation and reappropriation that is the heartbeat of African American and American culture. To put it differently, the African American swing stylist reclaimed, renewed, and reblued the rhythmic motif and pentatonicism that the Russian American composer had borrowed.

Besides playing it during his sets, Young quoted "Lester Leaps In" at the beginning of his solo on "Exactly like You," as well as in "Poundcake," "Blues in C," "Lavender Blue," and "Lester's European Blues." Other musicians followed suit—for example, on the Basie recording "Easy Does It," Harry Edison ends his trumpet solo with such a quote, taking it up from the sax section, which has played it softly behind him several times.[57]

Other saxophonists often paid homage to Young by quoting this melody. Gene "Jug" Ammons was one who literally went on record with his considerable respect for the tenor stylist, referring to "Lester Leaps In" on at least two occasions—in "Woofin' and Tweetin'" and in his own composition "Juggernaut," which sounds quite a bit like "Lester Leaps In." Dexter Gordon also admired Young and at the beginning of his solo on "The Steeplechase" quoted Pres's most famous tune. Both Sonny Stitt and Wardell Gray did so as well—Stitt while playing baritone at the end of "P. S. I Love You" and Gray on "Jackie," by the Los Angeles pianist Hampton Hawes.[58] More recently, Carlos "Patato" Valdez, a famous Afro-Cuban *conguero* and bandleader, has explored the same rhythms in "Yo Tengo Ritmo," paying homage simultaneously to the Gershwin and Young compositions by quoting the latter while taking his title from the former.[59]

In addition to "Lester Leaps In," some of Young's other early combo recordings propelled listeners up out of their seats and onto the dance floor to perform the athletic and strenuous routines of jitterbugs or Lindy hops, as they were known. Most spectacular were the "air steps" that required male dancers to hurl their partners through the air in what seemed like reckless abandon but was in fact a careful and painstaking choreography. Many, if not most, of the Lester Young Quartet and Kansas City Seven recordings were "jump" tunes or peppy, swinging selections; all included piano, and the larger ensemble added Buck Clayton on trumpet and Dicky Wells on trombone.

At times Young's combos inspired bebop as it would be developed by Charlie Parker, Dizzy Gillespie, Thelonious Monk, Kenny Clarke, and other musicians during the war; certain tunes by them also foreshadowed and paralleled the rhythm-and-blues hits of Louis Jordan and His Tympani Five and presaged the work of several combos modeled after Jordan's in the postwar years. "Jo-Jo," by the pianist Joe Bushkin, is one such embryonic rhythm-and-blues; "Afternoon of a Basie-ite" and "Six Cats and a Prince" are two others in this category. As critics have noted, Young's tone on these recordings is no longer the soft, sweet sound of the 1930s; it is fuller and sometimes even harsher, more reminiscent of Hawkins and Evans, particularly on "Four O'Clock Drag," "I Never Knew," and "After Theatre Jump." Now and then his sound anticipates that of Sonny Rollins a decade later.[60]

In the 1940s, these recordings met with considerable critical acclaim in the jazz press, and since then many have been elevated to the status of special classics. Nat Hentoff, for example, expressed his high regard for the Kansas City Six recordings years after they were first released: "[They] are among those half dozen collections I'd grab for if the building started to burn," he mused. These "exceedingly rare works of man," he asserted, "do not become stale." For Young's clarinet playing, Hentoff said he "would trade stereo and the collected works of Stan Kenton, Maynard Ferguson, and . . . even Benny Goodman."[61]

Ten years after they were issued, Ross Russell compared "Shoeshine Boy," "Lester Leaps In," and "Dickie's Dream" to recordings by Armstrong's Hot Five and the Charlie Parker Quintet. In each case, he said, the "records preserve a body of music at once fresh and mature, which went on to dominate jazz for a good decade to follow." He also praised some of the Basie big-band selections, singling out "Poundcake" and "Rock-a-Bye Basie" in particular.[62]

It was Russell's contention that the roots of Young's style "extend[ed] in many directions." First of all, he said, they were "undisputably in the reed tradition of the early clarinetists who emphasized the melodic and lyrical qualities of jazz and thought in terms of the blues scale." Russell claimed, in fact, that "the Kansas City style [spreads] the language of the New Orleans clarinetists."[63]

But Young, he believed, drew "equally from sources of a much different nature—Debussyian harmony, light intonation and the spiritual qualities which are attached to the white jazz tradition of Bix Beiderbecke and Bud Freeman." In what was probably news to the tenor stylist, the critic maintained that his playing synthesized "opposing attitudes and ideologies—the profound tradition of the blues combined with the infusion of European harmony and white romanticism"; it was this that "[gave] Lester Young's music its special appeal." Russell did not explain exactly what white romanticism was, but he asserted that "the foundations of modern saxophone style have been correctly traced back to Lester Young."[64]

Like other critics, Russell reserved his highest praise for the combo recordings of "Lester Leaps In" and "Dickie's Dream" which he deemed "at least [comparable to] many distinguished performances in the genre." They stood as singular testimony to the "perfection of the small ensembles" popularized by Teddy Wilson, Lionel Hampton, and Benny Goodman with Charlie Christian. The musicians on "Dickie's Dream," Russell wrote, "achieved an ideal equilibrium . . . and creativity flows onto a new level of subtlety and tonal achievement."[65]

Raymond Horricks likewise credited Young with paving the way for future developments in music. He characterized the tenor saxophonist's playing in the late 1930s and early 1940s as "audacious in construction, cool and relaxed in expression, pure in tone, suavely swinging . . . [it] confirmed Lester as perhaps the most assured and consistently creative jazz musician in operation [during] this period." Moreover, Horricks observed, Young was "a figure whose work formed a bridge between the gradually ailing swing school (already suffering from the interest of the white bands and their commercial traps) and the still underdeveloped modern trends."[66] Over the next decade, from 1939 to 1949, many critics would acknowledge Young as one of the leading saxophonists of the day.

Despite the growing critical acclaim they enjoyed, Young and the other Basieites knew from personal experience that in the commercial music arena white businessmen and musicians reaped most of the financial rewards. When John Hammond read Basie's Decca contract, in late 1936, he was shocked to learn that the band would earn no royalties from its recordings for the three years it was with that label. The Basieites did not even receive union scale until certain provisions of the contract were amended by the New York union. Meanwhile, white bandleaders such as Benny Goodman were becoming famous—and rich—by recording Black arrangers' originals, to the point where the covers became accepted as the standard version.[67]

Accounts of Young's and Basie's rise have rarely detailed the racism and economics of the big-band and popular-music business. At precisely the same time that the Basie band was struggling to attain national recognition, the bandleader Noble Sissle, praised by the *Kansas City Call* as a proud race man, was criticizing the new music corporations that dominated the economic life of jazz bands. Sissle conceded that white backing was essential for the success of Black bands—as was the publicity that went along with it—but he charged that the big corporations that provided that backing "get under contract several large orchestras and other theatrical stars . . . [and get] the big end of the dough." Black bands faced serious disadvantages in the recording studios, where they were usually "required . . . to make recordings in groups of twenty and thirty for which they received the minimum compensation." Then, too, white orchestras were given better material to work with: they routinely recorded the most popular songs, while "only occasionally are popular compositions recorded by Negro orchestras." Young's recordings with Billie Holiday and Teddy Wilson illustrated Sissle's point: they were "throwaways," second- or third-rate songs, that still managed to turn into gold for the record companies.[68]

Bound by the terms of the Decca contract, the Basieites had to scuffle for the first three years after they left the Midwest. In Kansas City, they had endured low wages as well as discrimination in white nightclubs. Buck Clayton reported that the salary Basie offered him at the Reno was far less than he had been earning in Los Angeles; furthermore, because management refused to pay him, Clayton had to depend on contributions from other band members at first. Earle Warren recalled that though he learned from his union local that sixty dollars a week was scale for a musician on the road, when he joined Basie in 1937, he "was earning $6.25 a night . . . [then] seven . . . the nights we worked." Such details help us to understand the reality of the racism that affected the Basieites, and suggest why success meant so much to them.[69]

While Basie's stints on Fifty-second Street were certainly a sign of success, it is important to note that bookers " 'cooperated' with the management of the Famous Door to enlarge those premises to serve as a showcase for [the record companies'] rising bands." Thus the club became a launching pad not only for Count Basie but also for Woody Herman and Charlie Barnet, thanks in part to MCA's backing and in part to the Famous Door radio broadcasts, which also helped to publicize the place.[70]

As a rule, African Americans did not benefit from the "two principal sources of prestige and financial reward" available to musicians of the era: jobs in prominent hotels and regular spots on commercial radio programs. Although Black bandleaders prospered through dance-hall jobs, theater engagements, and records, "they [could] never hope to equal the fabulous earnings of Goodman, Shaw, or Glen Miller," the last of whom grossed some $700,000 in 1940. Nor could Black sidemen—even standout talents such as Lester Young—ever "hope to attain the degree of public prominence which Gene Krupa enjoyed when he received $500 a week from Benny Goodman."[71]

Young and his fellow Basieites felt this racism and were only too aware of the practical effects it had on their lives, as it forced them to travel in order to publicize the band. If they had had more club dates with radio hookups, they would not have needed to be on the road so much; but as it was, even their two Famous Door stints did not exempt them from subsequent touring. They spent the early part of 1940 alternating between New York and Boston, for two to three weeks at a time, then traveled in late March and again in May; starting from Bluefield, West Virginia (where the Blue Devils had been stranded), on May 1, they snaked their way through that state, Ohio, Kentucky, and Pennsylvania for two weeks before heading back to the Apollo Theater in Harlem for a week's stay. Their touring continued at this pace until the end of the year.

Partly in reaction to discrimination, the Basie band members, including Young, formed especially close bonds with one another. They were united in their opposition to racism and cooperated by various means to aid one another and reinforce everyone's sense of self-esteem. They lived together, shared meals, and developed distinctive styles of dress (the porkpie among them), an argot or jive slang, and jokes and tales in which they had featured roles. The Basieites introduced their styles and ways to other African Americans wherever they traveled, often relying on personal ties and racial loyalties to help them overcome obstacles in finding meals and accommodations.[72]

Black culture and the resulting solidarity assisted them in defending themselves against the harmful effects of racism, commercialism, and economic exploitation. Particularly between 1936 and 1939, when the Basieites struggled hardest to make ends meet, they formed friendships that would last for decades. The band members' fraternal bonds gave them a special style, a mystique matched only by Duke Ellington's sidemen. "There was a personal style about everything these two bands did, including their dress, their slang, their humor, and the relationships within the personnel," one Basieite reminisced.[73]

To cite just one example of their closeness, Basieites relied upon a special signal to call one another, a whistle and a phrase. Lester Young devised or introduced the whistle's melody and lyric—"I want you to get way back, babe." Years later, when Earle Warren encountered Buck Clayton at New York City's union office, he "put the whistle on him," he said, and Clayton "cock[ed] an ear, because everybody from the old Basie band will recognize that whistle, even if they're in Istanbul."[74]

The Basieites became models of sartorial splendor on the bandstand not long after their arrival in New York. The support of John Hammond and his business associates permitted the purchase of short, fitted jackets, gambler-striped pants, and dark suits to document their shared identity. Onstage and off, high-waisted slacks, belted or suspendered (sometimes both) and reaching to just below the armpits, were worn by Young and other musicians; coats were often unbuttoned to reveal the high waist and the wide, flowing trousers, a style that must have been very comfortable, especially for jitterbug dancers. In a 1938 newsreel, Basie band members are shown wearing short, waist-length yellow Eton jackets that contrast with their black slacks and cummerbunds; white formal dress shirts complete the ensemble (see photo insert).[75]

Band uniforms confirmed the musicians' unity when they were performing, but their offstage clothes also took on special meaning, given the theatrical dimension and the importance of physical appearance in Black urban culture. With his six-foot-plus frame, Young looked good in the Basieites' onstage and offstage uniforms, the latter typically being a stylish two- or three-piece suit, perhaps high-waisted, often topped with a hat somewhat individualized to the wearer's personal tastes. Harry Edison recalled, "You had to wear what was in style and be most extreme in that style." African Americans recognized show-business people by the way they dressed: "You could see [a woman] walking down the street and immediately say, 'She's a singer, she's in show business.'" In a sense, performers never left the stage; as Edison explained, "Every time you go out on the street, you're on display, whether you know it or not." A strong sense of pride encouraged the bandsmen "to get up and get sharp" every time they went out.[76]

Early on, Young was a target of the ridicule his fellow Basieites employed to encourage conformity with their offstage wardrobe style—a campaign that abated only when he agreed to stop wearing his one old suit and purchased six new ones. Buck Clayton remembered, "We were feeling pretty good about that, but shortly after, on a theater booking down south, someone left the window open to our dressing room." The thief stole all Young's suit pants, leaving him with six jackets. Upset by the loss, he joked to his friends, "'I was happy with one suit. Now look what you got me into. Six coats!'"[77]

In 1939, when the band was in Memphis, "the long black coat Prez always wore with his pork pie hat" was stolen (along with Freddie Green's "brand-new coat," Buck Clayton remembered). Young would wear similar dark, ankle-length overcoats for decades; the style dated from the territorial days, when traveling musicians needed protection from the fierce winter winds that blew across the prairies and plains. It is not clear if other Basieites adopted the fashion in the late 1930s, but Buddy Tate also reportedly wore such a coat when he came to New York City in April 1939 to join Basie, after three years in Nat Towles's Omaha-based outfit. The coat was a badge of pride, a symbol of a musician's roots in the territorial tradition; moreover, it was a practical piece of outerwear.[78]

Young also started to wear his trademark porkpie around this time. Freddie Green, who was the next-best thing to a native New Yorker, was the first Basieite known to have worn this style of hat; in late January 1937 he sported a porkpie during the Wilson-Holiday recording session, at which Young, Benny Goodman, Jo Jones, and Walter Page served as sidemen. Young subsequently made the style his own; he and Harry Edison would wear versions of the hat in the film short *Jammin' the Blues,* shot in 1944, by which time the fad would have spread from coast to coast.[79]

Young popularized a number of new styles, if he did not introduce them. For example, he was among the very first to wear sunglasses on the bandstand to protect his eyes from the glare of the stage lights or the sun. Soloing with the Basie band at the Randalls Island Jazz Carnival in late May 1938, he struck the classic pose: saxophone outthrust as if he were about to take flight out of this world, head tilted slightly to the side, aviator sunglasses shading his eyes. Walter Page was another band member who wore sunglasses on this occasion. The newsreel coverage of the event dramatized the change in Young's life, from anonymity in a territorial band to stardom in one of the nation's leading swing bands, appearing on movie screens throughout the land. This new visual image of Young poised against the bandstand, his saxophone soaring, remains within American popular culture an icon of a new kind of hero—not just any musician, but the jazz sophisticate or hipster (see photo insert).[80]

The Basieites' shared style of dress was as an outward indication of their solidarity.[81] As to their deeper bonds, Edison explained, "We were all very close. . . . Buck [Clayton] was a very good friend. Freddie Green is about the closest friend I have. Basie is a good buddy to me, and I always looked upon him as a father." Earle Warren maintained that members of the old band "became almost like brothers in our every day living and shared each other's troubles and heartaches as if they were our own."[82]

The band members looked after one another; as Edison noted, Basie was a father figure. "Because I had no fatherly advice when I left home," Edison said, "[I] used to listen to him [Basie]." The pianist took him "every place in New York" and introduced him to a number of musicians—including Duke Ellington, Don Redman, Benny Carter, Chick Webb, and James P. Johnson—as well as dancers.[83]

The friendship that developed among Young, Billie Holiday, and

Buck Clayton was legendary. Holiday had lived in New York City since her early teens and was known everywhere in Harlem; she and Young had first met in New York in 1934, when he was with Henderson. "You sure couldn't ask for a better chaperone than Billie," Clayton recalled. "We'd go to all the joints in Harlem and if we couldn't make them all in one day then we'd start again the next and go to all of the pads that we had missed." They dubbed themselves " 'the Unholy Three' when we were together in some pad in Harlem."[84]

Although she herself did not like saxophone battles, Holiday defended Young when fans and writers suggested that he had lost in a jam session. In her autobiography she detailed a battle he had with Chu Berry, and on another memorable occasion she felt sufficiently concerned about a Coleman Hawkins session to write to *Down Beat* about the outcome. The event occurred in Puss Johnson's Harlem tavern, where in late 1939 Young, the rising upstart, competed against the veteran tenor saxophonist shortly after the latter's return from more than five years in Europe. Fats Waller's sidemen witnessed the contest and judged Hawkins the winner. Holiday disagreed, informing the musicians' trade journal, "Young really cut the Hawk . . . and most everyone there who saw them tangle agreed on that."[85]

Young returned such loyalty in kind, and for that he would be admired and appreciated for decades. For example, he took Buddy Tate under his wing when he joined Basie. The new recruit recalled that he had been eagerly anticipating the band's arrival in New York after a string of one-nighters early in 1939, but at Penn Station the other Basieites deserted him in their hurry to see their wives, families, and friends. "I was standing there with a pocket full of money, not knowing where to go, when I saw Prez standing in a corner," Tate remembered. The saxophonist observed dryly, " 'I knew you didn't know where to go. . . . The ladies [i.e., the bandsmen] are excited. They haven't seen their Madame Queens for a long time. You understand?' " Young, said Tate, "looked after me, carried me along in his cab, got me a kitchenette right next to him and Mary at the Woodside Hotel."[86]

On the road, the female singers prepared meals for their colleagues and performed other domestic chores. "Billie was always very helpful," Warren noted, adding, "She was a great cook." Holiday enjoyed preparing soul food, including red beans and rice, which must have particularly endeared her to Young. Likewise, Helen Humes would "sew buttons on, and cook for [the band], too"; she "used to carry pots and a little hot plate around, and . . . fix up some food backstage or in places where it was difficult to get anything to eat . . . down south."[87]

These home-cooked meals contrasted sharply with the appalling living conditions the Basieites were forced to endure on some tours. During the period when they were playing mainly colleges and amusement parks in small towns, their accommodations were typically, in Warren's words, "little old crummy places. . . . I got eaten up by bedbugs, and you had to keep one eye open all the time to keep from having your stuff stolen." It was a welcome relief to lodge with families in private homes, where they could "set up cooking quarters and have our meals collectively."[88]

Band members shared kitchen privileges in Harlem as well. Earle Warren remembered that when he was told that the band would be staying in the Woodside Hotel on its arrival in New York, "I pictured a big, palatial place with a circular driveway in front." So when the Basie bus pulled up to the establishment in June 1938, Warren said he "almost died." Much to his disappointment, "it was a third-rate hotel . . . in a much congested area."[89]

Located in Harlem, at 141st Street and Seventh Avenue, the hotel immortalized by the Basie anthem "Jumpin' at the Woodside" typified traveling musicians' accommodations. "A lot of show people" lived there, including Lester and Mary Young (and their dog Pimpy), the Mills Brothers' sister and her husband, and Jack Washington, trumpet player Ed Lewis, and Jimmy Rushing and their wives. Earle Warren remembered, "There were cooking facilities in some rooms, and a big kitchen where people could cook and take food up to their rooms." More important, "it was like a music house, and we rehearsed in the basement."[90]

In Boston, Young and Basie band members lived in similar surroundings. Buck Clayton described the city as "our second home" and noted, "we made many friends there that have remained true friends even until today." The Blue Goose, their transport bus, "practically became our second home" thanks to the long hours spent on it talking, joking, gambling, and sleeping.[91] To survive the hardships, the Basie bandsmen sustained themselves with the hope that they would soon be famous and prosperous. One Woodside tenant recalled, "Whenever I broke a dollar, I'd save three dimes in my little piggy bank in order to be able to eat later." Earle Warren remarked on the irony of their situation, recalling that "sometimes I didn't have a nickel to ride the subway, although I was with Count Basie's band."[92]

Holiday and Young grew quite close during these years, as their musical affinities and shared experiences in New York and on the road with Basie engendered a mutual admiration that would last for the rest of both their lives. In the summer of 1958, when an interviewer, Chris Albertson, informed him, "You're [Holiday's] favorite soloist," the saxophonist responded, "She's mine too. . . . So that's a draw." He explained, "Sometime I would sit down and listen to myself and it would sound like two of the same voices."[93] Holiday discovered that she and Young were similar in certain ways. He was, like her, very sensitive to slights and to the fact that some people thought he was cocky and arrogant. "You can hurt his feelings in two seconds. . . . I found out once that I had," she said. "We've been hungry together, and I'll always love him and his horn."[94]

Jazz fans thought the two were lovers, and in an *Ebony* article, the vocalist herself contributed to the rumor that she and her favorite accompanist were more than friends when she claimed, "I fell for his music, [and] nearly fell for him." Buck Clayton, however, pointed out that the guitarist Freddie Green was really the man she loved.[95]

At one point, the problems of urban life in Harlem caused Young to move in with Holiday. While he himself maintained it was in 1934, it may have been later. One morning, after a jam session, they returned to her place "to get some of [Holiday's mother's] early breakfast specials." Young told the two women that a rat had recently jumped out of a dresser drawer in his room in "a well-known Harlem hotel," leaving him "almost a nervous wreck." Another incident he related involved his having to use the water from a toilet bowl to get some hair straightener out because the water had suddenly been turned off; if he had not resorted to this emergency procedure, the straightener would have burned his scalp. Young's recitation of the difficulties he faced "as a young man living alone in a New York hotel" brought laughter to the breakfast table, and it was then that he asked to move in with the pair.[96]

The singer described this Harlem apartment as "a big railroad flat, two flights up, with two entrances off the hallway." The front door either was just off or actually opened into her bedroom, with another "little room off it we used to call my playroom, where I kept my records and a beat-up old piano." Her mother's room was in the back, near the living room, and Young lived in the middle room, next to the air shaft. Holiday explained, "It wasn't fancy, but it beat that damn hotel."

Young added a kind of finishing touch to the household: "It was wonderful having a gentleman around the house," Holiday recalled. More than just a home, the place was "a combination YMCA, boardinghouse for broke musicians, soup kitchen for anyone with a hard-luck story, community center, and after after-hours joint where a couple of bucks would get you a shot of whiskey and the most fabulous fried-chicken breakfast, lunch, or dinner anywhere in town."[97] Evidently Young enjoyed the company of the visitors as much as he did the food and companionship provided by the mother and daughter. In a way, everyone benefited from the homey atmosphere that they re-created in Harlem in the depths of the Depression.

It was around this time that Young's and Holiday's nicknames, Pres and Lady Day, became widely known among fans and fellow musicians. Despite their often-quoted claims that they gave each other these titles, the real story is more complicated; as we have seen, some of the Blue Devils called the tenor stylist Pres in the early 1930s, and it is likely that he told Billie Holiday that when they first met, in 1934.

On one occasion, Holiday gave the title's origins an interesting twist that was in some ways reminiscent of Blue Devil Abe Bolar's explanation, insofar as both traced the nickname to an esoteric element of Black culture. "I named him the President," she said, "and actually I was also Vice President . . . of the Vipers Society, you know. We were the Royal Family of Harlem." To complicate matters even further, Carmen McRae testified that Young in fact gave the name Lady Day to Billie's mother, only to have the daughter take it for herself.[98]

Young and Holiday's shared love of marijuana bonded them in their own little group within the Basie band. So did their drinking, a habit that Young seems to have picked up about the time he met her. Prior to that he did not drink, according to the testimony of several people. Edison insisted, "Pres . . . didn't drink at all when he first came to New York, when I first joined the band [1937], [and] he didn't smoke cigarettes. He didn't drink nothing." Edison was not sure when he started drinking, but Charlie Carpenter, who recalled Young's drinking milk at the Earl Hines audition, queried him about it after the saxophonist came to New York with Basie. Young maintained that he had begun to drink when he started associating with Billie Holiday: "I just started. I take a drink now and then."[99]

When traveling with the Basie orchestra on one-nighters, Edison contended, "everybody had to take a drink of something, because you were so tired most of the time . . . that you had to have something to give you that feeling." The saxophonist Earle Warren recalled that Young drank what was known as "top and bottom—wine and gin." Holiday also liked this mixture.[100]

Young also continued to drink milk—perhaps as a folk remedy or a means of atoning for consuming too much alcohol. Warren remembered that when they toured, "I'd see him sit back there in that bus and drink a whole quart of milk . . . in the morning, and clean his system, and he'd be all right, and then maybe [for] two or three days, he [wouldn't] do [drink] nothing." Young's drinking never affected his playing, Warren said: "He never faltered on that bandstand. What he did for his own pleasure wasn't what he did when he got on the bandstand."[101]

As we shall see, Young and Holiday additionally shared a dislike for John Hammond, which may itself have stemmed from the similarities in their music philosophies and outlooks on life. In their view, the recording executive was manipulative. Still, he gave Holiday's career a boost in early 1937 by providing the money for Basie to hire her on with his band; Hammond felt the orchestra needed a female soloist to complement Jimmy Rushing.[102]

In 1939, the vocalist cited Young's musical influence on her performances: "I don't think I'm singing. I feel like I am playing a horn. I try to improvise like Les Young, like Louis Armstrong." Performing the song differently each time was another musical conception the two shared. Holiday admitted, "I hate straight singing. I have to change a tune to my own way of doing it."[103]

She heard a singer in Young's saxophone playing, she said—thereby offering evidence that instrumentalists imitated the human voice in the jazz clubs of the 1930s, just like their counterparts in traditional and modern Africa. "Lester sings with his horn," Holiday contended. "You listen to him and can almost hear the words."[104] Very possibly this quality also resulted from Young's hearing his father teach voice to legions of singers and choirs during his teen years; for someone who paid little attention to written music, the human voice provided an alternative mode of conceiving and phrasing sounds and rhythms.

Again echoing the tenor stylist, Holiday insisted that everyone should sing or play in his or her own individual way: "If you copy, it means you're working without any real feeling. And without feeling, whatever you do amounts to nothing." The African American aesthetic and principle of artistry could hardly have been stated more simply.[105]

The singer much preferred the informality of the recording studio of the 1930s to the complicated band arrangements of the swing era and the exacting recording procedures of the 1950s. She detested written arrangements, long rehearsals, and numerous retakes. "Nowadays you have this talk and bull and nothing's happening," she would observe in later years. Like Young, she particularly liked the kind of improvisation typical of the blues: "In the old days, if we were one side short on a date, someone would say, 'Try the blues in A flat,' and tell me, 'Go as far as you can go, honey.' I'd stand up there and make up my words as I went along."[106]

The close personal relationship between Young and Holiday carried over into the music, just as the fraternity of the Basie band had a positive effect on its members' musical cohesiveness. The singer favored this saxophone stylist for his singular ability to "fill up the windows" when backing her, underplaying while she sang and bringing his sound to the fore when she stopped. Buck Clayton, the other member of the Unholy Three, explained how he managed this when *he* was her accompanist: "I would watch her mouth and when I saw that she was going to take a breath or something I knew it was time for me to play between her expressions."[107]

Their shared music philosophy enabled Young and Holiday, sometimes with Clayton, to produce classics, often from the raw material of second-rate American popular tunes such as "Sailboat in the Moonlight," "This Year's Kisses," and "Mean to Me." While these were all Holiday-Wilson recordings, Young's contributions—sometimes playing the introduction, and constantly weaving in and out of Holiday's lyrics, adorning them with riffs and fill-ins—were unforgettable. Of these sessions, Young himself once said, "I remember them well."[108]

Occasionally the saxophonist discussed their collaborations. He cited "Sailboat in the Moonlight" and "Back in Your Own Backyard" as his "personal favorites" among the songs he had recorded with Holiday, Clayton, and Wilson. He especially liked the "foghorn" effect he had achieved on the former song, suggesting the importance of visual images and atmosphere in his aesthetic and reminding us of Budd Johnson's comment that music echoes the sounds around us—in this instance, recreating the feeling of sailing at night. In the same interview, the saxophonist designated "Taxi War Dance," his own number based on "Willow Weep for Me," as his favorite Basie recording and "Tickletoe" as his best composition.[109]

Although later in life Young would aver that he did not listen to his records for fear that he might repeat himself, this was not the case while he was in the Basie band. Young and Clayton "sometimes . . . would get dollars-worth of nickels as the jukeboxes only took nickels at that time, and pull up two chairs and listen to what we [had] recorded, sometimes for hours, one nickel after the other." They were quite serious about their "studies," Clayton explained: "We wouldn't allow anybody to talk while we were digging ourselves." They preferred to frequent nightspots with jukeboxes, where "we would listen to ourselves on as many as we could find."[110]

Holiday later reminisced about Young, "I used to be crazy about his tenor playing; wouldn't make a record unless he was on it." She liked the fact that he "didn't try to drown the singer." Her use of the past tense here may have been related to the fact that she was discussing the years when they first met, or perhaps it was a concession, on her part, to the realities of show business: at the time, she was recording with the saxophonists Paul Quinichette and Ben Webster. She nonetheless maintained, "Some of my favorite recordings are the ones with Lester's pretty solos." Moreover, she added, "Lester's always been the President to me; he's my boy."[111]

Besides playing and sharing meals and homes, Basie members enjoyed another pastime: softball. Other swing bands had teams, too. "Basie's Bad Boys" were a "wonderful baseball team," according to Earle Warren, who played shortstop and occasionally third base. Herschel Evans excelled at hitting home runs and was the first baseman; Jack Washington held down second; Harry Edison covered short center field; and Lester Young invariably insisted on pitching. "Prez naturally wouldn't think of letting anyone else pitch than himself . . . [and he] was a pretty good softball pitcher," in Warren's estimation. He threw "a backspinning ball which made the [batter] hit the ball on the ground. Pres could do anything in ball!" They often played by the side of the road down south and in California, and whenever the Blue Goose was undergoing repairs. The game served as an emotional outlet and a welcome respite from the boredom of days passed pent up in the bus; it not only reflected but reinforced the Basieites' sense of solidarity. Softball, Earle Warren quite astutely noted, "was an attempt to give us relaxation and also to sort of draw the fellows closer together in teamwork, whether on the bandstand or on the playing field."[112]

In fact, the sport was a favorite pastime of the saxophonist's: he was a fan of the New York Giants and not only enjoyed pitching but displayed considerable skill at it. Lee Young also commented on his brother's love for the game back in Albuquerque in the late 1920s. He recalled that nothing could ever get Lester to hurry on the base paths, which he always ran slowly. It was a trait that would characterize Young his entire life: he was never known to rush anything.[113]

Young had a comedic side that was unique among the Basieites and has never been fully appreciated by writers. "Lester, of course, was generally the cut-up at all the sessions and kept everyone in a jovial mood." Both he and Holiday, actually, were described as being "always jovial and entertaining, very seldom moody or obstinate."[114]

But the tenor stylist was at the same time "a great critic," according to Sweets Edison. Young would ring a little bell "when you stood up to play if after a couple of choruses you didn't really start some fire back there." He was aided in this effort by the band's guitarist: "If Freddie Green had that disapproving look, the guy was on his notice then." Young, however, "had many ways of expressing disapproval, and in no uncertain manner."[115]

What was more, there was a group within the band known as the Vigilantes, who took it upon themselves to correct things. "When there was something in the band we didn't like, we would get rid of it quick," Edison explained. Not even Freddie Green was exempt from the Vigilantes' measures. When the guitarist started playing solos with an amplifier, the other band members felt that "the whole rhythm section [fell] apart." Concluding that something must be done about it, Edison removed the plug from the amp one night, and then the next night Young would do the same. As soon as it was fixed, Evans would break one of its wires—and so on, until finally they decided "to take all the guts out of the amplifier." When Green went to play a solo and couldn't, he was furious, "but nobody paid him any attention." Stung, the guitarist announced that he would not play any more solos, a statement that Edison said "rang a bell with us: 'Great,' you know."[116]

It was difficult for bandsmen not to take such obvious criticism personally. For example, Young disliked Earle Warren's singing; when the alto saxophonist sang "Where Are You?," the entire band backed him like a "choral group," except for Young, who "would stand on tiptoe, [and] . . . make out like he was singing very soulfully." The rest of the band would begin laughing while Warren continued singing, hating such antics. Behind Young's comedy lay a serious purpose: to ridicule someone or something he didn't like to the point that that person or thing was removed from the show.[117]

One idea that earned the tenor saxophonist's disdain was Basie's notion of closing the show with a popular song, in the manner of Tommy Dorsey, whose band was identified with the hit "Marie." "Goodnight Everybody," the choice that Basie settled on, was an old Moten song that was to be substituted for the band's traditional closing number, "One O'Clock Jump." It worked well enough in rehearsal, but when the time came to perform the tune publicly, many members of the band could not remember the lyrics. Young seized on the opportunity to rebel against this departure from the program he preferred: he burlesqued the song so, and received such laughs from the audience, that Basie immediately reverted to the old format.[118]

Young's delight in making people laugh was often coupled with a barely masked rebelliousness, a combination that typifies the satirical and serious features not only of minstrelsy but of most African American humor. The tenor stylist never respected the commercial side of his profession, so whenever Basie and Warren catered to the business people and their desire for popular numbers, Young always tried to find a way to return the band to what he thought of as the straight and narrow—primarily the blues or strictly instrumental ballads.

Despite the occasional wounding of pride, the comic antics generally cemented relations among band members rather than driving them apart or encouraging bad feelings. Dicky Wells explained, "It was like being part of a family. And all kinds of people liked Basie."[119] Some writers and fans have mistakenly assumed that the rivalry among the musicians, the jokes they played on one another, and the mischief they made were all evidence of the hostility that dominated their relationships. This was thought to be the case especially with regard to Young and Herschel Evans, both of whom were known for their mischief making. In actuality, however, it was Holiday who disliked Evans as much as she championed Young; Buck Clayton recalled that "from the very first day [Holiday and Evans] laid eyes on each other [they had] a deep dislike for each other." There does not seem to have been any rational reason for their antipathy; "they just couldn't stand each other." Perhaps because of her bias, Holiday advanced the idea in 1954 that the two tenor players had been bitter enemies: "Those cats really hated each other, and it kept them both blowing all the time," she contended. More than most of the other band members, the singer emphasized the animosity behind their rivalry: "They were forever thinking up ways of cutting the other one. You'd find them in the band room hacking away at reeds, trying out all kinds of new ones, anything to get ahead of the other."[120]

Young, for his part, likened himself and Evans to duelists, but more significantly, he summarized their relationship with the admission, "We was nice friends and things. . . . He was a nice person. I was the last one to see him die. In fact, I paid the doctor for his bill and everything." Young was not alone in asserting that he and Evans had actually been good friends.[121]

Several Basieites downplayed the alleged bad blood between the rival tenor stylists and occasionally tried to explain the real nature of their relationship. Buck Clayton stressed, "I know that they respected each other even though they didn't talk to each other very much," adding that when they sat "back to back in the reed section, it wasn't any kind of an indication that they didn't respect each other."[122]

Earle Warren emphasized the good feelings between the star soloists, maintaining that "little things that happened between [Evans] and Young were of no great consequence." As for their sitting at opposite ends of the section and not speaking to one another, Warren dismissed it as "a lot of hogwash" as far as indicating any real animosity between them. Dicky Wells observed that they were "the best of friends" regardless of whether or not they were speaking to each other. Jo Jones was convinced that "there was no real friction" between the two and drew attention to the fraternal aspect: "What there was was almost like an incident . . . [that] could exist between two brothers." Indeed, "no matter what[,] there was always a mutual feeling there." Fans who told Young he did not have the right tone, Jones added, contributed to any friction that existed.[123]

In addition to correcting the folklore concerning the rivalry between Young and Evans, the Basie sidemen knew Young well enough as a musician and as a person to reveal other aspects of his playing and personality that reviewers and writers have missed. Some noted that while his tone did not blend well, he improvised so brilliantly, so consistently, that this seeming disadvantage was of no real consequence.

The band's sax-section leader, Earle Warren, made an assessment typical of the opinions voiced by all the sidemen: "He played very well *constantly.* I never heard Pres, during my time with him, play bad." Moreover, "Pres had so many mixtures of things to play, and that's the way he was mentally." His blues solos also impressed Warren, as did his knowledge of chords and harmony, a mastery not often attributed to Young or other jazz virtuosos. "He was a master at playing chord changes and at playing his own interpretation," Warren testified.[124]

The tenor stylist was not simply an intuitive genius, that comfortable racial stereotype that many Americans picture when they think of jazz musicians; the foundation for his musical knowledge was solid, grounded as it was in his father's meticulous instruction. Eddie Durham, an outstanding composer-arranger and pioneer of the electric guitar, played in Basie's orchestra in late 1937 and early 1938 and believed that the saxophonist learned quite a bit about harmony from him; he recalled, "Lester thought I was the greatest arranger in the world . . . because I used to help him out a lot." Young gave him the nickname Poundcake, as in "*very* good"; they hung out at night, Durham said, "and I'd play chords on my guitar and he'd learn to run them." The guitarist tried to teach the tenor saxophonist the proper names for the chord progressions: " 'That's the diminished so-and-so,' [but Young would] say, 'I don't care what it is, I just want to hear it.' "[125]

If Young was indifferent about learning harmonic terminology, however, he could nonetheless "run a chord"—that is, find his own equivalent notes when he heard someone play a chord. Durham accounted for Young's relaxed or "lag-along" style—and unwittingly provided a possible explanation for the title of Young's most famous composition—by saying, "That's why he used to play after [the] beat. You hit something, he heard it . . . he'd leap in . . . then and fast." Durham maintained that Herschel Evans did much the same thing.

In deference to his unique tenor sound, Durham gave Young a specific place in the reed-section arrangements that he wrote for Basie. "You could do anything you wanted with your baritone [concerning a chord]," he explained, "but never [put] Young under that other tenor." Durham outlined the reed section's arrangements: "Lester didn't play down in there [with Evans]. Lester was another way." Young "had that C-melody sound," he said, "so when I made arrangements for him, like *all* the numbers I made for Basie, I had to use Lester on top." If he put

Evans on top, "it didn't blend good and you didn't get that weary [?] sound, that jazz sound." This need to place Young according to his tone "made Basie's reed section different from any [other] reed section."

Durham provided a telling insight into Young's soaring popularity during this period when he observed that the saxophonist "played what the public could hear." He was like Armstrong in this respect. Both musicians' playing would "always go," Durham suggested, whereas "a lot of [other] guys play over the public's head."[126] Sweets Edison made a similar point, averring, "[Young's] sound was simple, and it was simplicity that made him such an artist and such an innovator on the tenor saxophone." Edison compared this quality in Young's playing to good humor, which "is not complicated . . . the average man can understand . . . humor. . . . If it's simple . . . the gardener can stop and listen, and laugh at it." It was, he concluded, just "like a song. If you write a complicated song the average person can't hum it along with you, but if it's simple" it becomes another matter entirely.[127]

The trumpet stylist proclaimed his good friend the most daring as well as the most influential of all tenor saxophonists: "He will try anything on the bandstand. . . . Anything that he thought he wanted to try, he would try." Young, Edison said, "maintained that if you didn't try it on the bandstand, where you going to try it?" For Young as well as for others, the bandstand was a proving ground where experiments were tried and new techniques tested out—an important consideration for artists who were always learning and attempting to develop and extend the musical traditions that were such a vital part of their cultural heritage.[128]

Remarking on the quality of his roommate's playing, Edison referred to Benny Carter's contention, almost a cliché: "'It's not the notes you put in a solo that makes it effective, it's the notes that you leave out'—that makes it effective." When Basie's tenor star soloed, "every note that he made there was a purpose for that note, and it was put in the right place at the right time." In Edison's opinion, Young was a master craftsman who wasted no effort—every note he played had its rationale.[129]

Other Basie sidemen revealed that some of the traits noted in Young in earlier years persisted into the late 1930s. He was not a conversationalist, Earle Warren recalled: "If he was just sitting in [a] room, you would never know he was sitting here, because he would never have that much to say." And "he never went into big long conversations, hardly with anybody." But when he did speak or comment about something, it kept his companions laughing. He was carefree, lacking what Earle Warren termed "great stability."[130]

Even before he joined Basie, the tenor stylist had either suffered from insomnia or perhaps been possessed of inordinate amounts of vitality and energy, as well as a love of playing for its own sake. The bandleader Andy Kirk remembered that Young "was never ready to go to sleep" when he rode with the Clouds of Joy. Kirk's guitarist and the tenor saxophonist "would get together in the back of the bus, and they'd, just the two [of them]," play for hours on end.[131]

However much they loved Lester's sound, Basieites also had considerable regard for Evans's style and influence. Dicky Wells noted that Evans "had a first tenor sound that made a real contrast with Lester's," and Buck Clayton recalled that he "was intensely proud of being a tenor sax man from Texas." Wells insisted that both Evans's conception and his playing were highly original: "Herschel was playing that way before he ever heard Hawk in person." Jo Jones, not one known for lavishing praise, believed that Evans "was a natural. He had a sound on the tenor that perhaps you will never hear again"—in fact, in Jones's view, he "played [his tenor] the way it was supposed to be played."[132]

In Wells's opinion, the presence of the two tenors was a distinguishing feature of the Basie orchestra, and such an integral part of the first band that duplication in later years was impossible. While praising the quality of Buddy Tate's playing, Wells argued, "It's pretty hard to duplicate the original, especially when the original is perfect—and that it was." Luck, Wells thought, also played a role in accounting for the band's perfection; Basie, he said, "could never get that flavor after Lester left."[133] Jo Jones believed that Evans's playing influenced Young, and that that influence became particularly apparent after Evans's sudden death, on February 9, 1939: "Even in Lester's playing today," he said years later, "somewhere he'll always play two to four measures of Herschel because they were so close in what they felt about music."[134]

Persistent rumors about animosity between Basie's two tenor players served to enhance the importance of the musical statements they made when they soloed and to highlight the differences between them. But the quality of their playing also undoubtedly caused audiences to clamor for more. Wells claimed to have heard the two competing at the Cherry Blossom in Kansas City when he was with Fletcher Henderson.[135]

The trombonist dated the tenor players' show-stopping effects to a date at the Paradise Theatre in Detroit. "As soon as Herschel stood up, before ever he went down front, the people would start yelling. The same when Lester stood up," Wells recalled. He believed "that started the tenor sax duet within a band." Prior to that time (the Detroit date cannot be verified), it was mainly cornetists (later trumpeters), such as King Oliver and Louis Armstrong in the early 1920s, who dueled with one another.[136]

Basie's battling tenors started a trend in other orchestras as bandleaders gradually enlarged their saxophone sections. However, Basie was not the first to feature a pair of tenors. Buck Clayton's Los Angeles band boasted two in the mid-1930s: interestingly, they were Evans, a Texan, and Hubert "Bumps" Myers, a West Virginian who had grown up in California. Myers went with Buck Clayton's band to Shanghai in 1934 and was to play with the Young brothers in 1941 and 1942.[137]

But if the Basie orchestra was not the first to include two tenors, it did begin the custom of placing them at opposite ends of the sax section instead of together, like the altos. Young, Eddie Durham reported, wished to sit apart from Evans "because he didn't like that vibrato in Herschel's tone." Durham explained, "That's what started everybody doing it, even though they didn't know why they were doing it."[138]

By 1939, when the orchestra finally won plaudits and awards from trade journals, it had jelled; many of its members were to remain with it for several more years. By considering the band as an evolving entity, however, and Young as its catalytic soloist and the provider of statements for its riffs and new compositions, we can better grasp the history and significance of each. He was also, of course, part of the larger jazz community, which had its heroes, its name bands, its striving-to-make-it musical aggregations, its dancers, and its fans, who—almost like Masons—achieved rankings based upon their lineage, acquired knowledge, and length of association.[139]

Young acquired a national following as an important tenor stylist with Basie at precisely the time when Coleman Hawkins and the alto saxophonist and arranger Benny Carter were living in Europe, in the mid- and late 1930s. Their absence made it easier for new players to gain recognition. Young's alleged rivalry with Herschel Evans dramatized the competing schools of tenor saxophone playing, made for climactic moments in performances, and distinguished Basie's orchestra from others. Up until Evans's death in early 1939, it was not clear which of the two audiences preferred, but after that tragedy, Young's style became more popular. His frequent solos on Basie recordings between 1936 and 1944 are often regarded as the best of his career, and Basie's band during this period is generally considered to be the standard for comparison with later versions of the orchestra.[140]

Through their solidarity and their distinctive music, style, and aura, the Basieites band had a pronounced effect on African American urban culture and on city dwellers of various races and classes. Band members caused Black music culture's hip variant, with its attendant values, aesthetic, and associations, to become more southern in character, as more and less recent African American migrants and urban natives alike congregated in nightspots, theaters, and clubs in their own districts. Appearances by Basie's orchestra helped to popularize big-band blues, dress fads, and jazz lingo, not only in New York but in Chicago and other northern cities as well as down south and out west—wherever the band went.[141]

By 1940, the magic of the Basie years was over for Young. While friendships among band members usually survived the problems of racial discrimination and the opinions and behavior of management and bookers, professional relationships were often less resilient; sometimes the result was the loss of key entertainers or the breakup of a band. For example, men such as John Hammond were to blame for Holiday's leaving the Basie band in 1937, according to the singer. Some critics charged that she was unreliable, but the real issue was that Holiday, like Young, did not like businessmen's meddling in artistic matters. On one occasion, the singer and the tenor saxophonist even initiated a job action: they felt sufficiently strongly about the injustice of their salaries and working conditions in the band to protest and threaten to resign. They ended up getting raises and staying on.[142]

Holiday, however, ended up leaving the band after several months. "The Count and I got along fine," she explained in late 1939, "and the boys in the band were wonderful all the time." The problem, she said, was that "Basie had too many managers—too many guys behind the scenes who told everybody what to do." The bandleader, for his part, maintained that he felt it was "easier to work without a girl singer" because of the vast distances the band had to cover on its one-nighters; MCA supported his position. This contention would seem more credible had Helen Humes not subsequently replaced Holiday. Years later, Basie would suggest, "I think Billie left because she got a chance to make more money than we could afford to pay at that time."[143]

The bassist Gene Ramey, a good friend of Lester's, claimed that Hammond tried to manipulate both Young's and Holiday's careers, a misstep that also contributed to the tenor stylist's departure from the Basie band, at the end of 1940. "[Young] said he left Basie because he wanted a hundred and twenty-five dollars a week," Ramey recalled, "and he [Hammond] said he wasn't worth it, or something like that." Whenever the recording executive came to a club or theater where the Basieites were playing, he "would sit there with a smile on his face, and on many occasions he really made efforts to regain Prez's friendship, but he never did." Moreover, every time the singer and the saxophonist got together, "all they'd talk about was [Hammond], and how he tore that band asunder when it was on its way to make it." Young's nickname for Hammond, "Tommy Tucker" (actually the name of a bandleader), seems to have indicated his dislike for the man and perhaps hinted at his genteel social origins. Mary Lou Williams was another one who kept her distance from Hammond because of his penchant for placing the musicians he favored in the bands he sponsored.[144]

A quite different view of Hammond's involvement was expressed by Willard Alexander, Basie's manager, who insisted that the recording executive not only "got Billie the job with Count Basie, . . . [but] was responsible for Basie keeping her. . . . If it hadn't been for John Hammond, Billie would have been through six months sooner." Alexander, the MCA executive, took full credit for Holiday's departure; he dismissed her, he said, because "we just couldn't count on her for consistent performances." Her deportment and "wrong attitude" were used against her then, just as Young's would be used against him two decades later; in fact, this idea of "proper attitude" probably harked back to an age-old theme in race relations, whereby proud African Americans suffered at the hands of powerful whites who permitted more accommodating Blacks to work and even prosper.[145]

Young's and Holiday's stints with Basie's band ended because of differences of opinion between the artists and their management, who did not see eye to eye with them on many different matters—the need for racial equality, the worth of the artist, and the merit of popular songs, for example. Even the goodwill of well-meaning integrationists tended to be canceled out by the exigencies of the marketplace; it took more than an expressed desire for racial integration to convince the skeptical victims of racism.

While white swing musicians also complained about the unfairness of the big-band business, their relationships with management were not usually very much affected—if at all—by white racism. There were many more successful white imitators than there were Black originators in the world of swing. Young's and Holiday's employment with Basie, and eventually the careers of both artists, were among the casualties that inevitably resulted when Black artists' concerns with racism and their own dignity were placed second to their marketing to the public. The story of racism in popular music from ragtime to the present, and of its effects on innumerable careers, has yet to be told in its entirety, but Young's years with Basie's band afford a glimpse of the problems that Black artists faced.

Through his performances with Basie, Young became a major influence on the music as well as a folk hero to African American and jazz audiences, who knew him as one who stuck resolutely to his artistic conception throughout some trying times. Since the 1940s his significance has been overshadowed somewhat by the attention accorded Charlie Parker and bebop, not only in music circles and folklore but in trade journals and books and through recent popular films such as *Bird.* Before Parker, however, Young's tenor style changed the very conception of how the instrument should sound, and shaped musicians' ideas about line and rhythm. Moreover, Young influenced musicians on all instruments, which is remarkable enough in itself. And finally, he composed (or co-composed) a number of tunes that would later become standards, including, most notably, "Lester Leaps In" and "Dickie's Dream," as well as "Taxi War Dance" and "Tickletoe."[146]

It was Young's own belief that he did not receive sufficient credit for his contributions to the Basie orchestra—a belief that ultimately culminated in his departure from the band in late 1940. Until then, however, Young enjoyed playing with Basie as much as the other musicians did. He had finally made it to the big time in a name orchestra that was doing well in the major metropolises, and his section mates respected him and valued his playing. A swing-era musician could hardly ask for more.

CHAPTER 11

Watts Eyes

Paying Dues, 1941–1943

LESTER Young and the Basie band faced a major problem when Herschel Evans succumbed to a heart attack while they were on the road. He was said to have suffered one the year before, too, without ever being aware of it. Although he was originally from North Texas, he had family in Los Angeles, and he had spent the early 1930s there before joining Basie; accordingly, southern California musicians played at his service in front of the Angelus Funeral Home. The Basie band had to settle for paying its last respects to Evans—its sax-section mainstay, featured soloist, and member since the Kansas City days—in Chicago, where his body, en route by train to the West Coast, reposed for a brief period.[1]

Young was never quite the same after Evans's death. Jo Jones suggested that for the tenor stylist, it "was just like a twin dying. Soon after, Lester would be so restless that he would keep his coat and hat underneath the music stand and other guys would have to pull him back down to his seat to keep him playing." It was around this time that Young began drinking heavily. The loss of his friend and rival may also have been a contributing factor in his splitting with Basie at the end of 1940 to form his own combo. After spending a few wintry months in New York City in early 1941, he moved to Los Angeles and joined his brother's band that spring. They would play together for nearly two years.[2]

But in the immediate aftermath of the Evans tragedy, in addition to having to deal with the emotional problems caused by the sudden death of their barely thirty-year-old tenor saxophonist, the Basieites needed to fill his spot in the band. Several other saxophonists played in his style, but in a choice indicative of Young's influence, his candidate, Buddy Tate, another Texan, was finally selected as Evans's replacement. Tate received a telegram from Basie asking him to meet the orchestra in Kansas

City in the late winter (1939); he recalled that when he arrived in town for the audition, early one morning, Young was waiting in the hotel lobby to greet him, while everybody else was upstairs sleeping off the effects of the big welcome-home party. "'They had too much last night,'" Young told him. "'Come on, let's go and have breakfast.'"

Young ordered for the two of them, and over plates of red beans and rice, according to Tate, he asked, "'Have you been keeping up? Have you been listening?' I say, 'Well—I've been listening. I don't know how up I am.'" Young ignored Tate's modesty: "'If you're playing anywhere near as good as you were last time I heard you, it will be your engagement.'" Employing the distinctive slang for which he was known, he then added, "'A lot of ladies want the job. Miss Webster wants it, Miss Berry wants it, but you'll be the one.'"

Tate auditioned, and Basie hired him, but the other band members felt surer after he played "Blue and Sentimental," Evans's specialty, to their satisfaction in Lawrence, Kansas. Tate related what happened next in an anecdote that illustrates Young's compulsion to differentiate himself from the other Basieites: "I swear to God everybody in that place stood up. Everybody on the bandstand shouted, 'Look no further, he is the one!' Young did not join in, however; he didn't stand up. He'd never do what everybody [else] did." After touring the Midwest, the band returned to New York, where Young found a room for Tate at the Woodside.[3]

Despite the Basie band's successful recordings and acclaim on both coasts, Young left the orchestra at the end of 1940; he would play mainly in small combos until he rejoined Basie in the autumn of 1943. There has been much speculation as to the reason for his leaving the band, but he himself rarely discussed the topic, even with his closest associates. His supposed reluctance to record on Friday the thirteenth—the usual explanation given for the rupture—has been discounted; Basie, for example, labeled that theory "ridiculous" in his autobiography. Young's biographer Lewis Porter, too, has questioned this account.[4]

As Porter observed, the bandleader's financial problems with his booking agency, MCA, should receive greater attention as a contributing factor in the separation. Basie was unhappy with MCA because it made a practice of booking the band on strings of one-nighters requiring lengthy bus trips. Then, too, he was disappointed that so few of the clubs he and his orchestra played had radio hookups. Moreover, his personal debt and the band's amounted to seven thousand and five thousand dollars, respectively. Rumors began going around at about this time that Basie was planning to break up his orchestra and join Benny Goodman. Young may have left the band, therefore, because its future—financial and otherwise—seemed in doubt. Basie's financial issues with MCA were evidently resolved when the William Morris Agency paid twenty thousand dollars to release him from his contract in the winter of 1941.[5]

The orchestra's star soloist had been wanting to lead his own group for some time, according to Count Basie, who also believed that Evans's death played a role in Young's departure. Gene Ramey maintained that Young asked for higher pay—$125—but producer John Hammond thought that was too much money, given the financial straits Basie and his band were in. A Mrs. Lester Young—presumably Mary Dale—wrote a letter to *Down Beat* in which she addressed the matter, insisting that her husband had not been fired but not divulging what lay behind the separation: "He quit for reasons of his own," she stated. Young's refusal to discuss the break underlined his insistence on privacy when it came to matters of a personal or business nature.[6]

After leaving Basie, Young attempted to capitalize on his former status as the band's star soloist. Many others were launched from large bands as leaders in their own right, including Armstrong and Hawkins and later Parker and Dizzy Gillespie. Writers, critics, and fans who questioned the wisdom of Young's quitting Basie and emphasized his subsequent "decline" seem to have been indifferent to the simple fact that with the singular exception of Ellington, few bandleaders succeeded in holding on to their star soloists. Even Ellington lost his premier alto saxophonist, Johnny Hodges, and others, though they frequently returned.

Early in 1941, Young led his combo for a few weeks at Kelly's Stable, on Fifty-second between Sixth and Seventh avenues, and made several recordings with the singer Una Mae Carlisle, among them "Blitzkrieg Baby," which reminded audiences out for a good time of the war in Europe. Young's guitarist, John Collins, a native of Montgomery, Alabama, provided a vignette of the saxophonist's character and playing at this time, offered some insights into the formation of his combo, and explained the reason for its breakup. Collins first heard the tenor stylist in Chicago when he was with Fletcher Henderson, and then saw him perform again in late 1936 or in 1937, when Basie's band passed through. Young later jammed with Collins and Roy Eldridge at the Three Deuces, where the guitarist and trumpeter worked regularly. Collins reminisced, "I got to know Pres very well because we would play *every* night . . . [in]

different clubs . . . anyplace that would let us jam . . . and that was going all night. And I really got to know Pres, who encouraged me to come to New York."

Collins, Lester and Mary, and the third member of the combo, drummer Harold "Doc" West, all rented apartments at the Woodside. When the three of them played at Kelly's Stable, Collins said, Young's playing was "*all* truth and beauty. Simplicity." There were "no gymnastics," no technique for its own sake; "it was just straight *here* and it was just straight *there* beauty. . . . That was his life." Collins described the saxophonist as "just earth, pure earth." Hawkins's playing was "marvelous . . . and he did the tricks . . . , but Lester would grab at your *heart,*" Collins emphasized. "It wasn't what he said, it was *how* he said it. It wasn't his technique as much as it was his soul."

It was the guitarist's impression that John Hammond had a hand in Young's first attempt at being a bandleader: "Hammond was really the cause of Pres forming this group," he recalled. The promoter had "in the back of his mind . . . [that this should be] Billie Holiday's group . . . with Pres' band . . . but he didn't tell Pres this until he heard the group, and he liked it, and he tried to put Billie Holiday [in it] . . . under her name and Pres wouldn't go for it." When the saxophonist realized what the recording executive was up to, the two went their separate ways: "[Young] said, 'Well, I love Lady Day, but this is my band . . . not Lady Day's band. This is my band.'" In light of his belief that Hammond had destroyed the old Basie band, Young may very well have decided that this was the last straw.

Young conceived his first band as a pianoless one, a concept he and Roy Eldridge shared. Collins noted, "When I worked with Roy, when he wanted the piano to leave, he would say, 'Strollers.' That meant just guitar, bass, and drum. Well, Pres liked that very much." This shared affinity may very well have stemmed from Young's fond memories of strolling musicians, singers, and marching bands in New Orleans, or it may simply have reflected his liking for stringed instruments and subtle rhythmic backing, but in any case, it was the shape he initially wanted his own band to take. Yet he was hardly inflexible on this point; in fact, when the pianist Clyde Hart, a friend of Collins's and a veteran of Hezekiah "Stuff" Smith's combo, sat in with the others at a rehearsal, Young liked his playing so much that he made him a member of the band.[7]

Less than three weeks into the gig at Kelly's Stable, however, Young quit the place, believing that he had been slighted by an employee. According to Collins, "The bandstand was right by the aisle that led to the kitchen, which meant that the waiters had to come right by the bandstand all night long, and Pres played . . . a beautiful solo, and he stepped off the bandstand, and one of the waiters bumped right into him." After an exchange of words, "Pres quit that night . . . and so we [were] out of work . . . [because] he thought that the man had insulted him, and the boss didn't back him up." As Collins explained it, the boss or the waiter, or both, "had hurt [Young's] feelings, and so that was enough for him to quit, and he would *starve* before he would compromise . . . *one bit!*" Such demonstrations of pride were an integral part of his character, and they no doubt helped him develop a reputation as the prototype of the proud, hip Black urbanite whose artistic output was recognized and imitated from coast to coast.[8]

In the spring of 1941, the saxophonist moved to Los Angeles after telephoning his brother to inquire about playing in his band. He was willing to relocate because his family was there, but also because so many of his friends and fellow musicians had migrated to southern California—not only his former sidemen Le Roy "Snake" Whyte and Eddie Barefield, but also Nat "King" Cole and George "Red" Callender. The trend had begun some time before. After World War I, a number of New Orleanians, including Thomas "Mutt" Carey and Edward "Kid" Ory, had settled in the area; they had been preceded there by others from Louisiana, among them the nucleus of the Original Creole Jazz Orchestra, a decade earlier.[9]

The Young family's roots in the city went back to 1929 or 1930, when Lester's father, the professor, left Phoenix and took his younger son, Lee, to Los Angeles, to be joined a little later by Sarah, Irma, and Irma's young daughter, Martha. By then Lester was recently married and had gone out on his own. It may have been Willis Young who was listed in the City Directory for 1930 at 5608 South Broadway; in 1932 he and Sarah resided at 1651 Essex, a few miles south of downtown, where they stayed for about three years. By 1936, probably because of Professor Young's involvement in the music business, they moved into a large two-story frame house at 1706 Central, next door to the local union of African American musicians (at number 1710). Outside of New York City, musicians' unions were segregated in the United States in those years.[10]

The household swelled during that decade. At some point Mary Hunter (Aunt Mamie or "Sugar Pie") came to live with them, as did the professor's loyal mechanic and driver, Mr. White, who looked after his car. Lee and Irma eventually moved out on their own, but in 1936 several of the professor's grandchildren from Louisiana—the Tolberts, children of his daughter Alice—were sent out to stay in the Central Avenue house after their mother was seriously injured in an automobile accident. Lillian, Alice's sister, brought the children out to southern California and stayed on herself. Irma Young's second child, Crawford Brown Jr., subsequently enlarged the household and the number of recruits under the professor's regimen. "Brownie's" father was a musician who died in a car accident before his son was born.[11]

Even before his move to Los Angeles in 1941, the saxophonist considered the Central Avenue house his home. When he was with Basie in New York City, for example, he gave his parents' Los Angeles address on his application for a Social Security card. In the autumn of 1939, as Europe plunged into war, he visited his family when he came to town with the Basie band. Local musicians knew his entire family, if only by reputation. His saxophone playing must have impressed the Central Avenue musicians on one 1936 visit—probably his first—because "the other night at the Breakfast Club the cats decided to get together and have a real old eastern jam session in [his] honor." The Breakfast Club was an after-hours spot (above the famous Club Alabam) on Central Avenue that offered fried chicken with biscuits and honey, served liquor, and featured jazz. Freddy Doyle, a former Chicagoan and himself a musician, reported on the tenor stylist's jam session, on the other former Los Angelenos in the Basie band, and on their successes as they struggled for fame.[12]

Just as jazz had found a home in California cities in the early twentieth century, swing discovered southern California to be quite hospitable during the Great Depression. Some bands were fortunate enough to make brief appearances performing in movies; several nightclubs also promoted the music. In the early 1930s, the Club Alabam opened on Central Avenue, and Sebastian's Cotton Club was launched in Culver City. Near the Dunbar Hotel and all along Central Avenue, Black and white musicians and jazz lovers milled and fraternized, socializing in one nightspot and then another. Across town in Hollywood, the Famous Door, whose very name exemplified the habit of imitating New York resorts, showcased Fats Waller in late 1937, accompanied by musicians who would later play with Lester Young: Lee Young, Caughey Roberts, and Gardner Paul Campbell.

New residents Red Callender and Roy Porter, native Los Angeleno

Hampton Hawes, and sojourner Buck Clayton all depicted the Central Avenue milieu in their autobiographies. The Alabam was, in fact, the old Apex, where Lee Young had danced as a teenager and which had itself succeeded the Club Araby; functioning as the show room of the Dunbar Hotel, it was owned by two Italian brothers, but Curtis Mosby, a former Kansas Citian, had a hand in managing "the mecca for music lovers and devotees of the dance" and may very well have owned it himself at some point. Its address was 4015 South Central Avenue (later, when the city renumbered its streets, to become 4215). Irma Young, "Stompy," and Ernestine Porter played there in 1933; the Mills Brothers and the comedian Stepin Fetchit also performed, as did Buck Clayton and his Fourteen Gentlemen from Harlem.[13]

Young's prior visits to Los Angeles no doubt played a role in persuading him to make the move to southern California to play in his brother's band. He stayed with Lee until early 1943, then toured military bases in Al Sears's USO band for a few months before rejoining Basie at Jo Jones's invitation in the autumn of that same year. He made some classic recordings with Nat "King" Cole on piano and Red Callender on bass in the summer of 1942, and with the Kansas City Seven, including Basie and several of his musicians, in early 1944. In the late summer of the latter year, the saxophonist went to the Warner Brothers studio to be filmed by Gjon Mili for Norman Granz's classic *Jammin' the Blues.* The first image on the screen, a close-up shot of the top of Pres's porkpie, then a pan down to his face, with him playing his own composition "The Midnight Symphony," a slow blues, remains frozen for eternity in the minds of jazz and film buffs alike.[14]

The 1940s were a high point in Young's career in terms of both his importance among musicians and his wider recognition as a popular-culture hero. A *Metronome* poll ranked him third on "hot tenor" in its All-Star Band in early 1940; he garnered 323 votes, behind Eddie Miller (660) and Charlie Barnet (558). It is not terribly surprising that two white musicians outpolled him; more significant is that his chief rivals, Coleman Hawkins and Leon "Chu" Berry, lagged behind, with 261 votes each. He achieved a special status when he appeared in the pictorial weekly *Life*, which designated him as "probably the best tenor sax player out of uniform anywhere in the world today." *Ebony*, *Life*'s African American counterpart, contended that he was likely the single most photographed jazz musician, and informed readers that Norman Granz, the man behind Jazz at the Philharmonic (JATP), regarded him as "a completely original artist."[15]

These were good years for Young, and in retrospect they would appear particularly rewarding because of their sharp contrast with his tragic army experience and the severe illness that would plague him in the 1950s. He was at the top of his form in the early 1940s; "Teddy Bear," his nickname for a close friend, claimed that he could play anything he could hear—one of the ultimate goals of the creative musician. But beyond that, there were other reasons for his confidence and his sense of success, as a look at his family in Los Angeles will reveal.[16]

In the late 1930s, the Los Angeles Black community, and notably the *California Eagle*, a local African American weekly, were as much aware of the contributions of Professor Young and his offspring as they were of the growing status of Count Basie's star soloist. Lester was the exemplar of family music traditions and certainly the professor's best-known pupil, and the Youngs celebrated his rise. They listened to evening radio broadcasts of Basie's orchestra, probably from the Famous Door, and when Martha saw her uncle with the band in a newsreel at the local movie house, she raced home to deliver the news. "I came home excited about seeing Uncle Bubba in the newsreel and [Papa Young] went to the show, *just* to see the newsreel," she recalled; the clip was very likely from the Randalls Island Jazz Carnival. She reminisced, "When Uncle Bubba was coming home . . . he was [to the kids] . . . a king." They got to stay up late with him, playing pokeno. Martha was also a pupil of Willis Young's, but she "was . . . too [much in] awe of Lester . . . I would never let him hear me play."[17]

Lucille Tolbert was similarly awed by her uncle Bubba: "He could do no wrong. Whenever he was in town, I carried his bag. It must have weighed about eighty-five or ninety pounds, and I was a little bitty thing." He also let her carry his horn, another indication of her exalted station: "The horn was in a black velvet bag, with a drawstring at the top . . . and the whole thing used to have to hang over back here and I would hold it up under here with the neck of it back there and I would carry it everywhere."[18]

Young enjoyed his status in the family, an enlarged kinship group of three generations that was typical for many African Americans. He was the elder son who had come home, a glowing success after years of scuffling in the territorial bands and with Count Basie, to resume his close ties with his father, stepmother, aunt, brother, and sister, whom he had seen only once or twice since 1930, and to get to know his nieces and nephews. His half-sister Emelda, Lizetta's daughter with Levi Gray, also migrated to Los Angeles around this time. Mary Dale, Lester's second wife, either came with him to the West Coast or joined him there later. Beatrice, his first wife, also resided on the city's East Side in 1942.[19]

After more than a decade on the road, the tenor stylist's new life with his parents, siblings, and relations was especially meaningful for him. Young relished not only the home-cooked meals but the jokes and tales that were spun as they all relived the days of the Busy Bees and the New Orleans Strutters, and as he regaled the others with stories of his adventures in the Southwest and in the major metropolises.[20] Of particular importance to him were the affective ties. Martha Young would later claim, "I loved my childhood. I like thinking about my childhood . . . and music played a great part in it." Her recounting would underline the close relations among family members, and point to one source of Young's mischievousness and humor: "We had a lot of humor in the house as well as some music; it was a lot of humor," she recalled. Papa Young had a little routine he would go through with his adoring grandchildren: "Whoever went to the store for him to get his handpacked ice cream would be the one that got ice cream out of the hand pack, OK? And . . . Papa would set up there and he'd scrape the bottom of the box like it wasn't enough in there [laughs] and seems like he'd eat up all the ice cream, but he wouldn't be that way. He'd always leave you a nice corner." There were other games as well—for example, "at Eastertime we played games with eggs, who would crack the egg. [If] he cracked your egg you had to give it to him, and if you cracked his you get it back." And at Christmas it was nuts—"guessing how many nuts I had in my hand, and if you guess it you got it."[21]

Although she was his stepmother, Lester was extremely devoted to Mama Young, who was described by one family member as "an imposing, beautiful Black lady who played baritone horn [saxophone] like you have never heard," and as "a very, very aristocratic lady, very tall, very *dark* . . . , soft-spoken and sweet . . . [with] very, very long, tapered fingers." With several grandchildren to look after, she played a vital role in the extended family. Her leg had been amputated below the knee due to complications from diabetes; it is not clear which year the operation took place, but it was sometime after the family moved to Los Angeles. She watched the whole time the surgeon was sawing, and instructed him,

" 'Now, don't you take off any more than what you said you were going to take off.' " When she returned from the hospital, Papa Young joked "with her, telling her that he was carrying her across the threshold for the second time." He cut down a dining-room chair and put rollers on it, and "she'd roll all over the house."[22]

The two were so close that they agreed that when one died, the other should not remain in the world of the living for too long: "Daught," the professor reportedly said, using his pet name for his spouse, "now if I leave here before you, you better come on. You know I don't want you hangin' around here after I leave." He promised to do the same if she died before him. His Sarah was as good as her word: she died just a few weeks after he did, in early 1943. "She was a very strong woman, so her dying as quickly as she did after . . . my grandfather died was what she wanted to do," Martha asserted. "She didn't want to live; that's the same conclusion the doctors [came] to because she was too strong [to die otherwise]."[23] This deep well of spirituality influenced Lester Young in his relations with his kin and loved ones.

Lee and Lester came to know each other as adults and as musicians at this time. Although only four and a half years separated the brothers, as Lee pointed out, their "lives and . . . life-styles had been so *different.*" Lester claimed not to have known his father at all before he was ten, and Lee had been too young to remember much about those New Orleans years. Whereas Lee did not get to know his birth mother, Lizetta, until he was grown, Lester associated her with his memories of New Orleans. Lester did not learn music or go on the road until he was ten; Lee was onstage and traveling by the age of five or six. While Lester was touring in the Midwest and Southwest, Lee had been living in Los Angeles and attending Lafayette Junior High and Jefferson High School. Lester's formal education had ended around the fourth grade.

There were other significant differences between them. While Lester, a married man, had often barnstormed, Lee, as an adolescent and young adult, had stayed in one place, bearing responsibilities that were a considerable burden for a teenager during the Depression. He had worked nights at the Apex, run by Curtis Mosby ("the biggest emcee in town"), until the Labor Commission intervened, objecting because of his youth. Nevertheless, his father had continued to find singing and dancing jobs for him in the evenings and on weekends while he was still in junior high, because the Youngs depended upon his earnings. As much as he liked sports ("I wanted to be out playing baseball and basketball," he would recall), he had to take work seriously; as his stepmother explained to him, he "was the only one in the family that was earning any money. . . . 'You are now taking care of the family. So you have to bring your money home.'"[24]

The younger brother abstained from smoking and drinking and other vices associated with the nightlife, even as the elder, based on the opposite coast, became deeply enmeshed in drinking, smoking, and taking barbiturates to enable him to perform during the marathon series of one-nighters endured by the Basie band. Lee Young stayed off the road because he had had enough of that life as a child. He admitted that he "never did like traveling. . . . When you can make a living in the studios and stay at home, all that running around on the roads is so much tinsel." Moreover, after he got married, he wanted to raise his children and fulfill other family responsibilities. Lester, in contrast, loved the road (where "there's always something new," he said). The brothers' differences led to disagreements about, for example, Lester's drinking habit.[25]

In the Los Angeles combo, the Youngs assumed roles that suited their respective interests and abilities. Lester wanted to concentrate on the music alone, so he became the featured soloist, while Lee played drums and sang in addition to taking care of the business end of things and leading the unit. Although the older brother abhorred practice sessions, the younger insisted on rehearsing at least six times a week, either in the rehearsal room above the union offices or in the front room of their parents' home next door.

The band used arrangements by the bassist, Red Callender; by Billy Strayhorn, Ellington's famous arranger; and by trumpeter Gerald Wilson and Dudley Brooks, of Alton Redd and Cee Dee Johnson's band. The constant practice and learning one song a day enabled the musicians to play for several hours without referring to sheet music. According to Lee, "The reason for us rehearsing every day [was that] we didn't read music at night. . . . We would stand up there and play arrangements all night[;] that was the uniqueness of the band." This approach amazed some listeners, who knew the bandsmen were playing arrangements but marveled that they had memorized so much.[26]

Lester shared the tenor spot with Hubert "Bumps" Myers, which not only reminded listeners of Basie's two tenors but also gave the band a bigger sound. Lee Young explained, "I wanted two tenors because I knew how big that would make the band sound, with a guitar. . . . [With arrangements] you could spread the harmonies, the chords." Besides

Lester and Lee, the other musicians, who varied over the nearly two-year lifespan of the combo, were Gardner Paul Campbell (also "Red Mack," McClure Morris), on trumpet; Louis Gonzales on vocals and electric guitar; Arthur Twyne (and later Jimmy Rowles and then "Sir Charles" Thompson) on piano; and Red Callender on bass. The band offered four-part harmony, and its repertoire included swing or "jump" instrumentals, "Bugle Boy Blues" and "Lester Leaps In," the standards "After You've Gone" and "Body and Soul," and popular ballads and vocals such as "Imagination."[27]

Until his union membership was transferred out west, Lester was only a featured soloist, sitting outside in back while the band played, then coming in to join in on three songs per set. This restriction lasted for about six weeks. They played different clubs around Los Angeles—including the Capri in Hollywood, at La Cienega and Pico (later to become Billy Berg's), and the Trouville—and then, in a major breakthrough for the band, were booked into Café Society in downtown New York City in late 1942. Slim Gaillard and Slam Stewart (Slim and Slam), Joe Turner, the Spirits of Rhythm, and Billie Holiday were among those who played and sang opposite them in Los Angeles. Lee did most of the vocals; the *Eagle* reporter wrote that his singing "rated as tops," and, moreover, judged him to be "one of the finest drummers in southern California." The band was said to be "the talk of the town" shortly before the United States declared war on Japan and Germany.[28]

At this point in his career, Lester Young was still an avid participant in jam sessions. A notable one took place at the Capri in the early summer of 1941: "Every musician of note in town was there. Lunceford and Duke men had a chance to cut each other and knock everyone else out," according to Wilma Cockrell of the *California Eagle.* Among the tenors, Ben Webster, Joe Thomas, Bumps Myers, and Lester "battled for a while." Reportedly, Myers "sent everybody in the joint, including Lester"; Webster "as always went six stories below the basement, to dish up his particular brand of dirty tone"; and "Young honked away and played some magnificent breaks." The bassist Jimmy Blanton, the duo of Slim Gaillard and Slam Stewart, Nellie Lutcher, and Rex Stewart also took part. Lee Young was given credit "for getting together such a fine group of musicians.[29]

The Trouville was another site for Sunday jam sessions. Nat "King" Cole often played piano there with Lee, Lester, Red Callender, and Bumps Myers. From time to time Lionel Hampton and Jimmy Blanton stopped in. The tenor saxophonist Carlos "Don" Byas, of Muskogee, Oklahoma, who had known the Youngs in the Southwest in the 1920s, was joined by another tenor player to make four on this instrument (with Lester and Bumps) one Sunday, and "on the next Sunday," Lee Young recalled, "we had Willie Smith, Johnny Hodges, and two other alto players." Eventually Norman Granz, who had befriended Lee Young, took an interest in these sessions; a few years later he would develop the idea of formalizing a similar gathering of top artists and combos and sending it out on tour. "That's how the Jazz at the Philharmonic [came to be]," Lee explained. "I started giving Norman names of the guys to call and Norman took it a step further." The producer of *Jammin' the Blues* "went to the different clubs, and he used to have sessions at the 331 Club on a Monday night, he'd have one at the Trouville on Sunday afternoon, and then he'd have a session someplace else. And I'm certain this is how he came up with Jazz at the Philharmonic."[30]

The combo was at the Capri for most of 1941 before going to the Trouville. The following summer, the band also headlined at the Lincoln Theater, sharing the bill with Billie Holiday. She sang at the Trouville as well that year, opposite the Young combo, before being replaced by Marie Bryant. In late 1942 the Young brothers went east with their band and had settled into playing at Café Society in New York when they received word that their father was seriously ill. Lee returned to Los Angeles while Lester remained in New York. After Willis passed, in February, Lee attended to the funeral and started managing the family's affairs. Lester, for his part, "did not want to see his father in a coffin" because "he didn't want to think of him as being dead." Their band was another casualty; after it broke up, the brothers rarely performed together and followed separate paths. Lee played drums for movies, including Louis Armstrong's and Mae West's *Every Day's a Holiday,* and taught Mickey Rooney how to handle the drumsticks for *Strike Up the Band.* He also held other studio jobs, among them a three-and-a-half-year contract position at Columbia Pictures, where he was the first African American to be on staff. In 1946, at Jazz at the Philharmonic, Lee and Lester Young jammed together on the bandstand. Beginning in 1953, Lee would tour for several years with Nat Cole.[31]

Before we consider the effect that Willis's and Sarah's deaths had on Lester, we need to clarify his other sources of emotional support. His reluctance to discuss aspects of his personal life was a reflection of his intensely private nature, a trait he shared with many other public figures.

Yet it is important to our understanding of his life to know that both Beatrice Young and Mary Dale Young apparently resided in Los Angeles in 1942. Paradoxically, even though she was said to be white, Mrs. Lester Young (Mary Dale) was listed in *The Official California Negro Directory, 1942–1943* as residing at 1233 East Fiftieth Street, on Los Angeles's East Side. A Mary Young, possibly the same person, was also listed at 922 East Forty-fifth Street. After the war, Mrs. Lester Young remained at the same address on East Fiftieth, while Mary Young was listed as living at 1635 East Forty-third Street. If they were not the same person, one of them was probably the Mary D. Young who bought a house with Lester in the spring of 1947.[32]

Then there was Teddy Bear, a close friend who urged Young to settle down and take studio jobs, but to no avail. A Canadian of African American and Native American parentage, she described Young as an unusually sensitive romantic. They first met in Nebraska when he was with Basie, but it was not until she moved to Los Angeles that they began to spend time together as a couple. Teddy Bear provided one of the first portraits of the tenor saxophonist at home as well as on the bandstand. She recalled how he loved his dog (a black German shepherd named Tonics), enjoyed home-cooked meals, adored his new friend, and showered her with flowers and gentlemanly attentiveness.[33]

Both were married when they met, she to a saxophonist who played like him. She moved to Los Angeles sometime around 1939 and broke up with her spouse; Young saw her again when the Basie band went out there on tour, probably in early October 1939. "He was playing at the Paramount [at 325 West Sixth Street], and I worked on Broadway, and our back doors looked right into each other, so I was at the theater and back and forth. . . . We really got together right away," she recalled. "So we saw each other, and we were . . . fond of each other." He stayed "out here six or eight weeks . . . then he came out again . . . and then he quit Basie and he came out, and Lee formed the band." The second visit was probably in August and September of 1940, when the Basieites played the Paramount for nearly three weeks.[34]

After he moved to California, Young rented a furnished "two-bedroom back-house" (that is, a house at the back of a lot, behind the main dwelling) around Fifty-second Street, "right off Central," where he and Teddy Bear lived together for a time. (This may have been before Mary Dale came out to Los Angeles; the chronology is not clear.) Pres's utter devotion to his lover was such that despite his nocturnal habits, he "started getting up at eight o'clock every morning [and] taking two buses with me to go to work, and he stayed up all *day.*" Young rode the bus again to pick her up from work in the evening. During the day he played pool at the Dunbar Hotel, hung out in the barbershop, and bought her flowers. After she moved to new quarters near the Capri Club, at Pico and La Cienega, where he and Lee played, "I'd come home from work and there'd be this beautiful vase of fresh gardenias on the coffee table," she remembered, "and I'd make pot roast, and I *still* went to work with him" and also to the jam sessions. "He really got domesticated fast, and Saturday and Sunday mornings there'd be fresh fruit and a beautiful breakfast."

She reminisced about his sensitive nature and his love of the comforts of home. Evidently Young was tired of catch-as-catch-can meals and life on the road; Teddy Bear mused, "I don't think he had ever had many good meals in his life." He "*loved* the pot roast. Everything—prime ribs . . . heavy-duty down-home cooking." She told the story of when they went to the movies to see the classic *Wuthering Heights,* and "he started crying in the show. And so I gave him a handkerchief . . . and he said, 'Oh, this isn't *Wuthering Heights,* this is *Smothering Heights.*'" From then on, "anything that would get to him he would say, 'Oh, man, I was so smothered!'"

His attentiveness toward her was part of his chivalry: "He would pull out a chair for me . . . and he'd dust it off with his handkerchief before I sat down." Likewise, there "was never a door that I could touch" before he opened it for her. "Tenderness," she testified, "was just his way of life." When they "would sit on the porch and a butterfly flitted around and landed on his hand . . . he cried." He referred to such incidents as telegrams—"That was a telegram," he would say, meaning that "somebody loved him. . . . Everything was a telegram. . . . If you knocked your drink over . . . that's a telegram . . . somebody trying to tell you something."

As they walked home at night from the bus stop, "before we got this little house . . . there would be a mockingbird that would sing. And [Pres] would do the same riffs in the same key. And he would *call* the bird," Teddy Bear recalled. "*That* smothered him: 'Oh, baby!'" On other occasions during their nocturnal walks, "we'd play all kinds of little dramas . . . under the street lights, just twaddling away the time." Once she challenged him by suggesting, "Oh, you really don't love me, do you?" To prove his sincerity, "he jumped over a hedge and—this was a full moon—and went into a yard and brought me a *full-bloom* yellow rose, that big! I cried. . . . And [he] bowed, and gave it to me."

He did not like having visitors, so no one came to their house. After all, he had to deal with the public on the job, and besides, he was married—to someone else. "He was just that private," Teddy Bear said. "He didn't want nobody to come over and hear records or nothing." Explaining his feelings on the matter, he would sing, " 'Just me,' " snapping his fingers. He also "loved to dance." With her, he talked about his early days in show business and recalled the sometimes humiliating acts the entertainers had presented just to get laughs.

Whenever she went to hear him perform in a club, he insisted that she listen closely while he played, because he was doing it solely with her in mind: "Anywhere he was playing, he'd always send me a telegram. . . . If he was playing a chorus or something, I *couldn't* talk to nobody, he wanted *undivided* attention from me. [He claimed,] 'I'm playing this . . . for you.' " The standard "Crazy 'bout Me," whose lyrics included the line "I've never had nothing, and no one to care," was the song "he played for me all the time," she said. Young's music evidently sprang from private sources of inspiration and was a very personal means of communicating his inner thoughts and feelings, particularly to those he loved.

His lover knew about the other women in his life, so conceivably he talked to her about them. As for his Italian-American wife, Mary Dale, Teddy Bear was under the impression that he eventually returned to New York to go back to her, though, as we have noted, a Mary D. Young was in Los Angeles as late as 1947. Teddy Bear believed that Lizetta, Young's mother, thought Mary was a better choice for her son—"She wasn't on my side," she charged. His mother "got Mary out here after coming to Los Angeles." Mary Dale had worked and taken care of Young in New York—"She had been good to him"—and part of the reason he rarely had any money on the West Coast was that "all the time he worked at the Capri or anywhere, he had to send money home to her."

For most of the time they spent together, music enveloped them. Teddy Bear reminisced, "He'd like to go down on Main Street and set in on Okie groups and listen to that kind of music . . . see old men playing guitars on the street. He'd give them his last dollar . . . and stand there an hour." At their home, often "he would just get up and pick up his horn, and sit down, and blow for about an hour." He would announce that he was going to play something pretty, "and he would, and I would tell him how *important* he was, and what a *force* he was in the world, it would never be forgotten, because I don't believe anything's ever lost. . . . I would tell him, 'Your sound will be going round and round and round the world . . . for an eternity.' " The recordings he made with Nat Cole in the summer of 1942—"Indiana," "I Can't Get Started," "Tea for Two," and "Body and Soul"—indicate how well he was able to express the tenderest of emotions and sensibilities.

Even while Young slept, he listened to the radio. "Some nights he'd decide to put on a great big symphony," Teddy Bear said, "and that disturbed my sleep, and I would get up and turn it down." But "the minute I turned it down, that woke him up. I mean not *off*. Just *down*." He was always listening to music: "I mean he was really into it . . . and he would listen and he would say, 'Man! Listen at them cats sawing and trembling there!' "

Another expression that Young used constantly, "I've paid my dues," referred to his union dues as well as his years of struggling. The union's strict control over these matters meant that a musician's dues had to be paid before he or she could play and earn money, and scraping together the fee was a constant problem for the tenor saxophonist during this period. Once he was unable to play at the Philharmonic because of unpaid dues. "And so the main project with Lester was paying his dues. 'Cause he . . . never had any money," recalled Teddy Bear. Sometimes he had to pawn his horn or a suit.

Besides having to pay dues and send money to Mary, he had another, perhaps more serious problem: "He just had no idea of what money was about. All he wanted to do was play his horn." Despite being photographed so frequently and coming in near if not at the top in music polls on his instrument, Young, Teddy Bear maintained, "never made any big money" while she knew him, "even with Basie."

She also claimed that Young suffered from a serious medical condition: epilepsy. "He . . . had several attacks," she said. His father was epileptic, too, she contended, though the professor's death certificate gives no indication of that, citing only kidney problems and ulcers, and death from stroke and pneumonia. One of Young's seizures reportedly occurred in the Club Alabam restroom around noon one day; he was with Ellington's arranger, Billy Strayhorn, Teddy Bear said, "and they brought him home, and I didn't know it . . . but he had chewed his tongue all up." He did not go to a doctor; Teddy Bear fed him Cream of Wheat for a day until he recovered. She believed he had at least three such episodes—"I was never with him, though." Two of the seizures happened when he was in Los Angeles, she contended. "He was upset about it. Very upset about it."

Her testimony is corroborated by others who agree that Young suffered from attacks—though whether from epilepsy or from some other cause is unclear. Teddy Bear's statements about other health matters—that his tonsils caused him problems, for example, and that he had asthma as a child—have been supported by other sources. In fact, nothing she said has been disproved, so we may consider it a likely possibility that he did suffer from some kind of fainting spells, if not actually from epilepsy; perhaps this explains his later reluctance to seek medical help.[35]

Young's close relationships with loving women did not spare him from the grief he felt upon the deaths of close friends and family. It is likely that he had been shocked years earlier by the tragic death of Bess Cooper, the mother of his daughter, Beverly, in Minneapolis. But around the time of Herschel Evans's death, he also endured several other losses. Margaret Johnson, known as the Countess, a pianist from Kansas City with whom Young had been linked romantically, succumbed to tuberculosis at the age of twenty in the late summer of 1939. The deaths of his former sideman Clyde Hart and of Jimmy Blanton and Charlie Christian, also from tuberculosis and all within a few years of one another, were especially sobering and underscored the grim realities faced by African Americans, who sustained a higher mortality rate from the disease than whites.[36]

No previous account of Young's life, either formal or anecdotal, has considered how he was affected by these deaths or, most important, those of Willis and Sarah. His unwillingness to return to California for his parents' funerals cannot simply be attributed to the distance, nor can it be understood as indifference to death. If Evans's passing affected him deeply, surely the same must have been true for his father's and stepmother's passing within a few weeks of each other. Personal misfortunes with women, and then the deaths of those closest to him, must have been profound tragedies for someone as sensitive and ultimately as introverted as the tenor stylist; such events no doubt diminished the luster of his professional success. Few other people would be permitted to penetrate the void left by his parents' deaths.

Even these personal tragedies, however, might have been bearable for Young had it not been for the gnawing racism that dogged his steps at every turn. The critic who maintained that the saxophonist "may have carried the force of his own destruction within him, but it took civilization to energize that force" was at least half right.[37]

White racism plagued Lester Young and other Black musicians in California in the early 1940s. One memorable letter to *Down Beat,* headed "Why Hollywood Won't Ever Do an Authentic Movie on Negroes [and] Jazz," pointed out that "to be a real jazz story [a film] would have to [have a] mostly full if not completely full cast of Negroes to portray men like [Buddy] Bolden, [Freddy] Keppard, [Joe] Oliver, [Johnny and Warren] Dodds, and Louis [Armstrong]." Unfortunately, the writer contended, "the only Negro musicians to ever get in the movies have been Louis Armstrong and Cab Calloway. Because they are funny men" who "show the whites of their eyes and their teeth and act like a 'Hollywood coon' is supposed to act."[38]

In Oakland, ballrooms offered "white-only" and "colored-only" nights as late as 1946, and the police department "unofficially endorsed this 'Jim Crow–Crow Jim' policy." In Los Angeles, the *California Eagle* frequently complained about restrictive practices in local clubs and ballrooms, including Sebastian's Cotton Club in Culver City, the Pan-Pacific ballroom, and the Palomar. As we have noted, there was segregation even in the musicians' union, with separate white and Black union locals in Los Angeles; again, studio jobs, the very best of the pickings, were reserved exclusively for white musicians. Lee Young lost his position as the only African American playing in the (white) orchestra on a Hollywood network program due to "outside pressure" in 1943. According to the trumpet player Art Farmer, who moved west from Phoenix, Arizona, during the war, "Young black musicians caught hell in Los Angeles in the late forties and early fifties. White musicians had the work at the few clubs sewed up, and it wasn't easy getting into the studios, even if you were good enough."[39]

With the death of his parents, the breakup of his and his brother's band, and the Tolbert children leaving the household as they matured, Young's Los Angeles moorings loosened. In the winter of 1943 he played with Dizzy Gillespie in New York City, and then with the Gillespie-Pettiford band at the Onyx on Fifty-second Street in the spring of that year; after moving down the street to the Yacht Club, Gillespie's combo played opposite a band that included Lester and Trummy Young backing the vocalist Billy Eckstine. Then the tenor stylist appeared with Al Sears's band at several Harlem nightspots before touring with this unit for the USO. As a civilian he played at bases all over the United States, likely never dreaming that in little more than a year he himself would be a soldier.[40]

The Basie band still held considerable appeal for him, and at the urging of Jo Jones, he rejoined it in late 1943. No doubt the Basieites provided him with a sense of family, and New York and the road soon became his familiar home again. In their midst he was with close friends and could experience once more their warm camaraderie. Given World War II and the policies of the draft boards, however, this situation could not last.

CHAPTER 12

D.B. Blues

Tribulation and Trial, 1943–1945

THE Basie orchestra would be Young's home for a little less than a year this time. These were glory days for Young and his colleagues, thanks to the popularity of dance bands and entertainment in U.S. cities during World War II. The draft took its toll, though, inducting bassist Walter Page in the late summer of 1943 (before Young returned) and then saxophonist Jack Washington. The orchestra found replacements as necessary, traveled widely, and made some important records. The Basieites played the Blue Room in the Hotel Lincoln, a significant engagement for a Black band, for fifty-seven consecutive dates in November and December of 1943. The glory of this engagement was marred only by the drafting of Buck Clayton in mid-November.[1]

After its last date at the Lincoln, on January 1, 1944, the band actually got a night off before touring until the middle of the month. Weeklong bookings in Newark, Pittsburgh, Detroit, and Milwaukee were followed by two nights in Cincinnati and a series of untraceable one-nighters over ten days in February; after another week in Philadelphia, it was back to New York City's Roxy for twenty-five consecutive nights. A Fats Waller memorial concert at Carnegie Hall on April 2, 1944, preceded several more weeks in the Lincoln Hotel's Blue Room. In early June the Basieites were off to New England before spending ten days at Chicago's Regal Theatre.[2]

Thereafter, Basie's orchestra resumed its ceaseless travel, alternating week's stints in big cities with one-nighters—from Chicago to Columbus, Cleveland, and Youngstown, Ohio, then to Kansas City—before ending up in Los Angeles in late July. The Count Basie Stars, namely "Lefty" Young, Jo Jones, Dicky Wells, and Harry Edison, were featured at the second Jazz at the Philharmonic concert, on Sunday afternoon, July 30. Two weeks at the Orpheum Theatre were followed by a week at the Golden Gate Ballroom in San Francisco, after which the Basieites went across the bay to the Orpheum in Oakland for the last week of August. After two nights at Sweet's Ballroom in early September, they stayed in one place, Los Angeles, for a time, playing at the Club Plantation in Watts for twenty-eight consecutive nights.[3]

Young and the rest of Basie's entourage enjoyed their popularity as only bandsmen who had scuffled for years could. The crowds loved them, and they received rave reviews, especially in Los Angeles, where one critic noted, "Proof that the current stage show at the Orpheum this week is made to order for the hepcats and hepchicks, is the fact that the good Count Basie and his band and revue [have been] held over for a second week." This was quite an honor, one that had been accorded to no other band "in all Orpheum history." Furthermore, the *California Eagle* predicted, "This is the show that will go down in Orpheum books as the greatest in Orpheum history." Only once before, for Lena Horne, had "crowds stood three and four abreast for nearly a block waiting to get anything that looked like a seat."[4]

The Club Plantation engagement was touted as one "that will most assuredly go down in nightclub history as the hottest and grooviest thirty-day stint ever played on the nightclub circuit." The fact that Joe Morris's club did not practice racial discrimination, plus the air conditioning, ensured a positive experience for fans, who included "the average wage earner." The reviewer asserted that no mere description could do justice to the Basie orchestra, which "must be heard in person to be fully appreciated." The club's nightly floor shows showcased "two mad characters of comedy, Pork Chops Paterson and Jackson Shorts Davis," the singer Thelma Carpenter, and other acts, but the "magnet that will draw the hepcats and hepchicks is Count Basie." The band played "mostly on the jump side, but it is also a band whose playing doesn't give you cauliflower ears." Its music "had the . . . hepcats and hepchicks literally rockin' in rhythm." Another selling point was that "their playing makes conversation, while dancing, possible."[5]

Young was no doubt featured when "the Kansas City Seven came down from their respective chairs in the bandstand to beat out a couple of torrid tunes." One night the audience was pleasantly surprised "when Tommy Dorsey, seated at a ringside table with Pat Dane, Dave Rose,

Buddy Rich, and Gloria DeHaven, came out on the floor, borrowed a trombone from one of the boys in the band, and blew up a mess o' sharps and flats."[6]

Mention of the Dorseys and other white musicians such as Buddy Rich, as well as the movie star Gloria DeHaven, highlighted the fact that the club was integrated and thereby not only drew working Blacks but also regularly attracted white fans and entertainers, leaders of bands in their own right, and Hollywood types. A photograph of Basie posing with Mr. and Mrs. Dorsey, club owner Joe Morris, DeHaven, Rose, and others dramatized the integrated atmosphere as well as the high times. On the band's last night at the club, a valediction party was held, with guest artists including Art Tatum, Tommy Dorsey, Buddy Rich, and the famous dance team of the Nicholas Brothers.[7]

For Young, being in southern California meant that his brother, sister, nieces and nephews, and wives and lady friends—Beatrice, Mary, and Teddy Bear—could hear him play, and he could visit with them. Then there were the jam sessions and opportunities to meet with friends. But the much-publicized and long-term stint in Los Angeles also proved to be his undoing: in late September 1944, Young's draft board caught up with him and sent a federal agent to the Club Plantation.

Young had several reasons to think he might not be drafted. Buddy Tate was sure that the army would never take someone who drank a quart of Old Granddad whiskey a day. Budd Johnson toured with Young in Al Sears's USO band in 1943 and recalled that the saxophone stylist drank first thing in the morning, all day long, and just before going to sleep. He bought five or six bottles at a time, explaining to Johnson, "'I never want to lose this feeling . . . [that] I had when I made it with the horn, all the records with Basie and everything.'"[8]

The military's zeal and methods were illustrated by the means it resorted to in ordering Young and Jo Jones to report for induction. One night a young white zoot-suiter bought the Basie band members drinks at the Club Plantation and made a point of befriending Young and Jones. As Buddy Tate recounted the scenario, "He came on . . . [and] we just thought he was one of the . . . hip boys. . . . [But then] at the end of the night, he pulled his coat back like this, told Pres and Jo Jones where to be at nine o'clock that next morning, says, 'F.B.I. . . . If you aren't there, we will come after you.'" Tate recalled, "It really got Pres. . . . He was kind of sensitive, and man, that high voice really came out: 'Man' [Pres exclaimed], 'ain't that a bitch? . . . Well, goddamn . . . [the] little guy gained my confidence. . . . I liked the little son of a bitch. . . . You know, I started to turn him on.' "[9]

Young and Jones reported for induction on September 30, 1944, and while others' memories of precisely what transpired are hazy, the tenor stylist's behavior suggested that he probably did not expect to be drafted. Lee Young, who had been excused from service because of back problems, remembered that his brother showed up at the draft board with his saxophone case and a bottle of liquor. Young told the examining doctors that he smoked marijuana. When it became clear that the army was in fact going to take him, he fled the base. Lee Young testified that at some point during this period he took his brother "down on Eighth Street to be inducted, and he . . . went to Fort MacArthur, but that night he was sitting right in the front row when I opened up and started playing [at the Downbeat]." Lee informed him that he was in serious trouble. Shortly thereafter, Lester was arrested and hauled before a judge in Pasadena, who would not accept his excuse that the required spinal would prevent him from playing his horn.[10]

Jo Jones and Young were together for a time during basic training. After several weeks of that grueling training in California, the tenor stylist was transferred to Fort McClellan, in the northeast corner of Alabama, near the birthplace of the Ku Klux Klan, where he suffered a minor injury and had to be hospitalized. Upon his release, he was immediately assigned to duty. From the beginning it was obvious that he would not make a good soldier, but as other musicians pointed out, some officers could be very stubborn about making new recruits conform. A photo of Young and Jones playing their instruments in a jam session at Fort Ord appeared in *Down Beat,* but it was just a publicity stunt; fellow musicians, including his brother, expressed the opinion that Pres was not capable of ascertaining the proper procedure by which to make a request to get into a band unit.[11]

One day early in 1945 an army officer discovered marijuana on Young's person, and the saxophonist admitted to being high. A thorough search of his belongings turned up some pills. In the aftermath of the antimarijuana shocker *Reefer Madness,* a film that presented smokers as perverts and fiends, Young was put under detention, court-martialed, convicted, and ordered to be dishonorably discharged following a term of imprisonment at hard labor. He served the sentence and in late 1945 was released at Camp Gordon, near Augusta, Georgia.

Young's military experience, tragic though it was, was not all that different from many others'. At the war's outset, white bands were drafted as units to entertain servicemen, but the same was not true for Black bands. The shortage of musicians due to the draft meant that young Black band members could get better jobs, and veteran sidemen could work venues previously monopolized by whites. Buck Clayton explained that during the war, the Basieites "were just beginning to make money, 'cause we [had] made fourteen dollars a week in Kansas City . . . and we were just [now] getting to the point where we were making pretty good money." The new opportunities, he said, were such that "nobody [i.e., no Black musicians] wanted to go into the Army"—something of an exaggeration, but one that nevertheless had some substance.[12]

The economic opportunities afforded them by the war and by the drafting of white bands made Black musicians want to earn as much money as they could *while* they could. Setting aside the nation's, the military's, and the music industry's traditions of racism, the chance to make a decent salary for once was a sufficient incentive to dodge the draft. Especially during the early years of the war, Bootsie, the cartoon character created by Ollie Harrington, tried to avoid the draft by means that were laughable, but he accurately represented one line of thought in contemporary African American culture.[13]

Given the rare opportunities that had opened up for them, Black musicians' lack of enthusiasm for the military was understandable, as their sudden prosperity resulted from the spending of money that had been out of circulation during the Depression. While some African Americans dodged the draft, others, on reporting for induction, relied on various stratagems to escape service. Malcolm Little (later Malcolm X), for example, feigned a kind of lunacy manifested by an eagerness to join up and "kill . . . crackers." Buck Clayton reminisced that when other inductees went "down to be examined . . . they'd have on women's underwear, and someone would try to pass as gay, they'd have lipstick and stuff on. Others would try to be sick. They'd take Benzedrine, mix it up with Coca-Cola, and then you can't sleep. I did that, I know. I couldn't sleep for four nights. [At the physical] my heart was just pounding, and I had such a headache that they took me anyway, 'cause they knew it wasn't normal for my heart to be beating so."[14]

Lee Young shed some light on Black musicians' antipathy toward the army and the draft when he remarked that in California, "all the white musicians from out here were based right at Santa Ana air base." Black musicians learned just how malicious the military could be in its deployment of troops: Young contended that Black northerners were invariably sent to the South, while Black southerners were sent north to be "broken."[15]

The army probably did not harbor a grudge against Basie band members, though it certainly seemed that way at times. When Buck Clayton lost his draft card, he wrote for a new one to keep from going to jail, and it was then that he received his induction notice. In his autobiography, Clayton recounted how some officers made his life difficult because they knew he had been in Basie's orchestra. When he performed as a soldier with Sy Oliver and Mercer Ellington in New Jersey camps, he was often required to play late into the night, only to be forced to get up again at five in the morning.

Still, Clayton conceded, "I was . . . lucky . . . very lucky. Lester wasn't that lucky. . . . At my induction, there were three fellows that I knew very well, and they were musicians. They happened to be in the office of the reception center, and . . . whenever they'd get a roster, they'd have to call off all the names and put these people on the boat. . . . The only reason that I wasn't shipped over [to Europe] . . . was because they wanted me to stay to play in the [recruitment center's] band."[16] His luck and the fact that he was stationed so close to New York City meant that Clayton was able to make the best of his situation, earning money at jobs in the Empire City and participating in jam sessions.

Many musicians easily dodged the draft, at least for a while, because they were in constant motion. When Jay McShann heard of his board's desire to draft him, he asked that his papers be forwarded first to New York and then to California, after he headed out to the West Coast. Despite his flat feet, the board ordered his immediate induction because he kept missing his notices. Assigned to antiaircraft training, the shrewd pianist volunteered to play at the officers' club, and the officers in turn protected him, informing him of upcoming bivouacs and permitting him to hide and get out of such military excursions. Other officers had biases against certain soldiers. These "eager beavers," McShann recalled, would "do unheard of things[, saying,] 'I'll make this cat a soldier, I'll make him do [such and such].'" The guitarist John Collins charged that the army "could destroy a person," especially one who did not stand up for himself. Collins himself "did an awful lot of extra duty" as punishment for avoiding training. He was eventually transferred to a band unit, but not before being assigned to unload boxcars and, when he balked, wash windows on Thanksgiving Day.[17]

Lester Young's military career reflected the racism and "antidrug" atmosphere of the times, but it also revealed his uncompromising character and refusal to give in. It is important to note, in this context, that he was basically nonviolent—"the most nonviolent person you ever met," according to Red Callender. Rodney Richardson, Basie's bassist after Page was inducted, recalled that Young "wasn't a fighting person. Loved everything. I couldn't imagine Pres shooting somebody." If he had been more ideologically oriented, he might have filed for conscientious-objector status, though that, too, would also have entailed a jail sentence—the fate of such different individuals as the civil rights activist Bayard Rustin and the head of the Nation of Islam, Elijah Muhammad.[18]

While Young himself rarely discussed the episode, some independent documentation exists. Most significant are the transcript of the trial and court-martial records (available under the Freedom of Information Act), which shed light on the workings of the military as well as on Young's character, specifically his refusal to lie or to compromise, and the possibility that he knew precisely what he was doing and had good reasons for serving the sentence imposed on him. The transcript also contains Young's own explanation of why he took pills and smoked marijuana daily. Beyond these official reports, we also have the testimony of a few of the saxophonist's close associates.

In 1946 Young would describe his experience of the previous year as "a nightmare, man, one mad nightmare." Although his records indicate that he was stationed in Alabama, Young maintained, "They sent me down south, Georgia. That was enough to make me blow my top. It was a drag, Jack." He could not or would not recall details; "all he remembers," an interviewer noted, "was hating the army with a furious intensity, hating the brass, reveille, injustice to Negroes and the caste system in the South. . . . [The] disciplinary center in Savannah [*sic*] . . . was sheer hell."[19]

The army's evaluation and testimony during Young's court-martial reveal something of the nature of the American military and its procedures, as well as giving a glimpse into this particular soldier's character. On February 16, 1945, Young appeared before the court-martial, charged with "violation of the 96th Article of War": "On or about 30 January 1945, [he did] wrongfully have in his possession habit-forming drugs, to wit, about one ounce of marijuana and about one ounce of barbiturates, said drugs not having been ordered by a medical officer of the army." Given Young's testimony as to their use, the alleged "barbiturates" were probably not that, as barbiturates are "downers"; these were more likely "uppers," of the sort that truck drivers and students often take. Much of the testimony was matter-of-fact, though the inordinate attention paid to particular details of evidence, the complete disregard of other important matters, and Young's total cooperation with the authorities combined to lend a surreal quality to the trial.[20]

Apparently the military intended to proceed with business as usual, prosecuting Young without giving any consideration to the more difficult issues raised by his case. Army records described Private Young's "previous military service [basic training] as poor." His unit had rated him as the "worst sort and very unsuited for the military." After three weeks' stay in the hospital in early January 1945, during which time he was given medication several times a day, Young was diagnosed by Captain Luis Perelman, the chief of the Neuropsychiatric Service, as being in a "Constitutional Psychopathic State, manifested by drug addiction (marijuana, barbiturates), chronic alcoholism and nomadism." Furthermore, the captain classified the private as "purely a disciplinary problem and [recommended] that disposition should be effected through administrative channels."[21]

This assessment of Young, based on his records and his own testimony, noted that he had had a "poor [school] record" and "poor family adjustment." He had been arrested several times on minor charges before his induction. Taking into account his "excessive drinking and drug addiction for [the] last ten years," the captain suggested that "his undesirable traits and inadequate personality [render him] unlikely to become a satisfactory soldier."[22]

Whether or not the army was seeking to make an example out of Young is not altogether clear. More interesting is that the court-martial did not follow up on the lead he provided as to who had given him the barbiturates; did not clarify whether he was sent out with a pack before or after the discovery of the "narcotics," as the army repeatedly called them; and did not settle the issue as to whether the hospital had deemed him sufficiently recovered to go on military maneuvers.

Captain William C. Stevenson's testimony that he "had suspicioned [Young's use of pills or marijuana] when he first came in the company," a little after December 1, 1944, is noteworthy. He had said nothing at the time, he explained, because Young "had good control of himself." Stevenson was suspicious of Young because of "his color . . . and the fact that his eyes seemed bloodshot and he didn't react to his training as he should." Several weeks later, after Young's release from the hospital, Stevenson found him sitting in the day room "when he should have been outdoors training." The testifying officer's earlier suspicions had been confirmed by "a statement [received] right from the hospital," and he took the opportunity to question Private Young about his use of "narcotics." Young conceded that he used them but insisted that he had none in his possession. The captain testified that he then informed the private that the habit was "injurious to his health" and warned him to refrain from using drugs. On cross-examination, Stevenson admitted that he did not advise Young to "go on sick-call, report to the hospital,"[23] or seek counseling. In this respect, the officer was derelict in his duty.

Two days later, Young was "on assignment to battalion headquarters and . . . didn't seem to be in a very good condition." When Captain Stevenson asked him if anything was wrong, "[Young] said that he was 'high.'" When questioned further, the private produced some pills. Then his clothing and possessions were searched. "Several small white pills . . . three red capsules and some marijuana cigarettes . . . [and] two bottles of pink liquid . . . one with a very raw smell . . . [or] sensation . . . like . . . alcohol" were discovered. On January 30, 1945, the evidence was turned over to a chemist from the Atlanta Narcotics Division, who "happened to be here [Fort McClellan] on that same day." Tests performed on the samples substantiated the army's suspicions.[24]

On February 5, 1945, Private Lester Young was examined by Lieutenant Joe B. Humphreys, the investigation officer, who advised him of his rights and talked with him for some time. Lieutenant Humphreys took down Young's statement; when asked to relate the testimony to the court, he did so from memory. The private had informed him, he said, that "he had been using—I believe he used the word 'dope,' for eleven years and smoking marijuana for ten"; as a saxophone player in Count Basie's orchestra and other bands, "he resorted to the use of marijuana smoking and called them 'sticks.'" On the day in question, Young "had gotten these barbiturates—I know he referred to the marijuana, and that he intended to hide it and I guess he got to feeling too good and he forgot to hide it before Captain Stevenson got it."

After consulting the written statement to refresh his memory, Lieutenant Humphreys continued. Young had told him, he testified, that though some doctors had given him drugs, he had no prescription from any army doctor; he observed, however, that at Fort McClellan "you could get [drugs] if you had the money to buy [them]." Private Young furthermore "stated that he had never harmed anyone, [and said that] he told the authorities before coming in about [habits]. He never harmed anyone."

On cross-examination, the lieutenant repeated Young's assertion that "he had never made any denial of having used drugs or smoking marijuana or either one." Evidently Humphreys had enjoyed their dialogue, or at least had learned a great deal from it "about the effects of marijuana and the places where people would congregate to smoke marijuana and the effect it would have." Like Stevenson, Humphreys admitted that he had never brought up the possibility of counseling or hospitalization with the private. In both instances, the army failed to act responsibly—in fact, in Stevenson's case, it could be argued that he actually contributed to the private's behavior by not intervening before it became a disciplinary matter.[25]

The private's defense counsel waived the right to make an opening statement, instructed the accused of his rights, and informed the court of his desire to testify. It is noteworthy and indicative of Young's steadfast honesty that he chose to take the stand after pleading not guilty. He was not required to testify. His lack of knowledge of army protocol was evident in his confusion in the face of a simple question intended to establish his grade in the army—which was, of course, private. Young explained why he had been taking "narcotics" for ten years: "In the band we would play a lot of one-nighters. I would stay up and play another dance and leave and that is the only way I could keep up." When asked if other musicians had similar habits, the private replied, "Yeah, all that I know."

Young detailed his initial encounter with the military in Los Angeles when questioned as to whether he had informed his draft board of his habits: "Before I went to join the army I had to take a spinal, and I didn't want to take it; and when I went down, I was very high, and they put me in jail, and I was so high they took the whiskey away from me and put me in a padded cell, and they searched my clothes while I was in the cell."[26] Apparently it was just the first in a series of humiliating experiences he would have courtesy of the army: his clothing was stripped off him to be searched. Asked what he had taken to get high that day, Young cited "whiskey and . . . marijuana and . . . barbiturates." He also reported that he had informed the army of his habits again when he was hospitalized in January, after injuring himself on an obstacle course.

The army might reasonably have provided some kind of treatment for

Young if it was so intent on turning him into a soldier. But it didn't—and what was worse, it in fact exacerbated the problem: an army physician, Captain LeBell, gave him barbiturates during his three-week hospital stay. No one at the trial pursued this line of questioning, however, perhaps because the court did not wish to implicate any officers. Another puzzling detail concerns whether Young was sent into the field immediately after his release from the hospital, and whether the hospital even considered him fit for bivouac. Nor does the court-martial transcript shed any light on whether he went on bivouac before or after the discovery of the "drugs." It would have been somewhat unusual for him to be sent out after a search turned up "narcotics" (the army's term for all of the items found) in his belongings.

Young's lack of knowledge of military terminology was apparent once again when he was questioned about the type of pack he had carried in the field: "[Did you] carry a full pack?" His response, "I don't know," occasioned a clarification: Had he carried a "light pack"? "A pack and a rifle," he answered. Asked what he meant by "being very high," he insisted, "That's the only way I know how to explain myself."

Without marijuana, he testified, "I don't want to do anything, I don't care to blow my horn and I don't care to be around anybody." When asked if he could train in the military without such help, he replied candidly, "No, sir. . . . I tried it, sir, I tried it truthfully." He also stated that he became nervous without "drugs." When asked, "Feel pretty nervous now?," the saxophonist answered, "I think about it all the time."

The defense turned the witness over to the prosecution, who asked if Young had obtained the drugs without a doctor's prescription. The private explained that in the hospital, Captain LeBell "was giving me the same pills you have there . . . one at nine o'clock in the morning and one in the afternoon and five at night and nine o'clock at night." When asked if "they" had told him why they were giving him "barbiturates," Young said, "No, sir, because I was in another hospital and they gave me some pills [without any explanation]."

Following this revelation, the defense asked whether the hospital had assigned him to military duties in the sick-book, to which the private responded, "That is not what they told me but when I got there I found out." He was asked to clarify this statement, but the prosecution objected, which led to a legal dispute about hearsay evidence. After that the questioning shifted to Young's having been sent out into the field with a pack and a rifle. Whether this had been proper procedure was never settled. The defense then turned the witness back over to the prosecution; after posing a few queries concerning his earlier testimony, the prosecution turned him over to the court, which declined to ask further questions. Young stepped down and resumed his seat, and the defense rested its case. The prosecution waived its opening statement, evidently confident of a conviction. No closing argument by the defense or final argument by the prosecution was reported in the transcript before the court was closed.[27]

That very day, the court reached the verdict of guilty. Subsequently, Lieutenant William S. Moffet Jr., the assistant staff judge advocate, wrote that in view of the evidence, "together with the possibility that his undesirable traits may be corrected by proper treatment and disciplinary training[,] it is recommended that the sentence [of one year] be approved" and that Young be remanded to the U.S. Disciplinary Barracks in Fort Leavenworth, Kansas. The punishment also included forfeiture of all pay and allowances and a dishonorable discharge, which was to be suspended until the sentence of one year's confinement at hard labor had been completed. While Young was to serve his term at Fort Leavenworth, his transfer there was delayed on February 27 "pending further orders"; he in fact ended up serving out his sentence in the post stockade at Fort McClellan, and possibly also at Camp Gordon, Georgia.[28]

Young's refusal to lie or dissemble may have bothered the army officers as much as anything else he did. His repeated statement that he had never hurt anyone suggested that he minded his own business and let others mind theirs. It is significant that the army did not ask Young whom he had purchased the pills from or, for that matter, what role Dr. LeBell had played in all of this. Moreover, the court did not clearly establish that the evidence presented was the same confiscated from Young. Nor was the Atlanta Narcotics Division chemist in court to testify that the "drugs" were really what the army claimed they were—a curious absence, especially considering that the man had been on the base when Young was searched and thus would logically be a credible witness. The small bottles containing an alleged alcoholic substance were not produced as evidence or even mentioned again after the first time. That the chemist did not return to testify and the army failed to adhere to the rules of evidence indicates that the trial was merely a formality.

Young's sentence seems quite harsh given that he had had no previous convictions in the military, a fact that the army documents mention more than once. The army's failure to provide medical help or counseling for Young, its refusal to follow up on the person identified by him as the source of the pills and to clarify whether he had in fact been fit to be sent out into the field, and the careless handling of the evidence—all of these suggest that the proceedings were a sham, that the decision had already been made about his fate, and the prosecution and defense were simply going through the motions.

There is one other very interesting angle to this story, however, and that is the possibility that Young knew exactly what he was doing. As a member of an infantry replacement unit, he was in line to be sent to either the European or the Pacific theater to take the place of a wounded or deceased soldier, and then likely be wounded or killed himself. The timing of the incident was significant, because training lasted six weeks, and he was placed under arrest after five. He may have figured that a year in the stockade—as a worst-case scenario—was preferable to combat, and that on his release he could return to the Basie band. A further disincentive was provided around this time by the Battle of the Bulge, with its high casualty rates on both sides, which seemed to foreshadow the kind of carnage that lay ahead for the Allies.[29]

The military experiences of another musician, William Woodman, afford some additional insights into Young's case. Woodman was from Los Angeles and, like Lester, had been a member of a family band led by his father. Having attended integrated schools in California, he detested racism; in his words, he "was very bitter against prejudice." When, during World War II, he had the misfortune to be drafted and shipped down south, he knew right away that he wanted out. Fortunately—if only to this end—he discovered that he suffered from narcolepsy, an illness that caused him to have sleeping spells. While he was truly prone to fall asleep when on duty, he also faked it at times, and in this way manipulated the system until he got a medical discharge. (Young, in contrast, was not capable of this sort of subterfuge.) Half a century later, Woodman would assert his belief that if he had had to stay in the service down south, he either would have been seriously hurt by racists or would have become a dope addict.[30]

While the military focused on Young's use of "narcotics," others have maintained that it was the fact that he had a white wife that led to his court-martial, or at least spurred the army's zeal to prosecute him. Gene Ramey stated that Young had actually brought Mary Dale down south with him, while Jo Jones was under the impression that the discovery of her photo during the search of Young's belongings had enraged one of the officers involved. Jones further claimed that a major had framed Young and that the original sentence had been for five years, at hard labor. "Later on, when the truth came out," he explained, "to save face for the major, they didn't reverse the decision entirely, but reduced it to one year . . . [in] the detention barracks."[31]

This aspect of the case did not surface in the trial, but it is significant that these two musicians, both good friends of Young's, believed that racism had played a role in the court-martial. But even if it was not triggered by Mary Young's presence or by her photo, racism was undoubtedly a factor in the case, since Young's behavior and, significantly, his insistence on absolute honesty—two byproducts of his devout and strict upbringing in an African American household in the Deep South—seemed to be enough to cause the army officers to seek his conviction.

The military, however, could also make life difficult for white soldiers who defied segregation. The recording executive John Hammond, for example, got into considerable trouble in the service because he insisted on promoting integrated musical affairs and visiting Black sections of the bases to hear good musicians. He was repeatedly rebuked, forced to justify his actions, and transferred because of his defiance of southern Jim Crow laws and customs. On one occasion he came close to being court-martialed himself for insubordination. After being upbraided and assigned to KP for fraternizing with a Black soldier, Hammond recalled, "I had begun my defiance, my well-ingrained refusal to go along when the situation conflicted with my own convictions of fairness." This white grandson of a Union general "could never quite remember that I was [a] private . . . in a military hierarchy whose patterns of behavior had nothing to do with my principles." Again and again he defied the military brass, but family connections—a cousin by marriage was a major general, and his brother-in-law was another ranking officer—and his white skin saved him every time.[32]

Young's experiences in the detention barracks were obscured by both his reticence to talk and conflicting testimony. A few associates, however, reported his difficulties. Ramey claimed that drunken soldiers beat the tenor stylist: "Every night those guards would get drunk and come out there and have target practice on his head." Moreover, Ramey added, "I think he had lots of blows on his skull" that subsequently affected his coordination. His bassist, Rodney Richardson, asserted that Young "never did want to talk [about it]. . . . But he did tell me he almost got killed in the army. Someone saved him."[33]

Jo Jones said he was one of Young's guards at Fort McClellan, and recalled the tenor saxophonist's asking him to bring him his horn. The drummer reported that once, when Young was sent out on a detail to build a bridge, he fled, only to return again. Buddy Tate contended that Young was detained under terrible conditions until Norman Granz intervened, insisting, "'You've got to let this man out of here.'"[34] Fortunately for Young, the war ended, and he was released in 1945, after nearly fifteen months in the army. The effects of his stint in the military and his incarceration were probably blunted by a surge in his popularity after the war and a life with new family responsibilities.

Young's army experience is invariably cited as a significant turning point in his career because it allegedly changed his personality and also his playing. Richardson, for example, felt that "before he went in the army, he was bubbly. He was an extrovert in that sense. . . . And when he came out he was always backing up, [and] he backed up till the end. He died backing up." Writers and musicians have so frequently emphasized Young's supposed postwar decline that it has become an integral part of the legend about the loss of creativity suffered by this great American jazzman. More recently, scholars such as Lewis Porter, as well as Young's brother, Lee, have called into question the notion that Pres's creativity declined, and some of his musicians have also viewed the usual portrait with skepticism.[35]

That racism in the military was little different from racism in the rest of American society—and within the music industry itself—has for some reason seemed too unpleasant a possibility for many observers to consider. Likewise ignored is that McCarthyism after the war may have influenced some in the music business to regard a musician with a dishonorable discharge as a pariah. As we shall see, the narrow-minded thinking of recording executives and promotional people, and changes in the industry, probably affected Young's career far more than his time in the U.S. Army.

1. *Billy Young's jazz band, Minneapolis, 1927, with Lester's father, Willis, conducting, and Lester (far right) on alto sax. (Dr. Alice T. Plummer)*

2. *Lester's mother, Lizetta Young, and her three children lived in one side of a double shotgun dwelling, such as the one above, in New Orleans back-o'-town neighborhoods around World War I.*

3. Bayou Lafourche, southwest of New Orleans. Willis Young hailed from nearby Thibodaux.

4. Professor Willis Handy Young played all instruments and featured his children on saxophones in the 1920s. (Mary Young Collection)

5. Sarah Young, Lester's stepmother, played baritone saxophone and led the "show" for which the professor's band performed. (Lucille T. Bland)

6. "She sure loved Lester," recalled Lester's sister, Irma. This tender portrait of Lizetta and Lester suggests their close relationship. (Mary Young Collection)

7. The New Orleans Strutters, Lexington, Kentucky, 1924, with musicians including Sarah Young (front left) on baritone sax, Willis Young (center) on trumpet, and (at Willis's right) Lester on tenor sax. The Strutters outfit included a "show" of blackface comedians, dancers, and singers, shown here behind the musicans. (Mary Young Collection)

8. Left to right: Austin "Boots," Mary, William H., and William "Sport" Young, uncle and cousins of Lester, c. 1914. (Larry Young)

9. *"Boots" Young, Tom (last name unknown), "Sport" Young, and Lester (on C melody), Galveston, Texas, c. 1921. (Mary Young Collection)*

10. *The New Orleans Strutters, Minot, North Dakota, c. 1928, with Otto "Pete" Brown (trombone), and Lester's sister, Irma Young (alto saxophone), at left. Lee Young (in blackface) is seated on the steps with Sarah Young. The infant, Martha, is Irma's daughter. (William Young)*

11. Mary Elizabeth Hunter ("Aunt Mamie"), the professor's elder sister, widow of a minister, who lived with her younger brother and his family in Los Angeles. (Crawford W. Brown)

12. Herb Cowens (standing), drummer, and his close friend, reedman, and leader Henry "Buster" Smith, former Blue Devil and coleader of the Reno Club band, Dallas, 1986.

13. Pres performs with Count Basie. (IJS)

14. Pres listens to Basie. (Mary Young Collection)

15. Star soloist in the Basie orchestra, the saxophonist takes command of the moment, propelling bandsmen and listeners to heights of ecstasy at the Festival of Swing, Randalls Island, New York City, 1938.

16. Lee and Irma Young, c. 1940. (Crawford W. Brown)

17. Lester Young sideman Julian "Junior" Mance at the piano, c. 1950. (Le Roy Jackson Collection)

18. Lee Young during Nat "King" Cole tour, London, 1960. (Photograph © Val Wilmer)

19. *Kelly's Stable band, Manhattan, 1941. Left to right: Harold "Doc" West (drums), Shad Collins (trumpet), Pres, Nick Fenton (bass), Clyde Hart (piano), John Collins, guitar. (Mary Young Collection)*

20. *Lady Day and Pres. (Mary Young Collection)*

21. Pres in Paris, with an unidentified musician. (Photograph by Daniel Filipacchi, Paris, courtesy Val Wilmer)

22. *Pres in Paris. (Photograph by Daniel Filipacchi, Paris, courtesy Val Wilmer)*

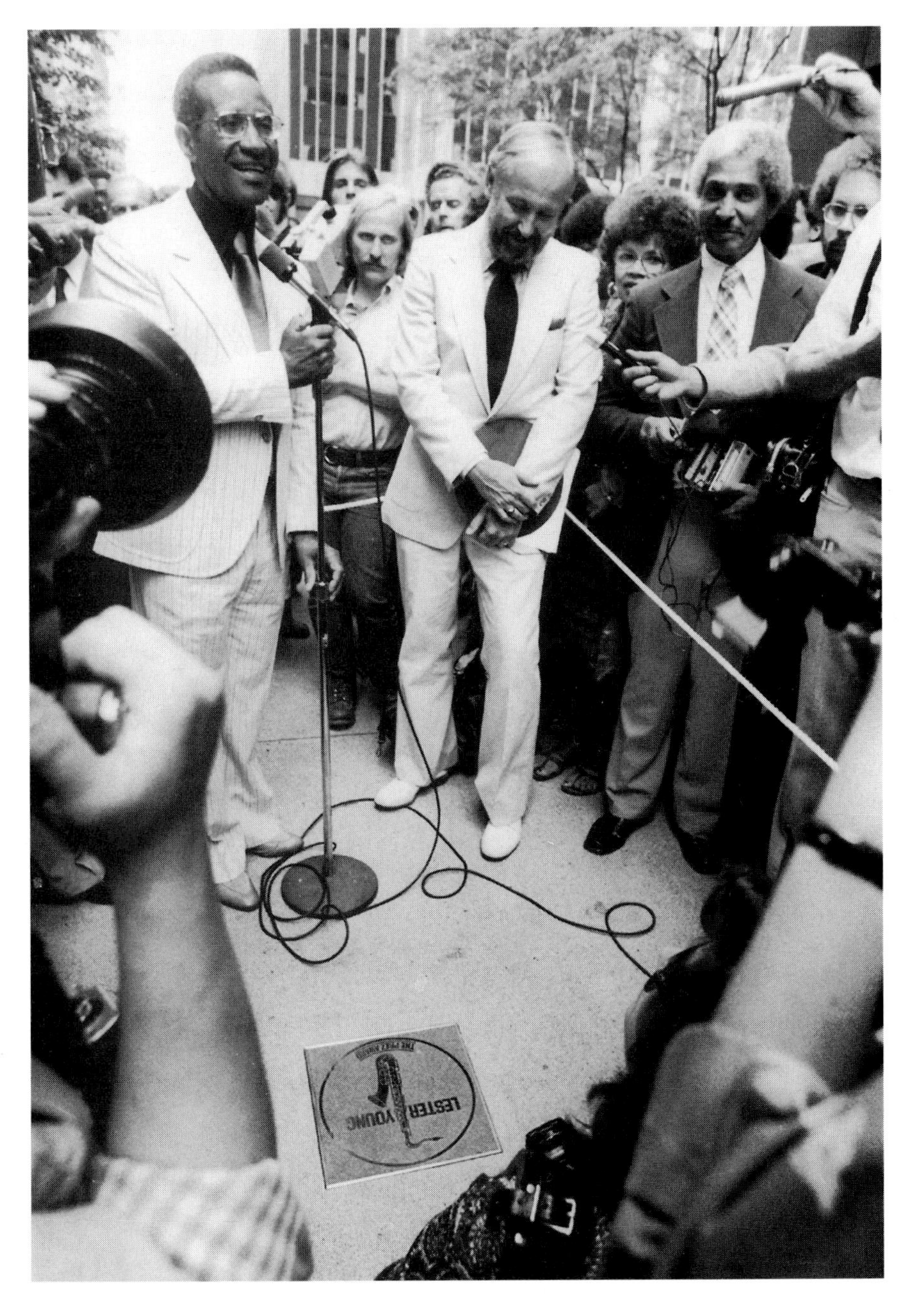

23. Drummer Max Roach (at microphone), fans, and reporters at the Prez Awards ceremony on Fifty-second Street, New York City. (IJS)

24. George "Red" Callender, bassist, composer, and leader, 1983.

PART III

Up Here by Myself

In [the] middle and late fifties before things got better . . . you had to go into another country to . . . be treated like a man if you were in a black band.

Marshal Royal, Jazz Oral History Project Interview, Institute of Jazz Studies, Rutgers University, Newark, New Jersey, vol. 3, p. 10

CHAPTER 13

Sax-o-Be-Bop

Life at the Top

YOUNG'S fifteen months in the military were a setback, to be sure, but nonetheless, even here he won some admirers for his unbending resolve to be himself rather than Private Young. As Connie Kay noted, some people would have gone insane if they had had to suffer what the tenor stylist endured. Less than a year after his court-martial, Young was on the West Coast again, recording in the studio; he had received his official (dishonorable) discharge sometime around December 1945.[1]

From 1945 on, though, many critics and some of their readers, as well as numerous promoters, club owners, and fans, would regard Young's post-Basie period as a never-ending spiral of declining musical abilities and physical health. Not everyone saw it that way, however; contemporary reviews of his performances, both live and recorded, offer another picture. His concerts, records, and successes were in fact regularly praised in the African American press, and he remained a cultural as well as a musical hero to many fans. He was also profoundly respected by countless musicians at precisely the same time that writers were describing his playing as passé.[2]

We can learn something of the gap between the world of the record reviewers for the trade journals and that of the jazz fans themselves by examining Young's career in the late 1940s and early 1950s. By paying greater attention to Black newspapers and to the opinions of musicians who knew Young and played with him, we can gain a better understanding than we could ever hope to do if we simply accepted the usual subjective portrayal of an older, eccentric musician on a downward trajectory. In the late 1940s, when he was often depicted as a has-been in the white press, Young was very clearly being heralded as a major innovator by both Black and white audiences at dates in posh nightclubs and corner bars, at Carnegie Hall concerts, and during jam sessions with dancers in tobacco barns down south. His career, in short, was flourishing.

(It is interesting to note, in this context, that no reference to Young's court-martial or imprisonment has ever been found in the mainstream press, in trade journals, or in African American newspapers of the 1940s. Conceivably, the absence of written material may have sparked rumors in show-business circles that were later rekindled by critics to account for changes in the saxophonist's playing and his behavior—and particularly for his eccentricities.)

In November 1945, shortly before his official release from the military, Young signed with Philo, a new independent label under the direction of Norman Granz and his associates (later to become Aladdin). Significantly, the army veteran decided to settle in Los Angeles because his wife, Mary Dale, lived there, as did his brother, his sister, and other relatives and friends. Another draw was the fact that the city was also home to Granz, who would come to play a singular role in Young's career, both by recording him and by persuading him to travel with his Jazz at the Philharmonic (JATP).[3] Originating in Los Angeles in 1944, JATP was one of the first large-scale attempts to make jazz respectable by showcasing its biggest names. Granz, its founder, conceived it as a unique entity and made it into a gathering of top talent that eventually grew from a Los Angeles–based operation that visited American cities into a traveling jazz concert that played all over Europe, in Canada, and as far away as Tokyo, Hong Kong, Manila, and Sydney, Australia.[4]

Granz had started holding jam sessions in Los Angeles clubs while he was still a philosophy student at UCLA; Lee Young had helped him in those endeavors. When he formed Jazz at the Philharmonic, named after the hall at 427 West Fifth Street where the show made its Los Angeles debut in April 1944, no one could foresee its future development. Granz himself, the musicians, and the fans all appreciated the tremendous solidarity and sense of goodwill that resulted from JATP. The cheering throngs in various cities were a part of it, certainly, but even more important were the camaraderie, friendly competition, bantering, and storytelling among the performers themselves, all of which provided another basis for enjoyment of the tour and for the fellowship unique to show-business circles.[5]

At war's end, many dance-band musicians regrouped and rejoined their old outfits, and for a time, *Pittsburgh Courier* readers entertained the hope that Young as well as other former Basie band members might follow suit. The bandleader himself was said to be anticipating "the early return to his band of several of his greatest sidemen who have been in Army service," and in December 1945 it was reported that Jo Jones, Buck Clayton, Ronald "Jack" Washington, and Lester Young had all "signified their intentions of returning to the Basie fold." The newspaper added that no other Black band had seen its ranks so depleted by the draft as Basie's.[6]

Regardless of his band affiliation, Young's reputation as a matchless musician had acquired considerable luster by 1945, when Leonard Feather, writing in *Metronome,* complimented Young, Harry Edison, Marie Bryant, Illinois Jacquet, and others who appeared in the film short *Jammin' the Blues,* which was nominated for an Academy Award that year. Like JATP, the film had an aura of informality about it, the air of an after-hours jam session for musicians and entertainers. As the opening credits roll over what is actually the top of Young's porkpie, the hat tilts back, and first his image and then a close-up of his face fill the screen as he plays "The Midnight Symphony" with the combo. The popular song "On the Sunny Side of the Street" features Bryant singing, followed by a Young solo that he takes seated in the foreground while Bryant looks on. On still another number, "Jammin' the Blues," she jitterbugs with Archie Savage in front of Young and his upraised horn; the rest of the combo is out of the frame for the moment. Often the camera shifts from the other musicians and the singer to Young, showing him lighting a cigarette or taking a seat—an indication of just how much he is the star of the film.[7]

Writing for *Time,* the journalist Walter Winchell hailed the short "as a new sort of camera teknik." He pointed out that *Jammin' the Blues* employed two kinds of lighting: "chiaroscuro, in which the line of a cheek, the wrinkle of a sleeve, the keys of a fingered saxophone, appear as if drawn in white ink on black paper; and its opposite, in which the musicians appear in almost featureless silhouette" against a blank white background. This "teknik" was new to Hollywood, though it had been "commonplace among advanced filmmakers for twenty-five years."[8]

Feather declared that "the best small-band music" he had heard on the West Coast was in this short film. He found it somewhat ironic that this cinematic jam session so far surpassed what he had encountered elsewhere live. Actually, the film's soundtrack was "source music," meaning that it was recorded in a separate session that the musicians then attempted to re-create for the camera; this was the custom at the time. This "best intimate jazz ever recorded for a movie" (in Feather's words) somehow managed not to be marred by a behind-the-scenes dispute over whether to conceal the white identity of guitarist Barney Kessel. In the end, those who wanted to placate southern racists got their way, and so Kessel was silhouetted with backlighting so his race would not be readily apparent. Such issues no doubt reminded Young that the political realities of race discrimination affected even the most seemingly innocuous facets of musicians' performances.[9]

Feather's enthusiasm for the soundtrack was rare praise in print for Young at a time—in the spring of 1945—when, ironically, he sat imprisoned in the army's detention barracks in the Deep South. Record reviews of Young's work with pickup musicians would later be among the most critical reports of the alleged diminution of his abilities, but even they occasionally mentioned superior efforts on his part. A case in point was the series of records Young made that December in Los Angeles with Vic Dickenson, Dodo Marmarosa, Freddie Green, Red Callender, and Henry Tucker Green, some of whom he had recorded with before. They performed "D.B. Blues," "Lester Blows Again," "These Foolish Things," and "Jumping at Mesner's," the last selection named for an Aladdin record executive and associate of Granz's.[10]

Down Beat offered faint praise, observing that "few of [Young's] adherents, some as fanatical as Gillespie's, will be disappointed." The reviewer added, however, that the more discerning might "find the sessions lacking in real excitement and brilliance." Noting a softer tone from the tenor saxophonist, the writer allowed that "his ideas [are] still creative, different, fresh," while carping that "none of them sound particularly inspired." *Metronome*'s review was likewise mixed: "All four sides are typical Lester but sound as though they were made in a hurry . . . with ragged ends and no coordination."[11]

The several Aladdin recordings that Young made in Los Angeles in the late winter and summer of 1946 included a mix of standards—"It's Only a Paper Moon," "Lover Come Back to Me" and "You're Driving Me Crazy"—and traditional Young material such as "Lester Leaps In." He also tipped his hat to the new music with "Lester's Be-Bop Boogie," which is more boogie than bop. The other horns were Vic Dickenson, Howard McGhee, and Willie Smith; a rhythm section composed of Wesley Jones, Curtis Counce, and Johnny Otis completed the septet.[12]

Late in the summer *Metronome* reviewed "It's Only a Paper Moon," "After You've Gone," "Lover Come Back to Me," and "Jammin' with Lester," rating each a C+. Again the reviewer criticized the "slap-happy method of recording," contending that "After You've Gone" ended "as if half the band expected another chorus, then expected to drop out." "Jammin'" was cut short as well, "as if the engineer became tired of recording." (In truth, both endings *are* rather sudden.) Some pointed criticism was reserved for the tenor star—"Lester goes through the usual somewhat drab gyrations"—with the reviewer finally speculating, "Guess he's just made too many records and we've reached [the] saturation point." Even after all that, *Metronome* concluded that "good moments [could be found] on all sides."[13]

In the fall of 1946, "You're Driving Me Crazy" and "Lester Leaps In" were reviewed in *Metronome,* which noted that the tenor stylist had once played the first selection as the classic "Moten Swing" with Basie. On this date, however, the reviewer suggested that Young "sound[s] so lethargic during his solos that you wonder whether the turntable is running right." The other selection, in contrast, ranked as an "important event." After praising pianist Joe Albany and guitarist Irving Ashby, the writer betrayed his lack of knowledge of the saxophonist and his music when he declared, "Whether Lester is currently in a groove or just a rut is anybody's guess."[14]

Critics seemed to make a habit of disparaging Young's Aladdin recordings. *Down Beat*'s reviewer was lukewarm on "She's Funny That Way" and "Lester's Be-Bop Boogie," both of which were recorded with Joe Albany (piano), Irving Ashby (guitar), Red Callender (bass), and Chico Hamilton (drums). The trade journal congratulated Young on his "better knit ideas," though it also noted that on these selections "he isn't playing as well as usual." In rating a Jazz at the Philharmonic record featuring Young, Parker, Willie Smith, Al Killian, Howard McGhee, and Lee Young, the reviewer spread the faint praise around, observing that the "solos all have some good spots, but none of them are in the best manner of each of the names."[15]

Mike "Mix" Levin of *Down Beat* actually paid Young a (backhanded) compliment on his performance on *Jazz at the Philharmonic, Volume 6,* which consisted of several discs, two of "JATP Blues" and one devoted exclusively to "Slow Drag." Pointing out that Young took considerable time warming up on "JATP Blues," Levin noted that "many evenings he doesn't get there," and then conceded, "But this time he does." For this critic, instrumentalists were contestants, to be compared with one another as if they were street fighters. Tenor saxophonists were to be considered only in pairs, as were altoists, to emphasize the rivalries between certain stylistic leaders on their instruments: Young and Hawkins on one side, and Willie Smith and Charlie Parker on the other. In the battle between the tenors, the reviewer proclaimed, "For my money, [Hawk] gets slashed here by Young." On "Slow Drag," however, "it's a toss-up as to who plays better."[16] This latter selection took up both sides of a disc, exemplifying a new format Granz had introduced—a way of going beyond the standard three-minute time limit to permit the musicians to develop their solos fully, as they would in a jam session.

Even Levin had to admit that these records warranted the new treatment, which was designed to take advantage of the spontaneity of the music and capture it on disc. "At long last Granz has made an album which justified the idea of JATP," "Mix" enthused, adding that the result was "jazz of a type you don't often hear these days on wax." In a review of *JATP, Volume 4,* Levin had acknowledged the success of Granz's efforts, though he was also very critical: "Despite its very bad editing, execrable balance, abortional taste, and poor surfaces, there are spots . . . which justify the concert theory of recording at least in part."[17]

Late in 1947, Young went into Aladdin's studios with Gene Di Novi (piano), Chuck Wayne (guitar), Curley Russell (bass), and Tiny Kahn (drums). Two songs from this collaboration, "East of the Sun, West of the Moon" and "Sheik of Araby," were reviewed favorably by the *Chicago Defender.* The rarity of reviews in the *Defender* at this time suggests that this may have been more of a publicity piece, but in any case, the selections were reported to be "finding favor with jazz lovers throughout the nation." Young's "saxophone artistry" was praised, and the record touted as an essential purchase for record collectors.[18]

An entirely different rating was awarded by *Down Beat,* however. Levin (again) conjectured that "somewhere between good swing and bad bop a great tenorman has got lost in a morass of conflicting styles and ideas." He castigated Young for "his honky, faltering, out-of-tune meanderings" and complained that they were "characteristic" of the saxophonist at the time. Again the reviewer caught "a glimpse of what used to be" on "Sheik," but he concluded that such "prize moments are few." He failed to mention the fact that this was not Young's regular combo.[19]

Di Novi subsequently revealed details about the session that illustrated Young's take on it, as well as demonstrating his inevitable rebellion and frankness. It began when Di Novi and Kahn were waiting outside the studio, and Young came up and greeted them, saying, "'Hey, man, you're gonna make records with Prez!' " Di Novi himself admitted that the date was "the greatest thing that ever happened to us."

For "East of the Sun," they agreed beforehand on a sixteen-bar introduction without the saxophonist, after which he was to join in. They started in, but to Di Novi's dismay, Young remained seated on the other side of the studio, away from the microphone. By the fifteenth and sixteenth bars, the guitarist was thinking, "God, he's never going to come in because the mike is clear over here." But then, on the second beat in the sixteenth bar, the saxophonist "like a gazelle . . . jumps into the air and comes flying over to the mike and sinks into a low A flat concert as his first note which is a strange beginning!" In other instances as well, Young "proceeded to do things like that."

At one point the saxophonist surprised the sidemen with his candor. The critic Leonard Feather was acting as the producer on this date, and he made a few suggestions about what they should play and how—only to have Young promptly step up to the mike and interrupt, "If Prez's kiddies were here, they would know what to play behind Prez!" The musicians felt "crushed" by Young's rejoinder, but Di Novi later realized that Young was "simply telling Leonard that he would have preferred to have been there with his own rhythm section." Despite these "funny goings-on," the guitarist pronounced it "a beautiful experience to be near [Young] and to play with him."[20]

Record reviewers did not usually have access to this kind of background and often did not take into account the unrehearsed and essentially improvisatory nature of the music. Nor did they consider, in this case, whether Young was recording with sidemen he had never met before or with members of his own combo. Indeed, perhaps the sessions were not his best—but they were nonetheless evaluated as if every session always "clicked." This in itself suggested the degree to which critics used the wrong standards—and Eurocentric ones, at that—to judge on-the-spot performances by musicians who did not always play together. After all, these were not standardized selections presented by rehearsed orchestras (or combos) in concert halls, but very often jam sessions with pickup musicians or, as Granz was wont to assemble, star performers from different bands.

Young formed a regular band in 1946. Sadik Hakim (then Argonne Thornton), the composer of "Jumpin' with Symphony Sid," found them in the Spotlite, Clark Monroe's club, on Fifty-second Street in Manhattan; Kenny Kersey was on piano, Shadow Wilson played drums, Rodney Richardson was on bass, and Bennie Harris, a trumpeter, rounded out the group. Later in the year the tenor stylist's band consisted of Maurice "Shorts" McConnell (trumpet), Sadik Hakim (piano), Lyndell Marshall (drums), and Fred Lacey (guitar); in the fall of 1947 Dennis "Tex" Briscoe and Roy Haynes became his bassist and drummer, respectively. Young and his combo recorded on several occasions in subsequent years, notably at Town Hall in Manhattan, opposite Sarah Vaughan, late in 1947.[21]

Because studio time was expensive, Young's postwar recordings were often made live, as at Town Hall, or under severe constraints. The demands on the musicians could be extreme: on one occasion when they made an Aladdin recording in Chicago in the autumn of 1946, bassist Rodney Richardson remembered "the guy coming out of the control room [and] saying to Pres, 'Lester, do you have something goes bomp; bomp; bomp bomp bomp bomp bomp bomp bomp,' and he goes and he did it. Just fabulous. . . . 'Sax-o-Be-Bop' [was the result]."

Then, too, recordings were usually done in only one take, no matter the condition of the personnel: pianist Sadik Hakim complained that some of the Aladdin records were made on a day when all the musicians were exhausted, having just arrived from the coast after the Esquire Awards concert, on no sleep. For Granz, it was all part of the appeal: from the *Jammin' the Blues* film to the Philo and Aladdin recordings, he attempted to capture the unrehearsed element of surprise that was such an essential part of jazz. If any record reviewers actually tracked musicians in a systematic way—listened to their live performances, for example, or tried to distinguish good recording sessions from superior ones—they did not report this activity.[22]

But even when Young recorded with his own sidemen in these years, trade-journal reviewers gave him mixed ratings. The Basie anthems "One O'Clock Jump" and "Jumpin' at the Woodside," recorded by Young's combo in the winter of 1947, earned an especially scathing review from *Down Beat*'s "Mix" Levin, who suggested that the piano on "'Jump' sounds as though it's been tuned with boxing gloves [and] recorded in a hayloft." The tenor stylist, for his part, was described as "managing to get lost several times on the reverse [side]." The conclusion drawn by Levin was that the record held "nothing of interest"—a clue to just how subjective such evaluations could be.[23]

Unlike Young's recordings between 1946 and 1949, his live performances were ranked quite highly by reviewers. That the reviews of such dates do not corroborate the blanket assessment of his recordings as lacking in inspiration becomes particularly significant when one considers that, as Leonard Feather noted, "most bands sound their worst on the stage, where they play strictly for squares; and they sound best on records."[24]

The first notice of a live postwar Young performance was published in the *Los Angeles Sentinel* a few weeks after his discharge from the army. The next appeared in the *Chicago Defender* in April 1946. The tenor saxophonist played on Chicago's South Side between JATP dates. He performed for one night only at the Pershing Ballroom on May 28 with Jesse Miller and his band; a few weeks later, he "fronted a local band for a new house record at the Pershing."[25]

Young's and JATP's success at a prior Chicago performance justified their return, the *Defender* declared. When the saxophonist was pitted against Coleman Hawkins in mid-May, the crowd response was such that Granz's touring jazz concert was booked for another Chicago date in late June. The May JATP show had been described by critics as "the most successful series of concerts ever given." Significantly, a photograph of Lester Young was used in *Defender* ads for JATP. To the promoters, Young was clearly the star of the show.[26]

In Philadelphia the next summer, an old-fashioned jam session featured Young along with local tenor stalwarts, who "almost blew Les Young out of his title" as "king" of the tenor sax. The *Philadelphia Afro-American*'s review was written along the lines of earlier accounts of Young's showdown with Hawkins at the Cherry Blossom. In the 1947 session, held at Town Hall and sponsored by the Jazz Festival Society, Young reportedly "fought to retain sovereignty over tenor men, and barely emerged with his crown." Of interest here is the fact that he succeeded; this was not a portrait of an artist past his prime. Also important to note is that the event was primarily symbolic—that is, the "strife" was mainly friendly. First Young and his sextet performed, then the local tenor men played with their respective bands, and then the saxophonists all came out together for "Lester Leaps In," the grand finale. Even though one Philadelphia sax man, "cool, little Jimmy Oliver[,] play[ed] the Lester Young style so faithfully," the king of tenors was "a better technician, and probably has more experience on his horn."[27]

Unconvinced, *Down Beat* stuck to its obsession concerning Young's decline. In December 1947, it found fault with his performance at the

Town Hall concert in New York City for which he shared billing with Sarah Vaughan. The trade journal summarized the two stars' respective performances in a headline: "Vaughan Great, But Lester Slips." Young was described as having "wallowed around the stand . . . played out of tune and without ideas and in general justified every idea the lay public has about jazz musicians." His trumpet player, Shorts McConnell, was said to have "consistently cut" him; the reviewer also criticized pianist Hakim and bassist Briscoe. "Mix" Levin blamed Young's poor performance on his being subpar physically, calling his efforts "pitiful . . . not only inadequate, but a flat proof . . . that you have to be in perfect physical condition to play good sax." He did not elaborate on whatever he may have known about Young's health at the time; nor were opinions of musicians reported, with one rather singular exception.[28]

In a rare instance of a musician's replying to a critic in a published letter, Young addressed Levin's evaluation of his performance. The note appeared at the end of the critical article. "I think that was the greatest concert I ever played in my life," Young protested, in an uncharacteristically immodest assessment. While "other people did criticize the band," he conceded, "the only people that didn't like my playing were you [Levin], my manager Charlie Carpenter and Shorts McConnell." Perhaps with tongue in cheek, Young claimed that such a verdict was incomprehensible to him, "because the rest of my friends told me it was real mad." This was probably the only occasion when the tenor stylist responded directly to an unfavorable review.[29]

Newspaper reports on his live performances indicated that Young was well received in the various cities he played with his combo in 1947 and 1948. He opened at the Argyle Lounge in Chicago sometime around Thanksgiving 1947, a date that the *Down Beat* columnist labeled as important because of the saxophonist's appearance. He then vacationed in Los Angeles for two weeks—presumably visiting with his brother, sister, and other relatives—before heading back to New York City.[30]

By this time the combo had jelled and was very likely playing better as a unit. Ralph Gleason reported on its Bay Area appearance in the winter of 1948 and praised the singing of the bassist and guitarist—Briscoe and Lacey, respectively—on some numbers. Such vocals are nowhere captured on record, though the band itself did go into the studio. (In fact, there are no male vocals on any of Young's records, other than some singing by guitarist Freddie Green on "Them There Eyes" and some clowning on the saxophonist's part on two rare recordings.) A Caribbean rhythm on one selection was also an indication, along with the singing, of the band's attempt to appeal to popular tastes. Young recorded "Lavender Blue" with just such a rhythm at a time when Afro-Cuban music was in vogue.[31]

No doubt contributing to Young's success after the war was his newly stable family life. This aspect of the saxophonist's biography has been closely examined only by Robert August Luckey, who interviewed Young's third wife in the course of his doctoral-dissertation research. The tenor stylist married Mary Berkeley sometime in 1946 or 1947; their son, Lester Junior, was born in the autumn of 1947, and around 1950 the family moved into a residential neighborhood in East Elmhurst, on Long Island. They also lived for a time with Ella Fitzgerald. Then, in the spring of 1952, the Youngs purchased a home in Jamaica, Queens County, New York City. Yvette, their daughter, arrived late in 1956.[32]

Significantly, Young started this new family within three years of the deaths of his father and stepmother. From it he drew the kind of support he needed, and providing for his wife and children in turn gave him a focus and purpose. Sometimes he even managed to combine his road tours with his family life, as when his wife accompanied him on a JATP tour of Europe. Nor was Young the only jazz veteran to find contentment and security in a new marriage in these years; Billie Holiday, who had recently wed, was reported to be demonstrating "a new sense of responsibility and cooperativeness" by 1952.[33]

Information about Young's private life was not readily provided even to his close associates—further indication that he regarded his marriages and domestic situation as profoundly personal matters. For instance, no one in his family, not even his brother, knew what had become of Lester's first two wives, Beatrice and Mary Dale. Several musicians mentioned that the tenor saxophonist worried about problems he was having with women before he wed for the third and last time, but no details were forthcoming. Sadik Hakim reported that when he played with Young after the war, the saxophonist would visit his "waybacks"—in this case meaning old girlfriends—but again, this seems to have been before he married Mary Berkeley. Even after 1958 or so, when he left his wife and children to live in the Alvin Hotel across the street from Birdland, the famous Manhattan nightclub, Young stayed in touch with them because they were such an important part of his life.

The story of his relationship with Mary Berkeley began in the late 1930s, when she heard him on Count Basie records. A native of Rockford, Illinois, ninety miles west of Chicago, she was the daughter of migrants from Tennessee and Mississippi. Like Young, she grew up surrounded by a rich African American musical heritage. Her cousin owned records by Fats Waller, which she enjoyed, and her uncle played blues guitar; the family was also active in the Baptist church, whose services accorded music a vital role.

On first hearing a record featuring Young, she was struck by "this beautiful tenor solo . . . [though at the time] I didn't even know what instrument that was." Its very tone deeply moved her, however, so when "finally somebody told me who it was and identified the instrument," she started purchasing Basie records. After church, she and other teenagers would meet in a small restaurant in Rockford where they would play the jukebox and listen to Basie numbers; her particular favorite was "Sent for You Yesterday." After she moved to Chicago to study at the Hughes Cosmetology School, she recalled, "one day I was on the el[evated train] . . . and as we were going downtown, I see this big poster of Lester. . . . I didn't even know if I had ever seen a picture of Lester [before] . . . but there was this big poster on a building." It was an announcement for an upcoming JATP concert. She had missed seeing him when the tour came through earlier in the year, probably in the spring of 1946; of that lost chance, she said, "I was so mad, because it would have been my opportunity to see and hear and meet him."[34]

Eventually, of course, she did meet the saxophonist, through a girlfriend who knew one of the JATP musicians; the proper protocol was very important to her. Before he came to town, she had written him a letter in care of the Pershing, a popular South Side hotel. "I want[ed] everything to be legitimate, I want[ed] someone to introduce us," she remembered. Thinking he had read her letter, she said very little when they met, hoping he would take the lead. He had not yet read it, however, and he, too, said very little upon meeting her backstage. "He didn't talk and I didn't talk," she reminisced. "Neither of us were big talkers." She was disappointed and thought, "Maybe he doesn't like me." She watched the performance from near the front of the bandstand that evening.

One Sunday he called and left a message asking her to meet him that night at the Wonder Bar, a South Side nightspot near Sixty-third Street and Cottage Grove, where he was going to be jamming. She was not in when he called, but before returning home, she stopped in at the Circle Inn, "a great big bar shaped like a circle," with a girlfriend who needed to use the telephone. While waiting, she heard Young jamming, working his way down to the Wonder Bar. She remembered this as occurring in April 1946.

After that meeting, he gave her his itinerary so she would know where he was going to be, and when. Her visiting him in Detroit later that year signaled a deepening relationship between them. While she met the other band musicians, she and Young "didn't do any socializing"—an indication of how much they enjoyed each other's company and valued their privacy. "Lester didn't like the socializing," she explained. "We said hello [to others] . . . but that was about it." A few years after they were married, she moved to New York with their young son, and they stayed in various Manhattan hotels and apartment buildings before relocating to Long Island. Lester Junior would later recall playing on the roof of one of those city buildings, a place where children and others customarily gathered in nice weather.[35]

These new family ties provided the tenor saxophonist with the warmth, stability, and security he had lost with the successive deaths of Willis and Sarah, his induction into the army, and his imprisonment in the detention barracks. Prior to this, in fact, he had never really enjoyed the comforts of a settled existence, apart from those hardscrabble years in Minneapolis with Beatrice. Clearly, home came to mean a great deal to him: he spent Christmas with his family nearly every year after 1946.

His relationship with his wife was a rich one. She picked out his clothes and did his hair, and he even wore a wedding band, not a common practice for Black men in the United States in that era. In the 1950s Mary would help him to maintain his image as a well-dressed and debonair elder statesman of jazz. Most important, Young's new prosperity permitted him to support his family with a degree of ease and in a style that must have given him considerable satisfaction.[36]

Nevertheless, as late as 1949, he could make a statement suggesting that he was not yet ready to settle down. He may have been referring not so much to his new family responsibilities, however, as to where they would all end up living when he confided, "When I do [settle down], I'll stay in California." His preference for southern California, he explained, was related to its weather; then, too, he owned a house there, and not only his brother and sister but also their mother, Lizetta Gray, resided in Los Angeles. Still, the lure of the road remained strong for the saxophonist: "There's always something new," he said of that life. In this respect, he was much like both his father—for whom family and employment as a traveling musician had always been the most important things—and *his* mother, the missionary.[37]

It took a few years for the couple to make the transition from hotel residency and apartment-dwelling to home-owning. They lived in the Marden, a Forty-fourth Street Manhattan hotel, in 1949, and it may have been there that Leonard Feather interviewed Young one late-spring or summer day. He described the rather cluttered surroundings: "The room was large, bare, but littered with a fantastic assortment of odds and ends"; the "long mantelpiece . . . [held] innumerable figurines, many of them religious." On a table were "several soiled plates, a bottle of gin and another of sherry."

As Feather questioned him, Young "fooled with a beat-looking all-metal clarinet" that needed repairing, while the record player replayed Kay Kyser's "Slow Boat to China" over and over again. The hand of his wife was not evident, but she may simply have been away at the time. The religious figures reminded visitors, and Young himself, of the Christian traditions of his childhood.[38]

One other holdover from Young's Black cultural heritage, and specifically from his southern Louisiana upbringing, has gone unremarked in accounts of his life. Lester Junior remembered his father's tending tomato plants on the roof of the New York apartment building where they lived in around 1950. Raising tomatoes was hardly a common hobby for a traveling musician; in and of itself, it indicated a settled state. Moreover, in this case, it was related to an interest in cooking. Like many southerners, and other former Blue Devils, Young liked to prepare savory dishes. One of his favorites harked back to his Louisiana roots: crab gumbo. He used to make it on special occasions; his son recalled that it was hot (with pepper) and that he was warned, as a child, that he was too young to try it. The important place that gumbo held in Black American culture would be reflected in a 1957 *Jet* article containing two recipes, one provided by the gospel singer Mahalia Jackson, who grew up in New Orleans.[39]

In the mid-1950s, Young sometimes permitted reporters to interview him in Queens, where he resided on a quiet, tree-lined street and spent his time "enjoying his lovely wife and sprouting son, his modest brick home, [and] his mid-afternoon nap," according to one. It was just a short walk to the local elementary school and to neighborhood stores. There was some continuity between his previous and his current life one reporter noted, but where before there had been the comings and goings of musicians visiting his hotel room, and the attendant greetings, tale swapping, and reminiscing, now there was "the constant and sometimes simultaneous din of television set and record player." The saxophonist was also said to enjoy playing ball with his son and eating home-cooked meals.

One of his favorite pastimes was putting golf balls into a cup; he practiced constantly. He was also quite a good pool player and had a table in the basement, which was fixed up as a recreation room/den. A television set enabled him to follow sports events, including the Giants and Dodgers baseball teams, as well as the progress of other bands. After one program he complimented the bandleader: "That Bob Crosby . . . he's still wailing."[40]

The tenor stylist spent his last decade in New York City. His presumed desire to settle down does not explain why he chose the East Coast over the West—where he had purchased a Los Angeles home in the spring of 1947, shortly after his career took off—or even the Midwest. In 1946 and 1947, he was often in Chicago with Mary Berkeley; then, too, his manager after 1947, Charlie Carpenter, was a Windy City native. But very likely the convenience of being near his agents' offices and New York's radio and recording studios was a determining factor in Young's change of coasts.

Much of the saxophonist's postwar success could be attributed, first, to Moe and Tim Gale, formerly managers for the late bandleader Chick Webb, who opened their talent agency in New York in 1940; and second, to the managerial skills of Norman Granz and then later Charlie Carpenter. The Gale brothers sought to improve conditions for Black performers after learning through firsthand experience what poor bookings they were forced to accept. Having signed up Ella Fitzgerald, Cab Calloway, and the Ink Spots, the Gales "discovered, groomed and built over twenty-five special stars into the six-figure income bracket." Young was one of these. And beyond the financial benefits, he must have particularly approved of "the pattern of integration that ran through every phase of the business from road managers to secretaries in [the Gale] office," in the words of one press release/newspaper article.[41]

Charlie Carpenter was probably Young's first manager besides Granz, though he did not exactly jump at the chance to take the job. The Gale Agency, which handled all Young's bookings, asked him to manage the tenor stylist for one night only—New Year's Eve 1946—but Carpenter declined. Subsequently he learned that his friend Shorts McConnell was in the band, and he "thought about how nice Lester was, and Frank [Sands, of the Gale Agency,] told me how everybody had been stealing from him." So he changed his mind and acted as Young's manager one night when an audience of four thousand turned out to hear the band in Newark, New Jersey. He was quite surprised at the large turnout, and even more taken aback to learn of the tenor saxophonist's highly personal but antiquated business methods shortly after the set: Carpenter figured the earnings by percentage and gave the money to Young, who counted it, wadded it up into six balls, and gave each man his share; when Carpenter unwrapped his wad, "It was . . . twenty-five dollars!"[42]

The two talked on the train back to New York. Young remembered Carpenter from his audition for Earl Hines back in 1935. "You know," he said, "I like the way you do things. . . . You want to keep managing me?" Carpenter stipulated his condition: "We don't work without a contract." Young objected, "I'm not going for that signing . . . but I just thought you might like to work with me after I go to Chicago"—probably aware that Carpenter came from that midwestern city and would welcome a trip to visit his family and friends. After the Midwest tour, the saxophonist finally relinquished the wariness he had acquired through long experience and told his prospective manager, "I've been watching you and everything, and I've been thinking. You get your contract and I'll sign it." Several weeks or months elapsed between Carpenter's joining Young and formally becoming his manager, a position he would hold until 1956 or 1957.[43]

The contract was at length drawn up and signed. Young's career continued to improve, and he began even to prosper. His new manager was well known and respected in music circles; as a teenager he had been befriended by Louis Armstrong and Earl Hines, neighbors of his on Chicago's South Side in the 1920s. He was also a World War II veteran, so he must have had an idea of what the army had put Young through. Moreover, through his connections, Carpenter was able to document Young's popularity in the late 1940s, countering the critics' assertion that the tenor stylist's improvisatory talents were on the wane.

The Chicagoan was probably behind a number of articles that appeared in various African American weeklies, introducing the popular tenor artist and relating his views on music and style in general. These articles ran for several years and presented Young in a very different light than the reviews did; it is tempting to wonder whether the record reviewers read them. Young was featured in *Jazz Record* in the summer of 1946, then in *Down Beat* interviews with Pat Harris in the spring of 1949 and with Leonard Feather in the summer of 1950. Significantly, it was only after his *Jazz Record* interview with Allan Morrison and after the Black newspapers publicized him that the larger trade journals "discovered" Young.[44]

His first interview, entitled "You Got to Be Original, Man," appeared in *Jazz Record* in July 1946. The very title of the piece promised that Young's thoughts and language would be the focus and medium of the article—a radical departure from the usual procedure, wherein the musician was "interpreted" by the all-knowing reporter. In as fine an interview as one could hope to find, Morrison re-created the mood one spring day in Chicago around the time of the JATP tours and Young's Pershing Ballroom appearance. Perhaps Young required just such a relaxed setting before he could feel comfortable with the inquiries of a reporter.[45]

Morrison, a Black journalist, chatted with the tenor stylist "under the best circumstances for such talk—a smoky hotel room lighted by a single pale-green bulb." The setting as described has a surreal quality, suggesting that it may not have been merely tobacco smoke that filled the room. The mood was set by a report on the weather conditions: "The skies were gray and a fine rain sprayed gently through the open window." From the record player, "the husky, sensuous voice of Billie Holiday flowed all around the room and did soothing things to the ears of the men who listened." Unnamed musicians asked the questions, adding an informality to the interview.

Young epitomized relaxation, lying on his back, "his belt unbuckled, his half-closed eyes looking up at the ceiling." The saxophonist made "funny little humming sounds" as he followed the music, "always in perfect tempo." When Vic Dickenson soloed, possibly on a recent Aladdin recording, "bold trombone choruses shook [Young] out of a luxurious lethargy and made him write crazy patterns in space with his forefinger."[46] Otherwise, Young's facial expressions were minimal—though at one point "his eyes opened wider . . . and he gestured slightly"—and long before Miles Davis, or Marlon Brando, or James Dean relaxed with reporters instead of assuming a more formal demeanor, he felt sufficiently at ease with Morrison that "he lay back on the bed and closed his eyes."[47]

The dialogue finally began when "someone broke the long silence" to ask Young if he had been born in California. Morrison noticed that the tenor stylist's response, in which he admitted that his birthplace was

Mississippi, included "a tinge of embarrassment in the way he said it." Pride supplanted embarrassment, however, when Young discussed life in his father's band, traveling the circuit, and getting his start on drums; he had switched to alto, he explained, because he was "lazy" and did not like having to pack up the drums and lug them around. Clearly he was proud that his father had played every kind of instrument, proud that he himself had mastered the saxophone so quickly, proud of having survived the territorial years, and proud of his originality.[48]

This was the first time the source of Young's singular sound was identified in print: "His approach to tenor playing was essentially an alto approach . . . [which was] unique, new, exciting." But then Morrison detected a bit of contempt in his voice when one of the musicians brought up Coleman Hawkins. Young, of course, denied having been influenced by the older saxophonist, asking, "Must a musician always get his ideas from another musician?" He stated flatly, "I never did have a favorite tenor." Young reviewed his experiences with Basie and Herschel Evans, summarized his thinking on the importance of originality, and recalled his army months as "one mad nightmare." "D.B. [Detention Barracks] Blues" was placed on the turntable, a kind of commentary on Young's account of his army life, and the stylist smiled in recognition. With that, the article ended.[49]

It is conceivable that given his show-business connections Carpenter put Morrison in touch with the saxophonist, though by his own recollection he did not team up with Young until later that year. Perhaps, then, the Gale Agency was responsible for the introduction. In any case, such an interview, appearing in an important jazz publication, could potentially boost Young's career by summarizing his life and clarifying his thoughts. He was probably glad to draw a Black reporter as his first interviewer; the ease he so obviously felt with Morrison would set the tone for future such sessions, which often took place where he was most relaxed, in his own hotel room or at home, sometimes with Carpenter present.

If Carpenter was behind the short pieces published about Young in several Black newspapers in 1948, it says a good deal about both the manager's connections with the world of African American journalism and the newspapers' racial loyalties. These publicity articles often came out of either Chicago or New York City. Sometimes they touted Young's successes, but on other occasions they served as evidence of his sense of humor and willingness to engage in what, in at least a few instances, seem to have been put-ons.

Having been in show business all his life, Young was game to participate in publicity events, as when he battled Gene Ammons at Chicago's Pershing Ballroom. The "Battle of Saxes" was waged on New Year's Eve 1947 and highlighted the celebration of that special night. The encounter climaxed a period of anticipation, one newspaper announced, since a showdown between the two saxophonists had "long been sought but promoters [have been] unable to get them together." A "packed house" was expected to observe the "swingfest."[50]

But there was also a serious side to Young's promotional efforts, as when he gave his opinions on bebop and maintained that it was here to stay. More recently, other musicians, including Red Callender, have suggested that the differences between swing and bebop were exaggerated; after all, swing combos such as the Kansas City Six and the Benny Goodman Quartet had foreshadowed bebop years before with their riff-based melodies. Nevertheless, in the 1940s Charlie Parker, Dizzy Gillespie, Thelonious Monk, Tadd Dameron, and Kenny "Klook" Clarke were regarded as the vanguard of a new and daring music filled with long, riff-based lines, unusual harmonies and accents in unexpected places, and sudden explosions or "bombs" from the drums. Many of their compositions were in fact rooted in blues or based on popular melodies, but that was not immediately obvious to the uninitiated. The music captured the loyalty of younger musicians, who entered into a contentious debate with their elder counterparts—a debate that the press eventually began to take notice of.[51]

In the autumn of 1948, Young published his thoughts on this "new music" in two major Black weeklies in different cities. "Bop Here to Stay Argues Les Young" and "Lester Young Defends 'BeBop'" appeared in the *New York Amsterdam News* and the *Chicago Defender*, respectively, on the same date—October 2. In virtually identical articles, the tenor stylist asserted that bebop was part of an evolutionary process and that as he himself knew from personal experience, "any innovation . . . is bound to be controversial and be open to all types of criticism." Sometimes music had to become commercialized in order to survive, and Young had found in his touring that among the "thousands of people [who made up his audiences] the majority are on a bop kick." His band, he claimed, played "relaxed bop," as he did not care for "the more wild type of bop." Furthermore, he added, listeners could easily understand his combo's music—a criterion that may in part explain the inclusion of singing and Caribbean rhythms in the band's selections.[52]

With this pair of articles, the swing master publicly proclaimed his support for and understanding of this latest step in the music's evolution. Young undoubtedly witnessed and, by Jo Jones's account, played an important role in the birth of the music at Minton's in New York, either between tours with Basie or when he was playing with his brother's combo in late 1942. He was not the first of the swing generation to speak favorably of the new music. Count Basie had expressed his qualified admiration the year before—"It's real great if it's played right. . . . I have records that I play all the time, trying to understand," he noted—while Coleman Hawkins had made *his* stance known a few years earlier in recordings made with Howard McGhee. Fletcher Henderson, in contrast, denounced the music as a "phenomenon of cruelty."[53]

The interview that the bop articles were based on may have taken place in the late summer of 1948, when Young played Emerson's in Philadelphia. Located at Fifteenth and Bainbridge Streets, it was advertised as having an air-conditioned "Rainbow Room" and being "Philadelphia's Most Beautiful Sepia Spot." Both this site and the venues in which the articles appeared—African American weeklies—should remind us of Young's strong ties to the African American urban communities.[54]

Just a few weeks after these articles were published, Dan Burley, the influential *Amsterdam News* columnist, announced his own conversion to bop in his weekly column. Burley reported on a Carnegie Hall concert at which Illinois Jacquet—not usually viewed as a bopper—had performed: "I experienced something that has never happened to me before—a sort of ecstatic emotion, a surging of blood through my veins and a tingling of the spine."[55] Possibly the endorsement of an established swing master such as Young played a role in Burley's epiphany.

In 1948 and 1949, other noteworthy items about Young appeared in the African American press; one article concentrated on his style of headgear, while others focused upon his career. The former, especially, humanized the photogenic sax stylist and contradicted trade-journal portrayals of him as an aloof eccentric. Here, instead, was a jazzman all too happy to hip the unhip to the latest in fashions. *Ebony*'s pictorial essay "How to Make a Pork Pie Hat" showed a relaxed and smiling Young demonstrating exactly how he shaped his hat to meet his own high standards. The article included a photo of him playing a recorder and another in which he affectionately cradled Macaroni, his black cat.[56]

The accompanying text pointed out that "American jazz has always been peopled by an abundance of colorful personalities, many of them odd characters . . . [with] strange mannerisms or outlandish dress." In this category Young was joined by Charlie Parker and Dizzy Gillespie. A "typical rebel not only against orthodoxy in music but against conventional tastes in clothes," the tenor stylist was described as a "jazz sophisticate" who not only sported the porkpie but was "credited by many jazz musicians with originating it." His affection for animals evidenced a sensitive side not often associated with alienated and aloof hipsters. "He carries his cat with him on tours all over the country and frequently takes the animal to bed with him," the reporter noted. Young even made silk neckbands for his pets, giving them a bit of style to match his own.[57]

The article revealed an anti-Hawkins bias—and the probability that it was a glorified publicity piece for Young—when it reported that its subject "has influenced more young tenor saxophone players than any modern jazz reed instrumentalist." Moreover, it permitted a glimpse into both the current state of jazz criticism and the concerns of the public when it compared contending musical factions with the current international political scene: "In the midst of the cold war which has rent the jazz world into two contesting camps—bop and anti-bop—[Young] is one of the few instrumentalists on whom there is a general agreement from Dixielanders to Gillespieites." The final line of the piece indicated the outcome of the struggle between the competing tenor men: "By 1941 . . . [Young's] huge army of admirers . . . gave him the nod over the great Coleman Hawkins."[58]

Other articles in Black weeklies publicized Young's successes and offered evidence that undermined any notion of his decline. His date at New York's home for bop, the Royal Roost, was presented as "the climax of a year's work of building his crew into what he considers a top outfit." During his series of one-nighters, fans had "hailed it as the best band of his career." The *California Eagle* reported how much Young had earned in 1948 and suggested that this pointed to a significant resurgence in his popularity: "One year ago they were saying that tenor sax king, Lester Young, was all washed up and that he was through as a topflight attraction in the amusement field." Even skeptics shook their heads in amazement at his "tremendous surge to the front" and his band's gross of seventy-five thousand dollars for the year. In March 1949 he was touted as "one of the top band-leaders after having two unsuccessful years back in '45 and '46"; it was speculated that he might earn even more that year than he had in 1948, when "he copped five polls as favorite soloist."[59]

Some of these articles emphasized Carpenter's role in Young's ascendance. A former songwriter who was said to possess "one of the shrewdest band brains in the business," he was liked and respected by promoters. "In many instances of booking Young his verbal consent over the telephone was tantamount to a written contract," noted one African American weekly. This was termed "a marvelous feat in a business where many bookers even look suspiciously on a written contract."[60]

The years immediately following the war's end brought Young honors as well as some humorous press. He also fared well in the trade-journal polls. In 1946 he was ranked at the top by *Down Beat*, and the following year he came second only to Hawkins in an *Esquire* poll. The *Esquire* editors hardly seemed to be describing a "washed-up" musician when they testified that in the magazine's "All-American Jazz Band," Young "gave the Hawk a real battle all the way to the wire" (in fact, a mere six votes separated them). Don Byas, George Auld, and Flip Phillips, relative newcomers in comparison, were ranked in third through fifth places.[61]

In February 1949, Chicago's Roosevelt University designated Young "President of the Tenor Saxists" at its Cherry Tree Chop Ball, an occasion on which students celebrated the birthday of the nation's first president, George Washington. Joe Segal, a student and president of Roosevelt's jazz club, presented the saxophonist with an inscribed plaque. The honor underscored his popularity among the wider public, outside the African American community.[62]

In 1949 his influence on and significance in the evolution of jazz were recognized by *Metronome*, which voted him one of the "influences of the year," along with newcomers Sarah Vaughan and Lennie Tristano. The trade journal enthused that "a whole school of music, *the* school" of tenor saxophone, had sprung from his style of playing—no small accomplishment for an artist still a few months shy of his fortieth birthday. Furthermore, Young was not simply touted as "an influence," but praised as "more, . . . the sire and dam, almost the man who made bop come true."[63]

Black newspapers, meanwhile, represented him as a kind of folk hero and continued to publicize even the minor events in his life, as when, on a trip to Canada, his band members failed to realize that the red boxes resembling fire alarms were actually mailboxes; they returned home carrying the cards they had intended to post. Around the time Count Basie dismantled his big band, Young and Carpenter denied rumors that the tenor saxophonist intended to enlarge his sextet to sixteen pieces. "Young said that at least one hundred musicians had contacted him within the last two weeks with a desire to join any new band he might have in mind," one report claimed in early 1949. Again, like much of Young's publicity, the story came out of Chicago, where Young was performing on the North Side; the Blue Note was said to have "landed the tenor sax star after months of negotiating with Carpenter."[64]

Nor were the publicity pieces limited to the late 1940s. In the 1954 article "Prez Nixes Clown Deal, Just Blows Fine, Champ," the tenor stylist commented on the popularity of the young saxophonists who jumped up and down, literally walked on top of the bar, or fell down on the ground while playing. He explained—likely in jest, but not entirely so—that his contract always contained a clause exempting him from such exhibitionism. He had no respect for such musicians: "If I can't just stand up and play music that please the people who pay to see me . . . then I don't want the job," he insisted. The musician who had started out in vaudeville doing such stunts as a child, and then continued to hold his saxophone out in a theatrical fashion with the Basie band and afterward, rejected such showmanship when it was taken to what he considered to be an extreme. His statement sparked a debate on the topic among musicians.[65]

Young's reputation was such that photos of him were used in a number of advertisements between 1946 and 1956, for JATP and other concerts, including a benefit for the Bel Canto Foundation, a nonprofit organization established by the pianist-composer Mary Lou Williams "to provide a future home and place for recuperation of indigent jazz musicians." The ninety-piece Xavier Symphony and boxer Sugar Ray Robinson were also featured. The tenor stylist was also one of the most frequently photographed musicians of the swing era. In 1953, a photo of Young with Billy Eckstine, taken at a Birdland party for the singer, appeared in *Down Beat*, and in 1954, the *Baltimore Afro-American* ran a picture of him with Basie, after they performed together at Carnegie Hall.[66]

All too often in jazz biographies and histories of the music, subjective evaluations have trumped objective evidence to the contrary. This has certainly been the case with Young, who, far from suffering a decline after his time in the military, as many writers have suggested, in fact experienced considerable success and prosperity. Those who have adhered to the idea of his decline have chosen to either overlook this evidence or dismiss it as inconsequential.

Young's reputation unquestionably rested on his genuine artistry and creativity, but he was also lionized because he dared to defy traditional authorities and managed to survive doing so. At a time when the entire nation was living a regimented existence, he chose to submit to an army court-martial rather than conform to the military's rules. In the circles of the initiated, he was known as a nonconformist in terms of his music, his dress, his language, and his love of marijuana. Like-minded people saw in him a hero who served as an exemplar of new possibilities in the hip urban milieus of the mid-twentieth-century United States. That he was able to fulfill this role in an era of cultural conformity and intense political repression further underscores the difficulty of the challenges he undertook as an artist and as an individual. Yet through it all, he never lost touch with his fans.

Young's itinerary for late 1946 and 1947 reveals how hard he worked to maintain that bond. Beginning on Christmas Day of 1946, his schedule was as follows: December 25, Huntington, West Virginia; December 26, Richmond, Kentucky; December 27, Cincinnati, Ohio; December 29, Buffalo, New York; December 30, Trenton, New Jersey; December 31, Newark, New Jersey; January 3, Youngstown, Ohio. From February 13 through 17, 1947, he performed in Richmond, Bakersfield, El Centro, San Diego, and Los Angeles, California—a city a day. On the nineteenth he played in Salt Lake City, Utah. He opened in Washington, D.C., in early April, went to New York City in mid-May, and then performed in Boston in early June. After stopping in New York in the middle of June, he went to Cleveland, Pittsburgh, Asbury Park, New Jersey, New Haven, and Philadelphia in July. He then performed in Chicago, St. Louis, Kansas City, and Omaha on August 8, 9, 10, and 11, respectively.[67]

On several of Young's Royal Roost records, which were issued only after his death, the audience can be heard conversing and occasionally shouting at the musicians in the combo, urging them on while simultaneously socializing with their friends. Insofar as he always preferred to play for dancing, Young valued the interaction between performer and audience, an exchange so intimate as often to blur such role distinctions in Black America. His appearances at Christmas, New Year's Eve, and other holiday celebrations represented a high point for fans. He personified a certain kind of royalty among the urban citizenry, and his lack of pretense and loyalty to his African American roots made his elevation to that status all the more remarkable and exemplary of the democratic aspects of jazz society. During these special performances, fans and entertainers alike celebrated activities and features of jazz culture that were inspiring, joyful, and occasionally romantic or sad, as Young delivered romping tunes, love songs, and finally the blues in the course of a single evening.[68]

After the war, three of his records, "After You've Gone," "It's Only a Paper Moon," and "Lester's Be-Bop Boogie," were listed as hits in African American newspapers on both coasts. Two Aladdin ads for his records, each part cartoon and part photo image, appeared in trade journals and indicated his high profile in these years. In the *Metronome* ad he was depicted as a genie, his crowned head surrounded by a cloud of smoke issuing from a magic lamp in the hand of a cartoon Aladdin. In the *Down Beat* version, the "Esquire Award Winner" and "King of the Tenor-Sax" sat on a throne, a crown on his head, while a turbaned Aladdin knelt before him and served him a saxophone on a record platter.

Given that this was the period when his career really took off and when enthusiastic audiences boosted his earnings higher than ever before, reviewers' criticism of Young's playing in the late 1940s must be interpreted as a kind of character assassination. In fact, as we will see, the disparity between his actual success and critical opinion of him highlighted not Young's supposed decline, but rather changing conditions in the entertainment world, as racial prejudice, developments in the music industry, and new audiences all combined to mute his reception by music fans. In essence, by the early 1950s, critics, promoters, agents, managers, and the public itself were ready to see a decline in Young's talents because they *wanted* to brand him as eccentric and unmarketable.

CHAPTER 14

Lester Blows Again

Critics' and Sidemen's Views

At the end of the 1940s, for perhaps the first time in his adult life, Young was financially secure and enjoying considerable acclaim from his fans from coast to coast. Yet despite his popularity immediately following the war's end, jazz journals and newspapers were driven by developments in the music industry to emphasize the economic and social problems of jazz districts and to criticize both Young personally and his audiences.[1]

The tenor stylist's aloofness was the most frequent target of writers' and some fans' comments. It stemmed from his dislike of club owners, managers, and journalists. Sadik Hakim contended that Young "didn't like *no* managers . . . didn't like to talk to the club owners . . . and didn't like to be [interviewed] unless he *knew* you." Jo Jones agreed that "Lester hated critics and always jived them. The only time he talked straight with them was when they asked him who his inspiration was." In a later era, some musicians would express their hostility toward writers in a more direct way, but for those of Young's generation—excepting the Teddy Wilsons and Paul Robesons, of course—another kind of response was necessary to disguise the fact that one "wasn't really interested in answering questions."[2]

In contrast, Young's close relationships with his sidemen reflected his beliefs about how band members should be treated—in the antithesis, that is, of the characteristic behavior of most promoters and of white racists, who rarely passed up an opportunity to let others know their low opinion of them. For his part, Young made special efforts to deal with his sidemen as equals; he was, after all, a gentleman whose word was his bond and who tried to treat others the way he wanted to be treated, without regard for race or color.

Of course, he was not alone in his dislike of the business side of entertainment, though he probably did find it more difficult than some to conceal his displeasure. The noted critic Leonard Feather, who worked as a publicist in the late 1940s, would later conclude that "for the most part, working in publicity, despite its advantages of bringing me into contact with so many musicians I respected, was an unpleasant business, because it meant catering to so many sleazy gossip columnists and remaining at their mercy." He was happy to move on to other things, feeling that "the power [the columnists] exercised was frightening."[3]

The example of Buster Smith, Young's mentor in the Blue Devils, who left New York's limelight for his hometown of Dallas, may have passed through the tenor stylist's mind on those occasions when he considered the elusiveness of "big-time" success. As Smith explained it, "I saw nothing to it. The glamour only lasts briefly. I saw the big musicians—like Willie 'The Lion' Smith—made to pay to get in and hear other bands. You're forgotten easily and there's no place to go. The average life of a musician in bright lights is seventeen years. I'm a man who likes to go hunt and fish. All you hunt in New York is the rent dollar."[4] Other musicians—Charlie Parker, for one—rued the day they had left their hometowns to chase success in New York City. While Parker earned enormous critical acclaim as a founder of bebop and a legendary improviser, drug abuse and alcoholism compounded his reputation for being unreliable in regard to meeting job commitments, and led to his death at thirty-four, in the spring of 1955.[5]

Stan Getz, one of the most successful of the Young school of tenor saxophonists, expressed the frustrations of many when he stated that he wanted to escape the difficulties inherent in the jazz life of the 1950s. Getz claimed he "wished to become a doctor" because he was "just not able to cope with all the hassles that go with being a jazz player." He complained about "the average club owner. . . . If you're a musician, you can't trust [the owners]" or "the agents and all the rest of the characters that are part of the music business." That this sentiment came from a young white tenor saxophonist who won the trade-journal polls on his instrument every year from 1949 on—the kind of headliner club owners and agents dreamed of—gives some indication of just how difficult dealing with management must have been for an older, uncompromising Black tenor player.[6]

Roy Haynes leveled a similar charge at nightclub owners, pointing out what many musicians knew and few club managers appreciated: "Not all, but too many [nightclub owners] seem to regard musicians as somewhat less than . . . total human being[s] . . . to be . . . wound up like a clock a certain number of times a night and [accorded] no more consideration than that kind of inanimate object."[7]

Young nonetheless fared well in terms of salary: he was said to be getting a thousand dollars per gig just a year after his release from the army's detention barracks. When Carpenter took over as his manager and learned of this, he claimed that the figure "was unheard of and ridiculous." In 1946 and 1947, his best years up until then, Young made more than $75,000; within a few years, he was reputedly earning over $50,000 annually. During this period he purchased a row house in the Queens borough of New York City, where a number of other musicians—including Roy Eldridge, Count Basie, and Illinois Jacquet—lived; five- and six-room brick bungalows cost about $11,000 in those days.[8]

A brief review of the salaries of other entertainers of the era puts Young's income in clearer perspective. Tommy Dorsey, for example, contracted to receive $7,500 a week, plus bonuses, if, after proving his band, he could draw the requisite crowds to the Tropicana, outside Havana, Cuba, in early 1950. Nat Cole—"probably the highest paid instrumentalist in the pop music field," according to one contemporary magazine article—earned over $100,000 in 1945 and 1946; the two sidemen in his trio made more than $35,000 and $25,000 each. The singer Billy Eckstine grossed more than a million dollars from appearances, royalties, and his first movie in 1952. Women singers were the highest-paid Black entertainers at the time. The vocalist and movie star Lena Horne ranked first, commanding $8,000 to $10,000 weekly for nightclub appearances, followed by Billie Holiday, who "picks up about $250,000 a year." On either coast the controversial singer could count on netting $3,000 to $4,000 a week.[9]

While Young was never paid as much as these other stars, his poor business habits diminished what he actually did earn as well as what he might have earned. Young's handling of his business affairs was criticized by his longtime friend, Buddy Tate, who told him that when Norman Granz had offered him $500 per week, he should never have accepted that salary immediately (as he had in fact done), without requesting a higher sum: counteroffers were fairly standard procedure for musicians of Young's stature. Furthermore, Young had never requested a raise, perhaps because he felt he should not have to haggle or negotiate in this way. Tate informed Young that one of Granz's employees had stated that the saxophonist ought to have asked for $2,000 a week, considering his popularity and what other JATP performers received. Clearly, Tate said, Young's financial problems resulted from the fact that he was a poor businessman; accordingly, he agreed to take over this end of his friend's affairs. This conversation occurred in 1958, long past the peak of Young's earning power.[10]

Like Armstrong and Fats Waller, Young was known both for his lack of attention to business details and for his generosity toward his friends, but then, too, he lacked the vices or lavish lifestyle that drained others' incomes. His sidemen earned $125 a week when they were working, and Young gave them money in the form of "loans" when they were not, but he did not keep track of the amounts he doled out. Moreover, though he enjoyed a measure of security with Granz's JATP, or as a member of the Rhythm and Blues Show tour of 1953, or with the Birdland All-Stars a few years later, he found that these jobs also had their disadvantages, notably in precluding him from recording on other labels or taking other bookings, except between tours.[11]

Young also earned less than his white imitators, a matter of no small concern for him; nor were movie offers forthcoming, as the films of the mid-1950s either romanticized musicians—as with Glen Miller and Benny Goodman—or sensationalized them, as in *The Man with the Golden Arm,* which depicted the abuses of heroin addiction. As for the most famous jazz musician of the era, Louis Armstrong, Hollywood's plans to portray his life story never materialized.[12]

Young's difficulties with the music industry and with reporters can be best understood within the context of the series of attacks made during this period on integrated jazz circles. His oft-noted decline reflected changes in the music industry and a general hostility toward African Americans and their culture more than it did any deterioration in his health or his playing. The extent to which white racist officials aimed drug and vice raids and political reforms at Blacks who mingled with whites has gone largely unappreciated. Much of the press was also downright hostile to jazz fans and jitterbug dancers, if not to the mixed couples who were so much a part of the jazz world. Attacks on African American people and culture and on efforts at integration lay at the heart of the matter. Nor were these limited to the South; but while southern brutalities against Blacks have been well documented, the same is not true of racist activities and attitudes elsewhere.

Young's enthusiastic audiences and the special manner in which they interacted with him were often noted by writers. When he arrived at the London theater where he was scheduled to play with JATP in the late winter of 1952, for example, he "found his dressing room already besieged by fans." Indeed, "they brushed past Flip [Phillips], Barney [Kessel], and Oscar [Peterson—all JATP musicians] to Pres. And all day they were there." His following was so loyal, *Down Beat* reported, that his fans "always fill the halls," and even when he thought he had satisfied them, he "left the audience cheering for more."[13]

Trade-journal writers often joined with civic officials in expressing their dislike of jazz fans' actions, especially their yelling at concerts in such citadels of elite culture as Chicago's Civic Opera House, New York's Carnegie Hall, and Los Angeles's Philharmonic. This type of behavior was regarded as being symptomatic of still another problem: younger fans' rowdiness and criminal proclivities. In 1946, D. Leon Wolff maintained in *Down Beat* that "every hydrocephalic and congenital idiot in Chicago" had attended the JATP concert at the Opera House that autumn. After criticizing the performances, Wolff revealed his elitism with the statement "Maybe the enormous, almost cosmic, grandeur of the Chicago Civic Opera House is no place for a jam session." A few years later, *Down Beat* bemoaned "the hoots and howls from the hoodlum section at Carnegie," whose members were "allowed to shout and act like husky-voiced school kids being encouraged to show off." This contingent represented a new departure in Carnegie Hall audiences.[14]

These jazz denizens were not found only on the East Coast. In 1949 the *Metronome* critic Barry Ulanov deplored the takeover of the Los Angeles strip by "zoot-suited hoodlums from the East" and the closing of southern California nightclubs. The trend had begun some years earlier: in 1944, *Metronome* had discussed racial incidents on Manhattan's Fifty-second Street and declared that "similar tensions exist in Los Angeles, where white musicians are now afraid even to visit the Central Avenue section where they once hung out with their colored friends."[15]

The newcomers were blamed for all kinds of social problems. The insistence on the part of some owners that their clubs be integrated raised the specter of drug and racial issues in many writers' minds. In an article entitled "Zombies Put Kiss of Death on 52nd Street Jazz," Tom Piper of *Down Beat* complained that the jitterbugs were ruining the atmosphere of nightclubs from coast to coast, causing "the decent citizenry [to] avoid the spots like the plague." The jazz fans "come with their zoot suits, long haircuts, reefers and 'zombie' jive to night spots that feature top jazz talent. Soon they become the 'atmosphere' that pervades the spots," Piper chided. These newcomers, who were often relatives or friends of the musicians', attended private parties as well.

The *Down Beat* writer maintained that "no racial angle" was involved in his criticism of the "zombies" or in "decent" citizens' reluctance to frequent the nightclubs. The newcomers were said to be "composed of all colors." Furthermore, Harlem nightspots had suffered the same decline as midtown clubs. All law-abiding citizens, whatever their color, were reportedly shunning the resorts, unanimous in their rejection of these crime-ridden areas where insults, muggings, and police raids were allegedly daily occurrences.[16]

Leonard Feather believed that Manhattan's legendary "Street" in particular—the area of Fifty-second Street near Sixth Avenue—and jazz districts throughout the nation in general, had degenerated during the 1940s. "What was once a healthy meeting place for musicians and fans, a street on which racial barriers were broken down, by 1945 had turned into something that parallels the notorious Barbary Coast of San Francisco," he wrote, referring to the area that from the nineteenth century had been the most famous tenderloin district on the Pacific Slope. (In this fashion, Feather unwittingly acknowledged an earlier precedent for the very behavior he deplored.) He blamed the decline of Fifty-second Street on the high salaries demanded by the big names, their managers, and agents, on "rotten liquor . . . plus discourteous service and a general how-much-can-we-get-out-of-you-for-how-little attitude towards the customers," and on "the lowlife reputation . . . acquired [from the] fringe of dope-addicts, dope-peddlers, pimps, prostitutes, and assorted characters."[17]

Despite the disclaimers proffered by some officials and writers, race *was* a factor. One *California Eagle* headline, "Mixed Parties Target of Big Raids on Night Spots," made only too clear what was really taking place in Los Angeles in 1947: "Fraternization of the races in Central avenue night spots was the target of large-scale police raids . . . on Eastside establishments." Ostensibly these were crime-busting efforts, but "according to an oblique admission" by the assistant police chief, they "were aimed to discourage the visits of white women to the Eastside night spots." Police invaded the Casa Blanca Club, Café Society, The Club Joy, Lovejoy's Café, and Café Zombie to protect white women from the alleged ruses of Black men.

During these raids, police searched "most of the patrons," going through their clothing—even their shoes and hats—and finding marijuana in a guitar case. Although the Central Avenue raid made headlines, the charges were dismissed the next day—a fact not mentioned in the daily papers. Later that month the *Chicago Defender* observed that such raids discouraged white visitors from patronizing Black clubs, not only in Chicago but in Harlem as well (and here we can also add Los Angeles and other cities). By the 1940s, laws regarding "drugs" had changed, and police raids on nightclubs, along with newspaper coverage of the spread of heroin, confirmed the public's belief that such places should be eradicated.[18]

Articles on drugs and interracial mingling preceded reports on the decline of the jazz districts by at least two years and suggested the social and political dimensions of what was, by 1949, being viewed primarily as an economic problem. It is difficult to avoid the conclusion that an element of racism, as well as elitism, figured into the debate. For example, after two years of concerts, Los Angeles civic officials refused JATP permission to perform at the Philharmonic Auditorium. Mayor C. H. Brainard claimed that the refusal stemmed from the behavior of the crowd at an earlier concert, where members of the audience had "scorched carpets with cigarettes, started fights over relative merits of performers and behaved poorly," according to the *Sentinel*. Brainard rejected the allegation that racism had played any role in his decision, noting that "mixed couples have been prominent at each concert." Promoter Norman Granz disagreed, however, charging that "'reactionary views' against color [were] the main reason" for the city's stance. Himself a staunch integrationist, Granz had learned about racism through hard experience. In Jackson, Michigan, a local proprietor had refused to serve JATP musicians before their concert, and the local police had supported him; Granz had responded by taking legal action.[19]

In Los Angeles, Granz, Billy Berg, and Fran Kelly typified a new type of jazz promoter dedicated to racial equality. Kelly, with the aid of Lester Young, Ray Bauduc, Kay Starr, Lucky Thompson, Red Callender, Charlie Parker, Nat Cole, Benny Carter, and other artists, sought to foster racial tolerance by booking UCLA's Royce Hall for a performance to benefit the scholarship fund of the George Washington Carver Club, named after the famous Tuskegee scientist. A *Metronome* recap reported that Young and Parker offered "the best number of the program." All the musicians either donated their services or received a nominal fee, with proceeds going to the scholarship fund. This marked a first for UCLA, whose music department neither taught jazz nor encouraged students to play it. As the trumpet player/singer Clora Bryant recalled, "There was no such thing as jazz on the campus then. . . . It was strictly Western music, classical . . . all classical."[20]

A careful reading of certain musicians' and fans' autobiographies sheds light on the new audiences who so offended nightclub managers, journalists, and a portion of the public. They were young, often Black, had grown up during the hard years of the Depression, and supported the antiracist and integrationist sentiments that emerged in the 1940s. To judge from what is virtually an underground literature—that is, the autobiographies of Babs Gonzales and Norwood "Pony" Poindexter, not to mention the better-known works of Mezz Mezzrow, Malcolm X, and Billie Holiday—it is clear that these fans did not lack knowledge, as many journalists contended, but in fact showed considerable appreciation, and respect, for the music tradition, the musicians, and their latest records. It was not so much a question of musicians' reaching out to their fans, because they did that in any case; rather, it was a matter of precisely *which* fans they chose to befriend, and which valued them for who they were.[21]

The fact that some of these jazz urbanites sought to make business connections also rankled critics and management. They were specifically criticized for their economic enterprise—that is, for arranging record dates with independent, "fly-by-night" companies. Occasionally these ambitious entrepreneurs assisted the new, smaller labels in signing up artists, thereby attracting the condemnation of critics who worked for the older, more established record labels. The new businessmen sometimes demanded to be credited as composers on record dates, a common practice among promoters—who put their names down, they claimed, because it brought recognition and increased sales, qualifying the musician as well as the promoter for royalties.

Some writers and managers did not seem to care that young people of different racial, ethnic, and social backgrounds found considerable solidarity in the music. Yelling and other activities—standing on corners, for example, or strolling the boulevards—were not simply expressions of youthful exuberance, bad manners, or antisocial behavior, but vital means by which fans contacted and communicated with the musicians as well as one another. Ecstatic moments in a solo or during a conversation called for vocal exclamations or exchanges of "fives" (hand slaps) in recognition of such signal points in time; also, besides cheering for encores, loyal fans urged their heroes on, talking to them during concerts in a manner typical of African Americans, whose collective participation has traditionally been encouraged in performance situations, in theaters as well as in churches. Hand-clapping, foot-stomping, and dance were all integral aspects of music behavior shared by whites and Blacks in the jazz community, and had been so from the beginnings of the music. On some occasions, however, even JATP promoter and master of ceremonies Norman Granz judged things to have gone too far; at least once, he was so offended by the audience's behavior that he stopped the show. One year he printed up handbills detailing proper fan behavior and gave them out to audience members as they arrived.[22]

Their relative youth underlined the fact that the exuberant fans had grown up during the Depression and endured all the sacrifices entailed by those troubled times; subsequently their hopes had been buoyed by a wartime economy. Most of them were African Americans or the children of European immigrants, and few had had the opportunity to go to any college at all, and certainly not to the Ivy League schools that some writers and musicians had attended. They appreciated the economic opportunities afforded by jazz's popularity and the likelihood of making money by arranging bookings and recording dates with the new labels. For these young entrepreneurs, the successful careers of Louis McKay (Billie Holiday's manager-husband) and Norman Granz of JATP pointed the way.

Then, too, the fans found their heroes relatively accessible. They spoke the same language and enjoyed their company and having the chance to mingle with them backstage and at private parties. Whites and Blacks alike benefited from the integration of audiences in an era when racism was out of vogue, and they thought they could socialize and fraternize as they pleased. The defeat of Nazi Germany, the integration of the federal workplace by executive order, and the portent of a Jackie Robinson in major-league baseball served as inspirations for young audiences, who had seen their bands, too, become increasingly integrated by the 1940s.

In early 1949, a few years after the criticism of the musicians and audiences began, *Down Beat* analyzed the economic reasons for the music industry's decline. The analysis, of course, was based largely on the trade journal's materialist approach to the music. What music to record, the writer argued, constituted a "puzzle" precisely because of uncertainty as to what would sell well. Record producers who "selected material with an elementary musical pattern and an interesting lyric line . . . usually were home safe," but neither bebop nor swing fitted this definition, unlike rhythm and blues (and later rock and roll). *Down Beat* commented on the new scene: "Today, the public, glutted with the recorded chaff of the ban year, has come up with a strange edge on its musical taste."[23] Young was not the only musician to be tarred with this brush: not only Parker but Ellington, too, had been dismissed as out of touch as early as the 1930s. In some respects, it was a foreshadowing of what would happen to a number of swing musicians when they were shunted aside by rock and roll in the 1950s.

Changes in the music industry made dance-band and nightclub ventures risky propositions for everyone. Two recording bans, from 1942 to 1944 and again in 1948—the result of legal disagreements among various factions in the music business—sent shock waves through the recording industry. The influx of U.S. servicemen near urban areas during World War II led the U.S.O. centers to feature dance bands, which in turn whetted the general public's appetite for the music, even as the migration of war workers to burgeoning industries, especially in California, expanded the range of offerings for more varied musical tastes. Radio and television bands meanwhile afforded opportunities that kept a few talented and fortunate musicians from traveling, an option that appealed strongly to some road-weary performers.[24]

After the war, the dance-band decline had an impact on many musicians, including Young, who invariably played in a combo format except on those special occasions when he performed with the Basie band. Jo Jones maintained that the desire on the part of big business to control the music industry resulted in the demise of all but a few African American swing bands, leaving only those of Ellington, Basie, Calloway, and Lunceford. Contemporary newspaper accounts corroborated Jones's claim. In January 1949 it was reported that MCA had "recently announced the curtailment of its band department and would release from existing contracts only leaders who agreed to shift to the General Artists Corporation." The bands of Ellington and Basie, Buddy Rich, Charlie Spivak, and Claude Thornhill were all affected by the change. Basie did not want to make the switch, so the Morris Agency refused to release him from his contract; it soon became clear to the bandleader that he might have a contract with no bookings if he failed to cooperate. It was around this time that his orchestra disbanded (an event that sparked rumors that Young might start a new big band).[25]

This background on the writers, nightclub owners, and business scene is essential to our understanding of Lester Young's reputation as an eccentric. The police raids and newspaper attacks on the musicians and their fans, and the vicissitudes of the declining nightclub business, took a considerable toll on Young. The day-to-day problems of leading a band and dealing with club owners only exacerbated the situation. The intelligent and artistically conscious Young responded by withdrawing from society out of disgust at the crass materialism and shallowness that characterized it. Even when jazz fans wanted merely to spend a little time with the sax stylist, rumors of his shyness and various other idiosyncrasies, such as his habit of never leaving his hotel room before evening, prevented the ready accommodation of their wish.

Despite the public's acclaim, Young's unassertive manner ensured that he would never receive the kinds of rewards garnered by others—even by his younger and more aggressive imitators, for example, who earned as much as or more than their model and were in ample abundance by 1949. Nor did that acclaim permit the tenor stylist to experiment with other instruments such as French horns or strings, as he would have liked to do. In the 1950s Young had to rely on his reputation, his sidemen's loyalty, and his own charisma to draw other musicians into his orbit and hold them there.[26]

Critics' writings on Young reveal one dimension of the problem: the fact that the saxophonist usually kept them at a distance. When we contrast writers' with musicians' opinions of Young, the journalists' inevitable lack of understanding of the artist begins to acquire a distinctive clarity. Again, it was not just a matter of race. While fans, musicians, critics, managers, and businessmen both in and outside of the music industry might meet and socialize at concerts and in clubs, differing social and geographic origins, conflicting economic interests, and competing historical perspectives nonetheless divided their jazz world into separate spheres. The controversy surrounding Young's character was furthered by critics' and fans' expressions of confoundment at his behavior and his consistent use of jazz argot. An analysis of the critics' opinions, however, highlights the gulf that separated the African American component of the jazz world from that of the many writers, record executives, and fans who were in that milieu but not of it.

Music critics' professions of puzzlement over Young's behavior abounded in printed accounts of his career. Leonard Feather, for one, described the saxophonist as "a strange and complex character." In attempting to delineate Young's onstage presence, Feather wrote, "Often Pres would shuffle onto the bandstand with ridiculous mincing little movements, or move across the stand with crablike sidesteps until he reached his destination. Once he'd reached it, he'd stop and shiver slightly . . . like a chicken spreading its feathers."[27]

The *Down Beat* writer Pat Harris, for her part, noted Young's "well deserved reputation of being uncomfortably shy . . . content to gaze silently at his pigeon-toed feet rather than talk." The saxophonist's shyness was thought to be responsible for his reluctance to speak out, but reticence had not been much of a problem in the Morrison interview. A somewhat stymied *Metronome* writer expressed the opinion of many critics when he referred to Young as "the solemn, slow slouching enigma of jazz." One booking agency representative voiced a not-uncommon disdain for the leading tenor stylist when he branded him "an aloof goof . . . in a world all by himself . . . oblivious to people . . . a nut."[28]

The recording executive John Hammond suspected that communication was hindered by the color barrier. He actually believed that Lester—who had, after all, married a white woman, Mary Dale—"was either unwilling or unable to communicate with anyone of a different hue." Describing the sax player as "a strange creature," this heir to the Vanderbilt fortune observed that "music seemed to be his only stimulus, his sole reason for living." Furthermore, he maintained, "outside music, Lester lapsed into indifference as if the vital spark had left his body to seek refuge in a dream which left him untouched by the trivia of the world."[29]

An illustration of the misunderstandings or miscommunications that were so common between Young and businessmen such as Hammond was provided by the record executive when he reported that near the end of his life, the saxophonist approached him and said, "I like you and regret that we haven't seen more of each other these last years." From this remarkable statement, Hammond "concluded that Lester Young knew his end was near." Hammond does not seem to have appreciated the compassion of Young's statement, which acquires greater meaning in light of his dislike of the executive's meddling.[30]

Feather suggested that Young's behavior was "part of the masquerade, the massive characterization." He cited the tenor stylist's use of jazz slang as an example of the mask he wore, a resort to an "almost entirely personal language . . . which became standard jazz argot." Feather claimed that this habit became even more pronounced as the saxophonist grew older: "The more Pres declined in his battle with the forces of life, the more he depended on such hip talk." The purpose of the argot, Feather contended, was "to help exclude any intruders." While the writer, himself a staunch integrationist, was correct in seeing Young's behavior as a self-defense, he had little insight into precisely what it was that Young was blocking out.[31]

Nat Hentoff was no more successful in penetrating Young's "massive characterization," or as he termed it, his "mask." He interviewed the tenor stylist in 1956 after a hospital stay that, according to Hentoff, enabled Young to "integrate his personality," whatever that may mean. Perhaps as evidence of the change, Hentoff noted that Young "was much more relaxed than he usually is in interviews, and his answers were lucid and carefully thought out before they were delivered." Nonetheless, "Pres still wears a mask, although it is more often a cheerful one than the familiar phlegmatic, almost somnolent face and posture with which he faced strangers." The writer believed that there had been a racial dimension to this as well, for to this last sentence he added the phrase "particularly white strangers."[32]

Hentoff did see, however—or rather, the saxophonist permitted him to come sufficiently close to see—the humorous and teasing aspects of his subject's character. He observed that when Young talked, there was a light side as well as a serious one: "In his frequent, teasing, good-humored moods, his tone can be lightly mocking, though almost never malicious." The critic Derek Young also noted Young's "particular brand of humor and . . . gentle drawl." It was during Hentoff's interview that Carpenter remarked that the saxophonist did not like hillbilly music and radio and television jingles, marking the only time Young ever—if only indirectly—publicly expressed a dislike for any type of music.[33]

Still, even critics who marveled at Young's lack of desire or his inability to communicate with them, and at his other idiosyncrasies, unashamedly confessed to admiring his musical abilities and profound influence on other musicians. According to Benny Green, Young was "one of the most remarkable and inscrutable of creative artists," a musician who played in "one of the most startling original and highly literate styles in all jazz." Hammond was another avid fan, admitting that he "was nothing less than a worshipper at the shrine [of Pres]" and that, furthermore, his "enthusiasm for him knew no bounds."[34]

Whereas critics earned their living rating musicians' performances and abilities for the public, the performers themselves hardly ever revealed their opinions of the writers outside of certain closed circles. When they did voice their thoughts, they were frequently misunderstood, so they protected their livelihoods by not offending writers or members of the business world. Nonetheless, evidence of considerable differences in perspective between some writers and musicians has occasionally reached print.

Over the years, a few musicians have made some rather striking statements about writers, revealing not only a unique perspective but also the fact that these artists do not need anyone to interpret them to the world. Some of the differences of opinion have been rooted in political realities. Clora Bryant, for example, wrote, "Jazz criticism, in this country, hasn't really served a good purpose for Black music or Black musicians. Critics make it sound as though this is a political ploy, and they, the critics, are the candidates out stumping for their political party, be it traditional or modernist. They want to tell us the way we, as Blacks, should feel in creating and playing our music. They want to dictate how to shape and [present] our music in order for it to comply with their philosophy of what jazz should be or where it should evolve to. . . . From the very beginning, their only aim or purpose has been to confiscate our music and claim it as their own."[35]

Similarly, in the introduction to his autobiography, the New Orleans musician Danny Barker lambasted the judges for the awards given out by a men's magazine, and writers generally, for attempting to exercise control over African American artists and art: "The judges were a conglomeration of assorted leeches and self-appointed critics. I had, through the years, seen most of these characters come around bands I played with. They would sit and stand around annoying musicians . . . , cleverly setting up arguments and debates, while absorbing opinions. They would go and write articles the way they decided a musician should be remembered and read about."[36]

Despite their left-wing politics and integrationist stance, even the most well-meaning writers, with few exceptions, failed to understand the historical effects of racism on African Americans or the myriad forms race prejudice might assume in leaving its mark on specific personalities. Published views of Young thus often reflected the writers' specific social and class origins. Hammond, for instance, was a descendant of the Vanderbilts and had attended Yale, while Feather came from a "Jewish middle-class life" where sons were expected to " 'go into the [family] business.' "[37]

Most music critics and business types were northern-born or from Europe, again in contrast to Young and some of his associates, who not only were African American but had been born and raised in one of the most distinctive cultural regions of the United States: the Deep South. Jazz provided the means for writers to gain a firsthand acquaintance with Black cultural traditions, but it was nothing like being raised within that heritage from childhood. While many insisted that they were friends with some of the musicians—and clearly that was true in many instances—there would always remain barriers or divisions between them and African Americans, boundaries of which Blacks were acutely aware.

Some writers realized that Young's behavior might be part of an act. This was not an unreasonable conclusion, given the fact that the tenor stylist had spent most of his life in show business, beginning with his father's band. Young himself once acknowledged the influence of show-business traditions when he explained to the guitarist Jimmy Gourley what lay behind his mincing approach to the microphone: "Show biz, Lady Jimmy, it's show biz!"[38]

The multidimensionality of Young's onstage and offstage personae, and their blending of contrasts, were hardly unique: many entertainers have public personalities that are very different from their private selves. Even such inveterate and commanding (onstage) personalities as Cab Calloway and Ray Charles confessed to being shy, retiring, and uncommunicative—even loners—when they were not entertaining. Count Basie, it was said, "allowed very few people ever to get close to him." Likewise, Fats Waller, the proverbial funny man, and Thelonious Monk, who has frequently been portrayed as a distant, aloof hipster, both had alter egos that offered them refuge from a world that was in some respects distinctly foreign to them.[39]

For numerous Black musicians, assuming a "mask" was a way to keep people out of their affairs and to protect aspects of their personalities and private selves. The jazz argot, jiving, humor, and even the music itself represented an adaptation of African American entertainment and racial traditions within the jazz world. Southern Negroes, in particular, were known for closing their private lives off from outsiders, especially whites, and for employing wit and satire to that end and as an effective weapon in dealing with whites. This tradition was fundamental to Black minstrelsy, enabling African Americans to satirize whites onstage and even off, so long as it was within a clowning context. Fats Waller and Dizzy Gillespie exemplified this latter legacy.[40]

Thrust into the public limelight and overwhelmed by the accolades of audiences, fans, and colleagues from his teen years, Young discovered that except when he was with his family or his few close friends, he was always onstage. The heritage of show business and of the African American cultural tradition gave him ways of evading the probing of the public, the press, and music executives. He employed a mask or masquerade to keep strangers at arm's length, sometimes relying on a solemn or deadpan expression when he was being least serious, then adding more wit and humor overlaid on serious statements, asides, and insights, all jumbled together into a total act that expressed the complex nature of his sensibilities and his character. In fact, his playing *did* change, as change or growth was a part of his philosophy. As late as 1959, though he was still playing the same numbers he had played in the 1940s, he told one interviewer that he was considering adding new instruments to his repertoire, including a bass clarinet.

CHAPTER 15

Movin' with Lester

"Always Reaching . . ."

AFTER the demise or reorientation of many of the Fifty-second Street jazz clubs, a new nightspot, Birdland—the "Jazz Corner of the World"—took on particular importance in Young's career. Named after Charlie Parker, the long, dark, smoke-filled cellar club was the premier locus of the new music, and a model for clubs of the same name that soon sprang up in other cities. Birdland and other, similar clubs marked a departure in their new policies: they featured neither singers nor dancers, and to keep expenses down, they often hired singles such as Young, Coleman Hawkins, and Roy Eldridge and backed them with pickup rhythm sections. In New York City, drummer Willie Jones, bassist Gene Ramey, pianists Kenny Drew, Horace Silver, and John Lewis, and occasionally former Basieites accompanied the tenor stylist. On dates in Chicago and Washington, D.C., after 1955, he was usually backed by local sidemen. But the most important feature of the various Birdlands, in Leonard Feather's view, was "the incidence of 25 percent or more Negro patronage in most of these clubs where once they were either barred as patrons or at best represented a fragmentary segment of the business." In the bigger cities, some clubs claimed "as high as 50 percent colored trade for certain attractions."[1]

Despite its name, Birdland also showcased swing, as when Basie's band played the venue. In fact, on the club's opening night, in late 1949, four different combos exemplified successive epochs of the music, according to the program: Max Kaminsky represented Dixieland, while Young, of course, symbolized the swing era; Charlie Parker epitomized bebop, and Lennie Tristano stood for the newest wave in jazz.

Young could always be depended on to accept the offer of a gig at Birdland, for playing there allowed him to stay at home. He performed at this famous nightclub every December holiday from its opening in 1949 until 1956, when he moved to the Café Bohemia—still in New York City—at Christmastime. Art Blakey, Miles Davis, John Coltrane, and Clifford Brown were among those featured at Birdland during the 1950s, and in the next decade as well. In the last year of his life, Young stayed in the Alvin, a musicians' hotel across the street from the club, so that (he claimed) he could be near his friends.[2]

Considerable fraternity and loyalty persisted in jazz circles, in spite of police raids, arrests of musicians and their friends, the demise of Fifty-second Street as a jazz mecca, and the closing of nightclubs all over the nation. Swing-era musicians and fans of dance bands still felt very much a part of something significant, despite the popularity of rhythm and blues artists and rock and rollers such as Chuck Berry, Elvis Presley, and Fats Domino. When news of Billie Holiday's acquittal on narcotics charges in San Francisco reached the East Coast late in the spring of 1949, applause broke out on New York City's Broadway. The *Amsterdam News* reported that "every record shop from Forty-second Street to Columbus Circle began playing Billie Holiday records." Although the singer did not appear with JATP, similar support existed for and among the performers in that entourage; its fans were just as loyal to the saxophone stylist as Holiday's were to her.[3]

Throughout the late 1940s and into the mid-1950s, Young also played in a variety of other venues. It is indicative of his success during these years that he was booked into some of the top nightspots in the country, including upscale North Side clubs in Chicago, Tiffany's in Los Angeles, and the Blackhawk in San Francisco. That he toured with large assemblages of stars—JATP from 1946 on, and the Birdland All-Stars in 1956 and 1957—also stood as positive proof of the esteem in which he was held. At the same time, he retained tremendous loyalty among fans and fellow musicians by playing in African American theaters and resorts in Harlem, on Chicago's South Side, in Philadelphia, and in Baltimore, and by going on road tours down south and in the Southwest with, for example, the Big Rhythm and Blues Show, a 1953 extravaganza featuring the former heavyweight champion Joe Louis doing a song-and-dance routine.[4]

Before the publication of Frank Büchmann-Møller's work, it was difficult to track Young's whereabouts and performance dates in the early 1950s or to identify the personnel on his records—mainly because he played when and where he chose to play, calling on loyal sidemen and old friends as he needed them, and also because he often traveled as a single, picking up rhythm sections in the cities where he was performing. Even now it is not always clear whether or not he worked between jobs that were advertised in the Black press and listed in *Down Beat*'s "Band Routes."[5]

Charlie Carpenter took care of bookings, but it was Young and his sidemen who chose replacement musicians as the need arose. Sometimes the musicians would tell the saxophonist about a good candidate, and often—though not always—Young would hear him play and then invite him to join the band. His methods of selection were unquestionably based upon years of experience, but his technique was singular. Roy Haynes recalled how the saxophonist asked him to join his combo in 1947 after trying him out one night at the Savoy: "After two or three numbers, he slipped over to the drums and whispered, 'You sure are swinging, Pres. If you got eyes, the slave is yours.'" Haynes toured with Young for two years and left only when the tenor stylist "went with Norman Granz on the Jazz at the Philharmonic tour, without his band." He concluded, "For two years, man, it was enjoyable. I learned a lot from Pres."[6]

The year Haynes left seems to have been a turning point. Several sidemen were not certain that Young even *had* a regular band after 1949, the year Birdland opened. The piano player Junior Mance explained that because the saxophonist "was involved more with Norman Granz," the combo gigged only infrequently. In the 1950s, Young "never did really have a permanent group," Mance observed; "it was usually whoever was available." The pianist performed with the tenor saxophonist on just "a few odd jobs" in those years.

When not on tour, Young preferred to stay close to his new family. Mance remembered, "While I was with the band [in 1949–1950], most of the time we were based . . . in New York." They toured "New England, Boston, Hartford . . . around Boston. Baltimore and Washington we played quite a bit." He also recalled that there were times when the band was without work for a few weeks at a time. The pianist Gildo Mahones corroborated this, as did the trumpet player Jesse Drakes. After touring as a member of Young's combo with the Big Rhythm and Blues Show in the summer of 1953, Mahones found that jobs were rather scarce for the band, and so he worked with others when necessary. Still, he joined Young "whenever he called me." Mahones did not understand why the band did not have more bookings.[7]

At the beginning of their relationships with Young and throughout them, most of the regulars responded positively whenever the saxophonist called. Jesse Drakes, Connie Kay, Junior Mance, and Gildo Mahones were among those he most relied on from 1949 until the early or mid-1950s. Mance departed in about 1950; Kay left for the Modern Jazz Quartet early in 1955, and Mahones quit around the same time. Drakes stayed the longest, from 1948 to 1956, but he also joined Harry Belafonte's band and others from time to time. The bassist Le Roy Jackson played with Young both before and after his own two-year army stint—for a couple of years beginning in March 1949 and then again after his discharge, in the spring of 1953.

In the 1950s, critics in the United States were not generous to Young. They almost invariably criticized both his live and his recorded performances, though they also pointed to evidence that he had not lost his touch. In 1954 Nat Hentoff, writing for *Down Beat,* reviewed a Birdland date on which Young and Paul Quinichette—Pres and Vice Pres, respectively—had played opposite each other. Hentoff followed the script that seemed to have been ordained by previous writers when he asserted, "Pres retains his honored title more in the echo of past greatness than present achievement." While conceding Young's "superb sense of rhythmic subtleties," the critic charged that he "just doesn't seem to care very much any more in performance." The saxophonist's tone was also described as "grayed"—a subjective term for music if ever there was one. Nonetheless, Hentoff indicated that he was not altogether convinced that Young was finished, and suggested that the right milieu was important in inspiring superior performances when he added that reports from France (where Young had been touring) held that "Lester was as exciting as ever."[8]

When Bill Coss reviewed Young's Carnegie Hall performance in 1955, he, too, was critical, though he also voiced some regret. Coss expressed the opinion that "Prez made it clear that a lot of his emulators are more vital in sound and tone than he is. This is certainly not the Prez of old, but a shadow of what was the most exciting tenor sound of all." However, Coss noted, the stylist had shown a glimmer of his old talent on "I Didn't Know What Time It Was," a rendition that hinted at "what he had been and possibly could be again."[9]

As a rule, trade-journal reviews of Young's records drew unfavorable comparisons with his early Basie recordings while simultaneously finding reminders of those feats in his contemporary stylings. In a way Young could not win, since he was always competing against himself and the standard he had set when he first came on the scene. Much the same thing happened to Armstrong, who in the estimation of some critics would never again achieve the level of artistry he had attained in his Hot Five and Hot Seven recordings.

In the early 1950s, *Down Beat* compared some newly reissued 1944 recordings by Basie sidemen with some others made by Young's own band a few years later. The reviewer concluded that the former records featured "some of [Young's] loveliest and most sensitively insinuating tenor," while the latter betrayed a "difference in tone and conception [which was] tremendous." "Thou Swell" and "Let's Fall in Love" were also reviewed around this time, with the *Down Beat* critic making reference to Young's "expert meanderings"—a phrase that may have been intended as a compliment. After starting his solo on "Swell" with a "simple-but-swinging phrase," Young "opens up to ramble coolly through some impressive changes," according to the review. "In a Little Spanish Town" was said to consist of "sloppy work by Pres." Having noted that Young exhibited "few of the qualities that earned him justified fame" on "There'll Never Be Another You," the reviewer went on to praise "Almost like Being in Love" as a number "of much more presidential stature." The other selections on the record kept up the "continuity and mood throughout." Such ambivalence was typical of *Down Beat*'s reviews of the saxophonist's recordings.[10]

Occasionally, a *Metronome* reviewer would write favorably of Young, as Coss did in covering a Birdland date in the fall of 1951: "Lester showed up well, playing with more controlled vibrato and closer to the beat than I have heard him do for some time," he declared. With his combo, comprising Erroll Knight (piano), Aaron Bell (bass), Al Jones (drums), and Jesse Drakes (trumpet), Young "swung well, producing a well-ordered pleasant sound." The reviewer expressed his relief that Young had refrained from honking, a recent habit. After enthusing that Drakes "cut Dizzy to my mind if only in the consistency of his solos," the reviewer summed up, "Lester without Granz is a good combination."[11]

Other *Metronome* reviewers, however, were considerably less generous in the early 1950s; among these were the magazine's editors, George T. Simon and Barry Ulanov, who shared responsibility for the record reviews with Coss. After listening to "A Foggy Day" and "Down 'n' Adam," Simon lamented that "on neither is [Young] the outstanding tenor man we have known." On the former selection, he "seems to be unsure of the chords, as though somebody had just called them out to him before the take." The saxophonist sounded "more sure of himself," the reviewer asserted, on the latter selection. Simon's critique revealed a lack of familiarity with Young's work, as the stylist had made a live recording of "A Foggy Day" in 1949 at the Royal Roost (which would be released only after his death). While Simon could not be expected to know about that recording, he should have realized that the tune was a standard in Young's repertoire.[12]

At this point in Young's career, many writers went to hear him for the express purpose of ascertaining how much he had declined since his Basie days, instead of attempting to understand what he was actually doing *now*. Some critics and fans trivialized musicians' individual artistry by comparing them with one another as if they were home-run hitters or race horses. When *Melody Maker* asked "Is Lester Still the President?" in a headline, the writer Mike Nevard responded "I'll Take Flip Any Time" in the adjoining column (Flip Phillips was a tenor player who often toured with JATP). As far as Nevard was concerned, younger, more energetic tenor players had unseated Pres, whom he described as being "out of office." Moreover, he sniped, "on stage [Young] is a big empty shell of a man. Off stage he is a whisky-drinker who makes a lot of witty remarks." Even Young's fellow tenor man Illinois Jacquet joined the debate when taking Leonard Feather's blindfold test in 1953; asked to comment on Young's "Let's Fall in Love," Jacquet noted that "Pres doesn't sound like he used to in the Basie days, but he sounds good. The feeling is still there."[13]

Significantly, Allan Morrison and Charlie Carpenter both believed that alcoholism and illness had taken the luster off Young's musical performances. After the saxophonist's death, Morrison would write candidly of his friend's problems with alcohol; at one point, he reported, Young had been consuming twelve fifths a week. The writer referred to the tenor player's love of marijuana in veiled terms, as "other indulgences sometimes associated with musicians."[14]

Carpenter, for his part, would provide a reminiscence of the problems he had encountered in managing Young. He knew he was "in for trouble," he said, when he "went in the back door at Birdland, and [Young was] sitting right on the edge of his chair, rubbing his hands." The saxophonist greeted him:

> "Lady Carpenter . . . how are your feelings?"
> "I'm fine, Lester."
> "I want you to know I'm not high tonight."
> He was so high he was blind. He hadn't worked yet, hadn't perspired, hadn't started to show it. He had built up an immunity but the heat would get to him.

His manager did not appreciate Young's sense of humor, nor did he consider the possibility that the saxophonist was toying with him. He did, however, praise him as "the sweetest, kindest man who ever lived." Carpenter also contended that contrary to rumor, Young had "never" been a user of hard drugs. His sidemen might indulge, but "the minute they drew that stuff out, Pres would order them to leave his room: 'Out! When you get past a stick or a glass, you have passed Pres.' "[15]

Barney Kessel was one of the musicians who painted a classic portrait of an artist with diminished powers. He recalled the Young who performed with JATP in 1952 as a man who "had slipped quite a bit [and whose] . . . health had deteriorated." The guitarist remembered a healthier Pres from the days when they had filmed *Jammin' the Blues* together in Los Angeles. When they recorded in 1952 with Oscar Peterson and Ray Brown in New York City, the tenor saxophonist was having "a good day . . . he didn't have anything to drink that day, and he had a big steak . . . a very unusual thing, 'cause . . . there were months that went by that he didn't do that." On that date, when they recorded mostly standards—among them "Just You, Just Me," "These Foolish Things," "Stardust," and "I'm Confessin' "—Young "was playing better . . . than he usually did in that low period," but he was nonetheless "still way below . . . what he normally would have done in the older days." Kessel believed that the change in Young had been "gradual" and attributed it to negative "elements in the army and his personal life." The saxophonist "had had shocking things happen to him. And he was shocked . . . to where he lost his way. And he never got back," said Kessel.

"When I knew him in '52 [with JATP]," Kessel reminisced, "all he was doing was sitting in his room drinking." The guitarist seconded what others had suggested before him: Young "didn't have much orientation [then]. . . . He was heavily involved in alcohol. He either was an alcoholic, or certainly consumed a lot . . . about a fifth a day." He did not eat and "looked very pasty, and very ill." Kessel noticed that the stylist seemed "kind of out of it, most of the time, and most of the time when he played, he played strictly by reflex." Young "played from having played so long that something would come to him." Yet Irving Ashby's recollection of his condition that same year contrasted sharply with Kessel's: Ashby did not remember seeing him drink any alcohol while he roomed with him on the JATP tour of Europe that spring.[16]

Other musicians besides Kessel expressed opinions similar to those put forward by writers. The guitarist John Collins, for example, felt that Young played with less "fire"—that is, less spirit—in the 1950s. Bassist Le Roy Jackson stated that he noted a change between the time he first played with Young, in 1949, and their reunion in 1953: the saxophonist, he said, "wasn't playing as hard. . . . Pres was playing more cooler." Jackson explained that the saxophonist's teeth were a real problem for him: "Pres used to take a piece of gum and stick it on his teeth to keep it [them] from vibrating. . . . [They] used to bother him lots." Otherwise he did not seem to have any health problems, according to Jackson, aside from his drinking.[17]

Testimony from longtime associates and sidemen sheds far more light on Young's abilities as a performer, on the question of his decline, and on the state of his health in the early 1950s than do writers' speculations. In a matter on which others agreed so readily, it seems significant that some musicians did not notice any difference in Young's playing. Buck Clayton, in fact, argued that after the war the saxophonist "sounded better." His experience in "the army didn't affect . . . his playing, I don't think," said Clayton, who attributed the improvement to the fact that Young could play more in JATP, for example, than he had been able to in the Basie band.[18]

The tenor stylist's sidemen were never systematically questioned about their years with him. Most were born in the 1920s, so the survivors are now in their seventies and eighties; their memories and reflections constitute an important source for comprehending Young, his music, and the music scene in general after World War II. Perhaps they revered Young more than other musicians did, since they were young apprentices—in their twenties, for the most part—working with someone they had never dreamed they might one day play with when they first saw him with Count Basie. A number of them—Junior Mance, Roy Haynes, and Connie Kay are exceptions—do not have name recognition with the general public or with younger fans. But it is particularly important to consider the opinions of lesser-known musicians, simply because, like many fans, they identified so thoroughly with Young, and also because they have been interviewed only rarely, if at all. Irving Ashby, Jesse Drakes, Gildo Mahones, Sadik Hakim, Carl "Kansas" Fields, and Le Roy Jackson all have much to contribute to our understanding of the saxophonist they played with as young musicians.

While noting Young's unique tone and powerful musical vision, his sidemen did not differentiate those qualities from his rather singular persona, which impressed his fans as much as his fierce devotion to the music and to his ideals of beauty, sincerity, and truth. The drummer Carl "Kansas" Fields, who was living in Paris when Young visited that city in the 1950s, insisted that the saxophonist's character and style of playing were linked—a concept not easy to grasp, partly because it is based on aesthetics and a quite abstract conception of self and music. In this respect, the sidemen's views of their leader differed from those of many critics and writers, who wished to separate the music from the jazz life that produced it, and to focus on specific musical characteristics—"lethargic" playing or honking, for example—rather than on the meaning or significance of the art.[19]

Surely the bonds Young formed with his regular sidemen were noteworthy, if only because these musicians spent so much time playing and traveling with him; because he occasionally gave them advice on their music or their lives; and because he looked after them financially, even though he was never one to "ride herd" on his sidemen, as most other bandleaders were prone to do. Thus their admiration for and loyalty toward him, and the emotion they witnessed on the part of audiences, become a crucial key to what others found to be such an enigmatic figure.

Young's sidemen emphasized his sheer popularity with African American audiences and fans. He was idolized not only for having his own distinctive style in music and dress, but also for blending together Black musical and oral traditions, permitting nonmusicians, from their spots near the bandstand or in the crowd, to scat-sing his record solos while he played. The longest of his lines, whether melodies or solos, were singable. As teenagers, Harlemites Connie Kay, Gildo Mahones, and Jesse Drakes had attended Basie shows at the Savoy and the Apollo Theater, near their homes; Sadik Hakim had heard Young perform with Basie in Minneapolis. All had noted the particularly warm reception that audiences gave Young whenever the Basie band came to town. Connie Kay recalled, "When Lester used to come out and play them solos, it broke up everything, man, you used to go [up to the bandstand], and the cats would wait for Lester to come out and solo." These loyal fans "would be singing along with him" during the more ecstatic moments of the evening's performance.[20]

Chicago musicians revered Young no less than Harlemites, and he spent considerable time in the Windy City between 1946 and the mid-1950s. Leroy Jackson and Junior Mance listened to the Basie band at South Side nightspots when they were growing up. On one occasion, Sadik Hakim reported, an arrangement of roses in the shape of a saxophone was presented to Young as a token of fans' appreciation of his artistry. When he played at the Bee Hive Lounge at 1503 East Fifty-fifth Street, near Hyde Park's lakefront, in the early autumn of 1953, his appearance was said to have resulted from the repeated requests of "numerous patrons." The stint was hailed as his "first appearance on the South Side on a permanent job." A party was held to welcome him to town.[21]

Junior Mance, a native of Evanston, Illinois, frequented and played in South Side clubs, often with the tenor saxophonist Gene Ammons, son of the boogie-woogie pianist Albert Ammons, in the late 1940s. He remembered, "When I was coming up, Pres was like God, as far as jazz [was concerned]. I had listened to all his records; in fact, all the young musicians then were buying all of Pres's records and listening to them." Young "influenced everybody in Chicago! Everybody," Mance claimed. "Guys who weren't musicians . . . could hum any Pres solo, note for note. . . . Everybody was scat singing. On the corners even, . . . out in front of the clubs." Similarly, when a band of high school students, including Chicagoans George Freeman, Le Roy Jackson, and Johnny Griffin, played "D.B. Blues," "all the kids in the dance room used to hum the solo." Mance recalled that "every time a new Lester Young record came out . . . we just went out and bought [it]." He concluded, "This is the impact he had on the Chicago musicians then."[22]

Besides being admired for his saxophone artistry, Young was known for emitting an aura of mystery that enveloped members of his band. Sadik Hakim referred to him as having a certain "mystique" about him. Charlie Carpenter related how strange the saxophonist's entourage appeared, on first meeting, even to him—someone who knew the musicians' world from inside. "I found myself riding the train into Newark with five of the funniest-looking cats I ever saw in my life," he reminisced. Their attire, no doubt the latest in hip fashions, was partly responsible, but it was also their hilarity: "We're sitting on the train looking at each other, and I'm cracking up and they're cracking up," Carpenter remembered.[23]

By the late 1940s Young had developed a regular routine and habits not unlike the rituals that some athletes go through before a big game or event. Unique to the tenor stylist, however, was that he made these a way of life, following his rituals even when he was *not* about to perform. What seemed like mere eccentricities to some in fact revealed his values and, moreover, helped to account for the hold he had on the imagination of his sidemen and fans. In the privacy of his hotel room, he could be straightforward with everyone with whom he shared his singular brand of hospitality.

His sidemen were, of course, always welcome in Young's room. In this respect, he differed from other bandleaders; Sadik Hakim recalled that he "left his door open and everybody'd be in his room, all the time, wherever we'd be." After checking in and unpacking, they would "all file into Pres's room, and he'd be walking around in his shorts." (Here Hakim explained, "All the time I was with him, he always walked around [with] his shorts on until we went to work"; waiting till show time to finish dressing was a ritual common to many, if not most, people in show business.) Nor did his emphasis on equality and informality stop at his open door: "He was different from guys nowadays. Leaders. Everybody [goes] to a city and the leader stays in one hotel, and musicians stay in another hotel and wherever you want to," Hakim said, adding that with "Pres, we all stayed together, *all* the time." In this way, Young kept alive the Blue Devils' spirit of "All for one, and one for all."

In 1946 and 1947, the years of Hakim's stint with him, Young "incessantly smoked [marijuana] and drank." The sideman claimed that the saxophonist "didn't want to *talk* to nobody if they didn't smoke." When someone entered his room, without any preliminaries, "the first thing [he] would hand you would be a glass of gin and sherry wine mixed, and a big joint. Light green. So if you didn't smoke, he'd tell you, 'What's the matter, Pres, I feel a draft' "—meaning he was getting bad vibrations. In this way he separated avid fans from other hangers-on and those who felt uncomfortable with his hospitality. Sometimes he would go through a "big routine" when a nonsmoker lingered on. Hakim recounted how on such occasions Young would whisper cryptically to him, " 'Von Hangman is here—we'll have to go out.' So he'd tell this guy we were going out and we'd go with him and say good-bye, and then we'd go round the block and right back in again!"[24]

Young's drinking also became part of his legend, as was the case for Lionel Barrymore and others in show business who were notorious for their alcoholism. Initially Hakim knew about Young's prowess as a musician but was unaware of his love of strong liquor. "When I went out with him from New York the first time," he recalled, "I picked up this case, suitcase, I thought it had clothes [in it], and it come open and it was all full of gin and sherry wine . . . which he took on the road with him." Using these ingredients, Young mixed his beloved "top and bottom" cocktail.

Hakim maintained that Young ate very little—not uncommon among those who drink as much as he did. "All the time I knew him, he *never* did eat much," the pianist said. He related how Young's friends tried to persuade him to eat, ordering savory dishes for him that he would invariably only nibble at, leaving the food practically untouched. Hakim also observed that the saxophonist seemed to suffer from insomnia. The two musicians customarily talked in Young's hotel room for a while after a performance, and then Hakim would leave to go to sleep; when he returned hours later, Young would still be sitting there smoking, drinking, and listening to records on his turntable. "I don't know when he ever slept," the pianist mused. On other nights, Young would fool around with another reed instrument: "He'd play that clarinet to death," his sideman noted, adding that he would have played it more if he hadn't enjoyed the tenor sax so much.

Around 1947, Young refrained from going out either before or after the job; he stayed in his hotel room when he wasn't playing, instead of visiting friends or seeking opportunities to jam. Hakim explained that Young simply "didn't like to be around people who didn't do the same things he did." He declined invitations to go out, even to accept the hospitality of the Heath family and sample Mrs. Heath's home cooking, a favorite of musicians when they stopped in Philadelphia. Jimmy Heath recalled that Young preferred having his meals delivered to his room. "His style was cool, laid back, laid back. And he would come out at night . . . and go make his gigs."[25]

A seizure that Young suffered around this time may have played a role in his insistence on staying in. Hakim reported that one day, before a job at the Baby Grand in Harlem in the late spring of 1947, Young "just collapsed"; he hit his head upon falling and then began to chew his tongue. The pianist placed a spoon in his mouth to prevent him from doing serious damage, then called a doctor. That night, wearing dark glasses to hide the black eye that had resulted from his fall, Young "played really great."[26]

Connie Kay, Young's drummer on and off for about six years, drove him to and from club dates in the early 1950s. The saxophonist preferred to ride in autos, it was said, because once, on the subway, a drunken passenger had spotted his saxophone case and demanded that he play, harassing him so much, and calling him by such a derogatory name, that he pulled out the straight razor that he carried for protection. Young was arrested, and after that he always rode in private cars or taxis. Kay reminisced, "[We] were like buddies. . . . He was a sweetheart to me. He was very shy . . . didn't love crowds or to be around strangers, and . . . didn't like to eat." Kay vividly recalled "all that alcohol," and told how Young would "leave home for work with a fifth of Scotch every night and everybody in the band would work on it to keep Lester from getting too drunk." When the doctor advised the saxophonist to switch to cognac—"a *little* cognac[—]it was a whole bottle of cognac every night."[27]

Young's musical talents, rituals, and language solidified his bond with his sidemen, apprentices, and fans, creating a circle of hipsters around him who just adored him and who were, moreover, attuned to what was happening in music culture throughout the nation. Dexter Gordon admired Young so much that he used to practice his repertoire of his hero's mannerisms in the mirror. Sonny Rollins in New York City, Miles Davis in St. Louis, Gene Ammons and Johnny Griffin in Chicago, and Jimmy Heath and John Coltrane in Philadelphia were all avid admirers of the tenor saxophonist. They visited with Young or listened to him closely while he played, drawing inspiration from his music. Connie Kay claimed that Young's playing influenced his own drum soloing: "My solos are always short, which I learned from Lester Young. He never took more than two or three choruses, and neither did Charlie Parker, but they always managed to say all they had to say."[28]

In another instance, Jimmy Heath explained why he and John Coltrane watched Young's every move on the bandstand so closely. Whenever their idol came to Philadelphia, or they themselves were in New York, Heath said they went to see him "because Lester Young [was] . . . one of the *leading innovators* in saxophone fingering. . . . He had fingerings that are not in any books anywhere." What was more, "Lester had more fingerings that would give you different textures of notes than anybody I ever met. . . . I use that fingering. Sonny Rollins [does]. Trane [does, too]." Heath added that Young was also "what I would term . . .

'sneaky fast.' . . . He wasn't obviously a fast saxophone player like you hear some guys, . . . they sound like they're fast players, but Lester would play tempos that [were] fast and just glide over them so smoothly, it wouldn't seem like it was that much effort applied."[29]

Young's sidemen had still other reasons for admiring and respecting him. He genuinely cared about their wellbeing, regularly asking if they needed money to tide them over when there were few or no bookings. Hakim noted, "I've worked with many bandleaders [and] he's the only one that used to come around and ask you, . . . 'You all need some money?'" Hakim insisted, "I never heard no bandleaders . . . none of them do that." The saxophonist treated these advances as "loans," though the pianist reported that he would "*never write it* [the amount of the loan] *down*" and never ask to be repaid. Some people took advantage of him: "I guess he expected the cats would pay him, and some of the cats would never pay him," Hakim said, adding, "He was very generous." Irving Ashby also mentioned Young's generosity; during their European tour, he remembered, the tenor saxophonist loaned him money to purchase a camera case, then never mentioned it again.[30]

Other remarks made by sidemen and admirers provide insight into the singular impact Young had on them both musically and personally. Hakim, for example, became a Muslim while he was with Young, and he concluded that the tenor saxophonist was not only basically "a beautiful person" but also "more religious than *all* those people that do [attend church] just to be seen." Moreover, Hakim felt that Young was, "in his head, a religious man," even though he did not go to church. Although he did not talk about it very much, "his religion, he *believed* in this. . . . His manner . . . was religious."[31]

Long after he left the band, late in 1947, Hakim continued to visit with Young in New York City and listen to his music whenever he could. He considered the saxophonist "probably about the greatest jazz instrumentalist in the world . . . one of the greatest." For Hakim, "he's as important as . . . Thurgood Marshall, Andy Young, he's more important to our thing, to Black people than [those] kinds of celebrities." Like Armstrong, Young was "an ambassador . . . like his music put Black and white people together." Nor was Hakim alone in expressing such beliefs: many people thought music promoted racial integration and democracy in an era of civil rights achievements, a time when professional baseball and even the military were being integrated, to be followed by the famous Supreme Court case that put an end to legal racial segregation.[32]

But behind such lofty ideals lay the day-to-day business of making music. Young's sidemen pointed out that they never rehearsed for nightclub performances; nor did their leader ever discuss the music with them. He might briefly scat the melody as an intro, as he did on "Sunday" and "Movin' with Lester" one night at Town Hall in the autumn of 1947. When he arrived in Washington, D.C., in December 1956 to play with the house trio at Olivia Davis's Patio Lounge, pianist Bill Potts recalled that "rather than have a rehearsal, we had a 'talk over' and agreed on which tunes we knew in which key, tempo, etc."

On and off for about seven years, Jesse Drakes played with and learned from this stylist who seemed to approach everything in a strikingly original fashion. If things were not going well, he might give one of the musicians a peculiar look. Drakes explained, "When you were around Pres for a while, you could tell what Pres liked and what he didn't like. It was a feeling." He eventually concluded that "being prepared for Pres, nothing was unusual with me. . . . What a lot of people would say was unusual would be normal to me from Pres."[33]

Similar statements about Young, displaying ingenuity in their explanations as well as considerable loyalty, were made by other sidemen. The guitarist Barney Kessel, for example, found insightful ways of expressing the saxophonist's character and significance. Besides appearing with him in Granz's film short *Jammin' the Blues,* Kessel did a JATP tour (as a sideman for Oscar Peterson) at the same time as Young, in the spring of 1952, and recorded with him later the same year. The Muskogee, Oklahoma, native said in 1982, "Of all the musicians in jazz that I've ever heard on any instrument, Lester Young is the most profound. Of any instrument—right up to now."

Commenting on Young's economy, Kessel observed that "when he played, there was nothing thrown away, there [were] no asides . . . nothing parenthetical," adding, "It's a firm but gentle approach. And it's just the purity of it." He likened hearing Young play to "getting a good piece of cheesecake . . . [that is] not served on a particularly warm plate; there's not red lights going on and off like you're sitting in a movie . . . it's just straight cheesecake. . . . It's spiritual . . . the purity of it comes through. The essence of it comes through, linked to a person's soul." With Young, Kessel contended, in a statement that said as much about Young's music as it did about his character, "What he is speaks louder than what he says he is."[34]

Several musicians remarked on the special relaxed quality of Young's playing. While noting the emotion involved, Irving Ashby maintained that there was also an ironic aspect to it: "Pres is the only person I know that could play a song that *called* for fire and not put fire into it . . . not approach it that way." Thus, "even when he was playing something that was way up [tempo,] like 'Clap Hands, Here Comes Charlie,' it was still the cool approach." Furthermore, Young never ran out of ideas or lost control, like some other musicians, who would be soloing and then "all of a sudden, nothing's happening." Ashby insisted, "that never happened with Pres. . . . His solos flowed, just smooth as though he had sat down there and figured them out before the concert." Without exception, "the *message* was always there," Ashby noted. Then "tomorrow on the same song, he'd tell a different story."[35]

Gildo Mahones discussed Young's singular artistry and echoed Ashby: "Everything he did was like a new experience every time we went on the bandstand." He confirmed others' claims that Young's "solos were different every time." At first the young pianist had been unable to perceive or appreciate the differences from song to song, from night to night. But whereas other musicians played set lists of tunes and soon found they were repeating themselves, with Young, "no matter how many times we played the songs, it was different every time. Whatever he created around the song was always different." Mahones finally realized that "it didn't matter what the song was." People who complained of Young, "'He's playing the same tune' . . . were not listening to what he was doing [with] the song. That's the whole thing in jazz," Mahones summed up: "what you do with the music."[36]

Young's impact on other bands' repertoires was impressive as well: not only did he turn certain popular tunes into jazz standards, but he also made his interpretation the standard one. In the early 1950s, his combo additionally performed numerous blues and ballads. But even though "everybody was playing the same ballads," Junior Mance recalled that Young "would play them different from everybody else . . . [to the point] where they would sound like different tunes." According to the pianist, Young's interpretation of some songs became the preferred choice: "When musicians said, 'These Foolish Things,' the first thing they thought about was Pres, and not the popular tune the way it was written."[37]

Sadik Hakim made a similar observation regarding Young and other great stylists: "What they played was even better than the melody to the song; they were able to create a line even better than what the composer wrote. . . . Their improvisations were better." Young's solo on "These Foolish Things," for example, inspired Eddie Jefferson to write accompanying lyrics, which became the basis for his "Baby Girl." "Polka Dots and Moonbeams" was another song that Young made famous.[38]

Young's sidemen shed new light on the criticism leveled at him. Gildo Mahones stated, "To me he sounded *great* . . . [not compared to others, but] compared to *himself*." Jesse Drakes noted that because Young never played anything the same way twice, it was impossible to evaluate how well or badly he was playing on a particular night. If his soloing varied, it was because of "how he felt" and the problems he had with his teeth. In other words, critics and fans never took into account the fact that Young's playing was not only spontaneous but situational, depending a great deal upon the other musicians, the audience, and the surroundings, as well as the saxophonist's own health.[39]

Connie Kay's thoughts on the matter were similar to the other sidemen's. On the question of "bad" nights, Kay mused, "When you're playing with somebody who's a creator, how do you know when he's having a bad night?" He explained, "He's a creator . . . so, as long as he's playing the right changes . . . who am I to say he's having a bad night?" Taking issue with the critics' comparison of Young in his Basie years with the stylist of the 1950s, Kay then asked, "How do they know that the second time [he recorded something] he didn't want to play it different[?] . . . There's no sense in . . . making two records of the same tune and playing it the same way."

Expanding on this idea of creators and imitators, Kay noted, "With creators you can't compare; *I* can't. Now imitators, yeah, 'cause imitators, they're going to play the same thing all the time. So . . . you can say, 'This was a bad night,' if what you heard the first time was supposed to be his greatest; so if he comes back the second time and doesn't do it like that, if he's an imitator, then you say, 'Well, man, that cat didn't play as good as he did the first time.' " Kay likened Parker to Young in this sense, insofar as "I couldn't tell when Bird had a bad night. . . . Them kind of cats, man, you can't say they had bad nights. It's always happening [when they play]."[40]

The issue of Young's declining artistry cannot be easily resolved, though his biographer Lewis Porter has done an excellent job of addressing it from a musicological perspective. For example, he notes that Young's tone changed twice—once after 1942 and then "again around 1950." Then, too, over the years, the saxophonist's rhythmic approach altered in that he became more independent of the beat. After 1942, he developed different contour types, increased the harmonic tension, and relied on "more extroverted expressive devices" in his playing. As Porter rightfully observes, his later sound was different from, but not necessarily inferior to, that of his Basie days. (As for repertoire, that remained essentially unchanged, as Young continued to play the same mix of blues and popular songs he had always offered audiences.)[41]

Some musicians take an epistemological stance on this question, in that they ask how any outsider can possibly decide that a difference in and of itself means that one performance is better than another. If Connie Kay and Gildo Mahones—who certainly were not outsiders unfamiliar with the man's music—do not feel qualified to make this kind of evaluation, then how can critics, who heard Young only occasionally, be so certain of their opinions? It seems curious, too, that writers did not see fit to compare him to other saxophonists of his generation, such as Coleman Hawkins and Ben Webster, both of whom, like Young, suffered from alcoholism and, moreover, favored ballads in the 1950s. No critic ever devoted as much ink to Young's liking for ballads as was spent on his playing of Basie standards or differences in his tone. And that is a shame, for such preferences can tell us much about an artist; as the bassist Percy Heath once observed, "The way you play has to do with the way you feel that night," adding, "When that slave cried out in the field, he wasn't just making music, he *felt* that way."[42]

In 1947 and again in the 1950s, Young published his opinions in trade journals, in Black newspapers, and in radio interviews, but his comments were either ignored altogether by critics or not taken seriously. Given the lack of attention paid to Young's views during his lifetime, some of them are worth recounting here. They paint a picture of an artist conscious of the changes he was making, a musician constantly seeking to create new sounds. He was ever-evolving, like Duke Ellington and Miles Davis, two others who also suffered the criticism that they did not compose or play the way they once had done.[43]

In a series of interviews in the 1950s, Young clarified the ideas he had first advanced in the late 1940s. In late 1951, he reacted to unidentified selections played for him in a "blindfold test," and explained that his musical tastes were diversified, though he admitted to being partial to singers. Asked who his favorites were, he responded, "I like variety. I don't like to get hung up with one thing. Anything they play over the radio that I like, I'll get it." He concluded with a signature Young remark proclaiming the catholicity of his taste: "Just all music, all day and all night music. Just any kind of music you play for me, I melt with all of it."[44]

If the number of stars he assigned to the blindfold-test selections was significant (five was the highest possible mark), he did make some distinctions, but he also spoke favorably of nearly every tune. In particular, he praised the Four Brothers—saxophonists Stan Getz, Zoot Sims, Herb Steward, and Serge Chaloff—with Woody Herman's band, liking them so much that he gave them eight stars: "I don't think I ever heard any saxophones sound like that," he exclaimed. He compared the number to some Coleman Hawkins recordings made in a similar format in Europe, and concluded, "Well I'm just weak for saxophones anyway. . . . I can just hear that over and over and over."

Several other selections received four stars from Young, including "Corcovado," a composition by Darius Milhaud, performed by Artie Shaw with an orchestra; the saxophonist liked the rendition—"All the way! . . . It's beautiful music"—and confessed, "I never dig into the classicals, you know, I've heard very few records. I've never dug that deep." While he did not recognize Shaw, he vowed to work on his own clarinet playing. Basie, JATP, and Boyd Raeburn selections also rated four stars.[45]

In early 1956, as he sat in his Queens home giving a *Down Beat* interview to Nat Hentoff, he expounded on his ideas, detailing the composition of his "dream band" and outlining his approach to the music: what he tried to do each set, why he always gave his musicians a chance to solo, and what he thought about the rhythm section. Asked to describe his ideal, he said he would prefer a small combo to a big band. He would have a rhythm guitarist such as Freddie Green to augment the piano, bass, and drums; then trumpet, trombone, baritone sax, and himself; and finally a singer—maybe Frank Sinatra. As for arrangements, "There are a lot of people I'd like, but I'd have to think about it." The chances of his being able to put together such a group were, he concluded, very small.[46]

Moving on from such fantasies, Young reported, "I'd also like to make some records with strings, some soft ballads"—thus confirming his interest in experimenting along the lines of recent work by Billie Holiday and Charlie Parker. He noted that he had been scheduled to make such records in California, but the deal had fallen through, though the door was not completely closed on the matter. (Two years after what the press had touted as his "reconciliation" with Billie Holiday, he also observed,

"I'd maybe also like to make some more records with Billie, but that would be left up to her." While they in fact would never record together again, for reasons that are unclear, he would accompany her on her song "Fine and Mellow," on "The Sound of Jazz," a CBS television special, and then again a few times when they were both in Paris in the winter of 1959.) Along with ballads, dance traditions also figured into Young's music conception. In the comfort of his Queens home, he explained, "I play a variety of tempos. I set my own tempos and I take my time."[47]

Sounding remarkably at ease throughout the interview, he remained modest concerning his influences and refrained from singling out specific saxophonists. "Of the newer tenors, I like all them little youngsters," he said, though pronouncing himself particularly fond of the Four Brothers record. As to whether he thought he had influenced them, he allowed, "I hear a lot of little things from what I play," but then added with characteristic restraint, "but I never say anything. . . . I don't want to sound like I think I influenced everybody." No one, he emphasized when pressed, among the younger tenor saxophonists had named him as a model.[48]

His own clarinet playing, he said, had been hindered by the fact that "I never could find the one I wanted," referring to the metal instrument he had used on the Kansas City Six records, which had somehow gotten away from him. If he could find a similar clarinet to his liking, he might "pick up on it this year," he vowed. He expressed a preference for Jimmy Guiffre among the younger clarinetists: "He sure plays me, especially in the low tones." Among the older ones, "I have to put it right on Benny Goodman always, him and Artie Shaw."[49]

The saxophonist liked some of the younger trumpet players—Miles Davis and Jesse Drakes in particular. Having overcome his heroin addiction, Davis was being presented in the press as a comeback story in the mid-1950s, with a number of successful records under his belt, and a quintet that was touted as the best in the business. Young noted, "I've heard more of Miles than most and I like him." In addition to St. Louis and New York City encounters, Young would record with Davis later that year in Europe. Of his own sideman Jesse Drakes, he said, "I like him because he plays his own way and doesn't try to imitate nobody." Because they had been playing together for so long, Young could, in a manner reminiscent of Walter Page and the Blue Devils, "just call a number and we're gone." The leader observed that within a band, "things like that mean a lot."[50]

Asked to detail his expectations of his sidemen, he made it clear that "the piano should play little fill-ins . . . nice little full chords behind the horn." He spoke highly of his current pianist, Gildo Mahones: "He never gets in your way. Some pianists just run all over the piano when you're playing, and that's a drag." He also liked John Lewis of the Modern Jazz Quartet, and remarked of that combo, "They need a quiet place to be heard." The MJQ's music was original, he said: "The little things they play are their own . . . something new. I've never heard anybody play like that but them."

In his own group, the bassist "should play nice, four-beat rhythm that can be heard, but no slapping," which he detested. He liked "bowed work" on bass but stressed that "not all bass players can play good with a bow." Speaking as if he were thinking of Percy Heath of the MJQ, he asserted, "It's so nice to have one [a bass player] who can [play with a bow] in a small group." Johnny Ore was a bassist he liked who worked with him quite a bit.

The remaining member of the rhythm section, the drummer, should "be straight with the section." Those who dropped "bombs," as they were called, were guilty of "messing with the rhythm," in Young's opinion. Drummers in small groups should play "a little tinkely boom on that one cymbal, four-beats on the pedal. Just little simple things, but no bombs."[51]

His philosophy of cooperation could be summed up as: "I don't get in his way, and I let him play, and he shouldn't get in mine." Without such a protocol, he said, "your mind gets twisted." Young explained, "That's why I always let my little kiddies play solos. That way they don't bother me when I solo." Occasionally the saxophonist heard criticism from people who came to hear him play and felt disappointed because he allowed his sidemen to solo so much, but it was his contention that "if you're paying a man to play, and if that man is on the bandstand and can play, he should get a chance to tell his story."[52]

By giving his sidemen ample opportunity to solo, Young adhered to the New Orleans heritage of cooperation and goodwill among the musicians in a band. And in upholding this tradition, he conversely displayed considerable wisdom as a leader by letting his sidemen have a chance, thus helping to ensure that they would learn something from the experience, stay in good spirits, and continue to play with him when he called on them.[53]

Not one to listen to his own records, he nonetheless listed his favorites for Hentoff, even as he protested, "I feel funny listening to my own records. I think I enjoy them too well." He feared he might unintentionally repeat himself when he played, he said, "so I don't like to listen to them over and over," as he did with other records. "Lester Leaps In," "Clap Hands, Here Comes Charlie," "Every Tub," "Swingin' the Blues," "One O'Clock Jump," and his very first recording, "Shoe Shine Boy," were his choices.[54]

Although he liked some of his Basie recordings, he was not willing to compare the big band of his day with that of the 1950s. When he first joined the Basie band, he said, "it was very nice. Just like I thought it was going to be." Comparisons seemed to him unfair, because the 1936 band "was different from today's, a different style. . . . But the band [Basie] has now is very nice." While he had recently played with Basie's band at Birdland as a featured soloist, and toured with the band in the club's entourage, Young observed, "I myself . . . wouldn't like to play in a big band. You don't get a chance to play." A mere eight bars of solo at the mike left him unsatisfied, as did the big-band format in general: "[After your solo] you sit down. You're just sitting there and reading the music. There are no kicks for me that way."[55]

A few years later, he would concede that his own playing had changed with the times. His music was dynamic, not static; sustained creativity was the key element for him, as it was for Miles Davis and John Coltrane. "If I'm going to stay there and play that same stuff"—as he had done, for example, with Basie—"year after year, well, Jesus, I'd be an old man." He concluded, "I don't think like that [anymore], so I have to try to think of little new tricks and little new sounds and things like that." Anything else, he insisted, was "not progressive."[56]

Despite the evolution in his own playing, he still liked listening to big bands "[that play] a variety of music that people can dance to and [feature] good soloists." In fact, just at the dawn of the rock and roll era, he yearned for the days of the big bands, expressing his opinion that "they'll all be finally coming back to swinging and to dancing to music again." As for the current fads, "a lot of the things now," he maintained, "are just novelties. For me, the music has to swing first." Swinging still gave him considerable enjoyment, and while he no longer practiced on his horn ("I think I've been playing long enough"), he emphasized, "I love to play."[57]

His love of playing was matched by his love of change, which he considered essential for any true artist; otherwise, he charged, one was simply a "repeater pencil." Nor was this concept limited to music; it applied equally to fashion, jive talk, dance styles, and hip culture in general. Young believed that in order to evolve, he had to remain sensitive to obvious changes, such as bebop, as well as to the more nuanced evolution of the jazz life. He was known as a trendsetter in this regard, not only in his treatment of songs and his use of jazz slang, but also in other, more profound ways.

CHAPTER 16

Up 'n' Adam

The Cult of the Cool

THE last few years of Young's life were in a sense the most controversial. Regardless of his alleged decline in previous years, by 1956 or 1957 it was clear that alcoholism and illness were taking an enormous toll on him. Ill health plagued him—he was frequently described as suffering from bad nerves or exhaustion, or both, and hospitalizations often followed lengthy road tours—but aside from cirrhosis and its effects, the precise nature of his ailment is unknown. Beverly, his daughter from Minneapolis, noted, "Dad had a liver problem (serious, yes) [and] also an ulcer (which bled). There was also . . . a form of sleeping disorder which affected him in many ways." He refused to see a doctor but was hospitalized in late 1955 and then again a year later. One of these times doctors gave him about two years to live; of course, they recommended that he give up drinking. He collapsed following a coast-to-coast tour in late 1957 or early 1958 and suffered a heart attack in the summer of 1958. His wife and his sister Irma, who had moved to Manhattan in around 1955, both looked after him. Others concerned with his condition included Marshall Stearns, a professor of English literature who also wrote about jazz; Dr. Luther Cloud, a clinical psychiatrist; and Elaine Swain, a friend of Young's who appeared on the scene around this time and would be alone with him when he died.[1]

In 1956 or 1957, Young and his manager went their separate ways, for reasons that remain unclear. At first Jesse Drakes took over Carpenter's responsibilities, and then there was at least one other manager, named Gabby Hayes. Most of Young's regular sidemen had ceased playing with him by the mid-1950s; Drakes was the last to go. Young played mainly as a single, backed by pickup musicians, or toured with larger shows—JATP, for example, or as a special feature with Basie in the Birdland All-

Stars. In early 1958 or so, he left his wife and two children and moved into the Alvin, the musicians' hotel at Fifty-second and Broadway, across from Birdland. This was where Dr. Cloud and others visited him.[2]

For much of this period, JATP was an important part of Young's life and career—a safe haven, a bastion of racial equality, and, given that he traveled with it nearly every year, a guarantee of his prosperity, since he no longer had a regular combo. JATP promoted and enjoyed a renaissance in the 1950s as jazz became increasingly popular on college campuses and even with the U.S. State Department, which sent jazz bands overseas to symbolize U.S. democracy in the midst of the Cold War. The resurgence of the music was evident in the concert halls and at the festivals where the traveling entourages played. The first annual jazz festival in Newport, Rhode Island, held in 1954, encouraged camaraderie and attempted to impart a sophisticated and respectable dimension to the music. *Newsweek,* summarizing the music's history with a cliché before moving on to other clichés, observed that from its humble beginnings in New Orleans bordellos, jazz "has now reached the fabled social lawns of the Casino at Newport." Despite such elitist environs, the general tone of the affair seemed to be "social pedigree be damned." The seventy thousand or so fans thus "included Newport veterans with the air of retired steam yachtsman, masses of orderly jazz lovers of all colors, and young hep cats of the most raucous sort." The following year, *Time* described the fans as "cats, hipsters, vipers, and . . . a few moldy figs," and the occasion as one on which, in defiance of the setting, "neckties were not worn and tea was not drunk."[3]

The egalitarian emphasis of jazz festivals and JATP harked back not only to TOBA, the Blue Devils, and the Reno Club band, but also to the throngs of urbanites who had once milled on the sidelines of parades and funerals in cities such as Memphis, New Orleans, and Baltimore in the late nineteenth and early twentieth centuries. Granz insisted of his JATP troupe, "Wherever we go, we go together," mirroring the fraternity that Young emphasized with an open hotel-room door and shared solos. In Granz's case, however, it meant that he saw to it that the performers traveled in style, stayed in first-class hotels, were guaranteed equal treatment regardless of their race, and were not booked into southern cities where state laws required segregated performances and accommodations. To achieve his end of bringing respect to jazz and its musicians, he required nonsegregation clauses in all JATP contracts, a point on which he was unyielding.[4]

Beginning in 1952, Young periodically traveled with JATP to Europe. Such junkets served as material evidence of the music's international stature and importance during the Cold War. In 1956 the saxophonist visited the continent with the Birdland All-Stars. He was pleased by his favorable reception and the tremendous response accorded the music. "I like some of the musicians I played with in Europe," he later reported; after the concerts, he would often jam in two or three different clubs a night. "I was surprised because you hear funny things over here before you go, but when you get to Europe, you find they can play very good, too," he noted. The Birdland entourage also included Bud Powell, Miles Davis, and the Modern Jazz Quartet. That fall Young played at Nicole Barclay's Club in Paris for three weeks.[5]

Granz's commentary on JATP's European reception went a bit further than Young's appreciation of the music scene. Touting JATP's exemplification of American principles of government after one foreign tour, the promoter declared, "Jazz seems to be understood the world over and everywhere it means but one thing, friendship for America and democracy." Evidently the U.S. government agreed: in 1956 it enlisted Dizzy Gillespie and other bandleaders to serve as jazz ambassadors overseas, in an effort to win friends and disprove Soviet criticism of American racial segregation. This approach backfired, however, in the fall of 1957, when Louis Armstrong protested President Eisenhower's handling of the crisis surrounding the integration of Central High in Little Rock, Arkansas. His comments prevented him from being chosen by the State Department to tour the Soviet Union.[6]

Granz's beliefs concerning democracy and racial equality served him well, as jazz became for him an instrument by which to help those who were victimized by racism and an oppressive political milieu. One of the first JATP concerts, in July 1944, had raised funds for the Sleepy Lagoon Defense Committee, which assisted several Mexican-American youths charged with murder. Participating musicians on that occasion included J. J. Johnson, Illinois Jacquet, Jack McVea, Lee Young, Shorty Sherrock, Nat Cole, Les Paul, and Red Callender.[7]

Granz's very politics, not to mention his aggressiveness, made him anathema to some in the music business. Unlike the usual entrepreneur, he insisted that improving race relations was his primary objective; making money and presenting good jazz came next. He freely admitted, "I would rather sell mediocre jazz to nine thousand people and sell my pitch on race relations with it . . . than operate in a vacuum." His straightforwardness was welcomed by many musicians, Young among them, and what was more, it *worked:* southern racists had to capitulate to his demands or lose the opportunity to hear the premier jazz artists in the nation. When bookers in Houston reneged on their part of the deal, or police raided a backstage card game in the middle of a concert, Granz hired attorneys and fought and won in court.[8]

Young, Roy Eldridge, Coleman Hawkins, Flip Phillips, Oscar Peterson, and the others in the show all benefited considerably from both Granz's sense of loyalty toward them and, of course, his organizational abilities. He served as the show's emcee for a time, during which period his zeal became almost as renowned as the music. JATP was also a money-maker: its reputation for giving "people in Des Moines and El Paso the kind of jazz they could otherwise never see or hear" allowed it to gross almost $5 million in 1953. Despite his high principles, Granz himself contended, "If I didn't make $100,000 take-home pay a year, I'd quit."[9]

Yet for all that profitability, the schedule of JATP could be grueling and hard on the health of the entourage. In the spring of 1952, JATP played Göteborg, Copenhagen, Malmö, Paris, Brussels, Zurich, Geneva, Bern, and Frankfurt—one or two shows and one or two days per stop. Its very success led to new kinds of problems for the musicians: after one concert, it reportedly "took the performers forty-five minutes to fight their way through the ecstatic crowd outside." In 1953 JATP covered some eighteen thousand miles, appearing in fifty-eight cities—not only in the United States and Canada, but in Japan, Australia, and the Philippines—within just three months' time.[10]

The array of JATP artists varied somewhat from year to year, but the format usually remained the same. The show started with a jam session—several horn men performing with Young, for example, on a blues or ballad. In 1952 Pres was featured in a medley that he started off with "I Can't Get Started"; Charlie Shavers followed on "Summertime," then Flip Phillips performed "Sweet Lorraine," Roy Eldridge used "It's the Talk of the Town" for his improvisations, and Benny Carter closed out the set with "Cocktails for Two." Different combos led by Oscar Peterson or Gene Krupa played during the show's second set.[11]

In 1955 Young traveled first with JATP, in the late summer and early autumn, and then with the Birdland tour. Late in the year he was hospitalized—for what complaint remains unclear—but by early 1956 he seems to have regained his spirits and health. Clearly it was a stressful time for him, as various forces at work in the music business in the 1950s—including the rise of rock and roll and the formation of large road shows featuring myriad different acts—challenged Granz's dominance and perhaps ultimately accounted for the saxophonist's leaving JATP.

Part of the problem Young faced was the emergence of white tenor saxophone players who admired him, played in his style, and reaped the financial rewards that should have been his. They won polls regularly, toured with JATP and other shows, and booked the best club dates. True, some African American saxophonists were also playing like Young, and others were adding their own particular dynamics and energy to performances; a movie deal was even in the offing for one such tenor player as early as 1949. But even without the challenge posed by this new generation—which was, after all, a part of the tradition that every well-known musician must come to expect—competing touring shows, changes in the music industry, and new fads among audiences all tested Young's ability to persevere in his profession.[12]

The other touring jazz and rhythm-and-blues shows positioned themselves as direct rivals to Norman Granz's creation. In 1953, for example, the bandleader Stan Kenton headlined a "Festival of Modern American Jazz," which also featured Erroll Garner's trio, the singer June Christy, and the bands of Dizzy Gillespie, Stan Getz, Candido, and Slim Gaillard. In early 1954, Lee Konitz and Charlie Parker joined the revue, which toured New England, the Eastern Seaboard, the Deep South, the Southwest, and the Rocky Mountain states. Around the same time, the Gale Agency assembled a troupe comprising Nat "King" Cole, Sarah Vaughan, the Billy May Orchestra, and a complement of comedians and dancers; this entourage of top names performed up and down the East Coast and in the South.[13]

These shows evidenced the arrival on the national scene of "new" artists, such as Cole and Vaughan, who had been known as jazz musicians before they gained a popular following. They appealed just as much to some jazz aficionados as they did to listeners who liked their treatment of immediately recognizable popular songs. Such so-called jazz stylings ranked among the best-selling records in the nation in the mid-1950s, and performers who played the Newport Jazz Festival and dates on college campuses enjoyed even greater popularity. In late 1956, "easy listening" records by the Modern Jazz Quartet, Ella Fitzgerald, and Oscar Peterson were top sellers, edging out "progressive" jazz recordings by

Art Blakey and the Jazz Messengers, the combo of Max Roach and Clifford Brown, and Lennie Tristano.[14]

Blues bands also grew in popularity after World War II. This was one facet of a greater interest in country and folk songs among progressives as well as southerners and southwesterners. Singers such as Charles Brown, Buddy Johnson, T-Bone Walker, Wynonie Harris, and Ruth Brown toured the United States, offering soulful blues, popular songs, and rhythm and blues in African American theaters and clubs. Electric guitarists in particular, notably Muddy Waters, B. B. King, and Chuck Berry, popularized blues through their own compositions and tunes by Willie Dixon, the bassist.

Chicago's South Side clubs reflected such changes in fans' tastes, giving Windy City audiences a remarkable range of nightclub music to choose from on any given evening. In the summer of 1955, for example, Ray Charles, Illinois Jacquet, and blues musicians Big Maybelle, Memphis Slim, and Muddy Waters were all playing in various resorts on Thirty-fifth, Forty-seventh, and Fifty-fifth streets, presenting stiff competition for Young and Ben Webster as the two tenors and their respective combos alternated sets in yet another Chicago club. The pianist Ahmad Jamal and the bandleader Sun Ra were appearing at the Pershing Ballroom and Chicago's Birdland, respectively. The rivalry just among tenor saxophonists was fierce the following year, when Ben Webster, Eddie Harris, and Johnny Griffin performed in different Chicago clubs in the late spring. As the saxophonist and Chicago native Von Freeman recalled, "Tenor was the horn of choice in Chicago. . . . There must be three million people in Chicago, and two million of them must play tenor."[15]

Young, by now nearing fifty, also had to compete with the more energetic, crowd-pleasing tenor men who relied on honking, walking on top of the bar, and going out into the streets to play during their sets. Joe Houston, for one, found such tactics quite lucrative. In response to Young's disapproval, he explained that he had always had trouble getting bookings until one night when he slipped on the floor while playing; the audience thought it was part of his act and loved it. It marked a "turning point" in his career, he claimed, and after that he started walking the bar, lying on his back while playing, and screeching on the tenor. In the summer of 1954 he boasted of having best-selling records, offers for television appearances, and a salary of $1,500 weekly. The saxophonist "Big Jay" McNeely indulged in similar antics; on one occasion when McNeely played opposite Young's band, he not only went out into the street but jumped on a bus, playing his saxophone all the while. Proving the adage that everyone is a critic, police arrested him.[16]

One way for promoters to deal with the competing musical styles of the 1950s was to assemble them in a single package. This was the idea behind the Big Rhythm and Blues Show of 1953, which showcased Young, the big bands of Wynonie Harris and Buddy Johnson, the singers Ruth Brown and the Clovers, and, on the lighter side, the former heavyweight champion Joe Louis, who sang and danced in a comedy routine with his partner Leonard Reed. The music offered by many of these bands and singers would come to be known as rock and roll within a few years' time. But the tenor stylist and other Black jazz musicians faced more immediate problems than the encroachment of a new music.[17]

When the bandleader Phil Moore gave a presentation to the Independent Citizens Committee of the Arts, Sciences, and Professions in New York City in 1946, he entitled his talk "Discrimination against the Negro in Music." In it he maintained that "the few Negro groups which are hired steadily by radio stations across the country are not hired for their musicianship but because they are 'Uncle Toms.'" The following year, the singer-actress Lena Horne, another outspoken critic of racial discrimination, suggested, "A million dollars' worth of talent is being kept from the American public because of the Jim Crow practices of radio." This "lily-white policy" was extensive, she insisted: "Almost every network is guilty of discrimination against the colored performer." For his part, the trumpet player and bandleader Erskine Hawkins proposed a strategy for coping with the recording ban of 1948: he urged musicians —and particularly Black musicians—to make arrangements with club owners to broadcast over the radio. "Negro musicians must wage an aggressive fight against the tacit understanding[s] which have kept them off the air and out of the better theatres and location spots," he declared.[18]

Over the next decade, conditions for African Americans in the music business only worsened. Black journalists were well aware of the discrimination that Black entertainers experienced, and some produced incisive critiques of the music industry. A 1954 article by *Amsterdam News* columnist Joe Bostic, "Performers Now at Mercy of Juke Box, Disc Jocks," drew attention to alarming new developments in the entertainment industry. Live performances could hardly compete for the audiences created by radio and disc jockeys in the era of payola, when large record companies were actually paying or bribing radio deejays to promote certain records; in other words, the record companies themselves had become programmers. Bostic criticized the lack of imagination and resourcefulness of African American bookers and managers, whose inertia had turned Black entertainers into "abject slave[s] of the juke box industry . . . and [its] offshoot, the disc jockey."[19]

Bostic asserted, "There seems to be no disputing the fact that show business, so far as Negroes are concerned, is dead or dying in fact." He cited as one of the reasons for this the "loss of ownership," whereby Black entertainers were left "entirely at the mercy of . . . exploiters." Movies, radio, and television had made inroads into the industry, and this had contributed to the declining fortunes of Black musicians, singers, dancers, and comedians. Even in New York, the acme of Black entertainment since the late nineteenth century, "there is but one show business operation of long standing . . . for Negroes—the Harlem Amateur Hour [which] has been running for fourteen years." Where, Bostic asked, was the African American entertainer supposed to go after winning that contest? The only opportunities were controlled by the exploiters, he charged.[20]

Radio and television offered opportunities for some entertainers, but African Americans controlled very little in terms of radio, and virtually nothing with respect to the newer medium. "You get some idea of the seriousness of this situation," wrote another *Amsterdam News* columnist, "Chick" Webb, "when it is pointed out that not one of the eight [radio] stations in the [New York] Metropolitan area, that are making an active bid to clear the spending dollar of the Negro population, by airing programs supposedly directed to these listeners, has a Negro staff member." In fact, *one* radio station did employ Blacks; the sole exception was WNJR, which had a staff of Black announcers. Elsewhere, white men imitated Black speech patterns to sell jazz and rock and roll over the radio. Racism thus both shut Blacks out and humiliated them—first by not hiring them and then by patronizing and mocking them through the use of white imitators as disc jockeys. Of the Black disc jockeys working at smaller, outlying radio stations, Webb noted, "not a single [one] . . . can boast of [a] regular take-home paycheck of $350."[21]

Following a rock-and-roll concert broadcast by a local radio station and officiated over by one of the more popular white imitators, a deejay known as Moondog, Webb observed with justifiable concern, "For the decision by the local independent station to bring in an outsider—and a non-Negro at that—to conduct a show beamed at the Negro market pointed up, with stark realism, the vicious economic angle involved in the philosophy of the various station managements with one or two exceptions." As the writer saw it, "The implication in the hiring of Mr. ["Moondog"] Freedman is that not one Negro radio personality has either the appeal, talent or brains to successfully and entertainingly reach his own people." The fact that the industry had arrived at this sweeping conclusion concerning Black disc jockeys, every one of whom "[has] been one of the large minority group all his life; [has] spoken their language and colloquialisms; has lived with their mores and customs; has been one of them"—but *still,* in the industry's view, could not reach other Blacks over the microphone—was all the more insulting.[22]

Much the same scenario was being repeated in the field of jazz, where white imitators were becoming more popular than Black originators. This fact alone affected radio programming, the listening tastes of audiences, and their very conception of the nature and history of the music. Young was, as we've seen, one of the first casualties among tenor saxophonists. Then, too, nightclub owners and promoters blamed jazz musicians for the negative image they supposedly presented. It was around this time that Young was criticized for being unreliable; it is not clear exactly when or how the business began to level the charge at him, however, since no newspaper or trade-journal articles ever verified this criticism.

Jazz musicians were often stereotyped as undependable, which went along with their (inevitably) being drug addicts, or alcoholics, or simply incapable of looking after business details. The promoter George Frazier thought it was a matter of personal hygiene and attire; jazz musicians' style of dress was giving the music a bad name, he said, and it was time for them to pay more attention to their presentation and start behaving like "civilized men." In an *Esquire* article in the late summer of 1955, Frazier quoted George Wein, promoter of the Newport Jazz Festival, who contended that "the worst enemies of jazz . . . are often the jazz musicians themselves."[23]

Many others saw it differently, pointing to the greed and racism of club owners as the real problems. In early 1958, Nat Hentoff defended the patrons of jazz clubs in a response to a letter criticizing a recent article by him on the Café Bohemia. Hentoff likened the Bohemia's business tactics to "guerrilla warfare against its customers." Citing the unreasonable price of one dollar for a seven-ounce bottle of beer, he suggested that "after some initial accidental successes with jazz," many nightclub owners had made it a practice to "not only eat the green-legged [?] goose, but try to make soup out of its bones." He regarded such attitudes, he said, as "ingenious hubris." The Café Bohemia and similar clubs, the object of his criticism, "are now back to strippers, and deserve to be." He pointed out that club owners refused to comprehend that "the average jazz partisan is not a setup for a shell game—and is not on an expense account." Modern jazz, he concluded, "is to be listened to, not talked against."[24]

Given the rather considerable problems facing musicians of Young's generation, it is hardly surprising that some became alcoholics and, like Ben Webster and Don Byas—his fellow tenor men—went into permanent exile. By the 1950s, alcoholism in a jazz musician was, for some observers, as much an anachronism as a thing to be pitied. While critics and fans have been by turns obsessed with and mystified by Young's alcoholism, Hawkins and Webster—both of whom, as Sweets Edison noted, lost their appetite in their last years, like Young—have received comparatively less attention in this regard. Heroin and cocaine abuse, too, at least have the dubious virtue of seeming more exotic, thus somehow more alluring, than the alcohol and tobacco addictions that have claimed so many more lives.[25]

Dicky Wells, who himself drank constantly, maintained that during his years of travel on the road, especially in the segregated South, alcohol eased the hard life of touring. Whiskey was available even when food could not be obtained from Jim Crow restaurants. Wells explained how easy it was for the touring musician to become an alcoholic: "Day in and day out, your system begins to ask for it, and whiskey will tell you—which is one of the damnedest lies—that it's good and you don't need anything to eat." He added that being away from home only exacerbated his alcoholism. Young must have had much the same experience during his lengthy road tours.[26]

At least one alcoholic among the musicians, James Moody, from Savannah, Georgia, received help around this time, but he was of a later generation than Young. By the time he was twenty-three, in 1948, he was an international success; four years later he was grossing $100,000 yearly. But at thirty-two he was consuming "two gallons [of wine] a day to live with himself," and so he sought treatment at the Overbrook Sanitarium in New Jersey. The administration allowed him to record an album, *Last Train from Overbrook,* during his stay there. After eight weeks of treatment, he was released, vowing never to touch another drink. Others in show business were not so fortunate: Diana Barrymore and her husband, for example, went to Alcoholics Anonymous once and never returned.[27]

The 1947 article "Are You a Drunkard?" was one of the few thoughtful discussions of alcoholism published in the Black press. It pointed out that rather than being seen as a serious personal and social problem, alcoholism was often treated lightly, as the comic subject of innumerable songs and vaudeville productions. The hit "Open the Door, Richard" was just such a song, having originated in a vaudeville skit in which a drunk roomer has lost his key. Thirty thousand people in the United States nonetheless deemed their problems with alcohol serious enough to induce them to join Alcoholics Anonymous (AA) after World War II. Black chapters were formed in Washington, D.C., and St. Louis, and attempts were made to establish the first interracial chapter in Harlem in 1947.[28]

In an era when heroin addiction was more likely to capture the attention of the press, jazz fans, and, of course, law-enforcement officials, Young, Hawkins, and Webster were all ridiculed by junkies. Gene Ramey related how heroin addicts "[would] see Ben or Prez or Hawk half drunk and say, 'Man, you're a drag. You a damned drunkard.'" He pointed out the alcoholic's dilemma: "You couldn't turn around and tell a guy who was high and bent all out that he was a dope addict, because that would be squealing!" The drinkers complained, "Man, this guy's hitting me . . . and I can't fight back."[29]

For many musicians, the mid-1950s were a make-or-break time. As we have noted, Young's sidemen contended that there were often insufficient bookings for his combo in its latter years. Abe Bolar, the Blue Devil who had moved to New York City in the late 1930s, became a taxi driver in the 1950s before finally returning to Oklahoma City; he blamed rock and roll for the downswing. Jimmy Rushing thanked his luck in 1957, during the heyday of rock and roll, because he was still working, but other former members of the Henderson, Calloway, and Basie bands were less fortunate: Dan Minor, Ed Lewis, Hilton Jefferson, Harry White, and Walter Johnson were all forced out of the business for lack of work. Rushing, the former Reno Club singer, remarked ironically, "There are enough musician-cabdrivers in town to get up a couple of swinging bands."[30]

Considering the number of artists who chose to move to Europe rather than leave music altogether, we may reasonably wonder if Young ever saw this as an option for himself. After all, the New Orleans virtuoso and reedman Sidney Bechet and the trumpet player Bill Coleman both lived abroad and were married to European women; Don Byas and Ben Webster also left the United States, as did Young's friend the drummer Carl "Kansas" Fields, who emigrated to France in 1952. Billie Holiday also pondered overseas residency, especially in light of the difficulty she had obtaining a cabaret card in New York City.[31]

The baritone saxophonist Sahib Shihab would become an expatriate in 1961, explaining, "I had to leave the States before I became too cynical." Born in Savannah, Georgia, in 1925, he had a successful career with Thelonious Monk and Dizzy Gillespie before growing tired of New York City and, in particular, getting "fed up with club owners, most of whom are a sick lot, influenced solely by money." Shihab was weary of having to suffer through repeated bouts of unemployment, and "disgusted with certain record companies that tried to take advantage of you"; moreover, he "wanted to get away from some of the prejudice." He confessed he had no "time for this racial bit. It depletes my energies."[32]

If Young ever seriously entertained the idea of moving to Europe, he left no record of it. (He traveled there several times, of course, and would spend the last few weeks of his life in Paris. Even before he left on that final trip, however, word of changing conditions on the Continent with regard to racism had reached the African American weeklies; Young himself would tell François Postif that he had encountered discrimination in Paris that last winter.) Instead of fleeing, he stayed in the United States and continued to work, despite the difficult conditions of the 1950s, the fact that swing was considered passé by many fans, and the public's preference for rock and roll and raucous tenor men. He still ranked as a singularly important figure to many musicians, fans, and critics. Louis Jordan, the popular bandleader who had competed against Young in Greenville, Mississippi, in around 1924, defended his stance against the more energetic saxophonists in 1952. With reference to the honkers, Jordan contended, "The tenor sax isn't supposed to be played that way"; he believed that instead "it should have the tenor vocal sound and range." He regarded Young as "the greatest creative artist playing the tenor saxophone today." Similarly, when Ben Webster shared his opinions of fellow tenor saxophonists in 1955, he expressed respect for his former teacher "because he has his own sound and is always [chock-ful] of ideas."[33]

Significantly, European critics continued to praise Young during this period, with a number of them evaluating his contributions and reviewing his most influential recordings in *Jazz Journal* and *Jazz Monthly* in 1956. Among them were A. J. Bishop, Svein Haagensen, Jim Burns, and Raymond Horricks. Bishop asserted that Young was "one of the three tenor-sax players to establish an original style," adding that it had "become a truism now to say that Lester virtually created modern tenor style." Similarly, Guy Kopelowicz, writing of the Aladdin records, reminded readers that Young's superb improvisations accounted for his having captured the attention of younger tenor players such as Stan Getz and Al Cohn.[34]

American trade journals bestowed praise on Young up until the end, though they also ran the usual critical reviews. Bill Russo and Jerry Mulvihill, writing in *Down Beat,* observed that his "influence on jazz in general and on tenor saxophone jazz in particular hardly can be overestimated." Discussing the saxophonist's collaboration with Teddy Wilson in 1956, Nat Hentoff called his playing "clear, direct, and economical with that presidential sense of phrasing and of making inventive, balanced mobiles from time patterns." While conceding that the record was not Young's greatest effort, Hentoff assured fans that it "contains much from him of musical substance."

Reviewing a date on the 1957 Birdland tour, *Down Beat* complained that Young "flashed on and off in a too-short appearance to open the second half." His selections were "Lester Leaps In," with the Basie orchestra, and "Polka Dots and Moonbeams," which the reviewer described as "handsomely done, with a series of beautiful choruses built in the best Young tradition." When Joe Segal reviewed the show in Chicago later in the spring of 1957, he claimed that the "most swingin' music of the evening" had taken place between the first and second performances, when "Prez [jammed] with Phineas Newborn's bass player, just pleasing themselves." Segal regretted not having heard more of Young: "Too short time given Prez and the group with Zoot."[35]

Down Beat reviewed Young's recorded collaboration with Roy Eldridge, *Giants of Jazz,* only a few months before the tenor saxophonist died, and once again the reviewer made clear his ambivalence concerning Young's contemporary efforts in comparison with his early work: "The striking thing about the set is the deliberateness of Pres' playing, almost as if he were making a conscious [attempt] to recapture the fluidity of the Lester of a decade or so ago." On "Blues," the reviewer concluded, "he plays better than I have heard him in several years." The record itself was characterized as "good relaxed jazz by a group of men who have been left behind by fads."[36]

For someone supposed to have been "left behind," Young fared well in the polls in the mid-1950s. He came in second in *Metronome*'s All-Star Poll in both 1956 and 1957, and after losing out to Stan Getz in the three previous *Down Beat* polls of the critics, in 1956 he placed first. He was ranked third behind Getz and Charlie Ventura in *Playboy*'s 1957 All-Stars poll, and fourth in 1958, when Coleman Hawkins moved ahead of Ventura to occupy the second position behind Getz.[37]

In his last decade Young was profiled and interviewed several times. Ralph J. Gleason captured his significance in American culture better than any other writer ever had, and without making the usual comments about his decline. In the late winter of 1954, when Young and his combo played San Francisco's Blackhawk, at 200 Hyde Street, Gleason listened as the proprietor, Guido Cacciarti, expounded on the tenor stylist's role as a kind of cult leader. The audiences were youthful ones, and Cacciarti reflected that "these kids today . . . go for this jazz like it's a club or something." He explained, "Take . . . President Young . . . [who] blows a lot of horn but it's not only that these kids . . . go for. He sets a style with them. They copy the way he talks." Young's speech was described as being "out of this world . . . like a kind of shorthand." One night, for example, the saxophonist responded to the club owner's comments by protesting, "You're smotherin' me." Thinking that his headliner was feeling hot, Cacciarti turned on a fan, only to learn that what Young meant was that he was overwhelming him—causing him to laugh until his sides ached, for one thing.[38]

Gleason was probably making his own observations as well, but he quoted the Blackhawk proprietor on Young's behavior, allowing him to voice his belief that "he lives in a world of his own." When his sidemen played, the saxophonist "talks and sings to himself [on the stand] and then he goes up to the corner of the room where the fan is and cocks his head like he was listening to a voice from another world or something," Cacciarti testified. Then he added, "Maybe he is." Strange though Young's behavior might have seemed to a layperson, a fellow musician might have surmised that he was ascertaining how the music sounded in different parts of the club, or even responding to something musical at that moment. Nor was he the only one in his profession, who sang along softly with his sidemen; other musicians, notably Thelonious Monk and Bud Powell, also hummed along with the music, in both cases while playing piano.[39]

Jesse Drakes corroborated the Blackhawk proprietor's evaluation of the relationship between Young and his fans, noting the special aura or image the tenor saxophonist projected in the 1950s: "There was a cult about Pres . . . you could *feel* that there was a cult about Pres. . . . Some of the cult about Pres was almost to the point of insanity, because . . . people . . . loved Pres so much."[40]

A rare *Ebony* pictorial published in the winter of 1955 provided further insights into Young's character and his singular cultural influence on his fans, while also tracing traditions of "cool" that are older than they may appear. Although many musicians disapproved of the use of this term to refer to a certain type of jazz, applying it in quotation marks if at all, they were less reluctant to employ it in regard to matters of personal demeanor. The term has often been invoked by writers to describe Young's saxophone playing, and whether or not this specific descriptive is valid, musicians generally agree that whatever you call his style of playing, Young originated it, with many others taking it up in his wake. The behavior associated with "cool" was also frequently ascribed to him. In other words, he was linked to a distinctive Black urban aesthetic and philosophy that underscored not only his originality but his detachment from the concerns of the world, and from the persistent intrusions of a materialistic society into African American life. In his own way, Young played a major role in spreading this ethos to musicians and fans.[41]

Jazz musicians and others, including the various hipsters who appeared in the works of Allen Ginsberg, Jack Kerouac, and John Clellon Holmes, created an ethos regarding appropriate behavior and specific values within their own social circles. But despite the usual linking of the term *cool* with jazz journalism, the concept in fact had its roots in ancient African traditions. A West African aesthetic of balance—the combination of competing extremes or emotions in equilibrium—has found its way into the philosophy, religion, and mundane aspects of a number of societies. In this context, the term typically points to the opposing extremes that exist within a balanced relationship: a "cool" person is thus one who avoids the excesses of emotionalism and maintains his or her dignity as well as a sense of control.

Certain characteristics of traditional Yoruba dances, Professor Robert F. Thompson has suggested—including "the frozen facial expressions" assumed by the dancers—express "a philosophy of the cool, an ancient indigenous ideal: patience and collectedness of mind." Coolness is thus about "control and symmetry [and] seems [to be] a metaphor of the spiritual." This aesthetic or ethos penetrated Black urban culture in the United States and laid the foundation for the hipster's philosophy; the style as well as its context have been presented to the world in, for example, Malcolm X's and Iceberg Slim's depictions of urban culture.[42]

This hipster aesthetic also informed the "cool" school of music in the mid–twentieth century. Young, Dizzy Gillespie, Ahmad Jamal, Miles Davis, Stan Getz, and others were introduced in the *Ebony* pictorial as the leaders of the cool school; in trade journals, white West Coast musicians, in particular, were often cited as proponents of this new trend in the music (which today might be called "smooth" jazz). Whatever the problems with the term and its relevance to the music itself, Robert Thompson has found meaningful similarities between philosophies of cool on both sides of the Atlantic, noting, "Multiple meter essentially uses dancers as further voices in a polymetric choir. The conversation is additive, cool in its expressions of community." Moreover, the balance between "the meters and the bodily orchestration seems to communicate a soothing wholeness." A similar balance resulted from the organization of the music: "Call and response is a means of putting innovation and tradition, invention and imitation, into amicable relationships with one another. In that sense it, too, is cool."[43]

In his exploration of rhythms, Young achieved a balance with other musicians that was the embodiment of cool. Hearing his saxophone float above the Basie orchestra, or weave in and out of the accompaniment of his own band, one can only marvel at these intricate rhythms that are so central to African and African American music. His sidemen described Young's sense of rhythm as being flawless. Connie Kay explained, "A lot of good players don't have good rhythm . . . [and] got to primarily lay on the rhythm section to make sure that they keep within the context of that rhythm . . . or tempo." But with Young, "even if you heard him playing things in different rhythms, [and it] sounded like he was playing in off rhythms and things, you didn't have to say, 'Uh-oh, he's gone off somewhere, let me try to find him.' You didn't have to worry about that."[44]

Known and respected for his lack of exhibitionism in an age of honkers and shouters, Young was also noted for his self-control and totally relaxed demeanor both onstage and off as he grew older. Nat Hentoff wrote that "his features evinced not the slightest emotion and his whole being was concentrated in the music [when he performed]." Hentoff also observed that the saxophonist "has personified consummate relaxation in the art of creative improvisation," adding that "a large part of the essence of Pres . . . is the flowing quality of his phrases . . . a uniquely muscular ease of playing."[45]

Ebony interviewed a number of musicians for its "cool" article, including Young, Gillespie, Davis, and Jamal. The reporter observed that "few of the cool men are entertainers." (One of the rare exceptions, of course, was Gillespie, who often clowned in his own way.) Departing from the usual stereotype of the entertainer-minstrel, "many of them are introspective intellectuals who would rather read Gide and Sartre than venture" into dark, smoke-filled nightclubs. While this feature may have been something of a put-on, the specific masks worn and the behavior displayed during such an interview situation reveal something of the underlying cultural values. *Ebony* claimed that the latest development in jazz represented both an outgrowth and a rejection of bebop: "What was once called bop has broadened its base and subdivided into a fascinating assortment of cults and coteries each characteristically different but all essentially united by a rejection of hot jazz and a fervent devotion to modern harmonies and 'cool' sounds," the writer maintained.[46]

According to *Ebony*, the new term *cool* was applicable "not only [to] modern harmonies, but also [to the musicians'] reactions to the tribulations of an uneasy outside world." Photos of the jazzmen in various attitudes of repose, sometimes playing, purportedly documented how they lived and behaved according to a hipster ethos that mirrored the qualities embodied by their art. "The disciples of the cool way aim to play with the same ease and calmness [with] which they move, walk and generally live," readers were told. Balance and self-control constituted the essence of cool in Black urban America, and hipsters epitomized these qualities in their music and life-styles. The pictorial reported that "regardless of the tempo a cool man never loses his aplomb. He is supposed to remain in control of himself and the proceedings all the time." The cool man viewed "emoting visibly as . . . undignified."[47] This was not an easy stance to maintain in the rough-and-tumble of the music business, or amid fears of nuclear holocaust as the Cold War escalated.

Young's character and the respect accorded him stood out in the *Ebony* piece. "Considered the best of modern tenor players," Young was said to be regarded by colleagues "as an example of not only a 'cool' musician but also a 'cool' man when it comes to his reactions to life around him." In fact, many believed that "more than anyone else at the time, [he] augured the slow change-over from hot jazz to cool jazz." Although he looked accessible enough in the accompanying photograph, which showed him attired in plaid shirt and slacks, seated in a chair playing his tenor, his feet propped up on a stool, the saxophonist was described as having erected "an emotional wall between himself and the outer world which few persons can pierce."[48]

This detachment, the *Ebony* reporter noted, was manifest in Young's onstage demeanor. Besides being "unaware of all save the music in his small unit, . . . at times he turns completely around and plays with his back to the audience." (This habit was characteristically associated with Miles Davis rather than with Young; at this time the trumpet player was drawing considerable criticism for his tendency to turn around or walk off the stage during his sidemen's solos.) In addition, Young headed straight for the dressing room between sets to avoid people; there he sipped Scotch "in solitary serenity" and, on the occasion of this interview, explained his values, which actually seemed completely normal: "All I care about are my music, my kid and my home," he said. Another statement attributed to him sounded less like his own mode of expression: "The world stinks and I don't want it to bruise me more than it has."[49]

Jimmy Heath remembered going to hear Young when he played at Pep's in Philadelphia; for him, the tenor stylist gave meaning to the concept of cool, even validated it, by connecting it with a physical state of ease. Like numerous other musicians—Sadik Hakim, for example—Heath pointed out that Young was singularly relaxed when he played, a condition that was central to his music and probably to *any* good music. Young, Heath noted, seemed to have developed the ability to relax earlier in life than many other musicians, who acquired it only after years of playing. "He was like the coolest saxophone player around," Heath said, which meant, he explained, "that he was . . . one of the most *relaxed* musicians that I've ever run across."[50]

Expanding on his take on Young's relaxation, Heath added that the saxophonist "was never in a big hurry about his playing or into flash technique just for the sake of being very fast." The ability to relax, he maintained, resulted from "confidence in what you are playing, and [in] your style. . . . [Pres] was *definitely sure* that he was cool within his style. He had no pressure." This relaxed state went a long way toward helping an artist realize and express his or her creativity. In Young's case, a lack of concern for the cares and opinions of the world enabled him to focus on his music, and that composure in turn extended to his general attitude toward life: "Lester was kind of cool like as if he were a rich man that didn't need anything . . . just . . . coastin' through life. Making music."[51]

Young's state of relaxation, its sources, and its significance were thoroughly intertwined with his art and his personality, which were deep water for many people who knew him. Occasionally, however, glimpses of his character and even of the means of his relaxation were revealed by musicians. While interviewers noted that he watched televised baseball games at home, and musicians related how he used to love to pitch in their softball games when he was younger, the fact that he carried golf clubs and practiced putting in his hotel room has not been widely reported. Paul Quinichette remembered that between sessions they would relax by putting golf balls into Pet milk cans. Jesse Drakes recalled that "Pres always played golf. . . . He'd practice [putting] all over." His coordination and reflexes were superb; "he had a *very* good eye, a *very* good eye," Drakes added. As the very symbol of a relaxed, leisurely existence, golf was the epitome of cool, a pastime enjoyed by a number of Basieites, among them Freddie Green and Harry Edison.[52]

Remaining poised in the midst of turmoil seemed to be a way of life for some older musicians, who had played in one style when they were young and adopted another in their later years. Like Young, Hawkins and Webster had been known in their youth for their energy and verve and for the vigor of their attack, but by the mid-1950s both had become balladeers. The saxophonist Marshal Royal was another who lost his ambitiousness as he grew older, and found himself content to leave the proving ground to his juniors. In an oral-history interview conducted when he was in his midsixties, he explained, "I don't want to be competitive. I want to live cool."[53]

Discussing Young, Royal pointed out something most of the critics had missed, noting that the saxophonist's playing of ballads and slow blues in the 1950s was more difficult technically than the energetic kind of playing they preferred. He had traveled with the Basie band on a Birdland tour that featured Young's combo, and he stressed that "sometimes it is harder for a person in their older age to play *slow,* for the simple reason that it takes more concentration to play slow and you have to have better air control." Furthermore, he said, some older players performed much better at a medium-fast tempo, whereas "to play a slow, slow ballad is probably *twice* as hard as playing terrifically fast, . . . and you have to express yourself much more playing slow than you do playing fast."[54]

Young's seeming preference for ballads and slow blues, his demeanor, and his philosophy may all have been a response to the hectic pace of life on the road, a pace that surely contributed to the deterioration of his health. When, in the spring of 1953, an interviewer asked him about the JATP concert he just completed in England, the tenor stylist replied, "I'm tired of all this noise. I like to play cool." Although he had been the hero of numerous cutting contests in his youth, Young had come to dislike the staged jam sessions of JATP because he "didn't like the idea of saxophone players battling." His attitude was, "You play *your* little songs, and I'll play *my* little songs."[55]

A few months after this interview, traveling with the Rhythm and Blues Show, his band would do "a tour of sixty one-nights that covered . . . just about every state outside of North and South Dakota," according to Jesse Drakes. Young's touring schedule in 1956 would be just as grueling: a sojourn with the Birdland contingent in the winter would be followed by a Basin Street stint in New York City the first two weeks of March; then it would be on to Chicago's Bee Hive for two weeks, to Detroit for one week, and to Toronto for nine days. Later in the year he would play a series of European dates with Birdland.[56]

In early 1957, after a period of illness and recuperation, he headed out with Birdland again. The entourage would travel by bus for nearly two months. The tour began with a performance in White Plains, New York, in mid-February, and then a midnight show at Carnegie Hall that same night, followed by a Newark date the next day, with another midnight performance at Carnegie Hall that night; the night after *that,* they played in Boston. Those five concerts in three days marked the beginning of a string of one-nighters that took the performers from New England to New York, Virginia, the Carolinas, back through the Midwest, south to Kentucky and Missouri, then north to Chicago, Ohio, and Canada, followed by Brooklyn and the District of Columbia, and finally out to the West Coast, all in six weeks' time. Between April 27 and May 12, the Birdland tour played in Berkeley and Los Angeles, Texas, Colorado, Oklahoma, and Kansas, ending up in Kansas City, Missouri. Even someone in the best of health would have been taxed by such a marathon, and Young, by this time in his life, hardly fit that description.[57]

The saxophonist could not have missed the supreme irony in the fact that despite the initial East Coast rejection of his style, by the late 1940s his imitators were seen as legends in their own right. Such professional disappointments, together with his military imprisonment, the constant challenge of racial prejudice, the deaths of friends, and his own illnesses, had taken their toll on Young by the 1950s. Then, too, the pressures of commercialism and the demands of fans that he play as he had played before aggravated his sense of having been passed over and forgotten. And finally there was the humiliation of having people come up to him and exclaim, "Pres! I thought you were dead!" Nonetheless, Young insisted that he was still developing, experimenting with sounds, and remaining true to his values.[58]

Like the singers of spirituals, he faced life and death with equanimity. Bobby Scott, the pianist with the Gene Krupa combo that traveled with Young and JATP in 1955, later recalled the saxophonist's telling him that he drank because he was in pain, saying, "When I drink the pain goes." He knew he was terminally ill, and he gave Scott the news in a manner that was "kind of graceful." He seemed content about it, or perhaps just resigned, and was adamant that he would not die complaining, which Scott thought "may have been the measure of his accomplishment, that he felt that way." At times, Scott said, he had played in great pain, but even then not everyone could tell he was ill; in this respect he possessed a "strength not given to many people." When Scott himself was too sick to play, he felt ashamed to think of the conditions under which Young performed.[59]

At the very end of his life, Young was vexed to learn that one of his imitators, a white saxophonist, would be earning twice the money Young himself was making for a comparable gig at the same Paris nightclub. This painful reminder of the injustices of the commercial jazz scene only underlined the disillusionment he expressed around the same time to his interviewer François Postif: "They're so rough out here. . . . Everybody's so chickenshit. They want everybody who is a Negro to be an Uncle Tom, or Uncle Remus, or Uncle Sam, and I can't make it." Sighing, he added, "It's the same way all over, you dig? You just fight for your life, that's all, until death do we part, you got it made."[60]

Earlier in the 1950s, he had given up drinking for a time. With a measure of wit as well as an air of (perhaps feigned) indifference, he claimed he intended to stay on the wagon "until I'm well and strong enough to start drinking again." When he did, he is said to have proclaimed, with grim humor, "I like to drink and I'm going to keep on drinking if it kills me." Informed by friends of the certainty of his early demise if he continued this pattern, he responded, "OK, I'll quit drinking, but I intend to have a few more nips before I stop." On another occasion he is said to have quipped, "The sooner I drink myself to death the happier I'll be." Sadly for those around him, he would not live to turn fifty.[61]

While the last year of his life brought Young some rewards and recognition, including the fourth-place finish among tenor saxophonists in *Playboy*'s All-Stars poll in the winter of 1958, it was also a period marked by poor health and depression, according to Dr. Luther Cloud and others. Cloud, a psychiatrist and amateur student of jazz, had been approached one day by Marshall Stearns, who in addition to being a professor of English literature also taught a jazz course that the doctor was enrolled in. Cloud recalled, "I was down at Marshall's house . . . in the Village and he said, 'Lester Young is very ill and he needs a doctor.'" Knowing nothing about the saxophonist's condition, Cloud asked, "What is he ill with, and why [hasn't] he [been] to a doctor? I'll give him the name of a doctor." Stearns explained, "'No, he *hates* doctors, is afraid of them, is afraid of needles, and he doesn't like white people very much.'" His friends were at a loss over what to do, since he refused to seek medical attention. Despite this rather alarming buildup, Cloud agreed to go see Young.[62]

He soon learned that the tenor great had left his wife and family to move into the Alvin, across from Birdland, where he could occasionally be seen sitting on the fire escape outside of his room. This was very likely sometime between mid-February and early June of 1958. When Stearns introduced the two, all he said to Young was, "'This is Luther Cloud, he's *very* interested in music. And he's taken my course at New York University. And he loves your music.'" That was the first of what would be a series of regular visits paid by the doctor to the saxophonist, who at the time was drinking heavily and quite depressed.[63]

During these informal sessions, Cloud talked with Young and, with the assistance of Elaine Swain, tried to get him to cut back on his drinking, eat regular meals, and take vitamins. After a time he felt compelled to tell Young he was a doctor, but the saxophonist seemed unperturbed by the revelation: "He accepted it beautifully, which surprised me," Cloud recalled. "Surprised *all* of us, that he didn't throw me out." Young's health gradually improved as he gained some weight, began to leave his hotel, and showed a renewed interest in performing sometime in the spring of 1958.[64]

Dr. Cloud found Young to be a fascinating figure, if a bit strange—for example, in his insistence on referring to everyone as "Lady." He was particularly struck by the saxophonist's use of language: "It was poetry, it was so beautiful . . . [consisting of] very *complicated* rhymes, sometimes . . . double rhymes within rhymes . . . and they had rhythm and his obscenities had a rhythm." Mary, Lester's wife, visited him occasionally, but even that did not seem to help; Young appeared, at least at first, to have lost his desire to live. The doctor believed that the musician's "feeling in the beginning was that there is nothing [and] . . . that 'I'm going to *die,* and there is no way that I can ever return to playing, and there is no way that I can ever return home'—these kinds of things." Young was reportedly "bitter" about his imitators' success, charging, " 'They're me. They are taking me. [And] I'm not even dead yet.' " He was also said to feel "bitter about white people"—"Bitter about me," Cloud added, "except that after a while I think he forgot I was white."

Young was deeply troubled, too, by matters of religion, according to Cloud, who recalled a concern of the saxophonist's that was rather startling to one unfamiliar (as the doctor was) with his family's religious heritage. After they had been talking for several weeks, Young told him about an experience he had had as a child in a church in the Deep South, where the minister had sermonized about sinners, hell, and being saved, and then instructed the repentant to come forward; Blacks were not permitted to confess, however. Years later, as the saxophonist pondered this memory, he asked the doctor, " 'Why is there one God for the whites and one God for the Blacks?' " and " 'What do I have to do to get eternal salvation?' " A professional himself, Cloud recognized that it was time to seek help from another professional, so he asked the Reverend John Gensel, often called the jazz minister, to talk to Young about these issues, and he did.

The doctor believed that Young suffered from schizophrenia and, like many alcoholics, had "a very strong death wish." Unlike some, he did not find the saxophonist to be especially wise, but instead concluded that while he was obviously intelligent and had seen a great deal of life, he was unable to put it all together. According to Cloud, "The fabric [of Young's life] didn't make a lot of sense, or he would have been much more successful. A wise person doesn't drink himself to death. I don't care how many degrees [he has]. [He] may be *educated* and so forth, but to me wisdom has something to do with the way you *preserve* your life, the *dignity* of your life, and so forth. And on that basis I would say [Young] was not wise. That doesn't mean he was stupid!"

In late 1958, Young heard from his fellow saxophonist Benny Carter that there was work to be had in Europe. He discussed the possibility of a trip with Dr. Cloud, who gave his qualified approval, despite some misgivings about Young's health, and about his getting back together with his buddies in Paris and drinking heavily again. So, with his doctor's mixed blessing, Young went, and on one occasion called Cloud from Paris to check in. They talked about Young's health and how he was doing. Although he was not terribly happy about his sidemen, the doctor recalled, he professed to be all right otherwise—but "I knew he wasn't all right," Cloud said. He asked the saxophonist if he had been drinking, and after receiving the expected response, asked *what* he had been drinking. "'We get a lot of absinthe and brandy,'" Young replied. The former was a bad choice for someone in his condition; as Dr. Cloud explained, "There's nothing in the *world* worse than absinthe," whose impurities, or "conjures," are particularly bad for the liver.

At some point during his stay in Paris, Young began bleeding internally. According to Cloud, when the liver of an aging alcoholic begins to harden, it presses against the esophagus and can cause the veins to rupture. "Certainly you or I," he observed, "would be scared to death [in such a situation], and we would go to the nearest doctor." But Young was afraid of doctors, and so he "decided to come home." He called Elaine Swain to inform her that he was leaving Paris on Friday, March 13, and to ask her to pick him up at the airport in New York.[65]

In the plane on the way back, Young's bleeding worsened, to the point where he bit his lip in pain, and causing it, too, to bleed. When he deplaned, Swain asked him if he wanted to go to the hospital, but he said he would prefer to be taken to his hotel and requested that she get in touch with Dr. Cloud. They managed to make it back to the Alvin, where, early on the morning of March 15, Young died. Cloud had been out of town and unreachable the day the saxophonist flew home; he heard the news of his death over his car radio. The cause of death, according to Cloud, was a ruptured vein or artery of the esophagus.[66]

Young's old Basie colleague Jo Jones related how he was informed: from Los Angeles, Lee Young called him about the funeral and said, "You got it." Jones explained that he and Lester had "had a thing going about Saturdays." For a time Young would not come out of his room on Saturdays, but then later they would meet at the Magpie, the bar next door to the Alvin. "When I'd got through doing some things downtown, I'd come in and get a drink and 'Cheers' to him, you know, and then he'd hit double, meaning take another one. So I'd take another for him, drink his drink. I'd say, 'Give me another, I'm drinking Lester's drink,' and then I'm gone." That Saturday, Jones stopped in front of the hotel: "Jack, I'm going to pick up a paper and then go home. It's two-thirty. He's upstairs dying. I was right downstairs. I got the paper, went home, put my feet up, looked at the sports page . . . Brrrrrring! 'Lester Young's dead.'" Jones went "back across town and there he was, his hat and his horn." Mary Young had come, and she and Jones heard Swain explain that the tenor stylist had refused to go to bed that night until he had a drink. Jones recounted: "He got it and just laid down. . . . Bam! Gone."[67]

PART IV

The Legacy

He had the saddest eyes I ever saw.

Reginald Scott, remark to the author

CHAPTER 17

Good-bye Pork Pie Hat

THE family and friends of a saxophonist who had transformed American music paid their last respects to him in New York City on March 19, 1959, a sunny day just before the official beginning of spring. The funeral, arranged by his wife, Mary, with the assistance of Catherine Basie and Jo Jones, was quiet and somber, as relatives and friends from near and far attended services at Universal Funeral Chapel in Manhattan. The deceased's mother, Lizetta Gray, arrived with relatives from California. Besides his wife and children, the saxophonist's longtime friend Leonard Phillips was present. During the service, Tyree Glenn played a muted trombone solo on "Just A-Wearyin' for You," and Al Hibbler sang "In the Garden," which he had composed in Young's memory. The saxophonist was buried in Evergreen Cemetery in Queens.[1]

Allan Morrison, eulogizing Young for *Jet,* the African American weekly, attempted to shed some light on the saxophonist's character. He described him as a "lovable man with [a] sensitive soul, who wore flamboyant pork pie hats and a Bohemian mane of hair," and also as a rebel who "inhabited a world of his own making—remote, strange, inaccessible." Without providing details, Morrison drew a portrait of a genius who had had a "deprived childhood" and "two tragic marriages," the negative effects of which had been compounded by the "searing brutality" of the military's detention barracks and by a serious drinking problem that had accelerated his death. "No one," Morrison asserted, "really knew the true Lester" (presumably excepting his family). Save for the reference to his military debacle, no mention was made of the role that racism had played in the saxophonist's life and career.[2]

Ralph Gleason's tribute appeared in the San Francisco press; its title, "If They Built Statues to Jazz Men, There'd Be One for Pres," aptly summed up his appraisal. "If you don't know who Pres was," Gleason announced, "you've missed a great part of America in the past twenty years"—a statement that in its very simplicity had profound implications: Young had been important to the nation, not just to jazz. His music had "created sounds and phrases and melodies that are inextricably wound up in almost all of jazz music today," and along with Armstrong and Parker, he must be counted as "one of the three great instrumental soloists of jazz who changed the course of this music."[3]

But Young, Gleason continued, had been far more than a highly creative musician; he had been "a poet, sad-eyed and mystical, hurt that the world was not in actuality as beautiful as he dreamed." He had refashioned the world through his art, cleansing it until it fit his conception and then sharing it with others. He would live on in recordings, yes, but he had also chosen to give away much of his music "as freely as the wind," in every conceivable setting. This music was "the lost art of Lester Young." His significance could be found, too, in his memory, which would outlast that of other heroes, such as *Time*'s "Men of the Year," because "his music set up the ringing of chords in the minds of men that will last as long as the human race."[4]

Members of the French jazz press praised the tenor stylist in similar terms. Demetre Loakimidis termed him *"un étrange revolutionnaire."* The April 1959 issue of *Jazz Hot* published the famous François Postif interview (translated into French). Lucien Malson immortalized Young as a genius who, along with Louis Armstrong, Charlie Parker, and Thelonious Monk, had been *"le plus remarquable improvisateur, le plus étonnant soliste de l'histoire de jazz."* Malson detailed this gentle soul's final weeks in Paris, playing at the Blue Note and staying at La Louisiane, where his flask, his saxophone, and the alcohol stove on which he prepared his meals were his favorite companions (*"object d'election"*).[5]

Back in the United States, the Black newspapers' coverage of Young's death took another tack, revealing their editors' reluctance to see or treat him as a sympathetic human being. An item in New York's *Amsterdam News* typified the approach of these otherwise informative papers when it mentioned that "the genius of the tenor saxophone . . . loved his bottle as well as he loved his music."[6] The *New York Age* likewise emphasized his problems with alcoholism even as it cited his brilliance. Here and elsewhere, the press repeatedly used the same word to describe Young: *genius,* a term too seldom applied to Black Americans.[7]

In the articles and reviews that appeared in the first few years after his death, writers often stressed Young's artistic and physical decline following World War II. Record producer John Hammond's evaluation was typical: "[Young's] last fifteen years seem to me," he noted, "to have been a tragic waste of one of the few genuinely creative talents in jazz." Frank Driggs wrote that on his 1942 recordings with Nat "King" Cole and Red Callender, "Prez still had the flow that was noticeably lacking from the majority of his postwar work." And when Whitney Balliett reviewed some of Young's 1956 recordings in *The New Yorker* a month after he died, he described the selections as "reminders that toward the end of his life Young had slipped into the melancholy position of no longer being able to outstrip his multitude of imitators."[8]

Although record reviews and obituaries in the United States and abroad provide only a partial perspective on Young's musical career, his character, and his significance in the history of jazz, the breadth of publications in which his death was observed was in and of itself a tribute to an artist of commanding importance. Not only *Jet* but *The New Yorker, The Saturday Review, Playboy,* and most jazz journals remarked on his passing. Other New Orleans musicians who died that same year—including jazz pioneers Sidney Bechet and Warren "Baby" Dodds—were accorded much less ink. Even Billie Holiday's death just a few months later did not receive the kind of press attention that Young's did.[9]

Within a few years' time Young and Holiday, both singular artists who had struggled mightily during their lifetimes, would be elevated to a status as patron saints, martyrs in a world that made a business of such artists' creations. Many believed, with the singer Bonnie Bramlett, that "Billie died for all our sins." Other musicians had been granted similar status in earlier generations—among them Bix Beiderbecke, whose life was vaguely portrayed in the novel and movie, *Young Man with a Horn* —but few among the more recent artists had had such readily apparent personal failings. The most obvious example from the 1950s, of course, was Charlie Parker, whose immortality was championed in the "Bird Lives!" graffiti that sprang up on posters and subway walls in some American cities. Remarking on such hero worship, Leonard Feather observed that Billie Holiday's induction into *Down Beat*'s Hall of Fame in late 1961, while well deserved, might "also reflect the peculiarly American death cult that has earned for James Dean, Charlie Parker, Lester Young, and Hank Williams more publicity posthumously than they earned alive."[10]

The canonization of Saint Lester and others epitomized the tendency toward adulation of the departed American artist, but it was a phenomenon promoted largely by fans, not by critics. Aside from the occasional suggestion that the artists in question might have contributed to their own decline through alcohol, drugs, or simple poor judgment, the press and trade journals engaged in little serious debate on why the reputations of these entertainers seemed so changeable, or why praise was so often hoarded for eulogies.

After Young's death, articles on him and reviews of new releases and rereleases appeared sporadically in jazz magazines. Often these essays were, like the records themselves, reissues of earlier material, sometimes with little change. Writers operated within the interpretive framework established in the late 1950s, highlighting Young's tragic genius, his lovable but enigmatic character, his artistic decline. Eventually, however, new records and reevaluations began to alter opinions among some critics and fans. Those who came to accept the possibility that Young had been ever changing but always brilliant were personified by "C.W." of *Melody Maker,* who wrote in 1976 of *Lester Swings,* "Having lived with the album for a couple of weeks . . . , I am now prepared to believe that the thirties were not necessarily the golden years at all and that Lester had much more to say and give." Similarly, a *Coda* reviewer noted of *Prez in Europe,* "Those who casually put down Lester Young's postwar recordings and particularly his work in the closing years of his life should listen well to this remarkable set taped . . . at a Frankfurt club in 1956." On this record Young's eloquence and fluency were particularly evident on three very long cuts: "Lester Leaps In" (lasting nearly ten minutes), "There Will Never Be Another You" (almost seven minutes), and "Lester's European Blues" (more than nine minutes). Significantly, for this session he had relied on a rhythm section of Europeans, including Pierre Michelot on bass.[11]

As early as 1959, the critic H. A. Woodfin disputed prevailing opinions concerning Young's deterioration. In a review of his two recorded versions of "These Foolish Things," Woodfin remarked on the odd chronicling of the saxophonist's career by jazz critics and historians. While Young himself was "nearly unanimously credited as being one of the seminal creators in the history of the art," he noted, his greatest works were "seldom commented upon." Critics wrongly emphasized the quality of the Basie recordings, which had not been solely Young's creation. Woodfin advanced the thesis that Young's post-Basie recordings were in fact his "finest work," a blanket judgment extending "from *Afternoon of a Basie-ite* in 1943 to *This Year's Kisses* in 1956." Unlike many other writers, however, he introduced evidence in support of his thesis: the two different versions of the ballad.[12]

Woodfin suggested of the 1956 version of "These Foolish Things" that "it is very probable that Young had the earlier version well in mind," noting that the saxophonist actually began the rendition with a quote from the original. It was his opinion that the melodic development of the second version was "equal to [that of] the first version in beauty, and . . . in the last eight bars of the first chorus rises to a peak that is clearly superior to anything in the first version and that, to my knowledge, is not surpassed by anything else in Young's recorded work." Not only the melodic elements but also the rhythmic contrast and sonority marked "the greatness of this performance." Nor were the two versions of "These Foolish Things" the only evidence of Young's creative evolution; Woodfin argued that "one could cite such equally effective recordings as the splendid *Slow Motion Blues* and *Stardust.*" He went on to criticize, rightly, "the lack of spadework on the part of critics who are content to accept critical errors and clichés without investigation."[13]

Despite the frequent criticisms leveled at Young's later efforts, his remarkable influence on jazz's development, and specifically on cool and bop as well as swing, was duly noted by many writers. In an appreciation entitled "The Forgotten Boppers," for example, Jim Burns proposed, "Perhaps we ought to look back at the records that Lester Young made on clarinet if we are to arrive at the origins of the bop/cool style of the instrument." He was referring, of course, to Young's 1938 recordings when he contended that "his tone, and the mood he established did point towards the modern." Along with "B.J." and others, "H.P.," reviewing *Lester Young on Record, 1945–59,* observed that Young's "solos and some of his compositions are slightly tinged with bop." Around the same time (1963), Don Heckman claimed that the tenor stylist had influenced the avant-garde of the 1960s, positing that "the searing, probing melodic lines of Ornette Coleman and John Coltrane are directly descended from the rhythmically liberated solos of Young."[14]

Decisions by business executives, especially Norman Granz, played a role in the release and reissue of many Young recordings; the film *Lady Sings the Blues,* starring Diana Ross as Billie Holiday and based in some respects on the singer's life, also provided a powerful impetus to record reissue trends in the 1970s. (As for the film itself, one must view it in vain for any reference to Lester Young or his friendship with Lady Day.) Before the late 1970s, Young rereleases were usually from the 1940s and

1950s, but then Columbia dug into its vaults to produce the *Lester Young Story* in several volumes, featuring Holiday, pianist Teddy Wilson, and the Basie band. Gradually, a reevaluation of Young occurred.[15]

"C.W." observed in 1976, "It is rather foolish to expect an artist to continue in the same vein for the rest of his life and not to be affected by changing lifestyles and amassed experience." This reviewer then set forth the interesting idea that "perhaps [Young's] apparent decline was more due to neglect than any collapse of his musical drive." It was left to the reader to deduce who had done the neglecting.[16]

Five years later, *Down Beat* at last conceded that Young's "final two decades demonstrate[d] a difficult, often brilliantly successful, search for a deeper, more emotionally complex range of experience." Reviewing the albums *At the Famous Door*, *Mean to Me*, and *Pres in Washington, D.C.*, John Litweiler observed, "The most dramatic change in Young's art came between his buoyant 1944 jump band sides and the resignation, both sorrowing and sardonic, of his Aladdin dates the next year. Along with the blues elements that now dominated his solos, Young deliberately began to reorganize his methods of solo construction, experimenting again and again." By the early 1950s, he continued, "the flow of his line is often erratic, in general, phrases are shorter, longer rests add suspense, his tone is softer and thinner, entire choruses appear in his lower registers, and in place of his former high rhythmic activity he often plays long phrases comprised of half notes as a dramatic device." The saxophonist's phrasing during this period, Litweiler noted, seemed "dislocated, even stark" compared to earlier recordings, as "structural consciousness replaces some degree of spontaneity, and thematic improvisation rears its head." Acknowledging Young's versatility, the writer concluded, "it was in his last fifteen years that he became a profound ballad player and a blues riff'n ride star." Writing of "Up 'n' Adam," a standard of the saxophonist's repertoire in the 1950s, "C.W." claimed that one recorded version had "all the raw excitement that rock and roll claims as its own."[17]

By 1980, many critics had been entirely won over: bestowing fulsome praise on the stylist, they insisted that his alleged decline was a myth, "a well-worn canard." A reviewer of several Verve rereleases of recordings by Young, Parker, Holiday, Ella Fitzgerald, and others contended that "as a whole, this package includes some of the best work ever recorded by most of the jazz legends active in the 40s and 50s." Fans who bought the two-record sets, he suggested, would feel "not unlike a crew of archeologists finding extra verses of Revelations buried in the desert near Bethlehem." Of *The '46 Concerts—Jazz at the Philharmonic,* documenting the famous Pres-Bird encounter, the reviewer claimed that "the grooves within contain an education, spiritually enlightening moments that definitely qualify as history."[18]

Praise flowed freely for Columbia's *Lester Young Story, Volume 1.* "B.J." wrote that this was "jazz at its most Mozartean; full of subtleties of light and shadow; joy and tears inextricably intermixed, two sides of the same coin; nothing exaggerated or blatant, everything balanced and controlled yet full of life and inner vitality." The selections were masterpieces "not surpassed anywhere in jazz and not often outside it," and Young and Holiday's collaboration, in particular, was "something unforgettable." The reviewer proclaimed, "This is classic jazz, or if it isn't, there ain't no such thing." The album, in short, was "unreplaceable and indispensable."[19]

Dan Morgenstern reviewed "newly discovered" recordings of the tenor stylist's Royal Roost sessions from the late 1940s. Noting that the "lassitude" that had marred Young's later performances was not in evidence here, he praised the saxophonist's ability to "say it all in two gorgeous choruses" on "Ghost of a Chance." After mentioning Young's humor, Morgenstern characterized him as "a poet, a dancer, an acrobat and one of the blessed few artists whose every utterance is worth preserving." Reviewing a 1950 record, "B. McR." observed that Young "was still ahead in 1950, and [this] also explains why he is cited as a major influence on several hard boppers."[20]

Young's Washington, D.C., performances of December 1956, taped by his sidemen, received accolades and convinced some writers of the leader's towering presence in a nightclub setting as opposed to a JATP concert stage. Brian Case suggested that the usual explanations concerning the saxophonist's postwar decline were "due for re-examination in light of these marvelous [1956] discoveries." Here there were no "signs of inertia . . . —the dallying with tonalities to the detriment of narrative, the cursory rows of honks, the general sense that since anything can be changed into anything else, how about the flat minimum . . . ?" Instead there was "adventurous double-tempo . . . [placed] athwart the rhythm in interesting ways," and abundant other evidence of Young's "high spirits." For Young, Case maintained, less was more, and the oral tradition was predominant: he could "imply more emotion by moving up a semi-tone than most saxophonists can in the false upper register. . . . He always sounds like a human behind the horn." The reviewer summed up, "No one ever shared Lester's grace."[21]

As the reissues accumulated, the acclaim mounted. Young's recordings with Charlie Christian were touted as "a brilliant specimen of swing at its creative peak." Comparing Young to Parker, Jim Burns contended that "in some ways he epitomized the hipster attitude more than Parker." *Jazz Journal International* described him as "one of the more potent conveyors of emotion in his later years" when he made recordings featuring "improvisation of profound depth and miraculous simplicity." Gary Giddins hailed Young's legacy as "an exquisite body of saxophone music quite unlike anything else in jazz."[22]

If all those reissues did not furnish proof enough, further material evidence of the reevaluation of the saxophonist's significance could be found in 1978's "Prez Awards"—a series of plaques embedded in the sidewalk of "Swing Street," a section of Fifty-second near the Avenue of the Americas. Of course, Young received one; other honorees were Roy Eldridge, Art Tatum, Stuff Smith, Billie Holiday, Charlie Parker, Dizzy Gillespie, Coleman Hawkins, Kenny Clarke, Sarah Vaughan, Thelonious Monk, and Miles Davis.[23]

In 1979 the awards ceremony was attended by New York City Mayor Edward Koch, basketball player and jazz fan Kareem Abdul Jabbar, and drummer Max Roach. Red Norvo, Slam Stewart, Oscar Pettiford, Fats Waller, Erroll Garner, and Ben Webster were among the musicians singled out for recognition over the few years that the program lasted.

Around this time Young was also paid another kind of compliment, one accorded Charlie Parker previously. "Prez Conference," a band that based its repertoire on Young's more famous solos—along the lines of the Supersax band, which had featured Parker's solos—was formed by saxophonist Dave Pell. Bill Holman—who some years earlier had composed and arranged an instrumental also entitled "Prez Conference," for Woody Herman's band—transcribed Pres's solos and arranged them for three tenors, baritone sax, trumpet, guitar, bass, and drums. Joining Pell in the band was former Basieite Harry "Sweets" Edison. Their one LP included "Taxi War Dance," "I Never Knew," "Sometimes I'm Happy," "Lester Leaps In," "One O'Clock Jump," and other selections from Young's repertoire with the Basie band.[24]

In the late 1970s and early 1980s—two decades after Young's death—jazz festivals continued to pay him homage, demonstrating his singular influence. They often showcased his compositions (especially "Lester

Leaps In") and renditions of songs, presented either by older saxophonists who had known him during the territorial days, such as Budd Johnson and Buddy Tate, or by younger ones who played in his style—Zoot Sims, Al Cohn, and Stan Getz among them. One such "Salute to Pres" took place at Carnegie Hall in 1982 and featured not only these saxophonists but former Basie band members Sweets Edison and Vic Dickenson. Around 1980 the Black playwright OyamO wrote and staged *The Resurrection of Lady Lester,* a drama that drew on episodes from Young's life, including his childhood. Bernie Cash unveiled his *Prez — A Jazz Opera* in 1985.[25]

Rarely, if ever, has a Black musician received such extensive recognition in such different media. Also in 1985, the popular film *Round Midnight,* starring Dexter Gordon in the role of a musician whose character and mannerisms resembled Young's, was dedicated to the tenor saxophonist and pianist Bud Powell. The settings—Paris and New York City, their clubs and nightspots—and the plot, in which a saxophonist resolves to leave France for the United States, roughly corresponded to some of the events and milieus of Young's last year.

Songs honoring the saxophonist began to be heard as early as 1959; notable among these were Charles Mingus's "Goodbye Pork Pie Hat" and Wayne Shorter's "Lester Left Town." (The former would be reworked with lyrics by singer Joni Mitchell in 1979 on her tribute album to Mingus; it would also be recorded by the multi-instrumentalist Rahsaan Roland Kirk.) And the saxophonist Gary Bartz memorialized the tenor saxophonist with a number of his own, borrowing Pres's nieces' and nephews' nickname for its title: "Uncle Bubba."[26]

Young had always had a special fondness for vocalists, and singers were now among the artists who paid tribute to the tenor stylist. Lorez Alexandria dedicated *Lorez Sings Pres,* recorded live "at an intimate club," to Young; the selection of songs included "Fine and Dandy, "D.B. Blues," "You're Driving Me Crazy," "Polka Dots and Moonbeams," "No Eyes Blues," and "Jumpin' with Symphony Sid." Besides singing the lyrics, on many of these songs she also scatted.[27]

Honoring Young in yet another way were the singer Eve Zanni and the late Eddie Jefferson, both of whom wrote lyrics to some of his solos and compositions. Jefferson was not the first to do it, but he was nonetheless one of the pioneers in writing new lyrics to familiar songs, the most famous of which was saxophonist James Moody's "I'm in the Mood for Love," as performed by King Pleasure. Jefferson went on to write the lyrics for "Baby Girl," based on Young's 1947 recording of "These Foolish Things." The former dancer and singer recalled, "Lester was in the hospital at the time and these lyrics represent what I imagined him writing in a letter to his wife."[28]

Zanni also composed lyrics in tribute to Young, demonstrating the powerful influence he continued to exercise even years after his death. For a time she led a vocal trio named the Sweethots, which performed "close harmony swing vocal arrangements" of selections by the Mills Brothers, the Boswell sisters, and the Lunceford trio, as well as Zanni's own original arrangements; the aim, she explained, "was to re-create [the sound of the] . . . early Basie horn sections, Ellington [and the] Kansas City Six."

She wrote "Lester's Embrace" after hearing Young's version of "Embraceable You" played repeatedly on the radio over the course of several days. "Moved by the plaintive 'stories' I was hearing—the sentences and phrases full of feeling and truth," Zanni recalled that she "listened to each phrase emotionally, with half-closed eyes in order to tune in to the feelings Pres was expressing." She could "hear distinct 'sentences' full of feeling and invention, expressing an 'inner language' the way only Pres can, far better than words." The lyrics she selected to accompany it "seemed to come closest to the pain, passion, beauty and longing that came out of Pres's horn." When the lyrics were finally complete, she began thinking about the best setting for the vocal. One evening while relaxing, listening to the recording, she heard Young speak: "I swear I felt Pres saying to me, 'Well, Lady Parker got to record with strings. . . .' [And I thought] Yes, strings! I want to record this with strings for Pres."[29]

Perhaps Young's greatest influence, however, was on the sidemen who were also his friends—Jesse Drakes, Irving Ashby, Barney Kessel, and many others. Their collective testimony is the best evidence we have of Lester Young's character, vision, impact, and singular genius. Even decades after he died, these musicians still painted a vivid picture of the tenor stylist, in words whose immediacy and affective meaning cannot be adequately conveyed in paraphrase.

Pointing to Young's towering presence in his life, Jesse Drakes maintained twenty-four years after the saxophonist passed on, "When I start talking about myself it always comes to Pres. I don't know why that happens. . . . Maybe I feel that's the only music I ever played."[30]

Likewise, the guitarist Irving Ashby asserted that Young's sound had "reached a part of me that no other [musician's] had," adding, "I don't think there's ever been any saxophone that has . . . had that much of an impact on my life and my feeling." Every note the tenor man played, he said, "had a message all the time." His music furthermore had a sort of hypnotic effect: "When Lester put his horn in his mouth and started playing, everything around me just wasn't there."[31]

In 1983 Ashby testified, "I never got over the impact of the solos that he played. . . . The effect they had on me is with me right to this moment. So *that* was the beginning of my worshipping Pres." He clarified this last, rather strong statement by explaining, "I've had a—well, you could say a love affair with Pres's style of playing and with him as a person." Ashby's admiration was amplified as a result of the time he spent rooming with Young on the JATP European tour in the spring of 1952. "I didn't get to know him enough to develop the worship that I had for his playing, to apply that to *him,* . . . until [then]," the guitarist noted. As to his rather unusual use of the term *worship,* Ashby emphasized, "If there were any word that I could use that would be *stronger* than that, I would have used it."[32]

Young's fellow tenor saxophonist Johnny Griffin was impressed by the hardships his hero endured as well as his wisdom. Griffin's recollections depicted two extremes of emotion: he remembered seeing tears in Young's eyes as he complained about the musicians who had been chosen to play with him at Chicago's Beehive, a situation he tolerated only because he needed the money; and he recalled Young's lighter side. For Griffin, the stylist was in the elite company of Thelonious Monk as "one of the world's greatest humorists." Griffin liked to "tell young musicians who think that they are hip that I've only met two hip people in my life, and the rest were pretenders." Both Young and Monk, he noted, "could say certain things that would be right to the point without a bunch of b.s. It could be humorous or it could be ironic but really right on it."[33]

Perhaps the most faithful to Young's model were the reedmen. Brew Moore's adherence to his style extended to his holding his head to the side like Young, and to making such proclamations as "Anybody who doesn't play like Lester is wrong." He added that "if you're going to play tenor, you make a choice between Hawkins and Pres." But whereas the older saxophonist "took his style as far as you can go," Young was different, "progressive": "You can go on from there." As an example, Moore pointed to Parker: "Look what Bird did with it." In his own playing,

Moore maintained that he "used Lester's idiom to project [his] own ideas." And as for holding his head to the side while playing, it allowed him to hear better, he said.[34]

Moore identified Young as a forerunner of the "new" and "progressive" jazz of the late 1940s. He recalled that the connection between his hero and bebop had not been immediately apparent to him, "but then suddenly I realized [that] Bird came from Lester and Lester was the foundation of bop." Consequently, the saxophonist explained, "I knew I could keep playing in Lester's style and play with a bop band."[35]

Other saxophonists likewise acknowledged being influenced by Young at one time or another. Wardell Gray, Gene Ammons, Zoot Sims, Al Cohn, Stan Getz, and Paul Quinichette all profoundly admired the older tenor stylist. Those who had once liked Hawkins tended to forget him when they heard Young. Later stylists such as John Coltrane and Sonny Rollins would claim to synthesize the two approaches.[36]

Nor were saxophonists the only bebop musicians who respected Young, himself usually portrayed as a master of the swing idiom. The trumpet players Howard McGhee, Miles Davis, and Art Farmer all testified to his influence on their playing. Davis, whom Young nicknamed Midget—a loving insult—contended that "Lester had a sound and an approach like Louis Armstrong['s], only he had [them] on tenor sax." Analyzing the saxophonist's "running style of playing," Davis suggested that what made it outstanding was that "it floods the tone"; moreover, he said, "it has a softness in the approach and concept, and places emphasis on one note." While acknowledging his debt to Clark Terry, Freddie Webster, and Gillespie, the young trumpet player asserted, "I learned about that running style from Lester Young." Similarly, Art Farmer found at least one of his musical ideals in Young's example: "I try for . . . the melodically swinging, lyrical quality that is as much a part of Pres' playing today [1957] as it was yesterday."[37]

Bluesmen, too, felt Young's influence. The guitarist B. B. King, for example, had nothing but praise for the tenor stylist, who he said had "revolutionized the music." In King's opinion, "Prez invented cool"; musically, this meant that "rather than state a melody, he suggested it." Contradicting writers' charges that Young lacked good breath control, King insisted that when the tenor stylist barely breathed into his horn, he created "an intimacy that gave me chills." He concluded that "Prez was an abstract jazz man, and he taught me the beauty of modern art."[38]

Krupa pianist Bobby Scott (whom Pres called Bobby Socks or just Socks—a play on his name) maintained that in his entire life, only two other people had influenced him as much as Young. He also recalled that "nobody ever made so much fun so consistently, so hard, so freely." Young's powers were evidently considerable in this respect, almost as if he had been drawing upon years of experience as a comedian: "Sometimes, when he was on a roll, it went on for days. Not jokes or one-liners. . . . It was always situational and personal." Nearly a quarter century after the saxophonist's death, Scott wrote, "I can *hear* him again, hear the fake dramatic pauses, the ham acting, the truncated explanations he was known for and, most of all, the disarming sweetness."[39]

Young's commentaries and sense of humor rose to the challenge at every turn. On one occasion, when faced with the prospect of less-than-desirable accommodations, he cut a glance at Scott before getting off the bus, and said, "You know the story, morning glory." The reference to the popular Mary Lou Williams composition was typical of Pres's oblique comments on the perils of life on the road. Another dilapidated hotel earned Young's description as an establishment where the rats played basketball in the halls at night. In yet a third such place, he surveyed the room but saw no bed, and asked Scott if they were supposed to sleep on the table. In response, the pianist pulled down a Murphy bed from its closet. Young, somewhat taken aback, surveyed the bed coolly and then inquired, "But where's Murphy?," adding, "If I get in it . . . will the sucker pop up?"[40]

Scott recalled the special problems he and other band members had getting Young onto airplanes. He hated to fly—a trait he shared with Louis Armstrong, Nat Cole, Duke Ellington, and Ella Fitzgerald—so his sidemen had to ply him with drinks before he would agree to board an aircraft. If he saw an infant among the passengers, he would relax a bit, reasoning that God would not cause the death of an innocent child, but if he saw an older person in a wheelchair about to board, he would shrink back in (mock?) fear, exclaiming, "It's a Johnny Deathbed!"—that is, someone whose time was nearly up and who was therefore, in Young's view, more likely to die in an airplane crash.

As the plane taxied down the runway, the comic routine would continue. Young would snap his fingers faster and faster as the propellers whirred and whined, urging the plane on—"Go on, go on, get it, get it, get it"—until it lifted off the ground; then he would sigh and lean back in his seat, murmuring, "All right. All right." He would turn to Scott and explain, "We've got to have four lungs, Socks"—meaning propellers—as he disliked planes with only two.[41]

As young as he was then, Scott was particularly impressionable, especially in the company of someone whom years later he would recall as having been so complex that he could not be described in prose. Poetry, Scott averred, was better suited to Young, who had been "very elusive" and yet "maybe the most *special,* and certainly the most likable," of all the people he had known. Scott likened the tenor stylist to Laurence Olivier in terms of his stature.

In addition to his comfort with Scott, the fact that the saxophonist chose Irving Ashby to be his roommate on the spring 1952 JATP tour, and befriended Paul Quinichette—who said Young treated him like a kid brother—also indicates that he felt very much at ease with some of the younger sidemen. Like many others, however, Scott observed that few people ever got close enough to Young "to look through that rather deep water" that was his essential nature. Some of the saxophonist's behavior was a defense mechanism, Scott thought; he characterized Young as one who, rather than speaking out about some slight or hurt, "took away the wound with him and licked it somewhere else."

A certain moral dimension and religiosity pervaded Young's worldview. Scott, who studied theology as well as music, remembered, "In his words he expressed many attitudes—but never contempt." Instead, Young's moral posture was "refreshing and, surprisingly, rang of a pure Christian view in which offenders are seen as pathetic." He appeared to be "more concerned with *how* an offensive person got that way," and in fact could seem almost sympathetic toward bigots due to "his deepest understanding of what they had paid for their hatred and how unrewarding the whole exercise must be." In his pity for misguided souls, Young struck Scott as being "Gandhi-like," though even "more perceptive" than that champion of civil disobedience. "Prez," the pianist believed, "exhibited the bravery of the human spirit." Moreover, for Scott and others he became "a *Tao,* a way, a path." In this respect, too, he was singular: "Few artists in the twentieth century," Scott wrote, "have had so many surrogate vicars."[42]

It was Scott's contention that Young defied commonly accepted notions about reality, both through his music and in his life. His thinking "straddled time and eras." While his style was indeed fashioned during a specific period in history, and one could gauge him by that—or try to—

still "there was so much more to Prez than the notes that crept out of his horn." His warmth was "almost a vision . . . not a halo but some kind of a bubble." By means of his horn, Scott maintained, he brought all of life's contradictions into his bubble, and "not everyone can do that."[43]

One example of Young's vision, or "bubble," was the Wiggins Club that he spun entirely out of his imagination. He himself was the head of the club or, as he designated himself, Dr. Willis Wiggins—likely a reference to his father and maybe to the term *wig* ("head") or the expression *wig out* ("to be out of one's head," or "way out"). Other members were referred to as Dr. Willis Jr. Young spoke about himself in the third person in this context—for example, dryly observing of a particularly long bus ride between dates, "Dr. Willis is not going to like this." Such statements allowed him to complain without being aggressive or insulting.[44]

Both Jesse Drakes and Bobby Scott often found Young's ways a challenge. "Prez always had something that puzzled me and once I thought I had it figured out, he'd come and play it another way," explained the trumpet player. Moreover, he added, "what a lot of people would say was unusual would be normal to me [coming] from Pres." Scott expressed a similar sentiment: "Everything that I'd imagined to be way out and bizarre was living reality in Prez. And he gave me more food for thought than anyone I'd met, excepting my music teacher . . . and a Lutheran minister." Despite that comparison, Scott noted that "neither of them had the totality of Prez's person. He was a world, fully constructed with all the loose ends tied up"—a world, furthermore, that "reality could not and did not puncture; not even slightly." The saxophonist's "spectral being . . . cut through every tidy notion I had formulated about the meaning of this existence," the pianist averred; Young seemed, to him, "an actuated illumination," something like "a visitor from a small planet."[45]

Young's powers of discernment especially impressed the young pianist. On one occasion, while traveling down South, they realized they were not going to be waited on in a restaurant. Scott was ready to fight for their rights, but Young's attitude was "Let's go somewhere else"; he more or less stated, "It does not pay to do this. I frankly do not want to eat where I am not welcome." In an age of civil rights campaigns, Scott was taken aback by the saxophonist's stance: after all, numerous other musicians—including Lena Horne, Lionel Hampton, and Erroll Garner—went to court over discrimination in the 1950s, and some of them won.

As Scott considered Young's position over the ensuing years, however, he began to see that there was a certain amount of wisdom expressed in it—that sometimes it was *not* wise to push where one was not wanted. The pianist thought the idea not only commendable but "exportable"—so that, for example, if a bandleader felt uncomfortable with a particular musician on a gig, he was often better off simply paying him to leave, because otherwise the bad feelings would affect everyone adversely.[46]

Young's whole approach to life could be summed up, Scott said, by his expression "It's all in the *way* you look at it." In other words, reality existed on different levels, and one perspective was not necessarily better than another—as with fighting for the right to dine somewhere versus getting up and leaving. One offhand remark that Young made seemed to reinforce this notion, even as it acknowledged the grief that some Americans inflicted on others through discrimination and race segregation. On a long airplane trip across the vast heartland of the nation, after watching the landscape crawl by below them hour after hour, Young commented to Scott, "Sure as hell is enough room for everybody, ain't there?"

Another statement by Young that Scott found especially insightful and memorable was "You can't own . . . what ain't." Then there was his explanation of why he did not play like Charlie Parker: "He [Bird] plays those licks, I play my licks, you play your licks." And he had a way of chiding someone whose ego had swelled with pride: "They say your hat don't fit no more." On issues of race, Young could be either humorous, as when he renamed Krupa's bassist, Red Mitchell, "White Boy," or sarcastic, as in his reference to "the seven o'clock white folks' news." One interviewer recalled how Young "once disposed of me with withering sarcasm when I [said I] hoped a broadcast we were about to do would be fun."[47]

Scott vividly recalled how Young loved to root for the underdog, and remembered, too, that he could pick a winner in the boxing ring. When Rocky Marciano was slated to fight Archie Moore, other JATP musicians backed Moore, stressing his weight advantage, among other things. Young reminded them, "'This is the Rock [that Moore is up against]. *I* watched Rocky Marciano knock Joe Louis right through the ropes!'" Young bet on his champion and "was just in his glory" after the fight as he collected his winnings: "'Served them right! Who do they think was being sent in with Archie Moore, a little boy?'" He told Scott, "'*You* should have bet a lot o' money, Socks. They got off too easy.'"[48]

Sometimes Young's wisdom was manifested as kindness, as in several incidents recalled by his niece Martha Young, Irma's daughter. Once, when "Uncle Bubba" was in Los Angeles to play at the Hollywood Bowl, probably in August 1957, Martha, a pianist, invited him to come and hear her perform with Johnny Otis's band at the Club Oasis on Western Avenue. She had never liked for him to hear her play; until then, she remembered, "it would frighten me to death for him to come to [our] house. . . . If he'd find me there [at the piano], I'd just freeze, I couldn't do anything." When he arrived at the Oasis, Young found that his niece had reserved a table for him near the bandstand. She herself was surprised to learn, meanwhile, that Otis, the bandleader, intended her to play in a trio format instead of with the band—putting her under an even brighter spotlight in front of her famous uncle. After performing, she reminisced, "I was as wet as a dish rag, . . . with him sitting right there looking at me, and I came down and . . . said, 'OK, Uncle Bubba, how'd I do?'" He responded, "'It seems like I have to get a gig for me and my niece.'" The compliment stayed with her "for all of these years. . . . He was telling me I could play with him, and what more could I need?"[49]

On another occasion she played at a fraternity affair with the saxophonist Vi Redd, and "one of the fellows of the group, [his] parents were very good friends with Erroll Garner"; in fact, the pianist showed up that night to perform. Martha Young had grown up listening to Garner, among others, and felt intimidated when he "walked up on the stage and sat on the stool right next to me while I was playing." At intermission she called her uncle, who happened to be in town at the time; she was crying "and I was telling him about this man sitting up there on the stage and [how] I didn't think I could play anymore, I was too scared." Young asked her the man's name, and she said, "Erroll Garner." He then asked her her name, and she told him. "He said, 'Well, don't you forget it!' And that was it." She added that it might not "seem much to anybody else, and it's not saying that I'm greater than Garner or however the situation may be, but I am who I am and you are who you are and all you can do is what you can do. I don't give a damn who comes up there!"[50]

The pianist Nat Pierce told a somewhat similar story about a night he played Birdland with Young. The saxophonist was being feted on the occasion of his thirtieth year in show business; several jazz critics sat at a table, friends of the guest of honor were in the audience, and there was a cake "and the whole thing." Young had not played in a while, having suffered a probable heart attack earlier in the year, and he was cold sober. He and Pierce, Doug Watkins, Curtis Fuller, and Willie Jones were in the middle of "Jeepers Creepers" when, Pierce recalled, "two hands came over the back of my shoulders behind me—right over my shoulders—and a guy says, 'I'm Bud Powell, let me play.'" Not wanting to create a scene, Pierce stepped down. Young, unaware of the switch in personnel behind him, continued playing and came to the bridge, "and evidently Bud Powell didn't know that bridge or something, [because] he played something strange, and Lester turned around and looked at him, and he saw that I wasn't there." Young kept playing, and then when they came to the bridge again, "Bud Powell played some different chords in the bridge, [and] they were still not the right ones."[51]

At that point the tenor stylist "just put his horn down on the stand and went to the bar and (he hadn't been drinking at all) . . . he got a tray, and seven double Hennesseys . . . and sat down there with his tray" in a corner booth at the back of the club. While the other musicians continued to play, Pierce came over and joined Young, who asked him, "'Are you happy with your job?'" The pianist answered that he was, adding, "One of the thrills of my life is to play with you and everything." Young responded, "'OK. Answer this question for me. Why do guys come on *my* bandstand where I call the tunes, the keys, and the tempos, and play *their* music?'" Nearly three decades later, Pierce still deemed this "one of the most profound statements that anyone has ever said to me." In fact, "thinking about it retrospectively," he observed, made it even "*more* profound."

For Pierce, Young's question went right to the heart of the matter, because "when you think about that, it probably killed more great jazz musicians than booze, drugs, or anything else did: incompatibility with an accompaniment." The pianist likened it to "somebody trying to tell Charlie Parker, 'Here's how bebop goes on the drums.' . . . Telling the *inventor* about it. That's basically what they were doing to Lester Young."[52]

As a champion of the underdog, the saxophonist had particular affection for his fellow African Americans. Jo Jones claimed, "There has never been . . . one Black man that loved the Black race like Lester Young, nobody." Much as Bobby Scott had seen Young as being Gandhiesque, Jones compared him to civil rights leaders, reiterating that "nobody from Marcus Garvey up . . . ever loved the Black man like Lester Young."[53] Yet this did not mean that the saxophonist was anti-white, as some believed. Like the Christians who condemned the sin but not the sinner, he made a distinction between the crime of racial prejudice and its supporters.

Always and everywhere, however, music was the vehicle of Young's beliefs, whether religious or political, moral or humanitarian. Speaking at the Berlin Jazz Festival in 1964, Dr. Martin Luther King Jr. was to point out that Black music could be neither separated from life nor neatly classified into sacred and profane categories. King observed:

> God has wrought many things out of oppression. He has endowed his creatures with the capacity to create, and from this capacity have flowed the sweet songs of sorrow and of joy that have allowed man to cope with his environment in many situations. Jazz speaks of life. The blues tell the stories of life's difficulties, and if you will think for a moment, you will realize that they take the hardest realities of life and put them into music only to come out with some new hope or sense of triumph. This is triumphant music: Modern jazz has continued in this tradition, singing the songs of a more complicated urban existence. When life itself offers no order and meaning, the musician creates an order and meaning from the sounds of earth which flow through his instrument.[54]

If we view Young's creation of his own world in this light, we can begin to understand the tenor stylist's values and behavior as a cohesive expression of his life history and character rather than some random collection of idiosyncrasies. Although he did not make explicit public statements about his religious beliefs, other musicians thought him religious and recalled his speaking of God as "The Old Master"; like numerous other musicians, some of them no less "profane" than him, he found a spiritual dimension in the music.[55]

Among writers, the beats may have been among the first to recognize Young's stature; he provided inspiration for some of their most memorable work. Allen Ginsberg noted of his controversial poem "Howl," for example, that it was "all 'Lester Leaps In.' And I got that from Kerouac. Or paid attention to it on account of Kerouac, surely—he made me listen to it."[56]

In San Francisco in the mid-1950s, poets and writers and their followers, later to be called beatniks or beats, congregated in North Beach coffee shops and at one of their favorite bookstores, City Lights, run by Lawrence Ferlinghetti, the future publisher of "Howl." Collectively, they set the tone for literature, social consciousness, and the counterculture of the 1960s, not only in the Bay Area but throughout the nation. Jack Kerouac and his friend Neal Cassady, the hero of Kerouac's *On the Road,* were both avid Young fans and were probably in the audience for the tenor stylist's March 1954 date at the Black Hawk; the novelist had arrived in California late the previous month.[57]

For Kerouac as for other leaders of and participants in this literary and social movement, Young was the archetypal jazz musician as cultural rebel, and the ultimate hipster of the 1950s. In *On the Road,* which would be published late in the summer of 1957 and would soon become a veritable bible for beats, Kerouac described Young as "that gloomy, saintly goof in whom the history of jazz was wrapped . . . an artist . . . [who] blew the greatest; . . . and he blows cool and easy getout phrases."[58]

Like many musicians, the beats kept to their own society, often smoked marijuana, and spoke in hip slang; as a result, mainstream America regarded them as deviants or at the very least as outcasts possessed of the peculiar otherness that characterizes such pariahs. Kerouac first took notice of the saxophonist when he was a student at the Horace Mann School for Boys and then at Columbia University between 1939 and 1941. His future wife testified in the documentary film *Kerouac* that the writer once shared a taxi to Minton's—and, in the course of the ride, smoked a joint—with Young. No doubt it was an unforgettable moment for one of the most prolific authors of the beat generation.[59]

Kerouac related an amusing encounter that took place between Ginsberg and Young one night at the Five Spot in Greenwich Village, probably not long before the saxophonist's death. Young sat in the back kitchen between sets on this gig, and Kerouac recounted how his "buddy poet Allen Ginsberg went back and got on his knees and asked him what he would do if an atom bomb fell on New York." Likely taken aback more by Ginsberg's posture than by his question, Young responded with typical humor and a hint of rebelliousness, proclaiming that he "would break the window in Tiffany's and get some jewels anyway," and then inquiring of the poet, "What are you doin' on your knees?" For Kerouac, Young's question indicated that he did not realize he was "a great hero of the beat generation and now enshrined."[60]

Asked about the inspiration for "Howl," Ginsberg made explicit the debt it owed to "Lester Leaps In." He explained that "Lester Young, actually, is what I was thinking about" while writing the poem, and then he sang the song:

Dadada DAT DAT DA, dada DA da
Dadada DAT DAT DA, dat da Da da
Dadada DAT DAT DA, dat da Da da,
Dadada DAT DAT DA, dat da Da da,
Dadada
dadada
dada da dadah . . .

Here as elsewhere, Black music and speech patterns strongly influenced beat literature—even to its manner of composition, which was likened to oral improvisation. While European precedents and the work of Walt Whitman and others also shaped this new writing, Ginsberg would claim that Kerouac had "learned his line . . . directly from Charlie Parker, and Gillespie, and Monk," taking inspiration for his free-flight literature from "sitting in the middle of Manhattan listening to the radio and picking up vibrations of a new breath, from the spades [Blacks]."[61]

For further insight into why the beat writers so admired Young, we may turn to John Clellon Holmes, who was the first to use the word *beat* in print when referring to this milieu. His *Esquire* article "The Philosophy of the Beat Generation" contended that some groups—teenage gangs, for example, but also the beats—sought to "return to an older, more personal, but no less rigorous code of ethics, which includes the inviolability of comradeship, the respect for confidences, and an almost mystical regard for courage." Here Holmes could have been describing Young's values as well. In fact, he might have had the saxophonist in mind when he maintained that an indomitable will to survive persisted in the older hipster, "who moves through our cities like a member of some mysterious Underground, not plotting anything, but merely keeping alive an unpopular philosophy, much like the Christians of the first century."[62]

This hipster, however, had no political agenda; rather, "his aim is to be asocial, not antisocial," for he believes "that argument, violence and concern for attachments are ultimately Square." Indeed, the hipster "practices a kind of passive resistance to the Square society in which he lives, and the most he would ever propose as a program would be the removal of every social and intellectual restraint to the expression and enjoyment of his unique individuality."[63]

More acutely than most observers, Young, Kerouac, and Ginsberg saw through the hypocrisy of respectable society. Like one employee at

MCA in the 1950s, they understood that "the wood paneling, and old English hunting prints in the elevators, and the leather-bound sets of [Gibbon] and other classics in each reception room . . . the dress codes"—all of that respectability was "only a front," at once a mask and a metaphor for the insidious hypocrisy that characterized U.S. society at midcentury.[64]

If the saxophonist's influence on certain white writers was extensive, and explicitly acknowledged, his status among their African American counterparts before his death was less so, even though Sterling Brown, Langston Hughes, Zora Neale Hurston, and a number of younger poets all found their inspiration in the very same Black oral tradition that Young tapped. Several poems were written about him after 1959, but along with Ralph Ellison, Chester Himes seems to have been one of the few Black writers who made much of Young during his life. The child of teachers, Himes became a writer in prison and later worked at a number of jobs as a laborer, writing at night, before going into permanent exile in the mid-1950s. In his Harlem novels, records by Louis Armstrong, Bessie Smith, and Lester Young are heard at crucial moments. When the hero of *The Heat's On,* Detective "Coffin Ed," hears a sax solo by Young, "he didn't recognize the tune, but it had the 'Pres' treatment . . . like listening to someone laughing their way toward death . . . laughter dripping wet with tears. Colored people's laughter." In his autobiography, Himes recalled sitting in a German family's parlor one night, listening to classical music and feeling that he "would give all of Bach for eight bars of Lester."[65]

The poets ted joans and Amiri Baraka (LeRoi Jones) immortalized the tenor stylist and his artistry in "Lester Young" and "Pres Spoke in a Language," respectively. joans—who, like e. e. cummings, preferred to use lower-case letters for his name—described Young as seeming sometimes "cool like an eternal blue flame burning in the old Kansas City nunnery," and other times "happy" until he remembered his Jim Crow birthplace with its "blood stained clay hills"; mainly, however, "he was blowin' on the wonderful tenor sax . . . preachin' in very cool tones, shoutin'" to emphasize his point in his "blues message." As President of his instrument and minister "of soul stirring Jazz, he knew what he blew / and he did what a pres should do, wail, wail, wail." Death, joans suggested, had merely booked Young to play with Bird, Art Tatum, "and other heavenly wailers." The poet who admired Langston Hughes concluded with an affirmation: "Angels of Jazz—they don't die—they live / they live—in hipsters like you and I."[66]

Baraka's poem, published some twenty years after Young's death, paid tribute to the saxophonist's wit and creativity with language. It explained the meaning behind his use of "Ding Dong," likening the words to the typewriter's bell signaling the end of a line, and of the expression "No Eyes," to denote, something "lame" that he "cdn't dig." Young's life and music had been as unique as his language, Baraka noted: what he did was "translat[e] frankie trumbauer into / Bird'*s* feathers / Trane*s* sinewy tracks / the slickster walking through the crowd / surviving on a terrifying wit / its the jungle the jungle / we living in." "Cats like pres" succeeded in making it because "they, at / least, / had to, / to do anything else." Baraka ended the poem with the cryptic line "Save all that comrades, we need it."

The writer Al Young claimed kinship of a sort with the tenor saxophonist. He made note of Young's sadness, comparing it to the depth of feeling of the New Orleans trumpet king, Joe Oliver, who once sold "fruit and vegetables from a roadside truck for a living," and that of the composer Tadd Dameron, who gave up a medical career "because he thought the world was sorely in need of beauty," and even that of Coleman Hawkins, "colorist and shaper of horn poems." But in the end he concluded that such sorrow "was Lester's alone."[67]

Nonetheless, the writer maintained, the tenor stylist had also been the source of "a musical force that gave the world so much loving sound that it still hurts to play his final recordings or to remember how pitifully wasted he was during those declining Jazz at the Philharmonic concert years." Al Young echoed the opinion of some critics when he contended that near the end of the saxophonist's life, "much of his exuberance and genius had fled him, . . . [and] everything that he had to say on his horn sounded like variations on sighs of resignation." The writer recalled Young's earlier career as the time "of all that wondrous discourse that used to pour and trickle and skeet out of him like light from some heavenly reservoir." Toward the end, weary from telling his story every night, Pres "was ready to step aside and do his brooding in private." The writer stressed jazz fans' connection with the tenor stylist and made a pun on the name they shared—"We fish who swam his ocean keep him young" —adding, "I used to lie and say he was a distant cousin, but it was true."[68]

Larry Neal played on the title of Mingus's composition in his own tribute, "Don't Say Goodbye to the Porkpie Hat (*Mingus, Bird, Prez, Langston, and Them*)," which appeared in his collection of jazz poems, *Hoodoo Hollerin' Bebop Ghosts.* In this poem Young becomes the hat "that rolled along on padded shoulders / that swang bebop phrases / in Minton's jelly roll dreams." A dreamlike sequence follows its journey through African American worlds where it "reigns supreme," amid (in an allusion to Gillespie and Parker compositions) "tonal memories / of salt peanuts and hothouse birds." From the Deep South with its "redneck lynchers," "man with the mojo hand," and "dyke with the .38" to the place where "Stop-time Buddy and Creole Sidney wailed," "shape to shape, horn to horn / the Porkpie Hat resurrected himself / night to night." At last, "swirling in the sound of sax blown suns," the porkpie / Young goes "flying / fast / zipping / past / sound / into cosmic silences." For Neal, Young's playing was not only efficacious but political, as well as metaphysical and communal: "So we pick up our axes and prepare / to blast the white dream; / we pick up our axes / re-create ourselves and the universe." The sounds they played would soon be "splintering the deepest regions of spiritual space . . . blowing death and doom to all who have no use for the spirit." Pres was immortal, and we must not say farewell to the porkpie, Neal admonished, because "he lives, oh yes." And not only "Lester lives and leaps," but "Bird lives / Lady lives / Eric stands next to me . . . Lester leaps in every night." The poem ends with the chant or refrain "spirit lives / spirit lives / spirit lives / SPIRIT!!! / SWEEEEEEEEEEEEEEETTT!!!" and then finally the coda "take it again / this time from the top."[69]

Again and again, Young's jive talk was cited by writers, musicians, hipsters, and other members of this jazz society that knew no national boundaries. While the use of slang and the habit of giving people nicknames were common enough within the Basie band and throughout Black America, Young seems somehow to have made these practices his own, thereby leaving a singular stamp on jazz culture. Buck Clayton, for one, thought that Young was "more original" than other jive speakers: "Lester could make up a name for something, it would stick whatever you'd call it. I know a lot of things that people don't know that Lester started, which I believe he did. I never heard these words before he said them, and then five years later, everybody's saying them, and nobody knows who started them."[70]

The guitarist Barney Kessel and the pianist Bobby Scott, among others, agreed that Young coined a number of slang terms and phrases, including "That's cool" and "Don't blow your cool." Another favorite was "fuds" and then "fuzz" for "feds," or federal agents. Family members attributed "Dig" and "You dig?" to him. Many of these expressions were picked up by beat writers who popularized them and introduced them into general parlance. "Eyes," "Dig?," "You dig?," and "That's cool" are all still used by musicians, elderly beatniks, middle-aged hippies, and others who wish to give the impression of being "hip to the jive." Three decades after his death, a *New Yorker* article noted that the saxophonist's "aphorisms are so widely diffused that many of those who plagiarize him are unaware they are doing so."[71]

Young put familiar words together in new ways, often in the form of brief statements or questions. Some of these have since become standard usage in the jazz world and points beyond:

"I feel a draft." (I'm getting bad vibrations.)
"How's your feelings?" (How are you?)
"Can madam burn?" (Can you/she cook?)
"Startled doe, two o'clock." (There's an attractive doe-eyed woman off to the right.)
"Those people will be here in December." (My second child is scheduled to arrive this winter.)
"George Washington." (Play or solo on the bridge [B section] of the song.)
"How do the bread smell?" (How much does the job pay?)
"Smotherin' heights." (I am deeply moved.)
"You bruised me." (You hurt my feelings.)
"Letter A." (Come again? Start at the beginning / from the top.)
"I've paid my dues." (I'm certified or approved and have a right to play.)
"Ding dong." (Somebody goofed / made a mistake.)
"Doom!" (End of conversation.)

He also used song references as a kind of shorthand. "I Only Have Eyes for You" probably supplied him with the abbreviated "eyes" to indicate a liking for a person or thing. "I Didn't Know What Time It Was" gave him the expression "You don't know what time it is," signifying that someone was naive, unknowing, unhip. On the bandstand, Young would call out "Poker Chips" when he wanted his sidemen to play "Polka Dots and Moonbeams," while "Afternoon of a Basie-ite" became "Afternoon of a Baseball Player."[72]

More than two decades after Young's death, the man and his music began to be memorialized annually in Jazz Vespers at Manhattan's jazz church, on Lexington Avenue at Fifty-fourth Street. In mid-March of 1986 and succeeding years, the anniversary of his passing was observed at Saint Peter's, with the late Reverend John Gensel, known in some circles as the jazz pastor, presiding. This church was, and remains, a favored site for the funerals of New York–area musicians. In 1992, tributes to Young were offered by Adam Clayton Powell III, son of the Harlem congressman, and by Willie Jones, a drummer who used to play with the saxophonist. Prayers and Scripture readings alternated with spoken and musical homages; Eve Zanni sang her "Lester's Embrace," and a quintet featuring the baritone saxophonist Cecil Payne and the drummer Thelonious Monk Jr. played "Lester Leaps In," "D.B. Blues," and "Jumping with Symphony Sid." Lester Young Jr. was in attendance with his wife and son, and the pews were filled with jazz fans. The Wingate High School Gospel Choir also performed.[73]

While it is impossible to know, of course, what Young himself would have thought of this annual service, it stood as a fitting tribute by family, friends, musicians, and the congregation to one who had profoundly affected the lives of many. It linked him with the jazz tradition and with the community—to which the music was of vital importance, far surpassing the significance usually attributed to it by the popular-music industry—and bestowed upon the saxophonist a measure of the recognition and dignity that the business had so often withheld from him, his fellow African American musicians, and jazz people generally.

It was a particularly appropriate venue in which to remember someone who, from one perspective, had been a pious pilgrim on a mission, spreading joy and deep feeling through his interpretations of popular songs and blues. Young faced daunting challenges throughout his career, from the racism he witnessed as a teenager on the carnival circuit and the hardships of his stints in territorial bands to the critical scorn and health problems of his final years. He kept on, though, right through to the end—"just trying," as he explained in his last interview, "to get me some money for my *family*. And it's all clean, believe that."[74]

At the last, Young conformed to his own image of himself, as a trouper and a suffering spirit able to rise to every occasion. That he managed to return to performing after suffering a severe depression was remarkable;

when he urged Valdo Williams, his pianist at the Five Spot, to continue soloing, never to simply give up, he was speaking from considerable experience. In his last year, 1958, he recovered in time to play at Birdland late in the spring, at the Mosque in Newark, in the Chicago area in November, and at Manhattan's Five Spot after that. The invitation to perform in Paris early in 1959 presented another challenge that he could not resist, despite his precarious health. In this respect, his jazz life—to borrow the Reverend King's word—represented a triumph of humanity.[75]

Stories that circulated about Young both before and after his death recorded a string of smaller victories. Some were strictly family tales, while others reported something he had said and were often unprintable and not to be repeated in polite company. Many such anecdotes are still recounted by musicians as prologues to songs either written by or in some other way associated with Young. One memorable incident described by the family took place when he was hospitalized. He hated needles and got tired of having the nurse come around every day to administer his shot. One day the rebel in him surfaced, and he surprised her, threw her facedown on the bed, pulled up her dress, grabbed the needle out of her hand, and plunged it into her backside, exclaiming, "Now! How do *you* like it?" We can be sure that the authorities were called in on this occasion.[76]

From such accounts, and from stories about his jive talk and use of profanity, a legendary aura began to envelop Young, so that he seemed to loom larger after his death than he had ever done when he was alive. The Prez Awards, the creative tributes—the play, opera, music, and poetry—and the memorial church services all served as reminders of his stature as a rebel, an artist, and a man. When I marveled to the saxophonist Al Cohn one night at the Blue Note that people talked about Young as if he were still alive, he immediately responded, "That's because he is."[77]

Although other musicians surely shared Young's goals, he may have sacrificed more to remain true to his ideals. The extent to which he drew upon African American religious ideals of stoicism and keeping the faith was evident in his own retelling of episodes from his life. Viewed as a whole, his approach to every aspect of his existence indicated the fundamentally spiritual nature of the world he chose to inhabit.

In his life as in his hotel room, certain substances became transformed, thus taking on new meaning. The usual association of marijuana and alcohol with the profane world was stood on its head as the two became symbols of fellowship in Young's circle. His considerable compassion toward humans also extended to animals, suggesting his respect for life in any form. There are any number of tales about his befriending and caring for wounded or abandoned birds, dogs, and cats; one bird that he nursed back to health flew off, he claimed, after he gave it a nip of brandy—the implication being that this elixir possessed curative powers.[78]

Another object of alchemy was even more mundane. The porkpie hat was not just a trademark for Young; it was a veritable crown, a sign that its wearer was in command and in his element, like a pope or a king. Whereas most "polite" folk took off their hats to show respect for an occasion, setting, or person, many jazz musicians, both Black and white, often kept theirs on as a way of establishing their "territory," or their "turf," in jam sessions and other milieus. As a visible symbol of his authority, Young's porkpie invariably stayed on his head or—for some photo sessions—immediately at hand and visible.[79]

The trials Young endured while trying to establish himself as a stylist gave his character a deeper dimension. The tale of his struggles, and of his rising always to the challenge—managing both to succeed and to maintain his integrity—had real meaning for his fans. Such stories, spread by word of mouth among musicians, added to his reputation as a rebel with dignity as well as an original talent. And this image in turn accorded with Young's own vision of his entire life—a vision not unlike that of the Christian slave or freedman, who saw himself as a child in a troubled, unfriendly world, constantly tested but ultimately prevailing through steadfast adherence to his faith. Like the American slave's, Young's attitude toward life's vicissitudes was one of resignation, for he was confident that he would at last come through and receive his just reward.

One more feature of the belated recognition of the saxophonist should be mentioned here, an aspect of particular meaning for religious people, as it involves renewal, rejuvenation, rebirth, and other dynamic qualities associated with the phoenix of mythology—and, of course, with other, less secular figures. Young's continuing influence even decades after his death points to his ability to reemerge and to revitalize popular culture. Even his beloved porkpie has lately experienced a comeback among Black urban dwellers. In this respect, his memory parallels his music, which paralleled his life, manifesting the importance of a dynamic force suggested by the titles of several of his songs: "Lester Leaps In," "Movin' with Lester," and "Lester Blows Again."

His soul, some might say, operating through his music and in the minds of those who remember him, continues to reveal itself in a way that might have been reassuring to his devout forebears as evidence of permanent truths. This persisting quality of dynamic force reflected and was reflected in Black culture, which perpetuated itself in the face of historic oppression. It suggests yet another way in which Lester Young's contributions went to the very heart of the American cultural experience.

PERSONAL INTERVIEWS

Interviews with the following members of the Young family and musicians were tape-recorded and usually took place in their homes; the length varied from thirty minutes to a few hours, with most sessions lasting about two hours. Often the Postif interview was played for them at the end, and their reactions were noted. Occasionally such exchanges took place backstage, in a hotel, in a car between sets, or on the bandstand, and in some instances I returned at a later date to get further information. The interviewees often recommended other relatives and sidemen of Lester Young for me to talk to. In a few instances interview subjects provided background information on the jazz scene rather than specific data about Young.

Name	Date of Interview
Ashby, Irving	June 24, 1983
Barefield, Eddie	May 24, 1981
Blakeney, Andrew	October 13, 1983
Bolar, Abe	June 5, 1984, etc.
Brown, Crawford "Brownie" Jr.	December 27, 1996
Callender, George "Red"	June 16, 1982
Chadwick, Leonard	April 18, 1985, etc.
Clayton, Wilbur "Buck"	May 21, 1981, etc.
Cloud, Dr. Luther	September 12, 1983
Collins, John E.	January 9, 1982
Daniels, Benjamin	November 26, 1982
Davis, Bert Etta	August 26, 1981
Drakes, Jesse	November 15, 1982
Durham, Eddie	March 21, 1982
Edison, Harry "Sweets"	December 23, 1981
Fields, Carl "Kansas"	July 17, 1981
Gensel, Reverend John	September 23, 1984
Hakim, Sadik	May 28, 1981
Heath, Jimmy	May 26, 1981
Jackson, Le Roy	November 27, 1982
Kay, Connie	June 10, 1981
Kessel, Barney	October 25, 1983
Kirk, Andy	May 29, 1981
Mahones, Gildo	February 2, 1982

Mance, Junior	March 24, 1982
Manuel, Diane Young	September 1998
Marquette, "Pee Wee"	October 28, 1984
McGhee, Howard	June 19, 1984
Parham, Charles "Truck"	August 23, 1982
Phillips, Clarence	June 16, 1983
Phillips, Leonard	February 22 and April 13, 1983
Pierce, Nat	March 22, 1984
Quinichette, Paul	March 23, 1982
Rowles, Jimmy	June 1, 1983
Royal, Marshal	April 8, 1985
Sims, John "Zoot"	June 1, 1983
Smith, Henry "Buster"	August 26, 1982, etc.
Tate, George "Buddy"	October 28, 1984
"Teddy Bear"	May 5, 1984
Tolbert, Alvin	February 19, 1983
Tolbert, James	June 12, 1982, etc.
Tolbert, Lucille	December 28, 1982, etc.
Whyte, Le Roy "Snake"	August 26, 1985, etc.
Williams, Irv	June 10, 1983
Young, Beverly	April 20, 1985
Young, Irma	September 9, 1981, and January 4, 1985
Young, Reverend John W.	March 14, 1983
Young, Lee	June 16, 1982, etc.
Young, Martha	February 15, 1982
Young, Mary	April 4, 1987

NOTES

1. The President of the Tenor Saxophone

1. "Fats Waller, Pianist-Composer, Dies," *Long Island Daily Press,* December 15, 1943, St. Albans Vertical File, Long Island Room, Queens Public Library, New York City.
2. "A Great Is Gone," *Down Beat,* April 16, 1959, p. 11.

2. Shoeshine Boy

1. Author's interview with Irma Young. Woodville was the birthplace of the famous African American composer William Grant Still (1895–1978), who likewise left as an infant: Robert Bartlett Haas, ed., *William Grant Still and the Fusion of Cultures in American Music* (Los Angeles: Black Sparrow, 1972), 3.
2. *Woodville (Miss.) Republican,* June 28, 1974, p. D-3, clipping in Vertical File on Woodville, Woodville Public Library. Richard Aubrey McLemore, ed., *A History of Mississippi* (Hattiesburg, Miss., University and College Press of Mississippi, 1973), 1: 512; *Republican,* June 8, 1974, on the 150th anniversary celebration of the town's founding.
3. "Local Notes of Town and Country," *Woodville Republican,* August 21, 1909, p. 3; "Drouth [*sic*] in Five States," ibid., August 28, 1909, p. 1; on rattlesnakes and malaria, ibid., September 4, 1909, p. 3; "Institutes for Farmers," ibid., August 7, 1909, p. 1; "Cotton Crop Report" and "Local Notes," ibid., August 14, 1909, p. 1 (reporting that "the cotton crop suffered on the whole" in Mississippi); "Cotton Crop Doing Better" and "Local Notes," ibid., August 21, 1909, p. 1; "Local Notes," ibid., June 19, 1909, p. 3; S. A. Knapp, "War on the Boll Weevil," ibid., September 18, 1909, p. 2; "Will We Raise Cotton," ibid., October 2, 1909, p. 2; Allison Davis, Burleigh B. Gardner, and Mary R. Gardner, *Deep South: A Social Anthropological Study of Caste and Class* (Chicago: University of Chicago Press, 1941), 269.
4. Social Security application form of Lizetta Gray, New Orleans, Louisiana, December 26, 1936; a copy of this form was obtained under the Freedom of Information Act.
5. March 2, 1998, fax from Thomas C. Tolliver Jr., chancery clerk, Wilkinson County Courthouse, Woodville, Mississippi.

   Young's ambivalence about his Mississippi origins is suggested by an anecdote related by his sister: once when he was crossing the Canadian border, Lester was asked where he had been born, and he mumbled "Mississippi" so inarticulately that the official had to repeat the question several times (author's interview with Irma Young). Death certificate of Lizetta Gray (1888–1972), no. 707–018697; she died in Los Angeles after about thirty years' residence in southern California. Lee Young maintained that she moved out to live in Los Angeles in the 1950s (personal communication with the author). We know virtually nothing about Lizetta Johnson's parents, other than their names, William and Cornelia, and the fact that they did not own property.

6. Pamphlet brochure in Vertical File on Woodville, Woodville Public Library. "Rural County," one of the counties examined by these scholars, was actually Wilkinson County. The famous study referred to is Davis, Gardner, and Gardner, *Deep South;* see Ronald Bailey, "'Deep South' Revisited: An Assessment of a Classical Text," *CAAS Newsletter* (Los Angeles: Center for Afro-American Studies, UCLA) 11 (1988): 10–14. Quoted in "Local Notes of Town and Country," *Woodville Republican,* June 12, 1909, p. 3.

7. "Local Notes of Town and Country," *Woodville Republican,* July 24, 1909, p. 5: "This time is set apart for the white people in order that the ladies and children may enjoy this pleasure."

8. *Woodville Republican,* June 19, 1909, p. 2.

9. "Militia Called Out," *Woodville Republican,* August 28, 1909, p. 1; ibid., September 4, 1909, p. 2; see also "Oppose Negro Farmers' Union," ibid., August 7, 1909, p. 1, on the expulsion of a white Farmers' Union member who attempted to form a Black branch. See John Hope Franklin, *The Militant South, 1800–1861* (Cambridge, Mass.: Belknap Press of Harvard University, 1956).

10. Albert Murray, *Stomping the Blues* (New York: Da Capo, 1976), is probably the best analysis of the paradoxical qualities and social functions of the blues; Lawrence Levine, *Black Culture and Black Consciousness* (New York: Oxford University Press, 1975), 13, 99–101.

11. Clerk of the Court, Washington Parish, marriage records indicate that the license was obtained on November 28 and the couple married on December 1, 1908; as LaJulia Conerly, deputy clerk of the Mortgage and Conveyance Department, has pointed out, many people got married in Mississippi to avoid paying the surety required in Louisiana. I wish to express my gratitude to LaJulia Conerly for additional information on the A.M.E. church and the African American community in Washington Parish. Lester Young claimed that his mother was a schoolteacher and a seamstress; see Lewis Porter, ed., *A Lester Young Reader* (Washington, D.C.: Smithsonian Institution Press, 1991), 142. Lee Young vaguely recalled his mother's singing (personal communication with the author). New Orleans City Directory, 1926, p. 40, lists the Lizetta Gray School at 1307 Magnolia; this may have been a music school. In 1938 she is listed as a music teacher: City Directory, 1938, p. 1378.

12. Lester does not appear to have been called by his first name, Willis, by anyone in the family. He used it as a first name only once that we know of—on his marriage certificate in 1930. Irma Cornelia Young's application (SS-5) for a Social Security card on February 10, 1937, revealed her middle name. New Orleans scholars have pointed out that Algiers was not usually included in the City Directory. Bruce Raeburn, head of the William Ransom Hogan Jazz Archive, informed me of local researchers' lack of success in obtaining

information on the Young family from interview subjects and other sources (personal communication). A new index to the archives provides a key to the few times Willis Young was mentioned in interviews.

13. Porter, ed., *A Lester Young Reader*, 175–76.

14. Ibid., 142, 176.

15. Ibid., 176.

16. Algiers residents would not have been listed in the City Directory. Recorded April 24, 1914, the birth certificate lists Lizetta as the mother, age twenty-five, from Woodville, and Willis Young of Thibodaux as the father; his occupation is given as teacher. I would like to express my gratitude to Mr. and Mrs. Lee Young for sharing this birth certificate with me. The various owners of this double shotgun between 1907 and 1916 were John R. Williams, John J. Zollinger (a grocer), Thaddeus E. and Alphonse S. Holland, Victor Fournier (a mason), George A. Vatter, and Philip J. Burg (a physician), each of whom presumably acquired either one or both of the residences (New Orleans Conveyance Office fax of April 16, 1999). I wish to express my gratitude to Don Gunaldo for providing this information. Information on the owners' occupations was obtained from the City Directory, 1907, and the 1910 Manuscript Census. I wish to thank Cynthia Hayot for photographing this house, and Professor Karen Kingsley for providing information about the street-name change and the history of the neighborhood. Personal communication with Kevin Williams, archivist, Architecture Archives, Tulane University, New Orleans, Louisiana, concerning the Eighth Street address. It must be pointed out that the New Orleans City Directory, 1914, p. 1246, lists "Mrs. Lizzie Young" at 1028 Bordeaux, not at the address given on Lee Young's birth certificate; of course, it is possible that she moved that year.

17. City Directory, 1914, p. 1246; ibid., 1918, p. 1342; ibid., 1919, p. 1359. Jessie Poesch and Barbara SoRelle Bacot, eds., *Louisiana Buildings, 1720–1940: The Historic American Buildings Survey* (Baton Rouge, La.: Louisiana State University Press, 1997), 276–84, on the shotgun house in New Orleans; see also John Michael Vlach, *The Afro-American Tradition in Decorative Arts* (Cleveland: Cleveland Museum of Art, 1978), 123–31, on the form's West African and Caribbean origins. While Lee Young always insisted that his mother's name was Lizetta and not Lizzie, white census takers and record keepers may have not been so careful in this matter. Notably, in one instance (City Directory, 1926, pp. 40, 672), she was listed as Lizette.

18. City Directory, 1918, p. 1342; ibid., 1919, p. 1359; ibid., 1921, p. 1576, and 1922, p. 1605; ibid., 1925, p. 1677. By 1926 she had a school; ibid., 1926, p. 762. In the 1935 directory, she was listed as a teacher residing at 3836 Fourth (p. 616).

19. New Orleans Manuscript Census, New Orleans Parish, vol. 42, E.D. 220, sheet 5B, lines 68–71, and New Orleans Parish, vol. 40, E.D. 175, sheet 9, line 89. New Orleans City Directories for 1913 and 1914, pp. 595 and 604, respectively, list Mrs. Cornelia Johnson at 531 Berlin (today's General Pershing); Louisiana Division, New Orleans Public Library, letter of September 12, 2000, on this change of street names.

20. City Directory, 1918, pp. 950, 946. Austin Young and his family can be found in the 1920 Manuscript Census, New Orleans Parish, vol. 42, E.D. 220, sheet 5B, lines 68–71; Irma Young, vol. 42, E.D. 212, sheet 13, line 38. If this was our Irma, her age was listed incorrectly, but the census taker may have confused her age with that of another young child in the same household.

21. Willis Young's use of name variants—William and Billy—and his mobility both complicate the task of identifying him in the census; no Willis or William Young of the right age and occupation could be found in the New Orleans listings. The same problem exists with respect to Willis Lester Young (Lester's full name): no Willis Young could be found of the right age to be clearly identified as the future saxophonist.

22. U.S. Manuscript Census, 1920, Madison Parish, vol. 18, E.D. 65, sheet 17, line 27. Henry was the middle name of William, Willis's brother; the elderly head of this Madison Parish household may thus have been an uncle or other relative.

23. City Directory, 1920, p. 1212, lists Thomas J. Murley, a longshoreman, as living at 1120 General Taylor. Today this is a double shotgun uptown.

24. Author's interview with Irma Young.

25. Lee Young, IJS, vol. 1, p. 7. One obvious problem with the census data is that no one recognizable as a family member lived with the brother and sister. Nor could any Lee (or Leonidas, Lee's actual first name) Young be found in the 1920 census. Some of these difficulties may reflect the problematic nature of the census itself: enumerators invariably missed some people and had trouble obtaining information on others.

26. Herbert G. Gutman, *The Black Family in Slavery and Freedom, 1750–1925* (New York: Pantheon, 1976); Deborah Gray White, *Ar'n't I a Woman?: Female Slaves in the Plantation South* (New York: W. W. Norton, 1985). Louis Armstrong, *Satchmo: My Life in New Orleans* (reprint, New York: Da Capo, 1986), 8–9, 26–27, 52–56; Alan Lomax, *Mister Jelly Roll: The Fortunes of Jelly Roll Morton, New Orleans Creole and "Inventor of Jazz"* (New York: Grossett and Dunlap, 1950), 32–35.

27. Sidney Bechet, *Treat It Gentle: An Autobiography* (1960; reprint, New York: Da Capo, 1978); Danny Barker, *A Life in Jazz* (New York: Oxford University Press, 1986); *Jazz Odyssey: The Autobiography of Joe Darensbourg*, as told to Peter Vacher (Baton Rouge, La.: Louisiana State University Press, 1987); on Kid Ory, see Burton W. Peretti, *The Creation of Jazz: Music, Race, and Culture in Urban America* (Urbana, Ill.: University of Illinois Press, 1992), 18–20, 25–27, 31, 34–35, 70, 77, 79. Reid Mitchell, *All on a Mardi Gras Day: Episodes in the History of New Orleans Carnival* (Cambridge, Mass.: Harvard University Press, 1995), is a good introduction to the urban bonhomie and music culture; see in particular chapters 8, 10, and 12.

28. Author's interview with Irma Young. Porter, ed., *A Lester Young Reader*, 178; see also pp. 132, 138, 177. In the same interview (p. 177), Young mentions the family's going to Memphis, but the City Directory of 1920–1922 did not list any Willis Young in that city: letter of June 10, 1996, from Patricia

M. LaPointe, History Department/Memphis and Shelby County Room, Memphis Shelby County Public Library and Information Center.

29. Porter, ed., *A Lester Young Reader*, 133, 142, 158, 138, 178.

30. Ibid., 158. Interview with the author. Porter, *A Lester Young Reader*, 178. Lee Young, IJS, vol. 1, p. 18: "Everyone would hold the drumstick between their forefinger and their thumb. . . . [Lester] held it between his forefinger and his middle finger." He was referring here to the right hand; Lester held the drumstick in the conventional manner in his left. Lee Young claimed that in all his years of drumming, he never saw anyone else hold the stick this way. According to Porter, *A Lester Young Reader*, ed., 174, the Postif interview took place at the Hotel d'Angleterre.

31. Lee Young suggested that his brother's claim was an exaggeration (personal communication with the author). The saxophonist reminisced in the François Postif interview, "I wasn't sure which way I wanted to go . . . and I had these motherfucking records, and I'd play one of Jimmy's, I'd play one of Trumbauer's, and . . . I don't know nothin' about Hawk then, you dig?" (in Porter, ed., *A Lester Young Reader*, 181). While he is known to have cited saxophonist Jimmy Dorsey and Frankie Trumbauer as "influences," usually Young was reluctant to admit to being influenced by anyone at all (ibid., 158, 182).

32. I assume that it is rather unlikely that someone who ran a music school in her thirties and forties could have come to music late in life. Personal communication with Lee Young; author's interview with Irma Young. New Orleans City Directory, 1926, pp. 40, 672; she resided at 2421 Felicity, which still stands. In 1938, she was listed as a music teacher: City Directory, 1938, p. 1378.

33. J. H. Kwabena Nketia, *The Music of Africa* (New York: W. W. Norton, 1974) and *Our Drums and Drummers* (Accra, Ghana: Ghana Publishing House, 1968); Francis Bebey, *African Music: A People's Art*, trans. Josephine Bennett (New York: L. Hill, 1975); and John Miller Chernoff, *African Rhythm and African Sensibility: Aesthetics and Social Action in African Musical Idioms* (Chicago: University of Chicago Press, 1979), are good introductions to African music.

34. Interview with Paulo "Polo" Barnes, in Valerie Wilmer, *The Face of Black Music: Photographs by Valerie Wilmer* (New York: Da Capo, 1976), [n.p.]; Bechet, *Treat It Gentle*, 68: "The music . . . was the onliest thing that counted. The music, it was having a time for itself. It was moving. It was being free and natural." Also see excerpts from a Dodds drum booklet in *The Second Line*, March–April 1959, pp. 7ff.

35. Author's interviews with Clarence and Leonard Phillips. His full name was Benny Williams (Mitchell, *All on a Mardi Gras Day*, 156, 159). On Black Benny, Armstrong, *Satchmo*, 75–78, 128–30; Warren Dodds, *The Baby Dodds Story*, as told to Larry Gara (Los Angeles: Contemporary, 1959), 8. Morton also mentioned Black Benny (Lomax, *Mister Jelly Roll*, 12–13).

36. Nat Hentoff and Nat Shapiro, *The Jazz Makers* (New York: Rinehart, 1957), 22. Typewritten manuscript on Warren "Baby" Dodds in the Bill Russell

collection, p. 72; see also Dodds, *The Baby Dodds Story;* and Barry Martyn and Mike Hazeldine, comps. and eds., *New Orleans Style by Bill Russell* (New Orleans: Jazzology, 1994), 12–47, which contains much of the same material as the Dodds manuscript in the Russell collection (consulted by the author in Bill Russell's New Orleans apartment).

37. Martyn and Hazeldine, *New Orleans Style,* 47. Joe René interview, September 8, 1960, vol. 1, p. 4, Hogan Jazz Archive.

38. Dodds manuscript in Russell collection, pp. 11 and 13, and Martyn and Hazeldine, *New Orleans Style,* 19, contain all but the last two quotations in this paragraph. Mahalia Jackson, the famous gospel singer who spent her childhood in New Orleans, also appreciated the importance of this singular African American element in the music: "First you've got to get the rhythm until, through the music, you have the freedom to interpret it": Mahalia Jackson with Evan McLeod Wylie, *Movin' On Up* (New York: Hawthorn, 1966), 33. G. E. Lambert, *Johnny Dodds* (New York: A. S. Barnes, 1961), 70; Dodds ms. in Russell collection, p. 72. The saxophonist Sidney Bechet discusses movement on different levels with the statement "You just can't keep the music unless you move with it"; within the music itself, Bechet maintained, "there's this mood . . . a kind of need to be moving" (*Treat It Gentle,* 95). Bebop drummer Kenny Clarke insisted that rhythm was "the whole thing" (Kenny Clarke interview, IJS, vol. 5, part 2, p. 5). Dizzy Gillespie declared, "When jazz first started, it was just rhythm. It started with just rhythm, no instruments" ("A Visit to the King in Queens: An Interview with Dizzy Gillespie," *Metronome,* February 1961, p. 18).

39. Author's interview with Connie Kay.

40. *Lester Young—The Complete Aladdin Recordings* (CDP 7243 8 32787 2 5); *Lester Swings* (VE 2-2516); *"Prez" Leaps Again with the Kansas City Seven* (Soul Parade HHP-5015-B).

41. On the changing meaning of the term in history, see Virginia R. Dominguez, *White by Definition: Social Classification in Creole Louisiana* (New Brunswick, N.J.: Rutgers University Press, 1986).

42. Author's interview with Irma Young. Personal communication with Lester Young Jr.

43. While Lizetta's mother's maiden name, Gilopet (or Silopet), suggests a French or Italian heritage, her father's name, William Johnson, is of little help. This information concerning her parents' names is taken from Lizetta Gray's application for a Social Security number, obtained under under the Freedom of Information Act (letter of November 17, 1997, from Darrell Blevins, Freedom of Information Officer, Social Security Administration, to the author). Author's interviews with Irma and Lee Young. Personal communication with Professor Gérard Pigeon, Department of Black Studies, University of California, Santa Barbara. The New Orleans City Directory for 1926, p. 762, lists a "Lizette" Gray residing at 2421 Felicity. Several family members remarked in passing on her hair, including Lester Young Jr., Jimmy Tolbert, and Crawford Brown Jr. Jack Forbes, *Africans and Native Americans: The Language of Race and the Evolution of Red-Black Peoples,* 2d ed. (Urbana, Ill.: University of Illinois Press, 1993).

44. Norwood "Pony" Poindexter, *The Pony Express: Memoirs of a Jazz Musician* (Frankfurt, West Germany: J.A.S. Publikationen, 1985), 92–94. Lomax, *Mister Jelly Roll,* was one of the first works to discuss the Creole influence in jazz (pp. 98–100); George Malcolm-Smith, "Cuban Natives, Not Jelly-Roll Morton or Handy, Started Jazz in 1712," *Down Beat,* March 1939, p. 8, contends that swing originated in the Caribbean; see also Ernest Borneman, "Jazz and the Creole Tradition," *Jazzforschung,* 1969, pp. 99–113, which argues that the "Latin" or Creole influence has always been an integral part of jazz, if not its very foundation.

45. Ross Russell, "Be-Bop Reed Instrumentation," *Record Changer,* April 1949, p. 20.

46. Author's interview with Irving Ashby. In a letter of January 25, 1999, to the author, Dr. Erwan Dianteill, a specialist in Afro-Cuban religions, pointed out that concepts of "cool" and "hot" are "central to Afro-Cuban religions. While 'hot' is associated with sacrifice, blood, and alcohol (and virility), 'cool' is linked to water, the color white, and spiritual cleansing."

47. Author's interview with Irma Young; Lambert, *Johnny Dodds,* 70. Author's interview with Sadik Hakim. The saxophonist agreed with these musicians when he explained, "I tried to get the sound of a C-melody on tenor. That's why I don't sound like other people" (Porter, ed., *A Lester Young Reader,* 158). In 1959 Young claimed that he played bass clarinet (ibid., 186). In February 1958 he recorded on clarinet in New York City: "They Can't Take That Away from Me," *Lester Swings* (Verve 314 547 772-2), and on "Salute to Benny," *Laughin' to Keep from Cryin'* (Verve 314 543 301-2).

48. Tom Bethel, *George Lewis: A Jazzman from New Orleans* (Berkeley, Calif.: University of California Press, 1977), 128, typifies the statements made by writers who have viewed Lester Young as a Kansas City musician.

49. Karl Koenig, "The Plantation Belt Brass Bands and Musicians, Part 1: Professor James B. Humphrey," *The Second Line,* fall 1981, 33.

50. See Newbell Niles Puckett, *Folk Beliefs of the Southern Negro* (reprint, New York: Dover, 1969), 311–519, in which the author discusses "Positive Control-Signs," "Negative Control-Signs," and "Prophetic Signs or Omens." Jelly Roll Morton also believed in spirits: "I was very, very much afraid of those things. In fact I was worried with spirits when I was a kid" (Lomax, *Mister Jelly Roll,* 10). Levine, *Black Culture,* 3–135, 298–440; Daryl Dance, *Shuckin' and Jivin': Folklore from Contemporary Black Americans* (Bloomington, Ind.: Indiana University Press, 1978).

51. Author's interview with Irma Young. On folklore in Lafourche Parish, see Philip D. Uzee, ed., *The Lafourche Country: The People and the Land* (Lafayette, La.: University of Southwestern Louisiana Press, 1985), 76–87. On the uses of photography in African American history, see Deborah Willis, ed., *Picturing Us: African American Identity in Photography* (New York: New Press, 1994), and Douglas Henry Daniels, *Pioneer Urbanites: A Social and Cultural History of Black San Francisco* (1980; reprint, Berkeley, Calif.: University of California Press, 1991), introduction. François Postif, "Lester: Paris '59," *Jazz Review,* September 1959, p. 9. This is the sole published photo of Lizetta with one of her children.

52. Although in his first interview he admitted with "a tinge of embarrassment" that he had been born in Mississippi, in 1949 and in 1950 Young seems to have told Pat Harris and Leonard Feather, respectively, that he was a native of New Orleans; in 1956 and 1959, however, he set the record straight (Porter, ed., *A Lester Young Reader,* 132, 138, 158, 175). See Harnett Kane, *Deep Delta Country* (New York: Duell, Sloan, and Pearce, 1944), and Karl Koenig, *"The Plantation Belt": The Music History of Plaquemines Parish, Louisiana* (Abita Springs, La.: Basin Street, n.d.), for the music scene at the turn of the century. Sandra R. Lieb, *Mother of the Blues: A Study of Ma Rainey* (Amherst, Mass.: University of Massachusetts Press, 1981), 112. Cyril Daryl Forde, ed., *African Worlds: Studies in the Cosmological Ideas and Social Values of African Peoples* (New York: Oxford University Press, 1954); Marcel Griaule, *Conversations with Ogotommeli: An Introduction to Dogon Religious Ideas* (New York: Oxford University Press, 1965); Maya Deren, *Divine Horsemen: The Living Gods of Haiti* (New York: Book Collectors Society, 1952); Karen McCarthy Brown, *Mama Lola: A Vodou Priestess in Brooklyn* (Berkeley, Calif.: University of California Press, 1991); Joan Dayan, *Haiti, History, and the Gods* (Berkeley, Calif.: University of California, 1995). I would like to thank Professor David Rankin, History Department, University of California, Irvine, for information on Algiers, which was settled by freedmen after the Civil War; unlike the French Quarter, it is not associated with Creole residency.

53. Puckett, *Folk Beliefs,* 462, 503.

54. Author's interview with Irma Young. Jelly Roll Morton recalled, "When I was a young man, these hoodoo people with their underground stuff helped me along" (quoted in Lomax, *Mister Jelly Roll,* 223). Because "he did not feel grateful and . . . did not reward them for the help they gave," he paid dearly later in life, in his opinion (ibid., 223–25). Puckett, *Folk Beliefs,* 228. "Poundcake" was also Young's nickname for the guitarist-trombonist-arranger Eddie Durham, a former Blue Devil and a member of the Basie band after it went to New York (author's interview with Eddie Durham).

55. Author's interview with "Teddy Bear," a close friend of Young's in the early 1940s, who did not want her real name to be used.

56. Kane, *Deep Delta Country,* 220–27; in 1944, only a few years after the publication of Melville Herskovitts's *The Myth of the Negro Past* (New York: Harper and Bros., 1941), in which the significance of African heritage in the United States was recognized for the first time by a famous Euro-American scholar, Kane wrote, "To the Delta the Negroes have brought their superstitions, *largely from Africa*" (emphasis added).

57. Zora Neale Hurston, *Mules and Men* (Bloomington, Ind.: Indiana University Press, 1978), is an excellent collection of African American folklore; in *Tell My Horse* (Philadelphia: J. B. Lippincott, 1970), Hurston examines Jamaican and Haitian religion, history, and folklore. Roger D. Abrahams, *Deep Down in the Jungle* (Hatboro, Pa.: Folklore Associates, 1964), was one of the first texts to examine the folklore of northern African American urbanites. The Black nationalists Marcus Garvey and Malcolm X (the latter while he was in the Nation of Islam) espoused separatist philosophies pre-

cisely because of the limitations of American democracy; see Amy-Jacques Garvey, ed., *The Philosophy and Opinions of Marcus Garvey* (New York: Atheneum, 1969), and Malcolm X with Alex Haley, *The Autobiography of Malcolm X* (New York: Grove, 1965).

58. Porter, ed., *A Lester Young Reader,* 166, 181, 176–77, 188, 182. Whitney Balliett, "Jazz Records: The President," *The New Yorker,* April 18, 1959, p. 88. "Almost like Being in Love," on *Lester Young in Washington, D.C., 1956, Volume 4* (Pablo Live 2308–230). His expression for "take another solo chorus" evoked fond memories of hospitality and home. In 1959 he made a comment indicating the sole objective of his Blue Note engagement in Paris: "Just trying to get me some money for my family—and it's all clean, believe that" (Porter, ed., *A Lester Young Reader,* 191, 152, 166). J. L. Dillard, *Black English: Its History and Usage in the United States* (New York: Random House, 1972), is an excellent introduction to the linguistic distinction between a "pidgin," which results when people who speak different languages come into contact with one another, and a "creole," which develops from the same kind of interaction over generations.

59. The late tenor saxophonist John "Zoot" Sims actually used this expression to describe the charisma that Young possessed (author's interview with Sims). The late Buck Clayton was the first person I interviewed concerning Lester Young, and he was also the first to tell me about the saxophonist's humorous remarks.

60. Milton "Mezz" Mezzrow and Bernard Wolfe, *Really the Blues* (New York: Random House, 1946), discusses Armstrong's scat singing and jive slang (pp. 102–4, 187–203, 223); also see Mezzrow's insightful discussion of Black slang on pages 190–200. Armstrong, *Satchmo,* and Louis Armstrong and Richard Meryman, *Louis Armstrong—A Self-Portrait: The Richard Meryman Interview* (New York: Eakins, 1971), give readers a chance to hear the trumpet player speaking in his own voice. See, for example, Armstrong's letter of September 25, 1942, to Bill Russell, which begins, "I've done things a lots o times/And I've done them in a *Hustle*/But I break my neack [*sic*] almost every time/To write to my boy—Wm Russell . . . /Lawd Today"; the salutation is, "'How'Doo' Brother Russell" (Hogan Jazz Archive). See also the autobiography of another innovator in language: Cab Calloway with Bryant Rollins, *Of Minnie the Moocher and Me* (New York: Crowell, 1976); Douglas Henry Daniels, "Lester Young: Master of Jive," *American Music* 3 (fall 1985): 313–28. Author's interview with Benny Daniels. Clearly other residents—for example, the drummer Zutty Singleton—also hailed people in a creative fashion, popularizing such greetings as "Whatcha know, face?" "Face" was a term of address that covered everybody, and Singleton was one Crescent City citizen known for using it; compare this to Young's use of "Lady" and "Pres" for musicians (Daniels, "Lester Young: Master of Jive," 323).

61. Author's interview with Martha Young. Stanley Dance, *The World of Count Basie* (New York: Charles Scribner's Sons, 1980), 122; Buddy Tate, IJS, p. 69. As Lee Collins explained, many "kids were ashamed to let anybody know that they ate only red beans and rice for Sunday dinner because it was con-

sidered a dish for the poorer families" (Mary Collins, *Oh, Didn't He Ramble,* ed. Frank Gillis and John W. Miner [Urbana, Ill.: University of Illinois Press, 1974], 9).

62. New Orleans customs and superstitions seem to have affected the Youngs in other ways as well. In an interview with the author, Irma Young recalled that her brothers would collect for her the fake gold "doubloons" that were thrown from the floats during Mardi Gras (a custom that survives to this day). She also mentioned the practice of cleaning the floors with redbrick dust. George W. Cable, a late-nineteenth-century writer and popularizer of the Creoles and their traditions, also noted this custom, as did Louis Armstrong. Cable observed that the cypress floor of one house was "worn with scrubbing and sprinkled with crumbs of soft brick—a Creole affectation of superior cleanliness." Armstrong's testimony suggested how widespread the custom was: as a youngster, he said, he crushed bricks and sold the resulting dust. His customers sprinkled it over their front steps after cleaning them, believing that it "brought them luck Saturday night. That was their superstition." Brick was also used to undo others' conjuring. Author's interview with Irma Young; George W. Cable, *Creoles and Cajuns: Stories of Old Louisiana,* ed. Arlen Turner (Gloucester, Mass.: P. Smith, 1959), 23; Armstrong and Meryman, *Louis Armstrong—A Self-Portrait,* 13. "What he does—what nobody do—is nobody's business," and "Whatever they do, let them do that, and enjoy themselves—and get your kicks yourself": Porter, ed., *A Lester Young Reader,* 185–86.

63. Porter, ed., *A Lester Young Reader,* 138, 142, 132.

64. Lee Young, IJS, p. 45. (Carey probably confused Lee with Lester: Lee left the city at the age of five, and southern children usually started school at an older age.) In 1983, Lee Young maintained that this was the reason Black Louisianans stuck together to such a remarkable degree, even when they were a long way from home (author's interview with Lee Young). Personal communication with James Tolbert.

65. Porter, ed., *A Lester Young Reader,* 181, 186.

66. Pops Foster, *Pops Foster: The Autobiography of a New Orleans Jazzman,* as told to Tom Stoddard (Berkeley, Calif.: University of California Press, 1971), 19.

67. *Esquire's World of Jazz,* commentary by James Poling (New York: Esquire, 1962), 71–72. Armstrong's *Satchmo* abounds with instances in which loyalty, honor, and generosity shaped relations among his childhood heroes and friends; the same is true of his personal life, as witness his adoption of his cousin's child. In one memorable passage of *Satchmo,* he reflected on the night he and his mother made the rounds of the neighborhood honky-tonks: "We were having a fine time meeting the people who loved us and spoke our language. We knew we were among our people. That was all that mattered. We did not care about the outside world" (pp. 82–83, 200–1).

68. Hentoff and Shapiro, *The Jazz Makers,* 23.

69. Ibid.

70. Bechet, *Treat It Gentle,* 124.

71. Ibid.

3. The Professor

1. Lewis Porter, ed., *A Lester Young Reader* (Washington, D.C.: Smithsonian Institution Press, 1991), 142, 137–38. Willis H. Young died on February 6, 1943; California death certificate no. 1901–2306. Author's interview with Lucille Tolbert.

2. Val Wilmer (as told to), "The Lee Young Story," *Jazz Journal* 14 (January 1961), pp. 3–5; author's interview with Lee Young.

3. Dianne Young Manuel, the great-granddaughter of Jacob Young Jr., used this term in referring to the incident (personal communication with the author). I discuss this historical episode in "History, Racism, and Jazz: The Case of Lester Young," *Jazzforschung,* December 1984, pp. 87–103.

4. Author's interviews with Martha Young, Crawford Brown, and Alvin, James, and Lucille Tolbert.

5. Author's interview with the Reverend John W. Young.

6. Author's interview with Henry "Buster" Smith; Bill Coleman, *Trumpet Story* (Boston: Northeastern University Press, 1989), 9, notes that it was sometimes used jokingly. Charles Hamm, *Music in the New World* (New York: W. W. Norton, 1983), 291–96; on Sousa's connection with social dancing, see ibid., 305–6.

7. Young was born in 1872, and Joplin in 1868: Edward A. Berlin, *King of Ragtime: Scott Joplin and His Era* (New York: Oxford University Press, 1994); Susan Curtis, *Dancing to a Black Man's Tune: A Life of Scott Joplin* (Columbia, Mo.: University of Missouri Press, 1994). James Reese Europe, another pioneer in the new music, was born in 1880: Reid Badger, *A Life in Ragtime: A Biography of James Reese Europe* (New York: Oxford University Press, 1995).

8. In 1949 his elder son incorrectly gave his name as William in an interview. He was listed in the 1880 census as "Willie," whereas his older brother was always "William"—notably, on his marriage license, the record for which is located in the office of the Clerk of the Court, Seventeenth Judicial Court District, Parish of Lafourche. Willis's nephew the Reverend J. W. Young (the youngest son of his brother William) conceded that his father and his uncle Willis "both had practically the same kind of name." Adding to the confusion was that, according to the reverend, "they all referred to [Willis] as William." Moreover, his father was known as Bill (again, remarkably close to Willis's stage name, Billy). Author's interview with the Reverend J. W. Young. William H. Young was married on November 22, 1888 (no. 201); the second brother, Jacob Young Jr., wed on January 28, 1886 (no. 25); and on June 7, 1897, Willis H. Young married Amelia Rhoden (no. 123). These mar-

riage records can be quickly accessed in the Lafourche Parish, Louisiana, *Computer-Indexed Marriage Records* (Hammond, La., n.d.), part 1, p. 265, Washington Parish Library, Franklinton, Louisiana. U.S. Manuscript Census, 1880, vol. 6, E.D. 128, sheet 42, Second Ward. On his Louisiana marriage license, Willis gave his name as "W. H. Young," but on the Texas marriage document he was "Willis H. Young." In his IJS interview (vol. 5, p. 6), Lee Young at first stated that his father's name had been Willis, then wavered when asked if it hadn't in fact been William. Porter, ed., *A Lester Young Reader,* 137. William H. Young's marriage license and court documents give his middle name. On his death certificate, the professor's name was entered as William H., and his date of birth as November 8, 1886—both of which were incorrect. Author's interviews with Clarence and Leonard Phillips and Irma, Lee, and Martha Young.

9. Author's interview with the Reverend John W. Young. Lester mentioned that his father had attended Tuskegee and been a blacksmith in the Leonard Feather interview, in 1949 (Porter, ed., *A Lester Young Reader,* 142); Lee Young said he was a school principal near Bogalusa in his IJS interview (vol. 5, p. 3), and also a blacksmith in his interview with Val Wilmer ("The Lee Young Story," *Jazz Journal,* January 1961, p. 3).

10. His mother, sister, and brother appeared regularly in the manuscript census, but after an initial listing in 1880, when he was eight, Willis Young was listed only once, in the first of the next three surviving censuses—1900, 1910, and 1920 (the 1890 census was destroyed by fire). U.S. Manuscript Census, 1900, Lafourche Parish, vol. 19, E.D. 25, Second Ward, p. 4A, line 45; his brother and his family comprise lines 40–44.

11. Conveyance Books, Tangipahoa Parish, vol. 93, p. 211, and vol. 97, p. 381, Tangipahoa Parish Courthouse, Amite, Louisiana. Minneapolis City Directory, 1927, p. 2509; I would like to thank Dr. David Taylor for this information. Albuquerque City Directory, 1929, p. 470; ibid., 1930, p. 483. A "W. H. Young" was listed in the Los Angeles City Directory for 1930 (p. 2438); he resided at 5608 South Broadway. I assume this was the professor, who was not listed in either 1929 or 1931 in that city.

12. Marriage of Willis H. Young and Amelia Rhoden, June 7, 1897 (no. 123), Marriage Records, Clerk of the Court, Lafourche Parish. Conveyance Books, vol. 39, no. 445, Lafourche Parish Courthouse, Thibodaux, Louisiana. Amelia's maiden name is unclear; it may have been Rhodes. Tutorship of Charles E. Young et al., no. 1714 Probates, Twentieth Judicial District Court, Lafourche Parish, filed August 3, 1904. This series of documents indicates that the professor's older brother Jacob Rice Young died on June 18, 1899; see the document filed on July 20, 1904. Marriage license of Willis Young and Lizetta Johnson, November 28, 1908, Clerk of the Court, Franklinton, Washington Parish, Louisiana. Conveyance Books, vol. 45, p. 184, Lafourche Parish Courthouse, Thibodaux, Louisiana. Amy Quick, "The History of Bogalusa, the 'Magic City' of Louisiana" (M.A. thesis, Louisiana State University, Baton Rouge, 1942), reprinted in *Louisiana Historical Quarterly* 29, no. 1 (January 1946).

13. In a personal communication with the author, Lee Young explained that in

his day, many people wanted to make themselves out to be younger than they really were, and he was no exception. He usually gave 1917 as the year of his birth, though he had actually been born in 1914. On her Social Security card application (form SS-5), dated February 10, 1937, Irma Young listed her date of birth as July 18, 1913, but the year appears to have been corrected by officials to 1912; moreover, her son, Crawford, has verified the earlier date. SS-5 form obtained under the Freedom of Information Act; author's interview with Crawford Brown Jr.

14. Amos White interview, August 23, 1958, p. 5, Hogan Jazz Archive. Author's interview with Irma Young.

15. Marriage Records, Camp County District Clerk, Pittsburg, Texas, 1919, vol. 6, p. 405. Author's interview with Irma Young. Porter, ed., *A Lester Young Reader*, 158. In 1900 the Hunters were living in West Feliciana Parish (U.S. Manuscript Census, 1900, West Feliciana Parish, vol. 48, E.D. 114, sheet 14, lines 42 and 43), but before the decade was out, they moved to the outskirts of Bogalusa (U.S. Manuscript Census, 1910, Washington Parish, vol. 79, E.D. 126, sheet 4B, lines 63 and 64) and by 1920, they resided in Natalbany, in still another parish (U.S. Manuscript Census, 1920, Tangipahoa Parish, vol. 58, E.D. 123, sheet 16, line 30); Lee Young, IJS interview, vol. 5, pp. 10–11.

16. Author's interviews with Clarence and Leonard Phillips, who were born in 1904 and 1907, respectively. Author's interview with Irma Young. Albuquerque City Directory, 1929, p. 470; ibid., 1930, p. 483. Author's interviews with Irma and Lee Young on the family's years in the Southwest. It is not clear exactly when they were in Phoenix, but family oral traditions maintain that Lester Young and Ben Webster left them in that Arizona city to head back to the Midwest. Los Angeles City Directory, 1930, p. 2438; in the 1932 directory (p. 2331) they were listed as living at 1651 Essex, but within a few years they had moved a short distance away, to 1706 South Central, where the couple remained until they died, within weeks of each other, early in 1943.

17. Marriage of Willis H. Young and Amelia Rhoden, June 7, 1897 (no. 123), Marriage Records, Clerk of the Court, Lafourche Parish, Louisiana.

18. Alice Young wed Hezekiah Tolbert on June 18, 1919—two and a half weeks after her father married Sarah (Book no. 85, folio 276, Marriage Records, Louisiana State Archives, Baton Rouge, Louisiana). Author's interviews with Alvin, James, and Lucille Tolbert.

19. Author's interview with Martha Young, who recalled her grandfather's belief that the eyes were windows to the soul.

20. Author's interviews with Crawford Brown Jr. and Martha Young.

21. Marriage Records, Camp County District Clerk, Pittsburg, Texas, 1919, vol. 6, p. 405. I have been unable to locate any New Orleans divorce papers for Willis and Lizetta. The surname Pilgrim does not match that given for Sarah's father ("Smith") on her death certificate, suggesting that she had been married to someone else before the professor. Her hairdressing-license application (no. 5772, to the State Board of Cosmetology, Secretary of State; California State Archives, Sacramento) cited Pittsburg, Texas, origins and

led to an inquiry that located her marriage license, on which Willis Young was named as the groom. The photograph accompanying the application seems to me to resemble Sarah Young, though members of the Young family disagree. Her name change to Sarah remains a mystery, though it may have biblical implications, given that she never had children by Willis Young (or anyone else, so far as the family knows). Sarah Young died on March 1, 1943, just a few weeks after her husband (California death certificate no. 1901–3561, which lists her date of birth as August 27, 1896—meaning that she shared a birthday with Lester). Lee Young, identified as the informant on the certificate, gave her maiden name as Smith and listed San Antonio as her birthplace. Her race is noted as "Ethio[pian]."

22. Author's interviews with Martha Young and Alvin, James, and Lucille Tolbert.

23. Author's interview with James Tolbert. Lizetta Gray's Social Security Card application (form SS-5) provided her birthdate of October 3, 1888; Sarah's birthdate, August 27, 1896, is taken from her death certificate. Neither Sarah Young nor her husband seems to have applied for a Social Security number.

24. Alan Lomax, *Mister Jelly Roll: The Fortunes of Jelly Roll Morton, New Orleans Creole and "Inventor of Jazz"* (New York: Grossett and Dunlap, 1950); Rudi Blesh and Harriet Janis, *They All Played Ragtime: The True Story of an American Music* (New York: Alfred A. Knopf, 1950); Al Rose and Edmond Souchon, *New Orleans Jazz: A Family Album* (Baton Rouge, La.: Louisiana State University Press, 1967); Barry Martyn and Mike Hazeldine, comps. and eds., *New Orleans Style by Bill Russell* (New Orleans: Jazzology, 1994); Karl Koenig, *Thibodeax: The Music City on the Bayou* (Abita Springs, La.: Basin Street, n.d.).

25. Allen Chapel was formed after the Civil War; Jacob Young's name is honored on a plaque along with others in the current Allen Chapel in Thibodaux. Eileen Southern, *The Music of Black Americans: A History,* 2d ed. (New York: W. W. Norton, 1983), 223–28, 254–56; LeRoi Jones (Amiri Baraka), *Blues People: Negro Music in White America* (New York: William Morrow, 1963); Lawrence Levine, *Black Culture and Black Consciousness* (New York: Oxford University Press, 1975), 30–54 and 155–74, on spirituals; Hamm, *Music in the New World,* 133–39, 256–58, 374–79, on spirituals.

26. Levine, *Black Culture,* 190–297 on secular song; William J. Schafer, *Brass Bands and New Orleans Jazz* (Baton Rouge, La.: Louisiana State University Press, 1977), 12–13, 29. Hamm, *Music in the New World,* 279–91, on brass bands in the United States in the late nineteenth century.

27. Schafer, *Brass Bands,* 12–13.

28. Porter, ed., *A Lester Young Reader,* 142; author's interview with Irma Young. Inquiries made at Tuskegee produced no evidence that Willis ever attended that institution, though he may have been a member of one of the first classes, for which documentation is scarce. See Louis Harlan, *Booker T. Washington: The Making of a Black Leader, 1856–1901* (New York: Oxford University Press, 1972), 150 (noting that a quartet of Tuskegee singers helped raise money in New England).

29. Booker T. Washington's *Up from Slavery: An Autobiography* (Garden City, N.Y.: Doubleday, 1901) is the classic expression of his philosophy of industrial education, self-help, race pride, and economic uplift. Koenig, *Thibodeax*, 276, 279, 12, 277. Ibid., 279, quotes the *Napoleonville Pioneer;* see also Dr. Koenig's *Trinity of Early Jazz Leaders: John Robichaux, "Toots" Johnson, Claiborne Williams* (Abita Springs, La., n.d.) on bandleaders from the bayou country.

30. Quoted in Koenig, *Thibodeax*, 76: "Perhaps we are reading of the demise of the brass band movement in Thibodaux. Seldom is a local brass band mentioned [in the local newspaper]. We find more and more the string band, a smaller group and more able to play for dances. Seldom do we find an activity that uses a brass band." This photo was reproduced in Porter, ed., *A Lester Young Reader*, opposite page 130.

31. Karl Koenig, "The Plantation Belt Brass Bands and Musicians, Part 1: Professor James B. Humphrey," *The Second Line*, fall 1981, 24–40; on Robichaux, see Frederic Ramsey Jr., "Vet Tells Story of the Original Creole Orchestra," *Down Beat*, December 15, 1940, pp. 10, 26.

Statements similar to those made about the regimen and discipline of Professor Willis Young were made about other bandmasters and professors, including Major N. Clark Smith of Kansas City, Captain Walter Dyett of Chicago, and Zelia Breaux of Oklahoma City, all of whom emphasized reading, mastery of fundamentals, and classical training rather than improvisatory skills. On Smith, see Reginald T. Buckner, "Rediscovering Major N. Clark Smith," *Music Educators Journal*, February 1985, 36–42; and, for further information, "Major N. Clark Smith Testimonial at Odeon Monday Night," *St. Louis Argus*, June 21, 1935, p. 3, and Smith's obituary in the *Kansas City Call*, October 11, 1935, pp. 1, 8; also see ibid., January 3, 1936 (city edition), p. 2, and ibid., January 17, 1936 (city edition), p. 3. On Walter Dyett, see "Johnny Griffin," *Bebop and Beyond*, March–April 1986, p. 23, characterizing Dyett as "a well-trained musician . . . [who] had studied extensively . . . also a disciplinarian. He'd take all of these little nappy-headed kids off the streets and mold them into musicians . . . so [they'd] be well trained and well equipped to step out in life and hold [their] own." But let his students beware: "Captain Dyett didn't tolerate any mess, not at all. He was like a father figure." On Zelia Breaux, see Ron Welburn, "Ralph Ellison's Territorial Vantage," *The Grackle*, no. 4, p. 5; also author's interview with Leroy Parks, who attended Frederick Douglass High School and played in the band under the direction of Breaux.

32. William M. Banks, *Black Intellectuals: Race and Responsibility in American Life* (New York: W. W. Norton, 1996), 43. Author's interviews with Irma and Martha Young, who claimed that Mercer Ellington had once taken trumpet lessons from the professor, though Lee Young disputed this (personal communication with the author). In his IJS interview, Lee Young noted that Cootie Williams, Ben Webster, and Clarence Williams were among his father's former pupils (vol. 1, p. 5, and vol. 5, p. 7).

33. Ramsey, "Vet Tells Story," 10. James Weldon Johnson, *Along This Way* (New York: Penguin, 1990), 145–62. Jane Julian, "Magnolia's Music," *The Missis-*

sippi Rag, July 1974, pp. 7–8, for information on how bands were established in Plaquemines Parish, south of New Orleans; I wish to thank Dr. Karl Koenig for bringing this article to my attention.

34. Koenig, "The Plantation Belt Brass Bands and Musicians," 33. Rose and Souchon, *New Orleans Jazz,* 109. See also Karl Koenig, *"The Plantation Belt": The Music History of Plaquemines Parish, Louisiana* (Abita Springs, La.: Basin Street, n.d.), on this area of Louisiana south of New Orleans.

35. Samuel Barclay Charters, *Jazz: New Orleans 1885–1963, An Index to the Negro Musicians of New Orleans,* rev. ed. (New York: Oak Publications, 1963), 7–9, 30, 79, 98; John Curran's May 8, 1953, interview with Oscar Celestin (Hogan Jazz Archive) identifies Donaldsonville, Louisiana, as Celestin's birthplace, though Peter R. Haby, "Oscar 'Papa' Celestin, 1884–1954," *Footnote,* June–July 1981, p. 4, cites Napoleonville, as does Rose and Souchon, *New Orleans Jazz,* 25; on Lewis James, see Austin M. Sonnier Jr., *Willie Geary "Bunk" Johnson: The New Iberia Years* (New York: Crescendo, 1977), 72–73.

36. Charters, *Jazz: New Orleans,* 30; Charters refers to the Youka Brass Band, but Koenig (*Thibodeax,* 117) points out that it was the Eureka. Charters, *Jazz: New Orleans,* 30, gives the lineup of the Eureka Brass Band. On Clay Jiles, see ibid., 33. Haby, "Oscar 'Papa' Celestin," 4, claims that in Orrin Keepnews and Bill Grauer Jr., *A Pictorial History of Jazz: People and Places from New Orleans to Modern Jazz,* rev. ed. (New York: Crown, 1966), Willis Young is listed (p. 11) as having been a member of Red Allen Sr.'s band. There is a photograph of the band, but Willis Young does not seem to be in it, despite the fact that others have placed him there—including Martin Williams, writing in *Jazz Masters of New Orleans* (New York: Macmillan, 1967), 258–59. In Whitney Balliett, *Such Sweet Thunder* (Indianapolis: Bobbs-Merrill, 1966), 346, Red Allen Jr. is quoted as recalling that Lester's father "and my father played together in New Orleans." John Chilton, *Ride, Red, Ride: The Life of Henry "Red" Allen* (New York: Continuum, 1999). C. L. Reynolds, registrar, New Orleans University, states in a letter to the author (October 4, 1982) that "there is nothing on record to indicate that [Willis Young] attended Dillard as a student or worked here as a professor."

37. Charters, *Jazz: New Orleans,* 7–8; Ramsey, "Vet Tells Story," 10; Sonnier, *"Bunk" Johnson,* 72; Lomax, *Mister Jelly Roll,* 72. Allan Barrell, "About Lee Collins," *Footnote* 5, no. 5 (1954): 8; Pops Foster, *Pops Foster: The Autobiography of a New Orleans Jazzman,* as told to Tom Stoddard (Berkeley, Calif.: University of California Press, 1971), 13, 41–42. Charters, *Jazz: New Orleans,* 7–9, and Ramsey, "Vet Tells Story," 10, 26; Foster, *Pops Foster,* 43–44, 86.

38. Albert Jiles interview, June 15, 1960, p. 3, Hogan Jazz Archive.

39. Jiles interview, February 24, 1961, Hogan Jazz Archive; Charters, *Jazz: New Orleans,* 30.

40. Charters, *Jazz: New Orleans;* Koenig, "The Plantation Belt Brass Bands" and *Thibodeax.*

41. Ted Vincent, *Keep Cool: The Black Activists Who Built the Jazz Age* (Boulder, Colo.: Pluto, 1995), 43, 59–60, and 88, on the creation of TOBA.

42. New Orleans City Directory, 1913, p. 1225; ibid., 1920, p. 1812. Ibid., 1932, lists him (p. 1462) as a musician living at 2014 Poydras, and places his brother, also a musician, at the same address (p. 1464). Austin F. Young and William H. Young Jr. were born in January 1890 and November 1898, respectively; they were listed in the U.S. Manuscript Census, 1910, Sixth Ward, Assumption Parish, vol. 3, E.D. 8, sheet 3A, lines 25–29, as living with their father, William; their mother, Rebecca; and Francis, a woman who may have been Austin's wife at the time, on Foley's plantation. Austin Young is also listed in Baton Rouge in the same census (U.S. Manuscript Census, 1910, West Baton Rouge Parish, vol. 74, E.D. 137, sheet 17B, lines 60–63); he appears in the 1920 Manuscript Census in New Orleans, at 3509 Tonti (vol. 42, E.D. 220, sheet 5B, line 68). An "Austin Young, musician," is listed as residing at 625 Bernard in the City Directory, 1947, p. 1340.

This biographical material comes mainly from Bill Russell, who interviewed Austin Young in 1944 and very kindly permitted me to examine his notes, and from family oral traditions; Rose and Souchon, *New Orleans Jazz*, 130–31; Charters, *Jazz: New Orleans*, 126. Some of Russell's interviews have been published (though not the one with Austin Young), in Martyn and Hazeldine, *New Orleans Style*.

43. Joe René interview, September 8, 1960, vol. 2, p. 3, Hogan Jazz Archive. Josiah "Frog" Waldren interview, July 10, 1961, vol. 1, p. 5, Hogan Jazz Archive. Earl Foster interview, March 22, 1961, vol. 1, p. 3, and vol. 2, p. 6, Hogan Jazz Archive. See also interviews with Father Al Lewis, February 21, 1972, vol. 2, p. 7; Ernie Gagnolatti, April 5, 1961, vol. 3, p. 4; and Josiah "Cie" Frazier, December 14, 1960, vol. 2, p. 9, all in the Hogan Jazz Archive, for more information on Austin Young. This biographical information was graciously shared with me by the late William Russell.

44. Biographical information on Austin Young provided by Bill Russell; Josiah Waldren, interview, January 10, 1961, vol. 1, p. 5, Hogan Jazz Archive.

45. William Russell interview with Austin Young. Another recording on the American Music label was with "Big Eye" Louis Nelson DeLisle (AM Records LP No. 646); they recorded "Dinah," "B-Flat Blues," "Clarinet Marmalade," "Basin Street Blues," and "Holler Blues." Russell's recordings were part of the New Orleans revival, as well as an attempt to document the early music. See Tom Bethell, *George Lewis: A Jazzman from New Orleans* (Berkeley, Calif.: University of California Press, 1977), 122–38, for more information on these sessions. See also Bruce King, "A Reassessment of New Orleans Jazz on American Music Records, Part 3," *Jazz Monthly*, April 1959, pp. 6–11, noting that Austin Young plays bass with Wooden Joe's New Orleans Band (American Music 640) on the compositions "Shake It and Break It," "Careless Love," "Eh La-Bas!" and "Blues." According to Worthia "Showboy" Thomas (interview of December 1, 1961, vol. 1, p. 4, Hogan Jazz Archive), William Young toured the United States with Robert Taylor's Knee High (Nee-hi) Review in 1927.

46. Foster, *Pops Foster*, 86 and 77.

47. Author's interview with Irma Young. Porter, ed., *A Lester Young Reader*, 159; author's interview with Martha Young. James Tolbert claimed that his grandfather played jazz.

48. Author's interview with Lucille Tolbert: the professor conducted the choir at St. Paul's Baptist Church at 1385 East Twenty-first; Los Angeles City Directory, 1935, p. 1517. He also conducted the Young family band for Father Divine's Peace Mission on Adams. Martha Young, the professor's granddaughter (Irma's daughter), learned that he did not approve of jazzing church music when he caught her doing it and punished her by striking her hands with a ruler; this was, she recalled, the only time he ever struck her (author's interview with Martha Young).

   On Father Divine, see Robert Weisbrot, *Father Divine and the Struggle for Racial Equality* (Urbana, Ill.: University of Illinois Press, 1983), and Jill Watts, *God, Harlem U.S.A.: The Father Divine Story* (Berkeley, Calif.: University of California Press, 1992). Author's interviews with James and Lucille Tolbert and Martha Young.

49. Interview with Lawrence Douglas Harris, June 6, 1961, vol. 1, p. 5, Hogan Jazz Archive.

50. Ibid.

51. Foster, *Pops Foster*, 6.

52. Ibid., 120; Foster also cited the guitarist Lonnie Johnson—"the only guy we had around New Orleans who could play jazz guitar"—and Johnson's violin-playing father as being notable among the street-corner musicians in that city; "most of the street corner players came out of the woods or some little town someplace" (p. 92). On Handy's experiences with blues, see Arna Bontemps, ed., *Father of the Blues: An Autobiography by W. C. Handy* (New York: Da Capo, 1991), 74–77. In Lomax, *Mister Jelly Roll*, 20–21, Morton discusses an influential New Orleans blues singer named Mamie Desdoumes; he recalled that "it was Mamie first really sold me on the blues." In his memoir *Satchmo: My Life in New Orleans* (reprint, New York: Da Capo, 1986), 101, 114–15, 198, Louis Armstrong writes that he invariably associated blues with the prostitutes who came into the honky-tonks to celebrate late at night after work.

53. See Paul Oliver, *Blues Fell This Morning: The Meaning of the Blues* (New York: Horizon, 1960); Charles Keil, *Urban Blues* (Chicago: University of Chicago Press, 1966) and Albert Murray, *Stomping the Blues* (New York: Da Capo, 1976), for the centrality of this idiom to American pop music; Levine, *Black Culture*, 217–38; see also Hamm, *Music in the New World*, 379–87, 403–4, 526–28.

54. Mahalia Jackson with Evan McLeod Wylie, *Movin' On Up* (New York: Hawthorn, 1966), 36. Jackson notes that New Orleans was very blues-conscious when she was a child: "You couldn't help but hear blues . . . up and down the street in the colored neighborhoods—everybody played it [on their record players] real loud" (ibid., 29–30). Balliett, *Such Sweet Thunder*, 349; Lomax, *Mister Jelly Roll*, 89.

55. Haby, "Oscar Celestin," 6; on Claiborne Williams, who was born in 1868, see Koenig, *Trinity of Early Jazz Leaders,* 120–81. The quote about DeLisle is taken from promotional literature accompanying the Russell recording (American Music LP No. 646), given to me by Mr. Russell. This record features Austin Young along with "Big Eye" Louis Nelson DeLisle, Johnny St. Cyr, and others. See Lomax, *Mister Jelly Roll,* 89, for DeLisle's statement on blues and jazz. For autobiographies of other New Orleans musicians, see Danny Barker, *A Life in Jazz* (New York: Oxford University Press, 1986); Sidney Bechet, *Treat It Gentle* (1960; reprint, New York: Da Capo, 1978); Barney Bigard, *With Louis and the Duke: The Autobiography of a Jazz Clarinetist,* ed. Barry Martyn (New York: Hill and Wang, 1986). Mary Collins, *Oh, Didn't He Ramble,* ed. Frank Gillis and John W. Miner (Urbana, Ill.: University of Illinois Press, 1428,974).
56. Author's interviews with Irma, Lee, and Martha Young, Crawford Brown Jr., and Alvin, Lucille, and James Tolbert.
57. "I Can't Give You Anything but Love," on *Lester Young with the Oscar Peterson Trio* (Verve 314 521 451–2), provides one example of Young's different "voices" alternating in a responsorial fashion. "I Cover the Waterfront" (both takes), on *Lester Young Trio* (Verve 314 521 650–2), is another example. The saxophonist-composer Jimmy Heath mentioned Young's fingering technique, the purpose of which was to obtain the effect of the human voice (author's interview with Jimmy Heath).
58. Author's interview with Clarence Phillips.
59. Ibid.
60. Author's interview with Irma Young.
61. Author's interviews with Lee Young and James Tolbert.
62. Author's interview with Clarence Phillips. Personal communication with the author. Lee Young, IJS, vol. 5, p. 3.
63. Personal communication with Crawford Brown Jr. and James Tolbert.
64. Author's interviews with Alvin, James, and Lucille Tolbert and Martha Young.
65. Author's interviews with Lucille and James Tolbert and Martha Young.
66. Author's interview with Lucille Tolbert.

4. Big Top Blues

1. The Phillips brothers met the professor and his family in late 1923 or early 1924: author's interviews with Clarence and Leonard Phillips and Irma Young.
2. Arna Bontemps, ed., *Father of the Blues: An Autobiography by W. C. Handy* (New York: Da Capo, 1991), is one of the best accounts of a life in minstrelsy and popular music. Ted Vincent's *Keep Cool: The Black Activists Who Built the Jazz Age* (Boulder, Colo.: Pluto, 1995) is quite good on TOBA. For the adaptive nature of minstrelsy, see Glenn Shirley, *Pawnee Bill: A Biography*

of Mayor Gordon W. Lillie (Albuquerque: University of New Mexico Press, 1958), 160–76, and Victor Weybright and Henry Sell, *Buffalo Bill and the Wild West* (London: H. Hamilton, 1956), 178–84; both provide examples of the evolution of the Wild West shows, which added European soldiers, Cossacks, and Asian impersonators to their usual complement of cowboys, Native Americans, and circus and carnival characters at the turn of the century. On the evolution of jazz from this popular-culture milieu, see Bruce Bastin, "From the Medicine Show to the Stage: Some Influences upon the Development of the Blues Tradition in the Southwestern United States," *American Music,* spring 1984, pp. 29–42; William Howland Kenney, "The Influence of Black Vaudeville on Early Jazz," *The Black Perspective in Music,* fall 1986, pp. 233–48; Sandra R. Lieb, *Mother of the Blues: A Study of Ma Rainey* (Amherst, Mass.: University of Massachusetts Press, 1981).

3. Eric Lott, *Love and Theft: Black Minstrelsy and the American Working Class* (New York: Oxford University Press, 1993), is one of the more controversial and insightful examinations of the institution. For earlier studies of minstrelsy, see Carl F. Wittke, *Tambo and Bones: A History of the American Minstrel Stage* (Raleigh, N.C.: Duke University Press, 1930), and Robert C. Toll, *Blacking Up: The Minstrel Show in Nineteenth-Century America* (New York: Oxford University Press, 1974). Thomas Cripps, *Slow Fade to Black: The Negro in American Film, 1900–1942* (New York: Oxford University Press, 1977), 24; for the treatment of African Americans in Hollywood films, see also Donald Bogle, *Toms, Coons, Mulattos, Mammies, and Bucks: An Interpretive History of Blacks in American Films* (New York: Oxford University Press, 1974).
4. Black minstrels traveled as far as San Francisco before the Civil War: Douglas Henry Daniels, *Pioneer Urbanites: A Social and Cultural History of Black San Francisco* (Berkeley, Calif.: University of California Press, 1991), 125. See Ann Charters, *Nobody: The Story of Bert Williams* (New York: Macmillan, 1970), on Williams and Walker, the famous comedians who originated the road shows that Bing Crosby and Bob Hope would capitalize on decades later. Eileen Southern, *The Music of Black Americans: A History,* 2d ed. (New York: W. W. Norton, 1983), 298–300.
5. Jo Jones, IJS, p. 20.
6. Lester Young's nostalgia is noted in Allan Morrison, "You Got to Be Original, Man," in Lewis Porter, ed., *A Lester Young Reader* (Washington, D.C.: Smithsonian Institution Press, 1991), 132; Mary Lou Williams, IJS, pp. 20, 23. Harry O. Brunn, *The Story of the Original Dixieland Jazz Band* (Baton Rouge, La.: Louisiana State University Press, 1960).
7. Lee Young, IJS, pp. 9 and 26; author's interview with Lee Young.
8. Lee Young's IJS interviews are good for these years; the author's interviews with Irma Young and Leonard and Clarence Phillips also helped re-create this period. Leonard Phillips's IJS interview is of interest here as well. Southern, *The Music of Black Americans,* 293–99. Leonard Phillips, IJS, p. 8, 19–20. See George Wright, *Racial Violence in Kentucky, 1865–1940: Lynchings, Mob Rule, and "Legal Lynchings"* (Baton Rouge, La.: Louisiana State University Press, 1990), on race relations in Kentucky.

9. Wren Brown, Lee Young's grandson, provided the information that the cousin was hiding and that Lester, a youngster at the time, managed to get him a gun (personal communication with the author). See also Douglas Henry Daniels, "History, Racism, and Jazz: The Case of Lester Young," *Jazzforschung*, December 1984, pp. 87–103, on the racism and prejudice encountered by Young and other Black musicians of his era. Lee Young mentioned the intense racism of the Deep South, particularly Texas, on several occasions, but did not provide further details (personal communication with the author). Bontemps, ed., *Father of the Blues*, 44.

10. Leonard Phillips, IJS, p. 17.

11. Ibid., 34, 38. On this theater, see "The 81 Theatre, Atlanta, Ga.," *Indianapolis Freeman*, January 22, 1916, p. 5. I wish to thank Lucelia Flood-Partridge, manager, Reference and Research Division, Auburn Avenue Research Library, Atlanta, Georgia, for the address of the 81 Theatre. On TOBA, see Vincent, *Keep Cool*.

12. Leonard Phillips, IJS, p. 41.

13. Ibid., 46.

14. Author's interview with Lee Young. Lee Young, IJS, vol. 3, p. 27. Leonard Feather, *From Satchmo to Miles* (reprint, New York: Da Capo, 1987), 119. Porter, ed., *A Lester Young Reader*, 176.

15. Author's interview with Irma Young.

16. Ibid. It was not unusual for a "Junior" such as Willis Lester Young to be called by his middle name. No one who knew Young in the 1920s (or later)—neither his siblings nor the Phillips brothers—ever referred to him by his first name in interviews with the author; in fact, his brother, Lee, was the only one who even brought up the subject. Lester Young Jr. described his father's relationship with his sister Irma as "very, very, very close" (personal communication with the author). In particular, Irma Young disliked the way publications referred to her brother's "drug" problem, when in actuality all he indulged in was alcohol and marijuana (author's interview with Irma Young).

17. Author's interviews with Clarence and Leonard Phillips and Irma and Lee Young.

18. Author's interview with Leonard Phillips. Lee Young, IJS, p. 27. I wish to express my gratitude to the late Leonard Phillips for providing me with this photograph; he and his brother Clarence, as well as Irma Young, helped with the identifications. The photo was taken in June 1924.

19. Leonard Phillips, IJS, pp. 20–22. Author's interview with Irma Young.

20. Lee Young, IJS, pp. 9–10. "Pal Williams and Jack Wiggins Together in the Dixie Bells," *Indianapolis Freeman*, November 1, 1919, p. 5. Wiggins, a singer and dancer, was known for his fashionable style of dress. Wren Brown told me about Jack Wiggins's teachings, which he learned of from his grandfather (personal communication with the author). Perhaps it was this name, together with his father's (and his own given name), that provided Lester with the title of his "club," the Willis Wiggins Society, which "inducted" members who were then appointed to offices such as "Junior Wiggins." The

club was probably a parody of Black social clubs and fraternal organizations.

21. "Program of J. C. Rockwell 'Sunny South' Co., Inc." *Indianapolis Freeman,* February 21, 1920, p. 12.

22. Williams and Walker's "Senegambian Carnival" appeared in Brooklyn, New York, in December 1898: *Indianapolis Freeman,* December 10, 1898, p. 5. Southern, *The Music of Black Americans,* 298–300.

23. For another show by the same company, this one set in Haiti, see Salem Tutt Whitney, "Seen and Heard While Passing" ("Hilarious Musical Spree at the Prospect This Week"), and Lew Hall, "The Smart Set Company—Salem Tutt Whitney a Star," *Indianapolis Freeman,* March 6, 1915, p. 6; the show was entitled *His Excellency, the President.* Georges Michel, *Charlemagne Péralte and the First American Occupation of Haiti,* trans. Douglas Henry Daniels (Dubuque, Iowa: Kendall/Hunt, 1996). " 'The Smart Set' Closing on July 26," *Indianapolis Freeman,* August 2, 1919, p. 9. See also the "Smarter Set Company" full-page ad, ibid., December 20, 1919, p. 9. *Bamboula* advertisment, ibid., July 17, 1920, p. 6; Salem Tutt Whitney, "Seen and Heard While Passing," ibid., December 27, 1919, p. 6 ("It is in the field of music that we have made the most consistent progress"); Salem Tutt Whitney, "Seen and Heard While Passing," ibid., March 20, 1920, p. 5. "Smarter Set Company," full-page ad, ibid., December 20, 1919, p. 9. See G. Stanley, "Smarter Set Company Murat Engagement Brilliant Success," ibid., May 22, 1920, p. 5, for a brief synopsis of the plot of this show, and also Sylvester Russell, "Musical and Dramatic," ibid., November 27, 1920, p. 5, for a review of its Chicago run. Like Williams and Walker's and Bob Hope and Bing Crosby's road shows, *Bamboula* featured trips to exotic locales.

24. In 1909, a new expression of civic consciousness, the National Association for the Advancement of Colored People (NAACP), today the nation's oldest civil rights organization, was formed. One of the chief architects of this new consciousness was W. E. B. Du Bois, whose *Souls of Black Folk* (New York: A. C. McClurg and Co., 1903) was one of the most influential books of the century. Mary White Ovington was another founder of the organization; see her *Black and White Sat Down Together: The Reminiscences of an NAACP Founder* (New York: Feminist Press at the City University of New York, 1995).

25. The tenor saxophonist Allie Brown delighted the public as early as 1898 with his specialty ("The Stage," *Indianapolis Freeman,* August 27, 1898, p. 5); he also played the tenor while on the slackwire ("The Stage," ibid., August 10, 1898, p. 5). In addition, Brown played the flute (ibid., August 13, 1898, p. 5). His photograph can be found in ibid., December 24, 1898, p. 5. Will Marion Cook's Memphis Students included the saxophone in their band in 1905; Tom Brown's Sax Sextet, a novelty group that performed in clown outfits, featured the instrument around World War I; and San Francisco's St. Francis Hotel orchestra used it during the World War I years. The Six Musical Spillers also showcased a xylophone ("Six Musical Spillers," ibid., January 22, 1916, p. 5). James Weldon Johnson, *Black Manhattan* (New York: Atheneum, 1977), 120–25. "The Saxophone Was Invented by Accident!," *Down*

Beat, February 15, 1940, pp. 12–13, provides an excellent summary of the instrument's history. See "The People's Band" (photo), *Indianapolis Freeman,* July 31, 1915, p. 5, a saxophone orchestra managed by Herbert Willis, a drummer. See also Bontemps, ed., *Father of the Blues,* 100, 104. The bandleader Andy Kirk discusses his introduction to the instrument in *Twenty Years on Wheels* (Ann Arbor, Mich.: University of Michigan Press, 1989), 38–39, as does Joe Darensbourg in Vacher, *Jazz Odyssey: The Autobiography of Joe Darensbourg,* as told to Peter Vacher (Baton Rouge, La.: Louisiana State University Press, 1987), 35–36.

26. Author's interviews with Lee and Irma Young; Lee Young, IJS, p. 12. My identifications of the personnel pictured in this photograph differ from those given in John McDonough, *Giants of Jazz: Lester Young* (Alexandria, Va.: Time-Life, 1980), 4; my information came from Irma Young. Leonard Phillips, IJS, pp. 28–29.

27. Lee Young, IJS, p. 27: "The acts that they really loved, they would [really] buy the photographs."

28. Others were also experimenting with new sounds and instruments. Jasper Taylor, for example, joined W. C. Handy in Memphis in 1915 and played xylophone in the Memphis Blues Band of Harry Pace and Handy some fourteen years before Lionel Hampton attempted the instrument at Louis Armstrong's suggestion ("Stage Gossip [Stage Notes]," *Indianapolis Freeman,* July 31, 1915, p. 5). Indeed, Jasper Taylor is credited with having taught Hampton to play the xylophone; see George Hoefer Jr., "The Hot Box," *Down Beat,* September 1, 1944, p. 11. Californian Reb Spikes performed in vaudeville with a musician who played xylophone around 1915 (Reb Spikes, IJS, p. 13); see also Bontemps, ed., *Father of the Blues,* 101, 172, 174. "The Memphis Blues Band, Inc." (photograph), *Indianapolis Freeman,* December 20, 1919, p. 14, includes Jasper Taylor as well as Handy; William Grant Still, the famous composer, was the band's arranger. Handy's band performed a famous trombone number, "Yellow Dog Blues," in which the musicians laughed on cue, "followed by the famous trombone laugh." One laugh produced another—first the musicians', then the onomatopoeia of the trombone, and finally the audience's response. "Laughing Trombone" was a specialty at a time when jazz musicians cried, whinnied, laughed, and talked through wind instruments: "They All Laughed," ibid., February 28, 1920, p. 5, and Ron Welburn, "Ralph Ellison's Territorial Vantage," *The Grackle,* no. 4 (1977–78), p. 5.

29. Lee Young, IJS, pp. 28–29. Leonard Phillips, IJS, p. 88.

30. Lee Young, IJS, p. 29; author's interview with Irma Young.

31. Lee Young, IJS, pp. 12, 17; author's interview with Lee Young. The professor also discouraged Irma from pursuing a career as a dancer, claiming that eventually her legs would give out and arguing that then she would need to play an instrument (author's interview with Irma Young). Lee Young, IJS, pp. 4, 8; author's interview with Lucille Tolbert.

32. Lee Young, IJS, pp. 4, 6.

33. Ibid., 5, 23.

34. Leonard Phillips, IJS, pp. 22–24.

35. Author's interview with Leonard Phillips.

36. Author's interview with Clarence Phillips. Cootie Williams, IJS, 43, 46–47.

37. Lee Young, IJS, pp. 12–13.

38. John Chilton, *Let the Good Times Roll: The Story of Louis Jordan and His Music* (Ann Arbor, Mich.: University of Michigan Press, 1994), 15, places the competition (ironically) in Woodville, Mississippi. Author's interview with Clarence Phillips.

39. Lee Young, IJS, pp. 4, 8; author's interview with Irma Young.

40. Author's interview with Lee Young.

41. Lester related the incident in interviews; see Porter, ed., *A Lester Young Reader,* 142, 182–83. Similarly, Louis Jordan's father, another bandleader and professor, physically chastised his son when he caught him clowning in the band. The effect on Jordan was the same as that on Young (Chilton, *Let the Good Times Roll,* 8).

42. John P. Noonan, "Hampton Tinkered with Xylophone—And a Vibe Artist Was Born," *Down Beat,* November 1938, p. 25. Lee Young, IJS, pp. 11–12; Val Wilmer, "The Lee Young Story," *Jazz Journal,* January 1961, p. 3. Then, too, the professor made certain that his children progressed in school by having them read their lessons aloud to him (author's interview with Irma Young).

43. Dan Morgenstern, "Little Jazz: The Fire Still Burns," *Down Beat,* February 4, 1987, p. 14; the IJS interviews with Marshal Royal, Gene Ramey, Eddie Durham, and Buddy Tate vividly portray these years. Buddy Tate, IJS, p. 5; Bill Esposito, "Buddy Tate," *Jazz Magazine,* summer 1979, p. 56. Britt Woodman played in a family band in Los Angeles; see his oral-history interview, Central Avenue Sounds, Special Collections, UCLA Research Library.

44. Leonard Phillips, IJS, pp. 12–13.

45. Ibid., 13. Author's interview with Leonard Phillips.

46. Cootie Williams, IJS, pp. 43–45; author's interviews with Clarence and Leonard Phillips and Irma Young. On Cootie Williams, see Leonard Feather, *The Encyclopedia of Jazz* (New York: Horizon, 1960), 462–63: entry for Charles Melvin Williams, born in Mobile, Alabama, on July 24, 1908.

47. Author's interview with Irma Young; "teddies" were described by Louis Armstrong as being "all silk, like baby bloomers only transparent" (Louis Armstrong and Richard Meryman, *Louis Armstrong—A Self-Portrait: The Richard Meryman Interview* [New York: Eakins, 1971], 12).

48. Jo Jones, IJS, p. 16.

49. See Lee Young's comments on this education, wherein he notes that as a child he traveled to nearly every state in the United States (IJS, pp. 24–25). Author's interview with Leonard Phillips.

50. Lee Young, IJS, pp. 23–24.

51. Author's interview with Irma Young; Joe Darensbourg played in a minstrel show as a young musician and in his autobiography mentions the special rail-

road car with the sleeper: "You carried all your equipment in one part of the car and the entertainers stayed in the other part" (Darensbourg, *Jazz Odyssey,* 35). Joseph Husband, *The Story of the Pullman Car* (Chicago: A. C. McClurg and Co., 1917), 27–35.

52. Author's interview with Irma Young.

53. Lee Young, IJS, pp. 32–33; author's interview with Irma Young.

54. Author's interview with Lee Young.

55. Ibid. Porter, ed., *A Lester Young Reader,* 142.

56. Author's interview with Irma Young; I recall this same punishment being used for primary school girls when I taught in Tanzania, East Africa, in the 1960s.

57. Author's interview with Leonard Phillips.

58. Ibid.

59. "Bill Robinson's Troupers Show Folk Only on Stage," *Kansas City Call,* June 23, 1933, p. 7-A. Lee Young remembered seeing Bill Robinson, as well as other Black stars, on the TOBA circuit (IJS, 7–8).

60. Porter, ed., *A Lester Young Reader,* 133, 138, 142, 158, wherein Young invariably stresses his having repeatedly run away from home.

61. Author's interview with Irma Young; Freddy Doyle, "Musicians and Orchestras," *California Eagle,* October 9, 1936, p. 10, mentions Young's visit with his family in Los Angeles. Personal communication with Jimmy Tolbert and Crawford Brown Jr., the saxophonist's nephews.

62. Porter, ed., *A Lester Young Reader,* 142; author's interview with Leonard Phillips. Clarence Phillips had already left to play with the blues singer Ma Rainey (author's interview with Clarence Phillips).

63. Nat Hentoff and Nat Shapiro, *The Jazz Makers: Essays on the Greats of Jazz* (1957; reprint, New York: Da Capo, 1979), 256, mentions Young's "mask."

64. McDonough, *Giants of Jazz: Lester Young,* 11, reports that Lester once helped his cousin Sport escape from a southern lynch mob. Lee Young recalled this incident as having taken place in Mississippi.

65. As a youngster, Lee Young witnessed Bill Robinson running backward in races, always defeating men who raced the regular way, and also saw Ida Cox (IJS, 38, 26–27); he noted that the singer Ethel Waters, the comedy team of Butterbeans and Susie, and the Whitman sisters traveled the circuit as well (ibid., 8).

66. Eddie Durham maintained that circus trombones suggested the response part ("ah! ah! ah! ah!") of the popular jump blues "One O'Clock Jump." He further stated that carnivals and minstrel shows "were the foundation of that stuff. I'm playing some of the same stuff now [1982]" (author's interview with Eddie Durham).

67. "Ellington Speaks Out on Jazz," *Los Angeles Sentinel,* February 3, 1955, p. 10A. Nathan Huggins, *Harlem Renaissance* (New York: Oxford University Press, 1971), chapter 6, discusses the psychological ramifications of minstrelsy and slumming for whites.

68. Discussing the role that different institutions played in shaping Black music,

Ellison contended that jazz was not taught well in academia because the schools and the music teachers "were not of its spirit and it was not part of their background." Rather than complaining about this, however, the writer argued that formal training would have imposed "too many thou-shalt-nots." Ellison believed that the example of Oklahoma City's legendary Blue Devils provided ample evidence that "dance halls and jam sessions along with recording are the true academy for jazz." Of course, the same applied to vaudeville and minstrelsy. Welburn, "Ralph Ellison's Territorial Vantage," 6–9; see also Rudi Blesh, *Combo: U.S.A., Eight Lives in Jazz* (1971; reprint, New York: Da Capo, 1979), 164.

69. Esposito, "Buddy Tate," 50. Cab Calloway with Bryant Rollins, *Of Minnie the Moocher and Me* (New York: Crowell, 1976), 81.

70. Calloway, *Of Minnie the Moocher and Me,* 81.

71. "Are Band Polls Important?," *Kansas City Call,* March 3, 1939, p. 16.

5. Jump Lester Jump

1. Leonard Phillips, IJS, p. 88; Phillips was under the impression that the professor came from Hammond, Louisiana, suggesting that he knew of Willis Young's winter residency in that town but not of his Thibodaux birthplace.

2. Author's interview with the Reverend John W. Young, son of William H. Young and brother of Austin ("Boots") and William Junior ("Sport").

3. Lot no. 87, tract no. 7127, Los Angeles County Recorder's Office; the office where Young's property records were found by the author and Mr. James Tolbert is in Norwalk, Los Angeles County, California. Liber 6336, p. 102, Queens County Property Records.

4. Letter from LaJulia Conerly, deputy clerk, Clerk of the Court, Franklinton, Washington Parish, Louisiana, June 11, 1996, and letter from Carolyn Williams, deputy clerk, Clerk of the Court, Tangipahoa Parish, June 10, 1996: no property was owned by the Hunters in either parish until the widow bought a lot after her husband's death. Two brothers, Weston and John Buckhalter, owned the farms on either side of the Hunters in 1910 (U.S. Manuscript Census, Washington Parish, vol. 79, E.D. 126, sheet 4B, lines 55–67); they were African Americans. For Willis Young's property, see Tangipahoa Parish Conveyance Books, vol. 98, p. 299, Amite Courthouse, Tangipahoa Parish, Louisiana.

5. Lee Young, IJS, vol. 5, pp. 110–13.

6. U.S. Manuscript Census, 1920, Tangipahoa Parish, vol. 58, E.D. 123, sheet 16, lines 30–34, taken on January 27, 1920. Willis Young's family was not enumerated in his mother's house in the 1920 census, though they might be expected to be there, considering that the data were gathered in the winter; Willis himself was not, in fact, listed in any census at all after 1900. Although all the evidence points to Louisiana origins for the family, the Youngs' close connections with the adjacent state of Texas are suggested by the presence of

this visitor, a boardinghouse keeper from the Lone Star State; by the birth of William and Jacob Young, Willis's two elder brothers, in that state; and by the fact that Sarah Young, stepmother to Lester, Irma, and Lee, came from there.

7. See, for example, the François Postif interview, reprinted in Lewis Porter, ed., *A Lester Young Reader* (Washington, D.C.: Smithsonian Institution, 1991), 178.

8. 14th U.S. Census, 1920, 1: 226–27; 3: 400.

9. 14th U.S. Census, 1920, 3: 397; John V. Baiamonte Jr., *Immigrants in Rural America: A Study of the Italians of Tangipahoa Parish, Louisiana* (New York: Garland, 1990), 66, 64–96, 91.

10. As in most, if not all, of Louisiana's parishes, the vast majority of the people designated as nonwhite would have been African American, and so with the 239 nonwhite proprietors in Tangipahoa. 14th U.S. Census, 1920, vol. 6, *Agriculture,* part 2, pp. 596, 599, 601, 613; Baiamonte, *Immigrants in Rural America,* 86.

11. Tangipahoa School Board Minute Book no. 3, pp. 266, 269, 350, 358–59, Tangipahoa School Board Office, Amite, Louisiana. James D. Anderson, *The Education of Blacks in the South, 1860–1935* (Chapel Hill, N.C.: University of North Carolina, 1988), 138–40, sets the Tangipahoa Parish Training School within the context of northern philanthropy and industrial education; see, in particular, the photograph on page 139.

12. Leonard Phillips, IJS, p. 31.

13. Porter, ed. *A Lester Young Reader,* 142. Lee Young claimed that his father attended New Orleans University and worked as a principal in Bogalusa, Louisiana (IJS, vol. 5, p. 3); in an interview with the author, Irma Young likewise stated that Willis was a school principal in that same town.

14. Tangipahoa School Board Minute Book no. 3, pp. 266, 269, 350, 358–59.

15. The difference was significant: $36,918 in parish tax dollars went to whites, and a mere $3,665 to African Americans. Tangipahoa Parish Conveyance Books, vol. 98, p. 299, Amite Courthouse, Tangipahoa Parish, Louisiana.

16. 14th U.S. Census, 1920, 3: 396–97, on Negro illiteracy in Tangipahoa (33.9 percent). For foreign-born whites, the rate was 50.9 percent; for native whites, 6.6 percent. The illiteracy rate for Blacks in New Orleans was 15.7 percent.

17. Letter of February 27, 1997 from the reference librarian, Louisiana Division, New Orleans Public Library; this information is based solely upon the address of Lizzie Young (and presumably Lester Young as well) taken from City Directories. A Black child attending school from 1028 Bordeaux would have gone to McDonogh #6, at 926 General Pershing; from 517 Third Street, the James Lewis School, at 2624 Chippewa; and from 2309 Second, Thomy Lafon, at 2916 South Robertson. The addresses of these schools are taken from the City Directory, 1919, pp. 1590–91.

18. Porter, ed., *A Lester Young Reader,* 139.

19. Irma Young recalled attending the Grant Street School (interview with the author), but school records indicate that in fact she went to Blaine, which

Lee Young has corroborated; he also dated the Minneapolis schooling in his IJS interview (pp. 32–40). Leonard Phillips defined the Minneapolis years as beginning in November or December 1926 and ending in January 1929 (IJS, p. 75). According to Minneapolis school records, Irma enrolled in the Blaine School on December 29, 1926, and left on April 18, 1927. Letters to the author from Elaine Kottke, Student Accounting, Minneapolis Public Schools, December 30, 1996, and December 19, 1997, state that no Willis (Lester's actual first name) or Lester Young could be found in the school records. Blaine was located at Twelfth Avenue North, at the corner of Third. In a private conversation with the author, Lee Young confirmed their attending Blaine.

20. Porter, ed., *A Lester Young Reader,* 177. In 1949 Young claimed that he had gone to school in Minneapolis (ibid., 138); Leonard Phillips also maintained that he and Young had attended school in that city (IJS, p. 21).

21. Author's interview with Leonard Phillips.

22. Author's interview with Irma Young. "School . . . was not my thing," Count Basie explained in his *Good Morning Blues: The Autobiography of Count Basie,* as told to Albert Murray (New York: Random House, 1985), 29. Ross Russell, *Bird Lives!: The High Life and Hard Times of Charlie (Yardbird) Parker* (New York: Charterhouse, 1973), 36–37, 69.

23. Porter, ed., *A Lester Young Reader,* 142: "Mother was a seamstress and a schoolteacher." Ibid., 139. Author's interview with "Teddy Bear" (the nickname of a friend of Young's who did not want her real name used). Years later, a chance remark he made onstage to Oscar Peterson was picked up by the microphone, and the entire auditorium heard his off-color language; after the concert Young remarked, "Norman [Granz] is going to keep me after school" (to have a few words with him): Bobby Scott, interview with Bruce Fredericksen, circa 1985. I would like to thank Mr. Fredericksen, who made a video biography of Lester Young, *Song of the Spirit* (1988), based upon this and other interviews, for providing me with a copy of his Scott interview.

24. John Avery Lomax, *Negro Folk Songs as Sung by Lead Belly* (New York: Macmillan, 1936); Alan Lomax and Moses Asch, eds., *The Leadbelly Songbook* (New York: Oak Publications, 1963); Alan Lomax and Sidney Robertson Cowell, *American Folk Song and Folk Lore* (St. Clair Shores, Mich.: Scholarly Press, 1977). See also John Wesley Work and Frederick J. Work, *Folk Songs of the American Negro* (Nashville: published by the authors, 1907); James Weldon Johnson and J. Rosamond Johnson, *The Book of American Negro Spirituals* (New York: Viking, 1925).

25. Author's interview with "Teddy Bear"; Porter, ed., *A Lester Young Reader,* 151.

26. Charles K. Wolfe, *The Life and Legend of Leadbelly* (New York: HarperCollins, 1992); Michael Joseph Morgan, "'Just a Real Song': Huddy Ledbetter (Leadbelly) and African American Oral Tradition" (Ph.D. diss., UCLA, 1993). Alan Lomax, *Land Where the Blues Began* (New York: Pantheon, 1993). See Lomax's Library of Congress recordings—for example, *Afro-American Spirituals, Work Songs, & Ballads* (Rounder CD 1510) and

Southern Journey, Volume 3: 61 Highway Mississippi (Rounder CD 1703).

27. Author's interviews with Clarence and Leonard Phillips. The published census also provided data on the importance of lumbering in these regions. See Amy Quick, "The History of Bogalusa, the 'Magic City' of Louisiana" (Master's thesis, Louisiana State University, Baton Rouge, 1942), reprinted in *Louisiana Historical Quarterly* 29, no. 1 (January 1946). F. H. and A. C. Goodyear, of Buffalo, New York, decided that the area that was to become Bogalusa was a good location (ibid., 23).

28. Author's interview with Irma Young. The size of these logging communities is noteworthy because of their similarity, in terms of their relatively small populations and the importance of personal relationships in conducting business, to the professor's hometown of Thibodaux. Population figures for Natalbany are unavailable, so Hammond will have to suffice. In each instance, the community's total population was quite small, permitting the professor to identify local leaders and serve the townspeople's musical needs. Other towns they resided in were larger: Bogalusa had 8,245 residents in 1920, and Albuquerque and Phoenix, where the family sojourned in 1929–1930, were bigger still, with 26,570 and 48,118 residents, respectively, in 1930. The Black population numbered at most a few thousand in each place, as the following table shows:

Town	1920		1930	
	Black Pop.	Total Pop.	Black Pop.	Total Pop.
Palatka, Fla.	2,634	5,102	3,000	6,500
Warren, Ark.	*	2,145	319	2,523
Bogalusa, La.	2,605	8,245	4,751	14,029
Hammond, La.	1,279	3,855	2,147	6,072
Thibodaux, La.	1,008	3,526	1,226	4,442
Albuquerque, N.M.	213	15,157	441	26,570

*Data not available

Source: 14th U.S. Census, 1920, vol. 3, *Population*, pp. 196, 400–1, 671; ibid., 1: 183, 226–27, for changes in population; 15th U.S. Census, 1930, vol. 3, *Population*, Part 1, pp. 196, 423, 979, 991–92; ibid., part 2, p. 243.

29. For population changes in southern Louisiana counties and parishes over the period 1910–1920, see the following table:

County or Parish	1910		1920		1930	
	Black Pop.	Total Pop.	Black Pop.	Total Pop.	Black Pop.	Total Pop.
Wilkinson	13,904	18,075	11,314	15,319	9,787	13,957
Lafourche	7,973	33,111	5,888	30,344	5,313	32,419
Assumption	10,105	24,128	7,487	17,912	6,319	15,990
Washington	5,458	18,886	7,391	24,164	9,719	29,904
Tangipahoa	9,135	29,160	8,892	31,440	15,644	46,227

Source: 13th U.S. Census, 1910, vol. 2, *Population*, pp. 782, 786–87, 1058; 14th U.S. Census, 1920, vol. 3, *Population*, pp. 393–98, 540; 15th U.S. Census, 1930, vol. 3, *Population*, part 1, pp. 974, 976, 978, 984, 1004, 1315.

For increases earlier in the century, see 12th U.S. Census, 1900, vol. 1, *Population*, pp. 22, 541–42. John Hope Franklin, *From Slavery to Freedom: A History of Negro Americans* (New York: Alfred A. Knopf, 1974), 369–70.

30. Quick, "The History of Bogalusa," 63–64.

31. Author's interviews with Irma and Lee Young. The bandleader visited the North in 1924, if not sooner. That year and the next, the New Orleans Strutters joined Billy Clark's Broadway Show and "traveled in the North, going through Indiana, Ohio, Illinois, Pennsylvania, [and Toronto,] Canada" (author's interview with Leonard Phillips). Until 1926, the show always closed in the South; that year, however, it folded in El Reno, Oklahoma.

32. Author's interview with the Reverend John W. Young. Lee Young, IJS, vol. 5, pp. 10–11. It is also possible that the disastrous flooding of the Mississippi River motivated the Youngs to relocate; see Pete Daniel, *Deep'n As It Come: The 1927 Mississippi River Flood* (New York: Oxford University Press, 1977). The Reverend John W. Young's twin brother, Richard, died in his teens.

33. Author's interview with the Reverend John W. Young.

34. Author's interview with Irma Young; no Cleo Young could be located in the 1920 Manuscript Census for Minnesota. Irma mentioned that the family traveled to Minneapolis on TOBA (interview with the author), a statement confirmed by her brother Lee (IJS, p. 11).

35. Val Wilmer, "The Lee Young Story," *Jazz Journal*, January 1961, p. 3.

36. Leonard Phillips, IJS, p. 121.

37. Elliot M. Rudwick, *Race Riot at East St. Louis, July 2, 1917* (Carbondale, Ill.: Southern Illinois University Press, 1964); William M. Tuttle Jr., *Race Riot: Chicago in the Red Summer of 1919* (New York: Atheneum, 1970); Scott Ellsworth, *Death in a Promised Land: The Tulsa Race Riot of 1921* (Baton Rouge, La.: Louisiana State University Press, 1982). Southern newspapers published articles about northern cities, intended to provide information for prospective migrants; see, for example, "Minneapolis–St. Paul and Their Differences," *Arkansas Gazette*, July 31, 1929. Minneapolis City Directory, 1923, introduction: the city also held the lead in grain, flour, and milk products, metalwork, clothing and textiles, printing and publishing, woodworking, and railroad construction. On Blacks in Minnesota, see David V. Taylor, "Pilgrim's Progress: Black St. Paul and the Making of an Urban Ghetto, 1870–1930" (Ph.D. diss., University of Minnesota, 1977), and idem, *Blacks in Minnesota: A Preliminary Guide to Historical Sources* (St. Paul, Minn.: Minnesota Historical Society, 1976).

38. Minneapolis City Directory, 1923, introduction. Even excluding its twin city, St. Paul, Minneapolis had a greater population than other cities more closely associated with jazz and with Lester Young. A total of 464,356 residents lived there in 1930, compared to 399,746 in Kansas City (then a major jazz center) and a mere 185,389 in Oklahoma City, the home of the Blue Devils. That the Young family and the show otherwise avoided such big cities suggests that some specific economic reason or family connection, or

both, must have played a role in the professor's decision to relocate there. 16th U.S. Census, 1940, vol. 2, *Population,* part 4, pp. 172, 449, 462; ibid., part 5, p. 927. 15th U.S. Census, 1930, vol. 3, *Population,* part 2, pp. 599, 570. Ibid., part 1, p. 1338. In 1940 Minneapolis still exceeded the other cities named above in total population, with 492,370 residents to Kansas City's 399,178 and Oklahoma City's 204,424. Minneapolis's African American population was considerably smaller than such populations in prairie cities to the south; both Kansas City (38,574) and Oklahoma City (14,662) were home to more Blacks than Minneapolis (4,646).

39. Minneapolis City Directory, 1927, p. 2509; regarding the Youngs' address, I wish to thank Dr. David V. Taylor for his assistance. Author's interview with Leonard Phillips.

40. I wish to express my gratitude to Dr. Gaye T. M. Johnson for identifying the owner of the home through research in the Real Estate Records Department of Minneapolis, and for verifying information in the City Directory. Information on the house can be found in the Department of Inspections, Office of the Inspector of Buildings (document no. 3167, "Permit to Wreck Buildings"), Minneapolis, Minnesota. An Inspector of Buildings form revealed that electricity was installed in the house in September 1926.

41. Information on the Haas brothers is taken from the City Directory, 1927, p. 948; the Majestic Music Shop, ibid., p. 1532; Leonard Phillips, IJS, p. 121.

42. Minneapolis City Directory, 1927, pp. 71, 66, and 69 for the churches; other Black social institutions are also identified in the City Directories and Minneapolis newspapers. I wish to thank Maggie Sloss, library assistant, Special Collections, Minneapolis Public Library, for providing information on these institutions from the City Directory (letter of November 22, 1996, to the author). See *St. Paul Northwest Bulletin Appeal,* January 14, 1925, p. 3. As for the fraternities, Lee Young said that his father had been a thirty-third-degree Mason and recalled that he and Lester had themselves joined a fraternal order at one point, somewhere in the South—possibly in Florida.

43. In 1920 a total of twenty-two Black circus roustabouts were arrested in Duluth, Minnesota. The white mob suspected six of them of rape, and confessions were extorted from some. Three were lynched before the National Guard arrived. Roy Wilkins, then a college student and later head of the NAACP, reported, "What bothered me most was the way those five thousand white Northerners had gotten together on the lynching" (Roy Wilkins with Tom Mathews, *Standing Fast: The Autobiography of Roy Wilkins* [New York: Viking, 1982], 42–44). Michael Fedo, *The Lynchings in Duluth* (St. Paul, Minn.: Minnesota Historical Society Press, 2000). Photos of the atrocity appear in James Allen et al., *Without Sanctuary: Lynching Photography in America* (Santa Fe, N.M.: Twin Palms, 2000), plates 28–30. The first anti-lynching law in the United States was passed in Minnesota; see David V. Taylor, "The Black Community in the Twin Cities," *Roots: Black Minnesotans* 17, no. 1 (fall 1988): 10. "Colored Citizens Protest against Separate Bureau," *St. Paul Appeal,* July 1, 1922, p. 2. "It Must Not Be!," ibid. (in which residents opposed a proposal for a segregated playground in St. Paul).

44. "Armed Negro Holds Crowd of 500 at Bay," *Minneapolis Morning Tribune,* June 21, 1922, p. 7. I wish to thank Dr. Gaye T. M. Johnson for this information.

45. See the ads in the *St. Paul Appeal,* May 1, 1920, p. 4, and May 8, 1920, p. 4. Abbey's Syncopated Orchestra was one of the first bands to recognize the new music in their names (advertisement, ibid., March 27, 1920, p. 4). For the Butler's Jazz Orchestra ad, see ibid., May 21, 1921, p. 2, and for the Railroad Men's Association ad, ibid., June 18, 1921, p. 4. Moore's Jazz Knockers ad, ibid., July 1, 1922, p. 3; see also ibid., July 1, 1922, p. 3. For Stevens's Jazz Canaries, see ibid., May 20, 1922, p. 2; Newland Jazz Orchestra Moonlight Boat Excursion ad for Gopher Lodge no. 105, ibid., December 2, 1922, p. 4. Ads for Professor Stevens's Full Jazz Band and for the Men's Episcopalian Club, ibid., June 30, 1923, p. 1.

46. 14th U.S. Census, 1920, vol. 3, *Population,* p. 523. St. Paul housed 3,376: ibid., 524. Author's interviews with Henry "Buster" Smith and Le Roy "Snake" Whyte. "'Shuffle Along,' New York's Delight, at Metropolitan Theater Next Week," *St. Paul Appeal,* October 20, 1923, pp. 1, 3. Nu-Way Jazz Hounds ad, ibid., 4. Noble and Sissle came the next year with another musical; for the Acme Palm Garden ad, see ibid., p. 3. Ibid., May 27, 1922, p. 4. Ad for "Grand Musical Festival" at People's Church, *Northwest Bulletin Appeal,* March 29, 1924, p. 2; ibid., February 14, 1925, p. 3. In 1925 the New York show's cast included pianists Blake and Sissle, trumpet player Valaida Snow, and the future dancer, singer, and comedienne of international renown, Josephine Baker, as well as a brass band and a symphony orchestra. On Blacks in Minnesota, see Taylor, "Pilgrim's Progress," and idem, *Blacks in Minnesota.*

47. Author's personal communications and interviews with Le Roy "Snake" Whyte; author's interview with Eddie Barefield. "Memories of the Jazz Age," reminiscences by Carl Warmington, 1988, p. 3; I wish to thank Maggie Sloss, reference librarian, Special Collections, Minneapolis Public Library, for bringing this typewritten manuscript to my attention. Eddie Barefield, IJS, pp. 33–34. Clinton Cox, "Old Man with a Horn," *New York News Magazine,* November 7, 1976, p. 7, Eddie Barefield Vertical File, IJS: in this article on Barefield, the saxophonist recalled Lester on alto, Irma on sax, Lee on drums, and Sarah on piano (p. 19). In Frank Driggs, "Eddie Barefield's Many Worlds," *Jazz Review,* July 1960, p. 20, the reedman maintained that Young performed on both alto and baritone saxes, and that Lee did not play, but danced; see also "The Eddie Barefield Story," as told to Albert J. McCarthy, *Jazz Monthly,* May 1959, p. 11. Author's interview with Le Roy "Snake" Whyte. Whyte dated the North Dakota meeting to a year or two earlier (1925 or 1926) than Barefield's estimate. Other Young sightings in the 1920s are detailed by Cootie Williams in IJS, pp. 42ff. The Minneapolis City Directory for 1927 listed a Roy Langford, porter, residing at 700 Sixth Avenue North; he may have fronted for other businessmen at the Nest, as there was no listing for any Siegal.

48. Gordon Parks, *A Choice of Weapons* (1965; reprint, New York: Berkley Medallion, 1967), 25–32.

49. "Dance Rowdies Must Go . . . ," *Minneapolis Times,* January 9, 1923 (morning edition); see also "Curfew Rings on Night Life," ibid., September 30, 1930; thanks to Maggie Sloss, Special Collections, Minneapolis Public Library.

50. Leonard Phillips, IJS, pp. 121–22. In "Grand Jury Asks New Law against Reckless Driver," *Minneapolis Times,* October 31, 1924 (evening edition), the ballroom is called the South Side Dance Hall. See also "Closing of Dance Halls Is Urged in Inspector's Report," ibid., August 30, 1928 (evening edition). In "Curfew Rings on Night Life; Police Watch," ibid., September 30, 1930 (evening edition), it is referred to as "the south side club, a black and tan café just off Washington Avenue South." These articles are in the morgue file in the Minneapolis Public Library.

51. In an interview with the author, Le Roy "Snake" Whyte said it was the Patterson Hotel. Author's interviews with Eddie Barefield and Le Roy "Snake" Whyte. Cootie Williams, IJS, pp. 42ff; the tenor saxophonist Buddy Tate recalled meeting the Young family in Texas in the mid-1920s (Brian Case, "Buddy and the President," *Melody Maker,* December 1, 1979, p. 37).

52. Author's interview with Le Roy "Snake" Whyte. The Minneapolis City Directory for 1930 listed Mr. Whyte and his wife, Cecile, as living at 2528 Chicago Avenue; thanks to Maggie Sloss, Minneapolis Public Library.

53. Leonard Phillips, IJS, p. 83. On Beiderbecke, see Ralph Berton, *Rememberin' Bix: A Memoir of the Jazz Age* (New York: Harper and Row, 1974).

54. Author's interview with Eddie Barefield.

55. Author's interview with Leonard Phillips.

56. Druie Bess interview, page 10, the Jazz Oral History Project of the Joint Collection, Western Historical Manuscript Collection, St. Louis, and the State Historical Society of Missouri Manuscripts at the University of Missouri, Kansas City, Missouri (hereafter referred to as UMoKC); these interviews have been edited and published in part in Nathan W. Pearson Jr., *Goin' to Kansas City* (Urbana, Ill.: University of Illinois Press, 1987).

57. Leonard Phillips, IJS, pp. 82, 71.

58. Ibid.; see also ibid., 21–22, 28, 50, 71, 122.

59. *Hot Jazz, Pop Jazz, Hokum and Hilarity* (RCA Victor LPV-524), *The King of New Orleans Jazz: Jelly Roll Morton* (RCA Victor LPM-1649), and *Mr. Jelly Lord* (RCA Victor LPV 546) showcase Jelly Roll Morton's classic Hot Peppers and feature such compositions as "Wolverine Blues," "Mr. Jelly Lord," "Wild Man Blues," "Hyena Stomp," "Freakish," and "Red Hot Pepper Stomp," all recorded in 1927 and 1928.

60. Author's interview with Leonard Phillips.

61. Advertisement in the 1928 Metropolitan Opera House Program Book, Special Collections, Minneapolis Public Library; I wish to thank Maggie Sloss, library assistant, Special Collections, Minneapolis Public Library, for bringing this to my attention.

62. The Minneapolis City Directory for 1928 lists only two musicians from Billy Young's band: Gurvas Oliver, musician, at 509 Lyndale Avenue North; and

Clyde V. Turrentine, 3621 Fourth Avenue South. I am grateful to Maggie Sloss, library assistant, Special Collections, Minneapolis Public Library, for providing me with this information.

63. Author's interview with Leonard Phillips. Leonard Phillips, IJS, p. 23.

64. Leonard Phillips, IJS, p. 84.

65. Thomas Joseph Hennessey, "From Jazz to Swing: Black Jazz Musicians and Their Music, 1917–1935" (Ph.D. diss., Northwestern University, 1975), argues: "In two short years, 1929–31, jazz bands, and particularly black bands, had become a major element within the established structure of the national entertainment industry" (pp. 430ff). Leroi Ostransky, *Jazz City: The Impact of Our Cities on the Development of Jazz* (Englewood Cliffs, N.J.: Prentice-Hall, 1973).

66. Charles R. Townsend, *San Antonio Rose: The Life and Music of Bob Wills* (Urbana, Ill.: University of Illinois Press, 1976), and Lawrence Welk with Bernice McGeehan, *Wunnerful, Wunnerful: The Autobiography of Lawrence Welk* (Englewood Cliffs, N.J.: Prentice-Hall, 1971), reveal how two bandleaders adapted to the tastes of audiences in their areas—primarily Oklahoma and Texas for Wills, and mainly the northern states for Welk, though both traveled extensively.

67. 15th U.S. Census, 1930, vol. 3, part 2, p. 427.

68. Leonard Phillips, IJS, p. 124. Author's interview with Leonard Phillips.

69. The following table gives 1930 population figures for towns where the Youngs played:

Town	Black Population	Total Population
Broken Bow, Neb.	9	2,715
Scottsbluff, Neb.	62	8,465
Lexington, Neb.	0	2,962
Grand Island, Neb.	120	18,041
Sioux City, Iowa	1,057	79,183
Des Moines, Iowa	5,428	142,559
Bismarck, N.D.	41	7,122
Minot, N.D.	65	10,476
El Reno, Okla.	533	9,384
Salina, Kan.	532	20,155
Wichita, Kan.	5,623	111,110
Amarillo, Tx.	1,600	43,132
Sherman, Tx.	2,014	15,713
Albuquerque, N.M.	441	26,570
Phoenix, Az.	2,366	48,118

Source: 15th U.S. Census, 1930, vol. 3, *Population,* part 1, pp. 153, 765, 766, 840; ibid., part 2, pp. 95, 96, 243, 427, 571, 972, 974.

70. Professor Brown of Omaha was probably one of those whom Professor Young knew and linked up with. Like Young, Brown had sons who were involved in music; one, Crawford, married Irma Young, and another, Eddie,

would be her partner in show business for several years; in fact, I was fortunate enough to meet him when I first interviewed Ms. Young. Author's interview with Professor Brown's grandson, and Irma's son, Crawford Brown Jr.

71. Cox, "Old Man with a Horn," 19; author's interview with Eddie Barefield.

72. Author's interview with Eddie Barefield.

73. *Northwest Bulletin Appeal,* December 13, 1924, p. 2. Minneapolis City Directory, 1927, p. 1532. Charles Haas, a repairman in the Majestic Music Shop, was the brother of the man who owned the house where the Youngs lived in 1927. The shop's proprietors were Arthur S. and Stanley B. Goldberg, who resided at 2707 Humboldt Avenue South, number 2 (ibid., 890–91).

74. Author's interview with Leonard Phillips.

75. Minneapolis City Directory, 1927, p. 1532; *Northwest Bulletin Appeal,* December 23, 1924, p. 12; ibid., March 11, 1922, p. 2; ibid., February 17, 1923, p. 4; see also ibid., February 24, 1923, supplement, for record ads.

76. Author's interviews with Le Roy "Snake" Whyte, Eddie Barefield, and Leonard Phillips.

77. Porter, ed., *A Lester Young Reader,* 142, 162. Buddy Tate, IJS, p. 12.

78. Porter, ed., *A Lester Young Reader,* 162, 133.

79. Author's interview with Leonard Phillips; Leonard Phillips, IJS, p. 63.

80. Porter, ed., *A Lester Young Reader,* 158–59. On Trumbauer, see Leonard G. Feather, *The Encyclopedia of Jazz* (1960; reprint, New York: Da Capo, n.d.), 445–46.

81. Leonard Phillips, IJS, pp. 58, 63, 61.

82. Ibid., 61.

83. Author's interview with Leonard Phillips; Porter, ed., *A Lester Young Reader,* 158.

84. Charles Hamm, *Yesterdays: Popular Song in America* (New York: W. W. Norton, 1979), appendix 5, 487–88.

85. Ibid.; these selections can be heard on *Lester Young/Lester Swings* (Verve VE-2-2516); *Masters of Jazz: Lester Young, Volume 7* (Storyville SLP-4107); *Lester Young in Washington, D.C., 1956, Volume 1* (Pablo 2308 219), *Volume 2* (Pablo Live 2308-225), *Volume 3* (Pablo Live 2308-228), and *Volume 4* (Pablo Live 2308-230); and *The President Plays with the Oscar Peterson Trio* (Verve 831670-2). These are merely examples of records or CDs that include the specified songs; there are many more. Statements about the number of times Young recorded a song are based on analysis of the "Song Index" in Frank Büchmann-Møller, *You Got to Be Original, Man* (New York: Greenwood, 1990), 507–15. Given the nature of the medium, Büchmann-Møller's song index is necessarily incomplete, insofar as individuals and record companies regularly issue previously unreleased recordings.

86. Porter, ed., *A Lester Young Reader,* 112, 168.

87. Hamm, *Yesterdays,* 487–88.

88. Author's interview with Leonard Phillips.

89. Cootie Williams, IJS, p. 43.

90. Lee Young, IJS, p. 31.

91. Ibid.; author's interview with Irma Young. Sidney Bechet, *Treat It Gentle: An Autobiography* (1960; reprint, New York: Da Capo, 1978), 95–110; Buck Clayton, *Buck Clayton's Jazz World* (New York: Oxford University Press, 1987), 25–26; Driggs, "Eddie Barefield's Many Worlds," 18; Whitney Balliett, *Jelly Roll, Jabbo and Fats: Nineteen Portraits in Jazz* (1983; reprint, New York: Oxford University Press, 1984), 52, 71. Daphne Duval Harrison, *Black Pearls: Blues Queens of the 1920s* (1988; reprint, New Brunswick, N.J.: Rutgers University Press, 1990), 201.

92. Lee Young, IJS, p. 32; Leonard Phillips, IJS, pp. 118–20.

93. Lee Young, IJS, p. 31.

94. Ibid., 33.

95. Author's interview with Irma Young. They may have left because they knew that the house they rented was shortly to be razed; see the Department of Inspections documentation in note 40 above.

96. On the Black Los Angeles music scene, see Lawrence Gushee, "New Orleans–Area Musicians on the West Coast, 1908–1925," *Black Music Research Journal* 9, no. 1 (spring 1989): 1–18; idem, "How the Creole Band Came to Be," ibid. 8, no. 1 (spring 1988): 83–100. The latter article points out that Will Johnson and his Creole band were in Los Angeles in 1907 (p. 93); by the end of 1913, four band members lived in that city (p. 94). See also idem, "A Preliminary Chronology of the Early Career of Ferd 'Jelly Roll' Morton," *American Music,* winter 1985, 389–412; Alan Lomax, *Mister Jelly Roll: The Fortunes of Jelly Roll Morton, New Orleans Creole and "Inventor of Jazz"* (New York: Grossett and Dunlap, 1950), 159ff; Bette Yarbrough Cox, *Central Avenue—Its Rise and Fall (1890–c. 1955), Including the Musical Renaissance of Black Los Angeles* (Los Angeles: BEEM Publications, 1996); Tom Reed, *The Black Music History of Los Angeles: Its Roots* (Los Angeles: Black Accent on L.A., 1992).

97. Author's interview with Le Roy "Snake" Whyte. An advertisement for the Nest, with photos, appeared in *Timely Digest,* April 1931; I wish to thank the late Dave Sletten, a Minneapolis jazz researcher, Brian Horrigan of the Minnesota Historical Society, and the Minneapolis Public Library for their assistance in locating a copy of it for me. For more on the Nest, see "Licensing Dance Halls Protested," *Minneapolis Times,* October 2, 1930 (evening edition); "Dance Hall Permit Delayed by Council," ibid., October 9, 1930 (morning edition); "Women Join Fight on Dance Permit," ibid. (evening edition); "North Side Dance Hall License Plea Refused," ibid., October 30, 1930 (evening edition); and "North Side Dance Hall Request Is Renewed," ibid., December 10, 1930 (evening edition). Relevant Cotton Club articles in the Vertical Files of the Minneapolis Public Library include "U.S. Court to Try North Side Mayor," *Minneapolis Times,* February 21, 1932 (morning edition); "'Mayor of North Side' Draws Workhouse Term," ibid., April 29, 1936; "Jailed in Attack on White Slave Witness," ibid., April 27, 1945; "Judge

Warns Slavers" and "Ganz Sentenced on 'Slave' Count," ibid., June 1, 1945. The location of the Kit Kat was provided to me by Le Roy "Snake" Whyte in a personal communication; at the time he lived across the street, at the corner of Aldrich and Sixth Avenue North.

98. From the Minneapolis Public Library morgue files: "Patron Wounded, 30 Rounded Up," *Minneapolis Times,* February 3, 1928 (evening edition); "Former Sheriff Is Sought . . . ," ibid., February 4, 1928 (evening edition); "Police Order Clubs to Close," ibid., February 5, 1928 (morning edition); "Policeman Wounded by Gunman," ibid., February 6, 1928 (evening edition); "Jury Begins Inquiry into Cotton Club," ibid., February 10, 1928 (evening edition); "Cotton Club Passes out of Existence," ibid., May 11, 1928 (morning edition); "U.S. Court to Try North Side Mayor," ibid., February 21, 1932 (morning edition); "Part Kid Cann Played in '28 Battle Studied," ibid., February 16, 1936 (morning edition); "Patrolman to Take Stand," ibid., February 17, 1936 (morning edition); "Federal Agents Nab Hess," ibid., March 26, 1936; " 'Mayor of North Side' Draws Workhouse Term," ibid., April 29, 1936.

99. Author's interview with Leonard Phillips on his and his friends' departure; author's interviews with Alvin, James, and Lucille Tolbert on the band in the 1930s.

100. I wish to thank the late Martha Young and her husband, William, for providing me with a copy of this rare photograph.

101. Porter, ed., *A Lester Young Reader,* 138.

102. Leonard Phillips, IJS, p. 78.

103. Ibid., 79.

104. Ibid., 79, 91. None of these musicians could be found in the Denver City Directory for 1930, except Art Bronson (p. 598).

105. Author's interview with Leonard Phillips. Leonard Phillips, IJS, p. 78.

106. Will Jones, "Paul Cephas . . . ," *Down Beat,* June 27, 1956, p. 17; in 1931, Cephas was listed in the Minneapolis City Directory as residing at 503 Colfax Avenue North (p. 232). I wish to thank Dr. Gaye T. M. Johnson for bringing this directory listing to my attention. Author's interviews with Eddie Barefield and Le Roy "Snake" Whyte. Theo Zwicky, "Lloyd Hunter's Serenaders and the Territory Bands, Part 2," *Storyville,* August 1979, pp. 207–13, lists some of the bands that played the northern prairie states, and suggests that Young was a member of some of these, including Eli Rice's Cotton Pickers.

107. Author's interview with Eddie Barefield.

108. Leonard Phillips, IJS, p. 75, clearly states that they played with the professor in the Minneapolis area from late 1926 to 1928. When the interviewer asked, "What part of 'twenty-eight was that?" Phillips responded, "December," suggesting that they joined Bronson around that time or perhaps in early 1929. Unfortunately, the interviewer then confused matters by inquiring, "So that band [Billy Young's] played all the way from December of 'twenty-six to January of 'twenty-eight [he should have said " 'twenty-nine"]?" to

which Phillips responded, "Yeah"—thereby contradicting his earlier testimony and giving the impression that they played with the professor a year less than they actually did. Albuquerque City Directory, 1930, pp. 482–83.

109. Albuquerque City Directory, 1929, p. 470. In 1928, the *Trend*'s editor was Arba Pollard; Albuquerque City Directory, 1928, pp. 430, 363; see also Albuquerque City Directory, 1929, pp. 645, 629. Ibid., 524. The Rio Grande National Development Society, Inc., listed its officers as "Henry Outley, pres., S. T. Richard, vice pres., & J. A. Lewis, sec-treas." (ibid., p. 391); listings for H. Outley (ibid., p. 365), Richard (p. 390), and Lewis (p. 298). Brenda Dabney, Mr. Outley's granddaughter, recalled that the society's real estate holdings were in the northeast section of the city (personal communication with the author). The offices of the *Trend*, under the editorship of Arba Pollard, appeared in Albuquerque city directories for 1928 (pp. 430, 363) and 1929 (pp. 645, 629). Barbara J. Richardson, *Black Directory of New Mexico: Black Pioneers of New Mexico, A Documentary and Pictorial History*, bicentennial ed., vol. 1 (Rio Rancho, N.M.: Panorama, 1976), contains information on Dr. Lewis, who opened the People's Sanitarium; S. T. Richards, who built the Ideal Hotel; and Henry Outley. Together the three community leaders built the Booker T. Washington Sanitarium.

110. Author's interview with Leonard Phillips. Welk, *Wunnerful, Wunnerful.*

111. Author's interview with Irma Young; see also Lee Young, IJS, pp. 30–31.

6. Red Boy Blues

1. Lewis Porter, ed., *A Lester Young Reader* (Washington, D.C.: Smithsonian Institution Press, 1991), 138; author's interviews with Leonard and Clarence Phillips. "I started playing drums then in Phoenix, and we had the band. We used to play at a place called West [actually East] Lake Park. . . . That's where Lester left": Lee Young, IJS, 1:30–31.

2. As early as 1959, Martin Williams was perhaps the first to acknowledge the fact that "contrary to common belief, Young spent as much time in Minneapolis during his formative years as he did in Kansas City" (quoted in Porter, ed., *A Lester Young Reader*, 25). When Young appeared in Minneapolis in 1954, the city's African American newspaper claimed that he was coming "home" ("Famous Musician Coming Back Home," *Minneapolis Spokesman*, July 16, 1954, p. 1). I wish to thank Brian Horrigan, curator, Minnesota Historical Society, for this information.

3. Author's interviews with Leonard Phillips and Le Roy "Snake" Whyte.

4. Albuquerque City Directory, 1930, pp. 482–83. Application for marriage license #9763, Bernalillo County Clerk's Office, Albuquerque, New Mexico; the certificate itself was also included with this case number. Date and place of birth were given on these marriage documents. Dr. Wiley W. Calloway and his wife, Verna, were listed at the Dartmouth address in 1929 (City Di-

rectory, 1929, p. 502); they did not appear in the directory the following year.

5. Max Jones, "Little Pres," *Melody Maker*, April 3, 1954, p. 2. On the marriage certificate filed with the city a few days after the ceremony, however, the clerk wrote down the name Willie. Young filled out his Social Security card application (form SS-5) under the name Lester Willis Young, on June 4, 1938, in New York City; significantly, he gave his parents' address in Los Angeles as well as the New York address of his employer, Count Basie. This is one of the rare documents bearing his signature (SS-5 form obtained under the Freedom of Information Act).

6. On his Social Security card application (SS-5), he gave his birthdate as August 27, 1909. In a letter to the author dated October 8, 1996, D. Hernandez, Office of the County Clerk, County of Bernalillo, stated, "Upon researching the 1923 chapter 100 amended sections 3427 section 3431 of the New Mexico statutes NMSA, 1915, we found that the legal age to marry for male applicants in 1930 without parental consent was twenty-one."

7. Personal communication with Lee Young. Eventually they must have learned about the marriage, but they do not appear to have met the bride until she moved to Los Angeles, in around 1941. Lee also recalled that he and his brother shared a room in a house in Albuquerque. Albuquerque City Directory, 1930, pp. 440 and 483. The professor was usually listed as "William" in City Directories; see, for example, Minneapolis City Directory, 1927, p. 2509. The fact that he was categorized as a "missionery [*sic*]" (p. 483) and a "Reverend" (p. 440) in Albuquerque suggests that he worked quite closely with the church.

8. Albuquerque City Directory, 1930, pp. 625–26, 483. Ibid., 1932, p. 184; thanks to John Vittal, Information Services, Albuquerque Public Library. A Reverend J. Cox had married the groom's uncle Jacob Young in Lafourche Parish in the nineteenth century; it is tempting to wonder if perhaps these ministers were related. A Reverend James O. Cox was listed in the directory, as were businessmen and teachers with the same surname: Edward J. Cox was vice president of the First National Bank and secretary-treasurer of the First Savings Bank and Trust Co.; Miss Louise Cox, a teacher, lived at the same address as Edward; and Orvis A. Cox was a chiropodist (City Directory, 1931, p. 184).

9. Porter, ed., *A Lester Young Reader*, 133. F[rank] S. Driggs, "Ed Lewis' Story," *Jazz Review*, October 1959, pp. 23–26; see Ross Russell, *Bird Lives!: The High Life and Hard Times of Charlie "Yardbird" Parker* (1973; reprint, New York: Da Capo, 1986), 74–75.

10. This timing of this sojourn in Albuquerque more or less coincides with the recollection of the pianist John Lewis, who grew up in the city and heard Young play there during this period. See Whitney Balliett, "Profiles: Room to Live In," *The New Yorker*, November 20, 1971, p. 92.

11. Albuquerque City Directory, 1921, p. 332. Both of John Lewis's parents died when he was a child; see article "John Lewis Wins High Acclaim," *Albuquerque Tribune*, July 19, 1973, John Lewis Vertical File, Albuquerque

Public Library. Lottie Burke lived at this address in 1928 (City Directory, 1928, p. 158); ibid., 1929, p. 166; ibid., 1930, p. 572. Alfred Adams owned the boardinghouse and lived at this address with Anna, a cook, in 1928; ibid., 1928, pp. 115, 544.

12. Author's interview with Le Roy "Snake" Whyte.

13. Minneapolis City Directory, 1935; Information Services of the Minneapolis Public Library provided this information on addresses; Kansas City City Directory, 1936; the Kansas City Public Library provided information on the Youngs' address in that city. Personal communication with Adolphus Alsbrook concerning Young's Minneapolis years from 1934 to 1936.

14. Thomas Joseph Hennessey, "From Jazz to Swing: Black Jazz Musicians and Their Music, 1917–1935" (Ph.D. diss., Northwestern University, 1973), 450. This work is an excellent source regarding changes in the bands; it was later published as *From Jazz to Swing: African-American Jazz Musicians and Their Music, 1890–1935* (Detroit: Wayne State University Press, 1994). Ross Russell, *Jazz Style in Kansas City and the Southwest* (Berkeley, Calif.: University of California Press, 1971), provides a good introduction to the music of the region; see also Nathan W. Pearson Jr., *Goin' to Kansas City* (Urbana, Ill.: University of Illinois, 1987), pp. 64–76.

15. Author's interview with Leonard Phillips. In an interview with Pat Harris in 1949, Young claimed that he ran away and joined the Bostonians at the age of eighteen (Porter, ed., *A Lester Young Reader*, 138), which would have been in 1926 or 1927; in the Morrison interview (ibid., 133) he stated that he left home in 1931. Of course, we know that he ran away more than once. Similarly, he sometimes joined and then left and then rejoined bands, which complicates the dating of his tenure with them; see Lewis Porter, *Lester Young* (Boston: Twayne, 1985), xvii. While Leonard Phillips maintained that Young had only one stint apiece with the Blue Devils and King Oliver (interview with the author), he concurred that the saxophonist ran away in 1926, when the family band was in El Reno; it is conceivable that Young played with the Bostonians then.

16. Phillips, IJS, p. 68: "He came back to us in 1930 . . . back to Bronson in 1930. And he was playing alto. . . . He started playing tenor after he went to Minneapolis. . . . He got started playing tenor again." Leonard Phillips, IJS, p. 178.

17. Porter, ed., *A Lester Young Reader*, 133–34.

18. Ibid., 138, 159, 178.

19. Author's interviews with Leonard Phillips, Eddie Barefield, and Le Roy "Snake" Whyte.

20. John Tynan, "Reminiscing with Benny Carter," *Down Beat*, May 1, 1958, p. 42; Leonard Feather, "Prez," *Playboy*, September 1959, p. 68. On Carter's distinguished career, see Morroe Berger, Edward Berger, and James Patrick, *Benny Carter: A Life in American Music* (Metuchen, N.J.: Scarecrow Press, 1982).

21. Stanley Dance, *The World of Earl Hines* (New York: Charles Scribner's Sons, 1977), 208.

22. Author's interview with Le Roy "Snake" Whyte.
23. Author's interview with Leonard Phillips; Leonard Phillips, IJS, 80.
24. Leonard Phillips, IJS, pp. 69, 54.
25. Ibid., 69. For Lee Young's account of the period with Ben Webster, see Val Wilmer, "The Lee Young Story," *Jazz Journal,* January 1961, in which he relates how he nearly drowned in the Rio Grande and Webster jumped in and saved him (p. 4). The very fact that he went swimming at all suggests that this episode took place in the warmer months, toward the middle of 1929.
26. Author's interviews with Le Roy "Snake" Whyte and Eddie Barefield. The Minneapolis City Directory for 1930 listed a Frank Hines, musician, residing at 1023½ Sixth Avenue North; the 1931 directory listed a Carl Ampey, porter, at 613 Lyndale Place. I wish to thank Maggie Sloss, library assistant, Special Collections, Minneapolis Public Library, for providing this directory information.
27. Author's interview with Le Roy "Snake" Whyte. The Minneapolis City Directory for 1932 listed an El Herbert, musician, residing at 532 Aldrich Avenue North. Whyte identified the musicians in the photo. Porter, ed., *A Lester Young Reader,* 25. The 1934 Minneapolis City Directory listed a Reuben "Rook" Ganz, musician, residing at 248 Fourth Avenue South.
28. Author's interview with Le Roy "Snake" Whyte.
29. Ibid.; author's interview with Henry "Buster" Smith.
30. Author's interview with Beverly Young. Jim Fuller, "'The Pres' Left a Different Set of Memories with His Daughter," *Minneapolis Times,* August 25, 1985, pp. 16ff; article in the morgue file, Minneapolis Public Library.
31. It is possible that the couple either never married or else wed in a small town in Minnesota. Charles "Truck" Parham recalled Young's having had a relationship with a white woman in Minneapolis but was vague on details (personal communication with author).
32. Stanley Dance, *The World of Count Basie* (New York: Charles Scribner's Sons, 1980), 53. Basie actually begins his autobiography with a reminiscence of this band: Count Basie, *Good Morning Blues: The Autobiography of Count Basie,* as told to Albert Murray (New York: Random House, 1985), 3–23.
33. Author's interview with Le Roy "Snake" Whyte.
34. Ibid.
35. Ibid.
36. Ibid.
37. Ibid.
38. Ibid.
39. Porter, ed., *A Lester Young Reader,* 177.
40. Author's interviews with Young's nieces and nephews Lucille and Jimmy Tolbert, Martha Young, and Crawford Brown. The Los Angeles City Directory, 1942, p. 2638, listed two Beatrice Youngs: one, a maid, at 100 South

Windsor Boulevard, and the other at 1222 East Forty-third. They may have been the same person, at work and home addresses. In Albuquerque in 1930, Bea Young was similarly listed at two addresses.

41. Useful interviews with Buster Smith, Ernie Williams, and other Blue Devils can be found in UMoKC. The author also interviewed several musicians from the region, including Abe Bolar, Henry "Buster" Smith, Le Roy "Snake" Whyte, Eddie Barefield, Leonard Chadwick, and George Hudson.

42. Pat Harris's interview, "Pres Talks," contains an editorial aside halfway through: "Don't try to make Lester's time estimates jibe. They don't" (Porter, ed., *A Lester Young Reader,* 138). Author's interview with Leonard Phillips.

43. John Hammond, "Count Basie's Band and 'Boogie-Woogie' Pianists Tops," *Down Beat,* May 1936, p. 6; "Kansas City a Hot-Bed for Fine Swing Musicians," ibid., September 1936, pp. 1, 9.

44. See interviews in Porter, *A Lester Young Reader,* ed., 138, 142, 159, 134.

45. Author's interviews with Eddie Barefield, Le Roy "Snake" Whyte, and Leonard Phillips; personal communication with Adolphus Alsbrook.

46. Author's interviews with Le Roy "Snake" Whyte and Leonard Phillips.

47. Ralph Ellison, *Shadow and Act* (New York: Signet, 1966), 206. Balliett, "Profiles," 92. Author's interview with Leonard Phillips; Rudi Blesh, *Combo: U.S.A., Eight Lives in Jazz* (Philadelphia: Chilton, 1971), 163–64, 170–71; Ron Welburn, "Ralph Ellison's Territorial Vantage," *The Grackle,* no. 4 (1977–78), p. 7. Author's interview with Paul Quinichette; Don Gazzaway, "Conversations with Buster Smith, Part 1," *Jazz Review,* December 1959, p. 22; Walter C. Allen, *Hendersonia: The Music of Fletcher Henderson and His Musicians* (Highland Park, N.J.: published by the author, 1973), 295; personal communication with Adolphus Alsbrook, in which the Rook Ganz bassist recalled that Young joined the band in the fall of 1934 and left in the spring of 1936. Tynan, "Benny Carter," 42. See also Basie, *Good Morning Blues,* 147–50, 159–61; Harold S. Kaye, "Francis 'Doc' Whitby," *Storyville,* December 1983–January 1984, pp. 51–53. I would like to thank Frank Driggs for informing me of the existence of Theo Zwicky, "Lloyd Hunter's Serenaders and Territorial Bands, Part 2," *ibid.,* August 1, 1971, 207–11, which provided information on Young's activities and whereabouts.

48. I wish to thank the Special Collections librarians of the Kansas City Public Library and the Minneapolis Public Library for this directory information. In Porter, ed., *A Lester Young Reader,* 25, Martin Williams mentions the difficulties of dating the Oliver years.

49. Robert O'Meally, *Lady Day: The Faces of Billie Holiday* (New York: Arcade, 1991); Billie Holiday with William Dufty, *Lady Sings the Blues* (1956; reprint, New York, Avon, 1976). Author's interview with Henry "Buster" Smith.

50. Author's interview with Le Roy "Snake" Whyte.

51. Author's interview with Leonard Chadwick; personal communication with Lee Young.

7. Blue Devil Blues

1. Lewis Porter, ed., *A Lester Young Reader* (Washington, D.C.: Smithsonian Institution Press, 1991), 134, 143, 159–60. See also François Postif, "Lester: Paris, '59," *Jazz Review*, September 10, 1959, 8, on the Reno Club band; the Postif interview is reprinted in Porter, ed., *A Lester Young Reader*, 173–91. Count Basie, *Good Morning Blues: The Autobiography of Count Basie*, as told to Albert Murray (New York: Random House, 1985), 156–77, and especially Basie's observations on the Blue Devils, pp. 3–23; Ross Russell, *Jazz Style in Kansas City and the Southwest* (Berkeley, Calif.: University of California Press, 1971), 133–46, 154–55. Archie Seale, in "Around Harlem," *New York Amsterdam News*, October 2, 1937, p. 18, spelled the trumpet player's name "Paige," which Henry "Buster" Smith asserted was correct (personal communication with the author).
2. Porter, ed., *A Lester Young Reader*, 134.
3. Author's interview with Henry "Buster" Smith. Don Gazzaway, "Conversations with Buster Smith, Part 1," *Jazz Review*, December 1959, p. 22 (Parts 2 and 3 appeared in January 1960, pp. 11ff, and February 1960, pp. 13ff); ibid., 22. Buster Smith reported Page's remarks in an interview with the author. Smith's version of Young's hiring was recounted during this interview: some of the Blue Devils approached Young, explaining that they "needed a hot tenor," but he declined, so later they tried again, having bought a new Ford before returning to Minneapolis, where "Lester was still playing there in the same place." By his own account as well as others', Page had left by this time; see, for example, Frank Driggs, "About My Life in Music by Walter Page," *Jazz Review*, November 1958, pp. 12–13.
4. Author's interview with Henry "Buster" Smith.
5. Ibid.
6. Henry "Buster" Smith, IJS, pp. 83, 86–87. Lee Young, in contrast, did not think that his brother played piano (personal communication with the author).
7. W. Royal Stokes, *Swing-Era New York: The Jazz Photographs of Charles Peterson* (Philadelphia: Temple University Press, 1994), 78–79. The photo was taken on December 29, 1940.
8. Russell, "Buster Smith and the Blue Devils," in *Jazz Style*, 74–87; Driggs, "Walter Page," 15. Nathan W. Pearson Jr., *Goin' to Kansas City* (Urbana, Ill.: University of Illinois, 1987), is based on a number of interviews by Pearson and Howard Litwak with territorial musicians, several of whom were Blue Devils.
9. Author's interviews with former Blue Devils Abe Bolar, Leonard Chadwick, George Hudson, Henry "Buster" Smith, and Le Roy "Snake" Whyte.
10. Author's interviews with Henry "Buster" Smith and Leonard Chadwick; I wish to express my appreciation to Professor James Campbell for information on the commonwealth bands.
11. On the businessmen's support, see Driggs, "Page," 13. "Social Whirl," *Okla-*

homa City Black Dispatch, February 12, 1931, p. 5, on the Elks engagement. The band was particularly special for African Americans in Oklahoma and elsewhere in the territories. Its very name was understood by this ethnic group as a color reference, according to Eddie Durham (interview with the author). Also, since the sharp barbs on barbed wire were called blue devils, the band's name carried the implication that its members looked and played sharp enough to cut; my thanks to Professor James Campbell for pointing out this connection. T. Terence Holder's Dark Clouds of Joy and Gene Coy's Black Aces likewise communicated their ethnicity to Blacks with their very names, using them to express pride in their color or race. The writer Ralph Ellison contended that "the term 'Blue Devils' is English and referred to a state of psychic depression, but during the range wars in cattle country those who were given to cutting barbed wire fences were called 'Blue Devils.' Perhaps Walter Page chose the name because of its outlaw connotations" (Ron Welburn, Ralph Ellison's Territorial Vantage," *The Grackle,* no. 4 [1977–78], p. 8; my thanks to Professor Welburn for providing me with a copy of this issue). Eugene Clark's Black Devil's Minstrel, a troupe that traveled with the John Robinson Circus, may have initiated the use of the name (see the *Indianapolis Freeman,* August 16, 1919, p. 6); Druie Bess mentioned Grant Moore's Black Devils and Eddie Randall's Blue Devils in his UMoKC interview (pp. 70–71). In baseball, too, there were the Memphis Black Devils (Margaret McKee and Fred Chisenhall, *Beale Black and Blue: Life and Music on Black America's Main Street* [Baton Rouge, La.: Louisiana State University Press, 1981], 63).

12. "Whites and Negroes Dance at Forest Park," *Black Dispatch,* May 26, 1932, p. 5. The event was described as "the first interracial dance ever staged in Oklahoma City"; it was also noted that Black men danced with white women and white men with Black women—and *publicly,* which was unheard of in the South up to that time (and beyond). "Forest Park" ad, ibid., May 12, 1932, p. 8. Two years later, another such event was sponsored by the Communists; see "'Reds' Stage Big Interracial Dance on East Side," ibid., May 3, 1934, pp. 1–2. Scott Ellsworth, *Death in a Promised Land: The Tulsa Race Riot of 1921* (Baton Rouge, La.: Louisiana State University Press, 1982).

13. Welburn, "Ralph Ellison," 8. See "Where to Go and What to See: Slaughter's Hall," *Oklahoma City Black Dispatch,* January 5, 1933, p. 5; Oran Page tried out his new English horn on this occasion, suggesting that the Blue Devils liked to experiment with new sounds in Oklahoma City. Also see "His Symphony on Air," ibid., November 22, 1934, p. 8, on Ralph Ellison's trumpet playing in Oklahoma City.

14. Author's interview with Leonard Chadwick.

15. Personal communication with Leonard Chadwick.

16. Quoted from the *Dallas Times Herald,* April 17, 1960, Dallas Public Library Vertical File on jazz. Smith's early years are also recounted in Gazzaway, "Buster Smith, Part 1," 22ff; see also Connie Hershorn, "Buster Smith Recalls Career as Jazz Musician," *Dallas Morning News,* August 28, 1978, and Don Safran, "Buster Smith: Dallas Musician Stirred the Move toward

'Swing,'" *Dallas Times Herald,* April 17, 1960, both in the Dallas Public Library Vertical File on jazz.

17. Eddie Barefield recounted his experiences in Frank Driggs, "Eddie Barefield's Many Worlds," *Jazz Review,* July 1960, p. 20, and in his own IJS interview (p. 25).

18. Author's interview with Leonard Chadwick.

19. Porter, ed., *A Lester Young Reader,* 159–60. Gazzaway, "Buster Smith, Part 3," 13–14, on Smith and Parker. See also Jack McDaniels, "Buster Smith," *Down Beat,* July 11, 1956, pp. 13–14.

20. Author's interviews with Le Roy "Snake" Whyte and Henry "Buster" Smith; Russell, *Jazz Style,* 196–205; see also Ross Russell, *Bird Lives!: The High Life and Hard Times of Charlie "Yardbird" Parker* (1973; reprint, New York: Da Capo, 1996), 94–95.

21. Author's interview with Henry "Buster" Smith.

22. Author's interview with Le Roy "Snake" Whyte.

23. Ibid.

24. Ibid.; author's interview with Leonard Chadwick.

25. Author's interview with Henry "Buster" Smith; Smith recounted this tale in nearly every interview he gave.

26. Author's interview with Le Roy "Snake" Whyte.

27. Ibid.

28. Ibid.

29. Ibid.

30. Ibid.

31. Author's interviews with Henry "Buster" Smith, Le Roy "Snake" Whyte, Leonard Chadwick, and Abe Bolar. Bolar thought Young acquired the name later, after he went to New York City with Count Basie.

32. Author's interview with Henry "Buster" Smith.

33. Author's interview with Leonard Chadwick.

34. Author's interviews with Henry "Buster" Smith and Leonard Chadwick. McDaniels, "Buster Smith," 13. Smith recalled that the quest to satisfy different audiences "kept me busy writing all the time" (quoted in Pearson, *Goin' to Kansas City,* 67). Snake Whyte also arranged for the band; some have claimed that he was selected as the leader, to replace Page, but he denied this (personal communication with the author).

35. Porter, ed., *A Lester Young Reader,* 182.

36. Russell, *Jazz Style,* 74–87; on repertoire, see Pearson, *Goin' to Kansas City,* 64–76, and McDaniels, "Buster Smith," 13. Author's interview with Abe Bolar.

37. Author's interview with Le Roy "Snake" Whyte; Gazzaway, "Buster Smith, Part 2," 13.

38. Author's interviews with Le Roy "Snake" Whyte and Leonard Chadwick.

39. Author's interviews with Le Roy "Snake" Whyte and Leonard Chadwick. Frank Driggs and Harris Lewine maintained that Jesse Stone wrote specific band arrangements in Kansas City in 1928 (*Black Beauty, White Heat: A Pictorial History of Classic Jazz* [New York: Da Capo, 1995], 155). T. Terence Holder was another southwestern arranger who arranged expressly for his musicians; for Holder's oral history, see UMoKC. See also John Chilton, *Who's Who of Jazz: Storyville to Swing Street* (Philadelphia: Time-Life Special Editions, 1978), 148. The Blue Devils' recordings were made in Kansas City on November 10, 1929; originally issued on Vocalion, they can be heard on *Territory Bands, Volume 2: 1927–31* (Historical HLP-26).

40. Gunther Schüller discussed their recordings in *Early Jazz: Its Roots and Musical Development* (New York: Oxford University Press, 1968), 296–98. See Russell, *Jazz Style,* for a discussion of "Toby" (p. 106), and for information on "One O'Clock Jump" (136–37); see ibid., chapters 9–11, for the Blue Devils and Moten. Bennie Moten recorded numerous times over several years, but never with Young; nor did either Andy Kirk or King Oliver record with his band when the tenor stylist was a member.

41. See *Count Basie in Kansas City: Bennie Moten's Great Band of 1930–1932* (RCA Victor LPV-514). Moten's band was stranded in the South shortly before its scheduled recording date and barely made it to the New Brunswick, New Jersey, studios in time to make those famous recordings of December 1932. Russell, *Jazz Style,* and Chilton, *Who's Who of Jazz,* as well as the record's liner notes, are useful for sorting out the musicians involved. In late 1932, for example, the Moten brass section included trumpet players Oran Page, who had been a Blue Devil and would be a star with Basie at the Reno, and Joe Keyes, later a Basieite; the trombonists included Dan Minor and Eddie Durham, both former Blue Devils and future Basieites. The reeds were Eddie Barefield, who played with nearly every major Black swing band; Jack Washington, who would become a Basie stalwart; and Ben Webster, the only one who would not later play with Basie, though he would be a regular with Andy Kirk and other territorial bands in the region. The Moten rhythm section comprised former Blue Devil Walter Page on bass; drummer Willie McWashington; Leroy Berry, a banjoist not usually associated with the Moten–Blue Devil–Basie dynasty; and, of course, Count Basie.

42. Author's interview with Henry "Buster" Smith.

43. Author's interview with Leonard Chadwick.

44. Ibid.

45. Author's interview with Henry "Buster" Smith. The band's demise has been discussed in several works, including Gazzaway, "Buster Smith, Part 1," 22; Pearson, *Goin' to Kansas City,* 72–75, and Russell, *Jazz Style,* 86–87.

46. Leonard Phillips, IJS, pp. 106–8.

47. Porter, ed., *A Lester Young Reader,* 143.

48. "Cotillion Club Program," *Bluefield Daily Telegraph,* October 20, 1932, p. 5. Driggs, "Eddie Barefield's Many Worlds," 21; Roscoe Dunjee, "Down the Chesapeake to the Ocean," *Oklahoma City Black Dispatch,* September 17, 1931, pp. 1–2, and "A Thousand Hallowed Spots," ibid., September 24,

1931, pp. 1–2; see also idem, "In the Blue Ridge Mountains of Virginia," ibid., October 1, 1931, pp. 1, 3. Author's interviews with Annis Lynch and James Rudolph Lynch, sister and brother of Reuben Lynch; Ernie Williams, UMoKC.

49. Porter, ed., *A Lester Young Reader,* 143; author's interviews with Abe Bolar and Henry "Buster" Smith. Leonard Phillips, IJS, pp. 113. Young himself said he went with Moten first, then with Basie (Porter, ed., *A Lester Young Reader,* 143–44).

50. Author's interviews with Le Roy "Snake" Whyte, Leonard Chadwick, Henry "Buster" Smith, and Abe Bolar for the Fats Waller and Zack Whyte episodes. For Waller in Cincinnati, see Maurice Waller and Anthony Calabrese, *Fats Waller* (New York: Schirmer, 1977), 105–21.

51. Quoted in Gazzaway, "Buster Smith, Part 3," 13.

52. Ibid. Moten used a form of the commonwealth system but kept two shares for himself. A different model along the lines of the commonwealth band emerged with the Modern Jazz Quartet in the 1950s and the Art Ensemble of Chicago in the 1960s.

53. Nat Hentoff and Nat Shapiro, *Hear Me Talkin' to Ya: The Story of Jazz, as Told by the Men Who Made It* (New York: Rinehart, 1955), 297.

54. Author's interviews with Abe Bolar and Henry "Buster" Smith. Druie Bess interview, UMoKC, pp. 41–42. Buster Smith also claimed that money was not a primary concern for musicians in the Kansas City area and the Southwest: "When they'd find a good bunch of fellows they'd just stay with them—like I stayed with the Blue Devils so long." He had offers to leave, "but I like[d] the boys, they were a bunch of regular fellows—just like brothers" (interview with the author). Other band members concurred, asserting that something very special had kept the Blue Devils together.

55. Jo Jones also paid tribute to Walter Page in his IJS interview (pp. 58–59); Raymond Howell, UMoKC, pp. 64–66; Driggs, "Walter Page," 12–13. Druie Bess, UMoKC, pp. 41–42; author's interview with Leonard Chadwick. Hentoff and Shapiro, *Hear Me Talkin',* 289; Robert C. Trussell, "Saluting a Blue Devil," *Kansas City Star,* January 31, 1986, pp. 80, 86; Pearson, *Goin' to Kansas City,* 68; Williams's remarkable life can be glimpsed in his UMoKC interview.

8. Big Eyes Blues

1. Leonard Phillips, IJS, p. 103. Walter C. Allen and Brian A. L. Rust, *"King" Oliver,* revised by L[aurie] Wright, with special contributions by Frank Driggs et al. (Chigwell, England: Storyville, c. 1987), is a thoroughly researched study of the bandleader that corroborates Phillips's testimony. The authors maintain that Whitby wanted a new, gold-plated Conn tenor sax; when he couldn't persuade Oliver to get him one, he quit, in May 1933 (p. 159). Harold S. Kaye, "Francis 'Doc' Whitby," *Storyville,* December 1983–

January 1984, pp. 52–53, questions whether Young was actually Whitby's replacement.

2. Leonard Phillips, IJS, pp. 113, 103. The tenor saxophonist's stint with the New Orleans band took place in the early 1930s. Author's interviews with Leonard Phillips, in which the trumpet player variously dated the start of Young's tenure to May 1933 and also late 1933. Scholars such as Lewis Porter, in *Lester Young* (Boston: Twayne, 1985), 9–10, 108 n. 10, generally accept the same year. However, in an interview with the author, Leonard Chadwick, who left the Blue Devils in Nashville in 1932 to join King Oliver until the spring of 1933, maintained that Lester was with Oliver's band before he was. He also recalled that Young played alto saxophone in that band, not tenor. See also Fred Moore, "King Oliver's Last Tour," in Art Hodes and Chadwick Hansen, eds., *Selections from the Gutter: Jazz Portraits from "The Jazz Record"* (Berkeley, Calif.: University of California Press, 1977), 86–89. Clyde E. B. Bernhardt, *I Remember: Eighty Years of Black Entertainment, Big Bands, and the Blues,* as told to Sheldon Harris (Philadelphia: University of Pennsylvania Press, 1986), 90–102.

3. Phillips, IJS, p. 109.

4. Sam Allen also contended that Young stayed in Kansas City and was replaced by Francis Whitby, whose place Young himself had taken earlier in the year (Allen and Rust, *"King" Oliver,* 323).

5. Leonard Phillips, IJS, pp. 133–34. See Young's account in Lewis Porter, ed., *A Lester Young Reader* (Washington, D.C.: Smithsonian Institution Press, 1991), 143.

6. Leonard Phillips, IJS, pp. 106, 104.

7. Neil Leonard, *Jazz: Myth and Religion* (New York: Oxford University Press, 1987), 118–19, 36–37. Allen and Rust, *"King" Oliver,* 329.

8. Author's interviews with Leonard Phillips and Leonard Chadwick.

9. Frederic Ramsey and Charles E. Smith, *Jazzmen* (New York: Harcourt, Brace, 1939), 59–94; Martin Williams, *King Oliver* (New York: A. S. Barnes, 1961); Dave Clark, "'Educated Cat Stole My Mute Idea'—Joe Oliver," *Down Beat,* March 1, 1940, p. 8. See the recollections of musicians in Arna Bontemps and Langston Hughes, eds., *The Book of Negro Folklore* (New York: Dodd, Mead, 1958), 455, 459–73, and in particular Joe Oliver's 1937 letters to his sister, 457–59.

10. "The Real Swing King Is Dead: Joe Oliver," *California Eagle,* April 21, 1938, p. 3B. Leon Hardwick, "'Nothing New about Swing Music,' Says Earl Hines," *Kansas City Call,* August 28, 1936, p. 14. Calloway maintained that "all of this talk about swing and its recent arrival into the musical world is just a craze, for swing has been in for some time" ("Cab Calloway Makes Hit . . . ," *Kansas City Call,* June 17, 1938, p. 17). For bandleader Don Redman's opinions on the music, see "Don Redman Seeks Test of Negro Jazz," *Oklahoma City Black Dispatch,* August 23, 1934, 8.

11. Allen and Rust, *"King" Oliver,* 148, 150, 153.

12. Newspaper advertisements in the *Oklahoma City Black Dispatch* do not help to date Young's presence in the various territorial bands. However, the

Chicago Defender places him in the Blue Devils in the spring of 1932 (see Frank Büchmann-Møller, *You Just Fight for Your Life: The Story of Lester Young* [New York: Praeger, 1990], 34), and his name surfaces again in New York and Chicago Black newspapers two years later, in the spring of 1934. No southwestern newspaper ever mentioned Lester Young before 1937. He was not listed as a member of the Bennie Moten band in *Black Dispatch* ads of January 5, 1933 (p. 5); January 12, 1933 (p. 5); March 16, 1933 (p. 3); October 19, 1933 (p. 3); February 8, 1934 (p. 8); or February 15, 1938 (p. 8). In an interview with the author, Henry "Buster" Smith recalled that he and Young were with Count Basie in Little Rock when the tenor saxophonist got the wire from Henderson. For the first newspaper references to Lester Young, Walter C. Allen cited the *Chicago Defender* and the *New York Amsterdam News*, April 14, 1934, p. 9 (Allen, *Hendersonia: The Music of Fletcher Henderson and His Musicians* [Highland Park, N.J.: published by the author, 1973], 294).

13. Author's interview with Leonard Phillips.
14. Leonard Phillips, IJS: "I'd been with King Oliver about a year or more before he came back" (p. 101).
15. For breakfast Oliver once ate, according to Leonard Phillips, half a dozen eggs, half a pound of bacon, a pot of grits, and two sticks of butter, with preserves or something similar on the side (IJS, p. 130).
16. Leonard Phillips, IJS, p. 127.
17. Ibid., 150, 149.
18. Author's interviews with Leonard Chadwick and Leonard Phillips. See also "The Real Swing King," p. 3B. Bernhardt, *I Remember*, 94–95.
19. Bernhardt, *I Remember*, 92.
20. Author's interview with Leonard Chadwick. In Frank Driggs, "Goodbye Fess," *Storyville*, October–November 1976, p. 17, we learn that one night in the 1920s, when he was in his prime, Oliver won a bet that he could play his passage differently on each break in the song—and seemed ready to continue on that way endlessly.
21. Bernhardt, *I Remember*, 92. Author's interview with Jimmy Heath. In reel 3 of his November 14, 1966, interview (Hogan Jazz Archive), Paul Barbarin mentions Oliver's "talking" abilities on the horn; see the King Oliver Vertical File at the Hogan Jazz Archive. Benny Green, "The Truth About Lester Young—And No Arguments," *Crescendo*, September–October 1962, makes the claim that "[Young's] habit of honking the same note on two or even three different densities of sound, by use of a set of false fingerings which he invented for the purpose, is now a mannerism which every modern saxophonist includes in his armory" (p. 5).
22. Bernhardt, *I Remember*, 94–96.
23. Ibid., 95. Young also took his sidemen aside when they showboated (author's interview with Jesse Drakes).
24. Moore, "King Oliver's Last Tour," 86; Bernhardt, *I Remember*, 91, 100.
25. Author's interview with Leonard Phillips. Nat Hentoff and Nat Shapiro,

Hear Me Talkin' to Ya: The Story of Jazz as Told by the Men Who Made It (New York: Rinehart, 1955), 32.

26. Bernhardt, *I Remember,* 97. Oliver may have had some influence on Young's use of profanity, which Professor Young would never have permitted within his hearing. The forbidden nature of such language may have made it all the more fascinating and alluring to Lester; we know that by the 1940s, if not earlier, he was frequently employing it. He did, however, tend to limit its use to occasions when he was in the company exclusively of men, and rarely swore in front of ladies or others who he thought might take offense (author's interview with Martha Young). Even so, when former Blue Devil George Hudson visited with Young during a St. Louis engagement in the 1950s, he found him so profane that he became embarrassed and left (interview with the author).

27. Bernhardt, *I Remember,* 92; author's interviews with Leonard Chadwick, Jesse Drakes, and Leroy Jackson. Leonard Phillips, IJS, 129–30. *Jet,* February 4, 1954, contains a short article to the effect that Young had lost his false teeth and had had to stop working until he could get a new set (p. 64).

28. Leonard Phillips maintained that Young had joined Oliver in May 1933 (IJS, p. 101).

29. Porter, ed., *A Lester Young Reader,* 159.

30. Quoted in Allen and Rust, *"King" Oliver,* 330.

31. Bernhardt, *I Remember,* 96.

32. Ibid., 92.

33. Quoted in Stanley Dance, *The World of Count Basie* (New York: Charles Scribner's Sons, 1980), 268.

34. Leonard Phillips, IJS, p. 130.

35. Bernhardt, *I Remember,* 91. Pat Harris, in Lewis Porter, ed., *A Lester Young Reader,* notes that Young's friends "find themselves in the peculiar position of trying to persuade him to tolerate the majority of musicians who can't meet his standards and, on the other hand, getting others to try and understand the Pres" (p. 137). She goes on to quote a fellow musician: "'Lester Young has been so misunderstood, underestimated, and generally shoved around . . . that he almost was pushed out of the field of top active jazz musicians.'"

36. *King Oliver in New York* (RCA Victor LPV-529).

37. Bernhardt, *I Remember,* 100. The Commodore Kansas City Six recordings can be found on *Giants of the Tenor Sax: Lester Young "Prez" and Friends* (CCD 7002). For "Sweet Georgia Brown," see *Lester Young: "Jammin' the Blues" (Soundtrack) 1944—The Apollo Concert—Harlem 1946* (30 JA 5110).

38. Albert Murray, *Stomping the Blues* (1976; reprint, New York: Da Capo, 1989), is one good account of the significance of blues among African Americans in the region. Connie Kay and Jesse Drakes, in particular, stressed Young's abiding love of the blues. Bernhardt, *I Remember,* 96. For more on Oliver's playing, see Gunther Schüller, *Early Jazz: Its Roots and Musical De-*

velopment (New York: Oxford University Press, 1968), 70–86. Author's interviews with Leonard Phillips and Leonard Chadwick.

39. Leonard Phillips, IJS, p. 150. An important difference between Oliver and Young lay in their treatment of the sidemen in their bands. Whereas Young would be known for his kindness and generosity, Oliver was a bully; he also spoke harshly to band members who were late or did not know their parts (Bernhardt, *I Remember*, 97–99).

40. Allen and Rust, *"King" Oliver*, 325.

41. Leonard Phillips, IJS, pp. 113–14. Except for "Tiger Rag," Oliver did not particularly like fast tunes, which distinguished his orchestra from many of the swing bands of the 1930s; see Lew Wright et al., "Ladies and Gentlemen . . . THE KING," *Storyville*, April–May 1973, p. 147.

42. Leonard Phillips, IJS, p. 116.

43. Ibid., 138–39.

44. Hardwick, "'Nothing New,'" 14.

45. Whitney Balliett, "Profiles: Room to Live In," *The New Yorker*, November 20, 1971, p. 96. See the photograph on the front of *Lester Young in Washington, D.C., 1956* (Pablo OJCCD-782–2 (2308–219). Author's interview with John Collins on Young's taste in shoes. A number of musicians recalled that he preferred soft shoes, like the ones we know as Hush Puppies.

46. Lew Wright et al., "Ladies and Gentlemen," reprints the photo on page 147. In his autobiography, Frank Marshall Davis described bellbottoms as "a new style of trousers with legs large enough for guests." A college student in the 1920s, Davis bought some biscuit-tan trousers, twenty-three inches wide from crotch to cuff in Wichita, Kansas (*Livin' the Blues: Memoirs of a Black Journalist and Poet,* ed. Edgar Tidwell [Madison, Wisc.: University of Wisconsin Press, 1992], 96).

47. See, for example, the photo of Lester Young in his father's band in Porter, ed., *A Lester Young Reader*, opposite page 130. Author's interview with Martha Young, Irma Young's daughter.

48. Author's interview with Leonard Chadwick. See the photo captioned "The 13 Original Blue Devils," in Ross Russell, *Jazz Style in Kansas City and the Southwest* (Berkeley, Calif.: University of California Press, 1971), photo insert.

49. Druie Bess, UMoKC, pp. 75–76.

50. Author's interview with Leonard Chadwick. Raymond Howell, UMoKC, p. 61. Douglas Henry Daniels, "Los Angeles Zoot: 'Race Riot,' the Pachuco, and Black Music Culture," *Journal of Negro History,* spring 1997, 201–20.

51. Dick C. Land, "100 Million Spent for Dance Music," *Down Beat,* December 5, 1939, p. 1. For a good discussion of the motion that is so essential to both African and Afro-American music, see Olly Wilson, "The Association of Movement and Music as a Manifestation of a Black Conceptual Approach to Music-Making," in Irene V. Jackson, ed., *More Than Dancing: Essays on Afro-American Music* (Westport, Conn.: Greenwood Press, 1985), 9–24.

52. Ron Welburn, "Ralph Ellison's Territorial Vantage," *The Grackle,* no. 4

(1977–78), p. 7. It would be worthwhile to compare jazz sessions with other African American rituals, not only in Protestant churches (where there are sequences of events, aesthetic experiences, and corresponding sensibilities for different cultural dimensions and distinct states of consciousness), but also in West Indian and West African religious worship; see Morton Marks, "Uncovering Ritual Structures in Afro-American Music," in Irving I. Zaretsky and Mark P. Leone, eds., *Religious Movements in Contemporary America* (Princeton, N.J.: Princeton University Press, 1974), 60–134.

53. Quoted in Margaret McKee and Fred Chisenhall, *Beale Black and Blue: Life and Music on Black's American Main Street* (Baton Rouge, La.: Louisiana State University Press, 1981), 34.

54. Max Jones, "Little Pres," *Melody Maker,* April 3, 1954, p. 2. Author's interviews with Irma Young.

55. Porter, ed., *A Lester Young Reader,* 160–61.

56. Author's interview with Connie Kay.

57. Author's interviews with Le Roy "Snake" Whyte, Abe Bolar, and Leonard Chadwick on jive talk; but listen to the Ernie Williams UMoKC interview for a real sense of hip slang.

58. James Lincoln Collier, *Louis Armstrong: An American Genius* (New York: Oxford University Press, 1983), 221, 134. Lester Grinspoon, *Marihuana Reconsidered* (Cambridge, Mass.: Harvard University Press, 1971), 12, 16–29; see also Richard J. Bonnie and Charles H. Whitebread, *The Marihuana Conviction: A History of Marihuana Prohibition in the United States* (Charlottesville, Va.: University of Virginia Press, 1984). On the herb's spread in Africa, see Brian M. du Toit, "Man and Cannabis in Africa: A Study of Diffusion," *African Economic History,* spring 1976, pp. 17–35. I wish to thank Professor Gerald Horne for this citation.

59. Albert "Budd" Johnson, IJS, vol. 2, p. 23; vol. 3, pp. 8, 5–6. In his article "Lester Young" (*Jazz: A Quarterly of American Music,* summer 1959), John Hammond recalled that a recording session with Holiday and Young "was nearly canceled when one of the top American Record Company officials walked in and sniffed the air suspiciously" (p. 183).

60. Some of these songs can be heard on *Tea Pad Songs, Volume 1* (Stash ST-103) and *Reefer Songs/16 Original Jazz Vocals* (Stash 100). The classic "Sweet Sue," in which Budd Johnson sang a chorus in the vipers' language, was recorded and reissued on *A Very Special Stash: The Best of Reefer Songs* (Stash 120). These songs provided amusement for the band and the proper degree of relaxation for the mood they sought to create. See Bonnie and Whitebread, *The Marihuana Conviction,* 32, 42–45, 92; "Start Crusade on Reefer Traffic," *Chicago Defender,* March 9, 1935, pp. 1–2; Robert Lucas, "The Real Truth About Marijuana," *Ebony,* September 1948, pp. 46–51. "Death Is My Partner . . . I Shall Not Want," *Down Beat,* November 1937, pp. 8, 14. Billie Holiday with William Dufty, *Lady Sings the Blues* (1956; reprint, New York: Avon, 1976), 44–45.

61. Bernhardt, *I Remember,* 92; Bonnie and Whitebread, *The Marihuana Con-*

viction, 92; Albert "Budd" Johnson, IJS, Vol. 2, p. 23; author's interview with Leonard Phillips.

62. Author's interview with Leonard Phillips.
63. Leonard Phillips, IJS, p. 131.
64. Milton "Mezz" Mezzrow and Bernard Wolfe, *Really the Blues* (New York: Random House, 1946), chapter 12 and appendix 2; see footnote 61.
65. Buck Clayton with Nancy Miller Elliott, *Buck Clayton's Jazz World* (New York: Oxford University Press, 1987), 45–46, 85, 91. Gary Giddins, "Satchmo," PBS special on Armstrong (1989). Mark Gardner, "Norman Simmons Talks to Mark Gardner," *Jazz Monthly,* October 1978, p. 7. Of course, musicians were not the only smokers to initiate others. The Mexican muralist Diego Rivera, for example, introduced the movie star Errol Flynn to marijuana to help him "hear" the colors of Rivera's artwork; see Errol Flynn, *My Wicked, Wicked Ways* (1959; reprint, New York: Berkley, 1974), 173–74.

9. No Eyes Blues

1. Author's interview with Leonard Chadwick. "Special Dance at Ritz Sunday Night," *Oklahoma City Black Dispatch,* March 9, 1935, p. 8. James Simpson, another former Blue Devil, managed Oklahoma City's Rhythm Club, the only nightspot "operated for colored this side of Kansas City" ("Rhythm Club," *Black Dispatch,* August 22, 1935, p. 8); the club was air-conditioned, and Charlie Christian's older brother, Edward, also a regular contributor to the *Dispatch,* provided the music. Author's interviews with Clarence and Leonard Phillips and Abe Bolar.
2. James E. Alsbrook, "Duke Ellington Calls Jazz a State of Mind," *Kansas City Call,* September 24, 1937 (city edition), p. 8.
3. See Albert Raboteau, *Slave Religion: The "Invisible Institution" in the Antebellum South* (New York: Oxford University Press, 1978), on Black religion and practices during the antebellum era.
4. Francis Bebey, *African Music: A People's Art* (New York: L. Hill, 1975), and John Miller Chernoff, *African Rhythm and African Sensibility: Aesthetics and Social Action in African Music Idioms* (Chicago: University of Chicago Press, 1979), 126.
5. J. H. Kwabena Nketia, *The Music of Africa* (New York: W. W. Norton, 1974), and Alan P. Merriam, *African Music in Perspective* (New York: Garland, 1982), clarify African music and the music-culture concept. On African religions in the New World, see Migene Gonzalez-Wippler, *Santeria: African Magic in Latin America* (Garden City, N.Y.: Anchor, 1975); Seth and Ruth Leacock, *Spirits of the Deep: A Study of an Afro-Brazilian Cult* (Garden City, N.Y.: Anchor, 1975); and Alfred Metraux, *Voodoo in Haiti,* trans. Hugo Charteris (1959; reprint, New York: Shocken, 1972). See Morton Marks,

"Uncovering Ritual Structures in Afro-American Music," in Irving I. Zaretsky and Mark P. Leone, *Religious Movements in Contemporary America* (Princeton, N.J.: Princeton University Press, 1974), 60–114, for an excellent analysis of similarities between New World cults, particularly jazz, and African ritual.

6. Lewis Porter, ed., *A Lester Young Reader* (Washington, D.C.: Smithsonian Institution Press, 1991), 186.

7. Author's interview with Eddie Barefield.

8. Albert "Budd" Johnson, IJS, vol. 5, pp. 42–43. Jo Jones voices similar ideas about the spirituality of jazz in IJS, vol. 1, pp. 54–56, and in Dan Morgenstern, "Taking Care of Business," *Down Beat,* March 25, 1965, p. 35.

See the quote on the frontispiece of Gary Giddins, *Riding on a Blue Note: Jazz and American Pop* (New York: Oxford University Press, 1981), which is excerpted from Duke Ellington, *Music Is My Mistress* (Garden City, N.Y.: Doubleday, 1973); author's interview with Eddie Barefield.

A number of bebop-era musicians, including the tenor saxophonists Dexter Gordon and Sonny Rollins and the pianist Hampton Hawes, the son of a minister, noted the rather serious dimensions of the musician's life. Hawes, for example, contended that there was a truth in all of us to be called out by the music: "I try to play for God . . . for the Creator . . . like my body is a tool, if I think deep enough and try to let the truth come out, then I can bring something to the audience." For Hawes, music was a means of communicating on a spiritual plane: "To me music is God so I play for God. . . . If [the audience] is thinking deep, the same shit will be coming out of them. . . . I believe everybody is God, everybody has God in him so just let it come out." Hawes's very language here resonates with a blending of the sacred and profane that recalls the same characteristic in West African culture and, closer to home, in the irreverent wit and rebelliousness of Lester Young. On Hawes, see Art Taylor, *Notes and Tones* (New York: Perigee, 1982), 182.

Dexter Gordon, for his part, maintained that "music is a philosophy. It's a way of life" (*Jazz Spotlite News,* fall–winter 1980, p. 33), while Rollins claimed that "music was sacred to him" (Nat Hentoff, "Sonny Rollins," *Down Beat,* November 28, 1956, p. 14, and Bret Primack, "Sonny Rollins," ibid., January 25, 1979, p. 12).

On "life forces," see Cyril Daryll Forde, *African Worlds: Studies in Cosmological Ideas and Social Values of African Peoples* (New York: Oxford University Press, 1960). Charlie Parker, one of the most creative artists of the bebop era, could recite Bible verses from memory as a youngster. He became a legend for his musical abilities but was also known for his aggressively antimaterialist stance. When asked what religion he practiced, he once responded, "I am a devout musician" (quoted in Ross Russell, *Bird Lives!: The High Life and Hard Times of Charlie [Yardbird] Parker* [1973; reprint, New York: Da Capo, 1986], 270).

Not only Young but southwestern music in general, and the Basie band in particular, were often characterized by musicians as having important humanistic and sometimes spiritual dimensions. The bassist Gene Ramey, a native of Austin, Texas, stressed the church origins of the western beat and the kind of social relations that prevailed among band members. The backbeat that he claimed distinguished the western rhythm, which allowed listeners to relax, "came from the camp meeting[s]" of the churches and tent revivals of the rural Southwest—and increasingly, in the early twentieth century, from the region's cities as well (Ramey, IJS, vol. 4, pp. 17–18).

9. "Self-taught musically . . . , [Duke] considers himself a missionary in his particular effort—the popularization of Negro music" ("Mae West Selected Duke's Band for 'It Ain't No Sin,'" *Kansas City Call,* May 18, 1934, p. 3).

10. Arna Bontemps, *Father of the Blues: An Autobiography of W. C. Handy* (1941; reprint, New York: Da Capo, 1970), 10. Alan Lomax, *Mister Jelly Roll: The Fortunes of Jelly Roll Morton, New Orleans Creole and "Inventor of Jazz"* (New York: Grossett and Dunlap, 1950), 225–26; Buck Clayton with Nancy Miller Elliott, *Buck Clayton's Jazz World* (New York: Oxford University Press, 1987), 86.

11. Leonard Feather, "Prez," *Playboy,* September 1959, p. 54; see also the classic Allan Morrison interview, "You Got to Be Original, Man," and the Nat Hentoff interview for the clearest expressions of Young's ideas (Porter, ed., *A Lester Young Reader,* 131–35, 157–64). The pianist Bobby Scott also discussed Young's goals, in "The House in the Heart," *Gene Lee's Jazz Newsletter,* September 1983, pp. 1–6.

12. Author's interview with Buddy Tate.

13. Author's interview with Sadik Hakim. Lee Young and his niece Martha both stressed that Lester was not religious in the usual sense.

14. Bobby Scott interview with video maker Bruce Fredericksen, circa 1985; I would like to thank Mr. Fredericksen for kindly sharing this interview with me. His video about Young is entitled *Song of the Spirit.*

15. Similarly, Hampton Hawes rebelled first against his parents' rules, by staying home on Sundays to play blues on the family piano, and then later against U.S. military discipline, when he was a soldier; see Hampton Hawes and Don Asher, *Raise Up Off Me: A Portrait of Hampton Hawes* (1974; reprint, New York: Da Capo, 1979). For examples of rebellious youngsters who became ministers, see Adam Clayton Powell Jr., *Marching Blacks: An Interpretive History of the Rise of the Black Common Man* (New York: Dial, 1945), and Malcolm X with Alex Haley, *The Autobiography of Malcolm X* (New York: Grove, 1965).

16. Author's interview with Barney Kessel. The guitarist contended, "I believe that not only jazz, but . . . all music, in its highest forms . . . is definitively spiritual." The saxophonist Lee Konitz also mentioned Young's "pure sound. . . . That real beautiful tenor sound" (quoted in Leslie J. Pythian, "Farewell to Prez," *Jazz Monthly,* June 1959, p. 29).

17. Author's interview with Paul Quinichette.

18. Dizzy Gillespie interview with Bruce Fredericksen, circa 1985; I wish to thank Mr. Fredericksen for providing me with a copy of this interview.

19. Author's interview with Harry "Sweets" Edison.

20. Ibid.

21. Author's interview with Earle Warren.
22. Author's interview with Buddy Tate.
23. Porter, ed., *A Lester Young Reader*, 131–34.
24. Ibid., 183, 133. When asked about Coleman Hawkins's influence in the course of the the Morrison interview, Young responded with a hint of irritation, as if he felt that his questioners had not been paying attention: "Must a musician always get his ideas from another musician? . . . I never did have a favorite tenor. I never heard much of Hawk except an occasional record" (ibid., 134).
25. Ibid., 188.
26. Ibid., 186.
27. Ibid., 168.
28. Ibid., 170, 181.
29. Louis Armstrong, *Swing That Music* (1936; reprint, New York: Da Capo, 1993), 121.
30. Author's interview with the saxophonist Bert Etta Davis.
31. Ralph Ellison, *Shadow and Act* (New York: Signet, 1966), 206. Ellison's dating of the event may be questioned. His observation that on this occasion Young "played with and against Lem Johnson, Ben Webster . . . and other old members of the Blue Devil Orchestra" does not seem to be consistent with the date he assigns it (1929). If Webster was learning saxophone from Professor Young and his elder son in 1929 and 1930, he would not likely have been battling Lester at that early date.
32. Ibid.
33. Ibid., 231; Rudi Blesh, *Combo: U.S.A., Eight Lives in Jazz* (Philadelphia: Chilton, 1971), 168–71. The Oklahoma City Directory for 1925 listed a Hallie H. Richardson living at 619 Kate Avenue; a George Richardson operating a rooming house at 721 Kelham Avenue; a Hardie Richardson who worked as a hallboy at Huckens Hotel; and several others. In the 1932 directory, Hallie Richardson was listed with the Elk Horn Shining Parlor and the Ready Cab Company; he and his wife, Georgene, lived in the rear of 434 NE Fourteenth Street.
34. Brian Case, "Buddy Tate and the President," *Melody Maker*, December 1, 1979, 37. One possible site for the jam session was the Booker T. Washington Hotel at 115½ North Main Avenue; according to city directories, a William I. and Edith Smith were associated with that establishment in 1929–1933, though no indication was provided of their status with the hotel—that is, whether they were the owners or managers. Letter of May 2, 1995, to the author from Directory Services, Tulsa Public Library.
35. Case, "Buddy Tate and the President," 37.
36. Buddy Tate, IJS, pp. 46–47.
37. Stanley Dance, *The World of Earl Hines* (New York: Charles Scribner's Sons, 1977), 209–10.
38. Author's interview with Eddie Durham.

39. Nat Hentoff and Nat Shapiro, *Hear Me Talkin' to Ya: The Story of Jazz, as Told by the Men Who Made It* (1955; reprint, New York: Dover Publications, Inc., 1966), 292–93; Mary Lou Williams dated the jam session to early 1934, "because Prohibition had been lifted and whiskey was freely on sale." Linda Dahl, *Morning Glory: A Biography of Mary Lou Williams* (New York: Pantheon, 1999), reports the version Williams gave in *Melody Maker* without criticism (p. 86).
40. Gene Ramey, IJS, vol. 2, p. 34.
41. Williams's recollections appeared in one of a series of articles entitled "The Battle of the Tenor Kings," *Melody Maker,* May 1, 1954, p. 11. Hentoff and Shapiro, *Hear Me Talkin',* 293. Walter C. Allen, *Hendersonia: The Music of Fletcher Henderson and His Musicians* (Highland Park, N.J.: published by the author, 1973), 293–94.
42. *Chicago Defender,* April 14, 1934, p. 9, and ibid., June 16, 1934, p. 8, both quoted in Allen, *Hendersonia,* 294–95.
43. Allen, *Hendersonia,* 290, 293–95. *Kansas City Call,* December 22, 1933, p. 5. However, the drummer Richard Dickert, like Mary Lou Williams, claimed that the event took place in January 1934 (Professor James Campbell, personal communication with the author). On the Cherry Blossom, see "Deluxe Night Club to Open April 3," *Kansas City Call,* April 7, 1933, p. 6A. According to Kansas City's City Directory, the Cherry Blossom was located at 1822 Vine Street (information provided to the author by the staff of the Kansas City Public Library). The Cherry Blossom had previously been the Eblon and was on the TOBA circuit. The ragtime composer James Scott was its musical director at one time (Ross Russell, *Jazz Style in Kansas City and the Southwest* [Berkeley, Calif.: University of California Press, 1971], 43).
44. Allen, *Hendersonia,* 586; *St. Louis Argus,* December 1, 1933, p. 3.
45. Count Basie, *Good Morning Blues: The Autobiography of Count Basie,* as told to Albert Murray (New York: Random House, 1985), 148.
46. Ibid., 148; Williams, "Battle of the Tenor Kings," 11.
47. Basie, *Good Morning Blues,* 148–49. Booker Pittman, grandson of Tuskegee president Booker T. Washington, made the point that it was often difficult to determine who had won a cutting session (UMoKC, p. 119).
48. Porter, ed., *A Lester Young Reader,* 144, 190.
49. Ibid., 190.
50. Leonard Phillips, IJS, p. 134.
51. Porter, ed., *A Lester Young Reader,* 139. As Young explained, "Moten was stranded, too, and all the men put him down; Count [Basie] had been playing piano with him, but they'd been squabbling, so Count cut out and took over most of the band while Bennie Moten and George Lee formed another group, and I went with them." Later he joined Basie (ibid., 143).
52. Case, "Buddy Tate and the President," 37.
53. Porter, ed., *A Lester Young Reader,* 139.
54. Ibid., 144, 160.

55. Ibid., 160.
56. Buddy Tate, IJS, p. 69. Frank Büchmann-Møller, *You Just Fight for Your Life: The Story of Lester Young* (New York: Praeger, 1990), 51.
57. See Gene Fernett, *Swing Out: Great Negro Dance Bands* (Midland, Mich.: Pendell, 1970), 79, on the exchange of saxophonists; quoted in Allen, *Hendersonia*, 295.
58. Bill Esposito, "Buddy Tate," *Jazz Magazine*, summer 1979, p. 56.
59. Ibid.
60. Porter, ed., *A Lester Young Reader*, 139.
61. Author's interview with Andy Kirk.
62. Dance, *Earl Hines*, 157.
63. Ibid., 157–58.
64. Charlie Parker had just such an experience; see Russell, *Bird Lives!*, 84–85. The trumpet player Robert Porter recalled that when he was young, a bandleader once asked him to sit in and play, but then, "after eight bars" of listening to him, gave him fifty dollars to leave the bandstand instead; Porter noted, "That was the most shocking thing that ever happened to me" ("Reflections of a Public Servant: Robert Porter," *California Jazz Now* 1, no. 7 [December 1991]: 5–15).
65. "Earl Hines' 'Jekyll-Hyde' Role," *Oklahoma City Black Dispatch*, March 15, 1934, p. 2.
66. Basie, *Good Morning Blues*, 3–84.
67. Porter, ed., *A Lester Young Reader*, 138–39. Young recounted his joining the Basie band in a number of interviews; see, for example, ibid., 177.
68. "Cab Calloway Band Mobbed at Memphis White Dance . . . ," *Oklahoma City Black Dispatch*, September 27, 1934, p. 8. Milton Hinton and David G. Berger, in *Bass Line: The Stories and Photographs of Milt Hinton* (Philadelphia: Temple University Press, 1988), 110, 122, 132–34, discuss some of the problems faced by Black bands traveling in the South.
69. Mary Lou Williams, IJS, pp. 85–86.
70. Roy Wilkins with Tom Mathews, *Standing Fast: The Autobiography of Roy Wilkins* (New York: Viking, 1982), 60–61.
71. Mary Lou Williams, IJS, pp. 85–86; Wilkins, *Standing Fast*, 63–70. In the 1930s, the degrading racist practices and custom of segregation on the U.S. Army post at Fort Leavenworth, Kansas, where the Tenth Cavalry was stationed, became public knowledge. The "Buffalo Soldiers," as they were known, were famous for the valorous service they had performed on the frontier in the Indian wars and in Cuba and the Philippines during the Spanish-American War; the racist treatment they were subjected to both on and off the post was to the shame of the cause they had served. See, for example, "Expose Discrimination against Tenth Cavalry at Leavenworth," *Kansas City Call*, September 16, 1938, pp. 1, 10.
72. Nelson Peery, *Black Fire: The Making of an American Revolutionary* (New York: The New Press, 1994), 29.

73. Ibid., 30.
74. Porter, ed., *A Lester Young Reader,* 177.
75. Kansas City City Directory, 1936, p. 1725; he did not appear in the directories for 1933 and 1934. I would like to thank the Special Collections staff of the Kansas City Public Library, Kansas City, Missouri, for this directory information.
76. Basie, *Good Morning Blues,* 167–68, 170. "Buster Smith, Saxophonist, New with Claude Hopkins," *Kansas City Call,* August 22, 1936, p. 15.
77. Basie, *Good Morning Blues,* 167.
78. Ibid.
79. Ibid.
80. Ibid.
81. Author's interview with Harry "Sweets" Edison.
82. Jo Jones, IJS, pp. 54–55.
83. Ibid.
84. Dom Cerulli, "Jo Jones," *Down Beat,* June 26, 1958, 17.
85. Author's interview with Buddy Tate.
86. Gene Ramey, IJS, vol. 3, p. 9.
87. If such noteworthy characteristics were limited to the Basie band, or even to certain southwestern bands, then one could fairly claim that along with a propensity for riff melodies and head arrangements, these identifying qualities of territorial bands were lacking in eastern bands. However, this does not seem to be the case. In commenting on his band's longevity at the celebration of its twentieth anniversary, Duke Ellington admitted, "A great amount of our success is due to the fact that the band has always been not just a business [venture] but more of a fraternal organization whose friendships are made and kept" (quoted in Buddy Howard, "Ellington Celebrates Twentieth Year in Music," *Down Beat,* April 1, 1942, p. 4). Ellington also encouraged particular social values that gave his music its distinctiveness. As in the Basie band, an atmosphere was maintained in which, with few words, each individual was expected to find his own way to musical and social harmony with the others. Like the southwestern musicians who preferred not to read music, Ellington took pride in his lack of formal conservatory training.

    His rehearsal style mystified the *Kansas City Call* (Tulsa edition) reporter in 1934 ("Mae West Selected Duke's Band for 'It Ain't No Sin,'" May 18, 1934, p. 3). Basieites stressed the emotional element in their band, as Ellington did in his own: "This music is 98 percent emotional and cannot be written down on paper," he explained. In this respect it was like good church music, a spontaneous manifestation of the spirit visiting at that specific moment, rather than a premeditated conception; according to the journalist, "cacophony" reined during the Ellington band rehearsals. Still, it was a cacophony with "a definite purpose—the establishment of individualism," with each band member adapting his part as he saw fit. Then "less discord [followed, then some] theme development, then a mood and finally an agreeable instrumental whole." Like Basie, Ellington refused to write out parts for his band members, though both were known to write out the melody as a guide (ibid.).

The very language that Ellington employed furthermore indicated that the jazz slang of Lester Young and his fellow Basieites was, like their music, a variation of an African American idiom rather than a unique and distinct phenomenon. It also suggested the church's influence: instead of requesting a solemn *andante,* Ellington revealed how close jazz remained to Black people's religious roots when he called out, "Come on, boys, go to church" to set the mood for a selection ("Duke Ellington's Trip Abroad . . . ," *Kansas City Call,* June 23, 1933, p. 3A).

88. Porter, ed., *A Lester Young Reader,* 191.

10. Poundcake

1. On the Basieites, see Stanley Dance, *The World of Count Basie* (New York: Charles Scribner's Sons, 1980). Many interviews quoted in this work were conducted for the National Endowment for the Humanities; they may be found in their entirety at the Institute of Jazz Studies (IJS), Rutgers University, Newark, New Jersey. Also see Dicky Wells, *The Night People: Reminiscences of a Jazzman,* as told to Stanley Dance (New York: Crescendo, 1971). Author's interview with Henry "Buster" Smith concerning his co-leadership, with Basie, of the Reno Club band. See John Hammond with Irving Townsend, *On Record: An Autobiography* (New York: Penguin, 1981), 165–68.

2. Count Basie, *Good Morning Blues: The Autobiography of Count Basie,* as told to Albert Murray (New York: Random House, 1985), 145–46. In a 1949 interview with Leonard Feather, Young explained that after the Blue Devils broke up, many band members left Moten, who was stranded, and went with Count Basie ("Here's Pres," *Melody Maker,* July 15, 1950, p. 3; the interview is reprinted in Lewis Porter, ed., *A Lester Young Reader* [Washington, D.C.: Smithsonian Institution Press, 1991]). Young first went with Moten and George Lee, but then rejoined Basie. By all accounts, Young was with Basie in early 1934. Basie could not later recall his first meeting with Young—"I cannot pinpoint the first time I became aware of him" (*Good Morning Blues,* 147)—but he did note that at one time the saxophonist had played in a band led by Bennie Moten and George E. Lee at Club Harlem in Kansas City (ibid.). Minneapolis's Cotton Club was one of a number of enterprises run by Ben Wilson, known as the "mayor" of North Minneapolis; it was located at 718 Sixth Avenue North in 1928 (information provided by the staff of Special Collections, Minneapolis Public Library).

For a Basie discography, see Chris Sheridan, *Count Basie: A Bio-Discography* (Westport, Conn.: Greenwood, 1986), appendix 1; Basie discusses the band's growth in his *Good Morning Blues,* 156–206. "Count Bassie's [*sic*] Band Heads New Bill at the Apollo Theatre," *New York Age,* June

5, 1937, p. 9, reported that the Music Corporation of America regarded "Basie's organization as the most prominent 'up and coming' colored band in America."

3. Porter, ed., *A Lester Young Reader,* 138.

4. Ibid., 159.

5. Basie, *Good Morning Blues,* 158.

6. Ibid., 158–59. Hammond, *On Record,* 165–68. Tom Palmer, "The Story of Count Basie and His Band," *Music and Rhythm* 2 October 1941, 22–23. On Jo Jones, besides the IJS interview with him, see Dom Cerulli, "Jo Jones," *Down Beat,* June 26, 1958, p. 17, and Richard Brown, "Ain't He Sweet? Jo Jones," *Down Beat,* February 8, 1979, p. 19; Earle Warren, "Earl Warren's Story," as told to Valerie Wilmer, *Jazz Journal,* August 1960, pp. 11–12ff. IJS interviews with Jo Jones, Harry Edison, Buck Clayton, Marshal Royal, Buddy Tate, Freddie Green, and author's interviews; on Walter Page, see Frank Driggs, "About My Life in Music by Walter Page," *Jazz Review,* November 1958, pp. 12–15, and Humphrey Lyttelton, "Walter Page—He Originated the Basie Sound," *Melody Maker,* January 11, 1958, p. 5.

7. Buck Clayton with Nancy Miller Elliott, *Buck Clayton's Jazz World* (New York: Oxford University Press, 1986), 84.

8. Basie, *Good Morning Blues,* 164.

9. John Hammond, "Lester Young," *Jazz: A Quarterly of American Music,* summer 1959, p. 182.

10. Basie, *Good Morning Blues,* 159, 5.

11. Ibid., 161. Shortly after Young died, Basie's depiction was a bit more fulsome: Young's sound, he noted, "was like nothing we'd ever heard. And it was consistent"—so much so, in fact, that he "never had a bad night" the whole time he was with Basie. The tenor stylist was the ultimate professional: "No matter what happened to him personally, he never showed it in his playing. I can only remember him as being beautiful" (quoted in Leonard Feather, "Prez," *Playboy,* September 1959, p. 68).

12. Dave Dexter, "Critics in the Doghouse," *Down Beat,* July 1939, p. 18; Palmer, "Story of Count Basie," 22–23. It is worth noting that Coleman Hawkins wondered why, if the Reno band was really as good as John Hammond claimed, it was necessary to enlarge it; see *Coleman Hawkins: A Documentary* (Riverside RLP 12-117/118). Among those who joined were midwesterners Harry Edison and Earle Warren, at least one easterner—Freddie Green, who had been born in South Carolina but had grown up in New York—and the small southwestern contingent of Eddie Durham and Ed Lewis.

13. Hammond, *On Record,* 168; Basie made the suggestion for the entertainers' dance to manager Sol Steibold. As the bandleader explained, this term for the breakfast dance "was an *in* jive word among entertainers those days. It didn't really have anything to do with color or ghosts directly." The term applied to people in show business—those Kansas Citians whom Basie invited to dine, to dance, and to enjoy the music (Basie, *Good Morning Blues,* 162).

14. John Hammond, "Count Basie's Band and 'Boogie Woogie' Pianists Tops," *Down Beat,* May 1936, p. 6.
15. "Six Bands to Play for Big Ball Monday," *Kansas City Call,* May 1, 1936, p. 9; "Musicians Union Will Stage Its Labor Day Ball at Labor Temple," ibid., September 4, 1936, p. 13; Basie, *Good Morning Blues,* 176.
16. Leon B. Hardwick, "Count Basie Going Good in the East," *Kansas City Call,* October 22, 1937 (national edition), p. 19; ibid., December 4, 1936, p. 9. The *Chicago Defender* used identical words in covering the band that same week in late 1936, suggesting that Basie's press agent supplied the information ("Count Basie to Play Roseland Ballroom" and "Famous Band Leaves Grand Terrace . . . ," *Chicago Defender,* December 5, 1936, p. 12). The commonwealth roots of these bandsmen may have resulted in the Basieites' assuming an important role in recruiting for the band; the prior experience of Smith, Page, and Clayton as leaders was also to the benefit of the band. Upon the recommendation of his fellow bandsmen, Basie signed on Herschel Evans (tenor sax) and Caughey Roberts (alto sax) in the fall of 1936; at that time, the saxophone section consisted of alto, baritone (Ronald "Jack" Washington, a Kansas City stalwart), and two tenors. Perhaps they were contacted when Young traveled to Los Angeles in Basie's car in the fall of 1936 to visit his ailing father. Later Basie would hire other musicians on the recommendation of his sidemen (Basie, *Good Morning Blues,* 169–70, 159, 192).
17. The *New York Age* referred to the band as "one of the outstanding radio orchestras" in the country; unfortunately, while advertising upcoming performances, Black newspapers frequently reported such events as financial endeavors rather than as cultural presentations ("Apollo Books New Orchestras," *New York Age* February 27, 1937, p. 9). Cheryl Lynn Greenberg, *"Or Does It Explode?": Black Harlem in the Great Depression* (New York: Oxford University Press, 1981).
18. Warren, "Earl Warren's Story," 11.
19. This is Buck Clayton's assessment; see Clayton, *Buck Clayton's Jazz World,* 95–96. He also claimed that "cheap and over-used instruments . . . made us play out of tune" (ibid., 100).
20. Author's interview with John Collins; the guitarist also jammed with Eldridge, Young, and others (both African Americans and whites) in Chicago's Three Deuces, a white club. "Count Basie, 'Swing King,' to Play," "Free Candy, Turkey at Party (Galaxy of Stars to Entertain You)," and "Billikens to Dance November 21 for Turkeys," *Chicago Defender,* November 14, 1936, p. 28. For Basie's, Clayton's, and Hammond's accounts, see, respectively, Basie, *Good Morning Blues,* 179–84; Clayton, *Buck Clayton's Jazz World,* 95–96; and Hammond, *On Record,* 172. Basie was under contract to Decca, whose representative, Dave Kapp, had heard about him in Kansas City and, claiming to be working with John Hammond, persuaded him to sign a contract, even though Basie had already made a verbal commitment to Hammond and Brunswick. The bandleader would later regret signing with Decca (Basie, *Good Morning Blues,* 167). Franklyn Frank, "Radio, Stage and Screen (Chicago's Congo)," *California Eagle,* November 20, 1936, p. 10.

21. For years the records were thought to have been made in October, but we now know that this was not the case; John Hammond provided the actual date of the recording session (letter of October 26, 1983, to Lewis Porter; my thanks to Professor Porter for this information). "Shoeshine Boy" and a variant, "Roseland Shuffle," are discussed in some detail in Professor Lawrence Gushee, "Lester Young's 'Shoeshine Boy,'" in *Report of the Twelfth Congress of the International Musicologist Society,* ed. D. Heartz and Bonnie Wade (Philadelphia: American Musicological Society, 1981), 151–63 (reprinted in Porter, ed., *A Lester Young Reader,* 224–254); Young's first recordings are analyzed in Lewis Porter, "Lester Leaps In: The Early Style of Lester Young," *The Black Perspective in Music,* spring 1981, pp. 3–23; and still other recordings have been reviewed in a computer analysis by Lewis Porter, the results of which may be found in his *Lester Young* (Boston: Twayne, 1985). Jan Evensmo, *The Tenor Saxophone and Clarinet of Lester Young, 1936–1949* (Oslo: Evensmo, Norway, 1983 ed.), focuses on the solos and lists the recordings; Jorgen Grunnet Jepsen, *A Discography of Lester Young* (Copenhagen: Karl Emil Knudsen, 1968), has been augmented by Frank Büchmann-Møller, *You Got to Be Original, Man: The Music of Lester Young* (New York: Praeger, 1990). Luc Delannoy, *Lester Young: Profession: President* (Paris: Denöel, 1987), also analyzes the saxophonist's life. John Hammond or Michael Brook, liner notes to Count Basie's *Super Chief* (Columbia CG 31224). For the review, see Paul Edward Miller, "Too Much Shoddy Sentiment . . . ," *Down Beat,* April 1937, p. 14. Basie, *Good Morning Blues,* 18–81.

22. John Hammond, "Goodman 'Killer' Arrangement Detracts from Band Musicianship," *Down Beat,* February 1937, pp. 7–9. The lineup in the band at the time (1936–37) was given as Cauchey [*sic*] Roberts, Harshell [*sic*] Evans, Lester Young, and Ronald Washington (saxes); W. O. Clayton, Carl Smith, and Joe Keyes (trumpets); Gerald C. Williams, Daniel Minor, and George Hunt (trombones); and Count Basie, Jo Jones, and Walter Page (rhythm) (Jack Ellis, "The Orchestras," *Chicago Defender,* November 21, 1936, p. 10). Hammond, *On Record,* 176–77.

23. Basie, *Good Morning Blues,* 187.

24. Hardwick, "Count Basie Going Good," 19.

25. Ibid. Dexter, "Critics in the Doghouse," 18; Palmer, "Story of Count Basie," 22–23. Count Basie and His Orchestra, *Do You Wanna Jump . . . ?* (HEP CD 1027) and *The Lester Young Story, Volume 4: Lester Leaps In* (Columbia 34843).

26. Refer to the CDs of Count Basie, *The Complete Decca Recordings* (Decca CGRD-3-611), and the records *Count Basie and His Orchestra—1937* (Jazz Kings QSR 2412) and *The Lester Young Story, Volume 3: Enter the Count* (Columbia C-3481 and C-3482).

27. Ross Russell, *"Bird Lives!": The High Life and Hard Times of Charlie (Yardbird) Parker* (1973; reprint, New York: Da Capo, 1996), 89–93. Idem, *Jazz Style in Kansas City and the Southwest* (Berkeley, Calif.: University of California Press, 1971), 141, 183.

28. "Chick, Basie Battle It Out in Swing Time," *New York Amsterdam News,*

January 22, 1938, p. 16; "Basie vs. Goodman," ibid., June 18, 1938, sect. 2, p. 8; "Votes Contradict Swing Critics," *Metronome,* February 1938, p. 20; "Ickie's Antics Submerge Goodman-Basie Battle," *Metronome,* July 1938, p. 7. Sheridan, *Count Basie,* appendix 1, 49–57. In "Count Basie to Broadcast to Europe," the *Kansas City Call* noted that "so far, no other Negro band has been signed by the British chain," though Ellington and Waller appeared on the series (July 15, 1938, p. 15). Interestingly, *Down Beat* chose to highlight the Famous Door's white singer when it reviewed the Fifty-second Street engagement: "The ace number in the show is . . . [a] white singer, who sends the band every night" ("Blind Musicians Plan Jazz Festival," *Down Beat,* August 1938, p. 28).

29. Author's interviews with John Collins and "Teddy Bear," who did not want her real name divulged. Personal communication with Lee Young.

30. See Paul Robeson, *Here I Stand* (1958; reprint, Boston: Beacon, 1988); Billie Holiday and William Dufty, *Lady Sings the Blues* (Garden City, N.Y.: Doubleday, 1956); and Hammond, *On Record.* In an article by Paul E. Miller about Duke Ellington, "The Music of My Race Is Going to Live," published in *Music and Rhythm,* May 1942, the famous composer claimed that Black music was "something more than the 'American idiom.' It is the result of our transplantation to American soil, and was our reaction in the plantation days to the tyranny we endured. What we could not say openly we expressed in music, and what we know as 'jazz' is something more than just dance music" (p. 13). See Roy Eldridge, "Jim Crow Is Killing Jazz," *Negro Digest,* October 1950, pp. 44–49, and " 'No More White Bands for Me,' Says Little Jazz," *Down Beat,* May 18, 1951, p. 1.

31. Fletcher Henderson, introduction to Paul Eduard Miller, *Down Beat's Yearbook of Swing* (1939; reprint, Westport, Conn.: Greenwood, 1978).

32. Leonard Feather, "Here's Pres!," in Porter, ed., *A Lester Young Reader,* 145. Dr. Luther Cloud, who would be introduced to Young by Professor Marshall Stearns in the late 1950s, recalled being told that the saxophonist liked neither white people nor doctors (interview with the author).

33. Author's interview with Lucille Tolbert. All the musicians I interviewed insisted that Young was intolerant of racial prejudice of any kind and, furthermore, could not understand it.

34. Young mentioned his likes and dislikes concerning singers in his 1958 interview with Chris Albertson, reprinted in Porter, ed., *A Lester Young Reader,* 169. Feather, "Here's Pres!," ibid., 146. In a "blindfold test" administered to Young ("Pres Digs Every Kind of Music," *Down Beat,* November 1954, p. 12), Leonard Feather expressed surprise at hearing the saxophonist "draw the racial distinction." Considering that Feather ranked among the better and most knowledgeable writers, it seems remarkable that he should have been taken aback by Young's response; but at the same time, his comments permit the observation that a bit of a misunderstanding occurred at this point in their interview. Nat Hentoff, "Pres," *Down Beat,* March 7, 1956, pp. 9–11. Feather's and Hentoff's pieces are also collected in Porter, ed., *A Lester Young Reader.*

35. Marshal Royal, IJS, vol. 3, p. 30.

36. Mary Lou Williams, IJS, p. 100.

37. Wilson asked, "How can you live in a Jim Crow town like this and do nothing about it?" He also confessed, "I would like to 'wake up' the masses of the Negroes to appreciate the true plight of the race. . . . That's one of my biggest ambitions" ("Swing Artists Visit Kaycee," *Kansas City Call,* September 30, 1938, p. 14, and J. E. Alsbrook, "Goodman Pianist Compares White and Negro Music," ibid., October 7, 1938, p. 17). "Billie Holiday Pays Visit to Mound City," ibid., October 21, 1938, p. 17. David Margolick, *Strange Fruit: Billie Holiday, Café Society, and an Early Cry for Civil Rights* (Philadelphia: Running Press, 2000). Dan Burley, "Backdoor Stuff," *New York Amsterdam News,* March 27, 1948, 15.

38. "Count Basie Defines 'Kultur' and 'Culture,'" *Kansas City Call,* December 30, 1938, p. 15. Typically Basie would not comment on the record when queried about or asked to support political candidates—refusing, for example, to endorse specific candidates in the late summer of 1940 in order to increase Black voter participation ("Basie Won't Throw Hat into Ring," *Down Beat,* August 15, 1940, p. 12).

39. Dan Burley, "Backdoor Stuff," *New York Amsterdam News,* April 24, 1936, p. 17. John Chilton, *Billie's Blues: A Survey of Billie Holiday's Career, 1933–1959* (London: Quartet, 1975), 15; Archie Seale, "Around Harlem," *New York Amsterdam News,* May 11, 1937, p. 18.

40. See "Du Bois Gets Rousing Welcome" (p. 9), "Robeson Amazed on Tour of Russia" (p. 11), and "Negro Population of 750,000 Faces Floods" (pp. 1–2), *New York Amsterdam News,* January 23, 1937; articles on Haile Selassie and Ethiopia may also be found in the January issues of this newspaper. Gerald Horne, *Red and Black: W. E. B. Du Bois and the African American Response to the Cold War, 1944–1963* (Albany, N.Y.: State University of New York Press, 1986); Langston Hughes, *The Big Sea* (New York: Knopf, 1940), and *I Wonder as I Wander: An Autobiographical Journey* (New York: Rinehart, 1956); and the autobiographies of James Weldon Johnson (*Along the Way: The Autobiography of James Weldon Johnson* [New York: Viking, 1933]) and Claude McKay (*A Long Way from Home* [New York: L. Furman, 1937]) are good on these years. Greenberg, *"Or Does It Explode?"*; Mark Naison, *Communists in Harlem during the Depression* (Urbana, Ill.: University of Illinois Press, 1983); Brenda Gayle Plummer, *Rising Wind: Black Americans and U.S. Foreign Affairs, 1935–1960* (Chapel Hill, N.C.: University of North Carolina Press, 1996).

41. Albertson interview, in Porter, ed., *A Lester Young Reader,* 167: "When I came to New York, in 1934 . . . I used to live at her house, with her mother . . . 'cause I didn't know my way around. And she taught me a lot of things." Author's interview with Harry Edison. Evidence of the Basieites' forming associations with specific political groups is slim, but more evidence may conceivably turn up in the future.

42. "Count Basie to Broadcast to Europe," *Kansas City Call,* July 15, 1938, p. 15; Sheridan, *Count Basie,* appendix 1, 49–56.

43. "Second (Hot Tenor) Sax," *Metronome,* January 1939, p. 14.

44. Sheridan, *Count Basie*, appendix 1, 59. *The Lester Young Story, Volume 4: Lester Leaps In* (Columbia 34843).

45. Danny Baxter, "Basie to Coast," *Kansas City Call*, September 15, 1939 (national edition), p. 16. For *Call* mentions of the band's success, see Chauncey W. Edgar, "Basie's 'Yes-Yes' a Sender," ibid., September 16, 1938, p. 16; "Harlan Leonard and Orchestra Soaring to Top," ibid., August 4, 1939, p. 16; "Chick Webb and Ella Fitzgerald 'Take' Kansas City," ibid., July 19, 1938 (Texas edition), p. 13; "Webb and Basie May Come Here," ibid., August 12, 1938, p. 15; "Count Basie to Play Here September 28," September 15, 1939 (national edition), p. 17. Sheridan, *Count Basie*, appendix 1, 51, 53. "Count Basie Congratulates Lester Young on His Choice of a Martin Frères Clarinet," *Down Beat*, April 1939, p. 5, and "Martin Frères Reaches New Peaks with the High Men in the Metronome Poll . . . ," ibid., August 1939, p. 26.

46. Frank Marshall Davis, "Rating—The Hot Records," *New York Amsterdam News*, August 26, 1939, p. 16.

47. Gordon Wright, "Four Basie Sides Highlight Lists," *Down Beat*, November 15, 1939, p. 14. "J. C. Hig. Waxes Great Blues," *Metronome*, June 1939, p. 18.

48. Julie Lyonn Lieberman, "Pro Session: Exercises for Improvisers—Lester Young's Solo on 'Jive at Five,'" *Down Beat*, March 1989, pp. 56–57.

49. *The Best of Count Basie* (MCA Records MCA 2-4050).

50. *The Lester Young Story, Volume 5: Evening of a Basieite* (Columbia 34850–34851); *The Lester Young Story, Volume 4: Lester Leaps In* (Columbia 34843); *"Prez" Leaps Again with the Kansas City Seven* (Soul Parade HHP-5015). Ross Russell, review of *Lester Young with Count Basie and His Orchestra* (Epic SAN 6031), *Jazz Review*, August 1960, pp. 25–26: Russell considered the Basie orchestra to be important for an understanding of subsequent developments in popular music, arguing that "within the Basie band, more than within the band of Goodman or Ellington, lay the sounds and rhythms of the jazz future"; these seeds, he contended, produced "bop [and] indeed everything that has developed along the main line since the days when America danced, in a thousand ballrooms now dark, across the land."

51. *Giants of the Tenor Sax: Lester Young "Prez" and Friends* (Commodore CCD 7002). The characterization of his tone as altolike is accurate with regard to certain numbers, but on "Every Tub" it sounds more like the tones of Hawkins and Evans—thicker, reedier, at least to this listener. Even the honks that critics disliked and dated from his Jazz at the Philharmonic period can be heard on the big-band version of "Oh Lady, Be Good" (*The Best of Count Basie* [MCA Records MCA 2-4050]). *Giants of the Tenor Sax: Lester Young "Prez" and Friends* (Commodore CCD 7002).

52. Milt Gabler, liner notes, *Kansas City Six and Five* (Commodore XFL14937); *Nat Cole Meets the Master Saxes* (Spotlite SPJ136); *"Prez" Leaps Again!: Lester Young with the Kansas City Seven* (Soul Parade HHP-5015). Martin Williams, *The Jazz Tradition* (New York: Oxford University Press, 1970), 115.

53. Author's interview with the guitarist John Collins, who recalled how much

Young liked the pianoless format, which he said reminded him of the "strollers." Of the MJQ, Young said, "The little things they play are their own. It's something new" (Porter, ed., *A Lester Young Reader,* 161).

54. Comments concerning the responsorial nature of the composition were made by Professor Michael White, Spanish Department, Xavier University, New Orleans, in his comments on my paper "Lester Young and New Orleans Traditions," delivered at the American Studies Association convention in New Orleans, November 1990; I wish to express my gratitude for his insights. *The Lester Young Story, Volume 4: Lester Leaps In* (Columbia 34843); *Count Basie and His Orchestra—1937* (Jazz Kings QSR 2412).

55. Deena Rosenbert, *Fascinating Rhythm: The Collaboration of George and Ira Gershwin* (New York: E. P. Dutton, 1991), 168, 190.

56. Ibid., 168, 182, 185–91, 230; "A Foggy Day" is one of the Gershwin compositions that uses the "I Got Rhythm" motif (ibid., 361).

57. *Count Basie and His Orchestra—1937* (Jazz Kings QSR 2412); *The Lester Young Story, Volume 3: Enter the Count* (Columbia JG 34840); *Lester Leaps In* (Jazz Line Serie Cicala BLJ8021); *The Lester Young Story, Volume 5: Evening of a Basieite* (Columbia 34850–34851); *Lester Young: Pres in Europe* (High Note HCD 7054).

58. *Gene Ammons All Stars* (Prestige LPOJC014 P-7050); Wardell Gray and Dexter Gordon / Paul Quinichette and His Orchestra, *The Chase and the Steeplechase* (MCA 1336). Sonny Stitt, *Genesis* (Prestige P-24044); Wardell Gray, *Central Avenue* (Prestige P-24062); Charlie Parker recorded an uptempo version on *"Bird" Is Free* (Charlie Parker Records PLP 401). Perhaps in homage to the tenor stylist, Benny Goodman would use Young's signature tune as a climactic riff in the 1950s, when one of the small units he led played a famous composition from 1939–1940, "Airmail Special"; at one point in the piece, the ensemble riffed "Lester Leaps In" to climax the song while Goodman soloed (*Benny Goodman Live at Basin Street, Volume 2,* The Yale University Music Library Series [MHS 5222772]).

59. Carlos "Patato" Valdez, *Rhythms at the Crossroads* (Redwood Records RRCD 9503). The identifying riff was so much a part of the idiom that the trumpet player Courtney Williams can be heard playing it in an early 1938 recording by Louis Jordan's combo, "Swinging in a Coconut Tree" (*Louis Jordan at the Swing Cats Ball* [MCAD-12044]).

60. *Kansas City Six and Five* (Commodore XFL14937); *"Prez" Leaps Again!: Lester Young with the Kansas City Seven* (Soul Parade HHP-5015). Gunther Schüller, *The Swing Era: The Development of Jazz, 1930–1945* (New York: Oxford University Press, 1989), 556.

61. Gabler, in his liner notes for *Kansas City Six and Five,* quoted Hentoff's statement about the value of these discs.

62. Russell, review of *Lester Young with Count Basie,* 25–26.

63. Ibid.

64. Ross Russell, "Lester Young," *Record Changer,* April 1949, pp. 6, 20.

65. Russell, review of *Lester Young with Count Basie,* 26.

66. Raymond Horricks, "Lester Young with Count Basie," *Jazz Monthly,* December 1956, p. 5.

67. Hammond, *On Record,* 171, 187. Goodman's hit "One O'Clock Jump" was a prime example of a swing "cover"—that is, a selection from a Black band that was capitalized on by a white imitator. By his own admission, Goodman was attempting to replicate the sound of the Henderson band; explaining his preference for five brass over the then more usual eight, he stated that "his goal was to assemble an organization like Fletcher Henderson's old band, only white." Significantly, by 1946 he seemed to have abandoned any efforts to integrate his band (Leonard G. Feather, "What's Happened to Benny Goodman?," *Esquire,* April 1946, p. 100). See also Benny Goodman and Irving Kolodin, *The Kingdom of Swing* (New York: F. Ungar, 1961), and Schüller, *The Swing Era,* 3–45.

68. "Noble Sissle Wins Favors of K.C. Dancers," *Kansas City Call,* March 12, 1937, p. 14. Other topics of note in Black newspapers included "Explorer Finds Jazz Origins in Jungle," ibid., December 18, 1934, p. 2; "Our Strongest Weapon," *California Eagle,* April 1, 1932, p. 8 (on the use of Black music as a means of "putting over our program for advancement"); "Don Redman Seeks Test of Negro Jazz," *Oklahoma City Black Dispatch,* August 23, 1934, p. 8 (on the future of Black bands).

69. Russell, *Jazz Style,* contends that separate facilities existed at the Reno (p. 23). See Hammond, *On Record,* 168, on the club's location in a "dingy building with a second floor which must have been a whorehouse, because . . . [of the] girls lounging on the stairway." Clayton, in *Buck Clayton's Jazz World,* recalls of the salary (fourteen dollars a week for six or seven hours' work per night), "I couldn't believe that. . . . I was really taken aback" (p. 88).

70. Irving Kolodin, "The Dance Band Business: A Study in Black and White," *Harper's,* June 1941, pp. 72–82. For more information on the history of this club, see Arnold Shaw, *The Street That Never Slept: New York's Fabled Fifty-second Street* (New York: Coward, McCann, and Geoghegan, 1971), 20; on the Famous Door, see chapters 6 and 7. I wish to thank Professor Cedric Robinson for bringing this work to my attention.

71. Kolodin, "The Dance Band Business," 79–80; on the importance of radio, see "Big Name Bands Today Are Built by Radio!," *Down Beat,* August 1938, p. 16, which maintained that the medium was "the lifeblood" of the big bands. See Zane Knauss, ed., *Conversations with Jazz Musicians* (Detroit: Gale Research Co., 1977), 160; see also Arnold Shaw, *The Street That Never Slept,* 120; "Is Radio a Dead End for Negro Bands?," *Music and Rhythm,* December 1941, p. 15. Sheridan, *Count Basie,* appendix 2, 1099–1101. Stanley Dance, *The World of Swing* (New York: C. Scribner's Sons, 1974), and *The World of Earl Hines* (New York: Charles Scribner's Sons, 1977), and Milt Hinton and David G. Berger, *Bass Line: The Stories and Photographs of Milt Hinton* (Philadelphia: Temple University Press, 1988), all yield musicians' views of the swing years and some of the racial problems they faced.

72. Wells, *The Night People,* and Basie, *Good Morning Blues,* are both good accounts of these days. See also Dance, *The World of Count Basie;* Clayton, *Buck Clayton's Jazz World.*

73. Author's interview with Harry Edison.
74. Quoted in Dance, *The World of Count Basie,* 82, 153.
75. See the photographs of the Basie sidemen in Frank Driggs and Harris Lewine, *Black Beauty, White Heat: A Pictorial History of Classic Jazz, 1920–1950* (New York: Da Capo, 1996), 295–96, 311. I would like to thank Frank Driggs for providing me with a copy of the photo of Young wearing sunglasses and holding his horn out to the side; it is a still from a newsreel clip on the Randalls Island Jazz Carnival, scenes from which may be seen in the Robert O'Meally and Toby Byron video *Lady Day: The Many Faces of Billie Holiday* (New York, 1991). Author's interview with Earle Warren.
76. Author's interview with Harry Edison.
77. Clayton, *Buck Clayton's Jazz World,* 110.
78. Ibid., 80, 112; see the photo of Young wearing such a coat in John Hammond, "Memories of Pres: Souvenirs de Lester Young," *Jazz Hot,* no. 292 (Mars 1973), p. 13. This probably occurred in February 1939; see "Orpheum Negro Band Pleases," *Memphis Press-Scimitar,* February 24, 1939, Vertical Files, Memphis Public Library. I wish to thank the staff of the Memphis Public Library for providing me with information on the band's appearance in Memphis.
79. Clayton, *Buck Clayton's Jazz World,* 98.
80. See the excerpts from the newsreel in the video *Lady Day.*
81. Author's interview with Buddy Tate.
82. Dance, *The World of Count Basie,* 104; Warren, "Earl Warren's Story," 12.
83. Dance, *The World of Count Basie,* 104.
84. Chilton, *Billie's Blues,* 2.
85. Holiday, *Lady Sings the Blues,* 47. "'Les Young Wasn't Carved'—Holiday," *Down Beat,* October 15, 1939, p. 4; it is interesting to note that *Down Beat* did not use the title "Pres" at this time. S[tanford] M[igdol], ". . . Harlem," *Metronome,* October 1939, p. 31, proclaimed Hawk the winner.
86. Dance, *The World of Count Basie,* 123; the "spring 1939" date comes from Sheridan, *Count Basie,* 1096.
87. Warren, "Earl Warren's Story," 12; Dance, *The World of Count Basie,* 132; Holiday, *Lady Sings the Blues,* 185.
88. Warren, "Earl Warren's Story," 12.
89. Sheridan, *Count Basie,* 1093. Dance, *The World of Count Basie,* 78.
90. Dance, *The World of Count Basie,* 78. Author's interview with John Collins, who mentioned Young's dog.
91. Clayton, *Buck Clayton's Jazz World,* 102, 95.
92. Dance, *The World of Count Basie,* 78.
93. Albertson interview, reprinted in Porter, ed., *A Lester Young Reader,* 167.
94. Holiday, *Lady Sings the Blues,* 59.
95. "Billie Holiday's Tragic Life," *Ebony,* September 1956, p. 47; Holiday, *Lady Sings the Blues,* 59; author's interview with Buck Clayton.

96. Holiday, *Lady Sings the Blues,* 48–49.
97. Ibid.
98. Young mentions the mutual naming in the Albertson interview, reprinted in Porter, ed., *A Lester Young Reader,* 167. Max Jones, "Lady Day Says: Lester Young Gave Me My 'Title,'" *Melody Maker,* February 13, 1954, p. 9; idem, "Holiday with Billie," ibid., February 20, 1954, pp. 7–10. Idem, *Talking Jazz* (1987; reprint, New York: W. W. Norton, 1988), reproduces the unexpurgated version on page 249. According to Holiday, *Lady Sings the Blues,* the singer was known as "Lady" before she met Young: "Back at the Log Cabin the other girls used to try and mock me by calling me 'Lady' because they thought I was just too damn grand to take the damn customers' money off the tables. But the name Lady stuck. . . . Lester took it and coupled it with the Day out of Holiday." (p. 50). O'Meally and Byron, *Lady Day.*
99. Author's interview with Harry Edison. Stanley Dance, *The World of Earl Hines* (New York: Charles Scribner's Sons, 1977), 158.
100. Author's interviews with Harry Edison and Earle Warren.
101. Author's interview with Earle Warren.
102. Holiday, *Lady Sings the Blues,* 48–49, 56–57. Author's interview with Earle Warren.
103. Dave Dexter Jr., "I'll Never Sing with a Dance Band Again," *Down Beat,* November 1, 1939, p. 4.
104. Holiday, *Lady Sings the Blues,* 59.
105. Ibid., 48.
106. Ibid., 60.
107. Clayton, *Buck Clayton's Jazz World,* 98–99.
108. Porter, ed., *A Lester Young Reader,* 163.
109. Ibid., 146.
110. Clayton, *Buck Clayton's Jazz World,* 98–99.
111. Jones, "Lady Day Says," 9.
112. Clayton, *Buck Clayton's Jazz World,* 105; Warren, "Earl Warren's Story," 12; author's interviews with Beverly Young and Earle Warren; Dance, *The World of Count Basie,* 79–80.
113. Bill Coss, "Lester Young," in Lewis Porter, ed., *A Lester Young Reader,* 155; Dance, *The World of Count Basie,* 79; author's interview with Earle Warren; Clayton, *Buck Clayton's Jazz World,* 105; author's interview with Lee Young.
114. Warren, "Earl Warren's Story," 12.
115. Max Jones, "Sweets Talk," *Melody Maker,* April 18, 1981, p. 34.
116. Ibid., 22, 34.
117. Warren, "Earl Warren's Story," 12.
118. Ibid.
119. Dance, *The World of Count Basie,* 87.
120. Clayton, *Buck Clayton's Jazz World,* 111; Jones, "Holiday with Billie," 7.

121. Porter, ed., *A Lester Young Reader*, 180.

122. Clayton, *Buck Clayton's Jazz World*, 94–95.

123. Dance, *The World of Count Basie*, 79, 87; Nat Hentoff and Nat Shapiro, eds., *Hear Me Talkin' to Ya: The Story of Jazz, as Told by the Men Who Made It* (New York: Dover, 1955), 309.

124. Author's interview with Earle Warren.

125. Author's interview with Eddie Durham. See also Joel A. Siegel and Jas Obrecht, "Eddie Durham: Charlie Christian's Mentor, Pioneer of the Amplified Guitar," *Guitar Player*, August 1979, 160.

126. Author's interview with Eddie Durham.

127. Author's interview with Harry Edison.

128. Ibid.

129. Ibid.

130. Author's interview with Earle Warren.

131. Author's interview with Andy Kirk.

132. Clayton, *Buck Clayton's Jazz World*, 111. Dance, *The World of Count Basie*, 90; Shapiro and Hentoff, eds., *Hear Me Talkin' to Ya*, 309.

133. Dance, *The World of Count Basie*, 90.

134. Shapiro and Hentoff, *Hear Me Talkin' to Ya*, 253.

135. Dance, *The World of Count Basie*, 89.

136. Ibid.

137. See Clayton, *Buck Clayton's Jazz World*, 81, for the trumpet player's comments on the two tenors who were in his Los Angeles band prior to his joining Basie: "I had two hell-of-a-tenor men—Herschel Evans and Bumps Myers."

138. Dance, *The World of Count Basie*, 68.

139. Earle Warren claimed that the orchestra "really started cooking in 1938" (quoted in Dance, *The World of Count Basie*, 78–79), but Clayton maintained that a booking at San Francisco's World's Fair, in late 1939, "was the real beginning of Basie's band" (Clayton, *Buck Clayton's Jazz World*, 112). In November 1938, *Metronome* picked Count Basie's sax and rhythm sections as the best in the business; the trade journal also rated swing bands and deemed Basie's the "most improved" of 1938 (January 1939, p. 17).

140. Hammond, *On Record*, 165. John Chilton, *The Song of the Hawk: The Life and Recordings of Coleman Hawkins* (London: Quartet, 1990); Morroe Berger, Edward Berger, and James Patrick, *Benny Carter: A Life in American Music* (Metuchen, N.J.: Scarecrow Press, 1982), 1: 140–65.

141. Nat Hentoff, "Garvin Bushell and New York Jazz in the 1920s," *Jazz Review*, January 1959, p. 12. See also Bushell's autobiography, *Jazz from the Beginning*, as told to Mark Tucker (Ann Arbor, Mich.: University of Michigan, 1988). Jack Schiffman, *Uptown: The Story of Harlem's Apollo Theatre* (New York: Cowles, 1971), and the entertainment pages of the *New York Age* provided insights into these developments. On Blacks in New York, their move to Harlem, and the Renaissance, see James Weldon Johnson, *Black Manhat-*

tan (New York: Alfred A. Knopf, 1930); Gilbert Osofsky, *Harlem: The Making of a Ghetto: Negro New York, 1890–1930* (New York: Harper and Row, 1963); and Nathan Huggins, *Black Renaissance* (New York: Oxford University Press, 1970).

142. Holiday, *Lady Sings the Blues,* 48–49.

143. Dave Dexter Jr., "I'll Never Sing with a Dance Band Again," 4. Basie, *Good Morning Blues,* 211; "Count Basie Eliminates Billie Holiday's Singing," *New York Amsterdam News,* February 26, 1938, p. 26. Basie, *Good Morning Blues,* 211.

144. Dance, *The World of Count Basie,* 27; Burt A. Folkart, "Tommy Tucker: Mellow Leader in Big Band Era," *Los Angeles Times,* July 15, 1989, part 1, p. 32. While she liked Hammond's political commitment, Williams felt "that the best way to be friends with him was not to be around him" (Linda Dahl, *Morning Glory: A Biography of Mary Lou Williams* [New York: Pantheon, 1999], 144–45).

145. Quoted in Chilton, *Billie's Blues,* 50–51.

146. Hammond, 165–69. Author's interviews with Barney Kessel and Sadik Hakim. Earle Warren was one who credited Young with creating riffs for the band's compositions; see Warren, "Earl Warren's Story," 12.

11. Watts Eyes

1. John Hammond, "Herschel Evans' Last Playing His Greatest," *Metronome,* March 1939, p. 17; "Musician Buried Here," *California Eagle,* February 16, 1939, pp. 1, 10A; Chris Sheridan, *Count Basie: A Bio-Discography* (Westport, Conn.: Greenwood, 1986), appendix 1, 64–69. The Los Angeles City Directory for 1941 lists a Herschel Evans, occupation watchman, and Martha Evans at 1034 West Forty-second Street (p. 724); they may have been the saxophonist's parents. Albert McCarthy, "Basie's Other Tenor: The Herschel Evans Story," *Jazz and Blues,* September–October 1971, pp. 8–10.

2. Leonard Feather, "Prez," *Playboy,* September 1959, p. 68.

3. Brian Case, "Buddy Tate and the President," *Melody Maker,* December 1, 1979, p. 37.

4. Lewis Porter, *Lester Young* (Boston: Twayne, 1985), 18–20. Sheridan, Count Basie, 111; Count Basie, *Good Morning Blues: The Autobiography of Count Basie,* as told to Albert Murray (New York: Random House, 1985), 245. Porter's contention is supported by a *Down Beat* report in early 1941 that "the split came as a terrific surprise to followers of Basie and the band" ("Lester Young, Count Basie Part Company," *Down Beat,* January 1, 1941, p. 14).

5. Buddy Tate could not explain the sudden end of Young's tenure with the band: "Everybody wondered and I've heard different things and I don't believe [them]. . . . Somebody said it was a Friday the thirteenth [record date

that he missed] . . . which I don't believe" (Buddy Tate, IJS, p. 27). "I'll Break Up My Band, Basie Says," *Down Beat,* November 15, 1940, pp. 1, 23; see also "Count Basie Pulling Out of 'the Red,'" *California Eagle,* March 27, 1941, p. 2B; "Basie Asks Petrillo Help in Squabble," *Down Beat,* December 1, 1940, p. 1; "Basie Band Won't Break Up," ibid., December 15, 1940, p. 1. On MCA and its business practices, see Dan E. Moldea, *Dark Victory: MCA, Ronald Reagan, and the Hollywood Mafia* (New York: Viking, 1986).

6. Basie, *Good Morning Blues,* 245; Gene Ramey, IJS, vol. 4, p. 24. Years later, John Hammond would maintain that financial disagreements between Basie and Young—over, for example, composer's royalties—had caused the split (October 26, 1983, letter to Professor Lewis Porter, to whom I am indebted for sharing this information with me). For a critique of John Hammond's attitudes toward Black musicians, see Freddy Doyle, "Orchestras and Musicians," *California Eagle,* November 4, 1936, p. 9A. "Lester Young Quit," *Down Beat,* March 1, 1941, p. 10. Lee Young said of his brother's break with Basie, "They had a misunderstanding." While "a lot has been written about it," it was all wrong, he insisted, adding, "We have a family [saying], 'You [don't] put your business in the street.'" He has abided by that principle himself, never discussing the details of the matter (personal communication with the author).

7. Author's interview with John Collins.

8. Ibid. See Bill Coleman's account of how the management of Kelly's Stable exploited his band: "Those guys had worked out a scheme where they would have three groups in on Tuesday nights under the pretext of auditioning for a job. [But since] the auditions did not pay anything, they were having one night a week of free music and making a nice profit" (Bill Coleman, *Trumpet Story* [Boston: Northeastern University, 1991], 127–28).

9. Wilma Cockrell, "Jam Session," *California Eagle,* May 22, 1941, p. 2B, is the first mention of the tenor stylist's presence in Los Angeles in 1941. He was playing at the Capri, with Lee on drums, Arthur Twyne on piano, Red Callender on bass, Tonie Gonzales on guitar, "Red" Mack on trumpet, and "Bumps" Myers on tenor. Author's interviews with Eddie Barefield, Le Roy "Snake" Whyte, and Lee Young; see also the Central Avenue Sounds Oral History Project interviews, Special Collections, University Research Library, UCLA (henceforth CAS), with Clora Bryant, William Douglass, Art Farmer, Gerald Wilson, William Ernest Green, Fletcher Smith, and William Woodman. The Los Angeles City Directory for 1942, p. 2553, listed a Leroy White [Le Roy Whyte] (Cecile) at 1161 East Thirty-fifth Street; Eddie Barefield lived at 1616 East Twenty-second (ibid., p. 108). The 1920 City Directory listed Thomas "Mutt" Carey on San Pedro; Edward "Kid" Ory was also in Los Angeles in the early 1920s, and turned up again in the 1941 City Directory (p. 1715), where he was listed as a janitor with the Santa Fe Railway, residing at 1001 East Thirty-third Street.

10. Los Angeles City Directory, 1930, p. 2438; ibid., 1932, p. 2331; ibid., 1934, p. 1839; ibid., 1935, p. 2617. The professor was always listed in these directories as William H. Young, even though his first name was really Willis; Lee

Young was listed at different addresses on Newton Street and at Naomi and Twenty-third streets. Clora Bryant et. al., *Central Avenue Sounds: Jazz in Los Angeles* (Berkeley, Calif.: University of California Press, 1998), 56.

Sarah Young, who gave her address as 9406 Baird in 1931, when she took a beautician's examination, had studied hairdressing at the Poro College in St. Louis and came from Pittsburg, Texas. The family did not know anything about Sarah's doing hair. Nevertheless, the photo in this file does resemble Willis Young's spouse, and most important, the evidence about her Pittsburg origins led to the location of the marriage-license application filed by the professor, who married Mattie Stella Pilgrim in June 1919. Admittedly, some information given in the beautician's application contradicts other known facts—for example, the applicant's admission that she had practiced her profession without a license in Los Angeles in 1923 and 1924 is difficult to reconcile with Sarah's documented presence with her husband in Arkansas and Louisiana during the same period. There is no record of the couple's presence in the St. Louis City Directory for these years. Such contradictions cannot be easily resolved. The application to the State Board of Cosmetology is in the California State Archives, Sacramento, California; quite by chance, it was one application that was preserved as a sample when others were discarded by the archives.

11. The Los Angeles City Directory for 1935 lists an M. Elizabeth Hunter, schoolteacher, residing at 1159 West Thirty-ninth Street (p. 875); she is also listed in the 1942 City Directory (p. 1187). Author's interviews with Crawford Brown Jr. and James Tolbert. In the 1935 City Directory, pp. 1908–9, Irma Young was listed at 923 Fortieth Place, and Leonidas Young, an entertainer, at 1125 East Twenty-third Street. "Leonidas" was Lee Young's given name. Author's interviews with Alvin, Lucille, and James Tolbert.

12. A copy of Lester Young's Social Security card application (SS-5) was obtained under the Freedom of Information Act. See mentions of the family in Freddy Doyle, "Musicians and Orchestras," *California Eagle,* October 9, 1936, p. 10; "Orchs. and Musicians . . . ," ibid., January 29, 1937, p. 10; and "Orchestras," ibid., September 25, 1936, p. 10. Fletcher Smith, CAS, p. 41, and Marshal Royal, CAS, pp. 86, 130. The Los Angeles City Directory for 1937 listed a Freddie Doyle at 4206 McKinley (p. 528); this may have been the reporter.

13. Buck Clayton with Nancy Miller Elliott, *Buck Clayton's Jazz World,* (New York: Oxford University Press, 1987), 29–65; Freddy Doyle, "Orchestras and Musicians," *California Eagle,* December 2, 1937, p. 10B. Red Callender and Elaine Cohen, *Unfinished Dream: The Musical World of Red Callender* (New York: Quartet, 1985); Hampton Hawes and Don Asher, *Raise Up Off Me: A Portrait of Hampton Hawes* (1974; reprint, New York: Da Capo, 1979); Roy Porter with David Keller, *There and Back: The Roy Porter Story* (Baton Rouge, La.: Louisiana State University Press, 1991); Club Alabam advertisement, *California Eagle,* December 22, 1933, p. 13; "Buck Clayton Goes into Apex," ibid., October 18, 1935, p. 4B; Marshal Royal, IJS, pp. 33–34. The Los Angeles City Directory for 1930 lists a Curtis Mosby, restaura-

teur, at 4015 (later 4215) South Central (p. 1651); the bandleader and saxophonist Benjamin Spikes was a business partner with Mosby at 4011 South Central. Ruth Mosby, his wife, ran a beauty school at 4206 South Central, and they resided at 1167½ East Forty-second Street (City Directory, 1940, p. 1405). On Black music in California, see Jacqueline Cogdell DjeDje and Eddie S. Meadows, eds., *California Soul: Music of African Americans in the West* (Berkeley, Calif.: University of California Press, 1998).

14. "The Norman Granz Story," *Metronome,* October 1955, p. 25. *Nat "King" Cole Meets the Master Saxes* (Spotlite SPJ136) and *"Prez" Leaps Again!: Lester Young with the Kansas City Seven* (Pickwick HHP 5015). See Lewis Porter's discography in his *Lester Young* (Boston: Twayne, 1985), 141–56. For music from the film on CD, *Lester Young, Volume 6: 1944* (Masters of Jazz MJCD 99).

15. "James Leads All-Star Band," *Metronome,* January 1940, p. 12. "Count Basie Congratulates Lester Young" (ad), *Down Beat,* April 1939, p. 5, and "Martin Frères Reaches New Peaks" (ad), *Down Beat,* August 1939, p. 26. "Swing," *Life,* September 25, 1944, p. 40. "The Jazz Scene," *Ebony,* November 1949, p. 24.

16. Author's interview with "Teddy Bear," who did not want her real name used.

17. Author's interview with Martha Young. Very likely this was the Randalls Island footage, from the late spring of 1938 or 1939; some brief portions are today in the possession of film collectors. I wish to thank the bandleader and saxophonist Loren Schoenburg for identifying this newsreel footage for me.

18. Author's interview with Lucille Tolbert.

19. Emelda Sheffie (California death certificate #0190-058298) was born in New Orleans in 1923, moved to Los Angeles in 1943, and died in 1975; she is buried next to her mother, Lizetta Gray, in the Evergreen Cemetery, Los Angeles. It is unclear how well Lester knew his half-sister. Conversation with Lee Young concerning Mary Dale's move to southern California. In an interview with Frank Büchmann-Møller, Harry "Sweets" Edison maintained that Young's second wife, Mary D. Young, was still living in Los Angeles as late as 1987 (*You Just Fight for Your Life: The Story of Lester Young* [New York: Praeger, 1990], 89). The Los Angeles Extended Telephone Directory for 1942 listed a Mrs. Lester Young at 1233 East Fiftieth Street (p. 1293); this was probably Mary Dale. See note 32 below. The Los Angeles City Directory for 1942 listed a Beatrice Young, maid, at 100 South Windsor Boulevard, with a residence at 1222 East Forty-third Street; this was very probably Young's first wife, as his niece Lucille Tolbert recalled that she lived across from Jefferson High School, which was located at 1319 East Forty-first Street.

20. Lee Young, IJS, vol. 1, p. 32.

21. Author's interview with Martha Young.

22. Ibid.

23. Ibid.

24. Lee Young's statement about their differences is taken from an interview with the author; Lee Young, IJS, vol. 1, pp. 41, 12.

25. Max Jones, "Little Pres," *Melody Maker,* April 3, 1954, p. 2. Pat Harris, "Pres Talks about Himself, Copycats," in Lewis Porter, ed., *A Lester Young Reader* (Washington, D.C.: Smithsonian Institution Press, 1991), 137. Lee Young, IJS, vol. 1, p. 32.

26. Lee Young, IJS, vol. 2, pp. 40–41; Sir Charles Thompson recalled that "most of the discipline or any words which were spoken . . . were done by . . . Lee. . . . Lester strictly was a jazz player" (IJS, pp. 204–5. Author's interview with Red Callender. Callender, *Unfinished Dream,* 47–54, recounts his years in the Young band. See Gerald Wilson's CAS interview, where he mentions Dudley Brooks and discusses the Los Angeles jazz scene when he arrived in around 1939 (p. 55). The Los Angeles City Directory for 1941 listed a Dudley A. Brooks Jr. as a musician residing at 1335½ East Twenty-eighth Street (p. 341). McClure Morris ("Red Mack") lived at 1215 East Forty-third Place (ibid., 1942, p. 1716).

27. Lee Young, IJS, vol. 4, p. 3; author's interviews with Red Callender and Jimmy Rowles. Recordings of the Kelly's Stable band and the Young brothers can be heard on *Historical Pres: Lester Young 1940–1944* (Everybody's EV-3002). The 1941 Los Angeles City Directory listed a Herbert E. Myers (and Orpha), musician, at two addresses, 3215 North Broadway and (his residence) 2622 Harcourt (p. 1639); a Louis J. Gonzales (and Mary), musician, 490 East Forty-ninth (p. 888); and a James Rowles, musician (p. 2073). The 1942 directory listed a George S. Callender (Emma), musician, at 1226 East Twentieth (p. 423), and an Arthur J. Twyne Jr., musician, at 1560 East Fifty-second (p. 2430).

28. See Lee Young, IJS, vol. 4, pp. 2–5, on the music in Los Angeles during these years. Cockrell, "Jam Session," May 22, 1941; Freddy Doyle, "Swingtime in H'Wood," ibid., November 27, 1941, p. 3B; see also Freddy Doyle, "Swingtime in H'Wood," Ibid. April 30, 1942, p. 2B. The 1941 Los Angeles City Directory listed the Capri Club, Inc., restaurant, at 8503 West Pico Boulevard (p. 415); ibid, 1942, listed Billy Berg's restaurant at the same address (p. 261).

29. Cockrell, "Jam Session," *California Eagle,* June 26, 1941, p. 2B.

30. Lee Young, IJS, vol. 4, pp. 6–7. Freddie Doyle reported on such a jam session in "Swingtime," *California Eagle,* July 2, 1942, p. 2B.

31. Cockrell, "Jam Session," May 22 and June 5, 1941; Doyle, "Swingtime in H'wood," November 27, 1941. In his "H'wood" column for January 8, 1942, Doyle reported that the band had "recently finished a very long engagement at the Club Capri" and was scheduled to open at Manhattan's Hickory House on Fifty-second Street. Ibid., April 30, 1942, p. 3B, and Freddy Doyle, "Billie Holiday Heads Lincoln Stage Show," *California Eagle,* July 2, 1942, p. 2B; this latter article also mentioned plans for the Young combo to play Café Society. Author's interview with Lee Young; Val Wilmer, "The Lee Young Story," *Jazz Journal,* August 1960, p. 5. See Freddy Doyle, "Orchestras and Musicians," *California Eagle,* February 3, 1938, p. 10A, on what

may have been Lee Young's first studio position: instructing six-year-old Billy Lee in drumming for a movie role. "Lee Young in Studios . . . ," *Down Beat,* May 20, 1946, p. 6. *Jazz at the Philharmonic/Bird and Pres: The '46 Concerts* (Verve VE2-2516). Author's interview with Lucille Tolbert.

32. Interviews with family members and close friends, especially James Tolbert, Lucille Tolbert, Martha Young, and "Teddy Bear," helped in the reconstruction of these years. Since the family does not know what happened to Beatrice after 1942, it is possible that she died in the 1940s. The fact that Jimmy Rowles and his wife told me that "Teddy Bear" was Lester's spouse when they first put me in touch with her suggests that his other relationships may have been unclear to his friends as well. *The Official California Negro Directory, 1942–1943* (Los Angeles: New Age Publishing Co., 1943?), p. 79; Pacific Telephone and Telegraph Co., 1947 Los Angeles Street Address Directory, Revised to April 18, 1949, pp. 764, 774. The fact that Mrs. Lester Young appeared in a Negro directory raises doubts as to whether it was Beatrice or Mary—since whites were not usually listed in such directories. On May 7, 1947, Lester W. and Mary D. Young purchased lot #87, tract no. 7127, according to records in the Los Angeles County Recorder's Office, Norwalk, Los Angeles County, California. When Mr. James Tolbert visited the location at the corner of Thirty-sixth and Edgehill Drive in around 1996 with the author, he recalled the house as having been his uncle's, though it had been enlarged considerably in the ensuing half century.

33. Author's interview with "Teddy Bear."

34. Ibid. Sheridan, *Count Basie,* appendix 2, pp. 1098, 1102.

35. Author's interview with "Teddy Bear."

36. "Death Stills Fingers of Colored 'Countess,'" *Down Beat,* August 1939, p. 3. Mercer Ellington with Stanley Dance, *Duke Ellington in Person: An Intimate Memoir* (1978; reprint, New York: Da Capo, 1979), 86–87; on the deaths of Blanton, Christian, and Hart, see John Chilton, *Who's Who of Jazz: Storyville to Swing Street* (Philadelphia: Chilton Book Co., 1972), 38, 68, and 136; also see Hart's obituary in *Metronome,* April 1945, p. 9.

37. Jack Maher, "Down T' Bunny's," *Metronome,* May 1959, p. 9.

38. Bob Troely, "Why Hollywood Won't Ever Do an Authentic Movie on Negroes, Jazz," letter to the editors, *Down Beat,* September 15, 1941, p. 10; see also "Movies Fix Merit by Color of Skin," ibid., July 29, 1946, p. 10.

39. Ralph J. Gleason, "Frisco Dancery Sets Up Two-Way Jim Crow Policy," *Down Beat,* June 30, 1950, p. 18; Freddy Doyle, "With Orchestras, Musicians," *California Eagle,* August 21, 1936, p. 10; idem, "Orchestras and Musicians," ibid., July 9, 1937, p. 4B; "Coast Ops Nix on Colored Bands," *Down Beat,* October 1, 1943, p. 6; "Color Loses Lee Young's Job," *Down Beat,* May 1, 1943, p. 1. Art Farmer is quoted in Whitney Balliett, "Profiles: Here and Abroad," *The New Yorker,* September 23, 1985, p. 52; I wish to thank Professor Elliot Brownlee for bringing this article to my attention.

40. Alyn Shipton, *Groovin' High: The Life of Dizzy Gillespie* (New York: Oxford University Press, 1999), 119, 129.

12. D.B. Blues

1. Chris Sheridan, *Count Basie: A Bio-Discography* (Westport, Conn.: Greenwood Press, 1986), 172–74, appendix 2, 1112.
2. Ibid., 172–74, appendix 2, 1112–13.
3. Advertisement, *California Eagle,* July 27, 1944, p. 12; Sheridan, *Count Basie,* appendix 2, 1114–15.
4. J. T. Gipson, "Count Basie Band Is Held Over by Popular Demand at Orpheum," *California Eagle,* August 10, 1944, p. 3.
5. "Basie Band Best in Swing Land Raves Editor GIP," *California Eagle,* September 7, 1944, p. 12; J. T. Gipson, "The Jump King of Swing Played to Capacity Crowds Every Night," ibid., September 28, 1944, p. 12. Idem, "Basie Band Sends Hepsters at Joe Morris' Plantation Club," ibid., September 14, 1944, p. 13. On the Club Plantation, see Earl Morris, "Joe Morris, of Club Plantation, Tells Earl Morris His Side," ibid., July 30, 1942, p. 5B ("The Club Plantation is owned and operated by Negroes and is a place for Negroes to enjoy themselves").
6. Gipson, "Basie Band."
7. Lena and DeVere, "Between Friends," *California Eagle,* September 14, 1944, p. 11; Lena and DeVere, "Curtain Falls on Another Joe Morris Club Plantation Triumph," ibid., October 5, 1944, sec. 3, p. 1.
8. Buddy Tate, IJS, pp. 33–36; Stanley Dance, *The World of Earl Hines* (New York: Charles Scribner's Sons, 1977), 214.
9. Buddy Tate, IJS, pp. 33–35.
10. Author's interviews with Lee and Irma Young. "Two Basie Sidemen Drafted by Army," *Down Beat,* November 1, 1944, p. 1, and "These Persons Figured in Recent News Stories," ibid., December 1, 1944, p. 2; they were inducted at the Presidio in Monterey, California.
11. See Lee Young, IJS, vol. 6, pp. 11–14, on the army; author's interviews with Irma and Lee Young. "These Persons Figured," p. 2. Young's military postings included McQuaide and Fort Ord, California; Fort McClellan, Alabama; and Camp Gordon, Georgia. According to his military records, he was discharged from Camp Gordon on December 15, 1945, but he may very well have been released earlier (information obtained from the Records Reconstruction Branch, National Personnel Records Center, St. Louis, Missouri, under the Freedom of Information Act).
12. Author's interview with Buck Clayton.
13. Ol[lie] Harrington, "Dark Laughter," *California Eagle,* May 22, 1941, p. 8A, and May 29, 1941, p. 8A. Young was at least somewhat familiar with the military and its regimen, having performed on military bases with Al Sears's USO band in 1943. A white jazz fan named Burt Goldblatt, then an eighteen-year-old recruit, sneaked into the Black section of the army post at Camp Sideret, Alabama, to hear his hero perform on the tenor sax in June of that year (personal communication with the author).
14. Malcolm X with Alex Haley, *The Autobiography of Malcolm X* (New York: Grove, 1965), 108; author's interview with Buck Clayton.

15. Author's interview with Lee Young.

16. Buck Clayton with Nancy Miller Elliott, *Buck Clayton's Jazz World* (New York: Oxford University Press, 1983), 117–21, provides a few more details than Clayton's IJS interview, vol. 3, pp. 13–14, 17–21.

17. Jay McShann, IJS, pp. 12–13; John Collins, IJS, pp. 210–11; see also Buddy Tate, IJS, pp. 33–35.

18. Author's interview with George "Red" Callender. Dale Smoak, "Rodney Richardson: Interview—Part One," *Cadence,* November 1989, p. 17. Bayard Rustin, *Down the Line: The Collected Writings of Bayard Rustin* (Chicago: Quadrangle, 1971), x. E. U. Essien-Udom, *Black Nationalism: A Search for an Identity in America* (Chicago: University of Chicago Press, 1962), 80–81. Karl Evanzz, *The Messenger: The Rise and Fall of Elijah Muhammad* (New York: Pantheon, 1999). The composer, bandleader, and pianist Teddy Powell was imprisoned for draft evasion in 1945; see "Teddy Powell on Prison Stretch," *Down Beat,* November 1, 1945, p. 13.

19. Allan Morrison, "You Got to Be Original, Man," *Jazz Record,* July 1946, 7–9, republished in Lewis Porter, ed., *A Lester Young Reader* (Washington, D.C.: Smithsonian Institution Press, 1991), 131–35.

20. *United States v. Lester W. Young, 397229502, Pvt. Company E, 2nd Bn. General Court Martial Orders No. 38, Headquarters Infantry Replacement Training Center, Fort McClellan, Alabama, February 27, 1945,* summarizes the trial, which took place on February 16, 1945. This material may be found in the Lester Young Vertical File at the Institute of Jazz Studies, Rutgers University, Newark, New Jersey. The various documents regarding the case, including the report of the Chief of Neuropsychiatric Service, will hereafter be referred to as Lester Young Court-Martial Records.

21. Captain Luis Perelman, Information Concerning Lester W. Young, Pvt., ASN 397229502, January 24, 1945, Lester Young Court-Martial Records.

22. Ibid.

23. Lester Young Court-Martial Records. I would like to thank Mr. Otis Madison, a lecturer in the Department of Black Studies, University of California, Santa Barbara, for his assistance in interpreting the Court-Martial Records. The idea that the officers should have offered Young an opportunity to seek counseling with regard to his problem was Mr. Madison's.

24. Report of the Neuropsychiatrist on Pvt. Lester W. Young, February 7, 1945, Lester Young Court-Martial Records.

25. Lester Young Court-Martial Records.

26. Ibid.

27. Ibid.

28. Ibid. While army records indicate that he was discharged from Camp Gordon, it is not clear whether he was there solely for the purposes of his discharge or whether he was actually in the stockade at Gordon for a period of time.

29. Howard E. Fuller, Brigadier General, U.S. Army, Notice of February 27, 1945, Headquarters, Infantry Replacement Training Center, Fort McClel-

lan, Alabama, Lester Young Court-Martial Records. That the punishment appeared unduly harsh for a first-time offender; that Young cooperated by providing the name of the doctor who had provided him with the pills; and that he may have been purposely trying to avoid being shipped overseas were all Mr. Otis Madison's observations. John Pimlott, *Battle of the Bulge* (Englewood Cliffs, N.J.: Prentice-Hall, 1983).

30. William Woodman interview, CAS, pp. 29–34; see also Clora Bryant et al., *Central Avenue Sounds* (Berkeley, Calif.: University of California Press, 1998), 108. Young's Minneapolis daughter, Beverly, claimed that her father suffered from this same malady (personal communication with the author).

31. Gene Ramey, IJS, vol. 5, pp. 37–39; Leonard Feather, "Prez," *Playboy*, September 1959, pp. 68, 106; Jones recalled this as taking place at Camp Gordon, which raises the possibility that Young may have spent at least part of his sentence in Georgia rather than in Alabama, where he was stationed. In the Morrison interview, Young also spoke of detention in Georgia (Porter, ed., *A Lester Young Reader*, 135).

32. John Hammond with Irving Townsend, *On Record: An Autobiography* (New York: Penguin, 1981), 245, 247, 249–50.

33. Gene Ramey, Trinity University (San Antonio, Texas) interview, side 1 of cassette tape. This and other interviews with Texas jazzmen and jazzwomen were conducted by Sterlin Holmesly. The same point is made by Ramey in Stanley Dance, *The World of Count Basie* (New York: Charles Scribner's Sons, 1980), 281, and in his IJS interview, vol. 5, pp. 37–39. Smoak, "Rodney Richardson," 17.

34. Lewis Porter, *Lester Young* (Boston: Twayne, 1985), 95–102.

35. See Porter, *Lester Young*. Smoak, "Rodney Richardson," 17. In his IJS interviews, Lee Young maintained that his brother had been "railroaded" by the army, but added that "maybe part of it was his [own] fault," mentioning the tenor saxophonist's sudden departure from Fort MacArthur; he did not believe that the army had "left . . . scars on Lester. . . . He was more intelligent than that" (vol. 6, pp. 12, 14).

13. Sax-o-Be-Bop

1. Author's interview with Connie Kay. Kay admired the tenor saxophonist with whom he played in the early 1950s, and suggested that anyone else forced to endure what Young suffered in the military might have been driven insane. According to his military records, Young was released on December 15, 1945, but he may have been let out earlier (records of Lester Young, Military Personnel Records, National Personnel Records Center, St. Louis, Missouri, National Archives and Records Administration).

2. This chapter and succeeding ones identify some of the writers who professed this belief.

3. "Lester Young Signs with Philo," *Down Beat,* November 15, 1945, p. 9. Hylton Davis, "Hollywood Periscope," *Metronome,* February 1946, p. 49; according to this brief mention, Young participated in some record sessions with just a rhythm section for Norman Granz. His first recordings after his release were in December 1945 with Dodo Marmarosa on piano, Red Callender on bass, and Henry Tucker on drums (*The Complete Aladdin Recordings of Lester Young* [Blue Note CDP 7243 8 32787 2 5]). A lavish reissue of his music by Time-Life (STL-J13) several years ago used the term *drugs* in the liner notes, probably referring to the pills he had had in his possession when he was arrested. Her brother's alleged use of "narcotics" was denied by Irma Young, who insisted that while he smoked marijuana, he had nothing to do with any other drugs.
4. "'Jazz at Philharmonic' Troupe to Tour Orient," *Jet,* September 10, 1953, p. 60.
5. "The Jazz Business," *Time,* March 2, 1953, p. 40. Author's interview with Lee Young. Los Angeles City Directory, 1942, p. 1901. "Norman Granz Presents *Down Beat* Award Winners Concert," *Los Angeles Times,* January 27, 1946, p. 2. Apparently Granz's Aladdin Recordings was housed in part of the Philharmonic, as the same address, 427 West Fifth Street, was given for both; see the ad for Philo Hits from Aladdin Recordings, *Metronome,* April 1946, p. 31.
6. "Basie's Key Men to Return," *Pittsburgh Courier,* December 1, 1945, p. 18.
7. The CD *Lester Young, Volume 6: 1944* (Masters of Jazz MJCD 99) includes recordings from the film.
8. *Time,* December 25, 1954, clipping in JATP file at the Margaret Herrick Library, Center for Motion Picture Study, Academy of the Motion Picture Arts and Sciences (my thanks to Wren Brown for information on this archive). It is apparent from its persistent popularity that the film has taken its place among such jazz classics as *Jazz on a Summer's Day* and *A Great Day in Harlem;* it is still shown at, for example, the Florence Documentary Festival and the Greenwich Village Jazz Festival Film Series in New York City (see *Variety* clippings, January 22, 1980, and August 30, 1983, ibid.).
9. Leonard Feather, "On Coast, You Hop before You Jump," *Metronome,* March 1945, pp. 8, 31; "*Jammin' the Blues,*" ibid., April 1945, p. 14. Author's interview with Barney Kessel on the separate recording session for the film. See Arthur Knight, "*Jammin' the Blues,* or the Sight of Jazz, 1944," in Krin Gabbard, ed., *Representing Jazz* (Durham, N.C.: Duke University Press, 1995), 11–53, for an excellent analysis of the film short. "Sweet Georgia Brown," "Blues for Marvin," and "If I Could Be with You" were also recorded.
10. *The Complete Aladdin Sessions, Volume 1: Lester Young* (Aladdin K18P 9256). Young also recorded with a band that backed Helen Humes on December 22, 1945. Granz produced all these recordings.
11. Don C. Haynes, "Diggin' the Discs with Don," *Down Beat,* March 25, 1946, p. 8; "Record Reviews by the Three Deuces," *Metronome,* April 1946, p. 33.

12. *The Complete Aladdin Sessions, Volume 1: Lester Young;* also, *Nat King Cole Meets the Master Saxes* (Spotlite SPJ136). Four Young recordings from 1942, with Nat "King" Cole on piano and Red Callender on bass, were issued in the spring of 1946, but I have been unable to find any reviews of them. The selections were "I Can't Get Started," "Body and Soul," "Tea for Two," and "Back Home in Indiana."

13. "Record Reviews," *Metronome,* August 1946, p. 37.

14. Ibid., October 1946, p. 34.

15. Mike Levin, "Diggin' the Discs with Mix," *Down Beat,* January 15, 1947, p. 19. In early 1947, Young did not fare much better in *Metronome* reviews; for example, in reviewing the *JATP No. 4* records (which were described as having "all the faults and merits of the previous albums"), the trade journal's critic contended that while Young "has some exciting moments . . . the Lester of the title [Pres] isn't there" (*Metronome,* January 1947, p. 34). The following month, the reviewer asserted that the "first shock" of Young's tone was "hard to get over," but then went on to praise him (ibid., February 1947, p. 34). In *Metronome's* December 1948 issue, the record reviewers complained about Young's "cardboard tone" and charged that he "sound[ed] very uncertain of his technique" on "East of the Sun" and "Sheik of Araby," which were both rated C (p. 46).

16. Mike Levin, "Diggin' the Discs with Mix," *Down Beat,* October 8, 1947, p. 15; ibid., December 31, 1947, p. 16; ibid., January 1, 1947, p. 7. In late 1947, Levin reviewed records that Young had made a few years earlier with Johnny Guarnieri, Slam Stewart, and Sid Catlett, and described him as "getting in some good sax bits" on "Sometimes I'm Happy." In this brief review, Levin praised the tenor stylist and ranked the records among his other "excellent" selections ("Diggin' the Discs with Mix," *Down Beat,* November 5, 1947, p. 14).

17. Levin, "Diggin'," October 8, 1947.

18. "Lester Young's New Disc Okay," *Chicago Defender,* September 18, 1948, p. 3. Frank Büchmann-Møller, in *You Got to Be Original, Man: The Music of Lester Young* (New York: Praeger, 1990), claims the records were made on December 29, 1947, despite other dates given on the records themselves (p. 289). Leonard Feather assembled these musicians (ibid.).

19. Tom Herrick, "Diggin' the Discs with Tom," *Down Beat,* November 17, 1948, p. 13.

20. "Musicians Talking: Gene Di Novi to Mark Gardner," *Jazz and Blues,* June–July 1971, p. 31. Dave Gelly, *Lester Young* (New York: Hippocrene, 1984), 63, attributes the suggestion about repertoire to DiNovi rather than Leonard Feather.

21. Frank Büchmann-Møller, *You Just Fight for Your Life: The Story of Lester Young* (New York: Praeger, 1990), appendix B, 252–53, claims that Hakim's stint ran from October 1946 to sometime in the fall of 1948, while Haynes's ran from October 1947 to July 1949. For the recording of the Young-Vaughan collaboration, "I Cried for You," refer to *Sarah Vaughan/Lester*

Young One Night Stand: The Town Hall Concert (Blue Note CD P 7243 8 32139 2 4).

22. Dale Smoak, "Rodney Richardson: Interview—Part One," *Cadence,* November 1989, p. 16. Büchmann-Møller, *You Got to Be Original,* 248–49, asserts that the recordings made in late December 1945 ("D.B. Blues," "Lester Blows Again," "These Foolish Things," and "Jumpin' at Mesner's") were unrehearsed; Büchmann-Møller also informs us that "Philo" records became "Aladdin" in 1946 (ibid., 249). Sadik Hakim WKCR (New York City) interview with Phil Schaap, April 9, 1976 (my thanks to Phil Schaap for providing me with a copy of this interview). See Jeff Levenson, "Sadik Hakim," *Down Beat,* April 1982, pp. 27–29.

23. Mike Levin, "Diggin' the Discs with Mix," *Down Beat,* January 14, 1948, p. 15.

24. Leonard G. Feather, "Jazz Is Where You Find It," *Esquire,* February 1944, p. 130.

25. "N. Granz Giving 'Jam Session' at Philharmonic, 18th," *Los Angeles Sentinel,* January 17, 1946, p. 2. Young performed in another JATP concert, featuring "The Battle of the Saxes" as well as Buck Clayton, in Los Angeles on April 22, 1946 (ibid., April 18, 1946, p. 19). Young's Chicago appearances were publicized in Al Monroe, "Swinging the Blues," *Chicago Defender,* April 27, 1946, p. 23, and in an ad on the following page; see also ibid., May 11, 1946, p. 25, on the May 14, 1946, JATP performance in Chicago, and Al Monroe, "Swinging the Blues," ibid., June 8, 1946, p. 24.

26. *Chicago Defender,* May 11, 1946, p. 25; "Coleman Hawkins Battles Lester Young at Opera House," ibid., June 15, 1946, p. 26; Al Monroe, "Swinging the Blues," ibid., June 22, 1946, p. 23. The trade journals were sometimes extremely critical of JATP concerts; see, for example, "Jazz at the Philharmonic," *Metronome,* July 1946, p. 42, and D. Leon Wolff, "Granz Bash a Caricature on Jazz," *Down Beat,* November 18, 1946, p. 3.

27. J. W. Wood, "Philly Sax Men Almost Blew Les Young Out of His Title," *Philadelphia Afro-American,* January 25, 1947, p. 11. That summer the *Baltimore Afro-American* praised Young, noting that "his brilliant saxophoning scored [him] an amazing personal triumph . . . when [he] played to a turn-'em-away crowd at the Zanzibar" one Friday night in July 1947. The fact that two days earlier a *California Eagle* item regarding the same date had employed identical language strongly suggests that the report came from a single source, either Young's manager or the Gale Agency ("Lester Young in Philly Triumph," *Baltimore Afro-American,* July 26, 1947, p. 6; "Les Young Is Hit in Philly," *California Eagle,* July 24, 1947, p. 18).

28. Mike "Mix" Levin, "Vaughan Great, But Lester Slips," *Down Beat,* December 3, 1947, p. 7 (a *Down Beat* misprint; it is actually p. 3).

29. "Lester Young Replies," ibid.

30. Ted Hallock, "Les, Muggsy, Herbie Chicago Openings Almost Too Much," *Down Beat,* December 3, 1947, p. 2 (a *Down Beat* misprint; it is actually p. 4). "Lester Young Returns to N.Y.," *California Eagle,* January 1, 1948, p. 18.

31. Ralph J. Gleason, "Lester Leaps to Town as Twin City Ops Merge," *Down Beat,* March 10, 1948, p. 9. On the 1942 recording "A Little Bit South of North Carolina," Young can just barely be heard singing (my thanks to Professor Lewis Porter for bringing this record to my attention; it was issued on Pres Box PB 01-22). See also Büchmann-Møller, *You Got to Be Original,* 167. The "Lavender Blue" selection can be heard on *Lester Young—Live Recording 1948 at the "Royal Roost" New York City* (Jazz Anthology 30 JA 5171); the other recording on which he sings (in a humorous fashion), "(It Takes) Two to Tango," is included on the CD *The President Plays with the Oscar Peterson Trio* (Verve 831 670-2).
32. Robert August Luckey, "A Study of Lester Young and His Influences upon His Contemporaries" (Ph.D. diss., University of Pittsburgh, 1982). Personal communication with Lester Young Jr.
33. Liber 6336, p. 102, Queens County Property Records. "'Is Lester Still the President?'—'I'll Take Flip Any Time!' Says Mike Nevard," *Melody Maker,* March 21, 1953, pp. 4–5, reprinted in Lewis Porter, ed., *A Lester Young Reader* (Washington, D.C.: Smithsonian Institution Press, 1991), 44, 152. Nat Hentoff, "Billie Holiday, Now Remarried, Finds Happiness, a New Sense of Security," *Down Beat,* January 11, 1952, p. 2.
34. Author's interviews with Sadik Hakim, Mary Young, Junior Mance, and Connie Kay.
35. Author's interview with Mary Berkeley Young. The saxophonist was in Chicago on May 14 and June 22 and from October 3 through December 1, 1946, according to Frank Büchmann-Møller (*You Just Fight,* 239). It is possible that Young and JATP played in Chicago, as Mary Young recalled, but she may also have been mistaken about the April date.
36. Büchmann-Møller, *You Just Fight,* 240–48. Photographs reveal that Young wore a wedding ring, while other married musicians did not. I myself recall that in the 1950s, when I was a youngster, wedding rings were thought to be primarily for women; it was somewhat unusual to see one on a man.
37. Pat Harris, "Pres Talks about Himself, Copycats," in Porter, ed., *A Lester Young Reader,* 136–39. Lee Young claimed that their mother did not move out to California until the 1950s (personal communication with the author).
38. Leonard Feather, "Here's Pres!," in Porter, ed., *A Lester Young Reader,* 140–47. Young also stayed at the Chesterfield and the Mark in New York City; see Stanley Dance, *The World of Count Basie* (New York: Charles Scribner's Sons, 1980), 279–80. Young's whereabouts in the summer of 1950 are unclear; see Büchmann-Møller, *You Just Fight,* 241.
39. Personal communication with Lester Young Jr. Young spent most of his summers in the New York area in the early 1950s (Büchmann-Møller, *You Just Fight,* 242–43, 251); and his son's recollection of the tomato plants can probably be dated to that period. "Mahalia Jackson, Louisiana Beauty Share Gumbo Secrets," *Jet,* April 18, 1957, pp. 42–43; the recipe of Rosita Tircuit (the "Louisiana Beauty" referred to in the article's title) was also included. When it comes to gumbo—and many other African American dishes, for that matter—different individuals often have their own highly distinctive and sometimes secret recipes.

40. Bill Coss, "Lester Young," *Metronome,* October 1955, p. 25 (reprinted in Porter, ed., *A Lester Young Reader,* 155–56). Personal communication with Lester Young Jr. on his father's putting; personal communication with Crawford Brown Jr., Irma's son, on his uncle Lester's pool playing. Nat Hentoff, "Pres," *Down Beat,* March 7, 1956, pp. 9–11 (reprinted in Porter, ed., *A Lester Young Reader,* 158).

41. "Gale Agency Boosted Many Negro Performers," *Pittsburgh Courier,* January 12, 1957, p. 19.

42. See Stanley Dance, *The World of Earl Hines* (New York: Charles Scribner's Sons, 1977), 157–59, on Young. In 1953 the Gale Agency managed Nat Cole, Sarah Vaughan, and Billy May's orchestra, along with other acts with which they were packaged; see "Vaughan, 'Nat' Cole Will Head 'Biggest Show' for This Year," *Chicago Defender,* April 11, 1953, p. 17. "Gale Agency Boosted Many Negro Performers," 19, mentions the agency's "big interracial staff." See Dance, *The World of Earl Hines,* 157–59, for Carpenter's account of his meeting Young. That the New Year's Eve date was in 1946 was corroborated in Nat Hentoff, "Pres," *Down Beat,* March 7, 1956, p. 9, an interview with Young during which Carpenter was present.

43. Aside from one member who quit the band because of Young's new manager, his sidemen revealed very little about Charlie Carpenter or Young's relationship with him; but see Porter, ed., *A Lester Young Reader,* 59–60, 95, 136. Nat Cole and his manager went without a signed contract in the 1940s (Leslie Gourse, *Unforgettable: The Life and Mystique of Nat King Cole* [New York: St. Martin's, 1991], 51).

44. See Dance, *The World of Earl Hines,* 142–57, on Carpenter's music background and association with Armstrong and Hines; he was also the lyricist for "You Can Depend on Me" and "Frenesi." This interview is reprinted in Art Hodes and Chadwick Hansen, *Selections from the Gutter: Jazz Portraits from "The Jazz Record,"* (Berkeley, Calif.: University of California Press, 1977), 225–29, as well as in Porter, ed., *A Lester Young Reader,* 131–35; citations in the notes that follow will be to this latter volume. These and other articles on Young are reprinted ibid., 136–47.

45. Porter, ed., *A Lester Young Reader,* 131–35. According to Büchmann-Møller, *You Just Fight,* appendix A, 239, JATP played Chicago on May 14 and June 22, 1946.

46. Porter, ed., *A Lester Young Reader,* 132; the Dickenson solo might have been from a recent release, recorded late in 1945 or early in 1946 and now available on *The Complete Aladdin Sessions, Volume 1: Lester Young* (Aladdin K 18P 9256).

47. Porter, ed., *A Lester Young Reader,* 132–34; Morrison recorded a number of errors, however. The years given are not correct, for example; Young left and returned to the family band several times, but he was very probably gone for good by 1931, which Morrison cites as the year of his departure. Nor were the Blue Devils still scuffling in 1934–1935. It may be, of course, that all these errors merely reflected Young's indifference to details such as dates.

48. Porter, ed., *A Lester Young Reader,* 132.

49. Ibid., 134–35.

50. "Lester Young to Battle Gene Ammons at Pershing," *Chicago Defender,* January 3, 1948, p. 9.

51. Author's interview with Red Callender; Scott DeVeaux, *The Birth of Bebop: A Social and Musical History* (Berkeley, Calif.: University of California Press, 1997).

52. "Bop Here to Stay Argues Les Young," *New York Amsterdam News,* October 2, 1948, p. 24; "Lester Young Defends 'Bebop' Which He Says Is Here to Stay," *Chicago Defender,* October 2, 1948, p. 8.

53. In Graham Colombé, "Jo Jones Speaks Out," *Jazz Journal,* December 1972, the former Basie drummer noted, "Another thing people don't know is that [pianist] Marlowe Morris and Pres used to be together when the people were jamming down at Minton's, [and] Pres picked a tune, 'How High the Moon,' and all the guys that used to run up on the bandstand didn't know what he was playing" (p. 6). Regarding Young's schedule in the early 1940s, see Chris Sheridan, *Count Basie: A Bio-Discography* (Westport, Conn.: Greenwood, 1986), appendix 2, 1099–115, which indicates that he was in New York City for extended periods in, for example, late January and early February, most of April, late October, and early December of 1940 alone. He returned to New York in 1942 with his brother's band. DeVeaux, *The Birth of Bebop,* 292.

Leonard Feather, "Basie's Blindfold Test," *Metronome,* July 1947, p. 33; John Chilton, *The Song of the Hawk: The Life and Recordings of Coleman Hawkins* (London: Quartet, 1990), 213–30. Hawkins explained his opinion of the new developments in music in terms quite similar to the ones Young used: "I don't think about music in the same way other people do. I don't think about music being new or modern. Music doesn't go seasonable to me" (*Coleman Hawkins: A Documentary* [Riverside RLP 12-117/118], as quoted by Chilton, ibid., 216). "Crazy Music Ridiculed by Band Leader," *Philadelphia Afro-American,* September 18, 1948, p. 8.

54. Ad for Emerson's Café, *Philadelphia Afro-American,* September 18, 1948, p. 9. Although the interview may have taken place in Philadelphia, sideman Jesse Drakes recalled Boston as the place where, in the course of a radio interview, Young mentioned that while he himself did not play bebop, his sidemen did—a comment that Young later regretted making because of the controversy that ensued (author's interview with Jesse Drakes).

55. Dan Burley, "Back Door Stuff," *New York Amsterdam News,* October 23, 1948, p. 29.

56. "How to Make a Pork Pie Hat," *Ebony,* August 1949, pp. 43–44.

57. Ibid. Gene Ramey recalled one of Young's pets: "He always talked about his cat. He called her Philharmonic. He said something one day that the cat didn't like, insulted her, and the cat jumped out the window from the eighth floor. He said it hurt him so badly" (quoted in Dance, *The World of Count Basie,* 280).

58. "How to Make a Pork Pie Hat," 44.

59. "Les Was Playing Be-Bop Long 'fore Be-Bop Was Born!," *California Eagle,*

November 11, 1948, p. 16, and "Lester Young and Crew Drew Down a Lotta Loot in '48," ibid., December 30, 1948, p. 15; "Lester Young at Broadway Roost," *Chicago Defender,* December 4, 1948, p. 17; "How Lester Fooled 'Em," ibid., January 1, 1949, p. 16; "Lester Is Back at Royal Roost," ibid., March 26, 1949, p. 25.

60. "Lester Is Back," 25, and "Lester Young and Crew," 15.

61. "*Esquire* All-American Jazz Band," *Esquire,* February 1947, p. 124; Don Byas, George Auld, and Flip Phillips, all relative newcomers compared to Young, were ranked next. *Down Beat*'s tenor poll for that year ranked him third (with 927 votes), behind Charlie Ventura (1,388 votes) and Flip Phillips (1,158) and ahead of Vido Musso, Corky Coran, and Bud Freeman; Hawkins was not listed (*Down Beat,* January 1, 1946, p. 18). In *Metronome*'s poll, Young came in seventh in 1946; Hawkins placed first, followed by Phillips, Georgie Auld, Ventura, Webster, and Don Byas (*Metronome,* January 1946, p. 34). Seven years later, *Metronome*'s All-Star Poll would rank Young in seventh place behind Stan Getz's first (*Metronome,* February 1953, p. 24).

62. "College Gives 'Pres' Title Again," *Down Beat,* April 8, 1949, p. 4.

63. "Influence of the Year," *Metronome,* February 1949, p. 18.

64. "Lester Young Gets Kicks," *Chicago Defender,* February 5, 1949, p. 6. "You Take the Big Band," *California Eagle,* February 24, 1949, p. 17; "Count Basie to Retire?," *Chicago Defender,* January 15, 1949, p. 16.

65. "Pres Nixes Clown Deal, Just Blows Fine, Champ," *New York Amsterdam News,* August 7, 1954, p. 22. See bandleader Joe Houston's response to Young, "Bandleaders Who Clown Criticized," *Baltimore Afro-American,* August 28, 1954, p. 7; Young's article appeared in the August 7, 1954, issue of the same paper (p. 7).

66. "Sat. Jazz Concert Will Aid 1956 Musicians," *New York Amsterdam News,* September 20, 1956, p. 15; "Here May 14" (photo), *Chicago Defender,* April 27, 1946, p. 24. See Linda Dahl, *Morning Glory: A Biography of Mary Lou Williams* (New York: Pantheon, 1999), 265–66, on the Bel Canto Foundation. *Down Beat,* September 23, 1953, p. 14S; "The Old Feud" (photo), *Baltimore Afro-American,* October 23, 1954, p. 7.

67. Al Monroe, "Swinging the News," *Chicago Defender,* December 28, 1946, p. 6; "Where They Are Playing," ibid., p. 8; "Band Routes," *California Eagle,* February 13, 1947, p. 18. "Band Routes," *Down Beat,* starting April 9, 1947, p. 21, permitted the tracking of Young's appearances; ibid., starting again July 16, 1947, p. 17; "Band Routes," *Baltimore Afro-American,* August 9, 1947, p. 6.

68. *Lester Young, Volume 2: Live Recordings 1948–1956* (Jazz Anthology 30 JA 5174A), side A; and *Lester Young, Volume 3: Live Recording 1949 at the "Royal Roost" New York City* (Jazz Anthology 30 JA 5214). Albert Murray, *Stomping the Blues* (New York: McGraw-Hill, 1976).

14. Lester Blows Again

1. "Records" ad for the Fegan Brothers employment agency; other than Andy

Kirk and possibly Nat Cole, Young was one of the few jazz artists, along with the Three Blazers, the Soul Stirrers, the Ink Spots, and Billy Eckstine. The *Los Angeles Sentinel,* July 4, 1946, p. 19, placed four of Young's records in the listing; see also "Harlem Juke Box Hits," *New York Amsterdam News,* December 7, 1946, p. 21. "Lester Young Exclusively with Aladdin" (ad), *Metronome,* April 1946, p. 31, and "Lester Young—King of the Tenor-Sax" (ad), *Down Beat,* February 12, 1947, p. 19.

2. Author's interview with Sadik Hakim. Chris Welch, "Jazz Albums: *The Lester Young Story, Volume 1,*" *Melody Maker,* May 28, 1977, p. 32; Val Wilmer, "The Lee Young Story," *Jazz Journal,* January 1961, p. 3.

3. Lee Young explained that his brother felt the day-to-day realities of fronting a band prevented him from focusing on his music; Wilmer, "The Lee Young Story," 3. Author's interviews with Lee Young and Sadik Hakim; Leonard Feather, *The Jazz Years: Earwitness to an Era* (London: Quartet, 1986), 74.

4. Don Safran, *Dallas Times Herald,* April 17, 1960, Vertical File on Jazz in the Dallas Public Library, Dallas, Texas.

5. Garry Giddins's video biography, *Celebrating Bird: The Triumph of Charlie Parker* (West Long Branch, N.J.: Kultur, 1987), includes an interview with Parker's first wife, Rebecca, who relates that near the end of his life, her ex-husband told her of his regret over having left her to go to New York City in pursuit of fame and success.

6. John Tynan, "Meet Dr. Getz," *Down Beat,* February 20, 1957, p. 13; see the polls in *Metronome,* February 1951 (p. 14), February 1952 (p. 13), February 1953 (p. 16), January 1956 (p. 19), and January 1957 (p. 17). Also see *Down Beat,* December 31, 1952, p. 3; December 30, 1953, p. 6; December 29, 1954, p. 6; December 26, 1956, p. 14; December 25, 1958, p. 17; and August 21, 1958, p. 13, for results of critics' polls. Donald L. Maggin, *Stan Getz: A Life in Jazz* (New York: William Morrow, 1996).

7. "Nat" [Hentoff], "Granz Wouldn't Let Me Record with Parker . . . ," *Down Beat,* April 4, 1952, p. 7. In 1950 Miles Davis expressed much the same sentiment concerning the business end of the music industry, singling out the nightclub operators in particular with a common complaint among his fellow artists: "They don't treat musicians with enough respect." Finding it easier to think stereotypically, the average club owner assumed that "all jazz musicians are irresponsible drunkards" (Pat Harris, "Nothing But Bop? 'Stupid' Says Miles," *Down Beat,* January 27, 1950, p. 19).

8. Stanley Dance, *The World of Earl Hines* (New York: Scribner's, 1977), 158; Leonard Feather, "Prez," *Playboy,* September 1959, p. 54; see the Hugo R. Heydorn real estate ad, *New York Amsterdam News,* January 8, 1949, p. 14, for typical prices of homes in St. Albans. At the time of his death, the saxophonist was reported never to have earned less than $25,000 per year after World War II (Allan Morrison, "Lester Young: Tragedy of a Jazz Genius," *Jet,* April 9, 1959, p. 61).

9. "New Outlet for U.S. Bands?," *Down Beat,* December 30, 1949, p. 1; Ralph J. Gleason, "Just Can't See for Lookin'," *Esquire,* January 1947, p. 107; "Amusement Row by Garlington: How Great Can an Artist Be?" *New York*

Amsterdam News, March 26, 1949, p. 24. "Ten Top Money-Makers in Show Business," *Jet,* February 26, 1953, pp. 59–60; included in the article were Lena Horne, Billy Eckstine, Nat Cole, Lionel Hampton, Louis Jordan, Louis Armstrong, the boxer Sugar Ray Robinson, Billy Daniels, Sarah Vaughan, and Pearl Bailey. In the late 1950s the singer Eartha Kitt would average $300,000 a year, though like other Black entertainers—Nat Cole, for example—she would also be harassed by the Internal Revenue Service for back taxes; see "Tax-Ridden Eartha Declares: 'I'm Rich, Yet I'm a Pauper,'" *Jet,* March 19, 1959, pp. 60–62. See "Hawk's Gross at Paramount Was Amazing," *Los Angeles Sentinel,* November 3, 1949, p. 6B, on Hawkins's earnings.

10. Buddy Tate, IJS, p. 115. In Whitney Balliett, "Pres," *The New Yorker,* February 23, 1981, Tate recalls this conversation's having taken place in 1958 (p. 99). Interestingly, Sadik Hakim reported nearly identical figures for Young and others, claiming that the tenor stylist earned $500 a week when others were making $1,500 (Sadik Hakim WKCR [New York] interview with Phil Schaap, April 9, 1976; my thanks to Phil Schaap for sharing it with me). After Carpenter left, Young would have other managers, including a Black man named Gabby Hayes (personal communication with Lester Young Jr.). See Frank Büchmann-Møller, *You Just Fight for Your Life: The Story of Lester Young* (New York: Praeger, 1990), p. 185, for further details on Young's negotiations with Granz.

11. Many of his sidemen—including Sadik Hakim and Connie Kay—voiced this opinion concerning what Young actually received versus what he should have received in the way of salary.

12. *Metronome* and *Down Beat* both ran articles featuring these films in the mid-1950s. "Plan Louis Armstrong Film Life Story," *Jet,* June 19, 1958, p. 60.

13. Lewis Porter, ed., *A Lester Young Reader* (Washington, D.C.: Smithsonian Institution Press, 1991), 44. Shirley Bentley, "Chicago Club Op Finds . . . ," *Down Beat,* September 21, 1955, pp. 35–36; Hannah Altbush, "Basie, Sarah Wail . . . ," ibid., November 3, 1954, p. 20. "Jazz at the Philharmonic," *Metronome,* July 1946, p. 42.

14. D. Leon Wolff, "Granz Bash a Caricature on Jazz," *Down Beat,* November 18, 1946, p. 3. He also described the audience as "a shade more repulsive than usual," and charged that "98 percent of [them] have absolutely no understanding of worthwhile jazz." "Jeg," "With a Hoot and a Howl, JATP Kicks Off Another," ibid., April 8, 1949, p. 12.

15. Barry Ulanov, "The Editors Speak . . . : Hollywood Hangover," *Metronome,* October 1949, p. 38. A few years earlier Ulanov had had nothing but praise for the rich jazz scene in the region; see Barry Ulanov, "Jazz in Los Angeles," *Metronome,* August 1946, p. 19. "Tension Mounts on Fifty-second Street," *Metronome,* August 1944, pp. 7, 28.

16. Tom Piper, "Zombies Put Kiss of Death on Fifty-second Street," *Down Beat,* February 25, 1946, p. 3. The use of the term *zombie* is interesting; besides suggesting the hipsters' drugged state, it also suggests that they were walking corpses who marched to a different beat than the rest of the public. Also, and despite the association of zombies with Haiti, these creatures have no

really significant racial designation, so the group could, at least in theory, be racially mixed.

17. Leonard Feather, "The Street Is Dead: A Jazz Obituary," *Metronome,* April 1948, pp. 16–17, 32–33. Feather also noted the widespread use of heroin as a major problem. He opened the article with an admission that he had begun writing it a year earlier but had "gleefully" torn up the previous effort after "an unexpected revival of jazz along Fifty-second Street." On the Barbary Coast, see Tom Stoddard, *Jazz on the Barbary Coast* (Berkeley, Calif.: Heyday Books, 1998).

18. Piper, "Zombies," 3. "Five Men Held As Drug Suspects; Seven Others Jailed," *California Eagle,* April 3, 1947, pp. 1, 8. Hal Holly, "L.A. Cops Garner Publicity in Sepia Hotspots Raid," *Down Beat,* April 23, 1946, p. 10. "Hot Spots Jump Sans Usual Ofay Trade," *Chicago Defender,* April 27, 1946, p. 26.

19. See Abe Hill, "Fifty-second Street New York's Real 'Melting Pot,'" *New York Amsterdam News,* July 15, 1944, pp. 1, 21; "Swinging Trailblazers Suffer from Invasion of Hellraisers," ibid., July 22, 1944, p. 11A; and "The Magic Wand of Swing Keeps Fifty-second Street Doors Ajar," ibid., July 29, 1944, p. 1; "Tension Mounts," 7, 28. "L.A. Symphony Hall Closed," *Los Angeles Sentinel,* May 21, 1946, p. 10.

"White Café Owner Prefers Fine to Serving Musicians," *Philadelphia Afro-American,* October 18, 1947, p. 8. Two years later, in Detroit, Billie Holiday's companion, a white musician, was beaten by other patrons for having the nerve to bring a Black woman into the club ("Musician Beaten by Dixie Thugs," *New York Amsterdam News,* October 29, 1949, p. 1).

20. "Jazz Goes to UCLA in Campus Concert," *Down Beat,* May 6, 1946, p. 16. "UCLA Jazz Concert," *Metronome,* June 1946, p. 38, suggested that Young and Parker's duet was "by far the best number of the program." In Los Angeles, one nightclub owner, Billy Berg, sought to treat the races equally. Having been raised with African Americans, he insisted that he recognized no difference between Blacks and whites. His club was described by *Ebony* as "the average man's idea of a democratic club." Berg reported that when curious customers (probably whites) queried him about the interracial seating—a marked contrast to the practices of other Los Angeles nightclubs outside of the Black district—he would inform them that it was the way he conducted his business ("Billy Berg's: Hollywood Jazz Temple Draws Stars and Hoi Polloi," *Ebony,* April 1948, p. 29; see also p. 32). "Norman Granz Turned Down Cash to Defeat Jim Crow at Jazz Concerts," *California Eagle,* February 12, 1948, p. 15. Clora Bryant, CAS, pp. 96–97.

21. Babs Gonzales, *I Paid My Dues: Good Times—No Bread* (East Orange, N.J.: Expubidence, 1967); Norwood "Pony" Poindexter, *The Pony Express: Memoirs of a Jazz Musician* (Frankfurt, West Germany: J.A.S. Publikationen, 1985); Milton "Mezz" Mezzrow and Bernard Wolfe, *Really the Blues* (New York: Random House, 1946); Malcolm X with Alex Haley, *The Autobiography of Malcolm X* (New York: Grove, 1965); Billie Holiday and William Dufty, *Lady Sings the Blues* (Garden City, N.Y.: Doubleday, 1956). Clora Bryant, CAS, pp. 103–4; Art Farmer, CAS, pp. 84–85.

22. Ralph J. Gleason, "Granz Has a Dynamic Talent for Making—and Breaking—Records," *San Francisco Chronicle,* October 6, 1957, p. 30.
23. "Ron," "Public's Tastes Puzzles Discers," *Down Beat,* January 28, 1949, p. 2.
24. David W. Stowe, *Swing Changes: Big-Band Jazz in New Deal America* (Cambridge, Mass.: Harvard University Press, 1994), 115–17, 196.
25. Russell Sanjek, *From Print to Plastic: Publishing and Promoting America's Popular Music, 1900–1980* (Brooklyn, N.Y.: Institute for Studies in American Music, 1983), is very good on the economic setting of the music industry. I wish to thank Bill Hassan, whom I met at a Smithsonian conference in Washington, D.C., in 1988, for providing me with a copy of the tape-recorded interview with Jo Jones. "New Ruling Hits Count," *New York Amsterdam News,* January 15, 1949, p. 21; "Count Basie to Retire?," *Chicago Defender,* January 15, 1949, p. 16; Basie discussed the move briefly in his *Good Morning Blues: The Autobiography of Count Basie,* as told to Albert Murray (New York: Random House, 1985), 281–83.
26. When Young complained to his interviewer François Postif that Norman Granz never let him record with strings, he was probably thinking of the fact that both Billie Holiday and Charlie Parker had made records with string accompaniment—the latter under Granz's direction. See the Postif interview, "Lester: Paris, '59," *Jazz Review,* September 1959, pp. 7–12 (reprinted several times, e.g., in Porter, ed., *A Lester Young Reader,* 173–92).
27. Leonard Feather, "Here's Pres!," *Melody Maker,* July 15, 1950, p. 3; Feather, "Prez," 53ff.
28. Pat Harris, "Pres Talks about Himself, Copycats," *Down Beat,* May 6, 1949, p. 15; Bill Coss, "JATP's Chief Executive: The President," *Metronome,* October 1955, p. 25; Nat Shapiro and Nat Hentoff, eds., *The Jazz Makers: Essays on the Greats of Jazz* (1957; reprint, New York: Da Capo, 1979), 244.
29. John Hammond, "Recollections," in "Two Views of Lester Young," *Jazz and Blues,* August 1973, pp. 8–19.
30. Ibid.
31. Feather, "Prez," 54.
32. Hentoff and Shapiro, *The Jazz Makers,* 256; Nat Hentoff, "Pres," *Down Beat,* March 7, 1956, p. 9.
33. Hentoff and Shapiro, *The Jazz Makers,* 256; Derek Young, "He Holds His Office Graciously," *Melody Maker,* March 21, 1953, p. 4 (reprinted in Porter, ed., *A Lester Young Reader,* 151–53). Hentoff, "Pres," 11.
34. Benny Green, "Lester Young: A Reflection," *Jazz Journal,* May 1959, p. 9; John Hammond, "Lester Young," *Jazz: A Quarterly of American Music,* summer 1959, pp. 181, 183.
35. Clora Bryant, "Liner Notes," *Bebop and Beyond* 4, no. 3 (1985): 3.
36. Danny Barker, *A Life in Jazz* (New York: Oxford University Press, 1986), v.
37. Leonard Feather, *The Jazz Years: Earwitness to an Era* (London and New York: Quartet, 1986), 6.
38. Luc Delannoy, *Lester Young: Profession: President* (Paris: Denöel, 1987), 245.

39. Cab Calloway and Bryant Rollins, *Of Minnie the Moocher and Me* (New York: Thomas Y. Crowell, 1976), 4. Ray Charles and David Ritz, *Brother Ray* (New York: Warner, 1979), 249. Alun Morgan, *Count Basie* (Spellmount, N.Y.: Hippocrene, 1984), 60. Dempsey Travis, *An Autobiography of Jazz* (Chicago: Urban Research Institute, 1983), and Milt Hinton and David G. Berger, *Bass Line: The Stories and Photographs of Milt Hinton* (Philadelphia: Temple University Press, 1988), are good introductions to the world of musicians more or less from insiders' perspectives. Maurice Waller and Anthony Calabrese, *Fats Waller* (New York: Schirmer, 1977); Bill Gottlieb, "Thelonious Monk—Genius or ??," *Down Beat*, September 24, 1947, p. 2; the subtitle of the article refers to Monk's being "elusive."

40. Lawrence Levine, *Black Culture and Black Consciousness: Afro-American Folk Thought from Slavery to Freedom* (New York: Oxford University Press, 1977), 13, 99–101. Waller and Calabrese, *Fats Waller.* Alyn Shipton, *Groovin' High: The Life of Dizzy Gillespie* (New York: Oxford University Press, 1999).

15. Movin' with Lester

1. Whitney Balliett, "Profiles: Room to Live In," *The New Yorker,* November 20, 1971, p. 63. Author's interviews with Jesse Drakes and Leroy Jackson. Frank Büchmann-Møller, *You Just Fight for Your Life: The Story of Lester Young* (New York: Praeger, 1990), appendix B, 252–53. Leonard Feather, "Birdlandish Bistros Boom; Make New Music Market," *Down Beat,* June 18, 1952, pp. 1, 19. "The First Ten Years of Birdland," ibid., December 10, 1959, pp. 18–22.

2. Büchmann-Møller, *You Just Fight,* appendix A, "List of Jobs and Engagements," 223–50.

3. Allan McMillan, "Allan's Alley," *New York Amsterdam News,* June 11, 1949, p. 25.

4. In 1957, the Gale Agency's offices were located at 48 West Forty-eighth Street ("Where They're Playing," *Down Beat,* May 30, 1957, p. 42). Moe Gale and his brother attempted to break down Jim Crow customs and promote the desegregation of audiences. The Gale Agency "boosted many Negro performers" and, furthermore, was manned by a "big interracial staff"; Tim Gale claimed to be "just interested in a client's talent and not his color or race" ("Gale Agency Boosted Many Negro Performers," *Pittsburgh Courier,* January 12, 1957, p. 19). John S. Wilson, "Birdland Applies Imagination to Jazz," *Down Beat,* January 27, 1950, p. 3. Birdland was located on the eastern side of Broadway, near Fifty-second Street; Basie and Young performed there for two weeks ("Basie, Les Young Top Action at Birdland," *Pittsburgh Courier,* January 10, 1953, p. 17). On this club, see Evelyn Cunningham, "New York's Famous 'Birdland,'" ibid., January 5, 1957, magazine sec., p. 3, and January 12, 1957, p. 5; and Robert Sylvester, "Night Life with Music," *Holiday,* February 1957, pp. 64ff. Max Kaminsky and V. E. Hughes, *My Life*

in Jazz (New York: Harper and Row, 1963). The Alvin was situated at the northwestern corner of Fifty-second Street and Broadway.

The Gale Agency also booked Joe Louis's tour; see the *Pittsburgh Courier,* June 6, 1953, p. 18. The tour covered Massachusetts, Ohio, Indiana, Missouri, Kansas, Oklahoma, Texas, Louisiana, Mississippi, Georgia, and Florida over thirty-one days; see "Big 'Big Rhythm, Blues Show' Opens Tour in Bean Town," "Where They're Playing," and "Real Headliners" (with accompanying photographs), ibid., July 25, 1953, p. 18. Author's interviews with Junior Mance and Gildo Mahones.

5. Büchmann-Møller, *You Just Fight,* appendix A, 223–50.
6. Bill Milkowski, "'The Father of Modern Drumming': Roy Haynes," *Down Beat,* October 1993, p. 21. Rodney Richardson, a former Basieite, was walking down the street in Chicago when he heard a familiar whistle. It was Pres and Shadow Wilson, in a taxi on their way to the airport and New York; Young asked Richardson to come to New York and join him, and shortly thereafter, he did (Dale Smoak, "Rodney Richardson: Interview—Part 1," *Coda,* November 1989, p. 16).
7. Author's interviews with Junior Mance, Leroy Jackson, and Gildo Mahones.
8. Nat Hentoff, "Caught in the Act," *Down Beat,* January 13, 1954, p. 4. Frank Tenot, "A la recherché de Lester Young," *Jazz Hot,* no. 76 (April 1953), p. 13, may have been the report to which Hentoff was referring. In the spring of 1955, Barry Ulanov, writing for *Down Beat,* gave high marks to a live performance by the tenor saxophonist at a Charlie Parker tribute. After drawing a connection between Bird and Pres—"These two musicians more than any other two made modern jazz what it is"—and emphasizing their historical significance, Ulanov praised Young's playing, which he said "reminded some of us that there were still giants in our midst." Nor was this the only occasion on which Young excelled; the editor recalled a similar night at Birdland when the saxophone stylist had played "more choruses of the blues than I could count or possibly remember if I had counted them. . . . It was the blues made moving, made melodic and tied together . . . to make one long statement of surpassing beauty." He asserted that "Young is one of the very few jazzmen playing today who [are] really entitled to that overworked adjective of the entertainment business, 'immortal'" (Barry Ulanov, *Down Beat,* May 18, 1955, pp. 34–35). In contrast, four years earlier, a *Metronome* critic had described a Lester Young combo performance as "a singularly graceless set of noises, following that most awful of jazz principles, a solo for every man in every number, save for Lester's breathy but cool solo [on] 'Ghost of a Chance'" ("B. H.," *Metronome,* May 1951, p. 24).
9. Bill Coss, "JATP's Chief Executive: The President," *Metronome,* October 1955, p. 25.
10. "Record Reviews," *Down Beat,* December 28, 1951, p. 18; ibid., March 21, 1952, p. 15; ibid., September 24, 1952, p. 13; ibid., March 11, 1953, p. 15-S. Nat Hentoff, "Jazz Reviews," *Down Beat,* March 24, 1954, p. 17, was a mixed review; another by Hentoff, "Jazz Review," ibid., September 22, 1954, p. 14, typified the ambivalence: "The performance [as] a whole would win any other tenor five stars. . . . For Lester, it's a good characteristic set, but on oc-

casion he can do better." See also Hentoff, "Jazz Review," ibid., October 16, 1954, p. 14 ("Neither side is Pres at his best . . . but Lester's still swinging"); idem, "Jazz Review," ibid., August 25, 1954, p. 14; and idem, "Jazz Review," ibid., May 5, 1954, p. 11, and May 19, 1954, p. 12, both praising Young's collaboration with Oscar Peterson.

11. B[ill] C[oss], "In Person," *Metronome,* October 1951, p. 21.

12. George T. Simon, "Record Reviews," *Metronome,* October 1951, p. 27: Simon claimed that "Down 'n' Adam," the second selection, a blues, "swings more," and that Young played "more interesting notes" on it. *Lester Young, Volume 3: Live Recording 1949 at the "Royal Roost" New York City* (Jazz Anthology 30 JA 5214).

13. Lewis Porter, ed., *A Lester Young Reader* (Washington, D.C.: Smithsonian Institution, 1991), 44, 152. Leonard Feather, "Illinois Takes Off His Jacquet," *Down Beat,* February 11, 1953, p. 16-S.

14. Allan Morrison, "'Prez' Swam against Current, Influenced 2 Jazz Generations," *Jet,* April 9, 1959, p. 61.

15. Ibid., 62. Stanley Dance, *The World of Earl Hines* (New York: Charles Scribner's Sons, 1977), 158–59.

16. Author's interviews with Barney Kessel and Irving Ashby. Oscar Peterson admired the saxophonist's simplicity: "Lester took the simplest path to where he wanted to get to, musically speaking. He always wanted [instrumental] backgrounds, and yet they had to remain inspirational." The pianist added, "I tried to simplify my playing to the point where he would always be comfortable" ("Oscar Peterson and Friends," *Chicago Tribune,* June 6, 1999, sec. 7, p. 4; I wish to thank my brother, Dennis, for bringing this article to my attention).

17. Author's interviews with John Collins and Le Roy Jackson.

18. Author's interview with Buck Clayton.

19. Carl "Kansas" Fields visited with Young in 1956 and 1959 in Paris, where the drummer lived for a number of years. Connie Kay thought that Young's uncompromising adherence to his values enabled him to survive his army experience. That alone won him the admiration of his fans. Kay stressed the necessity of appreciating "the way he [Young] grew up and where he came from and what he accomplished, plus what he went through as a Black person in the army . . . and [the fact that] he still came on out and played the saxophone." He continued, "A lot of cats might have wigged out . . . but Lester . . . had zest for life" (author's interview with Connie Kay).

20. Author's interviews with Le Roy Jackson and Connie Kay.

21. Sadik Hakim interview with Phil Schaap, WKCR, New York City, April 9, 1976; I wish to thank Mr. Schaap for providing me with a copy of this interview. "What the Cats Do While the Squares Sleep," *Chicago Defender,* September 23, 1953, p. 28; ibid., September 8, 1953, p. 28; "'Names' Take Over Local Nite Clubs," ibid., October 13, 1953, p. 28.

22. Author's interview with Junior Mance.

23. Author's interview with Sadik Hakim; Dance, *The World of Earl Hines,* 158.

24. Porter, ed., *A Lester Young Reader,* 94.

25. Author's interviews with Sadik Hakim and Jimmy Heath. Although initially Young was given credit for composing "Jumping with Symphony Sid," it is now known that Hakim deserved the credit.

26. Sadik Hakim interview with Phil Schaap. "Band Routes," *Down Beat,* June 4, 1947, p. 25, and June 18, 1947, p. 21, indicated that Young's combo was at the Baby Grand from June 12 to June 25, 1947.

27. Balliett, "Profiles," 84–86. Author's interviews with Irma and Martha Young and Connie Kay.

28. Balliett, "Profiles," 70.

29. Author's interview with Jimmy Heath.

30. Author's interviews with Sadik Hakim and Irving Ashby.

31. Author's interview with Sadik Hakim. See also Art Blakey's opinion, quoted in Art Taylor, *Notes and Tones* (1977; reprint, New York: Perigee, 1982), 240: "The musicians, entertainers and athletes are the ones who break down the race barriers."

32. Author's interview with Sadik Hakim.

33. Author's interviews with Jesse Drakes and Gildo Mahones. Bill Potts, CD notes, *Lester Young in Washington, D.C., 1956, Volume 1* (Original Jazz Classic CD 782-2 [2308-219]). *Sarah Vaughan/Lester Young One Night Stand: The Town Hall Concert* (Blue Note CDP 7243 8 32139 2 4).

34. Author's interview with Barney Kessel.

35. Author's interview with Irving Ashby. The saxophonist Lee Konitz described Young's playing in similar terms: "This is what I mean by playing warmly—I feel that it's possible to get the maximum intensity in your playing and still relax . . . what Lester did in the Basie days. To me, his work then is a perfect example of the essence of what I'm trying to do" ("Nat" [Hentoff], "Lee Konitz Moving into 'Valuable Property' Class," *Down Beat,* August 11, 1954, p. 8).

36. Author's interview with Gildo Mahones. Buddy Tate also stressed his friend's virtuosity, maintaining that "he never played the same solos [twice]" (Buddy Tate, IJS, p. 15).

37. Author's interview with Junior Mance.

38. Author's interview with Sadik Hakim. Liner notes, *The Jazz Singer: Eddie Jefferson* (Inner City 1016). The pianist Hampton Hawes, in the 1950s, and more recently the tenor saxophonist Pharaoh Sanders and the singer Lorez Alexandria are among the musicians who have recorded "Polka Dots and Moonbeams."

39. Author's interviews with Gildo Mahones and Jesse Drakes.

40. Author's interview with Connie Kay. See "Do Critics Really Know What It's All About?," *Metronome,* May 1937, p. 17: "All the silly, snippy smatterings of the reviewers' are just such because of one thing: THE LACK OF ACTUAL EXPERIENCE. They don't know WHY WHAT HAPPENS WHEN." The author insightfully observed that critics' opinions were in-

variably "based upon a view from the outside in, and usually a very warped view at that."

41. Lewis Porter, *Lester Young* (Boston: Twayne, 1985), 100.

42. Balliett, "Profiles," 106, 108.

43. John Hammond with Irving Townsend, *On Record: An Autobiography* (New York: Penguin, 1981), 132ff, and especially 137.

44. Leonard Feather, "The Blindfold Test: Pres Digs Every Kind of Music," *Down Beat,* November 2, 1951, p. 13 (reprinted in Lewis Porter, ed., *A Lester Young Reader* [Washington, D.C.: Smithsonian Institution Press, 1991], 150–51).

45. Ibid. Les Brown ("Blue Moon"), Bob Eberly ("But Not for Me"), the Ink Spots ("I Don't Stand a Ghost of a Chance with You"), and Bud Freeman ("Tia Juana") all received three stars; Young gave Mr. Google-Eyes, with Billy Ford's V-Eights ("No Wine, No Women"), two stars, his lowest rating, and explained, "It's kind of over my head. . . . I can't get with that [shuffle] rhythm."

46. Porter, ed., *A Lester Young Reader,* 162–63.

47. Ibid., 163. Frank Büchmann-Møller, *You Just Fight for Your Life: The Story of Lester Young* (New York: Praeger, 1990), 200–1, 215.

48. Porter, ed., *A Lester Young Reader,* 160.

49. Ibid., 162.

50. Ibid., 160.

51. Ibid., 161. See Gene Ramey's account of Young and the new drummers in Stanley Dance, *The World of Count Basie* (New York: Charles Scribner's Sons, 1980), 280; and another musician's recollection of Young's instructions to a young sideman on the dropping of bombs in "Norman Simmons Talks to Mark Gardner," *Jazz Monthly,* October 1970, p. 7.

52. Porter, ed., *A Lester Young Reader,* 161.

53. The New Orleans drummer Warren "Baby" Dodds noted, "As leader I felt that it was my place to let everybody else have a showing" (quoted in Nat Hentoff and Nat Shapiro, *The Jazz Makers: Essays on the Greats of Jazz* [1957; reprint, New York: Da Capo, 1979], 37). Dodds made this comment in the context of a specific recording session, and pointed out that his philosophy prevented him from soloing on that occasion because "by the time my chance came it was all over and the recording was finished. But I didn't care. . . . I was interested in being the leader and having my name on the records." This last part of his statement did not, however, negate Dodds's ideas about leadership.

54. Porter, ed., *A Lester Young Reader,* 163.

55. Ibid., 159, 163.

56. Chris Albertson interview, August 1958. François Postif interview, February 6, 1959, a tape of which can be found at IJS, Rutgers University, Newark, New Jersey; it was published as "Lester: Paris, '59," *Jazz Monthly,* February 1964, pp. 14–16, and is reprinted in Porter, ed., *A Lester Young Reader,* 173–91.

57. Porter, ed., *A Lester Young Reader,* 163.

58. Ibid., 186.

16. Up 'n' Adam

1. Beverly Young, letter of April 13, 1996, to the author. She spoke with both the doctor who was on the scene shortly after her father's death and the medical examiner at the hospital. "A Great Is Gone," *Down Beat,* April 16, 1959, p. 11, reported that the saxophonist had suffered a stroke in 1958 and had had "a succession of ailments, including a lingering kidney problem." Young's hospitalization is mentioned in "Strictly Ad Lib," *Down Beat,* January 25, 1956, p. 5 ("[He] has needed a rest badly. . . . He's progressing well and should be ready to play the Birdland tour." In ibid., February 8, 1956, p. 6, the magazine noted that the tenor man had left the hospital and was joining the Birdland tour. "Strictly Ad Lib," ibid., February 6, 1958, p. 8, noted Young's hospitalization at King's County Hospital; a January 4, 1958, clipping in the Lester Young Vertical File, IJS, Rutgers University, Newark, New Jersey, reported that he had collapsed a few days after a coast-to-coast tour and had recently broken with his manager, Charles Carpenter. For the 1957 Birdland tour with Basie, see "Birdland Tour Inks a Flock of Names," *Down Beat,* February 6, 1957, p. 9. Author's interviews with Marshal Royal, John "Zoot" Sims, and Dr. Luther Cloud; see also Allan Morrison, "Lester Young: Tragedy of a Jazz Genius," *Jet,* April 9, 1959, pp. 58–62. Dan Morgenstern, "Lester Leaps In," *Jazz Journal,* August 1958, p. 1.

2. Lester Young Vertical File clipping, January 4, 1958, IJS; author's interviews with Jesse Drakes, Leroy Jackson, Connie Kay, Gildo Mahones, and Dr. Luther Cloud. Drakes managed the band for a period when it traveled to California, while Carpenter was "going off with a *big* show." Morgenstern, "Lester Leaps In," 1.

3. "Jazz: North to Newport," *Newsweek,* August 2, 1954, p. 70; "Jam in Newport," *Time,* July 25, 1955, p. 65.

4. "The Granz Stand," *Metronome,* November 1953, pp. 21–22; "Norman Granz Slates Thirteenth Tour of JATP," *Pittsburgh Courier,* August 22, 1953, p. 19; "JATP Slates Fifty-eight Big Dates," ibid., September 10, 1953, p. 19. "Granz's Contracts Ban Segregation," *Baltimore Afro-American,* August 29, 1953, p. 6; Charles Emge, "How Norman Granz's Flourishing Jazz Empire Started, Expanded," *Down Beat,* December 15, 1954, pp. 3–4; "Granz Mapping Big Strides in Jazz Disk Field," *Billboard,* January 17, 1953, p. 28; Ralph J. Gleason, "Granz Has a Dynamic Talent for Making—and Breaking—Records," *San Francisco Chronicle,* October 6, 1957, pp. 29–30.

5. "Granz Tells Story of Tour," *Down Beat,* June 4, 1952, pp. 1, 17, on the first European tour; "Birdland All-Stars Will Play Europe," *Down Beat,* April 18, 1956, 11, on the Birdland tour; see also Alun Morgan, "Lester Young in Paris—1956," *Jazz Monthly,* December 1956, p. 27. Nat Hentoff, "Pres,"

Down Beat, March 7, 1956, p. 9. In idem, "European Jazz Lags Well behind Ours: Peterson," *Down Beat,* June 3, 1953, the pianist joined the debate about the state of jazz in Europe by emphasizing that in the United States, too many people regarded the music as "just entertainment," whereas Europeans tended to consider it an art form (p. 4). Recorded in two sessions in November 1956, *Lester Young: Pres in Europe* (High Note HCD 7054) permits us to hear him with both Europeans (René Utreger, piano, and Pierre Michelot, bass) and African American servicemen (Lex Humphries and Al King) stationed overseas. See Dan Morgenstern, liner notes to the 1974 LP *Prez in Europe* (Onyx 218), reprinted as "Prez in Europe" in Lewis Porter, ed., *A Lester Young Reader* (Washington, D.C.: Smithsonian Institution Press, 1991), 305–14.

6. "Granz Tells Story of Tour," 1, 17; see also "The Jazz Business," *Time,* March 2, 1953, p. 40. "World's Most Fanatical Jazz Artists Slated for Concert," *Los Angeles Sentinel,* September 27, 1956, p. 16. Alyn Shipton, *Groovin' High: The Life of Dizzy Gillespie* (New York: Oxford University Press, 1999), 280–85. James Lincoln Collier, *Louis Armstrong: An American Genius* (New York: Oxford University Press, 1983), 317–19.

7. "Los Angeles Jumps at Jazz Benefit," *Metronome,* August 1944, p. 9; I wish to thank Alice McGrath for bringing this information about JATP and Sleepy Lagoon to my attention (personal communication).

8. Bill Coss, "The Norman Granz Story," *Metronome,* October 1955, pp. 21, 25, 37. Emge, "Norman Granz's Flourishing Jazz Empire," 3–4. "Ella, Jazz Group Are Humiliated," *Dallas Express,* October 15, 1955, pp. 1, 9. On the dismissal of the "gambling raid" case, see "Dixie Charges against Ella, Granz Dismissed," *Philadelphia Afro-American,* December 31, 1955, p. 7.

9. Many JATP fans would have agreed with the opinion that "Norman Granz . . . is as great an attraction as the artists themselves" (" 'JATP' Comes to Carnegie," *New York Amsterdam News,* September 13, 1952, p. 23). *Metronome* characterized JATP's "usual trained seal act of induced hysteria" at the Carnegie Hall concert in 1956 as the "JATP stamp" ("JATP at Carnegie Hall," *Metronome,* November 1956, p. 28). On its grosses, see "The Jazz Business," 40.

10. Author's interview with Irving Ashby. "Granz Tells Story of Tour," 1, 17. "The Jazz Business," p. 40; Florence Cadrez, "Mostly About Musicians," *Los Angeles Sentinel,* September 17, 1953, p. B3; "Hip Nips Flip for Granz's 'JATP,' " *Variety,* November 11, 1953, p. 51.

11. *JATP—The Trumpet Battle* (Verve 8151512).

12. "In Person," *Metronome,* November 1957, p. 35. Illinois Jacquet, who had appeared with Young in *Jammin' the Blues* and played with Basie in the mid-1940s, became very popular and in early 1949 was said to be considering offers from Hollywood ("Illinois Jacquet Holds Out for Featured Movie Role," *Chicago Defender,* February 19, 1949, p. 17). On Jacquet, see also "Illinois Jacquet Youngest of Current Band Leaders," *Philadelphia Afro-American,* December 8, 1947, p. 10; "Jacquet and Sax Hits a Million—That's a Lick," *New York Amsterdam News,* June 26, 1948, p. 25; and "Jac-

quet Prepares for His Theatre Debut on Broadway," ibid., August 28, 1948, p. 25.

13. On Stan Kenton's Festival of Modern American Jazz, see *Philadelphia Afro-American,* October 31, 1953, p. 7; ibid., February 13, 1954, p. 6. On the Gale Agency's tour, see "Nat Cole Suffers Attacking During New York Concert," *Chicago Defender,* April 11, 1953, p. 17. Irving Granz, brother of Norman, presented Jazz à La Carte in late 1956 at the Shrine Auditorium; the show featured Sarah Vaughan, Mel Torme, the Hi Los, the Oscar Peterson Trio, the Lighthouse All-Stars, and Shorty Rogers and his band (advertisement, *Los Angeles Sentinel,* November 8, 1956, p. 10).

14. On the best-selling records in jazz, see *Down Beat,* August 8, 1956, p. 20. They ranked as follows: 1) MJQ, *Fontessa;* 2) Ella Fitzgerald, *Ella Sings the Cole Porter Songbook;* 3) Stan Kenton, *In Hi-Fi;* 4) an Oscar Peterson album; and 5) an album by Chris Peterson. Surprisingly, a record by Art Blakey's Jazz Messengers came in sixth; among the others in the top twenty were offerings by Lennie Tristano (11), and Max Roach and Clifford Brown (13).

15. "'Prez' Young, Charles, Webster Also on Beam," *Chicago Defender,* August 6, 1955, p. 28, and various nightclub ads, ibid., 30. On the Chicago jazz scene at this time, see "Jazz in Chicago: In the Beginning, There Was Dave Garroway," *Metronome,* May 1956, pp. 15ff. "Big Maybelle," *Ebony,* February 1955, pp. 104–5. Kevin M. Williams, "Chicago's Brawny Bebop Sound," *City Talk,* January 5, 2000, p. 9; I wish to thank my sister, Sylvia, for bringing this Chicago weekly to my attention. Dempsey J. Travis, *An Autobiography of Black Jazz* (Chicago: Urban Research Institute, 1983), is also good on Chicago jazz.

16. Critics referred to the "Getz-Young School" in "Saxophone Schools," *Metronome,* September 1951, p. 15. "The modern tenor sound . . . came mostly from Lester Young," the article claimed—but why then was it not referred to as the "Young School," or at the very least the "Young-Getz School" (especially since mention was made of the Eddie Miller, Charlie Parker, Johnny Hodges, Lee Konitz, and Coleman Hawkins schools)? "George Simon on the 'Cool Generation,'" *Metronome,* June 1954, p. 34; "The Cool School," *Ebony,* February 1955, pp. 74–78. "Bandleaders Who Clown Criticized," *Baltimore Afro-American,* August 28, 1954, p. 7; "No Clown Young Tells Promoters," ibid., August 7, 1954, p. 7. See also "'Wild Man' of the Saxophone," *Jet,* April 14, 1952, pp. 60–61, and ibid., back cover. On "Big Jay" McNeely, see "Big Jay McNeely," *Ebony,* May 1953, pp. 60–66; author's interview with Gildo Mahones. "Big Jay" McNeely interview, CAS, provides biographical details on the saxophonist.

17. "Joe Louis Begins New Career as Dancer," *Jet,* April 16, 1953, p. 59. "Joe Louis to Tour with 'Big Rhythm and Blues Show,'" *Pittsburgh Courier,* June 6, 1953, p. 18; the Gale Agency sponsored the show.

18. "Phil Moore Bemoans Lack of Chance Given Negroes in Radio and Music," *Chicago Defender,* April 27, 1946, p. 24. "Lena Horne, Victim, Flays Jim Crow Policy of Radio," *Philadelphia Afro-American,* September 20, 1947,

p. 6. "Erskine Hawkins Moves to Offset Ban on Recordings," *California Eagle,* January 1, 1948, p. 18.

19. Joe Bostic, "Performers Now at Mercy of Juke Box, Disc Jocks," *New York Amsterdam News,* August 7, 1954, p. 20.

20. Joe Bostic, "Is Show Business Influence Lost?," *New York Amsterdam News,* August 14, 1954, p. 22.

21. Alvin "Chick" Webb, "The True Significance of Moondog et al.," *New York Amsterdam News,* September 25, 1954, p. 24.

22. Ibid.

23. Jack Tracy, a former *Down Beat* editor, maintained that Young had indeed been undependable when he was questioned about this rumor in the late 1980s (personal communication with the author). I did not ask Mr. Tracy for clarification of what he meant, but in terms of Young's showing up for dates, his sidemen were unanimous in their recollection that he could always be counted on to appear before the scheduled hour. George Frazier, "Blue Notes and Blue Stockings," *Esquire,* August 1955, pp. 55–58; Wein's statement appears on page 56. See Norman Granz's insightful rebuttal, titled "Frazier versus Jazz at the Philharmonic," in the letters column, "Sound and Fury," ibid., November 1955, pp. 14, 16, 18.

24. Nat Hentoff, "A Civilian's Report," *Metronome,* January 1958, p. 5.

25. Harry Edison, IJS, pp. 4–9.

26. Dicky Wells, *The Night People: Reminiscences of a Jazzman,* as told to Stanley Dance, (Boston: Crescendo, 1971), 47–48.

27. "Alcoholism Cured, James Moody Waxes New Album for Comeback," *Jet,* December 25, 1958, pp. 58–59. Diana Barrymore and Gerold Frank, *Too Much, Too Soon* (New York: Henry Holt, 1957), 305–7.

28. "Are You a Drunkard?" *Philadelphia Afro-American,* February 22, 1947, p. M4; Dennis A. Bethea, M.D., "Alcoholism: A Social Disease," ibid., August 16, 1947, p. M8.

29. Stanley Dance, *The World of Count Basie* (New York: Charles Scribner's Sons, 1980), 280. "New York Dope Deaths Reach All-Time High," *Jet,* November 10, 1951, p. 54, reported seventy-seven deaths during a period of just eleven months.

30. Author's interviews with Carl "Kansas" Fields and Abe Bolar. Burt Korall, "I've Got to Get Close to a Blues," *Melody Maker,* September 7, 1957, p. 3; I wish to express my appreciation to Val Wilmer for bringing this interview to my attention.

31. Sidney Bechet, *Treat It Gentle: An Autobiography* (1960; reprint, New York: Da Capo, 1978), and Bill Coleman, *Trumpet Story* (Boston: Northeastern University Press, 1991). See Michael Levin, "'Don't Blame Show Biz!'—Billie," *Down Beat,* June 4, 1947, pp. 1, 6, in which Holiday mused, shortly before having to go to Lexington, Kentucky, for medical treatment, "After all this is over, maybe I'll go to Europe, perhaps Paris, and try to start all over." She added, "I'm a Negro. I've got two strikes against me and don't you forget it." Bill Moody, *Jazz Exiles: American Musicians Abroad* (Reno, Nev.: University of Nevada Press, 1993).

32. Jack Lind, "Sahib Shihab's Expatriate Life," *Down Beat,* March 14, 1963, pp. 17–18.

33. "Says Paris Is Not the Paradise of Old Since Americans Arrived," *Chicago Defender,* December 6, 1947, p. 30; Adam Clayton Powell Sr., "Bias Popping Up in Paris, Says Powell," *New York Amsterdam News,* December 8, 1951, pp. 1, 22. See "'New Trends in Tenor Sax': Louis Jordan," ibid., August 30, 1952, in which Jordan professed his admiration, too, for Paul Quinichette: "Those guys play the tenor the way it should be played" (p. 24). Webster, for his part, listed Coleman Hawkins, Don Byas, Stan Getz, and Sonny Stitt among the tenor men whom he "particularly admired" ("Ben Webster Plays That BIG Tenor," *Down Beat,* October 5, 1955, p. 13).

34. A. J. Bishop, "Lester Young: An Appreciation," *Jazz Journal,* June 1956, pp. 3–4; Svein Haagensen, "Lester Young with Billie Holiday," *Jazz Monthly,* December 1956, pp. 7, 31; Raymond Horricks, "Lester Young with Count Basie," ibid., 4; Guy Kopelowicz, "Lester Young on Aladdin," ibid., 8–10; Alun Morgan, "Lester Young on Clef," ibid., 11, 26; see also Alun Morgan's "Lester Young in Paris—1956," ibid., 27, and Charles Fox, "Lester Young: His Place in Jazz," ibid., 2–3. That the publication of *Jazz Monthly*'s December issue coincided with the Birdland European tour, in which Young took part, adds to its value rather than diminishing it—for why would a respected journal want to publicize an artist whose powers had declined, as many contended? There was no shortage of musicians on the 1956 Birdland tour, but none of the others had Young's stature.

35. Bill Russo and Jerry Mulvihill, "Jazz Off the Record—Lester Young," *Down Beat,* May 4, 1955, p. 7; Nat Hentoff, "Jazz Records," ibid., February 6, 1957, p. 34; "Birdland All-Stars Review," ibid., March 21, 1957, pp. 12, 35; Joe Segal, "Birdland Show in Chicago," *Metronome,* March 1957, p. 12. Bill Coss indicated that on the recorded 1957 Newport performance Young "does very well, particularly on the ballad ["Poker Chips"]. . . . The second track has better Lester . . . a powerful performance" ("Newport Jazz Festival on Record," *Metronome,* September 1957, p. 19). For critical reviews of Young recordings with Harry Edison, see Jack Maher, "Record Reviews," *Metronome,* November 1956, p. 38; see also "Dom" [Cerulli], "Newport Jazz 1958," *Down Beat,* August 7, 1958, pp. 14, 32, which criticized Young's placement rather than his playing that year, describing him as being "horribly out of place" in a Dixieland session and calling it "a dreadful waste of a jazzman to include him in this context." *Metronome* reviewed the 1958 festival and concurred with *Down Beat:* "Prez was supremely and evidently uncomfortable. This was perhaps the saddest part of the festival" ("The Newport Jazz Festival," *Metronome,* September 1958, p. 13).

36. "Record Reviews," *Down Beat,* October 16, 1958, p. 42. Young's collaboration with Roy Eldridge on this record was praised.

37. "All-Star Poll Results," *Metronome,* January 1956, p. 19; "All-Star Poll Results," ibid., January 1957, p. 17. "It's Basie and the MJQ," *Down Beat,* August 8, 1956, p. 11; among the critics who ranked Young in first place were Mike Butcher, Charles Delauny, Leonard Feather, John Hammond, Nat Hentoff, Allan Morrison, George E. Pitts, Tom Scanlan, Robert Sylvester,

Barry Ulanov, Erik Wiedemann, and Martin Williams. The stylist came in second on tenor in the "*Down Beat* Annual Readers' Poll," ibid., December 26, 1956, p. 14; *Playboy*, February 1957, p. 24; ibid., February 1958, pp. 35–41.

38. Ralph J. Gleason, "Some Pearls of Wisdom from the Dens of Equity." *San Francisco Chronicle*, March 19, 1954, p. 18. This popular nightclub would find itself the subject of controversy a few years later because of its policy permitting teenagers to sit in a segregated section and order soft drinks; see "War On! Jazz Spot Raided," *San Francisco Examiner*, January 27, 1961, pp. 1, 13; ibid., January 28, 1961, p. 3.

39. Gleason, "Some Pearls of Wisdom," 18. Jo Jones explained that he used to walk across the stage before a date and make "different sounds with my feet"—that is, take "soundings"—before deciding where to place his drums; he also contended that their sound changed with the seasons (quoted in Dom Cerulli, "Jo Jones," *Down Beat*, June 26, 1958, p. 42). Such humming can often be heard on records by Monk and Powell.

40. Author's interview with Jesse Drakes.

41. "The Cool School," 74ff; Douglas Henry Daniels, "Schooling Malcolm: Malcolm Little during the Golden Age of Jazz," *Steppingstones*, Spring 1983, pp. 45–58.

42. Robert F. Thompson, "An Aesthetic of the Cool: West African Dance," *African Forum*, fall 1966, pp. 85–86, 103; "Aesthetic of the Cool," *African Arts*, fall 1973, pp. 40ff; Malcolm X with Alex Haley, *The Autobiography of Malcolm X* (New York: Grove, 1965), particularly the chapters on his Roxbury and Harlem years; Jervis Anderson, *This Was Harlem: A Cultural Portrait* (New York: Farrar, Straus and Giroux, 1982), 307ff. Iceberg Slim, *Pimp: The Story of My Life* (Los Angeles: Holloway House, 1967); idem, *Trick Baby: The Story of a White Negro* (Los Angeles: Holloway House, 1967); idem, *Long White Con* (Los Angeles: Holloway House, 1987). Daniels, "Schooling Malcolm."

43. "The Cool School," 74ff. Thompson, "An Aesthetic of the Cool," 98. John Chernoff, *African Rhythms and African Sensibilities: Aesthetics and Social Action in African Musical Idioms* (Chicago: University of Chicago, 1979), presents a similar argument on pages 140 and 170.

44. Robert A. Perlongo, "Portrait of Pres," *Metronome*, May 1959, pp. 17–18, provides one example, as does the 1955 *Ebony* article. Author's interview with Connie Kay. Roy Haynes maintained, "I think the beat is supposed to be there within you, within everybody, once a tempo is established. You don't need anybody waving a stick at you, counting for you. If the beat is there, you just accompany the person" (Howard Mandel, "Roy Haynes Respect," *Down Beat*, November 1966, p. 20).

45. Nat Hentoff and Nat Shapiro, *The Jazz Makers: Essays on the Greats of Jazz* (1957; reprint, New York: Da Capo, 1979), 243.

46. "The Cool School," 74.

47. Ibid., 77.

48. Ibid., 74.

49. Ibid.

50. Author's interview with Jimmy Heath.

51. Ibid. Sadik Hakim's assessment of Young was almost identical: Young, he said, "never got what you'd call angry to the point of . . . [violence]"; sometimes he would be angered by things, "but . . . he had that cool relaxed attitude all the time . . . and he was such a nice man" (interview with the author). Jimmy Rowles recalled that Young carried a small whisk broom inside his jacket, and that whenever he was upset he would take it out and "sweep off his left shoulder" (quoted in Whitney Balliett, "Pres," *The New Yorker,* February 23, 1981, p. 97).

52. Author's interviews with Paul Quinichette and Jesse Drakes.

53. Marshal Royal, IJS, vol. 5, p. 33.

54. Author's interview with Marshal Royal.

55. Derek Young, "He Holds His Office Graciously," *Melody Maker,* March 21, 1953, p. 5; author's interviews with Jesse Drakes and Jimmy Heath.

56. Author's interview with Jesse Drakes; the touring schedule of the show was printed in the *Pittsburgh Courier,* July 25, 1953, p. 18. Despite Drakes's recollection that the tour lasted sixty-six days, according to the official schedule it was only about half that long. This schedule—assuming that it was the entire itinerary—did not include any states west of Kansas, Oklahoma, and Texas. See "Band Routes," *Down Beat,* February 22, 1956, p. 34; ibid., March 7, 1956, p. 34; ibid., April 18, 1956, p. 80; ibid., May 16, 1956, p. 40; ibid., June 27, 1956, p. 40; ibid., October 3, 1956, p. 50; ibid., December 12, 1956, p. 62.

57. "Band Routes," *Down Beat,* February 20, 1957, p. 42; "Birdland Stars of '57," ibid., 2.

58. Porter, ed., *A Lester Young Reader,* 189.

59. Bruce Fredericksen interview with Bobby Scott; Fredericksen produced a video, *Song of the Spirit,* about Young and very kindly loaned me a copy of the interview. Marshal Royal claimed it was obvious that Young was very ill during the Birdland tour (author's interview with Marshal Royal).

60. Author's interview with Carl "Kansas" Fields on the difference between Young's salary in Paris and that of the other musician; François Postif, "Lester: Paris, '59," in Porter, ed., *A Lester Young Reader,* 181.

61. Quoted in Allan Morrison, "Lester Young: Tragedy of a Jazz Genius," *Jet,* April 9, 1959, 61.

62. *Playboy,* February 1958. Author's interview with Dr. Luther Cloud. Stearns taught a course entitled "Giants in Jazz" at New York University in 1950 with the assistance of John Hammond and George Avakian ("Jazz Course at NYU," *Down Beat,* December 20, 1950, p. 1).

63. Young did not appear to have any playing dates between February 16 and June 2, 1958 (Frank Büchmann-Møller, *You Just Fight for Your Life: The Story of Lester Young* [New York: Praeger, 1990], 249). Author's interview with Dr. Luther Cloud.

64. Author's interviews with Dr. Luther Cloud.

65. Ibid.; author's interview with Jesse Drakes.

66. Author's interview with Dr. Luther Cloud. Both Dr. Cloud and Jo Jones remembered hearing the news on Saturday, March 14, but inexplicably, the death certificate and newspapers gave March 15 as the date of Young's death. Graham Colombé, "Jo Jones Speaks Out," *Jazz Journal,* December 1972, p. 6.

67. Quoted in Colombé, "Jo Jones Speaks Out," p. 6.

17. Good-bye Pork Pie Hat

1. Allan Morrison, "Lester Young: Tragedy of a Jazz Genius," *Jet,* April 9, 1959, pp. 58–62; Tom Dent, "Final Coda Sounds for Lester Young," *New York Age,* March 21, 1959, pp. 1, 3. "Bury Pres Thursday," *New York Amsterdam News,* March 21, 1959, p. 1, notes that an assistant minister of the Abyssinian Baptist church presided. Leonard Feather, "Prez," *Playboy,* September 1959, p. 107; Lucien Malson, "Hommage à Lester," *Jazz Magazine,* no. 48 (May 1959), p. 25. For other obituaries in the Black press, see "Saxophonist Les Young, Just Back from Europe Tour, Dies," *Chicago Defender,* March 17, 1959, p. 3; "'Pres' Young Dead at Fifty," *Philadelphia Afro-American,* March 21, 1959, p. 2; and the evaluation of Baker E. Morten, "Farewell to Lester, Truly a 'President,'" ibid., March 28, 1959, p. 7.

2. Morrison, "Lester Young," 61–62.

3. Reprinted from a San Francisco newspaper as Ralph Gleason, "Pres: Lester Young," in Lewis Porter, ed., *A Lester Young Reader* (Washington, D.C.: Smithsonian Institution Press, 1991), 119–21.

4. Ibid., 121.

5. Demetre Loakimidis, "Lester Young," *Jazz Hot,* no. 143 (Mai 1959), p. 7. François Postif, "La derniere interview de Lester Young," ibid., no. 142 (Avril 1959), pp. 11–13. This was published in English as "Lester: Paris, '59," *Jazz Review,* September 1959, pp. 7–12. Malson, "Hommage à Lester," 22–25, 38; both Malson and Morrison included photographs of the funeral in their reportage.

6. "Bury Pres Thursday," pp. 1, 9; see also Whitney Balliett, "The President," *The New Yorker,* April 18, 1959, pp. 87ff.

7. In sharp contrast, at the very time of Young's death, recordings by former Basie band members were being criticized in reviews; one reunion was described as "a wonderful idea" but deemed "unsuccessful" despite the presence of Basie sidemen. As for Young's recordings, on the same page of *The Jazz Review,* Frank Driggs pronounced the 1942 selections on *Lester Young: The King Cole Trio with Lester Young and Red Callender* "the most interesting" of the reissues, alongside the saxophonist's Aladdin sessions of the late 1940s (Frank Driggs, "Reviews: Recordings" [*Lester Young: The King Cole Trio with Lester Young and Red Callender* and *Basie Reunion*], *The Jazz Review,* July 1959, p. 25).

8. John Hammond, "Lester Young (1909–1959)," *The Saturday Review,* April 11, 1959, p. 53; Driggs, Review of *Lester Young,* 25. For one critic's claim that Young had declined after Basie, see Don Heckman, "Pres and Hawk: Saxophone Fountainheads," *Down Beat,* January 3, 1963, p. 20. Balliett, "The President," 88, 94. For more reviews, see also R. Brown, "Record Reviews," (*The Definitive Lester, Volumes 1–3*), *Jazz Journal,* June 1961, pp. 41–42; H. P., review of *Lester Young on Record, 1945–49, Jazz Monthly,* April 1962, pp. 23–24.

9. Hammond, "Lester Young (1909–1959)," 53. See note 1. An examination of jazz and other periodicals permits the conclusion that aside from the Black newspapers, few publications gave as much coverage to others who died in 1959 as they did to Young. For tributes to New Orleans musicians, see "In Memoriam," *Down Beat,* June 25, 1959, p. 14; "Sidney Bechet Dies in Paris," *The Second Line,* May–June 1959, pp. 3, 5, 18; "A Monument for Bechet," *Down Beat,* August 18, 1960, p. 14; and Bill Russell, "Warren 'Baby' Dodds," *The Second Line,* March–April 1959, pp. 7–8, 12, 15. On Billie Holiday, see J. B. Bush, "I'll Remember Lady," *Negro History Bulletin,* fall 1960, pp. 110–11; Richard Gehman, "Lady (for a) Day," *Saturday Review,* August 29, 1959, p. 39; Whitney Balliett, "Jazz Records," *The New Yorker,* March 26, 1960, pp. 89–90; "The Unmarked Grave," *Down Beat,* May 26, 1960, p. 13; and "A Stone for Lady Day," ibid., June 23, 1960, p. 14.

10. "Waxing On . . . ," *Down Beat,* July 14, 1977, p. 47; Leonard Feather, "Billie Holiday: The Voice of Jazz," *Down Beat,* February 1, 1962, p. 18. In a related expression of this tendency, years before the above-named cultural heroes died, *Down Beat*'s editorial "Good Die Young; Why Should They?" raised significant questions about the deplorable working conditions endured by musicians. It listed some of those who had died in their prime—Bix Beiderbecke, Glenn Miller, Chu Berry, Charlie Christian, and Jimmy Blanton among them—often due to the hazards of the traveling life, including occupational diseases, poor diet, and improper rest. The article stressed musicians' need for medical care, hospitals, and sanitariums and proposed issuing with every new subscription or renewal "an all-coverage accident insurance policy protecting the individual while traveling, working, or playing for loss of life, limb, sight or time" (*Down Beat,* January 28, 1949, p. 10).

11. C.W., "Jazz Albums: *Lester Swings,*" *Melody Maker,* July 17, 1976, p. 26. M.G., "Record Review: *Pres in Europe,*" *Coda,* April 1976, pp. 23–24, mentions Young's sensuality, a quality often noted in, for example, Johnny Hodges's playing, but not generally in Young's. *Pres in Europe* (High Note HCD 7054).

12. H. A. Woodfin, "Reconsiderations," *The Jazz Review,* July 1959, pp. 30–31; he also criticized Raymond Horricks, *Count Basie and His Orchestra: Its Music and Its Musicians,* with discography by Alun Morgan (London: Gollancz, 1957).

13. Woodfin, "Reconsiderations," 30–31.

14. Jim Burns, "The Forgotten Boppers," *Jazz and Blues,* June 1972, p. 4; H.P., review of *Lester Young on Record,* 24; Heckman, "Pres and Hawk," 22.

15. A few musicians who knew Holiday and were interviewed for the film later explained that they had tried their best to set the record straight and correct some of the false information about the singer, but the filmmakers had gone ahead with their own version, as if neither the musicians' testimony nor historical accuracy mattered.
16. C.W., "Jazz Albums: *Lester Swings*," 26.
17. John Litweiler, "Record Reviews: *At the Famous Door, 1938–1939* and *Mean to Me*," *Down Beat*, January 1981, pp. 40–42; C.W., "Jazz Albums: *Lester Swings*," 26.
18. Chris Sheridan, "Record Review: *Pres*," *Jazz Journal International*, August 1980, p. 30. Russell Shaw, "Waxin' On: *Pres, the '46 Concert*," *Down Beat*, July 14, 1977, p. 47.
19. B.J., "Record Review, *The Lester Young Story, Volume 1*," *Jazz Journal International*, April 1977, p. 39.
20. Dan Morgenstern, "Record Review, *Newly Discovered Performances, Volume 1*," *Down Beat*, May 22, 1975, p. 24; see also B[urnett] J[ames], "Record Review, *Lester Swings*," *Jazz Journal*, July 1976, p. 40; M.G., "Record Review, *Prez in Europe*," *Coda*, April 1976, pp. 23–24; B. McR., "Record Review, *Pres Lives*," *Jazz Journal International*, October 1977, pp. 55–56.
21. Brian Case, "New Light on Lester" (review of *Lester Young in Washington, D.C., Volume 3*), *Melody Maker*, September 12, 1981, p. 29. The pianist Bill Potts wrote insightfully about playing with Young on the liner notes of *Lester Young at Olivia Davis' Patio Lounge* (Pablo Records 2308-219).
22. John McDonough, "Record Review, *Count Basie/Lester Young and Charlie Christian*," *Down Beat*, November 2, 1978, p. 38; Jim Burns, "Lester Young's Postwar Years," *Jazz and Blues*, July–August 1971, pp. 4–6. Heckman, "Pres and Hawk," contended that Young was more revolutionary than Parker; forgetting about the swing craze and claims about the Kansas City jazz style, the writer asserted that "Young was not part of a highly publicized movement as was Parker, and explored his paths in solitude." "Imports from Japan: *Pres*," *Jazz Journal International*, August 1980, p. 30; Gary Giddins, "Riffs: Lester Young Grows Deeper" (review of *Lester Young in Washington, D.C.*), *Village Voice*, June 3, 1981, p. 59.
23. "Prez Awards," *Jazz Journal International*, August 1978, p. 36.
24. *Dallas Times-Herald*, June 27, 1979, clipping in Jazz File of Dallas Public Library; personal communication with Lester Young Jr.; "New Band Plays Only Pres Solos," *Billboard*, September 2, 1978, p. 50.
25. "Concert Reviews: 'Salute to Pres,'" *Variety*, July 7, 1982, p. 60; Gary Giddins, "The Unmaking of the Pres," *Village Voice*, November 18, 1981, p. 104; "The Return of Lady Lester," *Variety*, November 25, 1981, p. 104; Arnold Jay Smith, "'Lady Lester' Needs More Depth, More Pres Music," *Billboard*, December 5, 1981, p. 44; M. Hennessey, "Jazz Live: Jazz Opera *Prez*," *Jazz Journal International*, June 1985, p. 20. Both works have been broadcast on television.
26. Charles Mingus, *Better Git It in Your Soul* (Columbia G30628); Art Blakey

and the Jazz Messengers, *The Big Beat* (Blue Note 84029); Joni Mitchell, *Mingus* (Asylum Records 505-2). Rahsaan Roland Kirk, *The Return of the 5,000-lb. Man* (Warner Bros. Records BS 2918); I wish to thank Dr. Earl Epps for bringing this record to my attention. Gary Bartz, *Sphere* (Verve 314 557 796-2).

27. Lorez Alexander, *Lorez Sings Pres* (King KCD-565); I would like to thank pianist Gildo Mahones for telling me of this singer.

28. Leonard Feather, liner notes, *Eddie Jefferson: The Jazz Singer—Vocal Improvisations of Famous Jazz Solos* (Inner City IC 1016).

29. The recording was made at a JATP concert during which Charlie Parker also soloed on the song; Zanni pointed out that "Bird follows [Pres] and you can hear Bird's silence and humility and respect for several bars, then he quotes Pres several times in his solo" (Eve Zanni, letters of May 11, 1992, and June 1, 1992, to the author).

30. Bob Rusch, "Jesse Drakes: Interview," *Cadence,* March 1984, p. 19.

31. Author's interview with Irving Ashby.

32. Ibid.

33. See Dempsey J. Travis, *An Autobiography of Black Jazz* (Chicago: Urban Research Institute, 1983), 360, on Johnny Griffin, Gene Ammons, and Young at the Stage Door and Crown Propeller Lounge; "Johnny Griffin Interview," *Bebop and Beyond,* March–April 1986, p. 24.

34. John S. Wilson, "Brew Brews Bop on Pres Kick," *Down Beat,* July 1, 1949, p. 7. See also "A Tragic Figure in Jazz," *San Francisco Chronicle,* September 2, 1973, p. 28.

35. Wilson, "Brew Brews," 7.

36. Michael Levin and John S. Wilson, "No Bop Roots in Jazz: Parker," *Down Beat,* September 9, 1949, pp. 1, 12. Author's interview with John "Zoot" Sims; personal communication with Al Cohn. "Len," "'More like Pres Than Pres Himself': Meet Mr. Quinichette," *Down Beat,* September 10, 1952, pp. 7, 14. Theodore "Sonny" Rollins claimed that hearing Hawkins and Young was one of the things that made him decide to switch to tenor from alto (Nat Hentoff, "Sonny Rollins," *Down Beat,* November 28, 1956, p. 15). John Coltrane stated that he learned "simplicity" from Young; see Bill Coss's liner notes, *My Favorite Things* (Atlantic SD-1361).

37. Miles Davis with Quincy Troupe, *Miles: The Autobiography* (New York: Simon and Schuster, 1989), 99. Quoted in Burt Korall, "Art Is Farmer's Sake," *Metronome,* May 1957, p. 38: Farmer also liked "that light-footed grace and suggestion to his playing that is Pres and only Pres."

38. B. B. King and David Ritz, *Blues All around Me: The Autobiography of B. B. King* (New York: Avon, 1996), 105.

39. Bobby Scott, "The House in the Heart," *Gene Lee's Jazzletter,* September 1983, p. 5.

40. Bruce Fredericksen interview with Bobby Scott. Fredericksen produced the documentary *Song of the Spirit* on Lester Young; I would like to express my gratitude for his sharing this interview with me.

41. "Stars Who Won't Fly," *Jet,* September 16, 1954, pp. 60–62; Scott-Fredericksen interview.

42. Scott, "The House in the Heart," 2–5.

43. Ibid., 1; Scott-Fredericksen interview.

44. Scott-Fredericksen interview. Lee Young's grandson, Wren Brown, recalled his grandfather's telling him that he and his brother and sister were taught tap dancing by a Mr. Jack Wiggins; this may have been the source of the club's name (personal communication).

45. Rusch, "Jesse Drakes: Interview," 19; author's interview with Jesse Drakes. Scott, "The House in the Heart," 1.

46. "Chicago Restaurant Apologizes to Lena Horne for 1949 Jim Crow," *Jet,* March 5, 1953, pp. 58–59; "Erroll Garner Charges Bias at Baltimore Hotel," ibid., November 24, 1955, p. 55; "Lionel Hampton Cracks Color Bar at Detroit Café," ibid., July 22, 1954, p. 55; Scott-Fredericksen interview.

47. Scott, "The House in the Heart," 1–7. Clipping dated March 17, 1959, in Lester Young Vertical File, IJS.

48. Scott-Fredericksen interview; Scott, "The House in the Heart," 4. "Marciano, Floored in Second Round . . . ," *New York Times,* September 24, 1955, pp. 1, 37.

49. Author's interview with Martha Young. According to Lewis Porter, *Lester Young* (Boston: Twayne, 1985), 177, Young was featured at a Hollywood Bowl concert on August 22, 1957. On October 25 of that year, he played at the Shrine Auditorium (ibid., 177).

50. Author's interview with Martha Young.

51. Author's interview with Nat Pierce. Dan Morgenstern, "Lester Leaps In," in Porter, ed., *A Lester Young Reader,* 82–88; Morgenstern's account of the party originally appeared in *Jazz Journal,* August 1958, pp. 1ff.

52. Author's interview with Nat Pierce.

53. Jo Jones, IJS, pp. 91–95, on Young's character.

54. Joachim-Ernst Berendt, *Jazz, A Photo History,* trans. William Odom (New York: Schirmer, 1979), 22.

55. Sadik Hakim was one musician who thought Young was religious "in his heart" (author's interview). Carlos Ward, for example, acknowledged that many of his musical associates were religious, and explained, "This may not be a very practical concept, but anyone who decides to take up a musical instrument . . . they should first, or in their hearts, try to find God. . . . They should always be on their path to God, regardless of what kind of detours or how difficult it may be"; this accurately describes Young's career (quoted in Bill Smith, "Carlos Ward," *Coda,* June–July 1985, p. 25). The tenor saxophonist Sonny Rollins made this aspect of his musical career explicit: "I always try to inject my work with a spiritual quality. . . . I've studied Zen in Japan . . . Yoga in China . . . and I was born a Christian in America." He noted, "Spirituality is never far away from what I'm doing at any time" (quoted in Roy Durfee, review of *Sax Colossus, Coda,* February 3, 1987, p. 25). In addition to Rollins, Art Blakey, Hampton Hawes, Dizzy Gillespie, Mary Lou

Williams, John Coltrane, Pharaoh Sanders, and numerous others likewise found in their musical quests an important dimension that satisfied profoundly held religious beliefs.

56. Allen Ginsberg, *Composed on the Tongue,* ed. Donald Allen (Bolinas, Calif.: Grey Fox Press, 1980), 43.

57. Allen Ginsberg, *Howl and Other Poems* (1956; reprint, San Francisco: City Lights, 1964). Jack Kerouac, *On the Road* (New York: Viking, 1957). Carolyn Cassady, *Off the Road: My Years with Cassady, Kerouac, and Ginsberg* (New York: William Morrow, 1990), 231–36; Frank Buchmann-Møller, *You Just Fight for Your Life: The Story of Lester Young* (New York: Praeger, 1990), 245. See also the memoir of Kerouac's lover Joyce Johnson, *Minor Characters* (Boston: Houghton Mifflin, 1983).

58. Jack Kerouac, *On the Road* (1957; reprint, New York: Signet, 1982), 197–98. John Clellon Holmes's *The Horn* (New York: Random House, 1958), a novel in which two main characters are modeled after Lester Young and Billie Holiday, provides still another illustration of Young's influence on American literature in the 1950s. See also Kerouac's *Visions of Cody* (New York: McGraw-Hill, 1972) for the influence of Young and similarities between him and the book's title character, as discussed in W. T. Lhamon Jr., *Deliberate Speed: The Origins of a Cultural Style in the American 1950s* (Washington, D.C.: Smithsonian Institution Press, 1990), 166–67, 177, 178.

59. See Tom Clark, *Jack Kerouac: A Biography* (New York: Marlowe, 1984), in which the author notes that Kerouac wrote about Young and Basie for the *Horace Mann Record* (pp. 41, 227). *Kerouac: The Movie* (San Francisco: Roxie, 1985), was shown on television, and a copy exists in The Bancroft Library, University of California, Berkeley. Steve Turner, *Angel-Headed Hipster: A Life of Jack Kerouac* (New York: Viking, 1996), mentions Seymour Wyse, a friend who introduced Kerouac to Young and other musicians (p. 65). Wyse also persuaded Dizzy Gillespie to title one of his recorded numbers "Kerouac"; it can be heard on *Charlie Christian: Solo Flight* (Jazz Classics JZCL-5005). David H. Rosenthal, *Hard Bop: Jazz and Black Music, 1955–1965* (New York: Oxford University Press, 1992), contends that the incident between Young and Kerouac occurred in 1941 and that according to Kerouac, that was when "it all began for him" (pp. 17–18). Rosenthal also discusses the influence of jazz on Ginsberg's poetry on pages 18, 77–78.

60. Jack Kerouac, "New York Scenes," in *Lonesome Traveler* (New York: McGraw-Hill, 1960), 104–17, beautifully captures the city scenes and people of the 1950s. The incident was mentioned in Jim Burns, "Lester Young: The Postwar Years," *Jazz and Blues,* July–August 1971, 4. "Strictly Ad Lib," *Down Beat,* December 25, 1958, p. 44: The notation that "Lester Young was due back at the Five Spot" provides a possible time parameter for this event. One of his longtime sidemen expressed the opinion that whites' adulation was such that the tenor saxophonist "thought that Black people didn't like him. . . . It seems that the Black players . . . accepted Pres, but they would be between Coleman Hawkins or Ben Webster or somebody with that other type of sound. He seemed to think that maybe White players liked him more" (quoted in Rusch, "Jesse Drakes: Interview," 19). On the differences

between the literary climates in San Francisco and New York, see Ginsberg, *Composed on the Tongue*, 86–87.

61. Ginsberg, *Composed on the Tongue*, 41–44. In fact, Neal Cassady, one of the people to whom "Howl" was dedicated, wrote letters to Kerouac and Ginsberg utilizing a style that "put Kerouac on to his own literary style & taught him how to write modern prose modeled on natural speech, in certain Western rhythms" (Barry Gifford, ed., *As Ever: The Collected Correspondence of Allen Ginsberg and Neal Cassady* [Berkeley, Calif.: Creative Arts, 1977], 198). William Plummer, *The Holy Goof: A Biography of Neal Cassady* (Englewood Cliffs, N.J.: Prentice-Hall, 1981), also claims that Cassady's "spontaneous style" and "wild form" in his unpublished writings inspired Kerouac to write *On the Road* in twenty days in 1951 (pp. 86–88). See also Neal Cassady, *The First Third and Other Writings* (San Francisco: City Lights, 1971).

62. John Clellon Holmes, "The Philosophy of the Beat Generation," *Esquire*, February 1958, p. 38.

63. Ibid.

64. Johnson, *Minor Characters*, 142.

65. Chester Himes, *The Heat's On* (1966; reprint, New York: Vintage, 1988), 146; *My Life of Absurdity: The Autobiography of Chester Himes, Volume 2* (1972; reprint, New York: Thunder's Mouth, 1976), 95.

66. ted joans, "Lester Young," Arna Bontemps, ed., *American Negro Poetry* (New York: Hill and Wang, 1963), 171–72; Amiri Baraka, "Pres Spoke in a Language," in *Selected Poems of Amiri Baraka/LeRoi Jones* (New York: William Morrow, 1979), 320.

67. Al Young, "Goodbye Pork Pie Hat," in *Bodies and Soul: Musical Memoirs* (Berkeley, Calif.: Creative Arts, 1981), 102–3.

68. Ibid.

69. Larry Neal, *Hoodoo Hollerin' Bebop Ghosts* (Washington, D.C.: Howard University Press, 1974), 19–24. The appearance of OyamO's play *The Resurrection of Lady Lester* and of *Prez—A Jazz Opera* (reviewed by Mike Shera, *Jazz Journal International*, June 1985, pp. 20–21), as well as the observance of a memorial service at Saint Peter's in New York City on March 16, 1986, served as evidence of the saxophonist's enduring stature more than twenty-five years after his death. *Down Beat* dedicated a memorial issue to Young and Holiday in 1969; see "Pres and Lady" and Dan Morgenstern, "Lester Leaps In," *Down Beat*, April 3, 1969, pp. 17, 19–20.

70. Author's interview with Buck Clayton. For examples of his speech, see Allan Morrison, "You Got to Be Original, Man," *Jazz Record*, July 1946, pp. 7–9 (reprinted in Art Hodes and Chadwick Hansen, eds., *Selections from the Gutter: Jazz Portraits from the "Jazz Record"* [Berkeley, Calif.: University of California Press, 1977], 225–228), and Leonard Feather, "Blindfold Test: Pres Digs Every Kind of Music," *Down Beat*, November 2, 1951, p. 12; tape-recorded interview with Chris Albertson, August 1958, at IJS. The same institution also holds another, more famous tape-recorded interview with

Young, by François Postif, which has been printed and reprinted in edited, expurgated, and unedited versions in several publications. François Postif, "Lester: Paris, '59," *Jazz Monthly,* February 1964, pp. 15ff, is an edited English version; a longer version appears in French in *Jazz Hot,* nos. 362 (June 1979) and 363 (summer 1979). Most interviews with Young may be found in Porter, ed., *A Lester Young Reader.*

71. Robert A. Perlongo, "Portrait of Pres," *Metronome,* May 1959, p. 40. Sadik Hakim, "My Experiences with Bird and Pres," typewritten manuscript in the author's possession; author's interviews with Sadik Hakim, Jimmy Heath, Irma and Martha Young, and "Teddy Bear," a friend of Young's who did not want her actual name used. Bruce Fredricksen interview with Bobby Scott, circa 1985; Johnny Griffin also used *eyes* in this manner (Don Gold, "Blowin' In from Chicago," *Down Beat,* May 29, 1958, p. 17). Benny Green, "Lester Young—A Reflection," *Jazz Journal,* May 1959, p. 9; Whitney Balliett, "Pres," *The New Yorker,* February 23, 1981, p. 90.

72. Perlongo, "Portrait of Pres," 17ff, and Balliett, "Pres," 90ff. Author's interviews with Jimmy Heath and Sadik Hakim. The bassist Red Callender claimed that he used the numbering from a baseball double play—from shortstop, to second, to first—as a kind of code, too (personal communication with George "Red" Callender).

73. Program of "A Tribute to Lester Young," Jazz Vespers, the Liturgy at Saint Peter's (second Sunday of Lent), March 15, 1992; the Wingate High School Gospel Choir sang the entrance hymn, "Amazing Grace," and other selections, and there were readings from the Scriptures. "To Pres with Love," the Twelfth Annual Lester Young Memorial Celebration, on March 18, 1996, featured the Loren Schoenberg Ensemble and, among others, Jerome Richardson, Junior Mance, Lee Konitz, Tommy Flanagan, "Big Nick" Nicholas, the singer Eve Zanni, and speakers Phil Schaap and Benny Powell. The program also paid homage to a former Young sideman, the drummer Willie Jones, and Pastor John Garcia Gensel, as "the progenitors of this celebration." I wish to thank Lester Young Jr. for providing me with a copy of this program.

74. Postif, "Lester: Paris, '59," reprinted in Porter, ed., *A Lester Young Reader,* 191.

75. "A Great Is Gone," *Down Beat,* April 16, 1959, p. 11.

76. Author's interview with Martha Young.

77. Personal communication with Al Cohn.

78. Nat Hentoff, "Pres," *Down Beat,* March 7, 1956, pp. 9–11 (reprinted in Porter, ed., *A Lester Young Reader,* 158, mentions a seven-year-old Spitz named Concert. "How to Make a Pork Pie Hat," *Ebony,* August 1949, p. 44. The Lester Young Vertical File at IJS contains additional material on this.

79. Based on interviews with several musicians; for an example of Young photographed with his hat on while others have removed theirs, see the album cover of *Jazz at the Philharmonic: The Trumpet Battle, 1952* (Verve 815 152 1). During my interview with Eddie Barefield, Burt Clay and Dick Vance ex-

pressed their opinions on the significance of the wearing of hats, though they may not share my interpretation.

As for the parallel with Christian slaves, see Albert Raboteau, *Slave Religion: The "Invisible Institution" in the Antebellum South* (New York: Oxford University Press, 1978), 258: "In the religious consciousness of slaves . . . the most serious spiritual problem was not the battle versus 'old Satan' but the inner turmoil of a 'trebbled spirit.' "

SELECTED DISCOGRAPHY

Music mentioned in the text can be found on the following records and CDs.

Lester Young

The Best of Count Basie (MCA Records MCA 2-4050)
Count Basie, *Super Chief* (Columbia CG 31224)
Count Basie and His Orchestra, *Do You Wanna Jump . . . ?* (HEP CD 1027)
Count Basie and His Orchestra—1937 (Jazz Kings QSR 2412)
Giants of the Tenor Sax: Lester Young "Prez" and Friends (CCD 7002)
Historical Pres: Lester Young 1940–44 (Everybody's EV-3002)
Jazz at the Philharmonic: The Trumpet Battle, 1952 (Verve 815 152 1)
Lester Leaps In (Jazz Line Serie Cicala BLJ8021)
Lester Swings (Verve 314 547 772-2)
Lester Young, *The Complete Aladdin Recordings* (Blue Note CDP 7243 3 32787 2 5)
Lester Young, *Kansas City Six and Five* (Commodore XFL 14937)
Lester Young, *Laughin' to Keep from Cryin'* (Verve 314 543 301-2)
Lester Young, *Live Recording 1948 at "Royal Roost" New York City* (Jazz Anthology 30 JA5171)
Lester Young, *Pres in Europe* (High Note HCD 7054)
Lester Young, Volume 6, 1944 (Masters of Jazz MJCD 99)
The Lester Young Story, Volume 3: Enter the Count (Columbia JG 34840)
The Lester Young Story, Volume 4: Lester Leaps In (Columbia 34843)
The Lester Young Story, Volume 5: Evening of a Basieite (Columbia 34850-34851)
Lester Young—Volume 3—Live Recording 1949 at Royal Roost New York City (Jazz Anthology 30 JA 5214)
Lester Young Volume 6 1944 (Masters of Jazz MJCK 99)
Lester Young at Olivia Davis' Patio Lounge (Pablo Records 2308-230)
Lester Young in Washington, DC, 1956, Volume 1 (Original Jazz Classic CD 782-2 [2308 219])
Lester Young in Washington, DC, 1956, Volume 4 (Pablo Live 2308-230)
Lester Young with the Oscar Peterson Trio (Verve 314 521 451-2)
Lester Young Trio (Verve 314 521 650-2)
Nat Cole Meets the Master Saxes (Spotlite SPJ136)
The President Plays with the Oscar Peterson Trio (Verve 831 670-2)
"Prez" Leaps Again with the Kansas City Seven (Soul Parade HHP-5015-B)

Sarah Vaughan/Lester Young—One Night Stand (Blue Note CDD 723 83213924)

Other Musicians and Music of the Times

Lorez Alexander, *Lorez Sings Pres* (KING KCD 565)
Gene Ammons' All Stars (Prestige LPOJC014 P-7050)
Count Basie, *Kansas City Style—Young Count Basie with the Bennie Moten Orchestra* (AFM1-5180)
Leon "Bix" Beiderbecke, *Volume 1: Singin' the Blues* (Columbia CK 45450)
Billie Holiday with Lester Young (Giants of Jazz CD 0218)
The Blue Devils can be heard on *Territory Bands, Volume 2, 1927–31* (Historical HLP-26)
Benny Goodman Live at Basin Street, Volume 2, The Yale University Music Library Series (MHS 5222772)
Wardell Gray, *Central Avenue* (Prestige P-24062)
Wardell Gray and Dexter Gordon—Paul Quinichette and His Orchestra, *The Chase and the Steeple Chase* (MCA 1336)
Coleman Hawkins: A Documentary (Riverside RLP 12-117/118)
The Jazz Singer: Eddie Jefferson (Inner City 1016)
Louis Jordan at the Swing Cats Ball (MCAD-12044)
Jelly Roll Morton, *Hot Jazz, Pop Jazz, Hokum and Hilarity* (RCA Victor LPV-524)
Jelly Roll Morton, *The King of New Orleans Jazz—Jelly Roll Morton* (RCA Victor LPM-1649)
Jelly Roll Morton, *Mr. Jelly Lord* (RCA Victor LPV 546)
Joe "King" Oliver, *King Oliver in New York* (RCA Victor LPV 529)
Reefer Songs/16 Original Jazz Vocals (Stash 100)
Sonny Stitt, *Genesis* (Prestige P-24044)
Tea Pad Songs, Volume One (Stash ST-103)
Carlos "Patato" Valdez, *Rhythms at the Crossroads* (Redwood Records RRCD 9503)
A Very Special Stash: The Best of Reefer Songs (Stash 120)

ACKNOWLEDGMENTS

Although I have always loved reading biographies, I had never really thought of *writing* one before I began this book; it was just something I fell into. Of course, now I regard it as an exhilarating learning experience. When I began my research on Lester Young in the fall of 1980, I could not have guessed how long it would take me to see the project through. At the outset, I intended merely to examine the social history of swing-era musicians during my tenure as a Research Fellow at the Smithsonian's National Museum of American History in Washington, D.C. On my first tour of the museum, I viewed an exhibit that included Young's tenor saxophone, donated by his son, but I must confess I did not pay it much attention. Still, when I was invited to present a conference paper on a hero of Black popular culture, I chose as my subject Young, whose almost exclusive use of jazz slang became the focus of my research. After months of library work and some archival research, I interviewed Buck Clayton, the famous trumpet player and arranger. He in turn gave me the phone number of Lester Young Jr.

With the assistance of the saxophonist's son, I was able to contact and subsequently interview Young's sister Irma in the summer of 1981 and then his brother, Lee, in the late spring of 1982. I was particularly fortunate to have their help, and acutely aware that they were sharing with me family traditions that they had not readily discussed with other writers. Of course, there were also matters that remained private.

I could not have completed this biography without the intellectual and practical assistance of many friends, colleagues, and scholars. Two residents of the Washington metropolitan area, Will Calhoun and Dr. Donn Davis, helped me on several occasions at the beginning of my research, providing advice on living in that city as well as hospitality. Colleagues at the Smithsonian also assisted me in the initial stages of my work, and to them I wish to express my sincere gratitude: Michael W. Harris, James Piper, Joseph Corn, Brian Horrigan, and Roger Kennedy.

The late jazz critic Martin Williams and J. R. Taylor, both of the Smithsonian, kindly informed me of the existence of the Jazz Oral History Project at the Institute of Jazz Studies (IJS) at Rutgers; there, Dan Morgenstern, Ron Welburn, and their staff taught me how to work with transcribed interviews with musicians, as well as other materials in the institute's archive. In the several months it took for the transcripts to be prepared, I investigated resources at the Smithsonian and the Library of Congress, where Roland Grayson talked with me at length about the tenor saxophonist. Among other things, he showed me some new releases of recordings Young had made in Washington in 1956.

Thanks to the hospitality and friendship of Sam and Carolyn Williams and the late Dr. Jon Rashid, I had two places to stay—in Queens and Harlem, respectively—on the numerous occasions in the 1980s when I traveled to Newark to study the IJS interviews, or to New York City itself to track down musicians who had known and played with Lester Young.

This biography would not have been possible without the aid and encouragement of Lester Young Jr., who, in addition to putting me in contact with his uncle and aunt, also suggested that I interview his mother and mentioned some sidemen I should speak with. If I did not immediately appreciate where all this would ultimately lead, it was only because he and Buck Clayton wisely permitted me to discover for myself what I was getting into. Later he generously provided me with copies of a number of photographs from the family collection, some of which have never been published. Other Young relatives, including Irma's children, Martha and Crawford, and the Tolberts—Lucille, Alvin, and James—provided considerable assistance in reconstructing not only the saxophonist's life but also his family history, which can be traced to the Deep South on both his father's and his mother's side. Conversations with Larry Young and an interview with his father, the Reverend John W. Young, gave me a clearer idea of the family's history and traditions with respect to Lester's uncle William and his descendants.

I wish to express my gratitude to the late Nathan Huggins, then the W. E. B. Du Bois Professor at Harvard, chair of Afro-American Studies, and director of the Du Bois Institute, and the historian Richard Hunt, who directed the Mellon Fellowship Program, for their advice and assistance during my year's residency in Cambridge in 1982–1983. This and an NEH Summer Fellowship, as well as Faculty Career Development Assistance, Regents Humanities Fellowships, and Academic Senate Research Grants from the University of California, Santa Barbara, permitted me to visit archives and libraries and to interview musicians and Young's relations in principal cities of the East Coast, the Midwest, and the Southwest, and in small towns in the Deep South.

I am deeply indebted to Interlibrary Loan staff at the University of

California, Santa Barbara, without whose help this book could not have been written. I also wish to express my gratitude to the following: former Afro-American Studies staffers Marcelyn Dallis and Caren Betts at Harvard University, Cambridge, Massachusetts; Richard Allen, the late Curt Jerde, Bruce Raeburn, and Alma Williams of the William Ransom Hogan Jazz Archive at Tulane University, New Orleans, and the late music scholar William Russell of the same city; Richard Wang, who has been involved with a jazz oral-history project in Chicago; Samuel Johnson, at the time president of the Kansas City Mutual Musicians' Foundation; the late Horace M. Peterson III, executive director of the Black Archives of Mid-America Institute in Kansas City; David Boutros of the Joint Collection, Western Historical Manuscript Collection and the State Historical Society of Missouri, located at the University of Missouri, Kansas City, whose Jazz Oral History Project is an invaluable resource; Nina Jacobsen and Thomas Rosenblum of the Oklahoma Historical Society; Sterlin Holmesly, who interviewed San Antonio musicians and made those interviews available to me at Trinity College in San Antonio, Texas; Howard Dodson, chief of the Schomburg Center for Research in Black Culture; Professor Lawrence Gushee at the University of Illinois, Urbana; Professor Philip Uzee for important leads and corrections on New Orleans and Louisiana history; David Taylor and John Wright, professors at the University of Minnesota, Lewis Porter and Phil Schaap of the Institute of Jazz Studies, Rutgers University, Newark, New Jersey; and Brian Priestly and Loren Schoenberg.

Public libraries are an underappreciated national treasure trove; their Vertical Files of newspaper clippings, City Directories, and helpful staffs provided many precious details for this study. I would particularly like to thank the staffs of the public libraries in Albuquerque; Chicago; Dallas; Denver; Kansas City; Los Angeles, San Francisco, and Oakland; Minneapolis; New York City; Tulsa and Oklahoma City; Phoenix; New Orleans, Shreveport, Franklinton, and Thibodaux, Louisiana; and Woodville, Mississippi. The California State Library and the Minnesota and Oklahoma historical societies were also of invaluable assistance. Vital-records offices in New York City; New Orleans; Baton Rouge; Pittsburg, Texas; Sacramento; and Los Angeles supplied crucial information as well.

A number of graduate students and undergraduates assisted me in the course of this study. I am grateful to University of California, Santa Barbara, research assistants Victor Walker and Ula Taylor, who discovered material of considerable value. Tracy Thompson, Greg Freeland, and Mark Berman also pursued leads for me at Santa Barbara. Emmanuel Nordjoe helped with the research on Louisiana parishes. At Harvard University, Sarah Lazarus quickly and efficiently transcribed a number of interviews, allowing me to refer to them more readily, and Aaron Dean and Jeffrey Ferguson turned up useful material; Dr. Gaye T. M. Johnson, at the time a graduate student at the University of Minnesota, agreed to research property records in Minneapolis and performed that task admirably. Erin Edmonds assisted in editing and footnoting. Professor Gerald Horne read a draft of the manuscript and always encouraged me to see the project through. Professors Lawrence Levine, Leon Litwack, and William H. Kenney graciously read portions of the work, corrected errors, and made suggestions about its revision. Anneli Rufus offered especially helpful advice on the editing of some chapters.

To Dorothy Collins, at the time administrative assistant of the Department of Black Studies at Santa Barbara, I wish to express my gratitude for transcribing many of the interviews. She found the Young family history in particular so intriguing that she drew up, entirely on her own initiative, a family tree—a visual aid that enabled me to grasp the complex kinship network more readily. I am deeply indebted to Catherine McKinney for typing early drafts, and I would also like to thank Jessie Jones for her assistance in typing the manuscript in an even earlier stage. I wish to convey my gratitude to Deborah Chasman, editorial director of Beacon, and copyeditor Dorothy Straight, who helped immeasurably with the finalizing of the manuscript.

The advice and hospitality (they often go together) of numerous friends and relatives made this work possible. The following list is not exhaustive, but in addition to those previously mentioned, it must include my sisters, Sylvia and Cynthia; my brother and sister-in-law, Dennis and Marsha; my cousins Earl and James Bibbs; Howard and Jualynne Dodson, Gilberto Perez, Karen Kingsley, Shellie Williams, Bil Banks, Earl Epps, Barry and the late Judy Bloom, Nick Baines, Clarence Walker, Lorena Parlee, and my colleagues in the Black Studies and History departments at the University of California, Santa Barbara. Professor James Campbell provided invaluable advice and encouraged me to follow the route I had chosen. Professor William Banks and my uncle Benny Daniels helped me to reconstruct the back-o'-town neighborhoods of Black New Orleans, circa 1920. Finally, I wish to express my gratitude for the support of my parents, Henry and Eleanora Daniels; to all the descendants of Jacob and Martha Young for maintaining their profound family traditions and assisting me in this project; and to my wife, Claudine Michel, to whom this book is dedicated.

As for the musicians that I interviewed, I hope that this historical biography does justice to a highly creative tenor saxophonist, and that it will introduce them as well as others to one historian's way of viewing Lester Young, the man and the legend. The many musicians who so generously gave of their time in interviews made this work conceivable because they introduced me to the tangible as well as the intangible aspects of their history and their experiences, currently lived and kept alive in memory. To these performers, and their fans, I wish to express my deepest gratitude for helping me rethink the history of this music.

INDEX